The Anthropology of Media

Blackwell Readers in Anthropology

As anthropology moves beyond the limits of so-called area studies, there is an increasing need for texts that do the work of synthesizing the literature while challenging more traditional or subdisciplinary approaches to anthropology. This is the object of this exciting new series, *Blackwell Readers in Anthropology*.

Each volume in the series offers seminal readings on a chosen theme and provides the finest, most thought-provoking recent works in the given thematic area. Many of these volumes bring together for the first time a body of literature on a certain topic. The series thus both presents definitive collections and investigates the very ways in which anthropological inquiry has evolved and is evolving.

The Anthropology of Media

A Reader

Edited by

Kelly Askew and Richard R. Wilk

Blackwell
Publishing

© 2002 by Blackwell Publishing Ltd

BLACKWELL PUBLISHING
350 Main Street, Malden, MA 02148-5020, USA
108 Cowley Road, Oxford OX4 1JF, UK
550 Swanston Street, Carlton, Victoria 3053, Australia

First published 2002 by Blackwell Publishing Ltd
Reprinted 2004

Library of Congress Cataloging-in-Publication Data

ISBN 0-631-22093-3 (hardback); ISBN 0-631-220941 (paperback)

A catalogue record for this title is available from the British Library.

Set in 10/11.5 pt Sabon
by Kolam Information Services Pvt. Ltd, Pondicherry, India
Printed and bound in the United Kingdom
by MPG Books Ltd, Bodmin, Cornwall

The publisher's policy is to use permanent paper from mills that operate a sustainable forestry policy, and which has been manufactured from pulp processed using acid-free and elementary chlorine-free practices. Furthermore, the publisher ensures that the text paper and cover board used have met acceptable environmental accreditation standards.

For further information on
Blackwell Publishing, visit our website:
http://www.blackwellpublishing.com

Contents

Acknowledgments

We wish to thank Jane Huber, our series editor, for supporting this project from the beginning and improving it with her consistently insightful suggestions along the way. This book owes its existence to her. We also wish to thank Sarah Coleman, world's best editorial assistant, for her patience and good nature throughout the arduous process of pulling the pieces of this volume together. "Media Anthropology" would not exist were it not for the authors represented here and many more whose work could not be included due to limitations of space and scope. We thus thank them all and the anonymous reviewers whose comments and criticisms helped give the project sharper definition and scope. For the wonderful wire sculpture that adorns this book's cover, we thank Melvin Sithole of Cape Town, South Africa who created it and Michal Rahfaldt who found it. Kelly thanks her son Christopher who endured many a long night at the office and weekend day in the library with unfailing cheerfulness. Rick thanks Anne Pyburn who provided advice and support.

The authors and publishers gratefully acknowledge permission to reproduce copyright material as follows:

Elizabeth Hahn, "The Tongan Tradition of Going to the Movies" in *Visual Anthropology Review* 10.1, 1994; Don Kulick and Margaret Willson, "Rambo's Wife Saves the Day: Subjugating the Gaze and Subverting the Narrative in a Papua New Guinean Swamp" in *Visual Anthropology* 10.2, 1994; Purnima Mankekar, "National Texts and Gendered Lives: An Ethnography of Television Viewers in a North Indian City" in *American Ethnologist* 20.3, 1993; Richard R. Wilk, "'It's Destroying a Whole Generation': Television and Moral Discourse in Belize" in *Visual Anthropology* 5.3/4, 1993; all reproduced by permission of the American Anthropological Association and not for sale or further reproduction; Lila Abu-Lughod, "The Objects of Soap Opera: Egyptian Television and the Cultural Politics of Modernity" in Daniel Miller (ed.), *Worlds Apart: Modernity through the Prism of the Local*, published by Routledge, 1995, by permission of Taylor and Francis Ltd; John Berger, "The Ambiguity of the Photograph" in John Berger and Jean Mohr, *Another Way of Telling*, copyright © 1982 by John Berger and Jean Mohr, used by permission of Pantheon Books, a division of Random House, Inc. and in the UK by Writers and

Readers Publishing Cooperative; Vincent Van Gogh, *The Starry Night*, 1889, oil on canvas, Museum of Modern Art, New York/photo. Bridgeman Art Library – Giraudon; Erika Brady, "Save, Save the Lore" in *A Spiral Way: How the Phonograph Changed Ethnography*, published by the University Press of Mississippi, 1999; James C. Faris, "The Gaze of Western Humanism" in *Navajo and Photography: A Critical History of the Representation of an American People*, published by the University of New Mexico Press, 1996; Faye Ginsburg, "Mediating Culture: Indigenous Media, Ethnographic Film, and the Production of Identity" in *Fields of Vision: Essays in Film Studies, Visual Anthropology and Photography* ed. Leslie Devereaux and Roger Hillman, published by the University of California Press, 1995; Sut Jhally, "Image-Based Culture: Advertising and Popular Culture" in Gail Dines and Jean M. Humez (eds.), *Gender, Race and Class in Media*, published by Sage Publications, 1990; Catherine A. Lutz and Jane L. Collins, "The Color of Sex: Postwar Photographic Histories of Race and Gender" in *Reading National Geographic*, published by the University of Chicago Press, 1993; David MacDougall, "Complicities of Style" in *Transcultural Cinema*, copyright © 1998 by Princeton University Press, reprinted by permission of Princeton University Press; Marshall McLuhan, "The Medium is the Message" in *Understanding Media: The Extensions of Man*, published by MIT Press, 1994; Daniel Miller and Don Slater, "Relationships" in *The Internet: An Ethnographic Approach*, published by Berg, 2000; Hortense Powdermaker, "Hollywood and the USA" in *Hollywood and the Dream Factory*, published by Little, Brown, 1950, by permission of McIntosh and Otis; Ella Shohat and Robert Stam, "The Imperial Imaginary" in *Unthinking Eurocentrism: Multiculturalism and the Media*, published by Routledge, 1994; Stephen F. Sprague, "Yoruba Photography: How the Yoruba See Themselves" in *African Arts* 12.3: 52–9, 107, published by the University of California Press; Annabelle Sreberny-Mohammadi, "The Global and the Local in International Communications" in *Mass Media and Society* ed. James Curran and Michael Gurevitch, published by Edward Arnold, 1991; David E. Whisnant, *Rascally Signs in Sacred Places: The Politics of Culture in Nicaragua*, copyright © 1995 by the University of North Carolina Press, used by permission of the publisher; Raymond Williams, "The Technology and the Society" in *Television: Technology and Cultural Form*, published by Schocken Books, 1974 and in the UK and EU by HarperCollins Ltd.

The publishers apologize for any errors or omissions in the above list and would be grateful to be notified of any corrections that should be incorporated in the next edition or reprint of this book.

Timeline of Media Development

Year	Media-Related Event
100	Papermaking develops in China and spreads through Asia and the Arab world by the year 600
700	Arabs carry Chinese techniques for papermaking to the West
1000	Movable type made of clay is used in China
1400	Movable metal type is developed in Asia
1450	Gutenberg perfects movable metal type and handpress in Germany; the *Bible* is printed, 1456
1600	First "newspapers" appear in Germany, France, and Belgium
1702	London's *Daily Courant* is first daily newspaper
1833	Mass-circulation media begin with the first "penny press" newspaper, the *New York Sun*
1837	Telegraph is first demonstrated
1839	A practical method of photography is developed by Daguerre
1844	Samuel Morse sets up telegraph link between Washington and Baltimore
1876	First telephone message sent by Alexander Graham Bell
1877	Edison develops first phonograph
1879	Edison patents the electric light
1884	Eastman perfects the roll film
1895	Motion pictures are invented, and the first films are shown to the public
	Radio messages are transmitted by Marconi
1903	*Great Train Robbery* becomes model for storytelling with film

1920	First regularly scheduled radio broadcasting, by KDKA in Pittsburgh
1927	*The Jazz Singer* is first feature-length film with synchronized speech
1933	TV is demonstrated by RCA
1937	First digital computer is created from telephone parts
1941	First commercial TV is broadcast
1946	First mainframe computer is invented at the University of Pennsylvania
1947	First transistor is developed by Bell Labs as alternative to vacuum tubes
1948	Long-playing (LP) records, which rotate at $33\frac{1}{3}$ rpm, are introduced
1949	Network TV begins in the United States
1956	Videotape recording (VTR) is invented
1957	*Sputnik*, world's first communication satellite, is launched by the Soviet Union
1961	San Diego cable operator is first to import television signals from another city (Los Angeles) for distribution to subscribers
1969	First nodes of the computer Internet are created in Pentagon plan to establish a decentralized communications system that can withstand nuclear attack.
1970	Early (and expensive) videocassette recorders (VCRs) are introduced
1971	Invention of the microprocessor
1975	First microcomputer is marketed Fiber optics transmission begins HBO begins transmitting programming to cable TV systems by satellite
1977	Qube, the first interactive cable system, begins in Columbus, Ohio 200,000 VCRs sold; more affordable machines enter the market and sales boom
1990	World Wide Web (WWW) started as simple user interface for wide variety of data types
1997	Digital video discs (DVD) first introduced
1998	Digital television broadcasting begins

Source: David Croteau and William Hoynes, eds., *Media/Society: Industries, Images and Audiences*, 2nd. edn., Thousand Oaks, CA: Pine Forge Press, 2000.

Introduction

Kelly Askew

The saying that "we live in a media-saturated world" is now a truism-*cum*-platitude. Television screens adorn subway stations, international telephone communication via computer can be had for pennies a minute between Zanzibar and the USA, the Internet is producing countless marriage alliances, and this is but an early stage in what promises to be an ever-more technology-mediated century. Anthropology, long the self-appointed interpreter of and representative for cultural "Others," no longer holds privileged access to cross-cultural knowledge (not that it ever fully did). Nor do anthropologists serve as the primary interlocutors or advocates for the communities with whom we engage in experiments of mutual comprehension. Anthropologists remain committed to the pursuit of ethnographic knowledge and cross-cultural understanding, but it is CNN, Hollywood, MTV, and other global media that now present and represent cultures to the majority of our world. Local communities from Africa to America to Australia and everywhere in between catch their first glimpses of distant lifestyles through images in print, on television screens, and on celluloid. They hear unfamiliar musics and languages through radio broadcasts, music videos, and mass-produced (frequently pirated) cassettes. And they meet and interact with persons continents away by logging onto the Internet.

This volume introduces Media Anthropology as a legitimate subfield within anthropology and explores some of the theoretical and ethnographic issues that have captured the attention of scholars concerned with the entanglements of people and media technologies. Among other things, it will engage readers in an anthropological critique of how mass media are employed to represent and construct cultures, both Western and non-Western. Some qualifications are necessary: this volume is not about making ethnographic film or using media to do research (although both topics do arise along the way).[1] Nor is it weighted towards deconstructive analyses of media texts.[2] Recent decades have witnessed an explosion of fascinating critical approaches to the study of culture and media that interrogate in creative ways the all-too-common tendency to divorce media technologies and media texts from their social contexts. We seek to continue this trend by foregrounding the people taking pictures, listening to the radio, working behind and posing before the video camera, and examine how they manipulate these technologies to their own cultural, economic, and ideological ends.

The strength of anthropology lies in its concern with people and lived practices. What meanings do people construct out of mass-mediated images and sounds? How do they negotiate embedded ideologies, politics, and economics? What new forms of social interaction have media technologies enabled and how are existing social formations transformed? How are conceptions of space and time altered through engagement with media? And after acquiring the technology for themselves, can people previously excluded from media production use it to their own advantage within a prescribed world media order? Rather than focusing on the so-called "effects" of media technology "on" people (as it is so often put), all the contributors herein peel back the epidermal layer of mass mediation to expose the agents, aesthetics, politics, and economics behind the technologies. The term "mediation" – which together with "media" derives from the Latin *medius* meaning "middle" – assumes two or more poles of engagement. Media technologies do not mediate between themselves and people. Rather, they mediate between people and this is what defines them as a distinct variety of technology. The relationship – often superficially glossed as "producers versus consumers" – can be decidedly hierarch-ical or more egalitarian than credited at first glance. In some instances such as the Internet, pirate radio, and local community television stations (see Chapters 12 and 13, this volume; also Urla 1995) the dichotomy breaks down altogether. Only rarely is power held in equal measure by all participants, but how the inequities play themselves out varies from case to case to a startling degree.

Concerns such as these reverberate within and among the contributions to this volume. The chapters are arranged into thematic sections that tease out commonal-ities and differences *in* media experience and the *interpretation* of media experience across geographic region, technological format, and theoretical orientation. Each section commences with a brief overview of the issues confronted and suggestions for additional readings. This reader is designed to provide a representative taste of the ideas that have emerged from ethnographic studies of media and thus lays no claim to being a comprehensive assessment of the field to date. Many gaps will be noted and undoubtedly criticized, but limitations of space demanded that difficult decisions be made regarding content. East Asia, for instance, receives scant atten-tion, yet is a world region where media technologies clearly are widespread and wildly popular.[3] More attention might have been paid to gender issues, especially given the large literature devoted to gender/media.[4] Similarly, aural forms (such as radio and cassette technologies) are significantly underrepresented in comparison to contributions focusing on the visual genres of television, photography, and film. This in no way reflects a diminished global significance, for in fact radio and cassettes have penetrated a substantially larger percentage of the globe than the considerably more expensive media of television and CDs. But for reasons yet to be explored, they have attracted less academic interest than they deserve.[5]

The remainder of this introduction will prepare the reader for what follows by giving an abbreviated historical overview of approaches to the study of media and culture and by offering some thoughts on how these technologies serve a variety of social purposes, including (but not limited to) representation, communication, com-munity formation, imagination, and social action.[6] We envision the use of this book in tandem with one or two full-length media ethnographies (e.g., Powdermaker 1950; Kottak 1990; Heider 1991; Dickey 1993; Manuel 1993; Naficy 1993; Sreberny-Mohammadi and Mohammadi 1994; Pinney 1997; Mankekar 1999; Miller and Slater 2000; Spitulnik, forthcoming), so as to illustrate in greater detail the entanglement of media and society. This volume simultaneously casts the net of "media anthropology" further afield and closer to home than is the typical case with "visual anthropology." Media technologies are not restricted to visual forms. Some – like photography, film, and video – may entail a highly visual component, but to limit inquiry to those technologies alone would greatly impoverish anthropology's proven and continuing ethnographic contributions to the study of media. Continued allegiance to a strictly "visual" anthropology at the expense of media forms that are not predominantly visual – such as radio, cassettes, and the telephone – threatens to perpetuate and extend the visualist bias (what Jay (1991) calls "ocularcentrism") within Western culture that has been widely recognized and criticized.[7] It would also leave out in the cold the growing number of rich ethnographies and social analyses of aural and computer-mediated technologies (not to mention technological forms yet to be revealed). At the same time, however, media anthropology as we conceive it is re-stricted to the ethnographic study (and to a lesser extent the critical application) of *media* technologies – those that serve as intermediaries between people – and hence it would not concern itself with a social history of the toaster or microwave oven. This is a more narrowly conceived project than that espoused by contemporary visual an-thropology, which encompasses anything and everything perceived visually: body painting, tourist art, ritual, gendered performances, and much, much more, leading to some confusion as to what it excludes from its expansive embrace (see Henley (1998) for a thoughtful discussion of this issue). Media anthropology thus comprises ethnographically informed, historically grounded, and context-sensitive analyses of the ways in which people use and make sense of media technologies.

Genealogies I: Media Texts

Academic inquiry into the social consequences of media technology formed the basis of the relatively new disciplines of Communication Studies, Media Studies, Cultural Studies, Film Studies, Media Sociology, Visual Anthropology, and – we suggest with this volume – Media Anthropology. Although some would say anthropology came late to the study of media, at least one anthropologist tackled the subject head-on over a half-century ago, long before it became the fashionable thing to do. Hortense Powdermaker (1900–70) – labor organizer, Queens College anthropology professor, and student of Bronislaw Malinowski (the father of ethnology) – blazed a pioneering path in media anthropology that subsequently lay untrodden, forgotten, and over-grown for nearly fifty years. Despite her probing ethnographies of the Hollywood film industry, race relations in Mississippi, and industrialization and media in Zambia, Powdermaker is remembered most commonly for her memoir *Stranger and Friend* – a painful reflection of gendered stereotypes in academic production.[8] Media captured her academic attention during field research in Mississippi. In a small town where the primary source of entertainment was going to the movies, she started pondering the relations between Hollywood, the movies it produced, and the impact they had on audiences. Her fascination with the topic brought her to the belly of the beast: to Hollywood, where in 1946–7 she embarked on a year-long ethnographic study of the film industry encompassing everyone from writers, pro-ducers, and directors, to actors, set designers, and lighting crews. Her subsequent monograph *Hollywood the Dream Factory: An Anthropologist Looks at the Movie-Makers* (Powdermaker 1950), a selection from which is included in this volume (chapter 10), heralded her long-lived devotion to media scholarship. This devotion gave rise to an interdisciplinary seminar on mass communications that she chaired at the Wenner-Gren Foundation in 1951, and chapters on radio and film in her ethnography of a Zambian copper-mining town (see Powdermaker 1953, 1962).

Powdermaker conducted her Hollywood research at a time when the industry had recently consolidated into five dominant studios (Warner Brothers, MGM-Loew's, Twentieth Century-Fox, RKO, and Paramount) (Cherneff 1991: 435).[9] In light of these major changes, confessions of high anxiety and deep-seated job insecurity emerged as a repetitive theme in Powdermaker's data. Since success in Hollywood depends on luck as well as skill, such anxieties were well-founded, for luck is a fleeting and unreliable variable. Powdermaker located an additional source of stress in the profit motive that drives Hollywood efforts however much "art" is invoked in public discourse. Film is an industrial art form, one reputedly lauded by Lenin as the highest form of worker's art. The technical demands of producing a film typically require the labor of hundreds, even thousands of people, each of whom may hold their own personal artistic vision for the project. Negotiating all the competing visions can pose quite a challenge, which frequently results in the emergence of cinematic dictators who impose their vision on everyone else. Powdermaker explored the intersections of Hollywood economics, ideologies, politics, and psychologies in exquisite detail. She reached the conclusion that the industry's social system and overriding profit motive "mechanizes" creativity (Powdermaker 1950: 318), resulting in dehumanized, formulaic films that lull audiences into aesthetic conformity. Totalitarianism within the industry's social structure radiates outward, so she argued, from the silver screen to impose empty, distracting dreams ("the dream factory") on passive audiences:

Hollywood represents totalitarianism. Its basis is economic rather than political but its philosophy is similar to that of the totalitarian state. In Hollywood, the concept of man as a passive creature to be manipulated extends to those who work for the studios, to personal and social relationships, to the audiences in the theaters and to the characters in the movies. The basic freedom of being able to choose between alternatives is absent. (Ibid: 327)

The parallels between Powdermaker's conclusions and those of the Frankfurt School theorists (especially Max Horkheimer and Theodor Adorno) who were writing during roughly the same time are striking.[10] Compare the above quote with Adorno's description of the "culture industry," wherein "the progressive technical domination of nature, becomes mass deception and is turned into a means for fettering consciousness. It impedes the development of autonomous, independent individuals who judge and decide consciously for themselves" (Adorno 1997: 29). It is not inconceivable that their paths may have crossed, for Powdermaker's tenure at Queens College overlapped with the Frankfurt theorists' temporary relocation to Columbia University in 1933 in response to the ascension of Hitler. The experience of the war led them all to ponder deeply the phenomenon of totalitarianism and this emerges quite clearly in their respective work (see Bennett 1982: 41–7). In 1941 Horkheimer and Adorno left New York for Los Angeles, where they lived for eight years and where they produced their critical treatise on the culture industry, *Dialectic of Enlightenment* (see Jay 1973: 193–7). It was in the middle of those same eight years that Powdermaker came to Hollywood. She never cited them in her work, nor did they cite her, yet together they shared and promoted a view of the film world as a crass and brutal industry thinly disguised as art that used its technological advantage to objectify viewers and impose on them politically numbing cultural formulae.

This focus on the power of the media texts to shape attitudes and ideas was subsequently taken up by British cultural studies (especially Stuart Hall, David Morley, John Fiske, and Ien Ang), which emerged in the early 1970s. But whereas Powdermaker, Adorno, and others had concentrated their attention on media *production*, the turn towards cultural studies opened a window onto questions of media *reception*. Cultural studies theorists questioned and problematized the assumption of uncomplicated, unilineal transmission of media messages directly from producers to consumers. Discussions of the distribution of power remained central in their analyses, but power no longer was seen as monopolized entirely and exclusively by media producers. Informed by the writings of Antonio Gramsci and Michel Foucault, cultural studies scholars attributed some measure of power to the acts of viewing and listening, and in the process reconceptualized audience members as active subjects. Hall's famous "encoding/decoding" formulation allowed for multiple interpretations of media texts during both the processes of production and reception – an extension of reader-centered approaches in the field of literary criticism. But Hall simultaneously forced recognition and awareness of representational strategies prevalent in media practice that privilege certain interpretations ("preferred readings") over others:

All texts involve an economy of meaning: foregrounding certain interpretations and excluding others, seeking to plot a relatively unambiguous route through meaning. Ethnographic texts, more consciously than others perhaps, direct the reader towards a *preferred reading* since they must navigate the reader on a directed route through potentially complex and unfamiliar terrain. This preferred reading involves the dual process of unravelling certain meanings – *decoding* – but equally of selection and creativity which allows certain meanings to surface – *encoding*. A basket, for instance, might be decoded in many ways (the work of a particular artist; a fine exemplar; an ancient, unique specimen, etc.) but the accompanying text will encode it towards one or other of these, thereby guiding its interpretation and circumscribing its meaning. (Lidchi, in Hall 1997: 166–7)

Media audiences were thus, for the first time, elevated to a level of involvement above that of passive receptacle. Rather than mere *consumers*, audiences were accorded recognition as active *producers* of meaning. Yet Hall and his colleagues were quick to point out and reiterate – especially with regard to media texts concerning race, ethnicity, class, and gender – that media producers apply a host of strategies (e.g., stereotyping, essentializing, reductionism, naturalization, binary oppositions, erasure, fantasy, fetishism, disavowal) that predispose and guide audiences towards readings favoring existing power structures (Hall 1981, 1997; see also Mulvey (1989) for her analysis of the "male gaze").

This turn towards the reception, indeed active appropriation, of media texts – however guarded – proved a welcoming reentry point for anthropological approaches. Scattered about the globe in wide-ranging locales, anthropologists were ideally situated to test and disprove "hypodermic needle" models of text transmission. They offered many an unexpected reading of Western media products such as *Dallas* or *Rambo* (see chapter 16, this volume; also Ang 1982; Liebes 1984; Liebes and Katz 1990; Michaels 1994b; Miller 1992; Leuthold 1995) and showed how intended meanings often fell to the wayside during the process of reception. This emphasis on "active audiences" introduced an element of hope to counter Frankfurt School pessimism: the hope that media forms could be divorced from hegemonic elite or state projects. Granted, such efforts would no doubt prove difficult and challenging, but the possibilities of interpretive alternatives, evasion, resistance, and challenge now existed where they had been theoretically muted before.[11] As Hall explains:

Meaning can never be finally fixed. If meaning could be fixed by representation, then there would be no change – and so no counter-strategies or interventions. Of course we *do* make strenuous efforts to fix meaning – that is precisely what the strategies of stereotyping are aspiring to do, often with considerable success, for a time. But ultimately, meaning begins to slip and slide; it begins to drift, or be wrenched, or inflected into new directions. (Hall 1997: 270; emphasis in the original)

Ethnographic contributions from non-Western cultures prove a valuable complement to Western-based reception studies in demonstrating the strength and resiliency of local cultural norms and how they so often determine not only the *interpretation* of media texts but the very *experience* of media texts. Ethnographic studies such as those in this volume by Hahn (chapter 15), Kulick and Willson (chapter 16), Wilk (chapter 17), and Mankekar (chapter 18) show how meaning is actively invented during the process of reception – distorting, eliding, even reversing encoded meanings. These cases offer a strong rejoinder to strict "cultural imperialism" theorists who would have a hard time explaining the subordination of Western media products to local narrative demands and values.

Genealogies II: Media Technologies

Early attention to the technologies that enable interaction between temporally and/ or spatially distanced people marked the theoretical domain of Marshall McLuhan, his predecessor Harold Innis, and anthropologist/filmmaker Edmund Carpenter. In coining the phrase "the medium is the message" McLuhan shifted attention away from media content/texts to the technology that supplied them, insisting that it was the technology more than anything else that shaped human perception. So powerful, he argued, was the impact of media technologies that it constituted a revolution in social relations around the world, achieved through the compression of space and time and collapsing of social distance: the emergence of the "global village." And so powerful an impression did such technologies make, he further argued, that human perception has been indelibly and irrevocably altered. For McLuhan, the true "message" of any medium or technology is not to be sought in its content but rather in "the change of scale or pace or pattern that it introduces into human affairs" (McLuhan 1994: 8). He linked print media, for example, to increased individualism, social separation, continuity of space and time, uniformity of codes, and nationalism (ibid: 84, 19–20). McLuhan contended that each technological format has its unique characteristics and effects on human behavior. His book *Understanding Media* catalogues these characteristics and effects for each and every media format available when he wrote it in 1964.

McLuhan thus anticipated by two decades the work of Benedict Anderson (1983). In his analysis of nationalism, Anderson isolates print media as one of three factors necessary for the spread of nationalist consciousness. Print media disseminate nationalist thought and rhetoric via their content, but equally important they invite partici-pation into a practice shared more or less simultaneously by hundreds if not thousands and millions of people beyond one's immediate family and friends. By partaking in this experience, individuals obtain membership in an "imagined community" encompass-ing anonymous Others who over time cease to be strangers and begin to be fellow citizens (whether or not one ever meets them).[12] Following McLuhan's and Anderson's lead, several media ethnographers have focused on the role of media in the imagination of new social vistas and the construction/maintenance of communities. Conrad Kottak, for example, compared the social consequences of television viewing on com-munities in the US and Brazil in *Prime-Time Society: An Anthropological Analysis of Television and Culture* (1990). The contributions in this volume by Williams (chapter 2), Sprague (chapter 11), Miller and Slater (chapter 12), Ginsburg (chapter 13), Tacchi (chapter 14), Mankekar (chapter 18), and Abu-Lughod (chapter 22) all relate media to processes of community formation and transformation at multiple levels from the most local to the national and transnational (see also Yang 1997; Naficy 1993).

While philosophical arguments about the conscious and unconscious impact of media technologies on our psyche and daily routine continue unabated, an al-together different debate continues over the application of media technologies in ethnographic research. Despite contemporary visual anthropology's very inclusive scope, its roots lie in a positivist celebration of media technologies as scientific modes of cultural documentation. Margaret Mead and Gregory Bateson cham-pioned the use of the camera (both still and moving) in their 1930s research on Balinese culture and personality. Although they differed on exactly how to use it (as illustrated in chapter 3 of this volume), they agreed that the camera constituted a privileged medium for scientific research. Similarly, Franz Boas (among others) advocated the use of the phonograph for documentation purposes and sent numer-ous students out in the field to record as much as possible (see chapter 5, this volume). Technology was viewed as an objective and more accurate means of capturing reality, "a form of documentation directly apprehensible to the senses, presumably uncontaminated by the observer's inevitable categorical and perceptual biases" (Brady 1999: 69). Technology, so it was believed, could capture "the truth."

Concern with truth, science, and objectivity reflected the positivist orientation not only of early ethnography but any of a number of pursuits during the late nineteenth and early twentieth centuries. "Value-free science" remains a theoretical illusion, however, as some of the early and continuing applications of photography testify. Photography was enthusiastically enlisted in the categorization and classification of human subjects, especially the criminal, the mentally ill, and the culturally exotic.[13] Yet careful scrutiny of who was photographed and under what conditions reveals in every case a whole host of precursory judgments that negates the purported objectivity of the medium (see chapter 4, this volume; also Bazin 1967; Barthes 1977). Anthropology's love affair with the camera can perhaps be attributable in part to their entwined histories. As some scholars have pointed out, anthropology's emergence as a discipline coincided with the emergence of photography and film as technologies and modes of representation (see chapter 9, this volume; also Pinney 1992). A critical assessment of underlying assumptions about photographic and filmic practices threatened to evoke similar criticisms about anthropology and thus was best avoided altogether. Thus it wasn't until the late 1980s following anthropology's "crisis of representation" (Marcus and Fischer 1986; Rabinow 1986; Clifford 1988; Minh-ha 1989) that scholars began interrogating and problematizing the uses of technology in ethnographic research.

Opening the door on canons of realism and objectivity was akin to opening up Pandora's box. Suddenly one truth became many, objects became subjects, and subjects lost their assumed authority. Postmodernism posited the existence of multiple subjectivities. But the theoretical backlash that followed reasserted the importance of considering *context* – political, economic, and otherwise. Individuals are not subjects devoid of histories and cultures. While postmodernism injected a much needed dose of reflection on the ethnographic encounter, it evoked a resurgence of interest in context and it is to that final topic that we turn next.

Genealogies III: Media Contexts

Consider a pendulum. It swings from one side to the other before finally coming to rest in the middle. So it was within media studies in contemplating relations of power. As described above, early scholars accorded power to media producers who create and distribute media texts designed to promulgate dominant agendas. Then audiences were identified as free agents and producers of meaning, liberally appropriating media texts, emptying them of their original content, and filling them with new, locally relevant meanings. Emphasis had shifted from the power of the producers to the power of the consumers.

The swing towards audience agency and the open-endedness of meaning has come under attack. Critics and cynics argue that such unfettered optimism denies the cultural and historical, not to mention political and economic, conditions of both media production and consumption. Neo-Marxists, such as the Frankfurt School theorists, espoused the deterministic text-transmission models described earlier in large part because they were acutely aware of power differentials in the realm of media production and the world at large. Since they located the source of all power in the hands of media producers they thereby concluded that media existed for the sole purpose of facilitating the reproduction of existing social relationships (a mix of Marxism and functionalism). Media representations, in this perspective, inculcate false consciousness and misrecognition by masking the realities of economic and political inequality. One relevant case that has aroused considerable attention is media coverage of the Gulf War (discussed in chapter 8, this volume). The establishment of CNN as the authoritative voice on the war not only crowded out other voices but delegitimized them as well. Few realized that "the military view literally *became* the spectator's view [and] goes a long way towards explaining the massive public adherence in the US to the war" (Shohat and Stam 1994: 126).

McLuhan and other media enthusiasts advocated a far more sanguine position. They viewed media technologies as tools available to disenfranchised members of society that can be used to undermine existing power relations and instigate societal change. The contemporary strain of this perspective, known as liberal pluralism, links media to projects of "modernization" and "modernity" (Bennett 1982). Media is seen as a revolutionizing force in society that can be effectively harnessed for the betterment of everyone. Colonial regimes and modern nation-states have traditionally taken this position and run with it, establishing state radio and television stations and using them to promote various modernist agendas (see chapters 21 and 22, this volume; also Spitulnik 1998; West and Fair 1993).

In a context of rampant consumer capitalism, however, big business appropriated media technologies for the purposes of advertising their products. On radio, TV, the

Internet and in print media, companies construct desires and create needs that they seek to fulfill, at a price (see chapter 19, this volume). At times, the efforts are masked in humanist-sounding rhetoric, but more often than not constitute bald advances on consumer finances. The encroachment of multinational corporations on Third World countries from Western/Northern points of origin via Hollywood films, Marlboro cigarettes, MTV, Coca-Cola, CNN, Tommy Hilfiger jeans, cell phones, and McDonald's hamburgers evoke understandable fears of cultural, economic, and media imperialism (see Morley and Robins 1995a, 1995b; Appadurai 1990; Tomlinson 1991). But as Sreberny-Mohammadi points (chapter 20, this volume), there are too many examples of cross-cutting, non-Western cultural/economic/media expansions to justify the idea of a unidirectional American/European global takeover: Bollywood films, Mexican teleserials, and Japanese ownership of Columbia Pictures are but a few examples.

The marriage between global capital and Eurocentrism has spawned trends in media production that privilege partial, stereotypical, essentialized, and greatly condensed representations of cultures beyond and within America and Europe. The rich repertoire of representational strategies identified by Hall that construct Otherness have attracted a significant amount of scholarly attention.[14] One counter-strategy for undermining media constructions of Otherness is to identify and draw public attention to them (see chapters 6, 7, 8, and 9, this volume). A second counter-strategy is to produce alternatives to dominant constructions, including (but not limited to) self-constructions (chapter 13, this volume; also Hall 1981; Turner 1992a; Ginsburg 1994a). Real constraints in media production and distribution exist, however, that place media beyond the means of the majority. Film (16 mm and 35 mm) is an incredibly expensive medium, and getting licensing rights to broadcast television and radio signals is no easy task (Michaels 1994a). The costs vary by medium, but generally there are daunting start-up expenses, difficulties in first acquiring and then maintaining equipment, restrictions on access to existing channels of distribution, competition from established and well-endowed multinationals, and restrictive policies instituted by governments courting foreign investment. A number of "indigenous media" projects have put cameras in the hands of people who historically were relegated to roles as filmic objects – Navajo, Inuit, Kayapo, Australian Aborigines (Worth and Adair 1997; Ginsburg 1994a, 1994b, 1995b; Turner 1992a, 1995a). Efforts such as these seek to reverse the authority of ethnographic and popular representational practice and use media technologies as "vehicles for internal and external communication, for self-determination, and for resistance to outside cultural domination" (Ginsburg 1995a: 256). Yet nagging questions arise regarding "quality" (which is almost unilaterally defined in Western terms and according to Western aesthetic principles) and the degree to which media technologies are always bound within Western conventions. Faye Ginsburg asks: "Is it indeed possible to develop an alternative practice and aesthetic using forms so identified with the political and economic imperatives of Western consumer culture and the institutions of mass society?" (ibid: 256–7). James Faris cautions: "Western technologies are not benign . . . there is more West in Western products than has been carefully discussed" (Faris 1993: 12). Thus the extent to which self-representation via indigenous media productions has resolved problems of domination and agency or merely camouflaged them constitutes a topic of vigorous debate (see chapter 13, this volume; also Faris 1992a, 1992b, 1993; Michaels 1994a, 1994b, 1994c; Turner 1992a; Weiner 1997). In chapter 9 of this volume David MacDougall (ethnographer, theorist, and filmmaker) offers a view that potentially reconciles the two positions, namely the possibility that certain cultures "lend themselves to the codes of Western filmmaking" better than others due to inherent "complicities" (narrative, technical, psychological) in cultural style.

Media and Anthropology: Cultural Intermediaries

The value of anthropological approaches lies in a shared understanding of media as simply one aspect of contemporary social life, no different in essence from law, economics, kinship, social organization, art, and religion. All these categories of thought and behavior are socially conceived and socially enacted. Anthropologists categorically reject the common tendency to treat media as separate from social life and in ethnographic case after case highlight the interconnections between media practices and cultural frames of reference.

Some remarks should be made regarding the organization of this book. It is subdivided into five thematic parts.[15] Part one, "Seeing/Hearing Is Believing: Technology and Truth," questions the frequent description of media technologies as purveyors of reality, a.k.a. "truth." It begins with the oft-cited media theorist Marshall McLuhan and his highly influential statements on how media technologies created a "global village" and shape human perception (i.e., "the medium is the message"). Chapter 2 comprises a social history of media technologies by Raymond Williams, who stresses the social and cultural foundations from which they developed. Next comes an amusing debate between Margaret Mead and Gregory Bateson on the scientism of different camera techniques. The concerns they raise echo those within another debate in the discipline: does anthropology hold more in common with science or the humanities? Chapters 4 and 5 by John Berger and Erika Brady present critical and historical appraisals of photographic and phonographic takes on reality.

Parts two and three tackle the problem of representation from opposing perspectives. Part two, "Representing Others," dissects representational strategies of Difference and Otherness in a variety of contexts. In chapter 6 James Faris takes Western photographic representations of Navajo to task within a wider critique (à la John Berger) of photography. In a similar vein, chapter 7 by Catherine Lutz and Jane Collins offers an exhaustive survey of representations of race and gender in *National Geographic*, taking into account the poses, contexts, and relative percentages of photographs representing people of color and women. In chapter 8 Ella Shohat and Robert Stam focus their critical attention on the nostalgic longing with which Western media projects represent imperialist periods of history (past and present). Objects of their analysis include world exhibitions, imperial adventure films, Hollywood Westerns, contemporary action films, and news coverage of the Gulf War. In chapter 9 David MacDougall examines the culture shock that sometimes occurs during the reception of ethnographic films and offers some compelling suggestions as to why it happens in some films and not in others.

Part three, "Representing Selves," shifts attention to strategies of self-representation. It begins with chapter 10, a selection from Hortense Powdermaker's book on Hollywood and her analysis of how Hollywood films are structured (not necessarily by intent) by Hollywood social relations and ideologies. We then move to West Africa and Stephen Sprague's account in chapter 11 of how Yoruba photography is thoroughly Yoruba in aesthetic principles as well as content. In chapter 12 we shift from photography to cyberspace in Daniel Miller and Don Slater's analysis of Trinidadian engagements with the Internet. They show how the Internet has been fully incorporated into Trinidadian culture and how, among other things, it facilitates the maintenance of transnational Trinidadian identities and communities. Finally, in chapter 13 Faye Ginsburg discusses the promise and problems of "indigenous media," specifically as faced by Australian Aboriginal television productions. It leads her to query whether indigenous media are best assessed as a "Faustian contract" or the epitome of McLuhan's "global village."

Part four presents some cogent examples of anthropological attention to media reception and "Active Audiences." In chapter 14 Jo Tacchi examines how experiences with radio enable listeners to construct social identities in the physical presence or absence of sociality. In chapter 15 Elizabeth Hahn shows how going to the movies in Tonga is a peculiarly Tongan experience – something that would take many a Western moviegoer by surprise. Hollywood films fall prey to distinctly Papua New Guinean cultural concerns, as illustrated in Don Kulick and Margaret Willson's description in chapter 16 of how *Rambo* was interpreted within local parameters, emerging as an altogether different "text" than that conceived by its makers. In chapter 17 Richard Wilk explores how public discourse about the arrival of American television in Belize reveals a profound ambivalence that renders simplistic the wholesale fears of Western cultural imperialism. Finally, in chapter 18, Purnima Mankekar analyzes the construction of national and gendered identities through active engagement with Indian television serials. Both Wilk and Mankekar anticipate Part five of the book in showing how television can evoke nationalist sentiment in viewers, either intentionally via nationalist content or unintentionally by contrast with a foreign Other.

Part five, "Power, Colonialism, and Nationalism," presents a variety of perspectives on colonial, national, and global hegemonic projects and how they impact media practices. Chapter 19 by Sut Jhally presents a Marxist analysis of Western advertising and how it has produced a "visual image-system" that has colonized certain domains of life. In chapter 20 Annabelle Sreberny-Mohammadi critiques the globalization/localization dichotomy in First World/Third World media analyses and argues instead for a more nuanced understanding that recognizes a distribution – albeit an unequal one – of power, influence, and resources. Chapter 21 by David Whisnant focuses on how US–Nicaraguan relations during the Somoza regime enabled American media and consumer products (from Hollywood films to Quaker Oats and Disney comics) to penetrate Nicaragua with ease and tacit government support in a far-from-benign manner. Part five concludes with Lila Abu-Lughod's examination in chapter 22 of the production and active consumption of Egyptian soap operas, relating them to a wide variety of ideological agendas: modernism, nationalism, religious revivalism, and consumerism.

If media, by definition, translate/negotiate/intervene between parties to effect understanding (as the dictionary definition of "mediate" reveals), then they can be considered extensions of anthropology, a discipline devoted to the translation of cultures. Some varieties of media production may be lost forever to cultural misrepresentation for reasons of economic profit and political gain. But because anthropology passed through many stages of theoretical awareness before coming to terms with the challenges entailed in translating cultures in as ethical, sensitive, respectful, self-critical, dialogic, and collaborative a manner as possible, there is reason to hope that media practitioners will eventually reach a similar position. And the spread (plus decreasing costs) of media technologies all around the world may well be facilitating the process.

In her review essay "Anthropology and Mass Media" Debra Spitulnik stated "There is as yet no 'Anthropology of mass media'" (Spitulnik 1993: 293). Eight years later, the significant and growing literature represented by this volume indexes an existent, if still emergent, discipline. Media anthropology, the brainchild of Mead, Bateson, and Powdermaker, has finally come into its own.

NOTES

1   Readers interested in this topic should refer to Heider (1976); Collier and Collier (1986); Rollwagen (1988); Crawford and Turton (1992); Loizos (1993); Hockings (1995); Warren (1996); Barbash and Taylor (1997); MacDougall (1998); and Ruby (2000).

2   The term "text" is used here not in the sense of the written word but any cultural product (aural, visual, tactile, or otherwise) that is subject to interpretation.

3   See Leyda (1972); Ivy (1988); Yoshimoto (1989); Tanaka (1990); Lull (1991); Ching (1994); Rofel (1994); Skov and Moeran (1995); Zha (1995); Yang (1997); and Moeran (1996, 2001).

4   See Goffman (1976); Ang (1982); de Lauretis (1984, 1987); Pribram (1988); Gamman and Marshment (1989); Minhha (1989); Mulvey (1989); Tanaka (1990); Imam (1991); Press (1991); Traube (1992); Notar (1994); Bobo (1995); Pietropaolo and Testaferri (1995); Skov and Moeran (1995); Norris (1997); Willis (1997); Mankekar (1999).

5   Some notable studies on radio and cassette technologies are Eco (1978); Imam (1991); Manuel (1993); Miller (1993); Wong (1994); Sreberny-Mohammadi and Mohammadi (1994); Urla (1995); Gerdes (1998); Spitulnik (1997, 1998, and forthcoming); Douglas (1999); Eickelman and Anderson (1999); Hendy (2000); and Miller (forthcoming).

6   For a more comprehensive review of the literature up through the early 1990s, see Debra Spitulnik's *Annual Review of Anthropology* survey (Spitulnik 1993).

7   See Banta and Hinsley (1986); Crary (1990); Fabian (1983); Krauss (1988, 1993); Levin (1993); Tyler (1984).

8   For a critique of the propensity to marginalize female anthropologists to certain modes of academic production such as the memoir, see Visweswaran (1992). A helpful resource assessing the contributions of female anthropologists is Gaco, Khan, McIntyre and Weinberg (1989).

9   Universal, Columbia, and United Artists managed to hold on but the remaining small competitors were bought or forced out of business (Cherneff 1991: 435).

10 The group of radical intellectuals collectively known as the Frankfurt School had come together in 1923 with the establishment of the Institute for Social Research in Frankfurt, Germany. The combination of a critical outlook and predominantly Jewish background forced a relocation of the institute temporarily to New York, but it returned to Frankfurt in 1949. For more information, see Bennett (1982), Jay (1973), and Wiggershaus (1994).

11 There is quite a large literature devoted to debate over just how "active" audiences are. Some key texts are Drummond and Paterson (1988); Seiter et al. (1989); Gamman and Marshment (1989); Liebes and Katz (1990); Corner (1991); Fiske (1987, 1989, 1991); Gitlin (1991); Livingstone (1991); and Morley (1992).

12 While acknowledging the importance of Anderson's contribution to understandings of nationalism, some scholars argue for recognition of the significance of non-print media in the spread of nationalist consciousness, especially in parts of the world where literacy is not widespread (see Askew, forthcoming).

13   See Sontag (1990); Tagg (1988); Lutz and Collins (1993); Edwards (1992); Bate (1993); Faris (1993); Jenkins (1993); Webb (1995).

14   See Minh-ha (1989); Edwards (1992); Naficy and Gabriel (1993); Spurr (1993); O'Barr (1994); Shohat and Stam (1994); Campbell (1995); Webb (1995); Faris (1996); Rony (1996).

15   Readers should be aware that the theme defining a particular part may reappear in other parts due to the anthropological tendency to locate interconnections across conceptually disparate domains. Thus several of these chapters could just have easily been assigned to a different part than the one in which they appear.

Part I

Seeing/Hearing is Believing: Technology and Truth

Part one surveys a variety of social perspectives on the technologies of media. It spans discussions of media technologies in the service of social scientific research, critical analyses of how technologies "mediate" between reality and representation, and investigations of how media relate to wider social transformations. The chapters represent a range of disciplines, from communication studies (McLuhan), to cultural studies (Williams), to anthropology (Mead and Bateson), to art criticism (Berger), to folklore (Brady). In this respect Part one is atypical, as the rest of the book is heavily anthropological in affiliation.

We begin with two excerpts from Marshall McLuhan's widely cited book *Understanding Media: The Extensions of Man*, written in 1964. McLuhan, a Canadian professor of English literature, left his mark on the world by pronouncing the arrival of the "global village" and declaring that "the medium is the message." In *Understanding Media* he proposed the idea of media as "extensions of man" but also as sources of transformation in human relationships and perception. The book became a *cause célèbre*, landing him engagements on the US talk show circuit, winning him friends from Woody Allen to Andy Warhol, and leading the *New York Herald Tribune* to proclaim him "the most important thinker since Newton, Darwin, Freud, Einstein, and Pavlov."[1] His theories have gone in and out of style over the thirty-seven years since their publication, but have gained a new-found relevance and renaissance with the spread of cyber technologies. McLuhan is included here not merely because of the frequency with which he is referenced in writings on the media, but because he saw media as a social phenomenon that is at once cause and effect of social change. His work spawned a significant corpus of research, some of which sought answers to the question: "Is our world best characterized as a 'global village' or 'villagized globe'?"

The relationship between technology and social change is pursued by Raymond Williams in chapter 2, which is a selection from his book *Television: Technology and Cultural Forms*. Drawing inspiration from historical materialism, Williams relates the rise of media technologies and their subsequent applications to broader political and economic concerns. He seeks to redirect attention away from popular discourse analyzing media's "effects on" society to discussions of how they are "used by" people to support a wide variety of agendas. Taking issue with theorists and pundits who see these technologies as abstracted from society and somehow working their magic on humans without human involvement, he makes a compelling argument for the social origins of media technologies and their continued embeddedness in industrial capitalist concerns.

There follows in chapter 3 an amusing debate between Margaret Mead and Gregory Bateson, two eminent anthropologists who championed the use of cameras (still cameras and moving cameras) in ethnographic research. While Mead and Bateson concurred on the value of cameras, they differed on the question of application. Should ethnographic film data be conceived as first and foremost "ethnographic" – a scientific record? Or should an anthropologist approach ethnographic film first as a film, often an artistic medium that can be manipulated to reveal some things in greater detail than others? This discussion echoes another issue that continues to haunt anthropology, namely its intermediary position between science and the humanities.

John Berger (chapter 4) confronts the selectivity and ambiguity of photographic representation in his essay "The ambiguity of the photograph," taken from *Another Way of Telling* (written with Jean Mohr). An English art critic and novelist, Berger deconstructs the authority of visual representation and exposes some of its fundamental characteristics and limitations. He offers much food for thought in this excerpt and contributes a necessary critical perspective to any discussion of the relationship between technology and truth.

Erika Brady outlined the history of the use of phonographs in ethnographic research in her book *A Spiral Way: How the Phonograph Changed Ethnography*. In chapter 5 she introduces us to the Boasian enthusiasm for phonographs (in keeping with critical positivist concerns) and the lingering ambivalence of other researchers who variously felt that it denuded "real" performances of their vitality, was somewhat less than reliable, and was best confined to facilitating transcriptions. Brady concludes with an intriguing discussion of how the phonograph's authority could be appropriated quite unexpectedly by cultural informants. As with the camera, a direct consequence of the perceived "truthfulness" of the phonograph was its strategic employment in negotiations over power and struggles over representation.

NOTE

1   Lewis Lapham, in McLuhan (1994).

SUGGESTED READINGS

Banks, Marcus and Howard Morphy, eds. 1997. *Rethinking Visual Anthropology*. New Haven, CT: Yale University Press.
Banta, Martha and Curtis Hinsley. 1986. *From Site to Sight: Anthropology, Photography, and the Power of Imagery*. Cambridge, MA: Peabody Museum of Harvard University, Harvard University Press.

Barthes, Roland. 1977. "The rhetoric of the image." Pp. 32–51 in *Image-Music-Text*. London: Fontana.

—— 1981. *Camera Lucida: Reflections on Photography*. Trans. Richard Howard. New York: Hill and Wang.

Bate, David. 1993. "Photography and the colonial vision," *Third Text* 22: 81–91.

Berger, John. 1972. *Ways of Seeing*. Harmondsworth: Penguin/BBC Books.

Berger, John and Jean Mohr. 1982. *Another Way of Telling*. New York: Pantheon Books.

Bourdieu, Pierre. 1990. *Photography: A Middle-Brow Art*. Trans. Shaun Whiteside. Cambridge: Polity Press.

—— 1991. "Towards a sociology of photography," *Visual Anthropology Review* 7 (1): 129–33.

Brady, Erika. 1999. *A Spiral Way: How the Phonograph Changed Ethnography*. Jackson: University Press of Mississippi.

Collier, John, Jr. and Malcolm Collier. 1986. *Visual Anthropology: Photography as a Research Method*. Albuquerque: University of New Mexico Press.

Devereaux, Leslie and Roger Hillman, eds. 1995. *Fields of Vision: Essays in Film Studies, Visual Anthropology, and Photography*. Berkeley: University of California Press.

Edwards, Elizabeth, ed. 1992. *Anthropology and Photography, 1860–1920*. New Haven, CT: Yale University Press.

Henley, Paul. 1998. "Seeing is understanding. Review of *Rethinking Visual Anthropology*, ed. Marcus Banks and Howard Morphy," *Times Literary Supplement*, May 8, 1998.

Hockings, Paul, ed. 1995. *Principles of Visual Anthropology*, 2nd edn. The Hauge: Mouton.

Lutz, Catherine and Jane Collins. 1991. "The photograph as an intersection of gazes: the example of *National Geographic*," *Visual Anthropology Review* 7 (1): 134–49.

McLuhan, Marshall. 1994. *Understanding Media: The Extensions of Man*. Cambridge, MA: MIT Press.

Mead, Margaret. 1956. "Some uses of still photography in culture and personality." Pp. 79–103 in *Personal Character and Cultural Milieu*, ed. D. G. Haring. Syracuse, NY: Syracuse University Press.

—— 1968. "Anthropology and the camera." Pp. 166–85 in *The Encyclopedia of Photography*, vol. 1, ed. Willard Morgan. New York: Grestone Press.

—— 1975. "Visual anthropology in a discipline of words." Pp. 3–10 in *Principles of Visual Anthropology*, ed. Paul Hockings. The Hague: Mouton.

Mead, Margaret and Rhoda Metraux, eds. 1953. *The Study of Culture at a Distance*. Chicago: University of Chicago Press.

Miller, Toby. 1998. *Technologies of Truth: Cultural Citizenship and the Popular Media*. Minneapolis: University of Minnesota Press.

Piette, Albert. 1993. "Epistemology and practical applications of anthropological photography," *Visual Anthropology* 6 (2): 157–70.

Pinney, Christopher. 1992. "The parallel histories of anthropology and photography." Pp. 74–95 in *Anthropology and Photography, 1860–1920*, ed. Elizabeth Edwards. New Haven, CT: Yale University Press.

Scruton, Roger. 1981. "Photography and representation," *Critical Inquiry* 7: 577–603.

Sontag, Susan. 1990 [1977]. *On Photography*. New York: Anchor Books.

Spitulnik, Debra. 1993. "Anthropology and mass media," *Annual Review of Anthropology* 22: 293–315.

Tagg, John. 1988. *The Burden of Representation: Essays on Photographies and Histories*. Amherst: University of Massachusetts Press.

Walton, Kendall L. 1984. "Transparent pictures: on the nature of photographic realism," *Critical Inquiry* 11: 246–77.

Williams, Raymond. 1974. *Television: Technology and Cultural Form*. New York: Schocken Books.

1

The Medium is the Message

Marshall McLuhan

In a culture like ours, long accustomed to splitting and dividing all things as a means of control, it is sometimes a bit of a shock to be reminded that, in operational and practical fact, the medium is the message. This is merely to say that the personal and social consequences of any medium – that is, of any extension of ourselves – result from the new scale that is introduced into our affairs by each extension of ourselves, or by any new technology. Thus, with automation, for example, the new patterns of human association tend to eliminate jobs, it is true. That is the negative result. Positively, automation creates roles for people, which is to say depth of involvement in their work and human association that our preceding mechanical technology had destroyed. Many people would be disposed to say that it was not the machine, but what one did with the machine, that was its meaning or message. In terms of the ways in which the machine altered our relations to one another and to ourselves, it mattered not in the least whether it turned out cornflakes or Cadillacs. The restructuring of human work and association was shaped by the technique of fragmentation that is the essence of machine technology. The essence of automation technology is the opposite. It is integral and decentralist in depth, just as the machine was fragmentary, centralist, and superficial in its patterning of human relationships.

The instance of the electric light may prove illuminating in this connection. The electric light is pure information. It is a medium without a message, as it were, unless it is used to spell out some verbal ad or name. This fact, characteristic of all media, means that the "content" of any medium is always another medium. The content of writing is speech, just as the written word is the content of print, and print is the content of the telegraph. If it is asked, "What is the content of speech?," it is necessary to say, "It is an actual process of thought, which is in itself nonverbal." An abstract painting represents direct manifestation of creative thought processes as they might appear in computer designs. What we are considering here, however, are the psychic and social consequences of the designs or patterns as they amplify or accelerate existing processes. For the "message" of any medium or technology is the change of scale or pace or pattern that it introduces into human affairs. The railway did not introduce movement or transportation or wheel or road into human society, but it accelerated and enlarged the scale of previous human functions, creating totally new kinds of cities and new kinds of work and leisure. This happened whether the railway functioned in a tropical or a northern environment, and is quite independent of the freight or content of the railway medium. The airplane, on the other hand, by accelerating the rate of transportation, tends to dissolve the railway form of city, politics, and association, quite independently of what the airplane is used for.

Let us return to the electric light. Whether the light is being used for brain surgery or night baseball is a matter of indifference. It could be argued that these activities are in some way the "content" of the electric light, since they could not exist without the electric light. This fact merely underlines the point that "the medium is the message" because it is the medium that shapes and controls the scale and form of human association and action. The content or uses of such media are as diverse as they are ineffectual in shaping the form of human association. Indeed, it is only too typical that the "content" of any medium blinds us to the character of the medium. It is only today that industries have become aware of the various kinds of business in which they are engaged. When IBM discovered that it was not in the business of making office equipment or business machines, but that it was in the business of processing information, then it began to navigate with clear vision. The General Electric Company makes a considerable portion of its profits from electric light bulbs and lighting systems. It has not yet discovered that, quite as much as AT&T, it is in the business of moving information.

The electric light escapes attention as a communication medium just because it has no "content." And this makes it an invaluable instance of how people fail to study media at all. For it is not till the electric light is used to spell out some brand name that it is noticed as a medium. Then it is not the light but the "content" (or what is really another medium) that is noticed. The message of the electric light is like the message of electric power in industry, totally radical, pervasive, and decentralized. For electric light and power are separate from their uses, yet they eliminate time and space factors in human association exactly as do radio, telegraph, telephone, and TV, creating involvement in depth.

A fairly complete handbook for studying the extensions of man could be made up from selections from Shakespeare. Some might quibble about whether or not he was referring to TV in these familiar lines from *Romeo and Juliet*:

> But soft! what light through yonder window breaks?
> It speaks, and yet says nothing.

In *Othello*, which, as much as *King Lear*, is concerned with the torment of people transformed by illusions, there are these lines that bespeak Shakespeare's intuition of the transforming powers of new media:

> Is there not charms
> By which the property of youth and maidhood
> May be abus'd? Have you not read Roderigo,
> Of some such thing?

In Shakespeare's *Troilus and Cressida*, which is almost completely devoted to both a psychic and social study of communication, Shakespeare states his awareness that true social and political navigation depend upon anticipating the consequences of innovation:

> The providence that's in a watchful state
> Knows almost every grain of Plutus' gold,
> Finds bottom in the uncomprehensive deeps,
> Keeps place with thought, and almost like the gods
> Does thoughts unveil in their dumb cradles.

The increasing awareness of the action of media, quite independently of their "content" or programming, was indicated in the annoyed and anonymous stanza:

> In modern thought, (if not in fact)
> Nothing is that doesn't act,
> So that is reckoned wisdom which
> Describes the scratch but not the itch.

The same kind of total, configurational awareness that reveals why the medium is socially the message has occurred in the most recent and radical medical theories. In his *Stress of Life*, Hans Selye tells of the dismay of a research colleague on hearing of Selye's theory:

When he saw me thus launched on yet another enraptured description of what I had observed in animals treated with this or that impure, toxic material, he looked at me with desperately sad eyes and said in obvious despair: "But Selye, try to realize what you are doing before it is too late! You have now decided to spend your entire life studying the pharmacology of dirt!" (Hans Selye, *The Stress of Life*)

As Selye deals with the total environmental situation in his "stress" theory of disease, so the latest approach to media study considers not only the "content" but the medium and the cultural matrix within which the particular medium operates. The older unawareness of the psychic and social effects of media can be illustrated from almost any of the conventional pronouncements.

In accepting an honorary degree from the University of Notre Dame a few years ago, General David Sarnoff made this statement: "We are too prone to make technological instruments the scapegoats for the sins of those who wield them. The products of modern science are not in themselves good or bad; it is the way they are used that determines their value." That is the voice of the current somnambulism. Suppose we were to say, "Apple pie is in itself neither good nor bad; it is the way it is used that determines its value." Or, "The smallpox virus is in itself neither good nor bad; it is the way it is used that determines its value." Again, "Firearms are in themselves neither good nor bad; it is the way they are used that determines their value." That is, if the slugs reach the right people firearms are good. If the TV tube fires the right ammunition at the right people it is good. I am not being perverse. There is simply nothing in the Sarnoff statement that will bear scrutiny, for it ignores the nature of the medium, of any and all media, in the true Narcissus style of one hypnotized by the amputation and extension of his own being in a new technical form. General Sarnoff went on to explain his attitude to the technology of print, saying that it was true that print caused much trash to circulate, but it had also disseminated the Bible and the thoughts of seers and philosophers. It has never occurred to General Sarnoff that any technology could do anything but *add* itself on to what we already are.

Such economists as Robert Theobald, W. W. Rostow, and John Kenneth Galbraith have been explaining for years how it is that "classical economics" cannot explain change or growth. And the paradox of mechanization is that although it is itself the cause of maximal growth and change, the principle of mechanization excludes the very possibility of growth or the understanding of change. For mechanization is achieved by fragmentation of any process and by putting the fragmented parts in a series. Yet, as David Hume showed in the eighteenth century, there is no principle of causality in a mere sequence. That one thing follows another accounts for nothing. Nothing follows from following, except change. So the greatest of all reversals occurred with electricity, that ended sequence by making things instant. With instant speed the causes of things began to emerge to awareness again, as they had not done with things in sequence and in concatenation accordingly. Instead of asking which came first, the chicken or the egg, it suddenly seemed that a chicken was an egg's idea for getting more eggs.

Just before an airplane breaks the sound barrier, sound waves become visible on the wings of the plane. The sudden visibility of sound just as sound ends is an apt instance of that great pattern of being that reveals new and opposite forms just as the earlier forms reach their peak performance. Mechanization was never so vividly fragmented or sequential as in the birth of the movies, the moment that translated us beyond mechanism into the world of growth and organic interrelation. The movie, by sheer speeding up the mechanical, carried us from the world of sequence and connections into the world of creative configuration and structure. The message of the movie medium is that of transition from lineal connections to configurations. It is the transition that produced the now quite correct observation: "If it works, it's obsolete." When electric speed further takes over from mechanical movie sequences, then the lines of force in structures and in media become loud and clear. We return to the inclusive form of the icon.

To a highly literate and mechanized culture the movie appeared as a world of triumphant illusions and dreams that money could buy. It was at this moment of the movie that cubism occurred, and it has been described by E. H. Gombrich (*Art and Illusion*) as "the most radical attempt to stamp out ambiguity and to enforce one reading of the picture – that of a man-made construction, a colored canvas." For cubism substitutes all facets of an object simultaneously for the "point of view" or facet of perspective illusion. Instead of the specialized illusion of the third dimension on canvas, cubism sets up an interplay of planes and contradiction or dramatic conflict of patterns, lights, textures that "drives home the message" by involvement. This is held by many to be an exercise in painting, not in illusion.

In other words, cubism, by giving the inside and outside, the top, bottom, back, and front and the rest, in two dimensions, drops the illusion of perspective in favor of instant sensory awareness of the whole. Cubism, by seizing on instant total awareness, suddenly announced that *the medium is the message*. Is it not evident that the moment that sequence yields to the simultaneous, one is in the world of the structure and of configuration? Is that not what has happened in physics as in painting, poetry, and in communication? Specialized segments of attention have shifted to total field, and we can now say, "The medium is the message" quite naturally. Before the electric speed and total field, it was not obvious that the medium is the message. The message, it seemed, was the "content," as people used to ask what a painting was *about*. Yet they never thought to ask what a melody was about, nor what a house or a dress was about. In such matters, people retained some sense of the whole pattern, of form and function as a unity. But in the electric age this integral idea of structure and configuration has become so prevalent that educational theory has taken up the matter. Instead of working with specialized "problems" in arithmetic, the structural approach now follows the linea of force in the field of number and has small children meditating about number theory and "sets."

Cardinal Newman said of Napoleon, "He understood the grammar of gunpowder." Napoleon had paid some attention to other media as well, especially the semaphore telegraph that gave him a great advantage over his enemies. He is on record for saying that "Three hostile newspapers are more to be feared than a thousand bayonets."

Alexis de Tocqueville was the first to master the grammer of print and typography. He was thus able to read off the message of coming change in France and America as if he were reading aloud from a text that had been handed to him. In fact, the nineteenth century in France and in America was just such an open book to de Tocqueville because he had learned the grammar of print. So he, also, knew when that grammar did not apply. He was asked why he did not write a book on England, since he knew and admired England. He replied:

One would have to have an unusual degree of philosophical folly to believe oneself able to judge England in six months. A year always seemed to me too short a time in which to appreciate the United States properly, and it is much easier to acquire clear and precise notions about the American Union than about Great Britain. In America all laws derive in a sense from the same line of thought. The whole of society, so to speak, is founded upon a single fact; everything springs from a simple principle. One could compare America to a forest pierced by a multitude of straight roads all converging on the same point. One has only to find the center and everything is revealed at a glance. But in England the paths run criss-cross, and it is only by travelling down each one of them that one can build up a picture of the whole.

De Tocqueville, in earlier work on the French Revolution, had explained how it was the printed word that, achieving cultural saturation in the eighteenth century, had homogenized the French nation. Frenchmen were the same kind of people from north to south. The typographic principles of uniformity, continuity, and lineality had overlaid the complexities of ancient feudal and oral society. The Revolution was carried out by the new literati and lawyers.

In England, however, such was the power of the ancient oral traditions of common law, backed by the medieval institution of Parliament, that no uniformity or continuity of the new visual print culture could take complete hold. The result was that the most important event in English history has never taken place; namely, the English Revolution on the lines of the French Revolution. The American Revolution had no medieval legal institutions to discard or to root out, apart from monarchy. And many have held that the American Presidency has become very much more personal and monarchical than any European monarch ever could be.

De Tocqueville's contrast between England and America is clearly based on the fact of typography and of print culture creating uniformity and continuity. England, he says, has rejected this principle and clung to the dynamic or oral common-law tradition. Hence the discontinuity and unpredictable quality of English culture. The grammar of print cannot help to construe the message of oral and nonwritten culture and institutions. The English aristocracy was properly classified as barbarian by Matthew Arnold because its power and status had nothing to do with literacy or with the cultural forms of typography. Said the Duke of Gloucester to Edward Gibbon upon the publication of his *Decline and Fall*: "Another damned fat book, eh, Mr. Gibbon? Scribble, scribble, scribble, eh, Mr. Gibbon?" De Tocqueville was a highly literate aristocrat who was quite able to be detached from the values and assumptions of typography. That is why he alone understood the grammar of typography. And it is only on those terms, standing aside from any structure or medium, that its principles and lines of force can be discerned. For any medium has the power of imposing its own assumption on the unwary. Prediction and control consist in avoiding this subliminal state of Narcissus trance. But the greatest aid to this end is simply in knowing that the spell can occur immediately upon contact, as in the first bars of a melody.

A Passage to India by E. M. Forster is a dramatic study of the inability of oral and intuitive oriental culture to meet with the rational, visual European patterns of experience. "Rational," of course, has for the West long meant "uniform and continuous and sequential." In other words, we have confused reason with literacy, and rationalism with a single technology. Thus in the electric age man seems to the conventional West to become irrational. In Forster's novel the moment of truth and dislocation from the typographic trance of the West comes in the Marabar Caves. Adela Quested's reasoning powers cannot cope with the total inclusive field of resonance that is India. After the Caves: "Life went on as usual, but had no consequences, that is to say, sounds did not echo nor thought develop. Everything seemed cut off at its root and therefore infected with illusion."

A Passage to India (the phrase is from Whitman, who saw America headed Eastward) is a parable of Western man in the electric age, and is only incidentally related to Europe or the Orient. The ultimate conflict between sight and sound, between written and oral kinds of perception and organization of existence is upon us. Since understanding stops action, as Nietzsche observed, we can moderate the fierceness of this conflict by understanding the media that extend us and raise these wars within and without us.

Detribalization by literacy and its traumatic effects on tribal man is the theme of a book by the psychiatrist J. C. Carothers, *The African Mind in Health and Disease* (World Health Organization, Geneva, 1953). Much of his material appeared in an article in *Psychiatry* magazine, November, 1959: "The Culture, Psychiatry, and the Written Word." Again, it is electric speed that has revealed the lines of force operating from Western technology in the remotest areas of bush, savannah, and desert. One example is the Bedouin with his battery radio on board the camel. Submerging natives with floods of concepts for which nothing has prepared them is the normal action of all of our technology. But with electric media Western man himself experiences exactly the same inundation as the remote native. We are no more prepared to encounter radio and TV in our literate milieu than the native of Ghana is able to cope with the literacy that takes him out of his collective tribal world and beaches him in individual isolation. We are as numb in our new electric world as the native involved in our literate and mechanical culture.

Electric speed mingles the cultures of prehistory with the dregs of industrial marketeers, the nonliterate with the semiliterate and the postliterate. Mental breakdown of varying degrees is the very common result of uprooting and inundation with new information and endless new patterns of information. Wyndham Lewis made this a theme of his group of novels called *The Human Age*. The first of these, *The Childermass*, is concerned precisely with accelerated media change as a kind of massacre of the innocents. In our own world as we become more aware of the effects of technology on psychic formation and manifestation, we are losing all confidence in our right to assign guilt. Ancient prehistoric societies regard violent crime as pathetic. The killer is regarded as we do a cancer victim. "How terrible it must be to feel like that," they say. J. M. Synge took up this idea very effectively in his *Playboy of the Western World*.

If the criminal appears as a nonconformist who is unable to meet the demand of technology that we behave in uniform and continuous patterns, literate man is quite inclined to see others who cannot conform as somewhat pathetic. Especially the child, the cripple, the woman, and the colored person appear in a world of visual and typographic technology as victims of injustice. On the other hand, in a culture that assigns roles instead of jobs to people – the dwarf, the skew, the child create their own spaces. They are not expected to fit into some uniform and repeatable niche that is not their size anyway. Consider the phrase "It's a man's world." As a quantitative observation endlessly repeated from within a homogenized culture, this phrase refers to the men in such a culture who have to be homogenized Dagwoods in order to belong at all. It is in our IQ testing that we have produced the greatest flood of misbegotten standards. Unaware of our typographic cultural bias, our testers assume that uniform and continuous habits are a sign of intelligence, thus eliminating the ear man and the tactile man.

C. P. Snow, reviewing a book of A. L. Rowse (*The New York Times Book Review*, December 24, 1961) on *Appeasement* and the road to Munich, describes the top level of British brains and experience in the 1930s. "Their IQ's were much higher than usual among political bosses. Why were they such a disaster?" The view of Rowse, Snow approves: "They would not listen to warnings because they did not wish to hear." Being anti-Red made it impossible for them to read the message of Hitler. But their failure was as nothing compared to our present one. The American stake in literacy as a technology or uniformity applied to every level of education, government, industry, and social life is totally threatened by the electric technology. The threat of Stalin or Hitler was external. The electric technology is within the gates, and we are numb, deaf, blind, and mute about its encounter with the Gutenberg technology, on and through which the American way of life was formed. It is, however, no time to suggest strategies when the threat has not even been acknowledged to exist. I am in the position of Louis Pasteur telling doctors that their greatest enemy was quite invisible, and quite unrecognized by them. Our conventional response to all media, namely that it is how they are used that counts, is the numb stance of the technological idiot. For the "content" of a medium is like the juicy piece of meat carried by the burglar to distract the watchdog of the mind. The effect of the medium is made strong and intense just because it is given another medium as "content." The content of a movie is a novel or a play or an opera. The effect of the movie form is not related to its program content. The "content" of writing or print is speech, but the reader is almost entirely unaware either of print or of speech.

Arnold Toynbee is innocent of any understanding of media as they have shaped history, but he is full of examples that the student of media can use. At one moment he can seriously suggest that adult education, such as the Workers Educational Association in Britain, is a useful counterforce to the popular press. Toynbee considers that although all of the oriental societies have in our time accepted the industrial technology and its political consequences: "On the cultural plane, however, there is no uniform corresponding tendency." This is like the voice of the literate man, floundering in a milieu of ads, who boasts, "Personally, I pay no attention to ads." The spiritual and cultural reservations that the oriental peoples may have toward our technology will avail them not at all. The effects of technology do not occur at the level of opinions or concepts, but alter sense ratios or patterns of perception steadily and without any resistance. The serious artist is the only person able to encounter technology with impunity, just because he is an expert aware of the changes in sense perception.

The operation of the money medium in seventeenth-century Japan had effects not unlike the operation of typography in the West. The penetration of the money economy, wrote G. B. Sansom (in *Japan*, Cresset Press, London, 1931), "caused a slow but irresistible revolution, culminating in the breakdown of feudal government and the resumption of intercourse with foreign countries after more than two hundred years of seclusion." Money has reorganized the sense life of peoples just because it is an *extension* of our sense lives. This change does not depend upon approval or disapproval of those living in the society.

Arnold Toynbee made one approach to the transforming power of media in his concept of "etherialization," which he holds to be the principle of progressive simplification and efficiency in any organization or technology. Typically, he is ignoring the *effect* of the challenge of these forms upon the response of our senses. He imagines that it is the response of our opinions that is relevant to the effect of media and technology in society, a "point of view" that is plainly the result of the typographic spell. For the man in a literate and homogenized society ceases to be sensitive to the diverse and discontinuous life of forms. He acquires the illusion of the third dimension and the "private point of view" as part of his Narcissus fixation, and is quite shut off from Blake's awareness or that of the Psalmist, that we become what we behold.

Today when we want to get our bearings in our own culture, and have need to stand aside from the bias and pressure exerted by any technical form of human expression, we have only to visit a society where that particular form has not been felt, or a historical period in which it was unknown. Professor Wilbur Schramm made such a tactical move in studying *Television in the Lives of Our Children*. He found areas where TV had not penetrated at all and ran some tests. Since he had made no study of the peculiar nature of the TV image, his tests were of "content" preferences, viewing time, and vocabulary counts. In a word, his approach to the problem was a literary one, albeit unconsciously so. Consequently, he had nothing to report. Had his methods been employed in 1500 AD to discover the effects of the printed book in the lives of children or adults, he could have found out nothing of the changes in human and social psychology resulting from typography. Print created individualism and nationalism in the sixteenth century. Program and "content" analysis offer no clues to the magic of these media or to their subliminal charge.

Leonard Doob, in his report *Communication in Africa*, tells of one African who took great pains to listen each evening to the BBC news, even though he could understand nothing of it. Just to be in the presence of those sounds at 7 p.m. each day was important for him. His attitude to speech was like ours to melody – the resonant intonation was meaning enough. In the seventeenth century our ancestors still shared this native's attitude to the forms of media, as is plain in the following sentiment of the Frenchman Bernard Lam expressed in *The Art of Speaking* (London, 1696):

'Tis an effect of the Wisdom of God, who created Man to be happy, that whatever is useful to his conversation (way of life) is agreeable to him...because all victual that conduces to nourishment is relishable, whereas other things that cannot be assimilated and be turned into our substance are insipid. A Discourse cannot be pleasant to the Hearer that is not easie to the Speaker; nor can it be easily pronounced unless it be heard with delight.

Here is an equilibrium theory of human diet and expression such as even now we are only striving to work out again for media after centuries of fragmentation and specialism.

Pope Pius XII was deeply concerned that there be serious study of the media today. On February 17, 1950, he said:

It is not an exaggeration to say that the future of modern society and the stability of its inner life depend in large part on the maintenance of an equilibrium between the strength of the techniques of communication and the capacity of the individual's own reaction.

Failure in this respect has for centuries been typical and total for mankind. Subliminal and docile acceptance of media impact has made them prisons without walls for their human users. As A. J. Liebling remarked in his book *The Press*, a man is not free if he cannot see where he is going, even if he has a gun to help him get there. For each of the media is also a powerful weapon with which to clobber other media and other groups. The result is that the present age has been one of multiple civil wars that are not limited to the world of art and entertainment. In *War and Human Progress*, Professor J. U. Nef declared: "The total wars of our time have been the result of a series of intellectual mistakes..."

If the formative power in the media are the media themselves, that raises a host of large matters that can only be mentioned here, although they deserve volumes. Namely, that technological media are staples or natural resources, exactly as are coal and cotton and oil. Anybody will concede that society whose economy is dependent upon one or two major staples like cotton, or grain, or lumber, or fish, or cattle is going to have some obvious social patterns of organization as a result. Stress on a few major staples creates extreme instability in the economy but great endurance in the population. The pathos and humor of the American South are embedded in such an economy of limited staples. For a society configured by reliance on a few commodities accepts them as a social bond quite as much as the metropolis does the press. Cotton and oil, like radio and TV, become "fixed charges" on the entire psychic life of the community. And this pervasive fact creates the unique cultural flavor of any society. It pays through the nose and all its other senses for each staple that shapes its life.

That our human senses, of which all media are extensions, are also fixed charges on our personal energies, and that they also configure the awareness and experience of each one of us, may be perceived in another connection mentioned by the psychologist C. G. Jung:

Every Roman was surrounded by slaves. The slave and his psychology flooded ancient Italy, and every Roman became inwardly, and of course unwittingly, a slave. Because living constantly in the atmosphere of slaves, he became infected through the unconscious with their psychology. No one can shield himself from such an influence (*Contributions to Analytical Psychology*, London, 1928).

2

The Technology and the Society

Raymond Williams

It is often said that television has altered our world. In the same way, people often speak of a new world, a new society, a new phase of history, being created – 'brought about' – by this or that new technology: the steam engine, the automobile, the atomic bomb. Most of us know what is generally implied when such things are said. But this may be the central difficulty: that we have got so used to statements of this general kind, in our most ordinary discussions, that we can fail to realize their specific meanings.

For behind all such statements lie some of the most difficult and most unresolved historical and philosophical questions. Yet the questions are not posed by the statements; indeed they are ordinarily masked by them. Thus we often discuss, with animation, this or that 'effect' of television, or the kinds of social behaviour, the cultural and psychological conditions, which television has 'led to', without feeling ourselves obliged to ask whether it is reasonable to describe any technology as a cause, or, if we think of it as a cause, as what kind of cause, and in what relations with other kinds of causes. The most precise and discriminating local study of 'effects' can remain superficial if we have not looked into the notions of cause and effect, as between a technology and a society, a technology and a culture, a technology and a psychology, which underlie our questions and may often determine our answers.

It can of course be said that these fundamental questions are very much too difficult; and that they are indeed difficult is very soon obvious to anyone who tries to follow them through. We could spend our lives trying to answer them, whereas here and now, in a society in which television is important, there is immediate and practical work to be done: surveys to be made, research undertaken; surveys and research, moreover, which we know how to do. It is an appealing position, and it has the advantage, in our kind of society, that it is understood as practical, so that it can then be supported and funded. By contrast, other kinds of question seem merely theoretical and abstract.

Yet all questions about cause and effect, as between a technology and a society, are intensely practical. Until we have begun to answer them, we really do not know, in any particular case, whether, for example, we are talking about a technology or about the uses of a technology; about necessary institutions or particular and changeable institutions; about a content or about a form. And this is not only a matter of intellectual uncertainty; it is a matter of social practice. If the technology is a cause, we can at best modify or seek to control its effects. Or if the technology, as used, is an effect, to what other kinds of cause, and other kinds of action, should we refer and relate our experience of its uses? These are not abstract questions. They form an increasingly important part of our social and cultural arguments, and they are being decided all the time in real practice, by real and effective decisions.

It is with these problems in mind that I want to try to analyse television as a particular cultural technology, and to look at its development, its institutions, its forms and its effects, in this critical dimension. In the present chapter, I shall begin the analysis under three headings: (a) versions of cause and effect in technology and society; (b) the social history of television as a technology; (c) the social history of the uses of television technology.

(A) Versions of Cause and Effect in Technology and Society

We can begin by looking again at the general statement that television has altered our world. It is worth setting down some of the different things this kind of statement has been taken to mean. For example:

1   Television was invented as a result of scientific and technical research. Its power as a medium of news and entertainment was then so great that it altered all preceding media of news and entertainment.
2   Television was invented as a result of scientific and technical research. Its power as a medium of social communication was then so great that it altered many of our institutions and forms of social relationships.
3   Television was invented as a result of scientific and technical research. Its inherent properties as an electronic medium altered our basic perceptions of reality, and thence our relations with each other and with the world.
4   Television was invented as a result of scientific and technical research. As a powerful medium of communication and entertainment it took its place with other factors – such as greatly increased physical mobility, itself the result of other newly invented technologies – in altering the scale and form of our societies.
5   Television was invented as a result of scientific and technical research, and developed as a medium of entertainment and news. It then had unforeseen consequences, not only on other entertainment and news media, which it reduced in viability and importance, but on some of the central processes of family, cultural and social life.
6   Television, discovered as a possibility by scientific and technical research, was selected for investment and development to meet the needs of a new kind of society, especially in the provision of centralized entertainment and in the centralized formation of opinions and styles of behaviour.
7   Television, discovered as a possibility by scientific and technical research, was selected for investment and promotion as a new and profitable phase of a

domestic consumer economy; it is then one of the characteristic 'machines for the home'.

8 Television became available as a result of scientific and technical research, and in its character and uses exploited and emphasized elements of a passivity, a cultural and psychological inadequacy, which had always been latent in people, but which television now organized and came to represent.

9 Television became available as a result of scientific and technical research, and in its character and uses both served and exploited the needs of a new kind of large-scale and complex but atomized society.

These are only some of the possible glosses on the ordinary bald statement that television has altered our world. Many people hold mixed versions of what are really alternative opinions, and in some cases there is some inevitable overlapping. But we can distinguish between two broad classes of opinion.

In the first – (1) to (5) – the technology is in effect accidental. Beyond the strictly internal development of the technology there is no reason why any particular invention should have come about. Similarly it then has consequences which are also in the true sense accidental, since they follow directly from the technology itself. If television had not been invented, this argument would run, certain definite social and cultural events would not have occurred.

In the second – (6) to (9) – television is again, in effect, a technological accident, but its significance lies in its uses, which are held to be symptomatic of some order of society or some qualities of human nature which are otherwise determined. If television had not been invented, this argument runs, we would still be manipulated or mindlessly entertained, but in some other way and perhaps less powerfully.

For all the variations of local interpretation and emphasis, these two classes of opinion underlie the overwhelming majority of both professional and amateur views of the effects of television. What they have in common is the fundamental form of the statement: 'television has altered our world'.

It is then necessary to make a further theoretical distinction. The first class of opinion, described above, is that usually known, at least to its opponents, as *technological determinism*. It is an immensely powerful and now largely orthodox view of the nature of social change. New technologies are discovered, by an essentially internal process of research and development, which then sets the conditions for social change and progress. Progress, in particular, is the history of these inventions, which 'created the modern world'. The effects of the technologies, whether direct or indirect, foreseen or unforeseen, are as it were the rest of history. The steam engine, the automobile, television, the atomic bomb, have *made* modern man and the modern condition.

The second class of opinion appears less determinist. Television, like any other technology, becomes available as an element or a medium in a process of change that is in any case occurring or about to occur. By contrast with pure technological determinism, this view emphasizes other causal factors in social change. It then considers particular technologies, or a complex of technologies, as *symptoms* of change of some other kind. Any particular technology is then as it were a by-product of a social process that is otherwise determined. It only acquires effective status when it is used for purposes which are already contained in this known social process.

The debate between these two general positions occupies the greater part of our thinking about technology and society. It is a real debate, and each side makes important points. But it is in the end sterile, because each position, though in different ways, has abstracted technology from society. In *technological determinism*, research and development have been assumed as self-generating. The new technologies are invented as it were in an independent sphere, and then create new societies or new human conditions. The view of *symptomatic technology*, similarly, assumes that research and development are self-generating, but in a more marginal way. What is discovered in the margin is then taken up and used.

Each view can then be seen to depend on the isolation of technology. It is either a self-acting force which creates new ways of life, or it is a self-acting force which provides materials for new ways of life. These positions are so deeply established, in modern social thought, that it is very difficult to think beyond them. Most histories of technology, like most histories of scientific discovery, are written from their assumptions. An appeal to 'the facts', against this or that interpretation, is made very difficult simply because the histories are usually written, consciously or unconsciously, to illustrate the assumptions. This is either explicit, with the consequential interpretation attached, or more often implicit, in that the history of technology or of scientific development is offered as a history on its own. This can be seen as a device of specialization or of emphasis, but it then necessarily implies merely internal intentions and criteria.

To change these emphases would require prolonged and co-operative intellectual effort. But in the particular case of television it may be possible to outline a different kind of interpretation, which would allow us to see not only its history but also its uses in a more radical way. Such an interpretation would differ from technological determinism in that it would restore *intention* to the process of research and development. The technology would be seen, that is to say, as being looked for and developed with certain purposes and practices already in mind. At the same time the interpretation would differ from symptomatic technology in that these purposes and practices would be seen as *direct*: as known social needs, purposes and practices to which the technology is not marginal but central.

(B) The Social History of Television as a Technology

The invention of television was no single event or series of events. It depended on a complex of inventions and developments in electricity, telegraphy, photography and motion pictures, and radio. It can be said to have separated out as a specific technological objective in the period 1875–1890, and then, after a lag, to have developed as a specific technological enterprise from 1920 through to the first public television systems of the 1930s. Yet in each of these stages it depended for parts of its realization on inventions made with other ends primarily in view.

Until the early nineteenth century, investigations of electricity, which had long been known as a phenomenon, were primarily philosophical: investigations of a puzzling natural effect. The technology associated with these investigations was mainly directed towards isolation and concentration of the effect, for its clearer study. Towards the end of the eighteenth century there began to be applications, characteristically in relation to other known natural effects (lightning conductors). But there is then a key transitional period in a cluster of inventions between 1800 and 1831, ranging from Volta's battery to Faraday's demonstration of electromagnetic induction, leading quickly to the production of generators. This can be properly traced as a scientific history, but it is significant that the key period of advance coincides with an important stage of the development of industrial production. The advantages of electric power were closely related to new industrial needs: for mobility and transfer in the location of power sources, and for flexible and rapid controllable conversion. The steam engine had been well suited to textiles, and its industries had been based on local siting. A more extensive development, both physically and in the complexity of multiple-part processes, such as engineering, could be attempted with other power sources but could only be fully realized with electricity. There was a very complex interaction between new needs and new inventions, at the level of primary production, of new applied industries (plating) and of new social needs which were themselves related to industrial development (city and house lighting). From 1830 to large-scale generation in the 1880s there was this continuing complex of need and invention and application.

In telegraphy the development was simpler. The transmission of messages by beacons and similar primary devices had been long established. In the development of navigation and naval warfare the flag-system had been standardized in the course of the sixteenth and seventeenth centuries. During the Napoleonic wars there was a marked development of land telegraphy, by semaphore stations, and some of this survived into peacetime. Electrical telegraphy had been suggested as a technical system as early as 1753, and was actually demonstrated in several places in the early nineteenth century. An English inventor in 1816 was told that the Admiralty was not interested. It is interesting that it was the development of the railways, themselves a response to the development of an industrial system and the related growth of cities, which clarified the need for improved telegraphy. A complex of technical possibilities was brought to a working system from 1837 onwards. The development of international trade and transport brought rapid extensions of the system, including the transatlantic cable in the 1850s and the 1860s. A general system of electric telegraphy had been established by the 1870s, and in the same decade the telephone system began to be developed, in this case as a new and intended invention.

In photography, the idea of light-writing had been suggested by (among others) Wedgwood and Davy in 1802, and the *camera obscura* had already been developed. It was not the projection but the fixing of images which at first awaited technical solution, and from 1816 (Niepce) and through to 1839 (Daguerre) this was worked on, together with the improvement of camera devices. Professional and then amateur photography spread rapidly, and reproduction and then transmission, in the developing newspaper press, were achieved. By the 1880s the idea of a 'photographed reality' – still more for record than for observation – was familiar.

The idea of moving pictures had been similarly developing. The magic lantern (slide projection) had been known from the seventeenth century, and had acquired simple motion (one slide over another) by 1736. From at latest 1826 there was a development of mechanical motion-picture devices, such as the wheel-of-life, and these came to be linked with the magic lantern. The effect of persistence in human vision – that is to say, our capacity to hold the 'memory' of an image through an interval to the next image, thus allowing the possibility of a sequence built from rapidly succeeding units – had been known since classical times. Series of cameras photographing stages of a sequence were followed (Marey, 1882) by multiple-shot cameras. Friese-Greene and Edison worked on techniques of filming and projection, and celluloid was substituted for paper reels. By the 1890s the first public motion-picture shows were being given in France, America and England.

Television, as an idea, was involved with many of these developments. It is difficult to separate it, in its earliest stages, from photo-telegraphy. Bain proposed a device for transmitting pictures by electric wires in 1842; Bakewell in 1847 showed the copying telegraph; Caselli in 1862 transmitted pictures by wire over a considerable distance. In 1873, while working at a terminal of the Atlantic telegraph cable, May observed the light-sensitive properties of selenium (which had been isolated by Berzelius in 1817 and was in use for resistors). In a host of ways, following an already defined need, the means of transmitting still pictures and moving pictures were actively sought and to a considerable extent discovered. The list is long even when selective: Carey's electric eye in 1875; Nipkow's scanning system in 1884; Elster and Geitel's photo-electric cells in 1890; Braun's cathode-ray tube in 1897; Rosing's cathode-ray receiver in 1907; Campbell Swinton's electronic camera proposal in 1911. Through this whole period two facts are evident: that a system of television was foreseen, and its means were being actively sought; but also that, by comparison with electrical generation and electrical telegraphy and telephony, there was very little social investment to bring the scattered work together. It is true that there were technical blocks before 1914 – the thermionic valve and the multi-stage amplifier can be seen to have been needed and were not yet invented. But the critical difference between the various spheres of applied technology can be stated in terms of a social dimension: the new systems of production and of business or transport communication were already organized, at an economic level; the new systems of social communication were not. Thus when motion pictures were developed, their application was characteristically in the margin of established social forms – the sideshows – until their success was capitalized in a version of an established form, the motion-picture *theatre*.

The development of radio, in its significant scientific and technical stages between 1885 and 1911, was at first conceived, within already effective social systems, as an advanced form of telegraphy. Its application as a significantly new social form belongs to the immediate postwar period, in a changed social situation. It is significant that the hiatus in technical television development then also ended. In 1923 Zworykin introduced the electronic television camera tube. Through the early 1920s Baird and Jenkins, separately and competitively, were working on systems using mechanical scanning. From 1925 the rate of progress was qualitatively changed, through important technical advances but also with the example of sound broadcasting systems as a model. The Bell System in 1927 demonstrated wire transmission through a radio link, and the pre-history of the form can be seen to be ending. There was great rivalry between systems – especially those of mechanical and electronic scanning – and there is still great controversy about contributions and priorities. But this is characteristic of the phase in which the development of a technology moves into the stage of a new social form.

What is interesting throughout is that in a number of complex and related fields, these systems of mobility and transfer in production and communication, whether in mechanical and electric transport, or in telegraphy, photography, motion pictures, radio and television, were at once incentives and responses within a phase of general social transformation. Though some of the crucial scientific and technical discoveries were made by isolated and unsupported individuals, there was a crucial community of selected emphasis and intention, in a society characterized at its most general levels by a mobility and extension of the scale of organizations: forms of growth which brought with them immediate and longer-term problems of operative communication. In many different countries, and in apparently unconnected ways, such needs were at once isolated and technically defined. It is especially a characteristic of the communications systems that *all were foreseen – not in utopian but in technical ways – before the crucial components of the developed systems had been discovered and refined*. In no way is this a history of communications systems creating a new society or new social conditions. The decisive and earlier transformation of industrial production, and its new social forms, which had grown out of a long history of capital accumulation and working technical improvements, created new needs but also new possibilities, and the communications systems, down to television, were their intrinsic outcome.

(C) The Social History of the Uses of Television Technology

It is never quite true to say that in modern societies, when a social need has been demonstrated, its appropriate technology will be found. This is partly because some real needs, in any particular period, are beyond the scope of existing or foreseeable scientific and technical knowledge. It is even more because the key question, about technological response to a need, is less a question about the need itself than about its place in an existing social formation. A need which corresponds with the priorities of the real decision-making groups will, obviously, more quickly attract the investment of resources and the official permission, approval or encouragement on which a working technology, as distinct from available technical devices, depends. We can see this clearly in the major developments of industrial production and, significantly, in military technology. The social history of communications technology is interestingly different from either of these, and it is important to try to discover what are the real factors of this variation.

The problem must be seen at several different levels. In the very broadest perspective, there is an operative relationship between a new kind of expanded, mobile and complex society and the development of a modern communications technology. At one level this relationship can be reasonably seen as causal, in a direct way. The principal incentives to first-stage improvements in communications technology came from problems of communication and control in expanded military and commercial operations. This was both direct, arising from factors of greatly extending distance and scale, and indirect, as a factor within the development of transport technology, which was for obvious reasons the major direct response. Thus telegraphy and telephony, and in its early stages radio, were secondary factors within a primary communications system which was directly serving the needs of an established and developing military and commercial system. Through the nineteenth and into the twentieth century this was the decisive pattern.

But there were other social and political relationships and needs emerging from this complex of change. Indeed it is a consequence of the particular and dominant interpretation of these changes that the complex was at first seen as one requiring improvement in *operational* communication. The direct priorities of the expanding commercial system, and in certain periods of the military system, led to a definition of needs within the terms of these systems. The objectives and the consequent technologies were operational within the structures of these systems: passing necessary specific information, or maintaining contact and control. Modern electric technology, in this phase, was thus oriented to uses of person to person, operator and operative to operator and operative, within established specific structures. This quality can best be emphasized by contrast with the electric technology of the second phase, which was properly and significantly called *broadcasting*. A technology of specific messages to specific persons was complemented, but only relatively late, by a technology of varied messages to a general public.

Yet to understand this development we have to look at a wider communications system. The true basis of this system had preceded the developments in technology. Then as now there was a major, indeed dominant, area of social communication, by word of mouth, within every kind of social group. In addition, then as now, there were specific institutions of that kind of communication which involves or is predicated on social teaching and control: churches, schools, assemblies and proclamations, direction in places of work. All these interacted with forms of communication within the family.

What then were the new needs which led to the development of a new technology of social communication? The development of the press gives us the evidence for our first major instance. It was at once a response to the development of an extended social, economic and political system and a response to crisis within that system. The centralization of political power led to a need for messages from that centre along other than official lines. Early newspapers were a combination of that kind of message – political and social information – and the specific messages – classified advertising and general commercial news – of an expanding system of trade. In Britain the development of the press went through its major formative stages in periods of crisis: the Civil War and Commonwealth, when the newspaper form was defined; the Industrial Revolution, when new forms of popular journalism were successively established; the major wars of the twentieth century, when the newspaper became a universal social form. For the transmission of simple orders, a communications system already existed. For the transmission of an ideology, there were specific traditional institutions. But for the transmission of news and background – the whole orienting, predictive and updating process which the fully developed press represented – there was an evident need for a new form, which the largely traditional institutions of church and school could not meet. And to the large extent that the crises of general change provoked both anxiety and controversy, this flexible and competitive form met social needs of a new kind. As the struggle for a share in decision and control became sharper, in campaigns for the vote and then in competition for the vote, the press became not only a new communications system but, centrally, a new social institution.

This can be interpreted as response to a political need and a political crisis, and it was certainly this. But a wider social need and social crisis can also be recognized. In a changing society, and especially after the Industrial Revolution, problems of social perspective and social orientation became more acute. New relations between men, and between men and things, were being intensely experienced, and in this area, especially, the traditional institutions of church and school, or of settled community and persisting family, had very little to say. A great deal was of course said, but from positions defined within an older kind of society. In a number of ways, and drawing on a range of impulses from curiosity to anxiety, new information and new kinds of orientation were deeply required: more deeply, indeed, than any specialization to political, military or commercial information can account for. An increased awareness of mobility and change, not just as abstractions but as lived experiences, led to a major redefinition, in practice and then in theory, of the function and process of social communication.

What can be seen most evidently in the press can be seen also in the development of photography and the motion picture. The photograph is in one sense a popular extension of the portrait, for recognition and for record. But in a period of great mobility, with new separations of families and with internal and external migrations, it became more centrally necessary as a form of maintaining, over distance and through time, certain personal connections. Moreover, in altering relations to the physical world, the photograph as an object became a form of the photography of objects: moments of isolation and stasis within an experienced rush of change; and then, in its technical extension to motion, a means of observing and analysing motion itself, in new ways – a dynamic form in which new kinds of recognition were not only possible but necessary.

Now it is significant that until the period after the First World War, and in some ways until the period after the Second World War, these varying needs of a new kind of society and a new way of life were met by what were seen as specialized means: the press for political and economic information; the photograph for community, family and personal life; the motion picture for curiosity and entertainment; telegraphy and telephony for business information and some important personal messages. It was within this complex of specialized forms that broadcasting arrived.

The consequent difficulty of defining its social uses, and the intense kind of controversy which has ever since surrounded it, can then be more broadly understood. Moreover, the first definitions of broadcasting were made for sound radio. It is significant and perhaps puzzling that the definitions and institutions then created were those within which television developed.

We have now become used to a situation in which broadcasting is a major social institution, about which there is always controversy but which, in its familiar form, seems to have been predestined by the technology. This predestination, however, when closely examined, proves to be no more than a set of particular social decisions, in particular circumstances, which were then so widely if imperfectly ratified that it is now difficult to see them as decisions rather than as (retrospectively) inevitable results.

Thus, if seen only in hindsight, broadcasting can be diagnosed as a new and powerful form of social integration and control. Many of its main uses can be seen as socially, commercially and at times politically manipulative. Moreover, this viewpoint is rationalized by its description as 'mass communication', a phrase used by almost all its agents and advisers as well, curiously, as by most of its radical critics. 'Masses' had been the new nineteenth-century term of contempt for what was formerly described as 'the mob'. The physical 'massing' of the urban and industrial revolution underwrote this. A new radical class-consciousness adopted the term to express the material of new social formations: 'mass organizations'. The 'mass meeting' was an observable physical effect. So pervasive was this description that in the twentieth century multiple serial production was called, falsely but significantly, 'mass production': mass now meant large numbers (but within certain assumed social relationships) rather than any physical or social aggregate. Sound radio and television, for reasons we shall look at, were developed for transmission to *individual* homes, though there was nothing in the technology to make this inevitable. But then this new form of social communication – broadcasting – was obscured by its definition as 'mass communication': an abstraction to its most general characteristic, that it went to many people, 'the masses', which obscured the fact that the means chosen was the offer of individual sets, a method much better described by the earlier word 'broadcasting'. It is interesting that the only developed 'mass' use of radio was in Nazi Germany, where under Goebbels' orders the Party organized compulsory public listening groups and the receivers were in the streets. There has been some imitation of this by similar regimes, and Goebbels was deeply interested in television for the same kind of use. What was developed within most capitalist societies, though called 'mass communication', was significantly different.

There was early official intervention in the development of broadcasting, but in form this was only at a technical level. In the earlier struggle against the development of the press, the State had licensed and taxed newspapers, but for a century before the coming of broadcasting the alternative idea of an independent press had been realized both in practice and in theory. State intervention in broadcasting had some real and some plausible technical grounds: the distribution of wave-lengths. But to these were added, though always controversially, more general social directions or attempts at direction. This social history of broadcasting can be discussed on its own, at the levels of practice and principle. Yet it is unrealistic to extract it from another and perhaps more decisive process, through which, in particular economic situations, a set of scattered technical devices became an applied technology and then a social technology.

A Fascist regime might quickly see the use of broadcasting for direct political and social control. But that, in any case, was when the technology had already been developed elsewhere. In capitalist democracies, the thrust for conversion from scattered techniques to a technology was not political but economic. The characteristically isolated inventors, from Nipkow and Rosing to Baird and Jenkins and Zwyorkin, found their point of development, if at all, in the manufacturers and prospective manufacturers of the technical apparatus. The history at one level is of these isolated names, but at another level it is of EMI, RCA and a score of similar companies and corporations. In the history of motion pictures, capitalist development was primarily in production; large-scale capitalist distribution came much later, as a way of controlling and organizing a market for given production. In broadcasting, both in sound radio and later in television, the major investment was in the means of distribution, and was devoted to production only so far as to make the distribution technically possible and then attractive. Unlike all previous communications technologies, radio and television were *systems primarily devised for transmission and reception as abstract processes, with little or no definition of preceding content*. When the question of content was raised, it was resolved, in the main, parasitically. There were state occasions, public sporting events, theatres and so on, which would be communicatively distributed by these new technical means. *It is not only that the supply of broadcasting facilities preceded the demand; it is that the means of communication preceded their content.*

The period of decisive development in sound broadcasting was the 1920s. After the technical advances in sound telegraphy which had been made for military purposes during the war, there was at once an economic opportunity and the need for a new social definition. No nation or manufacturing group held a monopoly of the technical means of broadcasting, and there was a period of intensive litigation followed by cross-licensing of the scattered basic components of successful transmission and reception (the vacuum tube or valve, developed from 1904 to 1913; the feedback circuit, developed from 1912; the neutrodyne and heterodyne circuits, from 1923). Crucially, in the mid-1920s, there was a series of investment-guided technical solutions to the problem of building a small and simple domestic receiver, on which the whole qualitative transformation from wireless telegraphy to broadcasting depended. By the mid-1920s – 1923 and 1924 are especially decisive years – this breakthrough had happened in the leading industrial societies: the United States, Britain, Germany and France. By the end of the 1920s the radio industry had become a major sector of industrial production, within a rapid general expansion of the new kinds of machines which were eventually to be called 'consumer durables'. This complex of developments included the motorcycle and motor-car, the box camera and its successors, home electrical appliances, and radio sets. Socially, this complex is characterized by the two apparently paradoxical yet deeply connected tendencies of modern urban industrial living: on the one hand mobility, on the other hand the more apparently self-sufficient family home. The earlier period of public technology, best exemplified by the railways and city lighting, was being replaced by a kind of technology for which no satisfactory name has yet been found: that which served an at once mobile and home-centred way of living: a form of *mobile privatization*. Broadcasting in its applied form was a social product of this distinctive tendency.

The contradictory pressures of this phase of industrial capitalist society were indeed resolved, at a certain level, by the institution of broadcasting. For mobility was only in part the impulse of an independent curiosity: the wish to go out and see new places. It was essentially an impulse formed in the break-down and dissolution of older and smaller kinds of settlement and productive labour. The new and larger settlements and industrial organizations required major internal mobility, at a primary level, and this was joined by secondary consequences in the dispersal of extended families and in the needs of new kinds of social organization. Social processes long implicit in the revolution of industrial capitalism were then greatly intensified: especially an increasing distance between immediate living areas and the directed places of work and government. No effective kinds of social control over these transformed industrial and political processes had come anywhere near being achieved or even foreseen. Most people were living in the fall-out area of processes determined beyond them. What had been gained, nevertheless, in intense social struggle, had been the improvement of immediate conditions, within the limits and pressures of these decisive large-scale processes. There was some relative improvement in wages and working conditions, and there was a qualitative change in the distribution of the day, the week and the year between work and off-work periods. These two effects combined in a major emphasis on improvement of the small family home. Yet this privatization, which was at once an effective achievement and a defensive response, carried, as a consequence, an imperative need for new kinds of contact. The new homes might appear private and 'self-sufficient' but could be maintained only by regular funding and supply from external sources, and these, over a range from employment and prices to depressions and wars, had a decisive and often a disrupting influence on what was nevertheless seen as a separable 'family' project. This relationship created both the need and the form of a new kind of 'communication': news from 'outside', from otherwise inaccessible sources. Already in the drama of the 1880s and 1890s (Ibsen, Chekhov) this structure had appeared: the centre of dramatic interest was now for the first time the family home, but men and women stared from its windows, or waited anxiously for messages, to learn about forces, 'out there', which would determine the conditions of their lives. The new 'consumer' technology which reached its first decisive stage in the 1920s served this complex of needs within just these limits and pressures.

There were immediate improvements of the condition and efficiency of the privatized home; there were new facilities, in private transport, for expeditions from the home; and then, in radio, there was a facility for a new kind of social input – news and entertainment brought into the home. Some people spoke of the new machines as gadgets, but they were always much more than this. They were the applied technology of a set of emphases and responses within the determining limits and pressures of industrial capitalist society.

The cheap radio receiver is then a significant index of a general condition and response. It was especially welcomed by all those who had least social opportunities of other kinds; who lacked independent mobility or access to the previously diverse places of entertainment and information. Broadcasting could also come to serve, or seem to serve, as a form of *unified* social intake, at the most general levels. What had been intensively promoted by the radio manufacturing companies thus interlocked with this kind of social need, itself defined within general limits and pressures. In the early stages of radio manufacturing, transmission was conceived before content. By the end of the 1920s the network was there, but still at a low level of content-definition. It was in the 1930s, in the second phase of radio, that most of the significant advances in content were made. The transmission and reception networks created, *as a by-product*, the facilities of primary broadcasting production. But the general social definition of 'content' was already there.

This theoretical model of the general development of broadcasting is necessary to an understanding of the particular development of television. For there were, in the abstract, several different ways in which television as a technical means might have been developed. After a generation of universal domestic television it is not easy to realize this. But it remains true that, after a great deal of intensive research and development, the domestic television set is in a number of ways an inefficient medium of visual broadcasting. Its visual inefficiency by comparison with the cinema is especially striking, whereas in the case of radio there was by the 1930s a highly efficient sound broadcasting receiver, without any real competitors in its own line. Within the limits of the television home-set emphasis it has so far not been possible to make more than minor qualitative improvements. Higher-definition systems, and colour, have still only brought the domestic television set, as a machine, to the standard of a very inferior kind of cinema. Yet most people have adapted to this inferior visual medium, in an unusual kind of preference for an inferior immediate technology, because of the social complex – and especially that of the privatized home – within which broadcasting, as a system, is operative. The cinema had remained at an earlier level of social definition; it was and remains a special kind of theatre, offering specific and discrete works of one general kind. Broadcasting, by contrast, offered a whole social intake: music, news, entertainment, sport. The advantages of this general intake, within the home, much more than outweighed the technical advantages of visual transmission and reception in the cinema, confined as this was to specific and discrete works. While broadcasting was confined to sound, the powerful visual medium of cinema was an immensely popular alternative. But when broadcasting became visual, the option for its social advantages outweighed the immediate technical deficits.

The transition to television broadcasting would have occurred quite generally in the late 1930s and early 1940s, if the war had not intervened. Public television services had begun in Britain in 1936 and in the United States in 1939, but with still very expensive receivers. The full investment in transmission and reception facilities did not occur until the late 1940s and early 1950s, but the growth was thereafter very rapid. The key social tendencies which had led to the definition of broadcasting were by then even more pronounced. There was significantly higher investment in the privatized home, and the social and physical distances between these homes and the decisive political and productive centres of the society had become much greater. Broadcasting, as it had developed in radio, seemed an inevitable model: the central transmitters and the domestic sets.

Television then went through some of the same phases as radio. Essentially, again, the technology of transmission and reception developed before the content, and important parts of the content were and have remained by-products of the technology rather than independent enterprises. As late as the introduction of colour, 'colourful' programmes were being devised to persuade people to buy colour sets. In the earliest stages there was the familiar parasitism on existing events: a coronation, a major sporting event, theatres. A comparable parasitism on the cinema was slower to show itself, until the decline of the cinema altered the terms of trade; it is now very widespread, most evidently in the United States. But again, as in radio, the end of the first general decade brought significant independent television production. By the middle and late 1950s, as in radio in the middle and late 1930s, new kinds of programme were being made for television and there were very important advances in the productive use of the medium, including, as again at a comparable stage in radio, some kinds of original work.

Yet the complex social and technical definition of broadcasting led to inevitable difficulties, especially in the productive field. What television could do relatively cheaply was to transmit something that was in any case happening or had happened. In news, sport, and some similar areas it could provide a service of transmission at comparatively low cost. But in every kind of new work, which it had to produce, it became a very expensive medium, within the broadcasting model. It was never as expensive as film, but the cinema, as a distributive medium, could directly control its revenues. It was, on the other hand, implicit in broadcasting that given the tunable receiver all programmes could be received without immediate charge. There could have been and can still be a socially financed system of production and distribution within which local and specific charges would be unnecessary; the BBC, based on the licence system for domestic receivers, came nearest to this. But short of monopoly, which still exists in some state-controlled systems, the problems of investment for production, in any broadcasting system, are severe.

Thus within the broadcasting model there was this deep contradiction, of centralized transmission and privatized reception. One economic response was licensing. Another, less direct, was commercial sponsorship and then supportive advertising. But the crisis of production control and financing has been endemic in broadcasting precisely because of the social and technical model that was adopted and that has become so deeply established. The problem is masked, rather than solved, by the fact that as a transmitting technology – its functions largely limited to relay and commentary on other events – some balance could be struck; a limited revenue could finance this limited service. But many of the creative possibilities of television have been frustrated precisely by this apparent solution, and this has far more than local effects on producers and on the balance of programmes. When there has been such heavy investment in a particular model of social communications, there is a restraining complex of financial institutions, of cultural expectations and of specific

3

On the Use of the Camera in Anthropology

Margaret Mead and Gregory Bateson

Bateson: I was wondering about looking through, for example, a camera.

Mead: Remember Clara Lambert and when you were trying to teach her? That woman who was making photographic studies of play schools, but she was using the camera as a telescope instead of as a camera. You said, "She'll never be a photographer. She keeps using the camera to look at things." But you didn't. You always used a camera to take a picture, which is a different activity.

Bateson: Yes. By the way, I don't like cameras on tripods, just grinding. In the latter part of the schizophrenic project, we had cameras on tripods just grinding.

Mead: And you don't like that?

Bateson: Disastrous.

Mead: Why?

Bateson: Because I think the photographic record should be an art form.

Mead: Oh why? Why shouldn't you have some records that aren't art forms? Because if it's an art form, it has been altered.

Bateson: It's undoubtedly been altered. I don't think it exists unaltered.

Mead: I think it's very important, if you're going to be scientific about behavior, to give other people access to the material, as comparable as possible to the access you had. You don't, then, alter the material. There's a bunch of film makers now that are saying, "It should be art," and wrecking everything that we're trying to do. Why the hell should it be art?

Bateson: Well, it should be off the tripod.

Mead: So you run around.

Bateson: Yes.

Mead: And therefore you've introduced a variation into it that is unnecessary.

Bateson: I therefore got the information out that I thought was relevant at the time.

Mead: That's right. And therefore what do you see later?

Bateson: If you put the damn thing on a tripod, you don't get any relevance.

Mead: No, you get what happened.

Bateson: It isn't what happened.

Plate 3.1 Gregory Bateson and Margaret Mead, ca. 1938. Photograph by Conrad Waddington.

Mead: I don't want people leaping around thinking that a profile at this moment would be beautiful.

Bateson: I wouldn't want beautiful.

Mead: Well, what's the leaping around for?

Bateson: To get what's happening.

Mead: What you think is happening.

Bateson: If Stewart reached behind his back to scratch himself, I would like to be over there at that moment.

Mead: If you were over there at that moment you wouldn't see him kicking the cat under the table. So that just doesn't hold as an argument.

Bateson: Of the things that happen, the camera is only going to record 1 percent anyway.

Mead: That's right.

Bateson: I want that 1 percent on the whole to tell.

Mead: Look, I've worked with these things that were done by artistic film makers, and the result is you can't do anything with them.

Bateson: They're bad artists, then.

Mead: No, they're not. I mean, an artistic film maker can make a beautiful notion of what he thinks is there, and you can't do any subsequent analysis with it of any kind. That's been the trouble with anthropology, because they had to trust us. If we were good enough instruments, and we said the people in this culture did something more than the ones in that, if they trusted us, they used it. But there was no way of probing further into the material. So we gradually developed the idea of film and tapes.

Bateson: There's never going to be any way of probing further into the material.

Mead: What are you talking about, Gregory? I don't know what you're talking about. Certainly, when we showed that Balinese stuff that first summer there were different things that people identified – the limpness that Marion Stranahan identified, the place on the chest and its point in child development that Erik Erikson identified. I can go back over it, and show you what they got out of those films. They didn't get it out of your head, and they didn't get it out of the way you were pointing the camera. They got it because it was a long enough run so they could see what was happening.

SB: What about something like that Navajo film, *Intrepid Shadows?* [see Worth and Adair 1972].

Mead: Well, that is a beautiful, an artistic production that tells you something about a Navajo artist.

Bateson: This is different, it's a native work of art.

Mead: Yes, and a beautiful native work of art. But the only thing you can do more with that is analyze the film maker, which I did. I figured out how he got the animation into the trees.

Bateson: Oh yes? What do you get out of that one?

Mead: He picked windy days, he walked as he photographed, and he moved the camera independently of the movement of his own body. And that gives you that effect. Well, are you going to say, following what all those other people have been able to get out of those films of yours, that you should have just been artistic?

SB: He's saying he *was* artistic.

Mead: No, he wasn't. I mean, he's a good film maker, and Balinese can pose very nicely, but his effort was to hold the camera steady enough long enough to get a sequence of behavior.

Bateson: To find out what's happening, yes.

Mead: When you're jumping around taking pictures...

Bateson: Nobody's talking about that, Margaret, for God's sake.

Mead: Well.

Bateson: I'm talking about having control of a camera. You're talking about putting a dead camera on top of a bloody tripod. It sees nothing.

Mead: Well, I think it sees a great deal. I've worked with these pictures taken by artists, and really good ones...

Bateson: I'm sorry I said artists; all I meant was artists. I mean, artists is not a term of abuse in my vocabulary.

Mead: It isn't in mine either, but I...

Bateson: Well, in this conversation, it's become one.

Mead: Well, I'm sorry. It just produces something different. I've tried to use *Dead Birds*, for instance... [see Gardner 1964].

Bateson: I don't understand *Dead Birds* at all. I've looked at *Dead Birds*, and it makes no sense.

Mead: I think it makes plenty of sense.

Bateson: But how it was made I have no idea at all.

Mead: Well, there is never a long enough sequence of anything, and you said absolutely that what was needed was long, long sequences from one position in the direction of two people. You've said that in print. Are you going to take it back?

Bateson: Yes, well, a long sequence in my vocabulary is twenty seconds.

Mead: Well, it wasn't when you were writing about Balinese films. It was three minutes. It was the longest that you could wind the camera at that point.

Bateson: A very few sequences ran to the length of the winding of the camera.

Mead: But if at that point you had had a camera that would run 1,200 feet, you'd have run it.

Bateson: I would have and I'd have been wrong.

Mead: I don't think so for one minute.

Bateson: The Balinese film wouldn't be worth one quarter.

Mead: All right. That's a point where I totally disagree. It's not science.

Bateson: I don't know what science is, I don't know what art is.

Mead: That's all right. If you don't that's quite simple. I do. (To Stewart:) With the films that Gregory's now repudiating that he took, we have had twenty-five years of re-examination and re-examination of the material.

Bateson: It's pretty rich material.

Mead: It is rich, because they're long sequences, and that's what you need.

Bateson: There are no long sequences.

Mead: Oh, compared with anything anybody else does, Gregory.

Bateson: But they're trained not to.

Mead: There are sequences that are long enough to analyze...

Bateson: Taken from the right place!

Mead: Taken from one place.

Bateson: Taken from the place that averaged better than other places.

Mead: Well, you put your camera there.

Bateson: You can't do that with a tripod. You're stuck. The thing grinds for 1,200 feet. It's a bore.

Mead: Well, you prefer twenty seconds to 1,200 feet.

Bateson: Indeed, I do.

Mead: Which shows you get bored very easily.

Bateson: Yes, I do.

Mead: Well, there are other people who don't, you know? Take the films that Betty Thompson studied [see Thompson 1970]. That Karbo sequence – it's beautiful – she was willing to work on it for six months. You've never been willing to work on things that length of time, but you shouldn't object to other people who can do it, and giving them the material to do it.

There were times in the field when I worked with people without filming, and therefore have not been able to subject the material to changing theory, as we were able to do with the Balinese stuff. So when I went back to Bali I didn't see new things. When I went back to Manus, I did, where I had only still photographs. If you have film, as your own perception develops, you can re-examine it in the light of the material to some extent. One of the things, Gregory, that we examined in the stills, was the extent to which people, if they leaned against other people, let their mouths fall slack. We got that out of examining lots and lots of stills. It's the same principle. It's quite different if you have a thesis and have the camera in your hand, the chances of influencing the material are greater. When you don't have the camera in your hand, you can look at the things that happen in the background.

Bateson: There are three ends to this discussion. There's the sort of film I want to make, there's the sort of film that they want to make in New Mexico (which is *Dead Birds*, substantially), and there is the sort of film that is made by leaving the camera on a tripod and not paying attention to it.

SB: Who does that?

Bateson: Oh, psychiatrists do that. Albert Scheflen [1973] leaves a video camera in somebody's house and goes home. It's stuck in the wall.

Mead: Well, I thoroughly disapprove of the people that want video so they won't have to look. They hand it over to an unfortunate student who then does the rest of the work and adds up the figures, and they write a book. We both object to this. But I do think if you look at your long sequences of stills, leave out the film for a minute, that those long, very rapid sequences, Koewat Raoeh, those stills, they're magnificent, and you can do a great deal with them. And if you hadn't stayed in the same place, you wouldn't have those sequences.

SB: Has anyone else done that since?

Mead: Nobody has been as good a photographer as Gregory at this sort of thing. People are very unwilling to do it, very unwilling.

SB: I haven't seen any books that come even close to *Balinese Character* [see Mead and Bateson 1942].

Mead: That's right, they never have. And now Gregory is saying it was wrong to do what he did in Bali. Gregory was the only person who was ever successful at taking stills and film at the same time, which you did by putting one on a tripod, and having both at the same focal length.

Bateson: It was having one in my hand and the other round my neck.

Mead: Some of the time, and some not.

Bateson: We used the tripod occasionally when we were using long telephoto lenses.

Mead: We used it for the bathing babies. I think the difference between art and science is that each artistic event is unique, whereas in science sooner or later once you get some kind of theory going somebody or other will make the same discovery [see Mead 1976]. The principal point is access, so that other people can look at your material and come to understand it and share it. The only real information that *Dead Birds* gives anybody are things like the thing that my imagination had never really encompassed, and that's the effect of cutting off joints of fingers. You remember? The women cut off a joint for every death that they mourn for, and they start when they're little girls, so that by the time they're grown women, they have no fingers. All the fine work is done by the men in that society, the crocheting and what not, because the men have fingers to do it with and the women have these stumps of hands. I knew about it, I had read about it, it had no meaning to me until I saw those pictures. There are lots of things that can be conveyed by this quasi-artistic film, but when we want to suggest to people that it's a good idea to know what goes on between people, which is what you've always stressed, we still have to show your films, because there aren't any others that are anything like as good.

SB: Isn't that a little shocking? It's been, what, years?

Mead: Very shocking.

Bateson: It's because people are getting good at putting cameras on tripods. It isn't what happens between people.

Mead: Nobody's put any cameras on tripods in those twenty-five years that looked at anything that mattered.

Bateson: They haven't looked at anything that mattered, anyway. All right.

REFERENCES

Gardner, Robert, Director. 1964. *Dead Birds*. Peabody Museum, Harvard University. Color, 83 minutes. Available through New York Public Library.

Mead, Margaret. 1976. "Towards a human science." *Science* 191: 903–9.

Mead, M. and G. Bateson. 1942. *Balinese Character: A Photographic Analysis*. New York Academy of Sciences; Special Publications, II. (Reissued 1962.)

Scheflen, Albert E. 1973. *Body Language and the Social Order: Communication as Behavioral Control*. Englewood Cliffs, NJ: Prentice-Hall.

Thompson, Betty. 1970. "Development and trial applications of method for identifying non-vocal parent–child communications in research film." Ph.D. thesis, Teachers College.

Worth, Sol and John Adair. 1972. *Through Navajo* Eyes. Bloomington: Indiana University Press. [*Intrepid Shadows* was made by Al Clah, a 19-year-old Navajo painter and sculptor.]

4

The Ambiguity of the Photograph

John Berger

What makes photography a strange invention – with unforeseeable consequences – is that its primary raw materials are light and time.

Yet let us begin with something more tangible. A few days ago a friend of mine found this photograph and showed it to me [see page 48].

I know nothing about it. The best way of dating it is probably by its photographic technique. Between 1900 and 1920? I do not know whether it was taken in Canada, the Alps, South Africa. All one can see is that it shows a smiling middle-aged man with his horse. Why was it taken? What meaning did it have for the photographer? Would it have had the same meaning for the man with the horse?

One can play a game of inventing meanings. The Last Mountie. (His smile becomes nostalgic.) The Man Who Set Fire to Farms. (His smile becomes sinister.) Before the Trek of Two Thousand Miles. (His smile becomes a little apprehensive.) After the Trek of Two Thousand Miles. (His smile becomes modest.) . . .

The most definite information this photograph gives is about the type of bridle the horse is wearing, and this is certainly not the reason why it was taken. Looking at the photograph alone it is even hard to know to what use category it belonged. Was it a family-album picture, a newspaper picture, a traveller's snap?

Could it have been taken, not for the sake of the man, but of the horse? Was the man acting as a groom, just holding the horse? Was he a horse-dealer? Or was it a still photograph taken during the filming of one of the early Westerns?

The photograph offers irrefutable evidence that this man, this horse and this bridle existed. Yet it tells us nothing of the significance of their existence.

A photograph arrests the flow of time in which the event photographed once existed. All photographs are of the past, yet in them an instant of the past is arrested so that, unlike a lived past, it can never lead to the present. Every photograph presents us with two messages: a message concerning the event photographed and another concerning a shock of discontinuity.

Between the moment recorded and the present moment of looking at the photograph, there is an abyss. We are so used to photography that we no longer consciously register the second of these twin messages – except in special circumstances:

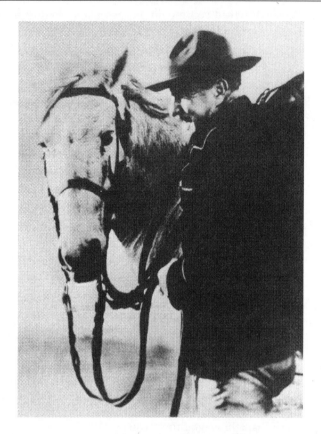

when for example, the person photographed was familiar to us and is now far away or dead. In such circumstances the photograph is more traumatic than most memories or mementos because it seems to confirm, prophetically, the later discontinuity created by the absence or death. Imagine for a moment that you were once in love with the man with the horse and that he has now disappeared.

If, however, he is a total stranger, one thinks only of the first message, which here is so ambiguous that the event escapes one. What the photograph shows goes with any story one chooses to invent.

Nevertheless the mystery of this photograph does not quite end there. No invented story, no explanation offered will be quite as *present* as the banal appearances preserved in this photograph. These appearances may tell us very little, but they are unquestionable.

The first photographs were thought of as marvels because, far more directly than any other form of visual image, they presented the appearance of what was absent. They preserved the look of things and they allowed the look of things to be carried away. The marvel in this was not only technical.

Our response to appearances is a very deep one, and it includes elements which are instinctive and atavistic. For example, appearances alone – regardless of all conscious considerations – can sexually arouse. For example, the stimulus to action – however tentative it remains – can be provoked by the colour red. More widely, the look of the world is the widest possible confirmation of the *thereness* of the world, and thus the look of the world continually proposes and confirms our relation to that thereness, which nourishes our sense of Being.

Before you tried to read the photograph of the man with the horse, before you placed it or named it, the simple act of looking at it confirmed, however briefly, your sense of being in the world, with its men, hats, horses, bridles...

The ambiguity of a photograph does not reside within the instant of the event photographed: there the photographic evidence is less ambiguous than any eye-witness account. The photo-finish of a race is rightly decided by what the camera has recorded. The ambiguity arises out of that discontinuity which gives rise to the second of the photograph's twin messages. (The abyss between the moment recorded and the moment of looking.)

A photograph preserves a moment of time and prevents it being effaced by the supersession of further moments. In this respect photographs might be compared to images stored in the memory. Yet there is a fundamental difference: whereas remembered images are the *residue* of continuous experience, a photograph isolates the appearances of a disconnected instant.

And in life, meaning is not instantaneous. Meaning is discovered in what connects, and cannot exist without development. Without a story, without an unfolding, there is no meaning. Facts, information, do not in themselves constitute meaning. Facts can be fed into a computer and become factors in a calculation. No meaning, however, comes out of computers, for when we give meaning to an event, that meaning is a response, not only to the known, but also to the unknown: meaning and mystery are inseparable, and neither can exist without the passing of time. Certainty may be instantaneous; doubt requires duration; meaning is born of the two. An instant photographed can only acquire meaning insofar as the viewer can read into it a duration extending beyond itself. When we find a photograph meaningful, we are lending it a past and a future.

The professional photographer tries, when taking a photograph, to choose an instant which will persuade the public viewer to lend it an *appropriate* past and future. The photographer's intelligence or his empathy with the subject defines for him what is appropriate. Yet unlike the story-teller or painter or actor, the photographer only makes, in any one photograph, *a single constitutive choice*: the choice of the instant to be photographed. The photograph, compared with other means of communication, is therefore weak in intentionality.

A dramatic photograph may be as ambiguous as an undramatic one.

What is happening? It requires a caption for us to understand the significance of the event. "Nazis Burning Books." And the significance of the caption again depends upon a sense of history that we cannot necessarily take for granted.

All photographs are ambiguous. All photographs have been taken out of a continuity. If the event is a public event, this continuity is history; if it is personal, the continuity, which has been broken, is a life story. Even a pure landscape breaks a continuity: that of the light and the weather. Discontinuity always produces ambiguity. Yet often this ambiguity is not obvious, for as soon as photographs are used with words, they produce together an effect of certainty, even of dogmatic assertion.

In the relation between a photograph and words, the photograph begs for an interpretation, and the words usually supply it. The photograph, irrefutable as evidence but weak in meaning, is given a meaning by the words. And the words, which by themselves remain at the level of generalization, are given specific authenticity by the irrefutability of the photograph. Together the two then become very powerful; an open question appears to have been fully answered.

Yet it might be that the photographic ambiguity, if recognized and accepted as such, could offer to photography a unique means of expression. Could this ambiguity suggest another way of telling? This is a question I want to raise now and return to later.

Cameras are boxes for transporting appearances. The principle by which cameras work has not changed since their invention. Light, from the object photographed, passes through a hole and falls on to a photographic plate or film. The latter, because of its chemical preparation, preserves these traces of light. From these traces, through other slightly more complicated chemical processes, prints are made. Technically, by the standards of our century, it is a simple process. Just as the historically comparable invention of the printing press was, in its time, simple. What is still not so simple is to grasp the nature of the appearances which the camera transports.

Are the appearances which a camera transports a construction, a man-made cultural artifact, or are they, like a footprint in the sand, a trace *naturally* left by something that has passed? The answer is, both.

The photographer chooses the event he photographs. This choice can be thought of as a cultural construction. The space for this construction is, as it were, cleared by his rejection of what he did not choose to photograph. The construction is his reading of the event which is in front of his eyes. It is this reading, often intuitive and very fast, which decides his choice of the instant to be photographed.

Likewise, the photographed image of the event, when shown as a photograph, is also part of a cultural construction. It belongs to a specific social situation, the life of the photographer, an argument, an experiment, a way of explaining the world, a book, a newspaper, an exhibition.

Yet at the same time, the material relation between the image and what it represents (between the marks on the printing paper and the tree these marks represent) is an immediate and unconstructed one. And is indeed like a *trace*.

The photographer chooses the tree, the view of it he wants, the kind of film, the focus, the filter, the time-exposure, the strength of the developing solution, the sort of paper to print on, the darkness or lightness of the print, the framing of the print – all this and more. But where he does not intervene – and cannot intervene without changing the fundamental character of photography – is between the light, emanating from that tree as it passes through the lens, and the imprint it makes on the film.

It may clarify what we mean by a *trace* if we ask how a drawing differs from a photograph. A drawing is a translation. That is to say each mark on the paper is consciously related, not only to the real or imagined "model," but also to every mark and space already set out on the paper. Thus a drawn or painted image is woven together by the energy (or the lassitude, when the drawing is weak) of countless judgments. Every time a figuration is evoked in a drawing, everything about it has been mediated by consciousness, either intuitively or systematically. In a drawing an apple is *made* round and spherical; in a photograph, the roundness and the light and shade of the apple are received as a given

This difference between making and receiving also implies a very different relation to time. A drawing contains the time of its own making, and this means that it possesses its own time, independent of the living time of what it portrays. The photograph, by contrast, receives almost instantaneously – usually today at a speed which cannot be perceived by the human eye. The only time contained in a photograph is the isolated instant of what it shows.

There is another important difference within the times contained by the two kinds of images. The time which exists within a drawing is not uniform. The artist gives more time to what she or he considers important. A face is likely to contain more time than the sky above it. Time in a drawing accrues according to human value. In a photograph time is uniform: every part of the image has been subjected to a chemical process of uniform duration. In the process of revelation all parts were equal.

These differences between a drawing and a photograph relating to time lead us to the most fundamental distinction between the two means of communication. The countless judgments and decisions which constitute a drawing are systematic. That is to say that they are grounded in an existent language. The teaching of this language and its specific usages at any given time are historically variable. A master-painter's apprentice during the Renaissance learnt a different practice and grammar of drawing from a Chinese apprentice during the Sung period. But every drawing, in order to recreate appearances, has recourse to a language.

Photography, unlike drawing, does not possess a language. The photographic image is produced instantaneously by the reflection of light; its figuration is *not* impregnated by experience or consciousness.

Barthes, writing about photography, talked of "humanity encountering for the first time in its history *messages without a code*. Hence the photograph is not the last (improved) term of the great family of images; it corresponds to a decisive mutation of informational economics."[1] The mutation being that photographs supply information without having a language of their own.

Photographs do not translate from appearances. They quote from them.

It is because photography has no language of its own, because it quotes rather than translates, that it is said that the camera cannot lie. It cannot lie because it prints directly.

(The fact that there were and are faked photographs is, paradoxically, a proof of this. You can only make a photograph tell an explicit lie by elaborate tampering, collage, and re-photographing. You have in fact ceased to practise photography. Photography in itself has no language which can be *turned*.) And yet photographs can be, and are, massively used to deceive and misinform.

We are surrounded by photographic images which constitute a global system of misinformation: the system known as publicity, proliferating consumerist lies. The role of photography in this system is revealing. The lie is constructed before the camera. A "tableau" of objects and figures is assembled. This "tableau" uses a language of symbols (often inherited, as I have pointed out elsewhere,[2] from the iconography of oil painting), an implied narrative and, frequently, some kind of performance by models with a sexual content. This "tableau" is then photographed. It is photographed precisely because the camera can bestow authenticity upon any set of appearances, however false. The camera does not lie even when it is used to quote a lie. And so, this makes the lie *appear* more truthful.

The photographic quotation is, within its limits, incontrovertible. Yet the quotation, placed like a fact in an explicit or implicit argument, can misinform. Sometimes the misinforming is deliberate, as in the case of publicity; often it is the result of an unquestioned ideological assumption.

For example, all over the world during the nineteenth century, European travellers, soldiers, colonial administrators, adventurers, took photographs of "the natives," their customs, their architecture, their richness, their poverty, their women's breasts, their headdresses; and these images, besides provoking amazement, were presented and read as proof of the justice of the imperial division of the world. The division between those who organized and rationalized and surveyed, and those who *were* surveyed.

In itself the photograph cannot lie, but, by the same token, it cannot tell the truth; or rather, the truth it does tell, the truth it can by itself defend, is a limited one.

The idealistic early press photographers – in the twenties and thirties of this century – believed that their mission was to bring home the truth to the world.

Sometimes I come away from what I am photographing sick at heart, with the faces of people in pain etched as sharply in my mind as on my negatives. But I go back because I feel it is my place to make such pictures. Utter truth is essential, and that is what stirs me when I look through the camera. (Margaret Bourke-White)

I admire the work of Margaret Bourke-White. And photographers, under certain political circumstances, have indeed helped to alert public opinion to the truth of what was happening elsewhere. For example: the degree of rural poverty in the United States in the 1930s; the treatment of Jews in the streets of Nazi Germany; the effects of US napalm bombing in Vietnam. Yet to believe that what one sees, as one looks through a camera on to the experience of others, is the "utter truth" risks confusing very different levels of the truth. And this confusion is endemic to the present public use of photographs.

Photographs are used for scientific investigation: in medicine, physics, meteorology, astronomy, biology. Photographic information is also fed into systems of social and political control – dossiers, passports, military intelligence. Other photographs are used in the media as a means of public communication. The three contexts are different, and yet it has been generally assumed that the truthfulness of the photograph – or the way that this truth functions – is the same in all three.

In fact, when a photograph is used scientifically, its unquestionable evidence is an aid in coming to a conclusion: it supplies information *within the conceptual framework* of an investigation. It supplies a missing detail. When photographs are used in a control system, their evidence is more or less limited to establishing identity and presence. But as soon as a photograph is used as a means of communication, the nature of lived experience is involved, and then the truth becomes more complex.

An X-ray photograph of a wounded leg can tell the "utter truth" about whether the bones are fractured or not. But how does a photograph tell the "utter truth" about a man's experience of hunger or, for that matter, his experience of a feast?

At one level there are no photographs which can be denied. All photographs have the status of fact. What has to be examined is in what way photography can and cannot give meaning to facts.

Let us recall how and when photography was born, how, as it were, it was christened, and how it grew up.

The camera was invented in 1839. Auguste Comte was just finishing his *Cours de Philosophie Positive*. Positivism and the camera and sociology grew up together. What sustained them all as practices was the belief that observable quantifiable facts, recorded by scientists and experts, would one day offer man such a total knowledge about nature and society that he would be able to order them both. Precision would replace metaphysics, planning would resolve social conflicts, truth would replace subjectivity, and all that was dark and hidden in the soul would be illuminated by empirical knowledge. Comte wrote that theoretically nothing need remain unknown to man except, perhaps, the origin of the stars! Since then cameras have photographed even the formation of stars! And photographers now supply us with more facts every month than the eighteenth century Encylopaedists dreamt of in their whole project.

Yet the positivist utopia was not achieved. And the world today is less controllable by experts, who have mastered what they believe to be its mechanisms, than it was in the nineteenth century.

What *was* achieved was unprecedented scientific and technical progress and, eventually, the subordination of all other values to those of a world market which treats everything, including people and their labour and their lives and their deaths, as a commodity. The unachieved positivist utopia became, instead, the global system of late capitalism wherein all that exists becomes quantifiable – not simply because it *can be* reduced to a statistical fact, but also because it *has been* reduced to a commodity.

In such a system there is no space for experience. Each person's experience remains an individual problem. Personal psychology replaces philosophy as an explanation of the world.

Nor is there space for the social function of subjectivity. All subjectivity is treated as private, and the only (false) form of it which is socially allowed is that of the individual consumer's dream.

From this primary suppression of the social function of subjectivity, other suppressions follow: of meaningful democracy (replaced by opinion polls and market-research techniques), of social conscience (replaced by self-interest), of history (replaced by racist and other myths), of hope – the most subjective and social of all energies (replaced by the sacralization of Progress as Comfort).

The way photography is used today both derives from and confirms the suppression of the social function of subjectivity.

Photographs, it is said, tell the truth. From this simplification, which reduces the truth to the instantaneous, it follows that what a photograph tells about a door or a volcano belongs to the same order of truth as what it tells about a man weeping or a woman's body.

If no theoretical distinction has been made between the photograph as scientific evidence and the photograph as a means of communication, *this has been not so much an oversight as a proposal.*

The proposal was (and is) that when something is visible, it is a fact, and that facts contain the only truth.

Public photography has remained the child of the hopes of positivism. Orphaned – because these hopes are now dead – it has been adopted by the opportunism of corporate capitalism. It seems likely that the denial of the innate ambiguity of the photograph is closely connected with the denial of the social function of subjectivity.

NOTES

1   Roland Barthes, *Image-Music-Text* (London: Fontana, 1977), p. 45.
2   John Berger, *Ways of Seeing* (London: British Broadcasting Corporation and Penguin Books, 1972), pp. 134, 141.

5

Save, Save the Lore!

Erika Brady

During the period in which the conventions of realist ethnography emerged, no ethnographer was more engaged by the dilemma of the paradigmatic versus the particular in presentation of fieldwork, and the issue of experiential authority, than Franz Boas, whose paternal relationship to the nascent discipline of anthropology is summarized affectionately in the nickname given to him by his students: "Papa Franz." Boas's work and teaching were characterized by a naturalist's attraction to text-based fieldwork collection; the body of work has been criticized by subsequent generations of scholars as more accumulative than evaluative – driven as a field-worker, he was deeply reluctant to theorize in advance of his data, and that mountain of data never achieved the critical mass he seems to have required to pronounce beyond his firm conviction in favor of diffusion as the dominant factor in cross-cultural expressive forms.

From the turn of the century through the early 1930s, most of the professional folklorists using the phonograph as a fieldwork tool were directly influenced in doing so by Franz Boas. Their use of the machine effectively fulfilled Boas's mandate to pursue "folklore" – that is "people['s] records of themselves in their own words" (Reichard 1943: 55). The results of their investigations in this area were most frequently published in the *Journal of American Folk-Lore*, which by 1908 the "Boasians" had effectively commandeered and would control for almost thirty years, edited by Boas himself (1908–24), Ruth Benedict (1925–39), and Gladys Reichard (1940) (Zumwalt 1988: 31–2). Such a mandate led many of Boas's colleagues and students, folklorists and anthropologists, to supplement their notebook and pencil with a phonograph in the field; Gladys Reichard, Paul Radin, Ruth Underhill, Clark Wissler, Robert H. Lowie, Helen Heffron Roberts, Martha Beckwith, Elsie Clews Parsons, and Alfred Kroeber among others all made significant cylinder re-cordings of field data. The reasons for this consistent methodological pattern are rooted in the emergent culture of anthropology at Columbia, including elements of ideology and an intellectual *Zeitgeist* as well as more practical persuasions.

Use of the phonograph satisfied the passionate urgency conveyed by Boas to his colleagues and students. Total immersion in a culture as a technique demands expertise, time, and interpersonal skills of a high order. Although Boas's fieldwork did tend at times toward what would later be called "participant observation" of general social patterns, the basis for his fieldwork was emphatically on collection of *texts* (Stocking 1974: 85). Verbatim textual transcription is exhausting for ethnographer, translator, and informant. With a phonograph, a collector could gather many times the quantity of linguistic and musical material possible using other means. Theodora Kroeber described her husband Alfred's experience with Boas as a teacher at Columbia at the turn of the century in terms he himself must have provided, since it was long before their meeting and marriage:

Virgin but fleeting – this was the urgency and the poetry of Boas' message. Everywhere over the land were virgin languages, brought to their polished and idiosyncratic perfection of grammar and syntax without benefit of a single recording scratch of stylus on papyrus or stone; living languages orally learned and transmitted and about to die with their last speakers. Everywhere there were to be discovered Ways of Life, many many ways. There were gods and created worlds unlike other gods and worlds, with extended relationships and values and ideals and dreams unlike anything known or imagined elsewhere, all soon to be forever lost – part of the human condition, part of the beautiful heartbreaking history of man. The time was late, the dark forces of invasion had almost done their ignorant work of annihilation. To the field then! With notebook and pencil, record, record, record. (Kroeber 1970: 51)

One might add "the phonograph" to "notebook and pencil." The importance of efficiency in field collecting and the usefulness of the phonograph in boosting productivity emerges with special clarity when one considers that, by today's standards, field trips were normally quite short during most of the cylinder era, seldom lasting longer than a couple of months at a time, and sometimes as brief as a mere day or two. Boas and his students, though considered quintessential fieldworkers, did not spend extended periods in the field in general – certainly not on the scale of later British anthropologists following the Malinowskian tradition. Rosalie H. Wax has pointed out that the nature of funding of early ethnographic work did not allow for long periods in the field, and in fact the nature of their data did not require it. They seldom achieved full fluency in the native languages, relying heavily on bilingual interpreters and informants. Boas himself made thirteen trips to the Northwest Coast, seldom spending more than two months at a time, and seems to have "worked" at least forty culture areas (Wax 1971: 31–2). The phonograph, for all its limitation, was a valuable tool in responding to the evangelical call to "record."

There may have been an ideological, even theoretical appeal to the use of the phonograph as well. Although Boas himself did not go as far as influential physicist Ernst Mach in adopting a pragmatic view of scientific laws as purely heuristic and potentially temporary constructs (Stocking 1974: 11), there is nonetheless in his anthropological work and teachings more than a whiff of Mach's radical sensationalist epistemology – the notion that knowledge must be rooted not in speculation but in experience, unimpeded by externally imposed paradigms and categories. The Machian epistemological revolution and the accompanying redefinition of knowledge in the wake of Charles Sanders Peirce's pragmaticism (especially the more diffuse interpretation and application found in William James's construct) can be seen in Boas's insistence on fieldwork incorporating direct observation and documentation of specific expressive forms; perhaps as well these intellectual trends exerted a negative influence affecting Boas's notorious reluctance to move beyond collection of texts to more expansive and theoretical works synthesizing the materials collected.[1]

There is a clear relationship between the critical positivism espoused by followers of Mach in many disciplines and the anthropological notion of cultural relativism pursued by Boas and his colleagues with missionary zeal:

We learn from the data of ethnology that not only our ability and knowledge but also the manner and ways of our feeling and thinking is the result of our upbringing as individuals and our history as a people. To draw conclusions about the development of mankind as a whole we must try to divest ourselves of these influences, and this is only possible by immersing ourselves in the spirit of primitive peoples whose perspectives and development have almost nothing in common with our own. (Boas 1974a [1889]: 71)

The relationship with Mach is largely implicit in Boas's writing and teaching but becomes explicit in the work and activity of students and coworkers such as Robert Lowie, Paul Radin, and Elsie Clews Parsons (Deacon 1997: 100–7).

But the very process of "immersion in the spirit" of peoples whose perspectives and development are utterly foreign is fraught with the risk of unconscious superimposition of the investigator's own native categories and constructs. The risk is greatest when the attempt is made at the most abstract and inclusive levels, as in the willy-nilly categorization of societies along an evolutionary continuum from "savagery" to "civilization" against which Boas campaigned so vigorously. The risk persists in the process of recording the most basic expressive forms, even inhering in the cross-cultural perception of as irreducible a form as linguistic phonemes. In an 1889 essay titled "On Alternating Sounds," Boas observes that fieldnotes even of scientists trained in supposedly objective systems for recording language demonstrate patterns of error – "mishearing" – consistent with their native tongue: "the nationality even of well-trained observers may readily be recognized" (Boas 1974b [1889]: 75).

The spirit of critical positivism energizing the American anthropologists clustered around Boas – the so-called Columbia school – supported the extensive use of the phonograph among the members of the group. It provided a form of documentation directly apprehensible to the senses, presumably uncontaminated by the observer's inevitable categorical and perceptual biases. Boas himself had experimented extensively with the phonograph in 1893 and 1895, recording Kwakiutl and Thompson River Indian material (Boas 1925: 319; Lee 1984a: viii); while not effusive concerning the experience, he continued to use the device intermittently throughout his career.[2]

Finally, there may be a practical and human reason for the attraction of the device for this group. "Critical positivism" was a thrilling approach to ethnology for neophyte Columbia anthropologists when the topic was on the agenda in the familiar intellectual give-and-take of Alexander Goldenweiser's discussion group, the now-celebrated Pearson Circle.[3] It was in this stimulating and urbane setting that Lowie and Radin in particular first grappled with the implications of the "new science" for anthropology. But the implementation of these insights in fieldwork represented a challenge of a different order. The "how-to" component in anthropological education at Columbia in the early years of the century was notably lacking. Papa Franz was a vigorous supporter of his students, but his pedagogy was notoriously unspecific; Boas's teaching style in this regard has been generously described by Herskovits as "subtle," more bluntly by Lowie as "odd" (Herskovits 1973: 22; Lowie 1959: 3).[4] Use of the phonograph created a body of data supposedly pure in

Machian terms; it also supplied a welcome degree of practical concreteness to the methodological problems posed by implementation of Boas's anthropological agenda. For insecure beginners in the field, armed only with the memory of Boas's lectures on linguistics and statistics, the phonograph provided a welcome focus and distraction as they found their feet.

They used the machine, but most of the Columbia ethnographers never overcame a certain ambivalence, even hostility, toward it, even after some of the technical shortcomings of the machine had been resolved and its price brought within their range. Granted, the phonograph was only suitable for the documentation of certain kinds of cultural phenomena: it was blind to nonverbal aspects of ritual and manifestations of material culture, as well as to intangible behavioral patterns such as kinship and social structure. The use of the phonograph automatically framed information as a presentation or performance, something set aside and special: brief, powerful, and permanent. As such it was best suited to record materials that were naturally and intrinsically "performances," formulaically defined and set off in the normal course of events from the usual flow of social expression – that is, songs, religious ceremonies, and narratives. But it was precisely these expressive forms that were of particular interest to ethnologists of the Boasian tribe; the source of their ambivalence must be sought elsewhere.

Folklorist Simon Bronner has characterized the late nineteenth and early twentieth century as a period in American intellectual history in the course of which examination of "time" and "space" in the sciences became professionalized: "Geographers and naturalists offered more exact descriptions of space, historians and geologists gave them for time" (Bronner 1986: 55). Ethnologists faced a more difficult dilemma: quantification of space and time in the arena of culture and tradition posed a challenge to both method and theory – a challenge to both scientific accuracy and humanistic values. The phonograph seemingly represented a useful if not ideal tool in this process of professionalization: it captured sound events objectively and with some degree of fidelity. Although cumbersome to pack into remote areas, it was not a significant burden in an era when even those travelers "roughing it" thought nothing of carrying with them an extraordinary amount of gear by today's standards. More burdensome than the literal encumbrance of the phonograph was the symbolic baggage that accompanied its use. Though it could be seen as a gleaming modern emblem of professionalization of ethnology – [Jesse Walter] Fewkes certainly regarded it as such – its presence in the fieldwork encounter could also imply a deficit on the part of the ethnographer: lack of full linguistic fluency, lack of training enabling swift and accurate linguistic or musical transcription, or, most damning of all, lack of the easy and full identification with the subjects that would lend fullest possible authority to the ethnographer's accounts. Its mechanical nature, at first glance an asset in the "measurement" of data representing cultural time and space, may have seemed uncomfortably reminiscent of inappropriate tools such as the calipers used for measurement of cranial capacity early in the careers of ethnographers such as Boas, Wissler, Lowie, and Kroeber, later to be recalled by some with regret. As a result, the relatively few evaluations of the usefulness of the phonograph surviving from the period suggest an ambivalence on the part of fieldworkers toward its usefulness that cannot be fully explained by its technical limitations or practicality.

For example, Paul Radin's 87 cylinder recordings made of Winnebago material in 1908 represent the earliest mechanically documented data available from that tribe, a significant and admirable accomplishment. Yet in reflecting some years later on the fieldwork of this period he underplayed the use of the machine, suggesting that, except for a few songs, he used the phonograph "sparingly," favoring instead either direct dictation or obtaining texts set down by the informants themselves in a syllabary adapted from that of the Sauk and Fox:

In 1908, when only the old Edison phonograph was known, this method had too many manifest drawbacks to warrant its use for anything but music. A text obtained in this fashion in 1908, one might suppose, and I did so suppose, would be markedly inferior to one procured in the two ways I have mentioned. However, this proved definitely not to be the case. The narratives recorded on the Edison phonograph cylinders were given by the best of my early informants, Charles Houghton. The circumstances were exceptionally unfavorable. I could use only the small cylinders and it must have been apparent to Houghton that I was in a great hurry. Yet, when compared with the narratives that Houghton had dictated to me directly, there was no evidence that this procedure, utterly new to him, had any perceptible effect on him. The style of narration, a highly individualistic one, differs, in no respect, from that found in Houghton's dictated texts. (Radin 1949: 5)

Curiously, Radin concludes from this reluctant experiment that all of the methods he chose – dictation by hand, transcription by the informant in syllabary, and recording with the phonograph – have *equal* merit. The disadvantages of the phonograph alluded to by Radin must have been a matter of inconvenience and perhaps his own discomfort with the device, since its performance was impeccable. Would Houghton have expressed a preference for the phonograph if consulted?

Similarly, ethnomusicologist Helen Heffron Roberts, a later student of Boas, made superbly effective use of the cylinder phonograph, notably in her collection of Northern California Karok and Konomihu music. These recordings represent possibly the finest single cylinder collection in the Archive of Folk Culture: technically high in quality and supported by splendidly accurate transcriptions and documentation. Her commitment to the cylinder phonograph as a tool led her to investigate the technical side of recording as well, consulting with Edison himself concerning problems of preservation and rerecording cylinders (Roberts and Lachmann 1963). Yet she too expressed reservations concerning the use of the phonograph:

Longhand notation is, of course, very much slower than record making and requires patience in all concerned. On the other hand, it has many merits. It affords excellent opportunities to the [collector] for observing the musical intelligence and ability of the singer, his variability in repetition to repetition in melody, form, text, etc., as would not be noted under the rather more strenuous and rapid recordings by the phonograph. It also affords an excellent chance for conversation by the way, for questions bound to arise which would never occur to the collector in the more perfunctory process of making records, and would only too late be put by the transcriber. Moreover, in this more leisurely pursuit, an informant may appeal to a bystander for assistance in recollecting, or arguments may arise which, to the alert collector, may furnish valuable additional data. Longhand notation is the best method possible for checking on impromptu composing and frauds. Phonograph records and long-hand notations of the same song may be compared with advantage. (Roberts 1931: 57–8)

Although the limitations of the phonograph were real, some of the difficulty experienced by ethnographers such as Radin and Roberts may not have related to the workings of the machine itself but instead to their adjustment to an unfamiliar process of documentation in which the oral nature of their material was retained rather than immediately reduced to written form. The historically shaped sensorium of ethnographers of the period was still essentially a post-Enlightenment environment in which meaningful sound was automatically spatialized – and specialized – in the form of the written word. In Walter Ong's terms, their frame of reference was fully "chirographic," centered on the preeminence of visual evidence, and the authority of text (Ong 1967: 87–8; 1982: 136). The contemporary era characterized by Ong as that of "secondary orality," in which the voice becomes newly alive and significant through electronic media, was being ushered in by the invention of the very machine the early ethnographers used with such obvious reluctance. Some of their hesitation may have had less to do with the limitations of the machine itself than with adjustment to an unfamiliar process of documentation in which the oral nature of their material was retained indefinitely, instead of being immediately reduced to written form. Despite their success with the phonograph, Radin and Roberts obviously hesitated to endorse it unreservedly as a tool – an attitude typical of Boas's students, reflecting both their experience and the opinion of Papa Franz himself.

Boas's influence on the course of ethnography, and the attention this influence indirectly drew to the usefulness of mechanical means of recording, predated and extended well beyond his circle of colleagues and students at Columbia. By the turn of the century, he had already systematically developed his agenda for the professionalization of American anthropology in ways that promoted the use of the phonograph in government-sponsored fieldwork. As early as 1887, he had corresponded with John Wesley Powell, director and founder of the Bureau of American Ethnology, concerning the publication of his first ethnological research in the Baffin Islands. By the early 1890s, he was fully engaged in the Byzantine politics of the organization and was offered a position directing editorial work for the Bureau (Stocking 1974: 59–60; 1992: 64–8). Although he turned down this offer, he benefited from the agency throughout the nineties in ways that he could not from other more archeologically oriented museums and institutions. The BAE indirectly subsidized his work on linguistics and mythology by purchasing his manuscripts and fieldnotes at a generous price. For his part, he did not hesitate to express his views concerning administration and policy both to Powell and to Samuel Langley, head of the Smithsonian Institution, of which the BAE was a part. In the course of Boas's prolonged "systematic self-professionalization" as an anthropologist, he had concluded that the growth of the field and the future of the BAE required that "those lines of human activity that do *not* find expression in material objects – namely language, thought, customs, and I may add, anthropometric measurements – be investigated thoroughly and carefully," a conviction he impressed upon Langley in correspondence concerning a possible successor to Powell in 1893 (Hinsley 1981: 251).[5]

Correspondence with Powell and his associate, William John McGee, in 1893 reveals Boas's early commitment to the essential importance of collection of full texts of cultural materials; we have seen that it was in this same year that he first experimented with the phonograph as an ethnographic tool. As the policy shift influenced by Boas drew the BAE collecting projects and publication initiatives ever more deeply into areas concerned with such nonmaterial aspects of culture as myth, music, narrative, and linguistics, the phonograph became an essential tool for the ethnographers employed by the BAE. As it happened, Powell retained control of the Bureau until his death in 1902, and although he was replaced by W. H. Holmes, no friend to Boas, the emphasis on nonmaterial forms of expression, especially linguistic and musical, remained strong. The Bureau publication of Boas's *Handbook of American Indian Languages* in 1911 bears witness to an influence that would continue for at least two more decades in the BAE's history (Stocking 1992: 60–91)....

The BAE's professional staff for the most part lacked formal ethnographic, musicological, and linguistic training, and they labored under impossibly restrictive time constraints in the field. They found the introduction of the phonograph as a tool to be a godsend in the collection of the full textual material that, through Boas's influence, became a standard requirement in their work in the 1890s and early decades of the next century. W. H. Holmes, Powell's successor, described the advantages and limitation of the phonograph in a 1906 letter:

I will say that the recording of phonetics of primitive languages by means of a phonograph of any construction is impossible, for the reason that the phonograph renders only the physical characteristics of the spoken sound, while the primary object we have to investigate is the physiological method of producing the sound. This can be obtained only by closest observation of the speaker.

On the other hand, the phonograph is of very great value in recording the characteristic rhythm and cadence of the spoken languages and it also is of greatest service in obtaining native texts, undistorted by the difficulties of recording the spoken word in writing, which always necessitates slow pronunciation and for this reason breaks up the syntactic unity of the sentences. I have applied successfully the method of having old people, well versed in the lore of the Indians, tell their stories into the phonograph. Then I had the same stories in the presence of the original informant repeated by the phonograph to an interpreter, who pronounced the sentences as they appear on the phonograph to me, and from this dictation I recorded the sentences, checking off the interpreter from the phonographic record. In these two respects the phonograph is the most useful instrument in linguistic studies. (Holmes 1906)

The device allowed them to record language, music, and ceremony – to "save the lore," in BAE ethnologist John Peabody Harrington's words – in a form from which they or others could later publish written phonetic and musical transcriptions, providing as well impressive quantifiable, artifactual evidence of their industry. Nearly a score of BAE consultants and staff made use of the phonograph from 1895 to the mid-1930s, creating an irreplaceable record of American Indian culture the value of which is still unfolding, as recordings of music and ceremony made during this era are recirculated among members of the communities in which they were originally recorded. This return of the recordings is not without irony, since both fieldworkers and often their subjects assumed that by the end of the twentieth century such communities would have long ceased to exist (Brady 1988: 35–44).

The anthropological folklorists who reluctantly embraced the phonograph as an ethnographic tool viewed the texts they collected as a key to the understanding of larger issues in the groups they studied – as artifacts of evolutionary development, as evidence for migration and diffusion, or as templates revealing in microcosm the significant cultural patterns that played out in many aspects of social life. But there were also scholars who, by temperament or training, gravitated toward textual and musically expressive forms in their own right, without necessarily generalizing from them concerning broader cultural questions about the cultures from which the materials were collected (Zumwalt 1988: 122). Musicologists and the scholars whom Rosemary Lévy Zumwalt labels "literary folklorists" both used the phonograph extensively in their work for reasons related to, but distinct from, the reasons

Plate 5.1 BAE ethnologist John Peabody Harrington at the Smithsonian, recording Cuna Indians Margarita Campos, Alfred Robinson, and James Perry. National Museum of American History, the Smithsonian Institution, Washington DC.

motivating the anthropological collectors of folklore. No less an authority than Béla Bartók stated unequivocally, "The father of modern folksong studies was Thomas Edison" (1950: n.p.).

The earliest investigations concerning the purely musicological usefulness of the phonograph were undertaken by psychologist Benjamin Ives Gilman, to whom Mary Hemenway entrusted the analysis of the Zuni cylinders made by Fewkes in 1890. Gilman's work on these cylinders earned for him credit from pioneer ethnomusicologist Erich Moritz von Hornbostel as "the first scholar to use the phonograph in a scientific approach to the study of music" (Lee 1984: vii). Gilman was primarily interested in the technical reliability of phonograph recordings and in their usefulness in comparative musicological studies. He scrupulously described his technique in transcribing the Fewkes cylinders. Using a harmonium tuned to concert pitch, he notated the programs of ten cylinders, having refrained from listening to any other Indian music so that his ear would be "clean." Despite the problems posed by fluctuations in the speed of recordings made with Fewkes's first machine, a treadle model, Gilman was enthusiastic about the accuracy of the phonograph:

The apparatus proves to be a means by which the actual sound itself of which a music consists may, even in many of its more delicate characteristics, be stored up by the traveler, in a form permanently accessible to observation.... [The recording] can be interrupted at any point, repeated indefinitely, and even within certain limits magnified, as it were, for more accurate appreciation of changes in pitch, by increasing the duration of notes. A collection by phonographic cylinders like that obtained by Dr. Fewkes forms a permanent museum of primitive music, of which the specimens are comparable in fidelity of reproduction and convenience for study, to casts or photographs of sculpture or painting. (Gilman 1891: 68)

Gilman's interest in the phonograph as a fieldwork tool was of the armchair variety: he was intrigued by the accuracy of the device because it suggested the possibility of a scientific study of comparative music. The machine raised "the hope that some proportion of the resulting close determinations of pitch might prove significant," revealing subtle "habitudes of performance" of different peoples and individuals (Gilman 1908: 25). He grasped the distinction between the notation of a performance, which he believed only possible through the use of an objective mechanical device such as the phonograph, and the notation of a piece of music, the result of taking down by ear, which is "a record of the observer's idea of what the performers of certain observed sequences of tone would have performed had their execution corresponded to their intention, or (perhaps) had their intention not wandered also from a certain norm" (ibid: 27). He concludes that notation made by ear from repeated hearings represents not observations but what he terms "a theory of observations" – the listener's paradigm for an ideal performance (ibid: 25).

Gilman's work indirectly demonstrated an aspect of phonograph use unremarked upon at the time but significant nonetheless. He was essentially an indirect participant in the ethnographic process: Fewkes's cylinders offered a scholar far from Zuni a body of apparently objective data to work with – a separation virtually impossible under any other circumstance. Gilman's role in the early history of the phonograph is defined by this curious quality of separation from the source. His most important legacy aside from his work with Fewkes's Pueblo recordings is his 1893 anthology of 101 cylinders containing "exotic music" that he recorded at the World's Columbian Exposition in Chicago, which included Javanese, Samoan, Turkish, and Kwakiutl performances, a collection inspired and financed by the generous Mrs. Hemenway (Lee 1984: viii).

Not all researchers were as impressed with the capacity of the phonograph to record musical performances. Musicologist H. E. Krehbiel, intrigued by Gilman's enthusiasm, pounced on the opportunity to test a machine on display at an exhibit in Frankfurt-on-Main. In a letter to the *Tribune* later printed in the *Musical Visitor*, he dismissed Gilman's assessment of the phonographic potential with an arch charm more deadly than any full-scale systematic critique: "I confess that I part with regret from the Zuni melodies which Dr. Fewkes imprisoned on his phonograph cylinder and Mr. Gilman transcribed for us (those quarter tones opened up such a delightful field for speculation); but since I toyed with a phonograph and pitch pipe at the Frankfurt exhibition yesterday they are banished from my collection" (Krehbiel 1891).

The dispute over the machine's usefulness in recording music remained unreconciled in Great Britain as well, but there the authoritative weight of opinion held against the phonograph. Like the American specialists in Indian linguistics, the British specialists in folksong placed great value on the skill required in making scrupulously accurate transcriptions – musical, in their case. It is perhaps no wonder, then, that Percy Grainger's vigorous recommendation of the phonograph as a tool met with such a cool reception on the part of the Folk-Song Society in 1908. In a letter commenting on a draft of Grainger's article "Collecting with the Phonograph" written for the Society journal, folksong doyenne Anne Geddes Gilchrist expressed her reservations to the equally eminent Lucy Broadwood:

In my own experience of seeing records being taken by my brother of the performances of singers, both cultured and otherwise, we have found it not absolutely reliable as a recorder (though a good instrument). It is faulty both as regards "dynamics" and timbre of the sounds recorded, and fails to reproduce sibilants – the initial "s" of a word particularly. As to pitch, I have also had some occasional doubts as to which instrument – the human or the artificial – was a little "out"! The chief weakness of the phonograph, I think (apart from the general slight or more than slight distortion of tone) is its limited range of piano to forte. (Yates 1982: 266)

For the trained musician, the fidelity of the phonograph clearly left something to be desired. The technical limitations led many collectors who used the machine to limit their performers to individuals whose vocal quality recorded well, and to restrict vocal mannerisms which would cause distortion (Hofmann 1968: 101–13).

Paradoxically, despite technical reservations such as those quoted above, both Gilchrist and Cecil Sharp also objected to the phonograph as a means of recording that was *too* precisely accurate. They believed that ultimately the subjective response of the human ear best caught and conveyed the content of a performance. Although Sharp was to make use of the cylinder phonograph from time to time, he disliked the machine, expressing his reasons at some length in a letter to Percy Grainger in 1908. After remarking that he felt that it made singers self-conscious, that it was useless for singers whose voices were too weak to register, and that he was not satisfied with the clarity with which it recorded words, Sharp makes clear his most strenuous objection: that in the documentation of folksong "it is not an exact, scientifically accurate memorandum that is wanted, so much as a faithful artistic record of what is actually heard by the ordinary auditor." He comments that just as a photograph is generally inferior to a painting in conveying a scene, a phonographic recording is inferior to an auditor's rendering of a performance in standard notation (Yates 1982: 269). This analogy was also drawn by Gilchrist, who passionately maintained that "the trained ear or eye of an artist is surely able to reproduce with more real *truth* – because with understanding and sympathy – the sounds or the sights impressing the sensitive surface – whether human or artificial – of an 'innocent' receptive medium" (Yates 1982: 267). . . .

Despite its many limitations, the phonograph represented a valued tool for many collectors in the early part of the century; it could expedite fieldwork undertaken under pressure, produce a body of data conforming to contemporary notions of scientific objectivity, and compensate for skills many collectors lacked in written transcription of music or phonetic texts. In addition, for many women collectors, it may have represented compensation of another order.

The typical role of women in the late nineteenth and early twentieth centuries located her at the protected center of the domestic nest – a role turned topsy-turvy in virtually every significant respect by the requirements of serious and extended field research. Indeed, this very inversion of gender expectations may account for the surprisingly large number of women who made substantive contributions in the area – women whose professional activities in anthropology and folklore included a social agenda, overt or covert. Whether or not they framed their involvement in fieldwork as revolutionary – and some did – the adventure of escaping the usual routine of women's lives of the period was intensely attractive to a wide range of temperaments, from indomitable Matilda Coxe Stevenson to gentle Helen Heffron Roberts.

Escape into a male-dominated professional sphere had its price. Franz Boas was exceptional in his encouragement of women as ethnographers, but his sponsorship was not an entree into the almost exclusively male precinct of institutional employment (Deacon 1997: 258–72). Relatively few women had had access to even the limited formal academic training available in fieldwork-related disciplines at the turn of the century, and they were further burdened with the expectation that their work would display an inappropriate level of "feminine" subjectivity. Perhaps reacting to these critical stereotypes, a striking number of women collectors used the phonograph expertly and extensively, including Alice Cunningham Fletcher, Elsie Clews Parsons, Constance Goddard DuBois, Helen Heffron Roberts, Laura Boulton, Natalie Curtis Burlin, Helen Hartness Flanders, Gladys Reichard, Theodora Kroeber, and the tireless Frances Densmore.

Not only was the phonograph a useful tool in preempting sexist assumptions concerning the nature of the data collected by women, but mastery of its technology also implied a satisfyingly "masculine" proficiency in mechanical matters usually considered a male preserve. Such symbolic appropriation of "manly" skill in emergent technologies was a notable feature of gender politics of the period – Jane Gay, Alice Cunningham Fletcher's companion in the field, wrote lively popular accounts of their adventures among the Nez Perce in which she habitually referred to herself in the third person as "she" when her role was that of "the Cook," but "*he*" when acting as "the Photographer" (Mark 1988: 185). The use of up-to-date equipment provided an emblem of competence for women in the field, allowing them to demonstrate facility in areas usually marked off as male territory.

[The previous material is excerpted from chapter 3 of Brady's book *A Spiral Way*. The following is drawn from chapter 4 of the same book.]

Implicit in most early ethnographic collections are three assumptions concerning interactions in the field: the collector is in control of the event, the full cooperation of the performer is achieved without reflection or negotiation, and unsatisfactory recordings are owing to shortcomings on the part of the performer, or, when the phonograph was used, nervousness over the mechanical process of recording or malfunction of the device. The phonograph itself represented a kind of emblem of authority for the collector; as its operator, he or she felt securely in control of the episode. Frances Densmore's 1940 instructions to a neophyte collector exude a quelling impression of the lengths to which some collectors would go to achieve a technically accomplished recording:

The psychology of managing the Indians so as to secure the best songs, sung in the desired manner, is the most important factor in the work, in my opinion. I will take pleasure in giving you the benefit of my experience in this regard. I had to formulate my own method, but I find it gives equally good results in all tribes....

Before actual recording is begun, it is sometimes a good plan to have an "open house" where everyone is shown the apparatus, sees it in use, and, perhaps, some test records may be made at this time – so all curiosity is satisfied. This may be followed by a promise that everyone can come again, and hear the records, if they will keep away while the work is in progress.

Only the interpreter and singer should be present when the songs are recorded unless they want a "witness" or someone to consult.

Only one singer at a time, unless the records are for "exhibition purposes," and to show concerted singing.

An Indian drum does not record well, and a rattle does not record at all. A short stick on a pasteboard box gives the percussion without resonance, which is all that is wanted unless the records are for exhibition use....

Each song should be sung through several times, followed by a distinct pause. Singers should not be allowed to *"run their songs together."*

It is safest to get information before recording the song. Translations can safely follow the recording.

All yells must be strictly forbidden, if the records are to be transcribed. It is also a waste of space on the blank to let them "talk," and announce the song in the native language, etc.

It does not pay to have them "rehearse" a song audibly – they should "run it over in their mind," then record it. Often, a "rehearsal," which is not recorded, is better than the recording.

The singer must never be allowed to think that he is in charge of the work. A strict hold must be kept on him.

Singers should be checked by general reputation. Loud voices are not essential, and men who sing at dances are apt to be too free-and-easy.

It is not wise to take too many songs from one singer, nor let a man sing too long at a time. (Gray 1988: ix)

Not all collectors using the phonograph were as rigid or systematic as Frances Densmore, but all had to evolve negotiating strategies to achieve cooperation from their singers, and all had to accommodate the technical limitations of the machine by adjustment of performers to an unnatural performance context.

Despite the apparent control of the encounter exerted by the collector as operator of the machine, the process of negotiation involved in its use may actually have altered the power dynamics in favor of the performer. Robert A. Georges and Michael Owen Jones have observed that, ... because fields for folklore and anthropology require fieldwork as a professional activity, folklorists and anthropologists are singularly vulnerable to their informants (1980). Fieldworkers depicted themselves in control of the collecting process, in Densmore's words, "managing the Indians so as to secure the best songs," but in practice the mechanical nature of the phonograph required a much higher degree of compliance, even collaboration, than documentation consisting of simple observation and note taking – a process in which the question might well be raised concerning who was in fact being managed. The performer and collector had to agree on a time and place to record – documenting social or ritual events *in situ*

Plate 5.2   Frances Densmore and Blackfoot singer Mountain Chief. National Museum of American History, the Smithsonian Institution, Washington DC.

was out of the question. The performer had to show up – no small matter in cultures in which the concept of "an appointment" was non-existent. Selections that would record effectively had to be agreed upon. And finally, in the process of recording itself, once the needle engaged the wax, the performer and the phonograph formed a dyad as intimate as that of two dancers; the attention and voice poured directly into the horn of the machine, effectively excluding the collector for the duration of the piece.

As she herself reported, Densmore was at least once outmaneuvered in a strategic duel centering on the use of the phonograph. When working among the Uinta and White River bands of Northern Utes at Fort Duquesne, Utah, in 1914, she found little initial cooperation. The Utes were unmoved by the offer of payment and the promise of preservation of the recordings, and made her work the object of open ridicule. Uneasily she insisted on a formal meeting with their chief, Red Cap, despite the fact that she had seen him and noted that "his face wore the smile I do not like to see on the face of an Indian." She prepared her borrowed office carefully, placing an American flag over the chair for the Chief. When he arrived, she addressed him with consciously assumed dignity, reminding him of her adoption by the Sioux chief Red Fox and warning that she would tell her Indian father of her rude treatment at the hands of the Utes.

Red Cap listened attentively through his interpreter, then informed her that he would ensure the cooperation of his best singer. He even remained for the duration of an entirely satisfactory session. But Red Cap had a countermove to play:

After the recording was finished, Red Cap said, "I have done as you wished. Now I want to ask a favor. I do not sing, as I said, but would like to talk into your phonograph. Will it record talking?" Guilelessly I said it would record any song.

"Well," said the wily old chief, "Then I will talk and I want you to play the record for the Indian Commissioner in Washington. I want to tell him that we do not like this Agent. We want him sent someplace else. We don't like the things he does. What we tell him does not get to the Commissioner but I want the Commissioner to hear my voice. I want you to play this so he will hear my words, and I want you to give him a good translation of my speech. We want to get rid of this agent." (Densmore 1968 [1917]: 39–43)

Densmore had received a favor from Red Cap and was obliged to agree to his request. Six months later she kept her promise to the chief – in part. She played the recording of his speech to Cato Sells, Commissioner of Indian Affairs. Alas for Red Cap's diplomacy: after an explanation from Densmore, the speech was played without comment or translation. Densmore concludes, "Numerous employees of the Indian Office were asked to hear the recordings, but no one understood the Ute language and the contents of the speech remained a mystery. The record has not been played since that day."[6] Despite the failed outcome of Red Cap's ploy, he controlled the encounter with Densmore masterfully, placing her in his debt before advancing his request and making canny use of the cylinder phonograph as a political tool.

The relationship between fieldworker and informant during the era of the cylinder phonograph must be reexamined in all its intricacy in order to evaluate the effect of the machine on the interaction. Many fieldworkers infantilized their subjects to an extent that not only insulted their hosts but disgusted white observers as well.[7] Objectionable in itself, this practice also placed the collectors at a disadvantage in evaluating the complex motives that led to cooperation in the documentation of native culture, effectively blinding them to the extent to which their performers were active collaborators in the ethnographic process.

In the end, both men and women accepted or rejected the phonograph for a variety of reasons. For some, it provided a convenient and practical means to document the forms of verbal and musical expression considered the essential units of a community's traditional culture; others considered it too cumbersome and intrusive to use on a regular basis. Some collectors welcomed the opportunity to make use of a dynamic new technological innovation; others saw the very novelty of the phonograph, and the social change its dissemination heralded, as a symptom of precisely that progressive force against which they were valiantly holding the line. Some regarded the device as a means to achieve a scientific objectivity in their work; others saw it as a cheap evasion of the skill in transcription essential to any well-trained ethnographer.

Then as now, every fieldworker engages not only in a professional process of documentation and analysis but also in an inner enactment of a privately composed drama as suspenseful, risky, and exhilarating as the hunt – a heroic drama in which we cast ourselves as protagonist. In the end, the choice each fieldworker made concerning the use of the phonograph often depended on a combination of practical and ideological factors – but depended as well on how readily he or she accepted the role of the phonograph as a dramatis persona in the fieldwork scenario. A clumsy prop? A steady supporting performer? Or even an upstaging scene-stealer? The phonograph could be any of these.

But the performers had strong feelings about the process, and their reaction to the use of the phonograph in recording their lore indicates that they cast both the device and its operators in unexpected parts in their own *mise-en-scène*.

NOTES

1   The influence of William James on more recent folklore scholarship through the work of George Herbert Mead is discussed in Bronner (1990).
    Boas's reluctance to pronounce on collected data is a persistent leitmotif in critical accounts of his influence. Marion Smith strikes a typically exasperated tone: "The exhaustive collection of data which seems at the time to have little or no connection with any specific problem is peculiarly a feature of [Boas's] approach... Masses of data may therefore be worked over with no clear knowledge of what's to be gained at the end. A new hypothesis or a new slant on an old problem will "emerge" or be "revealed" or "suggested." The data will "speak for themselves.... Boas was always too self-critical to rely completely on his own observations. He needed the documentation of the texts, the family history, to test his own precision" (Smith 1959: 54–6).

2   He remarked much later with regard to Frances Densmore's work, "the study of form is not easy, because in transcriptions made from the phonograph – and I presume that most of the material in Miss Densmore's book has been so transcribed – accents are not reliable, because mechanically accents are introduced on those tones that correspond to the rate of vibration of the diaphragm" (Boas 1925: 319).

3   The Pearson Circle was one of several memorable discussion groups established by Goldenweiser, a popular and charismatic student at Columbia, that were modeled on groups formed in Russian universities to study the emerging topics in psychology, philosophy, and history of sciences. The circle was named for Karl Pearson, author of the influential *Grammar of Sciences* (Deacon 1997: 99–101).

4   An excellent discussion of the intellectual climate of the early years of anthropology at Columbia can be found in Deacon (1997: 97–107).

5   The description "systematic self-professionalization" is Robert Lowie's (1943: 183).

6   Translated some years later, Red Cap's cylinder did not include a scathing indictment against the agent as Densmore feared but rather a message of approval concerning Densmore's activities and a plea to the Commissioner to allow the Utes free participation in the pastimes and religious ceremonies of their tradition; possibly the agent in question had interfered with these activities. The original transcript is in the National Anthropological Archives; a photocopy is in the files of the Federal Cylinder Project, American Folklife Center, Library of Congress. Two personal memoirs of this episode survive: a formal report sent to the BAE archives and reprinted in Hofmann (1968: 39–43), and a typescript dated June 6, 1943 containing a somewhat more detailed and circumstantial account. A photocopy of the latter version is in the files of the Federal Cylinder Project, American Folklife Center, Library of Congress; the original is in the National Anthropological Archives, Smithsonian Institution. In addition, Hofmann reprints a letter from Densmore to her sister, Margaret Densmore, briefly recounting the event on the evening it occurred, July 16, 1914 (ibid: 35–7).

7   Indian rights advocate D. A. Goddard, editor of the *Boston Daily Advertiser*, in 1886 wrote contemptuously of Alice Cunningham Fletcher's "wretchedly sentimental way of calling the Omaha her children – her babies – and such pet names" (Mark 1988: 107).

REFERENCES

Bartók, Béla. 1950. Liner notes, *Hungarian Folk Songs*. Folkways FE 4000.

Boas, Franz. 1974a [1889]. "The aims of ethnology." Pp. 17–24 in *Die Ziele der Ethnologie*. New York: Hermann Bartsch. Reprinted as pp. 1–20 in *The Shaping of American Anthropology: A Franz Boas Reader*, ed. George W. Stocking. New York: Basic Books.

—— 1974b [1889]. "On alternating sounds," *American Anthropologist* 2: 47–53. Reprinted as pp. 72–7 in *The Shaping of American Anthropology: A Franz Boas Reader*, ed. George W. Stocking. New York: Basic Books.

—— 1925. "Note: Teton Sioux music," *Journal of American Folklore* 28: 319.

Brady, Erika. 1988. "The Bureau of American Ethnology: folklore, fieldwork, and the federal government in the late nineteenth and early twentieth centuries." Pp. 35–45 in *The Conservation of Culture: Folklorists and the Public Sector*, ed. Burt Feintuch. Lexington: University Press of Kentucky.

Bronner, Simon. 1986. *American Folklore Studies: An Intellectual History*. Lawrence: University Press of Kansas.

—— 1990. "'Toward a common center': pragmatism and folklore studies," *Folklore Historian* 7: 23–30.

Deacon, Desley. 1997. *Elsie Clews Parsons: Inventing Modernity*. Chicago: University of Chicago Press.

Densmore, Frances. 1968 [1917]. "Incidents in the study of Ute music." P. 40 in *Frances Densmore and American Indian Music: A Memorial Volume*, ed. Charles Hofmann. Contributions from the Museum of the American Indian, vol. 23. New York: Heye Foundation.

Gilman, Benjamin Ives. 1891. "Zuni melodies," *A Journal of American Ethnology and Archaeology* 1: 63–91.

—— 1908. *Hopi Songs*. Boston: Houghton Mifflin.

Gray, Judith A. 1988. *Great Basin/Plateau Indian Catalog, Northwest Coast/Arctic Catalog*. Vol. 3: 3 of *The Federal Cylinder Project: A Guide to Field Cylinder Collections in Federal Agencies*, Dorothy Sara Lee, gen. ed. Studies in American Folklife, no. 3: 5. Washington, DC: American Folklife Center, Library of Congress.

Herskovits, Melville J. 1973. *Franz Boas*. Clifton, NJ: Augustus M. Kelley.

Hinsley, Curtis M. 1981. *Savages and Scientists: The Smithsonian Institution and the Development of American Anthropology, 1846–1910*. Washington, DC: Smithsonian Institution Press.

—— 1983. "Ethnographic charisma and scientific routine: Cushing and Fewkes in the American Southwest, 1879–1893." Pp. 53–69 in *Observers Observed: Essays on Ethnographic Fieldwork*, vol. 1 of *History of Anthropology*, ed. George Stocking Jr. Madison: University of Wisconsin Press.

Hofmann, Charles, ed. 1968. *Frances Densmore and American Indian Music: A Memorial Volume*, Contributions from the Museum of the American Indian, vol. 23. New York: Heye Foundation.

Holmes, W. H. 1906. Letter, National Anthropological Archives. Photocopy in files of Federal Cylinder Project, American Folklife Center, Library of Congress, Washington, DC.

Krehbiel, H. E. 1891. Letter. *Musical Visitor* 20 (10): 256–7. Reprinted in *Ethnomusicology* 2 (1958): 116–17.

Kroeber, Theodora. 1970. *Alfred Kroeber: A Personal Configuration*. Berkeley and Los Angeles: University of California Press.

Lee, Dorothy Sara. 1984. *Early Anthologies*. Vol. 8 of *The Federal Cylinder Project: A Guide to Field Cylinder Collections in Federal Agencies*, Dorothy Sara Lee, gen. ed. Studies in American Folklife, no. 3: 8. Washington, DC: American Folklife Center, Library of Congress.

Lowie, Robert H. 1943. "Franz Boas, anthropologist," *Scientific Monthly* 56: 183–4.

—— 1959. *Robert H. Lowie, Ethnologist: A Personal Record.* Berkeley and Los Angeles: University of California Press.

Mark, Joan. 1988. *Stranger in Her Native Land: Alice Fletcher and the American Indians.* Lincoln: University of Nebraska Press.

Ong, Walter, SJ 1967. *The Presence of the Word: Some Prolegmena for Cultural and Religious History.* New Haven, CT: Yale University Press.

—— 1982. *Orality and Literacy.* New York: Methuen.

Radin, Paul. 1949. *The Culture of the Winnebago: As Described by Themselves.* Special Publications of the Bollingen Foundation, no. 1. *International Journal of American Linguistics*, Memoir; no. 2. Bloomington: Indiana University Publications in Anthropology and Linguistics.

Reichard, Gladys. 1943. "Franz Boaz and folklore." Pp. 52–7 in *Franz Boas, 1858–1942*, ed. Alfred L. Kroeber. Memoirs of the American Anthropological Association 61. Menasha, WI: American Anthropological Association.

Roberts, Heleh Heffron. 1931. "Suggestions to field workers in collecting folk music and data about instruments," *Journal of the Polynesian Society* 40: 111–12.

Roberts, Helen Heffron and Robert Lachmann. 1963 [1935] "The re-recording of wax cylinders." *Zeitschrift für vergleichende Musickwissenschaft* 3: 75–83. Reprinted in *Folklore and Folk Music Archivist* 6: 4–11.

Smith, Marion. 1959. "Boas' 'natural history' approach to field method." Pp. 46–60 in *The Anthropology of Franz Boas*, ed. Walter Goldschmidt. Menasha, WI: American Anthropological Association.

Stocking, George W. 1974. "Introduction: the basic assumptions of Boasian anthropology." Pp. 1–20 in *The Shaping of American Anthropology: A Franz Boas Reader*, ed. George W. Stocking. New York: Basic Books.

—— 1992. *The Ethnographer's Magic, and Other Essays in the History of Anthropology.* Madison: University of Wisconsin Press.

Wax, Rosalie H. 1971. *Doing Fieldwork: Warnings and Advice.* Chicago: University of Chicago Press.

Yates, Michael. 1982. "Percy Grainger and the impact of the phonograph," *Folk Music Journal* 4: 265–75.

Zumwalt, Rosemary Lévy. 1988. *American Folklore Scholarship: A Dialogue of Dissent.* Bloomington: Indiana University Press.

Part II

Representing Others

To what extent are media producers responsible for promoting distortions and misrepresentations of cultures and how do such distortions emerge? These are the core questions addressed in Part two of this book. Following Stuart Hall's identification of the many representational strategies in media that exploit and magnify cultural/racial/ethnic/gendered difference at the expense of common humanity, the contributions that follow isolate ways in which non-Western peoples and marginalized Westerners are transformed into Others.

We begin with a chapter from James Faris's probing investigation of *Navajo and Photography: A Critical History of the Representation of an American People*. Echoing some of John Berger's criticisms of photographic representation (see chapter 4, this volume), Faris assesses Western photographic images of Navajo and the ideologies underlying them. He queries the assumed neutrality of media and proceeds to argue that there is a very limited set of conventional representations of Navajo that Westerners find acceptable. His analysis reveals that Western photographs of Navajo reveal far more about Westerners than they reveal about Navajo.

Photography is again under investigation in Catherine Lutz and Jane Collins's *Reading National Geographic*. In chapter 7 Lutz and Collins tackle the representation of race and gender in the highly popular *National Geographic* magazine. Their stated goal is to expose the ways in which images of racial and gendered Others are composed, framed, and distributed so as to place the analysis of racism and gender discrimination "in the realms of human agency and to emphasize the specificity of its historical forms" (Lutz and Collins 1993: 156). Examination of which types of pictures were prevalent in the magazine during which time period enabled Lutz and Collins to measure social attitudes and mark shifts in consciousness. Like Faris, Lutz and Collins conclude that despite all editorial claims to cross-cultural understanding, photographic explorations of non-Westerners or marginalized Westerners ultimately sustain and reinforce dominant Western ideologies of Self and Other.

In chapter 8 Ella Shohat and Robert Stam reach a similar conclusion by way of their analysis of popular film. Surveying an enormous quantity of films that intentionally or unintentionally embrace imperialist ideologies, they find that "The dominant European/American form of cinema not only inherited and disseminated a hegemonic colonial discourse. It also created a powerful hegemony of its own through monopolistic control of film distribution and exhibition in much of Asia, Africa, and the Americas" (Shohat and Stam 1994: 103). Nostalgia for empire is never benign (however much Hollywood and European film industries may claim otherwise) for imperialist projects necessarily entail the domination of other peoples. Therefore all imperialist films by definition perpetuate agendas of Otherness and Western social superiority. Shohat and Stam take their analysis through world exhibitions, imperial adventure films, Westerns, contemporary action adventure films, and media coverage of the Gulf War. Point for point, their analysis perfectly illustrates all the tropes of empire outlined by David Spurr (1993) in his book *The Rhetoric of Empire: Colonial Discourse in Journalism, Travel Writing, and Imperial Administration*.

Finally, any discussion of cross-cultural media representations would be incomplete without attention to ethnographic film. Ethnographic film, once the *raison d'être* of visual anthropology, has come under attack in recent years for exacerbating rather than minimizing cross-cultural distance and understanding. Wilton Martinez's pioneering work (Martinez 1990, 1992, 1996) on ethnographic film spectatorship led to rather dismaying appraisals of the state of the field. Were the films doing more harm than good? Did early filmmakers focus undue attention on the extraordinary and more bizarre aspects (from a Western point of view) of other cultures, thereby increasing a sense of alienation, distance, and culture shock? Indeed, Martinez's research among students in introductory anthropology courses with high ethnographic film content suggested that, contrary to filmmaker intent, ethnographic films were "perpetuating the devaluing and stereotyping of other cultures" (Martinez 1992: 132).

This debate over the success or failure of ethnographic film coincided (not coincidentally) with the "crisis of representation" that emerged in anthropology in the late 1980s (Rabinow 1986; Clifford 1988; Trinh 1989). Just as written anthropological texts came under scrutiny for loud assertions of authority that drown out the voices of those being represented, ethnographic films came under scrutiny for framing non-Western lives according to Western filmic and narrative principles. In chapter 9 David MacDougall, himself a noted ethnographic filmmaker, tackles these issues head-on and offers one interpretation for why some films and not others fail in communicating across cultures. He argues that when a culture's own narrative codes and style of self-presentation are compatible with those of the West it facilitates cross-cultural understanding. When, however, a culture's codes conflict with Western ones, culture shock and alienation result.

SUGGESTED READINGS

Allen, Tim and Jean Seaton, eds. 1999. *The Media of Conflict: War Reporting and Representations of Ethnic Violence*. London and New York: Zed Books.

Barbash, Ilisa and Lucian Taylor. 1997. *Cross-Cultural Filmmaking: A Handbook for Making Documentary and Ethnographic Films and Videos*. Berkeley, CA: University of California Press.

Bate, David. 1993. "Photography and the colonial vision," *Third Text* 22: 81–91.

Campbell, Christopher P. 1995. *Race, Myth, and the News*. Thousand Oaks, CA: Sage Publications.

Crawford, Peter I., ed. 1993. *The Nordic Eye (Proceedings from NAFA 1)*. Hojbjerg, Denmark: Intervention Press.

Crawford, Peter Ian and David Turton, eds. 1992. *Film as Ethnography*. Manchester: Manchester University Press.

Devereaux, Leslie and Roger Hillman, eds. 1995. *Fields of Vision: Essays in Film Studies, Visual Anthropology, and Photography*. Berkeley: University of California Press.

Edwards, Elizabeth, ed. 1992. *Anthropology and Photography, 1860–1920*. New Haven, CT: Yale University Press.

Faris, James. 1992a. "Anthropological transparency: film representation and politics," in *Film as Ethnography*, ed. Peter Ian Crawford and David Turton. Manchester: Manchester University Press.

—— 1992b. "A political primer on anthropology/photography." In *Anthropology and Photography 1860–1920*, ed. Elizabeth Edwards. New Haven, CT: Yale University Press.

—— 1993. "A response to Terence Turner," *Anthropology Today* 9 (1): 12–13.

—— 1996. *Navajo and Photography: A Critical History of the Representation of an American People*. Albuquerque: University of New Mexico Press.

Graham-Brown, Sarah. 1988. *Images of Women: The Portrayal of Women in Photography of the Middle East 1860–1950*. New York: Columbia University Press.

Hall, Stuart. 1980. "Encoding/decoding." Pp. 128–38 in *Culture, Media, Language: Working Papers in Cultural Studies, 1972–79*. London: Hutchinson.

—— 1981. "The whites of their eyes: racist ideologies and the media." In *Silver Linings: Some Strategies for the Eighties*, ed. George Bridges and Rosalind Brunt. London: Lawrence and Wishart.

—— 1989. "Cultural identity and cinematic representation," *Framework* no. 38.

—— ed. 1997. *Representation: Cultural Representations and Signifying Practices*. London: Sage Publications.

Heider, Karl G. 1976. *Ethnographic Film*. Austin: University of Texas Press.

Jenkins, David. 1993. "The visual domination of the American Indian: photography, anthropology and popular culture in the late nineteenth century," *Museum Anthropology* 17 (1): 9–21.

Kulick, Don and Margaret E. Willson. 1992. "Echoing images: the construction of savagery among Papua New Guinean villagers," *Visual Anthropology* 5 (2): 143–52.

Lutz, Catherine and Jane Collins. 1991. "The photograph as an intersection of gazes: the example of *National Geographic*," *Visual Anthropology Review* 7 (1): 134–49.

—— 1993. *Reading National Geographic*. Chicago: University of Chicago Press.

MacDougall, David. 1991. "Whose story is it?" *Visual Anthropology Review* 7 (2): 2–10.

—— 1998. *Transcultural Cinema*. Princeton, NJ: Princeton University Press.

Martinez, Wilton. 1990. "Critical studies and visual anthropology: aberrant vs. anticipated readings of ethnographic film," *Society for Visual Anthropology Review* (spring): 34–47.

—— 1992. "Who constructs anthropological knowledge? Toward a theory of ethnographic film spectatorship." Pp. 130–61 in *Film as Ethnography*, ed. Peter Ian Crawford and David Turton. Manchester: Manchester University Press.

—— 1996. "Deconstructing the 'viewer': from ethnography of the visual to critique of the occult." Pp. 69–100 in *The Construction of the Viewer: Media Ethnography and the Anthropology of Audiences (Proceedings from NAFA 3)*, ed. Peter I. Crawford and Sigurjon Baldur Hafsteinsson. Hojbjerg, Denmark: Intervention Press.

Morley, David and Kevin Robins. 1995. "Cultural imperialism and the mediation of Otherness." Pp. 228–50 in *The Future of Anthropology*, ed. Akbar Ahmed and Cris Shore. London: Athlone Press.

—— 1995. *Spaces of Identity: Global Media, Electronic Landscapes and Cultural Boundaries*. London: Routledge.

Mulvey, Laura. 1989. *Visual and Other Pleasures*. Basingstoke: Macmillan.

Naficy, Hamid and Techome H. Gabriel, eds. 1993. *Otherness and the Media: The Ethnography of the Imagined and Imaged*. Langhorne, PA: Harwood Academic Publishers.

Nichols, Bill. 1994. *Blurred Boundaries: Questions of Meaning in Contemporary Culture.* Bloomington: Indiana University Press.

Rollwagen, Jack R., ed. 1988. *Anthropological Filmmaking: Anthropological Perspectives on the Production of Film and Video for General Public Audiences.* Chur and London: Harwood Academic Publishers.

—— 1993. *Anthropological Film and Video in the 1990s.* Brockport, NY: The Institute.

Rony, Fatimah Tobing. 1996. *The Third Eye: Race, Cinema and Ethnographic Spectacle.* Durham, NC: Duke University Press.

Ruby, Jay. 2000. *Picturing Culture: Explorations of Film and Anthropology.* Chicago: University of Chicago Press.

Said, Edward. 1978. *Orientalism.* New York: Random House.

Shohat, Ella and Robert Stam. 1994. *Unthinking Eurocentrism: Multiculturalism and the Media.* London and New York: Routledge.

Sontag, Susan. 1990 [1977]. *On Photography.* New York: Anchor Books.

Spurr, David. 1993. *The Rhetoric of Empire: Colonial Discourse in Journalism, Travel Writing, and Imperial Administration.* Durham, NC: Duke University Press.

Steiner, Christopher B. 1995. "Travel engravings and the construction of the primitive." Pp. 202–25 in *Prehistories of the Future: The Primitivist Project and the Culture of Modernism,* ed. Elazar Barkan and Ronald Bush. Stanford, CA: Stanford University Press.

Taylor, Lucien. 1996. "Iconophobia: how anthropology lost it at the movies," *Transition* issue 69.

—— ed. 1994. *Visualizing Theory: Selected Essays from V.A.R., 1990–1994.* New York: Routledge.

Tomlinson, John. 1991. *Cultural Imperialism.* Baltimore, MD: Johns Hopkins University Press.

Traube, Elizabeth G. 1992. *Dreaming Identities: Class, Gender, and Generation in 1980s Hollywood Movies.* Boulder, CO: Westview Press.

Trinh T. Minh-ha. 1989. "The language of nativism: anthropology as a scientific conversation of man with man." Pp. 47–76 in *Woman, Native, Other: Writing Postcoloniality and Feminism.* Bloomington: Indiana University Press.

Troy, Timothy. 1992. "Anthropology and photography: approaching a Native American perspective," *Visual Anthropology* 5 (1): 43–61.

Webb, Virginia-Lee. 1995. "Manipulated images: European photographs of Pacific peoples." Pp. 175–201 in *Prehistories of the Future: The Primitivist Project and the Culture of Modernism,* ed. Elazar Barkan and Ronald Bush. Palo Alto, CA: Stanford University Press.

Weinberger, Eliot. 1994. "The camera people." Pp. 3–26 in *Visualizing Theory: Selected Essays from V.A.R., 1990–1994,* ed. Lucien Taylor. New York: Routledge.

Weiner, James F. 1997. "Televisualist anthropology: representation, aesthetics, politics," *Current Anthropology* 38 (2): 197–235.

Willis, Sharon. 1997. *High Contrast: Race and Gender in Contemporary Hollywood Film.* Durham, NC: Duke University Press.

Wright, Chris. 1998. "The third subject: perspectives on visual anthropology," *Anthropology Today* 14 (4): 16–22.

6

The Gaze of Western Humanism

James C. Faris

I want to see, that's all. This is my life. I want to see.
Leni Riefenstahl, on the occasion of her ninetieth birthday
(*Vanity Fair, September 1992*)

Photography as Enterprise

There are broad circumstances that characterized the intellectual organization of the social forms in which photography developed. The West had long privileged scopic enterprises and visual modalities, and by the mid-nineteenth century an observational visualist hegemony became a persistent focus of modernism in social, scientific, and aesthetic endeavors – and certainly of anthropology.[1] More specifically, photography came into being at a time when the notion of observation itself was in change in the West, as a complex interaction of technology, emerging mass culture, surveilling state institutions, and associated intellectual ferment.[2] This transition entailed a wholesale shift in vision itself and the rise of an assertive observational and perspectival paradigm that was matched locally by the United States's conquest and aggressive expansion in Navajoland. These are the intellectual, institutional, and disciplinary settings in which and by which Navajo were photographed.

The history of photography, especially given the recent sesquicentennial celebrations of its invention, has generated an enormous literature. More recently, there has begun to appear a literature specifically on photographic encounters with non-Westerners, both critical and introspective (cf. Graham-Brown 1988; Coombes 1994; Lippard 1992; Edwards 1992 and references therein; and Baker 1983, and Fergus 1991, for recent literary treatments of the topic) and celebratory, art historical, and aesthetic (cf. Fleming and Luskey 1993).

It is now increasingly accepted that photography's vision is peculiar and historical and can be divorced neither from specific developments in its history nor from the particularly Western milieu (a changing and sometimes contradictory one) in which it emerged. These considerations are compounded when photographic practices and discourses intersect with other cultural forms whose knowledges and practices are (or were) independent of photography and its history in the West. These encounters have been, of course, unequal, and conquest and oppression have usually warped the engagement. Photography evolved and matured in the same capitalist environment as did anthropology,[3] and both moved, with an expansionist West, into Navajoland at approximately the same time.

Navajo constitute both a generic as well as a unique and peculiar Other to photography's West and the West's photography. I will first consider photography as a practice of the West, then apply this analysis to the photography of Navajo. Much of what might be said about photography of Navajo can be said of the photography of all local minorities, but much is specific. I must echo some recent debate concerning photography and its limitations in order to outline some of the positions by which I will approach the photography of Navajo. Thus, in this chapter I discuss some of the possibilities and limitations, the framings and the exposures, of the depiction of Navajo by non-Navajo. After this initial commentary, I will examine specific photographic registers, modes and characters of representation, and concrete histories of photography in Navajoland.

Just what can be expected or understood from photographs? I will argue that, culturally, not very much can be understood about Navajo from photographs of them. But certainly something can be understood of photographers, of the various ways the West privileges photographs, and of the way Navajo photographically appear to the West. Photographs of Navajo mirror the West's desire and ambition, its obsession and pathology, and something of the specificity of social relations the West views as important (normal) and/or important for Navajo to have (marginal and/or normalized).[4] However, in addition to reading the West in its photography of Navajo, we also can read the limits and boundaries of how Navajo can appear in such representations and typical ways in which they do appear.

The focus became a black hole into which freedoms disappeared; frames become the limits and boundaries of representations. Photographs are gripping because they have boundaries and focus; the limits are clear, established. Framing is a device for speaking (showing) truth. Parameters are as vital as the "frame" of an ethnography – the table of contents, with its categories presented in some hierarchy, priority, unity, or totality. Of course, the severity of its framing and editing greatly limited any interactive possibilities.

But what is not represented? What is outside the frame? What is not focused? What are the silences to be listened (watched) for? To ask this is to displace intention and the founded field of representation; it is to pose a question not of vision but of project. It is, indeed, to critique – to disrupt the closure, the framing, the representation – by noting within the representation that which cannot be represented (by the photograph, by the white man, by the texts available to viewers). It is to deconstruct (or to challenge without program) the conceptual space, the rule of being, the representation. It is to subvert desire (perhaps for another one). Framing is, then, in this sense, censoring. It is not, however, a simple aesthetic gesture, for an alternative power might rest in what does not appear.[5]

Photography exposes another rigidly limiting feature – the strange notion that, by freezing the moment, it transcends temporality (or that which we allow in conventional Western wisdom). But in fact, quite the opposite is true. Photography represents a shutter stop/closing, a deliberate avoidance of any and all other notions of time. Positioning in time and space to allow discourse, allowing speech to subjects, is impossible. Photography is thus an index in but a single tense, one voice, and one time.[6] Photography makes present; it appears to transcend time. But this appearance, this presence, in photography's rigidly fixed single dimension obviously cannot transcend time, particularly if such time involves (as it always does) the possibility of an alternative historical discourse, completely opaque or invisible to photography. As Benjamin (1969: 226) noted, photographs "become standard evidence for historical occurrences, and acquire a hidden political significance. They demand a specific kind of approach; free-floating contemplation is not appropriate to them." Temporally, then, photography could only look back, could only be reactionary, and could only satisfy in terms of nostalgia, preservation, desire, and other nihilistic fixations from a single discursive view. The image exceeds both the photographer and the subject and is present in different time, open to different judgments and protocols. It no longer "represents" what might have been intended, and we are not sure what that might have been. We are not only *allowed* to read and assign meaning, we are required and forced to do so.

Through its ubiquitous extension as a mechanically reproduced commodity, photography soon succumbed to the gaze, as the world (especially the non-Western world) came to be an exhibition to silent consumers. Whereas "spectacles" (local events focused upon) once had specific audiences, they now became available to all individuals, though (ironically) increasingly privately, to the point of isolation. Photography made gazing upon events (thereby making them "spectacles") safe for voyeurs. This form of isolating and emphasizing events demanded an observational pacifism, and it was particularly important in photography's extension to distant peoples – now domesticated, made safe.[7] With the rise of hunting metaphors that dominated photographic production (the "shot," the "captured" image), photography thus became symbolic in the West's history of conquest, of defeat, of assimilation or disappearance, a force by which white men's power was validated. This aspect was particularly vital in photography that involved social relations with minorities and of subjugation. Such considerations give rise to a preservational motivation – things (cultures, peoples) only disappear as evidence of the West's own history. Nostalgic tendencies, so common in the repertoire of the photography of Native Americans, have come to signify desire for, at best, more liberal and generous white men and, at worst, the conqueror, the Indian fighter, the raw expansionist, the frontier tamer.

Photography introduced, as no other visual medium could, the "death effect," such that "the person who has been photographed is dead ... dead for having been seen" (Metz 1985: 85) – dead for having been stopped from breathing, speaking. Photographs mute; they render speechless, "for every photograph of the Other is a visual reduction of the Other – both a distancing and a muting" (Owens 1993: 106). They do not speak; they are "worth a thousand words" only if there is nothing to say, if all communication has already taken place, if every possible sign is already shared – i.e., if all texts are already accepted. The photograph is transparent only if we allow it to be.[8] This transparency produces a curious alienation, a strange appearance of unarguable reality whose monuments are photographs. We can have little idea about, say, Navajo social relations from photographs of Navajo except those the photographer or the viewer (whose expectations are themselves constituted in part by photographs) brings.

I am suggesting that photography has no undeniable, necessary, or essential characteristics. Though it emerged in a historical setting, a prepared field, a way of seeing, a set of visualist discourses, a saturated domain in and by which it was accepted, utilized, extended, and allowed, these were and are ever-shifting fields. Moreover, consumers of photography changed over time, and just as there is no existential production, neither is there a monolithic, pan-historical observer. On the contrary, viewers and subjects were immersed in specific and changing social, political, and aesthetic relations that helped shape photography's development and future quite as much as photography imposed itself on them. This instability is perhaps an important reason to remain optimistic in the face of an otherwise somewhat inimical critique.

Of course, there have always been claims that photography was a "neutral technology," for it was but simply (or complexly) a photochemical process that somehow candidly reflected the world on the other side of the photographer (albeit with a cultural component, especially if the camera were in the hands of the Other,[9] excluding all ethical issues). These insistences were often heard loudest from anthropological photographic practitioners,[10] for they were important in expediting the discipline's emergence as a social *science*.

The emergence of anthropology as a distinct field of inquiry with an abstract methodology coincided very closely with photography's rise.[11] The earliest anthropological methodology primers mention the importance of photography,[12] and by the late nineteenth century photography of non-Westerners, of the exotic, was very popularly consumed.[13] At this time the great imperialist powers were extending across the globe, and the United States was pushing toward the Pacific. The West's authorizing signatures – rhetorics, disciplinary apparatuses (Western humanism), history, knowledges – were commonly expressed in photography, culminating in banal "Family of Man" notions or the reformist propaganda of Farm Security Administration (FSA) photography projects, which began once everyone had been safely conquered. Photography of this sort came to be normalizing, and an Other was thereby established, an Other always measured off the West's Normal. The "perpetual ratio" (Foucault 1973: 378) was thus maintained, as the West became the only subject, the only eye. Native Americans could not be seen looking back; they could only be seen.

This coincidence itself deserves more commentary, for it derives from a social context of expansionism, a motion into the rest of the world, an imperialist acceleration. In the American Southwest, in Navajoland, this expansion was dramatic from the 1870s on, involving a series of government expeditions with explicit photographic agendas and the extension of the capitalist mandate and Manifest Destiny.

Early scholars denied the setting in which photography emerged (the deep and complex history of visualism) and was practiced (the shallow history of expansionist capital and imperialist conquest). As a result, two sorts of critical scholarship initially dominated the study of photography. The first type focused exclusively on aesthetics and the aesthetics of form.[14] Form aesthetics came to be relentlessly preferred above other levels of actual use and meaning. There was rarely any historical or cultural context outside the formal postures – just a transcendent aesthetic ideal. Photographs were to speak for themselves (indeed, to "say it all") only because viewers were all educated (or uneducated) to the same form assumptions – that photography was a neutral photochemical operation about which only assessments of form aesthetics were possible. This view precluded any other text, any introduced meaning, any critique at all. From this perspective, there could be, then, axiomatically fascist aesthetics, bourgeois aesthetics, where meaning was introduced *from* form, as if there were some intrinsic link between morality and aesthetics.

The second type of scholarship offered rudimentary political critique based upon a rather limited notion of representation.[15] It often argued that the photograph did not adequately represent or only represented partially, as if it were always a stereo-type and that a "real" representation could be achieved photographically – "seeing is believing," "photographs never lie." The problem here is not that representations are always inadequate (of course they are inadequate) but that they never produce a truer or more accurate view. Representation is compromised because it holds a complex relation to reality – sometimes contradictory, sometimes laced with desire, fear, sometimes jeopardized, filled with resistance.[16] Indeed, the relationship of reality to representation is not something that can even be satisfactorily approached in rationalist discourse.

With the traditional, limited conceptions of representation, one obvious solution was to put cameras in the hands of the "misrepresented" subaltern. There were and are now a number of experiments in this direction. But cross-cultural photography is very problematic, for unless it can manage to *enforce* a boundary cross-culturally, it normally drags the framing practices of the dominant photographer and the tech-nology along. As will be argued, placing the subaltern behind the camera is not a solution to the problems of representation, however much it may be vital to intro-ducing alternative discourses; it illustrates only the photographer's specific perti-nences. Photograph[er]s only present themselves – anything we think we see beyond them in the photograph is representation. I am not convinced that conventional indigenous photography gets around this problem.[17] Some less experienced or less introspective Navajo photographers acquired a reflective vision or double vision; they came to see themselves as others see them. Photography alone can never provide a truth (the real) to challenge power – that can only be an intellectual affair. It is quite as discursive as "nature," or "rights," or "law," or "poverty," or "theory," or the West's Other. But, as will be argued, for Navajo the images became the reality, and Navajo (real) emerged as imperfect or inadequate copies of their images.[18] This was a complicated issue, however, for the West's real Navajo were not exactly what they appeared. Photographs could only tell the whole story if accompanied by anthropology's text.

Navajo, Photography, and Anthropology

What, then, does it mean to be Navajo *in photographs*? This is not as sententious a question as it sounds, for photographic representations are critical in shaping responses to specific "meanings" of Navajo that have been persistently put forward. Indeed, photographs have been instrumental in bringing into being something of these "Navajo." "Reality" came to be (had to be) the representation, the photo-graphic image. These meanings change, of course, over time, but a stubborn stability characterizes them.

Photography of Navajo by definition leans on canons of realism, the opaqueness of the subject, the transparency of the photograph. Navajo are received as real, as existing independently of the technology, of the social relations that placed them in the photograph, and of their own social relations. But they do not exist, or at least not in any necessary or nontrivial way revealed in the photograph. As noted, photographs say less about Navajo than about photographers of Navajo – indeed, in the limited ways in which Navajo appeared, photographers used amazingly few tropes, and these are remarkably consistent over time. Navajo, by definition, are set in their alterity to white men, their distance of Other accepted without so much as a whimper from viewers. They appear unproblematic as Other, and the photograph functions as document, as presentation of Navajo alterity. Non-hostile Navajo are, after all, such attractive Others (and certainly vital to a vast tourist industry in the region). To be sure, some representations were clichés, some objectionable by later historical movements, some objectionable by later Western sensitivities. But never was the alterity dissolved, even by Navajo photographers (unless the latter avoided photographs of people). The tropes of photographs of Navajo people were always rigidly on Western terms; there has emerged as yet no setting in which instruments of gaze can present Navajo. Photography is not a medium that has a being in indigenous culture (or local presentation), though it may be used in explicit political ways by local artists.

I am not attempting to expose, reveal, or analyze a falsity about Navajo that has been perpetrated by photography. Photography is not a conspiracy; but, more important, there are no truth claims or determinant conclusions in this analysis. Of course, there are some clearly erroneous labels, claims, settings, and deliberate distortions in photography, as in Western texts, where Navajo are misunderstood, misinterpreted, or missing. But the task is to examine the nature of the entity constructed, not match it or compare it with a "real" entity it may have claimed to portray or with which it might be contrasted. Nevertheless, this register of representation is a vitally important one for the West, for it is how the West often "knows" it has knowledge of Navajo – Navajo are always framed, muted, always as the photographs show them.

To demonstrate, let us contrast the photography of another Southwestern minority group, the various Pueblo peoples, as evidence of their history and social relations with the photography of Navajo as evidence of another history and other social relations. Suffice it to say here that the West is prepared to accept in rough outline the antiquity of the Pueblo peoples to the region and thereby at least some of their claims to aboriginality and to the land on which they are found. It thus accepts Pueblo social relations in general (at least with respect to the land). Photographs confirm these claims and are considered evidential to them. This is not to say that photographers have never violated Pueblo peoples,[19] only that at least some Pueblo truths are considered in correspondence with Western truths.

Quite the contrary is true of photography of Navajo, which denies their status as aboriginals, as claimants, as indicators of their own social relations (though a naive minority popular discourse – among uninformed tourists, romantic Big Mountain supporters, etc. – regards Navajo as being in their place, as if they have always been there). Photographs are silent to any other discourse and certainly to a Navajo discourse. Anthropological orthodoxy and conventional wisdom deny them autochthonous or indigenous status, and photographs thus become evidences of their exotic and foreign origins, their hybrid and borrowed culture – Navajo as adapters.[20] In other words, Navajo exist in a space (as must all photographic subjects), but they also exist in a time (a dimension about which photography has very little to say, confined as it is to the instant past moment). Space is turned into time in the West's predatory grip on history, and thus Navajo space is denied them by the Western rewrite of their history, by the anthropological evidence of their late arrival, their adaptation, their alien and exotic character. Photography becomes a perverse asset in denying Navajo history, and they become subjects only of the West's history. The only Navajo social relations seen are those that can be placed into two visual dimensions. Metamorphic relations are not visible to photography, nor clan relations, nor healing relations, nor migrations, nor emergences from netherworlds, nor Navajo histories with European Americans. Though some of the specific Western history of Navajo is hidden to photographs by convention (for example, exploitation), so too are any and all Navajo claims to a history.

What, then, are the rhetorics of the Western photographic projects, the figures that allow us to recognize the master portrayals that forecast, that indicate something of the optical unconscious? I will argue that even though they change over time, even though one discourse penetrates and percolates into others, the projects are quite limited in number, and the same gestures appear again and again over time. There are a very limited series of frames. To extend much beyond these risks the West's "Navajo," whether or not any other "Navajo" is possible in photographic registers. Thus, there is not another history, another means of discussing photographic appropriations and inscriptions of Navajo by the West – Navajo inscriptions. Unlike ceremonial accounts involving many histories, photographs of Navajo allow for no alternative narratives. All histories are reduced to those of the West.

There is insufficient depth for much of an archeology of Navajo photography, as the stratigraphy is mixed and jumbled, interpenetrated by other layers, or not varied enough to enable us to discriminate. We can only distinguish the tropes that were there from the beginning, and in many cases, despite the commentary of their partisans, Laura Gilpin looks like Edward Curtis, Marcia Keegan looks like Curtis, John Running looks like Curtis, Joel Grimes looks like Curtis or Carl Moon, or Frederick Monsen. Thus, photography is even more impoverished than it might initially appear; it is not even in competition with an alternative. These limited photographic registers will be explored in some detail, but it is clear that Navajo appear only as another intention of the West, not because the "reality" of Navajo is not comprehensible but because it may well be impossible to approach in prevailing discourses of the West or in Western modes of visual representation. There certainly cannot be, in this circumstance, nonviolent representation – exposing the inability of Western humanism to adequately evince (represent) the non-West.[21] Certainly aesthetics of form dictate "success" or "interest" in many photographs from Navajoland. But Navajo, except as devices (as red rocks, trees, turquoise, silver, sheep, lichens), are irrelevant, nothing more than exotic props, colorful contrivances to Western projects.

The point is not just that Navajo social relations – Navajo texts – are ignored (though they are) but that there is no space available for them. The West cannot have its Navajo without having saturated the universe of possibilities, and the serious admission of Navajo discourse is simply impossible. Culture dictates appearance, and the West's culture has its own view of Navajo culture. A great many contemporary Western photographers accompany their photographic collections with Navajo memoirs (usually, of course, in English) or commentary. But such attempts to present Navajo "reality" presume the universalism of the predatory West. This universalism not only saturates the possible meaning of photographic referents (subjects) but also establishes "respect" – the way the West prides itself on the ostensible acceptance of its Other (a feeling of, "How good we are to 'know' them"). Of course, no direct link exists between the subject matter of the photograph and the text, revealing that this gesture is at base cynical – it constitutes an insulation, a wrap of liberal acceptance on the terms of the West (which dictates the texts worthy of inclusion). In the available examples, the relationship between the photographs and the texts are extremely problematic. Unless readers and viewers suspend judgment, the relations of text to photographs are not even clear or logical. The kind of respect or dignity offered in these efforts, however sincerely motivated, is only possible on Navajo terms.[22]

In some instances, of course, Navajo have sought out or solicited photographs. However, the sediments of Western narrative or Western discourse are present in all cases, evidence that Navajo behave "just like Americans." But this also says something about the very real limitations of photography. Though photography is considered innovative, in fact there is no room for innovation. Photography must lean on new subjects, new types of behavior, new things people will do in front of the camera. Its innovation depends upon how outrageous humans will be, how shameless or perverse photographers will be. As Navajo change, so, too, does the photographic subject, but because the West only has a limited series of ways in which it accepts Navajo images, photography must, in most circumstances, continually repeat itself. Navajo can only be accepted as exemplars of a tradition the West names for them (thus maintaining the tradition/modernity dichotomy so important to Western notions of progress and hierarchy), even (and especially today) if photographed in behavior considered ironic, used as pastiche, or thought humorous – herding sheep with motorized vehicles, shooting arrows with high-tech bows, participating in healing practices while wearing sneakers and t-shirts emblazoned with names of heavy-metal rock stars.

Photographs of objects of alternative social relations such as Navajo are curious. They enter Western discourse in familiar registers (what other registers might they enter under?), take on an evidential quality after so long a time, and become Western treasures, as the social relations that originally situated them are no longer very apparent, unknown, or perhaps even totally opaque. They are rather like the pyramids of Giza or the Bastille – that is, monuments of considerable beauty and character. Once the social relations that enabled their creation are no longer in place, a deliberate amnesia sets in, one that does not encourage history to be read critically. This has been called a "ruins aesthetic" in the museum world – the West neither wants to know what things might have looked like prior to the West, nor what social relations might have generated them, nor certainly which ones generated Western access. There is in this circumstance a slippery link between content and form – a link normally ironclad in the West, with its rationalist and materialist foundations. What social relations were necessary to build the Cheops pyramid or make possible the Bastille? Are Navajo as the objects and subjects of conquest (as represented photographically) themselves even necessary to their photographs? Can Navajo social relations (productive, in the Western view, of Navajo visual appearance) be photographed, be represented? Are non-Navajo photographs of Navajo nothing more than ruins, great monuments of the West's alienation, its contumaciousness? How do we account for the few very fine photographs taken by Westerners of Navajo – or is it, as Lippard (1992: 37) suggested, especially in the aftermath of genocide, "simply luck?"

Navajo History

A central thesis of this volume is that photography has been very important in the situating of Western perceptions of Navajo, not simply in superficial appearances and pastoral setting but also in the establishment of a specific Navajo history and a concrete conventional wisdom of Navajo character and being in time.

Several nonphotographic Navajo histories exist. At least one of these, broadly accepted by many Navajo, suggests that in a remote past *diné* ("people of the earth's surface") came to occupy the area that today (approximately) makes up greater Navajoland. This event occurred after the *diné diyinii* ("Holy People") had freed the earth from almost all the monsters that had inhabited it, and it appeared largely as it did prior to Europeans. The *diné* had emerged from netherworlds and metamorphosed from other forms. Various adventures characterized the *diné* as they learned to live in this world, and on occasion the Holy People taught some of them how they might help other *diné* to deal with some of the remaining monsters, such as sickness. For example, one individual, *bi'áhát'iní*, was taken by the Holy People and instructed in the healing system today known as the Nightway (*t'éé'jí*), which addresses maladies of the head. After the *diné* appeared on the earth's surface, the Holy People came to occupy, invisibly, the sacred places of Navajoland – the canyons, ruins, mountaintops, etc. – and remain there today. Several Navajo healing practices, such as the Nightway, include masked individuals impersonating some of the Holy People.

Although this history acknowledges that Navajo borrowed some traditions, the substance of Navajo culture came to be in this fashion, especially the orders – the proper social relations (*hózhó*) – that are so essential to Navajo health and beauty. The violation of these orders brings about sickness and death and thus necessitates the great healing system, which reestablishes the essential conditions of beauty and order, the proper social relations between people and between people and "nature" (though this dichotomy does certain violence to the actual Navajo conceptions, and though nature is certainly discursive in Navajo reckoning). This history makes little claim to account for other populations and establishes no priorities for alternative histories. It sets Navajo social relations and order and provides for their maintenance and their reorder. To violate, consciously or unconsciously, such social relations – such orders – is to become sick, disordered, ugly. Navajo causality, in direct reference to innovation, creativity, the new, suggests that the world was once ordered and cannot be added to without severe consequences for the established social relations. Indeed, in this view, knowledge is limited (or cannot be added to), and there is no room for innovation, addition, adaptation, assimilation[23] – the very opposite of the Western view of Navajo character and history (that is, the notions of Navajo as borrowers, Navajo as nonauthentic, Navajo as late, intrusive, mimetic, Navajo as adaptive).

Another history assigned to the Navajo stems from conventional European–American archeology and anthropology of the Southwest. This history, with some minor technical debate, argues that the Navajo are a people recently derived from Asia who arrived into approximately their present location (first a bit further north and further east) as late as the fifteenth century A D – essentially, just in time to greet the first Europeans moving north from Mexico. This history suggests that Navajo arrived with a cultural system substantially different from their current one, which in large measure has been borrowed subsequently – much of their lifeway and economy from European introductions, their great healing system from the Pueblo, weaving and silverwork and herding from elsewhere, and so forth. Navajo in this history are adaptive and assimilative. This history *does* prioritize other histories – the others, it argues, are wrong.

These two histories, at least, are in some conflict over fundamentals. It is not my purpose in this volume to debate their relative merits, nor certainly their truths and falsities. But photography becomes very important to one of these histories and is largely irrelevant to the other, and I will argue that this difference is vital to understanding some of the complexities of the photography of Navajo. To the history by which the West situates Navajo, photography is an important evidential apparatus and thus a tool of rationalist discourse. Navajo in this scheme are but information, but signs – gestures that can be captured by imaging devices. There is an established and firm hierarchy of observer, subject, representation, real, imaginary, object.

However, events that occurred long after the origins postulated in these opposing histories established the setting for photography's temporal appearance in the area. Because of claimed violations of agreements, claimed persistent raids on European–American settlers and herds – not to mention European–American expansionist needs, specifically coveted mineral deposits, nor the ambitions of redundant Civil War military men – the great majority of Navajo were rounded up in 1864 and forcibly marched ("The Long Walk" – *Hwéeldi*) from Arizona to Bosque Redondo (Fort Sumner) on the Pecos River in eastern New Mexico Territory. The first known

Plate 6.1 "Little Navajo Girl." David Burnett, photographer, n.d. (1992?), Monument Valley. "The Native Americans have a cagey relationship with the camera, but they know the value of a good picture" (Nicholson and Burnett 1993: 31). Certainly it is important for Westerners to have these attitudes, as if Native Americans have much choice. Why is one of their only means of earning income locally held in such contempt, and why is contempt not extended to those who make such activity desirable? The little girl seems uncertain and appears to be seeking instruction or support from elsewhere. Despite the "reality" of the landscape this photograph credits the thesis that Navajo are not aboriginal but only "adapters." Photograph © David Burnett/ Contact Press/Colorific.

photographs of Navajo date from and were taken at the incarceration at Fort Sumner.

The chronological history of the photography of Navajo begins with the first photographs of Navajo in captivity, taken in 1866. No known photographs of Navajo in their homeland were taken prior to that year. There was something diabolically prophetic about this, for it is a central thesis of this volume that Navajo have been essentially captive to photography ever since – to the majority discourses of photographers and to the commercial, scientific, humanist agendas of the West.

Let me close this segment by referring back to the epigram with which the chapter began.[24] This aphorism expresses something fundamental to the West's obsessions in general and is menacingly instructive to a volume on photography of non-Westerners – the "natural" privilege that should permit Westerners to be able to view, to see anything, anywhere, anytime and the consequent benefits to be gained if this vision is extended to those with the right artistic talent, character, and empathy (basically, Western Enlightenment philosophy). That this can be, and often is, a dramatically assumptive, racist, and predacious motivation never occurs to Riefenstahl, of course, nor probably to many photographers.[25] But the world of other humans is not simply available as fodder, either for photographic capture or for ethnographic predation, however compassionate the Westerner. The belief that vision must be accorded all privilege, that there exists some natural concession or fundamental freedom to extend sight everywhere, must be understood as a temporal and historical feature of expansion and power, not a biological or universally accruing human right.[26]

NOTES

1   Cf. Fabian (1983: 106); Faris (1992b); Tyler (1984). Some would argue this is a Western motion of even longer standing – all the way back to Plato and shadows on cave walls (cf. Rorty 1980) – or even a product of the projective activity of speech itself (cf. Derrida 1976; 1993). Tyler (in Clifford and Marcus 1986: 130) discusses well the implications of visualist ideology for referential discourse, its "presumption of representational signification," and the failure of the entire enterprise in ethnographic matters.

2   Cf. Crary (1990); Levin (1993). Photography was hardly a unique, singular invention. At the time of its emergence there were actually several different technical processes in experimentation simultaneously – that is, lots of photographies were competing for acceptance. Some (for example, Fox-Talbot) even had to be persuaded to pursue their experiments.

3   Cf. Pinney (1992).

4   This should be read not as an essentialist statement but as a critique of the view that a photograph speaks its subject by its reference – that it conveys a neutral image of what was in front of the lens. It is a critique of the view that photographs are opaque (or alternatively, transparent to reality), that photographers and photographic culture are not in every way the makers.

5   Postmodern photographers, somewhat like surrealists, attempt to obliterate those boundaries, whereas modernists toyed with them, flirted with the edges, deliberately called attention to them, or suggested them slightly differently – but never effectively transcended such boundaries nor established alternative power relations that might challenge the existence of such boundaries. Indeed, photography, as commonly practiced, cannot do so. In a new study, Krauss (1993) discusses this idea.

6 The medium of photography has been argued to be inherently pornographic, as – incapable of being an erotic art – it "presents us with the object of lust rather than a symbol of it"; it "gratifies fantasy of desire long before ... expressing the fact of it" (Scruton 1981: 602–3). Some feminists argue that because photography was normally a process of the symbolic order (rather than the real or the imaginary and rather than the signifying order), it could thus not escape the domination of the father.

7 See Sontag, in Goldberg (1981: 516).

8 Cf. Walton (1984).

9 See here especially Worth and Adair (1972), but also Faris (1992a, 1993).

10 Cf. Banta and Hinsley (1986: 127); Collier (1967: passim).

11 Cf. Pinney (1992).

12 Cf. Edwards (1992).

13 See also in this regard Albers and James (1988) and Coombes (1994).

14 There is considerable debate about photographic aesthetics – especially in the genre of "art" photographs. Soloman-Godeau (1985), for example, persuasively argues that if photography is going to lean on the world, on reality (to distinguish itself from, say, painting), it effectively jettisons the possibility of a genuinely photographic aesthetic.

15 Cf. Berger (1972, 1980, 1982).

16 Cf. Young (1990).

17 Cf. Faris (1992a, 1992b, 1993); Moore (1992); but see also Turner (1992), Ginsburg (1994).

18 They certainly have – see Lyon (1988).

19 A typical example is K. Brower (1967), a photographic book with abundant images of Anasazi ruins (considered by Western authorities to have been built hundreds of years before Navajo arrival in the area) but filled with quotations from Navajo healing texts and commentary from Navajo philosophy. This is all the more remarkable in that the text itself was organized by a leading academic authority on Navajo, Stephen C. Jett.

20 Indeed, as Todorov (1984: 71) has put it: "It is impossible ... to desire both cultural diversity and familiarity with culture other than our own; for familiarity is the final step toward the disappearance of that diversity. [This, in effect, requires us to face the prospect of being] anti-humanist, to oppose the intermixing of cultures."

21 Navajo have commonly been represented as bearers of a beautiful and meaningful culture. But once they are represented, there is no attempt (nor need, as it has been superficially established within a humanist discourse of acceptance on Western terms) to seriously consider that culture. In other words, the exercise is basically to establish them as human beings – the issue isn't that their cultural values or notions might be superior to the West's or preferable to the West's or even *different* from the West's. To do so, indeed, would be implicitly to criticize the West. How do Navajo critique the West? Rarely, for they are all too aware of the very significant power differentials. If they actually act, they are labeled terrorists and killed or jailed. Their only real way of criticizing the West that doesn't immediately bring down something on their head is to simply be themselves, to *do* their own culture. What if they banned cameras on the reservation? What if they declared everything save the main highways private property and prosecuted anyone found there or found taking photographs?

22 When once asked about the sources of his creativity and the inspiration for his painting, the surrealist Magritte remarked, "I do not feel I am 'adding' something to the world: where would I get what I am adding if not from the world?" [June 20, 1957] (Alexandrian and Waldberg 1980: 74–5). Magritte, in this sense, would have been quite comfortable with Navajo thinking. Perhaps, indeed, this is one of the reasons Magritte gave up painting, as he realized its limitations in "saying" anything – the inability of painting

(visual imaging) as a means by which to "discuss" these matters. This ever-changing/never-changing, creative/conservative axis is argued in more detail in Faris (1990). But it also points up here – in dramatic difference – photographic imaging and the "new" in Navajo cosmology and in Western cultural practice.

23   Riefensthal's plea, stemming from her long photographic experience, is described mostly in terms that feature her as innocent victim in her recent memoirs (Riefenstahl 1987; 1992 – but see also Faris 1988a, 1993a). Despite her grotesque propaganda heritage during the Third Reich, her outlook (pun intended) here reveals the rigidly Western motivations in her "quest for Great Art" and how very Western was the Nazi movement in its fundamentals, especially in many of its cultural expressions.

24   Cf. Ammann (1993) for a recent example.

25   There are today, of course, abundant experimental works in vision and film that attempt to call attention to the peculiarly Western "view" of sight and to discuss it further and/or transcend it (cf. Tyler 1984; Taylor 1993; Krauss 1993; Trinh 1989). For theoretical discussion, see Krauss (1988).

Some historians of ethnographic photography actually argue that the problem is that photography and visual inscriptions have been ignored for the written word and argue that the balance should be redressed (cf. Scherer 1988, 1990). Though not attempting to privilege the written, on the strength of the experience with the photography of Navajo, this study would clearly argue to the contrary, *against* photography's ascendancy or any further authority.

REFERENCES

Albers, Patricia C. and William R. James. 1988. "Travel photography: a methodological approach," *Annals of Tourism Research* 15: 134–58.

Alexandrian, Sarane and Patrick Waldberg. 1980. *René Magritte*. New York: Filipacchi Books.

Ammann, Karl. 1993. "Hostile places and sensitive subjects," *Outdoor Photography* 9 (3): 48–71.

Baker, Will. 1983. *Backward: An Essay on Indians, Time, and Photography*. Berkeley, CA: North Atlantic Books.

Banta, Martha and Curtis Hinsley. 1986. *From Site to Sight: Anthropology, Photography, and the Power of Imagery*. Cambridge, MA: Peabody Museum of Harvard University, Harvard University Press.

Benjamin, Walter. 1969. *Illuminations*. New York: Schocken Books.

Berger, John. 1972. *Ways of Seeing*. Harmondsworth: Penguin Books.

—— 1980. *About Looking*. New York: Pantheon.

—— 1982. *Another Way of Telling*. New York: Pantheon.

Brower, Kenneth, ed. 1967. *Navajo Wildlands*. Text by Stephen C. Jett. Photographs by Philip Hyde. San Francisco and New York: Sierra Club and Ballantine Books.

Clifford, James and George E. Marcus, eds. 1986. *Writing Culture: The Poetics and Politics of Ethnography*. Berkeley: University of California Press.

Collier, John C., Jr. 1967. *Visual Anthropology: Photography as Research Method*. New York: Holt, Rinehart, and Winston. Revised and expanded edition, Albuquerque: University of New Mexico Press, 1986, with foreword by Edward T. Hall, and Malcolm Collier as additional author.

Coombes, Annie E. 1994. *Reinventing Africa: Museums, Material Culture and Popular Imagination*. New Haven, CT: Yale University Press.

Crary, Jonathan. 1990. *Techniques of the Observer: On Vision and Modernity in the Nineteenth Century*. Cambridge, MA: MIT Press.

Derrida, Jacques. 1976. *Of Grammatology*. Translated by G. Chakravorty Spivak. Baltimore, MD: Johns Hopkins University Press.

—— 1993. *Memoirs of the Blind*. Translated by Pascale-Anne Brault and Michael Naas. Chicago: University of Chicago Press.

Edwards, Elizabeth, ed. 1992. *Anthropology and Photography 1860–1920*. New Haven, CT: Yale University Press and the Royal Anthropological Institute.

Fabian, Johannes. 1983. *Time and the Other: How Anthropology Makes Its Object*. Chapter 4: "The Other and the Eye." New York: Columbia University Press.

Faris, James. 1988. "'Southeast Nuba': a biographical statement," in *Anthropological Film-making*, ed. Jack Rollwagen. New York: Harwood Academic Publishers.

—— 1990. *The Nightway: A History and a History of the Documentation of a Navajo Ceremonial*. Albuquerque: University of New Mexico Press.

—— 1992a. "Anthropological transparency: film representation and politics," in *Film as Ethnography*, ed. Peter Ian Crawford and David Turton. Manchester: Manchester University Press.

—— 1992b. "A political primer on anthropology/photography," in *Anthropology and Photography 1860–1920*, ed. Elizabeth Edwards. New Haven, CT: Yale University Press.

—— 1993a. "Leni Riefenstahl and the Nuba peoples of Kordofan Province, Sudan," *Historical Journal of Film, Radio and Television* 13 (1): 95–7.

—— 1993b. "A response to Terence Turner," *Anthropology Today* 9 (1): 12–13.

—— 1996. *Navajo and Photography: A Critical History of the Representation of an American People*. Albuquerque: University of New Mexico Press.

Fergus, Charles. 1991. *Shadow Catcher*. New York: Soho Press.

Fleming, Paula Richardson and Judith Luskey. 1993. *Grand Endeavors of American Indian Photography*. Washington: Smithsonian Institution Press.

Foucault, Michel. 1973. *The Order of Things: An Archaeology of the Human Sciences*. New York: Vintage Books.

Ginsburg, Faye. 1994. "Culture/media: a (mild) polemic," *Anthropology Today* 10 (2): 5–15.

Goldberg, Vicki, ed. 1981. *Photography in Print*. New York: Simon and Schuster.

Graham-Brown, Sarah. 1988. *Images of Women: The Portrayal of Women in Photography of the Middle East 1860–1950*. New York: Columbia University Press.

Krauss, Rosalind. 1988. "The im/pulse to see," in *Vision and Visuality*, ed. Hal Foster. Dia Art Foundation Discussions in Contemporary Culture, No. 2. Seattle: Bay Press.

—— 1993. *The Optical Unconsciousness*. Cambridge, MA: MIT Press.

Levin, David Michael, ed. 1993. *Modernity and the Hegemony of Vision*. Berkeley: University of California Press.

Lippard, Lucy, ed. 1992. *Partial Recall*. New York: New Press.

Lyon, Luke. 1988. "A history of the prohibition of photography of Southwest Indians' ceremonials," in *Reflections: Papers on Southwest Culture History in Honor of Charles H. Lange*, ed. Anne V. Parry. Archaeological Society of New Mexico papers, no. 14.

Metz, Christian. 1985. "Photography and fetish," *October* 34: 81–90.

Moore, Rachel. 1992. "Marketing alterity," *Visual Anthropology Review* 8 (2): 16–26.

Owens, Craig. 1993. "Improper names." Pp. 101–10 in *Unsettled Objects*. Published in conjunction with the exhibition AMERICA *Invention* by Lothar Baumgarten. New York: Solomon R. Guggenheim Museum.

Pinney, Christopher. 1992. "The parallel histories of anthropology and photography." Pp. 74–95 in *Anthropology and Photography, 1860–1920*, ed. Elizabeth Edwards. New Haven, CT: Yale University Press.

Riefenstahl, Leni. 1987. *Memoiren*. Munich: Albrecht Knaus Verlag FmbH.

—— 1992. *The Seive of Time: The Memoirs of Leni Riefenstahl*. London: Quartet Books.

Rorty, Richard. 1980. *Philosophy and the Mirror of Nature*. Princeton, NJ: Princeton University Press.

Scherer, Joanna Cohan. 1988. "The public faces of Sarah Winnemucca," *Cultural Anthropology* 3 (2): 178–204.

—— 1990. "Historical photographs as anthropological documents: a retrospect," *Visual Anthropology* 3: 131–55.

Scruton, Roger. 1981. "Photography and representation," *Critical Inquiry* 7: 577–603.

Solomon-Godeau, Abigail. 1985. "Winning the game when the rules have been changed: art photography and postmodernism," *exposure* 23 (1): 5–15.

Taylor, Lucien, ed. 1993. *Visualizing Theory*. New York: Routledge.

Todorov, Tzvetan. 1984. *The Conquest of America*. New York: Harper and Row.

Trinh T. Minh-ha. 1989. *Woman, Native, Other*. Bloomington: Indiana University Press.

Turner, Terence. 1992. "Defiant images: the Kayapo appropriation of video," *Anthropology Today* 8 (6): 5–16.

Tyler, Stephen. 1984. "The vision quest in the West, or what the mind's eye sees," *Journal of Anthropological Research* 40 (1): 23–40.

Walton, Kendall L. 1984. "Transparent pictures: on the nature of photographic realism," *Critical Inquiry* 11: 246–77.

Worth, Sol and John Adair. 1972. *Through Navajo Eyes: An Exploration in Film Communication and Anthropology*. Bloomington: Indiana University Press.

Young, Robert. 1990. *White Mythologies: Writing History and the West*. London and New York: Routledge.

7

The Color of Sex: Postwar Photographic Histories of Race and Gender

Catherine A. Lutz and Jane L. Collins

Again and again, when the negative space of the woman of color meets the Age of Mechanical Reproduction or, worse yet, Baudrillard's "simulations," the resulting effect is...a form larger than life, and yet a deformation powerless to speak.

Wallace (1990: 252)

Race is, as Henry Gates has said, "a trope of ultimate, irreducible difference between cultures, linguistic groups, or adherents of specific belief systems which – more often than not – also have fundamentally opposed economic interests" (Gates 1985: 5). It is a trope that is particularly dangerous because it "pretends to be an objective term of classification." Gates points to the profoundly social nature of racial classification. Social groups engaged in struggle define racial boundaries in the contexts of that struggle; powerful groups then invoke biology in a post-hoc justification of the boundaries they have drawn. Those in power elaborate observable physical differences – no matter how subtle – into explanations, affirmations, and justifications for inequality and oppression. Once this work is done, and the boundaries are intact, racist theory produces full-blown descriptions of culture and personality that juxtapose powerful ego and degraded/dangerous alter, "lending the sanction of God, biology, or the natural order to even presumably unbiased descriptions of cultural tendencies and differences" (ibid).

As Gates and others have so eloquently pointed out, racial difference – and its supposed cultural concomitants – is thus not the *source* of the many contemporary conflicts where it is said to be at issue. It is never a simple matter of two groups in contact finding themselves so physically and culturally different that they just cannot get along. Rather, racial and cultural difference become coded ways of talking about other differences that matter, differences in power and in interests.[1] For this reason – however absolute and intransigent they may seem – racial/racist theories must retain flexibility and are frequently ambiguous. As Omi and Winant (1986: x) have said, race is an inherently unstable "complex of social meanings, constantly being transformed by political struggle." To work to uncover the social arrangements that give rise to and reproduce racism is to place its analysis in realms of human agency and to emphasize the specificity of its historical forms.

Tranquil Racial Spaces

Race theories form one of the most powerful and lethal systems in the world for communicating about difference. Zora Neale Hurston wrote, "Race consciousness is a deadly explosive on the tongues of men" (Hurston 1984: 326). It has justified the most heinous of social relations, including slavery, genocide, and apartheid. Yet, dangerous as they are, race theories have infiltrated the commonsense thinking of most people in the United States, profoundly influencing the ways they perceive and account for cultural difference. Like other forms of essentialist reasoning, racist thought has the appeal of simplicity, and it draws authority from invoking biology and nature. The hegemony of a theory of race that insists on two "bounded" human categories has been challenged in the 1970s and 1980s by new waves of immigration from Asia and Latin America, confronting white America with tremendous diversity in physical appearance and widely varying relationships between race and class, education and social standing.

National Geographic magazine is the product of a society deeply permeated with racism as a social practice and with racial understandings as ways of viewing the world. It sells itself to a reading public that, while they do not consider themselves racist, turn easily to race as an explanation for culture and for social outcome. The Geographic headquarters itself has had few black employees up to the present, despite the predominantly African-American citizenry of Washington, DC. It is not surprising, therefore, that while race is rarely addressed directly in the magazine, American racial categories powerfully structure the images contained in its pages.

One of the most powerful and distinctive tenets of racism in the United States is that "blackness" is an all-or- nothing phenomenon. Racial law through the period of the Civil War, and after, held that any "black" ancestry was sufficient to define one as black. As recently as 1983, this type of reasoning was upheld by the State Supreme Court of Louisiana, when it refused to allow a woman descended from an eight-eenth- century white planter and a black slave to change the classification on her birth certificate from "colored" to "white" (Omi and Winant 1986: 57). The laws in question and the cultural preconceptions upon which they were based insistently denied the reality of interracial sexual relations or of the sexual exploitation that so frequently accompanied the master/slave relation. They insisted on pure and un-equivocal categories with which to reason about difference. Such airtight categories were viewed as necessary to guard the privileges of "whites" as absolute and to justify the denial of equality to "blacks" as an impossibility.

Nevertheless, when Euramericans turned their eyes outside the borders of their own country, other forms of reasoning prevailed. Evolutionist thought dominated attempts to understand the human diversity of the non-European world. Such thinking needed a continuum, one that was grounded in nature. Skin color is obviously highly variable, only with some difficulty made to accommodate the simple binary classification "black"/"white" in the United States. A continuum of skin color was thus a perfect biological substratum on which to graft stories of human progress or cultural evolution.

Late nineteenth-century fairs and expositions frequently organized the world cultures they presented along an evolutionary scale. These almost always corresponded to a racial continuum, as Rydell (1984) has noted, from the "savagery" of the dark- skinned Dahomeyans, to the Javanese "Brownies," to the "nearly-white" Chinese and Japanese. As evolutionary trajectories were reproduced over the course of the twentieth century, in anthropological theory and in white popular consciousness, they were almost always connected to a scale of skin color, which was then construed, in many cases, as an independent form of verifying their correctness.

As we turned to *National Geographic* photographs, we hypothesized that it was this more differentiated scale – rather than the simple binary opposition called into play for analyzing American culture – that would inform the ways *National Geographic* would portray, and readers would interpret, images of the third world. Distinctions in popular stereotypes of the peoples of Northern and sub-Saharan Africa, or of Melanesia and Polynesia, indicated that Euramericans drew conclusions about others based on the *degree* of darkness of skin color. As we analyzed constructions of race in *National Geographic* photographs, we thus coded them in a way that would allow us to determine whether "bronze" peoples were portrayed differently from those who would be more commonly seen as "black"; to see, in other words, if simple binary constructions informed the images, or if more complex evolutionary schema structured their messages. This coding procedure was based solely on observable skin color (not cultural characteristics). We used a decision rule that deliberately maximized polarization of categories; that is, when it was difficult to decide whether an individual was "bronze" or white, we coded white. When it was difficult to decide between bronze and black, we coded black. We coded only individuals identifiable as native to the region portrayed, eliminating the few Westerners who appeared in the photographs.

The period for which we analyzed photographs – 1950–86 – encompassed times of great turmoil in racially defined relationships in the United States. The late 1950s and early sixties saw struggles to overturn racial codes that were more intense than any since the Civil War era. Participants in the civil rights movement sought to obtain basic civil liberties for African Americans; they used the egalitarian verbiage of federal law to challenge the restrictive laws and practices of states and municipalities. Such changes did not simply require a change in the legal codes and their implementation, however; they also demanded, as Omi and Winant (1986: 90) have argued, "a paradigm shift in established systems of racial meanings and identities."

Nonviolent tactics such as freedom rides, marches, attempts to desegregate key southern school districts and universities, and sit-ins at segregated lunchrooms characterized the period up until the passage of the 1964 Civil Rights Act and the voting rights legislation of 1965. By the mid-sixties, however, many who had worked and hoped for these changes were disillusioned. Changes in legislation had profound symbolic value, and materially benefited a small number of middle-class African Americans. But they did not alter the economic circumstances of the vast majority of blacks living in poverty, and they did not adequately challenge the tremendous and continuing burden of institutional racism. This led to an increasing radicalization of key branches of the civil rights movement and to angry rioting in places like Watts and Newark (Harding 1981; Carson 1981).

The civil rights movement contested white privilege and its counterpart, the institutionalized oppression of black Americans. It also contested the very meaning of race in American culture. As white Americans were deprived of one of the master tropes explaining their privileged position in the world, race became an uncomfortable topic for them. This discomfort was reflected in the pages of *National Geographic*. Clearly the magazine did not cover the turmoil in American cities during the period. At the same time, it sought to ease anxieties in its portrayal of the third world. As late as the early 1950s, the Euramerican reading public could comfortably view Asian and African peoples attending white explorers and photographers – carrying them across rivers, pulling them in rickshaws, carrying their packs and bags. By the late sixties, however, these images were too disturbing, the possibility of rebellion and anger too present. White travelers simply disappeared from the pictures, removing the possibility of conflictual relationships.

With this action, third world spaces were cleared for fantasy. Black and bronze peoples of Africa, Asia, and Latin America were shown going about their daily lives – happy, poor but dignified, and attuned to basic human values. The photographs themselves were not much different from those of previous decades; however, in the racially charged context of the fifties and sixties their meaning had changed. The implicit contrast with Watts and Newark, or even with Selma and Montgomery, operated behind the scenes. The third world was constituted as a safe, comfortable space, where race was not an issue and where white people did not have to reevaluate the sources of their privilege.

Plate 7.1 As late as the 1950s the Euramerican reading public could comfortably view images such as this – of Asian, African, and here New Guinea peoples attending white explorers. Images of Westerners, and so of racially mixed groups, declined sharply in the late 1960s. Photograph by E. Thomas Gilliard and Henry Kaltenthaler, National Anthropological Archives, the Smithsonian Institution, Washington DC.

Apparently, though, in the minds of *National Geographic* editors, too much of even a reassuring fantasy could be disturbing. Until 1961, the numbers of white, black, or bronze people appearing in any given issue of *National Geographic* was variable. In 1952, for example, only about 15 percent of people depicted in articles on the third world were dark-skinned; in 1958, the figure was about 46 percent. Beginning in 1961, however, a remarkably stable pattern began to appear. For the next 25 years the percentage of dark-skinned people in any issue held very constant at about 28 percent. People who could be categorized as bronze formed a fairly regular 60 percent of the total, with the remaining 12 percent constituted by light- or white-skinned third-world peoples. The intense stability of this pattern, and particularly the almost invariant proportion of dark-skinned people represented, suggests that editorial attention may have been focused on the issue.

This is admittedly indirect evidence. We did not find anyone at *National Geographic* who was willing to say that skin color *per se* was a consideration in putting together issues (although conversations in planning meetings suggest that it may well be). We do know, however, that *National Geographic*'s marketing department gathered significant amounts of data on the popularity of different kinds of articles and that Africa was by far the least popular world region. By marketing definitions, African peoples constituted a difficult topic; to the extent that market concerns drive content, one would thus expect some sort of regulation of their coverage.

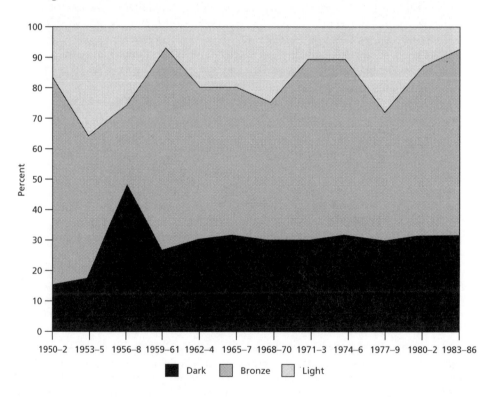

Figure 7.1   Skin color in photographs, 1950–1986.

In photographs where dark-skinned peoples were portrayed, there were interesting regularities – contributing to an overall image of contentment, industriousness, and simplicity. The activity level of individuals portrayed in the photographs, for example, clearly sorted out on an evolutionary scale marked by skin color. Individuals coded as black were most likely to be depicted in high levels of activity – engaged in strenuous work or athletics. People coded white were most likely to be engaged in low-level activity – seated or reclining, perhaps manipulating something with their hands, but rarely exerting themselves. Those coded bronze were most likely to be found engaged in activities that fell somewhere between the two extremes, such as walking or herding animals. In keeping with this pattern, people of color (both black and bronze) were most likely to be portrayed at work in the photographs we examined, while people with white skin were most likely to be found at rest.

The determinants of such a portrayal are complex, and the message it conveys is multifaceted. We cannot rule out the brute empiricist interpretation that what is portrayed is determined to some extent by events in the real world: that photographers found dark-skinned peoples at work more often than lighter-skinned peoples. Yet when we are dealing with sets of published photographs that are chosen out of a universe of tens of thousands that were taken, we are clearly dealing with a problem of representation as well.

Portraying people at work is in keeping with an editorial policy that demands a focus on the positive as construed in the United States, that is, the work ethic. It is possible to imagine that editors sought to counter images of the laziness of non-white peoples (in the Euramerican imagination) by deliberately presenting an alternative view. At the same time, in the contradictory manner characteristic of colonial/neocolonial mentality (see Bhabha 1983), it is also possible that deeply ingrained notions of racial hierarchy made it seem more "natural" for dark-skinned peoples to be at work and engaged in strenuous activity. White ambivalence toward the black male seems often to center on issues of strength: while vigor is good for the worker to have, it also has the threatening connotations of potential rebelliousness, and so some hobbling often follows the rendition of strength.

Few topics have occupied as much space in colonial discourse as the relationship of blacks to labor. As Euramericans sought to build wealth on the backs of colonized peoples and slaves, they sought to continually refine methods of maximizing the labor they were able to extract. Colonial administrators and plantation bosses continually reported on the success and failures of innovations in the process. The double mentality reflected in the reports was plain – while people of color were inherently suited to labor, they never wanted to work hard enough in the fields of their white masters. The image of a tremendous capacity for work, coupled with an unwillingness to actually work, gave rise to contradictory stereotypes. The heritage of these stereotypes and the labor relations that gave rise to them can be traced in the strenuously employed black bodies portrayed in the pages of *National Geographic*.

In equally regular ways, black and bronze peoples were more likely to be portrayed as poor and technologically backward. Individuals coded as white were more likely to be wealthy and less likely to be poor than other categories. Still, only 21 percent of black and 16 percent of bronze people were photographed in contexts of poverty. Fully 70 percent of the former and 72 percent of the latter were shown without any markers of wealth of poverty, and some of each group were portrayed as wealthy. There is clearly a tension at work in the photographs. The greater poverty of darker-skinned individuals may, in part, be empirically determined; it is also in keeping with popular Euramerican stereotypes of the degraded status of dark-skinned peoples. On the other hand, *National Geographic*'s policy of focusing on the positive and avoiding advocacy precludes too heavy an emphasis on impoverishment. Dark- skinned peoples have a somewhat greater tendency to be poor – one might construe the statistical weight of the photographs as saying – but in general, they live well.

Individuals coded white were most likely to be depicted with machines of one kind or another; black and bronze individuals were most likely to be shown with simple tools of local manufacture. Not surprisingly, people of color were more often depicted as engaged in ritual. This variable also sorted out along an evolutionary/ skin color continuum: the darker the skin color, the more likely to engage in ritual practices. In classic evolutionist terms, superstition (represented by ritual) and science (represented by technology) were counterposed. Similarly, the darker the skin color of an individual, the less likely he or she was to be depicted in western-style clothing. The darker the skin of the people portrayed, the less they were associated with things European, and the more exotic they were rendered.

Given these trends, it was somewhat surprising to find that dark-skinned peoples were not photographed in natural settings (that is, in landscapes or greenery) more often than their lighter-skinned counterparts. They were, however, more likely to appear in settings where surroundings were not clearly discernible. Such portrayals tend to aestheticize the materials on which they focus. In this case, they force attention to the lines, shapes, and colors of the bodies themselves, rather than providing information about the context in which the bodies appear. Because such photos were relatively numerous, dark-skinned people consequently appeared in *social* surroundings less frequently.

People coded black or bronze were more likely to be photographed in large groups than those coded white. They were less likely to be portrayed alone or in small intimate groups. People of color were therefore less often the subject of individualized photographic accounts, attentive to "biographic" features and life circumstances. They were more often portrayed as part of a mass, perhaps thereby suggesting to readers that they had relatively undifferentiated feelings, hopes, or needs. Individuals coded black and bronze were far more likely to be photographed gazing into the camera than individuals coded white – a stance that, while complex and sometimes ambiguous – frequently suggests availability and compliance.

Despite some Euramerican stereotypes, dark skin was not associated with evidence of aggression in the pages of *National Geographic* through most of the period we have examined. Aggression is generally taboo as a topic for *National Geographic* photographs, except in the highly specific case of depicting US military power. Additionally, however, to retain its status as a place where white US readers go to assuage their fears about race and cultural difference, *National Geographic* must studiously avoid photographs that might suggest a potential threat from colonized and formerly colonized peoples. To depict anger, violence, or the presence of weapons is to evoke the fear that they might be turned to retaliation. They serve as an uncomfortable reminder of a world given to struggles for independence, revolutions, and rebellions.

In the marketplace of images, *National Geographic* relies on two intertwined strategies. It relies on recognition – on offering readers what they already know and believe in new and appealing ways. Its reputation and sales also turn on the classic humanism with which it portrays the world. In its depictions of "non-white" peoples, the humanist mission – to portray all humans as basically the same "under the skin"[2] – comes into conflict with Western "commonsense knowledge" about the hierarchy of races.

The organization of photographs into stories about cultural evolution (couched in more "modern" terms of progress and development) provides the partial resolution of this contradiction. These stories tell the Euramerican public that their race prejudice is not so wrong; that at one point people of color *were* poor, dirty, technologically backward, and superstitious – and some still are. But this is not due to intrinsic or insuperable characteristics. With guidance and support from the West, they can in fact overcome these problems, acquire the characteristics of civilized peoples, and take their place alongside them in the world. In the context of this story, the fact that bronze peoples are portrayed as slightly less poor, more technologically adept, serves as proof that progress is possible – and fatalistically links progress to skin color.

At the same time, the "happy-speak" policies of *National Geographic* have meant that for people of color – as for others – the overall picture is one of tranquillity and well-being. We are seldom confronted with historical facts of racial or class violence, with hunger as it unequally affects black and white children, or with social movements that question established racial hierarchies. One photographer expressed this discrepancy poignantly, pointing to a photograph of an African family in a 1988 issue on population. "The story is about hunger," he said, "but look at these people. It's a romantic picture."

This is not to say that no one at the National Geographic Society is attentive to these issues. Dedicated photographers and editors worked hard in the 1970s to produce and push into print two deeply disturbing accounts of apartheid. And while this attempt engendered a repressive movement within the society's Board of Trustees, an article critical of South African black homelands appeared in February 1986.

The same strategies, however, pursued in different epochs, can have different meanings and consequences. The humanist side of *National Geographic* in the 1950s and 1960s denied social problems; it also provided images of people of color living their lives in relatively dignified ways. It gave short shrift to poverty and disharmony, but it permitted a certain amount of identification across racial boundaries. In a period when racial boundaries were highly visible and when African Americans were struggling for equal rights under the law, these images could be read, at least in part, as subtle arguments for social change.

The 1970s have been characterized as a period of "racial quiescence," when social movements waned and conflicts receded (Omi and Winant 1986: 2). Racial oppression did not cease, but it was not as openly contested. In turn, the 1980s saw a backlash in undisguised attempts to dismantle legislation protecting civil rights and nondiscriminatory practices. These moves did not require and, in fact, assiduously avoided, an explicitly racial discourse. Busing, originally implemented to desegregate schools, was overturned under banners of "community control" and "parental involvement." Rejections of racially balanced textbooks were couched in terms of battles against "secular humanism" and "political correctness." And in the 1988 presidential campaign, movements of people of color were recast as "special interests" (Omi and Winant 1986: 125).

In such a context, classic humanism takes on pernicious overtones. The denial of race as a *social* issue, in a society with a profoundly racist history and where institutional racism still exists, forecloses dialogue on the issues. *National Geographic* has not intentionally contributed to this foreclosure; it goes on producing pictures in much the same way it has for years. And yet the message that we are all alike under the skin takes on new meaning in a social context which denies that discrimination exists or that race has been used to consolidate the privilege of some and oppress others. The racism of the 1980s was not confrontational and defiant; it simply turned its back on the issues. The tranquil racial spaces of *National Geographic* can only contribute to this willed ignorance.

The Women of the World

National Geographic's photographs of the women of the world tell a story about the women of the United States in the post – World War II period. It is to issues of gender in white American readers' lives, such as debates over women's sexuality or whether women doing paid labor can mother their children adequately, that the pictures refer as much as to the lives of third-world women. Seen in this way, the *National Geographic*'s women can be placed alongside the other women of American popular culture: the First Lady, the woman draped over an advertisement's red sports car, the Barbie doll, the woman to whom the Hallmark Mother's Day card is addressed. Rather than treating the photos as simply images of women, we can set them in the context of a more complex cultural history of the period, with the sometimes radical changes it brought to the lives of the women who are the readers (or known to the male readers) of the magazine.

Research on the visual representation of women makes clear that female images are abundant in some domains (advertising) and virtually absent in others (photojournalism of political subjects). The invisibility extends much further for women of color. In popular images as well as the dominant white imagination, as Hull, Scott and Smith (1982) have so eloquently told us, "All the women are white, all the blacks are men," and black women are simply invisible. The photographs of *National Geographic* are indispensable because it is one of the very few popular venues trafficking in large numbers of images of black women. While the photographs tell a story about cultural ideals of femininity, the narrative threads of gender and race are tightly bound up with each other. In the world at large, race and gender are clearly not separate systems, as Trinh (1989), Moore (1988), Sacks (1989), and others have reminded us.

For the overwhelmingly white readers of the *Geographic*, the dark-skinned women of distant regions serve as touchstones, giving lessons both positive and negative about what women are and should be (compare Botting 1988). Here as elsewhere, the magazine plays with possibilities of the other as a flexible reflection – even a sort of funhouse mirror – for the self. The women of the world are portrayed in sometimes striking parallel to popular images of American womanhood of the various periods of the magazine's production – for instance, as mothers and as beautiful objects. At certain times, with certain races of women, however, the *Geographic*'s other women provide a contrast to stereotypes of white American women – they are presented as hard-working breadwinners in their communities. Primarily, however, the *Geographic*'s idealization of the world's people extends to women in egalitarian fashion. To idealize "the other woman" is to present her as like, or aspiring to be like, her American counterpart. The other woman is exotic on the surface (she is dressed in an elaborate sari and has a golden nose ring) but her difference is erased at another, deeper level (she is really just a mother, and like the American woman, interested in making herself beautiful through fashion). The woman's sameness in difference allows us to avoid the sense of threat that confrontation with difference presents and allows us to pursue the illusory goal of wholeness.

As with American women in popular culture, third-world women are portrayed less frequently than men: one quarter of the pictures we looked at focus primarily on women.[3] The situation has traditionally not been much different in the anthropological literature covering the non-Western world, and it may be amplified in both genres where the focus is on cultural differences or exoticism. Given the association between women and the natural world, men and things cultural (Ortner 1974), a magazine that aspires to describe the distinctive achievements of civilizations can be expected to highlight the world of men. But like the people of nature in the fourth world, women have been treated as all the more precious for their nonutilitarian, nonrationalistic qualities. Photographs of women become one of the primary devices by which the magazine depicts "universal human values," and these include the values of family love and the appreciation of female beauty itself.[4] We turn to these issues now, noting that each of them has had a consistent cultural content through the postwar period, during historical changes that give the images different emphases and form through the decades.

The motherhood of man

There is no more romantic set of photographs in the *Geographic* than those depicting the mothers of the world with their children. There is the exuberant picture showing the delight of a Kurd mother holding her infant. Filling much space, as an unusually high percentage of the magazine's mother–child pictures do, the photograph covers two pages despite the relative lack of information in it. Its classical composition and crisp, uncluttered message are similar to those in many such photos. They often suggest the Western tradition of madonna painting and evoke the Mother's Day message: this relationship between mother and child, they say, is a timeless and sacred one, essentially and intensely loving regardless of social and historical context – the foundation of human social life rather than cultural difference. The family of man, these pictures might suggest, is first of all a mother–child unit, rather than a brotherhood of solidarity between adults.[5]

For the magazine staff and readers of the 1950s, there must have been even more power in these images than we see in them today. The impact of the photos would have come from the intense cultural and social pressures on middle-class women to see their most valuable role, often their only one, as that of mother (Margolis 1984). The unusually strong pressure of this period is often explained as motivated by desires to place returning World War II veterans (and men in general) in those jobs available and by anxieties about the recent holocaust of the war and the potential for a nuclear conflagration, which made the family seem a safe haven (May 1988). As a new cult of domesticity emerged, women were told – through both science and popular culture – that biology, morality, and the psychological health of the next generation required their commitment to full-time mothering. This ideological pressure persisted through the 1950s despite the rapid rise in female employment through the decade.

The idealization of the mother–child bond is seen in everything from the warm TV relationships of June Cleaver with Wally and the Beaver to the cover of a *Life* magazine issue of 1956 devoted to "The American Woman" showing a glowing portrait of a mother and daughter lovingly absorbed in each other; all of this is ultimately and dramatically reflected in the period's rapidly expanding birth rate. This idealization had its counterpoint in fear of the power women were being given in the domestic domain. In both science and popular culture, the mother was criticized for being smothering, controlling, oversexualized, and, a bit later, overly permissive (Ehrenreich and English 1978; May 1988).

The *National Geographic*'s treatment of children can be seen as an extension of these ideologies of motherhood and the family. As the "woman question" came to be asked more angrily in the late 1950s, there was a gradual erosion of faith in the innocence of the mother–infant bond and even in the intrinsic value of children (Ehrenreich and English 1978), centered around fears of juvenile delinquency and the later 1960s identification of a "generation gap." The *National Geographic*, however, continued to print significant numbers of photographs of children, perhaps responding to their increasingly sophisticated marketing information, which indicated that photographs of children and cute animals were among their most popular pictures.

As the magazine has moved into depicting social problems through the seventies and eighties, however, the child has become positioned to tell the most poignant part of the story. In a wrenching photograph that Wilbur Garrett took in Laos, a Hmong

Plate 7.2 Photographs of women in *National Geographic* emphasize motherhood, as in this 1958 image of a Kurd mother and child. The third-world mother is often backgrounded and iconic, with emphasis placed on the child. © National Geographic Society, J. Baylor Roberts/NGS Image collection.

family sits on a bench, the mother breast-feeding a baby, the father holding a toddler who appears to be asleep (January 1974: 100–1). No one is smiling. The caption lets us know that the older child is dead, the parents grieving. Only then do we comprehend that the mother's hand is touching her child's shroud rather than his blanket and read the parents' faces as mournful rather than simply solemn or strained. While the caption begins lyrically with the magazine's standard infrastructure of balance, "Milk of life, shroud of death," it goes on to give the grim statistics for these people of 50 percent infant mortality rate, 35-year life expectancy.

Throughout the 1950s and 1960s, however, there were few poignant pictures of children, and they remain relatively rare. The more prevalent, pleasant pictures still play a fundamental role in raising the comfort level of those readers for whom articles on nonwhite peoples are the most unpopular type. For them, the loving mother and smiling child are a quick fix. Indeed, the black mother may be the *most* valorized kind of dark-skinned person for magazine readers, as in the culture at large, where one finds the "mammy" figure of film and literature and the stoic, capable single mother on whom documentaries of American life have often focused (Collins 1991: 67–90). Why has this woman been such an important figure? In part, it must be because the traditional maternal role is seen as teaching children to be polite, to be good citizens, to reproduce the status quo. If the most valued black person for white Americans will be the least threatening one, then the culturally constructed image of the black mother will fill the bill. The photo of a Bedouin mother and child can suggest, like a number of others, the mother's protectiveness as well as her own vulnerability or fear (December 1972: 838–9). We might ask if the perceived danger of things foreign increases the power of the mother to be portrayed as especially protective. Given the kindly intentions in editorial policy, the sympathetic other will often be a mother, protecting both her infant and the reader.

In pictures of mother and child, it often appears that the nonwhite mother is backgrounded, with her gaze and the gaze of the reader focused on the infant. The infant may in fact be an even more important site for dealing with white racial anxieties, by virtue of constituting an acceptable black love object. A good number of pictures in the postwar period have the form of these two: one a Micronesian infant and the other an Iraqi infant, from 1974 and 1976 respectively, each peacefully asleep in a cradle with the mother visible behind. The peacefulness constitutes the antithesis of the potentially threatening differences of interest, dress, or ritual between the photographed adult and the reader.

Women and their breasts

The "nude" woman sits, stands, or lounges at the salient center of *National Geographic* photography of the non-Western world. Until the phenomenal growth of mass circulation pornography in the 1960s, the magazine was known as the only mass culture venue where Americans could see women's breasts. Part of the folklore of Euramerican men, stories about secret perusals of the magazine emerged time after time in our conversations with male *National Geographic* readers. People vary in how they portray the personal or cultural meaning, or both, of this nakedness, some noting it was an aid to masturbation, others claiming it failed to have the erotic quality they expected. When white men tell these stories about covertly viewing black women's bodies, they are clearly not recounting a story about a simple encounter with the facts of human anatomy or customs; they are (perhaps unsus-pectingly) confessing a highly charged – but socially approved – experience in this dangerous territory of projected, forbidden desire and guilt. Such stories also exist (in a more charged, ironic mode) in the popular culture of African Americans – for example, in Richard Pryor's characterization, in his comedy routines, of *National Geographic* as the black man's *Playboy*.

The racial distribution of female nudity in the magazine conforms, in pernicious ways, to Euramerican myths about black women's sexuality. Lack of modesty in dress places black women closer to nature. Given the pervasive tendency to interpret skin color as a marker of evolutionary progress, it is assumed that white women have acquired modesty along with other characteristics of civilization. Black women remain backward on this scale, not conscious of the embarrassment they should feel at their nakedness (Gilman 1985: 114–15, 193). Their very ease unclothed stigma-tizes them.

In addition, black women have been portrayed in Western art and science as both exuberant and excessive in their sexuality. While their excess intrigues, it is also read as pathological and dangerous. In the texts produced within white culture, Haraway (1989: 154) writes, "Colored women densely code sex, animal, dark, dangerous, fecund, pathological." Thus for the French surrealists of the 1930s, the exotic, unencumbered sexuality of non-Western peoples – and African women in particular – represented an implicit criticism of the repression and constraint of European sexuality. The Africanism of the 1930s, like an earlier Orientalism, evidenced both a longing for – and fear of – the characteristics attributed to non-Western peoples (Clifford 1988: 61). The sexuality of black women that so entertained French artists and musicians in cafés and cabarets, however, had fueled earlier popular and scientific preoccupation with the Hottentot Venus and other pathologized renditions of black women's bodies and desires (Gilman 1985).

The *Geographic*'s distinctive brand of cultural relativism, however, meant that this aspect of black sexuality would be less written in by the institution than read in by readers, particularly in comparison with other visual venues such as Hollywood movies. Alloula (1986) gives the example of the sexualized early twentieth-century "harem" postcards of North African women. His thesis is that the veil fascinates a Western audience because it is read as a no-trespass message, and it is experienced by outside men as frustrating and attractive for this reason. It became an object of Western quest from a sense of the need to penetrate beyond it through, simultan-eously, the light of photography, the reason of enlightened social change, the know-ledge of science, and the desire of the flesh (compare Fanon 1965). One can also see the distinctive *Geographic* style in comparison with *Life* photography of non-Western women. We can see the stronger cultural viewpoint on race at work in a 1956 *Life* article on "other women," which ran next to an article on American women of various regions of the country. The two articles read as a kind of beauty pageant, with all the photographs emphasizing the sitter's appearance, sexuality, and passivity. Ultimately, the magazine's editors judged American women the better-looking set (many captions also noted the "natural," "healthy," wholesome – non-perverted? – quality of the American women), but the adjectives they used to caption the non-Western women described their sense of the more passive and sexually explicit stance of the other women. So they are variously praised for their "fragility," "great softness," "grace," "langorous" qualities, and eagerness "to please"; "the sensuous quality often seen in women of the tropics" was found in one Malayan woman. The hypersexual but passive woman here replicates the one found by many Westerners in their imaginary African travels throughout the last century (Hammond and Jablow 1977). In the *Life* article, all of the non-Western women except the one Chinese "working girl" (and many of the American women), touch themselves, their clothes, or fans in the usual pose for characterizing female self-involvement (Goffman 1979).

As in German photography at Bamum in central Africa, those who would communicate the message that non-Western others are enlightened felt the necessity to mute certain kinds of facts. Although King Nioya at Bamum had many wives, there is relatively little evidence of this in European photography of the court, and so, too, the *Geographic* rarely shows female or male sexuality in more explicit forms. Although emphasis on the veil has been strong throughout the *Geographic*'s history, it seems deployed more in a narrative about progress than one about sexuality, as we will see. The magazine and its readers are caught between the desire to play out the cultural fantasy of the oversexed native woman and the social controls of sexual morality, of science, and of cultural relativism.

If *National Geographic* trades on the sexuality of black women, it is less comfortable with that of black men. Men coded black were far more likely than those coded white to appear bare-chested in the pages of the magazine – often in poses that drew attention to musculature and strength. The *National Geographic* has apparently tried to include pictures of "handsome young men" (Abramson 1987: 143). For American readers, male muscles take the place analogous to female breasts as signs of gendered sexuality (Canaan 1984). Many pictures visually or through their captions draw attention to the rippling muscles of photographed men. A picture of a man from the Nuba mountains in the Sudan (November 1966: 699) fills the page, primarily with his torso rather than face or full body, accentuating his strongly defined musculature. The caption highlights his brawn and implicitly suggests that this physicality is at the expense of intelligence: "Muscles like iron, his leather arm amulet worn as insurance against disaster, a champion wrestler exudes confidence. In his world, a man's strength and agility count for much, and at festivals he earns the plaudits of his peers. But modern civilization – a force beyond his comprehension – threatens his primitive way of life."

The magazine has been extremely skittish, however, about portraying male genitals. As described earlier, a respect for the facts does not inhibit the careful erasure of all evidence of male penises from photographs. In cultures where men do not customarily wear pants, the magazine has relied on lengthening loincloths, drawing in shorts, or simply air-brushing offending body parts to avoid offending the white reading public. The fear of – and desire to erase – black male sexuality has a long tradition in Euramerican culture. It reached its fullest and most heinous development in the paranoid fantasies of organizations such as the Ku Klux Klan and in the castrations and lynchings of southern black men for real or imputed advances toward white women (Carby 1985: 307–8). Haraway (1989) and Torgovnick (1990) offer vivid examples and analyses of the evidence of miscegenation and black abduction anxieties in American popular culture materials, such as the Tarzan stories and movies. Masquerading as taste or propriety, however, the underlying anxiety also finds its place in the pages of *National Geographic*.

Like the nude and its role in Western high art painting (Hess and Nochlin 1972; Betterton 1987; Nead 1990), nudity in *Geographic* photographs has had a potential sexual, even pornographic, interpretation. Such interpretations would obviously threaten the magazine's legitimacy and sales, achieved through its self-definition as a serious, relatively highbrow family magazine. Pornography represents just the opposite values: "disposability, trash," the deviant, the unrespectable, the low class (Nead 1990: 325). Like fine art, science attempts to frame the nude female body as devoid of pornographic attributes. While art aestheticizes it, science dissects, fragments, and otherwise desexualizes it. The *National Geographic* nude has at times done both of these contradictory things.

The *Geographic* nude is first and foremost, in readers' attention, a set of breasts. This follows the culture at large, where the breast is made a fetish of, obsessed on. And the obsession is not just with any kind of breast. As Young (1990: 91) has pointed out, breasts are "normalized," leaving women to feel themselves inadequate for not having the culturally dictated "one perfect shape and proportion for breasts": young, large, round, but not sagging. If the *Geographic* is identified with the female breast, then a cultural history of the *Geographic* must take account of changing attitudes towards women's breasts and bodies over that period.

Unfortunately, significant change has been hard to come by. From the pinup (which still had some currency at the beginning of the period) to the large-breasted model recently heralded by fashion magazines as "back for the nineties," the obsession has continued unabated but for the Twiggy and braless moment of the late sixties and early seventies. If anything, the objectification of the breast has increased; it is now so radical that breast enlargement surgery was undergone by nearly a hundred thousand women in 1986 alone. The *Geographic* may reflect this trend when it increasingly exposed women's breasts in the seventies and eighties, taking them out of the shadows where they were more often found in earlier periods. The now foregrounded breasts are also strikingly more often teenage. A taboo that remains in place throughout this culture is showing old women's sagging or dimpled breasts. The *Geographic* has included these breasts, in the interest of veracity, but bows to cultural pressures by almost invariably printing them in smaller or dimly lit formats.

Two important stylistic changes can be identified in photos of women's bodies in the magazine, one related to changes in commercial photography of women and the other to the growing tolerance of "aesthetic" pictures in the *Geographic* of the eighties. Beginning in the late fifties, certain changes in the way women were photographed in commercials began to be reflected in *National Geographic* images.[6] In early advertisements of the period, women are shown directly involved in the use of a product, as when a woman with a fur stole is shown being helped into her 1955 Chrysler by the doorman of an obviously upscale building. By contrast, a 1966 Chevrolet ad shows a woman lying on the roof of the car putting on lipstick, with a small inset photo that has her sitting on the roof being photographed by a man. The ads of the 1950s show women as domestic royalty; the later ads place them in more straightforwardly sexual roles and postures.

In *National Geographic* documentary images as well, we find a shift, coming some years after that in commercial photography; the naked woman moves from being just an ethnographic fact ("this is the way they dress as they go about living their lives") to being presented as in part an aesthetic and sexual object. After 1970, naked women are less often shown framed with men, less often mothering, more often dancing or lounging.[7] The erotic connotations of the horizontal woman, drawn on by advertisers (Goffman 1979), and of the woman absorbed in dance, combine with more romantic, aesthetic styles to create photos which follow the inflation of sexualized images of women in the culture at large (Wolf 1991). Contrast the 1986 highly aesthetic photo of a Micronesian teenager, whose direct gaze invites the reader to make contact and whose hazy green background suggests tropical romanticism, with the more clinical 1970 shot of two women buying herbs at a market in Ethiopia. The breasts of the women are clear and central to the photo's narrative, but focus is also on the twigs being passed between the seller of herbs and one of the women and on the camels in the near background. The picture's composition and straightforward realism, as well as the informative caption tell us something ethnographic – that is, about something more than women's beauty or women's bodies.

The development of commercial styles elsewhere in the culture amplifies an effect of photographs of women noted by Pollock (1987); the addition of a woman to a photographed scene often succeeds, given cultural ideologies and history, in changing the scene from a still-life or object of contemplation to a purchasable commodity. This is because women have traditionally been seen as objects to be possessed, owned, or controlled, and as ornaments to the lives of men. In the case of the *Geographic*, that commodity is a potential tourist destination. Newly glossy images of women led the way in selling the third world to travelers.

A second explanation for changes in rendering the nude woman is found in the increasing tolerance of a more aesthetic rendering of all subjects in the *Geographic*. Aesthetic style, however, has special implications and nuances when the photos are of women. What arises after the fifties in the *Geographic* is not just a more self-consciously aesthetic style but a style whose uses elsewhere in the culture were centered on photography of women, as in fashion and other commercial work.

The cultural debate (however minor in scale and impact) over whether the nudity in the *Geographic* was or is appropriate follows shifting and conflicting definitions of acceptable portrayals of women's bodies (Nead 1990). At issue is not simply whether women's bodies are displayed, but what the cultural context of those images is (Myers 1987; Vance 1990); that context includes the sexualization of the breasts, the objectification of women, the racist understanding of black femininity, and the shame that inheres in American culture to sexuality itself.[8] Nonetheless, the still heavily white male photographic and editorial staff at the *Geographic* appears relatively unaffected by feminist critiques of the use of women's bodies or the critique of colonial looking-relations (Gaines 1988) that prompt both the frequent inclusion and a particular distorted reading by subscribers of the nude black woman's body. The African-American cabdriver who took one of us to *Geographic* headquarters was less sanguine, even angry, when he noted that the magazine's white women are well covered.

The kitchen debates in Africa: woman's place in the march of progress

In a subtly nuanced analysis of the genre of 1980s Hollywood success movies, Traube (1989) details the influence of the Reagan years and a particular moment of labor demography and consumer capitalism in the construction of the films' plots and styles. These films describe, among other things, the gender-specific dangers and possibilities of the world of managerial work for the middle-class youth who view these movies on their way to corporate work lives. Specifically, they include "warning of the feminizing effects of deference on men and, conversely, the masculinizing effects of ambition on women" (ibid: 291). The *National Geographic*'s women do not provide as easy an identifying anchor for the magazine's readers as do these movies' characters, but their image, too, has responded to changes in the politics and rate of American women's labor-force participation. They have also played a role in articulating longstanding cultural notions about the role of women in socioeconomic development overseas. We will now examine problems of the progress of women here and abroad.

Against the indolent native of colonialist discourse, the *Geographic*'s industrious native toils in response to an editorial policy which calls for a sympathetic other. The way women's work is portrayed, however, shows some culturally predictable differences from that of men's. As in the wider culture, women's work is sometimes presented as less intellectually demanding, more toilsome. Take the Melanesian man and woman set up on opposite pages (April 1969: 574–5). A male archer on the left is labeled "man, the hunter" and, on the right, a photo of a woman with child in a netbag carrying a large load of firewood, "woman, the laborer." The woman smiles under her burden, perhaps thereby evoking images long in circulation in Western culture: these are images that romanticize the hard-working black woman, often ignoring the difference between her enduring and enjoying (much less opposing) oppression (hooks 1981: 6). In this latter cultural discourse, the black woman could endure what no lady could and therefore revealed her more natural, even animal nature (ibid: 81–2). For many readers of the *Geographic*, it may be an easy step from the celebration of the strong working woman to her dehumanization as someone with less than human abilities to withstand those burdens.[9]

Cultural ambivalence toward women working outside the home has been profound during the postwar period, when employment for which women sixteen and older received wages grew from 25 percent in 1940 to 40 percent in 1960. More of this is accounted for by African-American women, half of whom were employed in 1950, with their wage-paying work continuing at high rates in the following decades. The ideological formulation of the meaning of women's work has changed. Working women in the fifties were defined as helpmates to their husbands. Only much later did women's work come to be seen as a means to goals of independence and self-realization (Chafe 1983), although even here, as Traube (1989) points out, messages were widely available that women's success in work was threatening to men. This ambivalence occasionally shows up in the *Geographic* when the laboring woman is presented as a drudge or when her femininity, *despite her working*, is emphasized. An example of the latter is found in a photograph of a Burmese woman shown planting small green shoots in a garden row (June 1974). Retouching has been done both to her line of plants and to the flowers encircling her hair. The sharpening and coloring of these two items lets the picture tell much more clearly a narrative about her femininity and her productivity and about how those two things are not mutually exclusive.

More often, however, the labor of women as well as other aspects of their lives are presented by the *Geographic* as central to the march of progress in their respective countries. Women are constructed as the vanguard of progress in part through the feminizing of the developing nation-state itself (Kabbani 1986; compare Schaffer 1988). How does this work? In the first instance, those foreign states are contrasted, in some Western imaginations, with a deeply masculine American national identity (Krasniewicz 1990; Jeffords 1989), a gendering achieved through the equation of the West (*in* the West, of course) with strength, civilization, rationality, and freedom, its other with vulnerability, primitivity, superstition, and the constraints of tradition. Once this equation was made, articles can be titled as in the following instance, where progress is masculinized and the traditional nation feminized: "Beneath the Surge of Progress, old Mexico's Charm and Beauty Lie Undisturbed" (October 1961).

Plate 7.3 Photographs of working women in the magazine are as ambivalent as their cultural context. Some portray the laboring woman as drudge, while others, like this June 1974 picture of a Burmese woman, emphasize her femininity *despite* her working. The flowers in her hair and the plants she works with have been brought forward by retouching. © National Geographic Society, Wilbur Garrett/NGS Image collection.

From the perspective of the colonial era, the symbolic femininity of the non-Western states would seem to have been solidly established, but this kind of rhetoric may have lost some of its power in the new world of social relations of the 1970s and 1980s. The more salient actors in US media coverage of the third world seem now to be male terrorists in the Middle East and male economic competitors in Japan and Korea. Starving ungendered children have some representational space, but female workers are still not visible. How the *Geographic*'s recent coverage articulates with other media representations of the shifting gender of the foreign remains to be studied.

Fanon (1965: 39) pointed out in his analysis of French colonial attitudes and strategies concerning the veil in Algeria that the colonialists' goal, here as elsewhere in the world, was "converting the woman, winning her over to the foreign values, wrenching her free from her status" as a means of "shaking up the [native] man" and gaining control of him. With this and other motives, those outsiders who would "develop" the third world have often seen the advancement of non-Western women as the first goal to be achieved, with their men's progress thought to follow rather than precede it. In the nineteenth century, evolutionary theory claimed that the move upward from savagery to barbarism to civilization was indexed by the treatment of women, in particular by their liberation "from the burdens of overwork, sexual abuse, and male violence" (Tiffany and Adams 1985: 8). It "saw women in non-Western societies as oppressed and servile creatures, beasts of burden, chattels who could be bought and sold, eventually to be liberated by 'civilization' or 'progress,' thus attaining the enviable position of women in Western society" (Etienne and Leacock 1980: 1), who were then expected to be happy with their place.[10] The *Geographic* has told a much more upbeat version of this story, mainly by presenting other women's labors positively.

The continuation of these ways of thinking into the present can be seen in how states defined as "progressive" have been rendered by both Western media like the *National Geographic* and the non-Western state bureaucracies concerned. Graham-Brown (1988) and Schick (1990) describe how photographic and other proof of the progress or modernity of states like Turkey and prerevolutionary Iran has often been found primarily in the lives of their women, particularly in their unveiling.[11] Indeed, as Schick points out, "a photograph of an unveiled woman was not much different from one of a tractor, an industrial complex, or a new railroad; it merely symbolized yet another one of men's achievements" (Schick 1990: 369).

Take the example from the *Geographic*'s January 1985 article on Baghdad. Several photographs show veiled women walking through the city streets. One shot shows women in a narrow alley. The dark tones of the photograph are a function of the lack of sunlight reaching down into the alley, but they also reinforce the message of the caption. Playing with the associations between veil and the past that are evoked for most readers, it says, "In the shadows of antiquity, women in long black abayas walk in one of the older sections of the city." A few pages earlier, we learn about the high-rise building boom in the city and the changing roles of women in a two-page layout that shows a female electrical engineer in a hard hat and jeans organizing a building project with a male colleague. The caption introduces her by name and goes on: "Iraqi women, among the most progressive in the Arab world, constitute 25 percent of the country's work force and are guaranteed equality under Baath Party doctrine." On the opposite page, the modern buildings they have erected are captioned, "New York on the Tigris." The equation of the end point (Manhattan) with the unveiled woman is neatly laid out.

The goal of progress through women and of women's progress might have been inferred by many viewers from a 1968 photo from Ecuador (February: 271) showing a family of four in the park, sitting in front of the man's abstract painting. This thoroughly modern nuclear family enjoys the clean and cultivated leisure brought by that progress, with the woman most easily understood as housewife and mother. With the bifurcation of the frame into two halves, one side containing the man's art-work, and the other the mother and her children, the symbolic dualism familiar to Western audiences of women/child/nature and men/independent/art is achieved. This couple has no further to go on the Great March. The photo also shows that the kindly-light policy makes a critique of patriarchy as problematic as a critique of anything else.

This celebration of simultaneous women's liberation and national progress is not the whole story, of course. The magazine also communicates – in a more muted way through the fifties and into the sixties – a sense of the value of the natural, *Gemeinschaft*-based life of the people without progress. Progress can be construed as a socially corrosive process as it was in the late nineteenth century, when non-Western women were seen as superior to their Western counterparts because too much education had weakened the latter, sapping vitality from their reproductive organs (Ehrenreich and English 1978: 114). The illiterate woman of the non-Western world still lives with this cultural inheritance, standing for the woman "unruined" by progress.

Another potential factor in the questioning of progress in gender roles is the feminization of natural landscapes. As Schaffer (1988) has shown for Australian culture and Tiffany and Adams (1985) for the Americas, the landscape has been culturally construed as female over the entire period since discovery. The one who comes to exploit and change it is male, and so the undeveloped third world/feminine can be construed as a repository of timeless (not political) wisdom about the values of a simple life, family, and living in harmony with nature.

An example of the contradictory place of progress is found in two photographs that draw attention to housewives. In the first, an Inuit woman wearing a fur-trimmed parka stands in front of a washing machine: "Unfamiliar luxury," the caption says, "a washing machine draws a housewife to the new 'Tuk' laundromat, which also offers hot showers" (July 1968). This picture is deliberately structured around the contrast between the premodern and the modern, with the evaluative balance falling to the luxurious present. It might have still resonated for readers with the image from 1959 of Nixon and Khrushchev arguing over the benefits of capitalism next to a freshly minted washing machine and dryer at the American National Exhibition in Moscow. In those debates, Nixon could argue that the progress of American society under capitalism is found in its ability to provide labor-saving devices to women. "I think that this attitude toward women is universal. What we want is to make easier the life of our housewives," he said. In the gender stories told during the cold war, family life and commodities provided what security was to be found in the post-Hiroshima, post-holocaust world (May 1988). The non-Western woman, too, could be deployed as proof of capitalism's value, of the universal desire for these goods, and of the role of women in the evolution of society.

From January 1971, however, an article entitled "Housewife at the End of the World" documents the adventures of an Ohio woman settling in Tierra del Fuego, and congratulates her on adapting to local norms of self-sufficiency and simplicity. The last photo's caption articulates the theme of the whole article: "Life in this remote land spurs inventiveness .... My special interests keep me so busy I have little time to miss the conveniences I once knew." The North American woman chooses to forgo the benefits of progress, in search of an authentically simple place, as her "younger sister" climbs the ladder in the other direction.

In stories of progress and/or decline, Western and non-Western women have often been played off against each other in this way, one used to critique the other in line with different purposes and in the end leaving each feeling inadequate. The masculine writer/image maker/consumer thereby asserts his own strength, both through his right to evaluate and through his completeness in contrast to women. Although non-Western men cannot be said to fare well in these cultural schemes, they are used less frequently and in other ways (Honour 1989) to either critique or shore up white men's masculinity.

In sum, the women of the non-Western world represent a population aspiring to the full femininity achieved in Western cultures, and, in a more secondary way, they are a repository for the lost femininity of "liberated" Western women. Both an ideal and thus a critique of modern femininity, they are also a measure to tell the Western family how far it has advanced. They are shown working hard and as key to their country's progress toward some version of the Western-consumer family norm. The sometimes contradictory message these pictures can send to middle-class women is consistent with cultural ideologies in the United States that by turns condemn and affirm the woman who would be both mother and wage earner. We can see the women of the *National Geographic* playing a role within a social field where the cold war was being waged and where social changes in kinship structures and gender politics were precipitated by the entrance of white women into the paid labor force in larger and larger numbers.

Conclusion

We have focused here on the rendition of racial and gender difference in the *Geographic*. We can now step back and remind the reader that the color of sex in the magazine emerges first from the photographer's work. The *Geographic* photographer has always been and predominantly remains, both literally and symbolically, a white man. And not just any white man, but the whitest and most masculine version possible: the great hunter/adventurer (Bright 1990: 137–8), free to roam the globe in search of visual treasure, flamboyantly virile in his freedom from observation and evaluation, and his bravery in entering the dangerous realms at the ends of the earth, in continents still dark for most of his audience.[12] While the photographs that we find in the magazine are often gentle, beautiful images of people construed as feminine, the image-maker – at least as many viewers imagine – looks out on this exotic world from that Marlboro Country where the jaws are all square with a tough growth of stubble and the Indians are all gone.

NOTES

1 This is not to deny that there are complex correspondences between culture and racial categories as socially deployed. Once race has been used to marginalize and isolate social groups, shared experiences of oppression, coping, and resistance may give rise to shared cultural premises. The "culture" or "cultures" that result, however, are at least partly a consequence of the deployment of racial categories and not evidence of the validity of the categories themselves.
2 In part because of its focus on everyday life, *National Geographic* does not trade in the standardized images of black people that have been common in Western art – some of which have been characterized by Honour (1989) as "heroes and martyrs," "the benighted," "the defiant," and "the pacified."
3 This proportion is based on those photos in which adults of identifiable gender are shown (N = 510). Another 11 percent show women and men together in roughly equal numbers, leaving 65 percent of the photos depicting mainly men.

4   The popularity of this notion in American culture, which *National Geographic* relies on as much as feeds, is also one wellspring for American feminism's focus on universal sisterhood, that is, its insistence, particularly in the 1970s, that Western and non-Western women will easily see each other as similar or sharing similar experiences.

5   The popular Family of Man exhibition also included a substantial section devoted to mothers and infants, unfortunately nicknamed "Tits and Tots" by the staff of photographers who organized it (Meltzer 1978). This exhibit, immensely popular when it toured, became a bestselling book.

6   For an example of the connection between *Geographic* and commercial styles, see the similarity between women's fashion photography of the period and the galleries of Polynesian beauties remarked on in chapter 5. One Tahitian woman is posed for a side portrait with her head pushed forward, accentuating a long neck and paralleling the elegance of the model of high- fashion photography of the 1950s.

7   This is based on the twenty photos in our sample of 592 where women are shown without shirts on; half of that number occurred from 1950 to 1969 and the other half from 1970 to 1986 (one would, of course, expect there to be somewhat fewer such photos as urbanization and change in dress styles spread across the globe). Some of the same phenomena noted here have been found in advertising in American family magazines (that is, a decrease in images of married women shown in child care and an increase in those showing them at recreation), although in the latter ads the trends begin earlier, in the later 1940s (Brown 1981).

8   The *Geographic*'s breasts should be seen against the broader background of the social changes in the industrial West relating to sexuality. Foucault (1978) has noted that those changes have been mistakenly associated with a "liberation" of sexuality. In fact, he suggests, with the emergence of the modern state and its regulatory needs has come an obsession with talking about and managing sex – through science, state policy, clinical medicine, and now photography.

9   That step may have been taken by white feminism as well, hooks points out: "When the women's movement was at its peak and white women were rejecting the role of breeder, burden bearer, and sex object, black women were celebrated for their unique devotion to the task of mothering; for their 'innate' ability to bear tremendous burdens; and for their ever-increasing availability as sex object. We appeared to have been unanimously elected to take up where white women were leaving off" (hooks 1981: 6). See Hammond and Jablow (1977) for an analysis of the particular strength of the notion of nonwhite women as beasts of burden in the case of African women; see also Collins (1991).

10 Western feminism in the 1970s may have simply transformed rather than fundamentally challenged the terms of this argument as well when it argued that the women of the world were oppressed by men and were to be liberated by feminism as defined in the West (see Amos and Parmar 1984).

11 Although feminist anthropology has analyzed and critiqued these kinds of assumptions, it has nonetheless often continued a basic evolutionary discourse in the assumption that Ong has identified: "Although a common past may be claimed by feminists, Third World women are often represented as mired in it, ever arriving at modernity when Western feminists are already adrift in postmodernism" (Ong 1988: 87).

12 The masculine part of this ethos is found in contemporary anthropology as well, as indicated by Okely (1975). The racially white part is noted by Said (1989).

REFERENCES

Abramson, Howard S. 1987. *National Geographic: Behind America's Lens on the World*. New York: Crown.

Alloula, Malek. 1986. *The Colonial Harem*. Minneapolis: University of Minnesota Press.

Amos, V. and Prathiba Parmar. 1984. "Challenging imperial feminism," *Feminist Review* 17: 3–20.

Betterton, Rosemary, ed. 1987. *Looking On: Images of Femininity in the Visual Arts and Media*. London: Pandora.

Bhabha, Homi K. 1983. "The other question – Homi K. Bhabha reconsiders the stereotype and colonial discourse," *Screen* 24 (6): 18–36.

Botting, Wendy. 1988. *Posing for Power/Posing for Pleasure: Photographies and the Social Construction of Femininity*. Binghamton, NY: University Art Gallery.

Bright, Deborah. 1990. "Of Mother Nature and Marlboro Men: an inquiry into the cultural meanings of landscape photography." Pp. 125–42 in *The Contest of Meaning*, ed. R. Bolton. Cambridge, MA: MIT Press.

Brown, Bruce W. 1981. *Images of Family Life in Magazine Advertising: 1920–1978*. New York: Praeger.

Canaan, Joyce. 1984. "Building muscles and getting curves: gender differences in representations of the body and sexuality among American teenagers." Paper presented at the annual meeting of the American Anthropological Association, Denver.

Carby, Hazel. 1985. "'On the threshold of women's era': lynching, empire, and sexuality in black feminist theory." Pp. 301–16 in *"Race," Writing, and Difference*, ed. H. Gates. Chicago: University of Chicago Press.

Carson, Claybourne. 1981. *In Struggle: SNCC and the Black Awakening of the 1960s*. Cambridge, MA: Harvard University Press.

Chafe, William. 1983. "Social change and the American woman, 1940–70," in *A History of Our Time: Readings on Postwar America*, ed. William Chafe and Harvard Sitkoff. New York: Oxford University Press.

Clifford, James. 1988. *The Predicament of Culture: Twentieth-Century Ethnography, Literature, and Art*. Cambridge, MA: Harvard University Press.

Collins, Patricia Hill. 1991. *Black Feminist Thought*. Boston: Unwin Hyman.

Ehrenreich, Barbara, and Deirdre English. 1978. *For Her Own Good: 150 Years of the Experts' Advice to Women*. Garden City, NY: Anchor Press/Doubleday.

Etienne, Mona and Eleanor Leacock, eds. 1980. *Women and Colonization: Anthropological Perspectives*. New York: Praeger.

Fanon, Frantz. 1965. *A Dying Colonialism*. New York: Grove Press.

Foucault, Michel. 1978. *The History of Sexuality*. Vol. 1, trans. R. Hurley. New York: Random House.

Gaines, Jane. 1988. "White privilege and looking relations: race and gender in feminist film theory," *Screen* 29 (4): 12–27.

Gates, Henry Louis, Jr. 1985. "Writing 'race' and the difference it makes." Pp. 1–20 in *"Race," Writing, and Difference*, ed. H. L. Gates. Chicago: University of Chicago Press.

Gilman, Sander. 1985. *Difference and Pathology: Stereotypes of Sexuality, Race, and Madness*. Ithaca, NY: Cornell University Press.

Goffman, Erving. 1979. *Gender Advertisements*. New York: Harper and Row.

Graham-Brown, Sarah. 1988. *Images of Women: The Portrayal of Women in Photography of the Middle East, 1860–1950*. London: Quartet Books.

Hammond, Dorothy and Alta Jablow. 1977. *The Myth of Africa*. New York: Library of Social Science.

Haraway, Donna. 1989. *Primate Visions: Gender, Race, and Nature in the World of Modern Science*. New York: Routledge.

Harding, Vincent. 1981. *There Is a River: The Black Struggle for Freedom in America*. New York: Harcourt Brace Jovanovich.

Hess, Thomas B. and Linda Nochlin. 1972. *Women as Sex Object: Studies in Erotic Art, 1730–1970*. New York: Newsweek Books.

Honour, Hugh. 1989. *The Image of the Black in Western Art. Vol. 4: From the American Revolution to World War I*. New York: Morrow.

hooks, bell. 1981. *Ain't I a Woman: Black Women and Feminism*. Boston: South End Press.

Hull, Gloria, Patricia Bell Scott, and Barbara Smith. 1982. *All the Women Are White, All the Blacks Are Men, but Some of Us Are Brave: Black Women's Studies*. Old Westbury, NY: Feminist Press.

Hurston, Zora Neale. 1984. *Dust Tracks on a Road: An Autobiography*, 2nd edn. Urbana: University of Illinois Press.

Jeffords, Susan. 1989. *The Remasculinization of America: Gender and the Vietnam War*. Bloomington: Indiana University Press.

Kabbani, Rana. 1986. *Europe's Myths of Orient*. Bloomington: Indiana University Press.

Krasniewicz, Louise. 1990. "Desecrating the patriotic body: flag burning, art censorship, and the powers of 'prototypical Americans.'" Paper presented at the annual meeting of the American Anthropological Association, New Orleans.

Margolis, Maxine. 1984. *Mothers and Such*. Berkeley and Los Angeles: University of California Press.

May, Elain Tyler. 1988. *Homeward Bound: American Families in the Cold War Era*. New York: Basic Books.

Meltzer, Milton. 1978. *Dorothea Lange: A Photographer's Life*. New York: Farrar Strauss Giroux.

Moore, Henrietta. 1988. *Feminism and Anthropology*. Cambridge: Cambridge University Press.

Myers, Kathy. 1987. "Towards a feminist erotica." Pp. 189–202 in *Looking On*, ed. R. Betterton. London: Pandora.

Nead, Lynda. 1990. "The female nude: pornography, art, and sexuality," *Signs* 15: 323–35.

Okely, Judith. 1975. "The self and scientism," *Journal of the Anthropological Society of Oxford* 6 (3): 177–88.

Omi, Michael and Howard Winant. 1986. *Racial Formation in the United States: From the 1960s to the 1980s*. New York: Routledge.

Ong, Aihwa. 1988. "Colonialism and modernity: feminist re-presentations of women in non-Western societies," *Inscriptions* nos. 3 and 4: 79–93.

Ortner, Sherry. 1974. "Is female to male as nature is to culture?" Pp. 67–88 in *Woman, Culture, and Society*, ed. M. Rosaldo and L. Lamphere. Stanford, CA: Stanford University Press.

Pollock, Grieslda. 1987. "What's wrong with 'images of women'?" Pp. 40–8 in *Looking On*, ed. R. Betterton. London: Pandora.

Rydell, Robert. 1984. *All the World's a Fair: Visions of Empire at American International Expositions, 1876–1916*. Chicago: University of Chicago Press.

Sacks, Karen. 1989. "Toward a unified theory of class, race and gender," *American Ethnologist* 16: 534–50.

Said, Edward. 1989. "Representing the colonized: anthropology's interlocutors," *Critical Inquiry* 15: 205–25.

Schaffer, Kay. 1988. *Women and the Bush: Forces of Desire in the Australian Cultural Tradition*. Cambridge: Cambridge University Press.

Schick, Irvin Cemil. 1990. "Representing Middle Eastern women: feminism and colonial discourse," *Feminist Studies* 16 (2): 345–80.

Tiffany, Sharon and Kathleen Adams. 1985. *The Wild Woman: An Inquiry into the Anthropology of an Idea*. Cambridge, MA: Schenkman.

Torgovnick, Marianna. 1990. *Gone Primitive: Savage Intellects, Modern Lives*. Chicago: University of Chicago Press.

Traube, Elizabeth G. 1989. "Secrets of success in postmodern society," *Cultural Anthropology* 4: 273–300.

Trinh, T. Minh-ha. 1989. *Woman, Native, Other: Writing Postcoloniality and Feminism.* Bloomington: Indiana University Press.

Vance, Carol. 1990. "The pleasures of looking: the Attorney General's Commision on Pornography versus visual images." Pp. 38–58 in *The Critical Image*, ed. Carol Squiers. Seattle: Bay Press.

Wallace, Michele. 1990. *Invisibility Blues: From Pop to Theory.* London: Verso.

Wolf, Naomi. 1991. *The Beauty Myth: How Images of Beauty Are Used against Women.* New York: Morrow.

Young, Iris Marion. 1990. "Breasted experience: the look and the feeling," in *Throwing Like a Girl and Other Essays in Feminist Philosophy and Social Theory*, ed. I. M. Young. Bloomington: Indiana University Press.

8

The Imperial Imaginary

Ella Shohat and Robert Stam

The colonial domination of indigenous peoples, the scientific and aesthetic discip-
lining of nature through classificatory schemas, the capitalist appropriation of
resources, and the imperialist ordering of the globe under a panoptical regime, all
formed part of a massive world historical movement that reached its apogee at the
beginning of the twentieth century. Indeed, it is most significant for our discussion
that the beginnings of cinema coincided with the giddy heights of the imperial
project, with an epoch where Europe held sway over vast tracts of alien territory
and hosts of subjugated peoples. (Of all the celebrated "coincidences" – of the twin
beginnings of cinema and psychoanalysis, cinema and nationalism, cinema and
consumerism – it is this coincidence with the heights of imperialism that has been
least explored.) Film was born at a moment when a poem such as Rudyard Kipling's
"White Man's Burden" could be published, as it was in 1899, to celebrate the US
acquisition of Cuba and the Philippines. The first Lumière and Edison screenings in
the 1890s closely followed the "scramble for Africa" which erupted in the late
1870s; the Battle of "Rorke's Drift" (1879) which opposed the British to the Zulus
(memorialized in the film *Zulu*, 1964); the British occupation of Egypt in 1882; the
Berlin Conference of 1884 which carved up Africa into European "spheres of influence"; the massacre of the Sioux at Wounded Knee in 1890; and countless other
imperial misadventures.

The most prolific film-producing countries of the silent period – Britain, France,
the US, Germany – also "happened" to be among the leading imperialist countries, in
whose clear interest it was to laud the colonial enterprise. The cinema emerged
exactly at the point when enthusiasm for the imperial project was spreading beyond
the elites into the popular strata, partly thanks to popular fictions and exhibitions.
For the working classes of Europe and Euro-America, photogenic wars in remote
parts of the empire became diverting entertainments, serving to "neutralize the class
struggle and transform class solidarity into national and racial solidarity."[1] The
cinema adopted the popular fictions of colonialist writers like Kipling for India
and Rider Haggard, Edgar Wallace, and Edgar Rice Burroughs for Africa, and
absorbed popular genres like the "conquest fiction" of the American southwest.
The cinema entered a situation where European and American readers had already
devoured Livingstone's *Missionary Travels* (1857); Edgar Wallace's "Sanders of the

River" stories in the early 1900s; Rider Haggard's *King Solomon's Mines* (1885); and Henry Morton Stanley's *How I Found Livingstone* (1872), *Through the Dark Continent* (1878), and *In Darkest Africa* (1890).

English boys especially were initiated into imperial ideas through such books as Robert Baden-Powell's *Scouting for Boys* (1908), which praised

the frontiersmen of all parts of our Empire. The "trappers" of North America, hunters of Central Africa, the British pioneers, explorers, and missionaries over Asia and all the wild parts of the world...the constabulary of North-West Canada and of South Africa.[2]

The practical survivalist education of scouting, combined with the initiatory mechanisms of the colonial adventure story, were designed to turn boys, as Joseph Bristow puts it, into "aggrandized subjects," an imperial race who imagined the future of the world as resting on their shoulders.[3] While girls were domesticated as homemakers, without what Virginia Woolf called a "room of their own," boys could play, if only in their imaginations, in the space of empire. The fantasy of far-away regions offered "charismatic realms of adventure"[4] free from charged heterosexual engagements. Adventure films, and the "adventure" of going to the cinema, provided a vicarious experience of passionate fraternity, a playing field for the self-realization of European masculinity. Just as colonized space was available to empire, and colonial landscapes were available to imperial cinema, so was this psychic space available for the play of the virile spectatorial imagination as a kind of mental *Lebensraum*. Empire, as John McClure puts it in another context, provided romance with its raw materials, while romance provided empire with its "aura of nobility."[5]

The Shaping of National Identity

Beliefs about the origins and evolution of nations often crystallize in the form of stories. For Hayden White, certain narrative "master tropes" shape our conception of history; historical discourse consists "of the provisions of a plot structure for a sequence of events so that their nature as a comprehensible process is revealed by their figuration as a story of a particular kind."[6] The nation of course is not a desiring person but a fictive unity imposed on an aggregate of individuals, yet national histories are presented as if they displayed the continuity of the subject-writ-large.[7] The cinema, as the world's storyteller *par excellence*, was ideally suited to relay the projected narratives of nations and empires. National self-consciousness, generally seen as a precondition for nationhood – that is, the shared belief of disparate individuals that they share common origins, status, location, and aspirations – became broadly linked to cinematic fictions. In the modern period, for Benedict Anderson, this collective consciousness was made possible by a common language and its expression in "print capitalism."[8] Prior to the cinema, the novel and the newspaper fostered imagined communities through their integrative relations to time and space. Newspapers – like TV news today – made people aware of the simultaneity and interconnectedness of events in different places, while novels provided a sense of the purposeful movement through time of fictional entities bound together in a narrative whole. As "bourgeois epic" (in the words of Georg Lukács), the novel inherited and transformed the vocation of the classical epic (for example the *Aeneid*) to produce and heighten national identity, both accompanying and crystallizing the rise of nations by imposing a unitary topos on heterogenous languages and diverse desires.

The fiction film also inherited the social role of the nineteenth-century realist novel in relation to national imaginaries. Like novels, films proceed temporally, their durational scope reaching from a story time ranging from the few minutes depicted by the first Lumière shorts to the many hours (and symbolic millennia) of films like *Intolerance* (1916) and *2001: A Space Odyssey* (1968). Films communicate Anderson's "calendrical time," a sense of time and its passage. Just as nationalist literary fictions inscribe on to a multitude of events the notion of a linear, comprehensible, destiny, so films arrange events and actions in a temporal narrative that moves toward fulfillment, and thus shape thinking about historical time and national history. Narrative models in film are not simply reflective microcosms of historical processes, then, they are also experiential grids or templates through which history can be written and national identity figured. Like novels, films can convey what Mikhail Bakhtin calls "chronotopes," materializing time in space, mediating between the historical and the discursive, providing fictional environments where historically specific constellations of power are made visible. In both film and novel, "time thickens, takes on flesh," while "space becomes charged and responsive to the movements of time, plot and history."[9] There is nothing inherently sinister in this process, except to the extent that it is deployed asymmetrically, to the advantage of some national and racial imaginaries and to the detriment of others.

The national situation described by Anderson becomes complicated, we would argue, in the context of an imperial ideology that was doubly transnational. First, Europeans were encouraged to identify not only with single European nations but also with the racial solidarity implied by the imperial project as a whole. Thus English audiences could identify with the heroes of French Foreign Legion films, Euro-American audiences with the heroes of the British Raj, and so forth. Second, the European empires (what Queen Victoria called the "imperial family") were themselves conceived paternalistically as providing a "shelter" for diverse races and groups, thus downplaying the national singularities of the colonized themselves. Given the geographically discontinuous nature of empire, cinema helped cement both a national and an imperial sense of belonging among many disparate peoples. For the urban elite of the colonized lands, the pleasures of cinema-going became associated with the sense of a community on the margins of its particular European empire (especially since the first movie theaters in these countries were associated with Europeans and the Europeanized local bourgeoisies).[10] The cinema encouraged an assimilated elite to identify with "its" empire and thus against other colonized peoples.

If cinema partly inherited the function of the novel, it also transformed it. Whereas literature plays itself out within a virtual lexical space, the cinematic chronotope is literal, splayed out concretely across the screen and unfolding in the literal time of twenty-four frames per second. In this sense, the cinema can all the more efficiently mobilize desire in ways responsive to nationalized and imperialized notions of time, plot, and history. The cinema's institutional ritual of gathering a community – spectators who share a region, language, and culture – homologizes, in a sense, the symbolic gathering of the nation. Anderson's sense of the nation as "horizontal comradeship" evokes the movie audience as a provisional "nation" forged by spectatorship. While the novel is consumed in solitude, the film is enjoyed in a gregarious space, where the ephemeral *communitas* of spectatorship can take on a national or imperial thrust. Thus the cinema can play a more assertive role in fostering group identities. Finally, unlike the novel, the cinema is not premised on literacy. As a popular entertainment it is more accessible than literature. While there was no mass reading public for imperial literary fictions in the colonies, for example, there *was* a mass viewing public for imperial filmic fictions.

The dominant European/American form of cinema not only inherited and disseminated a hegemonic colonial discourse, it also created a powerful hegemony of its own through monopolistic control of film distribution and exhibition in much of Asia, Africa, and the Americas. Eurocolonial cinema thus mapped history not only for domestic audiences but also for the world. African spectators were prodded to identify with Cecil Rhodes and Stanley and Livingstone against Africans themselves, thus engendering a battle of national imaginaries within the fissured colonial spectator. For the European spectator, the cinematic experience mobilized a rewarding sense of national and imperial belonging, on the backs, as it were, of otherized peoples. For the colonized, the cinema (in tandem with other colonial institutions such as schools) produced a sense of deep ambivalence, mingling the identification provoked by cinematic narrative with intense resentment, for it was the colonized who were being otherized.

While the novel could play with words and narrative to engender an "aggrandized subject," the cinema entailed a new and powerful apparatus of gaze. The cinematic "apparatus," that is to say the cinematic machine as including not only the instrumental base of camera, projector, and screen but also the spectator as the desiring subject on whom the cinematic institution depends for its imaginary realization, not only represents the "real" but also stimulates intense "subject effects." For Christian Metz, the cinematic apparatus fosters narcissism, in that the spectator identifies with him/herself as a "kind of transcendental subject."[11] By prosthetically extending human perception, the apparatus grants the spectator the illusory ubiquity of the "all-perceiving subject" enjoying an exhilarating sense of visual power. From the Diorama, the Panorama, and the Cosmorama up through NatureMax, the cinema has amplified and mobilized the virtual gaze of photography, bringing past into present, distant to near. It has offered the spectator a mediated relationship with imaged others from diverse cultures. We are not suggesting that imperialism was inscribed either in the apparatus or in the celluloid, only that the context of imperial power shaped the uses to which both apparatus and celluloid were put. In an imperial context the apparatus tended to be deployed in ways flattering to the imperial subject as superior and invulnerable observer, as what Mary Louise Pratt calls the "monarch-of-all-I-survey." The cinema's ability to "fly" spectators around the globe gave them a subject position as film's audio-visual masters. The "spatially mobilized visuality"[12] of the I/eye of empire spiraled outward around the globe, creating a visceral, kinetic sense of imperial travel and conquest, transforming European spectators into armchair conquistadors, affirming their sense of power while turning the colonies into spectacle for the metropole's voyeuristic gaze.

Cinema as Science and Spectacle

If the culture of empire authorized the pleasure of seizing ephemeral glimpses of its "margins" through travel and tourism, the nineteenth-century invention of the photographic and later the cinematographic camera made it possible to record such glimpses. Rather than remaining confined to its European home, the camera set out to "explore" new geographical, ethnographic, and archeological territories. It visited natural and human "wonders" (the Nile, the Taj Mahal) and unearthed buried civilizations (the excavations in Nubia), imbuing every sight with the wide-eyed freshness of the new machine. Yet the pioneers of the recorded image rarely questioned the constellation of power relations that allowed them to represent other lands and cultures. No one questioned how Egyptian land, history, and culture should be represented, for example, or asked what Egyptian people might have to say about the matter. Thus photographers making the grand oriental tour might record their own subjective visions, but in doing so they also drew clear boundaries between the subject looking and the object being looked at, between traveler and "traveled upon." Photographers such as George Bridges, Louis de Clercq, Maxime du Camp and filmmakers like Thomas Edison and the Lumière brothers did not simply document other territories; they also documented the cultural baggage they carried with them. Their subjective interpretations were deeply embedded in the discourses of their respective European empires.

The excitement generated by the camera's capacity to register the formal qualities of movement reverberated with the full-steam-ahead expansionism of imperialism itself. The camera was hired out to document the tentacular extensions of empire. Photographers and filmmakers were especially attracted to trains and ships, engines of empire that delivered raw materials from the interiors of Asia, Africa, and the Americas into the heart of Europe. Robert Howlett's photographs for the London *Times* of "The Bow of the Great Eastern" (1857) not only foreshadowed subsequent homages to the futurist aesthetics of the machine, but also documented the construction of an unprecedentedly large ship as a matter of national pride and a confirmation of British supremacy at sea.[13] The work of early photographers such as Felix Teynard, Maxime du Camp, Edouard-Denis Baldus, John Beasley Green, Louis de Clercq, and John Murray was supported, published, and exhibited by diverse imperial institutions. De Clercq, for example, was invited to accompany the historian Emmanuel-Guillaume Rey on a French government-sponsored expedition of 1859 to the Crusader castles of Syria and Asia Minor, a trip that generated the six volumes of *Voyage en Orient, Villes, Monuments, et Vues Pittoresques de Syrie*, along with the collection of historical artifacts now housed in the Oriental Antiquities Department of the Louvre. And Murray served in the East India Company army, where, like many Englishmen in India, he took up photography as a hobby. His work, first exhibited in London in 1857 during the "Indian Mutiny," was encouraged by the Governor-General of India, Lord Earl Canning, the same governor who suppressed the uprising and who, together with his wife Lady Charlotte Canning, was a major patron of photography in India.

Travel photographers did not just document territories for military and governmental purposes, their photos also registered the advances of scientific activities, for example the archeological excavations of Greece and Egypt. Fascination with ancient monuments was mingled with admiration for the camera's capacity to provide a vivid sense of distant regions and remote times: a photo in Du Camp's album *Egypte, Nubie, Palestine et Syrie* (1852) – "Westernmost Colossus of the temple of Re, Abu Simbel, 1850" – shows the photographer's assistant atop the crown of Rameses II, illustrating both relative scale and a moment of mastery and possession. If bourgeois travelers cherished photographic moments of their own exploring – as in Du Camp's photo of Flaubert in Cairo in 1850 – the colonized had to bear the weight of a generic ethnographic gaze, as in the anonymous photograph "Women

Grinding Paint, Calcutta, 1854." The camera also played a botanical and zoological role by documenting exotic fauna and flora. Louis Pierre Théophile Dubois de Nehant's "Another Impossible Task" (1854) shows the elephant "Miss Betsy," imported from India, in the Brussels Zoo, while Count de Motizon's photo (1852) captures Londoners admiring a hippopotamous captured on the banks of the White Nile. More than a servile scribe, the camera actively popularized imperial imagery, turning it into an exciting participatory activity for those in the motherland.

The social origins of the cinema were schizophrenic, traceable both to the "high" culture of science and literature and to the "low" culture of sideshows and nickelodeons. (At times the two cultures coalesced: the flying balloon in *Around the World in 80 Days*, designed to circle the world, is also the object of spectacle for enthusiastic Parisians.) The desire to expand the frontiers of science became inextricably linked to the desire to expand the frontiers of empire. The immediate origins of the cinema in Western science meant that filmic exhibition also entailed the exhibition of Western triumphs. The visible achievements of both cinema and science also graced the proliferating world fairs, which since the mid-nineteenth century had become the new "international" showplaces for the spectacular fruits of industrial and scientific progress.

The visualist inclinations of Western anthropological discourse[14] prepared the way for the cinematographic representation of other territories and cultures. The "ontologically" kinetic status of the moving image privileged the cinema not only over the written word but over still photography as well. It lent indexical credibility to anthropology, arming it with visual evidence not only of the existence of "others" but also of their actually existing otherness. Cinema in this sense prolonged the museological project of gathering three-dimensional archeological, ethnographic, botanical, and zoological objects in the metropolis. Unlike the more auratic and "inaccessible" elite arts and sciences, a popularizing cinema could plunge spectators into the midst of non-European worlds, letting them see and feel "strange" civilizations. It could transform the obscure *mappa mundi* into a familiar, knowable world.

Photography and the cinema represented alien topographies and cultures as aberrant in relation to Europe. Operating on a continuum with zoology, anthropology, botany, entomology,[15] biology, and medicine, the camera, like the microscope, anatomized the "other." The new visual apparatuses demonstrated the power of science to display and even decipher otherized cultures; dissection and montage together constructed a presumably holistic portrait of the colonized. Technological inventions, in other words, mapped the globe as a disciplinary space of knowledge.[16] Topographies were documented for purposes of military and economic control, often on the literal backs of the "natives" who carried the cinematographers and their equipment. In the colonial context, the common trope of the "camera gun" (Marey's "fusil cinématographique") resonated with the aggressive use of the camera by the agents of the colonial powers.[17] "Primitive" peoples were turned into the objects of quasi-sadistic experimentation. This kind of aggression reached a paroxysm in the 1920s films of Martin and Osa Johnson, where the filmmakers gleefully prodded Pygmies, whom they called "monkeys" and "niggers," to get sick on European cigars. In films such as *Trailing African Wild Animals* (1922) and *Simba* (1927), the Johnsons treated African peoples as a form of wildlife. The camera penetrated a foreign and familiar zone like a predator, seizing its "loot" of images as raw material to be reworked in the "motherland" and sold to sensation-hungry

Plate 8.1 *Simba: King of the Beasts.*

spectators and consumers, a process later fictionalized in *King Kong* (1933). There was no clue, in such films, as to how Europeans depended for their everyday survival in the field on the knowledge, intelligence, labor, and the "enforced subordination of people the white folk insisted on seeing as perpetual children."[18]

If cinema itself traced its parentage to popular sideshows and fairs, ethnographic cinema and Hollywoodean ethnography were the heirs of a tradition of exhibitions of "real" human objects, a tradition going back to Columbus's importation of "New World" natives to Europe for purposes of courtly entertainment. Exhibitions organized the world as a spectacle within an obsessively mimetic aesthetic.[19] In the US, at a time roughly coincident with the beginnings of cinema, a series of fairs – the Chicago Columbian Exposition of 1893, the Omaha Trans-Mississippi Exposition in 1898, the Buffalo Pan-American Exposition in 1901, the St Louis "Louisiana Purchase" Exposition in 1904 – introduced millions of fairgoers to evolutionary ideas about race in an atmosphere of communal good cheer. The Chicago Columbian Exposition spatialized racial hierarchies in a quasi-didactic fashion by having the Teutonic exhibits placed closest to the "White City," with the "Mohammedan world" and the "savage races" at the opposite end. Racism and "entertainment," as Robert W. Rydell points out, became closely intertwined.[20] The Omaha fair featured an exhibit on "the Vanquished Races," and in the Atlanta Exposition the Sioux were obliged to reenact their own defeat and humiliation at Wounded Knee. The Louisiana Purchase Exposition included a Filipino exhibit that made the Pacific Islands seem as much a part of "manifest destiny" as the conquest of the west. Such expositions gave utopian form to White supremacist ideology, legitimizing racial hierarchies abroad and muting class and gender divisions among Whites at home by stressing national agency in a global project of domination.[21]

Africans and Asians were exhibited as human figures with kinship to specific animal species, thus literalizing the colonialist zeugma yoking "native" and "animal," the very fact of exhibition in cages implying that the cages' occupants were less than human. Lapps, Nubians, and Ethiopians were displayed in Germany in anthropological – zoological exhibits.[22] The conjunction of "Darwinism, Barnumism [and] pure and simple racism" resulted in the exhibition of Ota Benga, a Pygmy from the Kasai region, alongside the animals in the Bronx Zoo.[23] A precursor to Epcott's global village, the 1894 Antwerp World's Fair featured a reconstructed Congolese village with sixteen "authentic" villagers. In many cases the people exhibited died or fell seriously ill. "Freak shows" too paraded before the West's bemused eye a variety of "exotic" pathologies. Saartjie Baartman, the "Hottentot Venus,"[24] was displayed on the entertainment circuit in England and France. Although her protrusive buttocks constituted the main attraction, the rumored peculiarities of her genitalia also drew crowds, with her racial/sexual "anomaly" constantly being associated with animality.[25] The zoologist and anatomist George Cuvier studied her intimately and presumably dispassionately, and compared her buttocks to those of "female mandrills, baboons... which assume at certain epochs of their life a truly monstrous development."[26] After Baartman's death at the age of twenty-five, Cuvier received official permission for an even closer look at her private parts, and dissected her to produce a detailed description of her body inside out.[27] Her genitalia still rest on a shelf in the Musée de l'Homme in Paris alongside the genitalia of "une négresse" and "une péruvienne"[28] as monuments to a kind of imperial necrophilia. The final placement of the female parts in the partriarchally designated "Museum of Man" provides a crowning irony.

As the product of both science and mass culture, cinema combined traveling knowledge with traveling spectacles, conveying a view of the "world itself as an exhibition."[29] The study of a hypersexualized "other" in scientific discourse was paralleled by the cinema's scopophilic display of aliens as spectacle. Hollywood productions abounded in "exotic" images of moving native bodies, at times incorporating actual travelogs dug up from the archives, deployed in such films as the *Tarzan* series. Thus in a "double standard" erotics, the Production Code of the Motion Picture Producers and Directors of America, Inc., 1930–4, which censored Jane's two-piece outfit into one in later *Tarzan* films, left intact the naked African women in the background, evoking a *National Geographic*-style prurient delight in unilateral native nudity. The portrayal of dance rituals in such films as *The Dance of Fatima* (1903), *The Sheik* (1921), *Bird of Paradise* (1932), and *Sanders of the River* (1935) displayed alien flesh to hint at the masculinist pleasures of exploration. Hiding behind a respectable figleaf of "science" and "authenticity," ethnographic films focused directly on the bouncing breasts of dancing women,[30] Hollywood films, under the surveillance of domestic moral majorities, relegated native nudity to the background, or restricted the imagery to minimal "native" garb. Formulaic scenes of dark frenzied bodies entranced by accelerating drum rhythms relayed a fetishized image of indigenous religions. Ceremonial possession (portrayed as a kind of mass hysteria) evoked the uncontrollable id of libidinous beings. Ethnographic science, then, provided a cover for the unleashing of pornographic impulses. The cinematic exposure of the dark body nourished spectatorial desire, while marking off imaginary boundaries between "self" and "other," thus mapping homologous spheres, both macrocosmic (the globe) and microcosmic (the sphere of carnal knowledge).

Projecting the Empire

The cinema combined narrative and spectacle to tell the story of colonialism from the colonizer's perspective. From the Lumière brothers' mocking portrayals of the culinary habits of North Africans in *Le Musulman Rigolo* (The Funny Muslim, 1902), through the adventure tales of *Tarzan*, to the Westerner-in-the-pot cannibal imagery of the 1980s version of *King Solomon's Mines* and the scientific missions of *Indiana Jones* (1981, 1984, 1989), dominant cinema has spoken for the "winners" of history, in films which idealized the colonial enterprise as a philanthropic "civilizing mission" motivated by a desire to push back the frontiers of ignorance, disease, and tyranny. Programmatically negative portrayals helped rationalize the human costs of the imperial enterprise. Thus Africa was imaged as a land inhabited by cannibals in the Ernst Lubin comedy *Rastus in Zululand* (1910), Mexicans were reduced to "greasers" and "bandidos" in films like *Tony the Greaser* (1911) and *The Greaser's Revenge* (1914), and Native Americans were portrayed as savage marauders in *Fighting Blood* (1911) and *The Last of the Mohicans* (1920).

Each imperial filmmaking country had its own imperial genres set in "darkest Africa," the "mysterious East," and the "stormy Caribbean." It was in this imperializing spirit that Thomas Alva Edison staged battles against Filipino guerrillas in the fields of New Jersey (with Blacks standing in for the Filipinos) and that J. Stuart Blackton staged the Spanish – American war using scale-model battleships in local bathtubs. Indeed, many of the early American one-reelers, such as *Cuban Ambush* (1898), *Roosevelt's Rough Riders* (1898), *Troop Ships for the Philippines* (1898), and *Landing of U.S. Troops near Santiago* (1902), glorified the imperialist binge in the Caribbean and the Philippines. Even filmmakers not conventionally associated with lauding imperialism betray a shared discourse of empire. Georges Méliès' filmography, for example, features a number of films related to expansionist voyages and orientalist fantasies: *Le Fakir – Mystére Indien* (1896), *Vente d'Esclaves au Harem* (1897), *Cléopatre* (1899), *La Vengeance de Bouddah* (1901), *Les Aventures de Robinson Crusoe* (1902), *Le Palais des Mille et une Nuits* (1905).[31] Similarly, in Méliès' *Le Voyage dans la Lune* (A Trip to the Moon, 1902; based on Verne's *From the Earth to the Moon*, 1865), the rocket's phallic penetration of the moon (the space frontier) recapitulates, on another level, the historical discourse of the other (imperial) "frontier." ("I would annex the planets if I could," Cecil Rhodes often said.) The film is structured like a colonial captivity narrative: spear-carrying skeleton creatures burst from the moon's simulacral jungle and capture the explorers, only to be defeated by the male explorers' gunlike umbrellas, which magically eliminate the savage creatures. Such a film, not in any obvious sense "about" colonialism, can thus be read as analogizing imperial expansion.

Many American films, for example *Beau Geste* (1939), filmed in Arizona but set in Morocco, praised the work of their imperial confrères in the French Foreign Legion. Between 1911 and 1962, France itself made over 200 feature films set in North Africa, many of them memorializing the exploits of the Legion against native rebels.[32] But the British especially became masters of the imperial epic, as in the Korda trilogy *Sanders of the River* (1935), *Drums* (1938), and *The Four Feathers* (1939) and in the films produced by Michael Balcon: *Rhodes of Africa* (1936), *The Great Barrier* (1936), and *King Solomon's Mines* (1937). At a time when roughly one-fourth of the human race lived under British rule, many films preferred a nostalgic look back at the "pioneering" days of "exploration" to a frontal examination of the quotidian brutality of latter-day imperialism.[33]

Cedric Hardwicke as Livingstone conducting an African choir in "Onward Christian Soldiers" in *David Livingstone* (1936), Cecil Rhodes planning the Cape-to-Cairo railway before a map of Africa in *Rhodes of Africa*, Reginald Denny laying down imperial law to a native ruler in *Escape to Burma* (1955), Tarzan performing deeds of valor in the imperial service; such are the filmic epiphanies of empire. What Jeffrey Richards describes as the "square-jawed, pipe-smoking, solar-topeed English sahib," standing at the ramparts, scanning the horizon for signs of native restlessness, crystallized an ideal imperial figure for cinematic consumption. Actors such as Ronald Colman, C. Aubrey Smith, Clive Brook, David Niven, Basil Rathbone, George Sanders, and Ray Milland incarnated heroic virtue in what amounted to a form of celluloid ancestor worship. *Rhodes of Africa*, for example, paints a hagiographic portrait of the imperial patriarch, constructed as an exemplum of foresight and benevolence. Both Korda and Balcon stress the austere stoic virtues and natural authority of the British on foreign strands. In *Sanders*, a film based on the popular Edgar Wallace series, a colonial District Commissioner (Sanders) puts down an uprising in Nigeria and brings British law and order to the River Territories. The usual colonial splitting pits the good Black Chief Bosambo (Paul Robeson) against the evil King Mofalaba. Colonialism, as incarnated by the authoritative and likeable Sanders, is portrayed as natural, eternal, beneficent. Africans themselves, meanwhile, were enlisted to enact their own caricatures. The exploits of figures like Sanders, Tarzan, and Quartermain brought home to the domestic public an idealized version of what abstract imperial theories meant "on the ground."

The imperial thrust of many of these films requires no subtle deciphering; it is right on the surface, often in the form of didactic forewords. *Sanders*, for example, is dedicated to the "sailors, soldiers and merchant adventurers... who laid the foundations of the British Empire [and whose] work is carried on by the civil servants – the Keepers of the King's Peace." The preface to *Rhodes of Africa* suggests that Africans themselves endorsed Rhodes's enterprise; the Matabele, we are told, regarded Sanders as "a royal warrior, who tempered conquest with the gift of ruling." Elsewhere imperial ideology is explicitly expressed through dialogue. Colonel Williams in *Wee Willie Winkie* (1937) tells Shirley Temple: "Beyond that pass, thousands of savages are waiting to sweep down and ravage India. It's England's duty, it's my duty, to see that this doesn't happen." *Farewell Again* (1937) begins:

All over the world, wherever the Union Jack is flown, men, from castle and cottage, city and village, are on duty... facing hardship, danger, death with only a brief glimpse of home. Each has his own joys and sorrows but a common purpose unites them – their country's service.

In such films, Britain's material interests in the imperialized world are masked by what Conrad's Marlowe would have called "redeeming ideas": the battle against savagery (*Wee Willie Winkie*), the struggle to abolish slavery (*Killers of Kilimanjaro*, 1959), the fight against fascism (*The Sun Never Sets*, 1940).

A positive image of empire was also encoded into law. The British in particular imposed censorship provisions throughout their empire. In Trinidad, the censorship code forbade "scenes intended to ridicule or criticize unfairly" British social life, "White men in a state of degradation amidst native surroundings, or using violence towards natives, especially Chinese, negroes and Indians," and "equivocal situations between men of one race and girls of another race."[34] In 1928 the Hong Kong censor told the American Consul-General that his duty was to uphold British prestige in "a small settlement of white men on the fringe of a huge empire of Asiatics." A United Artists agent in Hong Kong reported that banned subjects included "armed conflict between Chinese and whites" and portrayals of "white women in indecorous garb or positions or situations which would tend to discredit our womenfolk with the Chinese."[35] The British censorship codes applied to global audiences, pressuring American producers to respect them. In 1928 Jason Joy warned production personnel that the British would not permit "the portrayal of the white man and woman . . . in a way that might degrade him or her in the eyes of the native, nor will they permit anything in films tending to incite the natives against the governing race."[36] At the same time, colonial powers tried to prevent the development of rival "native" cinemas. The growing power of Egyptian national cinema in the Arab world was perceived as troublesome by the French, leading them to form a special department "responsible for setting up a production centre in Morocco whose official mission was to oppose the influence of Egyptian cinema."[37]

Hollywood films also rendered service to empire by reconstructing colonial outposts in southern California. In Samuel Goldwyn's *The Real Glory* (1939), for example, soldiers of fortune and the American army quell a "terrorist" uprising in the Philippines. Despite the US's own historical origins in anti-British revolt, Hollywood films often demonstrated as much enthusiasm for European colonialism as did the European films. Hollywood made more films than the French did about the French Foreign Legion,[38] and American films like W. S. Van Dyke's *Trader Horn* (1931) and *Stanley and Livingstone* (1939) glorified British colonialism in Africa. George Stevens's *Gunga Din* (1939), similarly, showed three heroic British soldiers battling savage Punjabis in nineteenth-century India.

Furthermore, the fact that American stars such as Spencer Tracy in *Stanley and Livingstone* and Charlton Heston in *Khartoum* (1966) played British colonial heroes virtually ensured the sympathetic identification of the Euro-American public, thus playing out on a thespian level the historical lap-dissolve by which the British-dominated imperialism of the nineteenth century faded into the US-dominated imperialism of the twentieth. In Henry Hathaway's *Lives of a Bengal Lancer* (1934), starring Gary Cooper, a handful of British officers hold back a native rebellion. The older officers are played by British actors, the younger by Americans, suggesting a kind of imperial succession. As Richards points out, Shirley Temple, the top box-office attraction in Britain and the US from 1935 to 1938, played a central role in the imperial films.[39] *Wee Willie Winkie*, based on a Kipling story, featured her as an American girl in India who learns about England's mission from her British grandfather, the commanding officer of a frontier fort. While the grandfather – a figure of British colonialism – is overly rigid, the American granddaughter is flexible and adept at mediation and at one point actually intervenes in a war to reconcile a rebel Khan to the British Raj. Thus the English–American family becomes enlisted in a kind of imperial allegory. Temple's diplomatic "in-betweenness" reflects the historical in-betweenness of the US itself, as at once an anticolonial revolutionary power in relation to Europe, and a colonizing, hegemonic power in relation to Native American and African peoples. Upon arriving in India, Temple confuses the Indians (natives of India) with American "Indians" – committing Columbus's error, but in reverse. In a film released just two years later, *Susannah of the Mounties* (1939), she intervenes between the Royal Canadian Mounted Police and an "Indian" tribe, suggesting the substitutability of the two kinds of "Indian." (Shirley Temple Black's later nomination as Ambassador to Ghana provides a further twist on this trope of substitutability.) Moreover, three of the epics of British India, *Lives of a Bengal Lancer*, *Four Men and a Prayer* (1938), and *Gunga Din*, were remade as westerns, entitled respectively *Geronimo* (1940), *Fury at Furnace Creek* (1940), and *Soldiers Three* (1951). The imperial epic also provided the model for westerns like *Santa Fe Trail* (1940) and *They Died with Their Boots on* (1941), while *Charge of the Light Brigade* (1938) was the model for *Khartoum*. Thus a kind of imperial circularity recycled the formulae of European supremacy *vis-à-vis* globally dispersed others, with the White European always retaining his or her "positional superiority" (Edward Said's term).

The studios' predilection for spinning-globe logos also translated imperial ambition. The Lumières' location shootings of diverse "Third World" sites, such as India, Mexico, Egypt, and Palestine, inaugurated this imperial mobility. The globe logo became associated with several studios (Universal, RKO), and with the British Korda brothers' productions, many of whose films, such as *Drums*, *The Four Feathers*, and *The Jungle Book* (1942), concerned imperial themes. The globe image symbolically evokes divine powers, since the created world implies a Creator. Later, TV news updated this trope of "covering the world." In the 1950s, John Cameron Swayze used the globe-trotting motif in his *Camel News Caravan* and contemporary news programs call attention to it through their spherical-line globes and illuminated maps. Recent TV coverage of international crises generated further elaborations of the trope. A Gulf War special, ABC's *A Line in the Sand*, had Peter Jennings walk on top of a colorful political map of the Middle East as a setting for a

Plate 8.2   Peter Jennings "striding the world like a Colossus."

pedagogical tour of the region's history, in a "covering" at once temporal and spatial. The North American TV commentator literally steps on, sits on, and looks down on the map, bestriding the narrow world "like a colossus."[40]

In both cinema and TV, such overarching global points-of-view suture the specta-tor into the omniscient cosmic perspective of the European master-subject. Incorpor-ating images of maps and globes, *Around the World in 80 Days* (1956), for example, begins with its omniscient narrator hailing the "shrinking of the world" which occurred during the period that Verne was writing his book. (The prelude to the film includes the mandatory globus prop made to spin for the camera.) The idea of "shrinking" materializes the confident, scientific perspective of upper-class British men. "Nothing is impossible," says the David Niven character: "when science finally conquers the air it may be feasible to circle the globe in eighty hours." Thus he implicitly links the development of science to imperial control, an idea reinforced by the character's recurrent association with the strains of "Rule Britannia." In recent science-fiction films such as *Return of the Jedi* (1983), globality embraces spheres yet to be charted by NASA. The conquest of outer space cohabits with an underlying imperial narrative in which the visualization of another planet conforms to the representational paradigm of Third World "underdevelopment." A Manichean struggle pits the hero against the new land and its natives. The exotic, teddy-bear-like "Ewoks" – whose language, as in most colonial films, remains unintelligible – worship the high-tech Euro-American hero and defend him against repulsive, evil, irrational creatures. The hero's physical and moral triumph legitimates the enemy's destruction and the paternal transformation of the friendly "elements" into servile allies, authorizing his right to establish new outposts (and implicitly to hold on to old ones). Like early adventure films, spectacular sci-fi and star-war video-games visualize progress as a purposeful movement toward global ubiquity; if in the early films traveling the ocean entailed no boundaries, in the recent ones the sky is no longer the limit.

The Western as Paradigm

If the imperial adventure film conveyed the pleasures and benefits of empire, the western told the story of imperial-style adventures on the American frontier. Indeed, the link between the two imperial adventures, in the continental US and outside of it, has usually been obscured, the word "imperialism" usually being restricted in refer-ence to the late nineteenth-century expansions beyond the continent into the Carib-bean and the Pacific. As has often been noted, the high proportion of westerns in Hollywood's costume-film output – roughly one-fourth of all Hollywood features between 1926 through 1967 – is so striking as to betray a kind of national obsession.[41] Although relatively few films treat the American revolution, Washington, Jefferson, and Franklin, countless films treat the conquest of the west, Kit Carson, Billy the Kid, and General Custer. The central place of the "myth of the frontier" in the American imaginary has been eloquently discussed by Francis Jennings, Richard Slotkin, Rich-ard Drinnon, Michael Rogin, John Cowelti, and others. Arguably the longest-lived of American myths, it traces its origins to the colonial period. The myth of the frontier has its ideological roots in some of the discourses addressed in the previous chapter: the competitive laws of Social Darwinism, the hierarchy of the races and sexes, the idea of progress. It gave exceptionalist national form to a more widespread historical process – the general thrust of European expansion into Asia, Africa, and the Americas. What Slotkin calls the "American-History-As-Indian-War" trope has consistently given a fantastical self-aggrandizing shape to "United Statesian" self-narration, with reverberations that echo through popular culture even today.

The western inherited a complex intertext embracing classical epic, chivalric romance, Indianist novel, conquest fiction, the paintings of George Catlin, and the drawings of Frederic Remington. It played a crucial pedagogical role in forming the historical sensibilities of generations of Americans. The western's macronarrative was doubly "condensed," both temporally and spatially: of a "New World" history of almost four centuries, these films focus on the last 200 years, thus repressing situations of first contact when American land and culture were more obviously Indian, and when non-genocidal collaboration with the Indians was still possible. Films like *Drums along the Mohawk* (1939) and *Northwest Passage* (1940), set before 1800, are in this sense the exception; westerns usually place us at a historical moment when the penetration of the frontier is already well under way, when the characters' point of origin is no longer Europe but Euro-America, and when there is little likelihood that Native Americans will mount a successful resistance to European occupation. That westerns are not "easterns" is no accident, since "easterns," set on the eastern seaboard of an earlier generation's contact with Native Americans, might have stressed the "un-American" foreignness of White Europeans, bringing up some of the intriguing "what ifs?" of history.

Hollywood's Native America, as Ward Churchill puts it, "flourished with the arrival of whites," then "vanished somewhat mysteriously, along with the bison and the open prairie," in a story with no "before" and no "after."[42] As a result, there is no cinematic recognition of what Churchill calls "a white-free and autonomous past," no Iroquois, Sioux, or Cherokee (not to mention Aztec or Inca) counterpart to *Cleopatra* (1934, 1963), *The Robe* (1953), or *Ben Hur* (1926, 1959). Furthermore, even within an already condensed spatiotemporality, these westerns privilege a period of roughly fifty years, and return time and again to particular sites and events. Although historical Native Americans generally avoided direct confrontation with the White military – according to the National Parks Service, there were probably only six full-scale attacks on US cavalry forts between 1850 and 1890 – the Indian raid on the fort, as the constructed bastion of settled civilization against nomadic savagery, nevertheless became a staple topos in American westerns.[43] Turned into aggressors, Native Americans became dispensable "pop-up targets for non-Indian guns."[44] The status of a hero, and indirectly of an actor, was defined by the number of Indians he could kill.[45]

Central to the western is the land. The reverent attitude toward the landscapes themselves – Monument Valley, Yellowstone, the Colorado River – occludes those to whom the land belonged and thus naturalizes expansionism. The land is regarded as both empty and virgin, and at the same time superinscribed with biblical symbolism – "Promised Land," "New Canaan," "God's Earth." A binary division pits sinister wilderness against beautiful garden, with the former "inevitably" giving way before the latter: "The sturdy plant of the wilderness," Thomas Farnham writes, "droops under the enervating culture of the garden. The Indian is buried with his arrows and bow."[46] The dry, desert terrain furnishes an empty stage for the play of expansionist fantasies. Nor is it usually explained that the native populations portrayed as an intrinsic part of the landscape were for the most part driven there by the White expropriation of more fertile lands farther east.

A Manichean allegory also papers over two diametrically opposed views of the land and the soil: for most Native American cultures, land is not real estate for sale but is sacred both as historically consecrated and as the "mother" that gives (and needs) nurture.[47] In many indigenous languages, the concept of "selling land" is literally unspeakable, because there are no words to convey it; whence the absurdity of imagining that Europeans "bought" Manhattan for $24 and a few trinkets. For the European, on the other hand, the land was a soulless conglomeration of exploitable resources, and the Indians a wandering horde without a sense of property, law, or government. "Civilization," as one Secretary of War put it, "entails a love for exclusive property." Progress, said Senator Henry Dawes, depends on not holding land in common, since "selfishness is the basis of civilization."[48] For Europeans, land existed to be transformed and monogrammed, as it were, by a human, societal presence. While for the Europeans land was a commodity that had to produce quickly or else be abandoned for greener pastures (or more golden mines), for the Native Americans land was a sacred trust irreparably damaged by conquest.

The very titles of westerns stress a mobile, and mobilizing, European claim on the land. A disproportionate number stress European-designed state borders – *Oklahoma Kid* (1939), *Colorado Territory* (1949), *The Texas Rangers* (1936), *California Conquest* (1952) – the irony of course being that a high proportion of American states (such as Alabama, Arizona), rivers (including the Ohio, Potomac), lakes (for example Huron, Ontario) and mountain ranges (the Adirondacks and Poconos, for instance) carry native names.[49] The titles themselves exhibit the Adamic/Promethean power to name: *El Dorado* (1967), *Northwest Passage* (1940), *The Last Frontier* (1956). A kind of occidentotropism ("Go West Young Man!") informs the films, conveying a thrusting, trailblazing purposiveness, a divinely sanctioned crepuscular teleology: *Red Sundown* (1956), *Union Pacific* (1939), *The Last Outpost* (1935, 1951), *Heaven's Gate* (1980). Other titles resonate more blatantly with westward-driving zeal – *Westbound* (1959), *Westward the Women* (1951), *The Way West* (1967). Such titles relay the "becoming" of the American nation, which reached its telos with the complete transmogrification of nature into culture, a point fully reached only in the age of cinema. The west was thus less a place than a movement, a going west, a moving horizon, a "vaguely realizing westward" in Robert Frost's phrase, a tropism in both senses of the word – a movement toward and a figure of speech.

The western projects a vision of wide-open possibility, a sense of vistas infinitely open in both space and time. Aesthetically, this vision is expressed in wide-screen perspectives and soaring crane shots accompanying stampedes and cavalcades. The title of *How the West Was Won* (1963), a spectacular epic that follows an emigrant family from the Erie Canal in the 1830s to a settled home in the west fifty years and four generations later, sums up the theme of conquest and settlement. Western films inherit the vocation of frontier painting, exemplified by the Currier and Ives lithograph *Through to the Pacific*, where an allegorical landscape rich in symbols of material progress includes a train moving through an industrial town in the foreground toward "undeveloped" land stretching to the Pacific in the background. John Ford's *The Iron Horse* (1924), whose title itself is an anthropomorphic "Indianism," narrates a similar progression from a rustic past (before the railroad was built, when Indians attacked the wagon trains) to a dynamic adventure-filled present (during the construction of the railroad, when the Indians attack the workers), and an implied felicitous future (with the linking of the two railroads, symbolically the realization of the nation's manifest destiny, and the disappearance of Indians from the scene). A nation with continental ambitions crystallizes on the screen as diverse groups coalesce around a common project. The wild land is domesticated and envalued, with progress embodied in its metallic avatar, the locomotive, a vehicle often metonymically (Lumière's train station) and metaphorically associated with the cinema itself. A differential mode of emplotment encodes Enlightenment values of progress and development, assigning a comic "happy end," under the sign of providence, for the characters representing the west, and a tragic "doomed to extinction" emplotment for the west's others. A narrative paradigm is enlisted to serve teleological notions of national progress and manifest destiny.

"Too bad," Duke Wayne says of Indian extinction in *Hondo* (1953); "it was a good way of life." The elimination of the Indian allows for elegiac nostalgia as a way to treat Indians only in the past tense and thus dismiss their claims in the present, while posthumously expressing thanatological tenderness for their memory. Here too the titles are revelatory of the idea that Indians live in historically condemned time: *The Vanishing Race* (1912), *The Last of the Mohicans* (1920, 1932, 1936, 1992), *The Last of the Redmen* (1947). An ambivalently repressive mechanism dispels the anxiety in the face of the Indian, whose very presence is a reminder of the initially precarious grounding of the American nation-state itself. For Native Americans, meanwhile, the memories were vivid and painful. In the filming of *The Indian Wars* (1914), traumatized Sioux were obliged to reenact their own historical defeat and humiliation at Wounded Knee:

The plan called for the battle to take place right over the Indian graves, which seemed to the Sioux a horrible desecration...the Indians were resentful, remembering how the white soldiers had massacred their tribesmen and the women and children.... The greatest difficulty in getting these men together was to convince them that the purpose of this mobilization was merely to reproduce the wars and not to annihilate them, for when they saw the Hotchkiss guns, the rifles, revolvers and cases of ammunition, there was a feeling of unrest, as though the time had come when they were to be gathered in by the Great Spirit through the agency of the white men.[50]

In a temporal paradox, living Indians were induced to "play dead," as it were, in order to perform a narrative of manifest destiny in which their role, ultimately, was to disappear.

We are not suggesting that all westerns were made in a single mold, or that there were never sympathetic portrayals of Indians, or that westerns were free of ideological tensions and contradictions. Enormous differences, obviously, separate William S. Hart's *The Aryan* (1916) from "pro-Indian" westerns like *Broken Arrow* (1950) or *Devil's Doorway* (1970), and the general run of westerns from a going-native western like *Little Big Man* (1970), a satirical western such as *Buffalo Bill and the Indians, or Sitting Bull's History Lesson* (1976), or an implicitly anti-Vietnam-war western like *Soldier Blue* (1970), which appropriates the 1864 Sand Creek massacre of Cheyenne and Arapahos to allegorize the My Lai massacre in Vietnam. Even within specific subgenres there were notable differences. A captivity narrative, for example, could either portray White assimilation to Indian ways or convey a racist horror of a sexual assault, avenged by "savage war." The western has also evolved historically, particularly since the 1960s when pro-Indian films began to promote identification, however condescendingly, with Indian cultural values. As Thomas Schatz points out, later westerns become reflective, projecting a less flattering vision of the expansionist project; the law-and-order heroes of the classic western give way to renegade antiheroes.[51] Post-1960s' "realistic" westerns depict the frontier as violent but unheroic, often presenting Native Americans with considerable sympathy.

Our point, then, is not to collapse differences among westerns, but rather to point to the genre's ideological premises and its general procedures for fostering identification. Generally speaking, the Hollywood western turned history on its head by making Native Americans appear intruders on their own land, and thus provided a paradigmatic perspective, as Tom Engelhardt points out, through which to view the whole of the non-White world.[52] Rarely do westerns show Native Americans as simply inhabiting the domestic space of their unthreatening daily lives, although it was *their* lives and habits that were brutally disrupted by western expansion. Native Americans are usually portrayed as mean-spirited enemies of the moving train of progress. The point-of-view in the western is premised on exteriority, within what Tom Engelhardt calls "an imagery of encirclement." The besieged wagon train or fort forms the focus of attention and sympathy, and from this center familiar figures sally out against unknown attackers characterized by inexplicable customs and irrational hostility: "In essence, the viewer is forced behind the barrel of a repeating rifle and it is from that position, through its gun sights, that he [*sic*] receives a picture history of western colonialism and imperialism."[53] The point-of-view conventions consistently favor the Euro-American protagonists; they are centered in the frame, their desires drive the narrative; the camera pans, tracks, and cranes to accompany their regard. In films such as *Drums along the Mohawk*, the point-of-view can be said to follow a structure of concentric circles. The inner humanized circle – often including women and children – is threatened by a second circle of attackers, until a final outer circle – the cavalry – rescues the besieged first circle by annihilating the middle circle. The outer circle, as colonial *deus ex machina*, executes an environing providential order – cinematic shorthand for genocide. The possibility of sympathetic identifications with the Indians is simply ruled out by the point-of-view conventions; the spectator is unwittingly sutured into a colonialist perspective.

Dominant narratives about colonial encounters suggest that "we," while imperfect, are at least human, while the non-European "they" are irrational and subhuman. The "colonial proportion" decrees that many of "them" must die for each one of "us," a pattern repeated in films of Zulus fighting the British, Mexicans fighting the US cavalry, American soldiers against Japanese kamikaze bombers, and, most recently, American pilots against Iraqi conscripts. But while "they" die disproportionately, "we" must believe that "they" pose an apocalyptic threat. Richard Drinnon traces the process by which White hostility toward premodern "savages" has been recycled throughout American history. The process began with the "protovictims," the Pequots massacred in 1637, when the Puritans made some 400 of them "as a fiery oven" in their village near the Mystic River and later finished off 300 more in the mud of Fairfield Swamp, in an early example of the "righteous massacres" that have so marked American history.[54] The founding arrogance of the Pequot massacre was subsequently expanded to the "Conquest of the West," after which it was extended to the Philippines during the "imperialist binge" at the end of the nineteenth century, where many of the commanding generals had fought in the

Plains and Apache wars.[55] "The pigments of Indian-hating," writes Drinnon, "shaded off into coolie-hating, the Chinese exclusion act (1882) and the 'Yellow Peril' hysteria at the turn of the century."[56] During the Philippine–American war, soldiers writing home stressed the comparison. An officer who served in the Philippines wrote reporter Henry Loomis Nelson:

We exterminated the American Indians, and I guess most of us are proud of it, or, at least, believe the end justified the means; and we must have no scruples about exterminating this other race standing in the way of progress and enlightenment, if it is necessary.[57]

Another Asian war, the Vietnam war, also reverberated with echoes of the Indian wars. The same Custer story that provided John Ford with the plot for *Fort Apache* (1948) also provided Arthur Penn and Sidney Salkow with allegorical material with which to denounce the imperial folly of the Vietnam war. According to Frances Fitzgerald in *Fire in the Lake* (1973), the American elite saw the war as the

painless conquest of an inferior race [just as to] the American settlers the defeat of the Indians had seemed not just a nationalist victory, but an achievement made in the name of humanity – the triumph of light over darkness, of good over evil, of civilization over brutish nature.[58]

The very names of some of the military operations in Vietnam – "Rolling Thunder," "Sam Houston," "Hickory," and "Daniel Boone" – resonated with the memory, and the attitudes, of the American frontier history relayed in the western. Troops described Vietnam as "Indian country," while General Maxwell Taylor justified escalation as a case of moving the "Indians" away from the "fort" so that the "settlers" could "plant corn."[59] For Lyndon Johnson, Vietnam recalled the Alamo. Even the "domino theory," according to Drinnon, "was an updated, internationalized version of the older fear of pan-Indian movements that went back beyond the Pequots and the Narragansetts."[60] And more recently General Schwarzkopf compared Iraq to "Indian territory."

The Late Imperial Film

The colonial/imperial paradigm did not die with the formal end of colonialism, nor is the western paradigm limited to the wild west. Indeed, one could speak of a "submerged" imperial presence in many films – the South African diamond mines in the background of *Gentlemen Prefer Blondes* (1953), the French presence in Morocco in *The Man Who Knew too Much* (1954), the neocolonial backdrop of Disney films set in Latin America (*The Three Caballeros*, 1945, for example),[61] or the French domination, again in North Africa, in René Clair's *Les Belles des Nuits* (1952). Such attitudes seep even into innocuous television entertainments such as *Gilligan's Island*, seen by 2.5 million people per day as late as 1986, where the island, as Paul Sellors points out, is perceived as surrounded by barbarian tribes.[62] The same Rider Haggard novels that inspired filmmakers in the silent period were adopted again throughout the sound period, sometimes more than once. *King Solomon's Mines* was filmed again, often recycling the same footage, in 1937, 1950, 1959 (under the title *Watusi*), and 1985. The 1937 film features Paul Robeson as the Zulu Umbopa and has the witchdoctor Gogoul trap innocent Whites inside a volcano; as they are about to be butchered, an opportune solar eclipse confirms their pretense of being gods. The 1959 Kurt Neumann film *Watusi* reuses footage from the 1950 film, and has a missionary's daughter saved from "savages." The 1985 *King Solomon's Mines* borrows shamelessly from *Raiders of the Lost Ark* and recycles the most classic colonialist imagery, such as hordes of spear-carriers and the venerable "Europeans-in-the-pot" cannibal motif. Made in Zimbabwe, the film, in an amalgam of Manichean narratives, suggests that the real colonial foreigners in Africa were not the British or the French but the Turks and the Arabs, along with the German Nazis.[63]

It would be impossible, even pointless, to inventory all the films that relay a colonialist or imperialist perspective, but we can examine a symptomatic example. Andrew McLaglen's *The Wild Geese* (1978) extends the western conventions to post-independence Africa. Based on a novel by Daniel Carney, a White man from Rhodesia (now Zimbabwe) and a former member of the South African police, the film glorifies the White mercenaries who once propped up White-minority rule in places like South Africa and corrupt Black rule in places like Zaire. The film, which centers on the mercenaries' armed rescue of a deposed Central African president, features highly popular actors playing the mercenaries. Richard Burton plays a tough Bogart-like commander who hides a sensitive heart beneath his cynical surface. Richard Harris is a brilliant military technician who regretfully tears himself away from his young son to join the "mission." Roger Moore is a playboy–pilot and Hardy Kruger a South African policeman. The mercenaries form the central focus of our sympathy; they win us with their flawed humanity, their quirky eccentricities, and their boisterous Hawksian camaraderie. Killing Africans en masse, the film implies, somehow brings out the mercenaries' latent humanity.

In the racist hierarchies of *The Wild Geese*, White males stand at the apex, White women are essentially dispensable, and Africans are playthings for Western plans. The film adroitly camouflages its racism, however: a token Black is included in the mercenary force – massacres seem more palatable when the perpetrators are "integrated" – and the entire operation is in any case performed on behalf of a Black leader repeatedly characterized as "the best there is." (The "best there is," unfortunately, is portrayed as sick, helpless, dying, literally carried on the backs of the Whites.) Within this White rescue fantasy, the Black leader of the 1970s speaks oddly like the Sidney Poitier of the 1950s. Pleading for love and integration, he calls on Blacks to "forgive the White past" and on Whites "to forgive the Black present," thus canceling out centuries of slavery and colonialism in the misleading symmetry of an aphorism.

Despite its flimsy integrationist facade, itself rather anachronistic in the 1970s, *The Wild Geese* conforms to the generic conventions of the western as colonialist adventure film. Even mercenaries, recruited from the flotsam and jetsam of English society, the film suggests, are suited to exercise power over African life. Whether gamblers, drunkards, or opportunists, they remain human; they are "us." African life, meanwhile, comes cheap. The film consistently obeys the "colonial proportion" in the body count; scores, even hundreds of Blacks die for each White mercenary slain. At the same time, the film exploits our instinctive sympathy for any group performing a "mission." We are induced to glory in the "surgical precision" of a task well done, whatever its political motivation. The European right to determine Africa's destiny is simply assumed. *The Wild Geese* enlists the gamut of cinematic devices in the service of the mercenary cause. The camera places us behind the barrels of mercenary guns, from which vantage point we see Africans fall by the hundreds.

History is neatly inverted, so that Africans, like Native Americans in the western, come to seem invaders in their own land. The cinematography, finally, celebrates the lyricism of warfare. Explosions are made beautiful and violent death graceful. Free-falling paratroopers float earthward in choreographed aerial shots: neocolonial war as *homo ludens*.

In the Reagan–Bush era, dominant cinema rediscovered the charms of the imperial/frontier narrative. *Red Dawn* (1984) returns to the encirclement imagery of the western, but this time it is the Cubans, the Soviets, and the (presumably Sandinista) Nicaraguans who take over the functional slot of the Indians. A literary eulogist of the Somoza regime in Nicaragua, Jack Coz, produced *The Last Plane Out* (1983), a defense of the dictator whom Roosevelt called "our son of a bitch." *Mountains of the Moon* (1989), meanwhile, recapitulates the Victorian explorer Richard Burton's search for the sources of the Nile, with weirdly colorful savages, presumably incapable of "discovering" the sources for themselves, as his witnesses. The Michael Caine vehicle *Ashanti* (1979) resurrects the venerable scenario of the British as the passionate enemies of slavery in Africa, seen also in films such as *Killers of Kilimanjaro* (1959) and *Drums of Africa* (1963). In *Dr No* (1962), the British exercise benevolent rule over good-natured West Indians.

The 1980s and 1990s have witnessed a wave of elegiac narratives about the closing of the imperial period. The Raj nostalgia genre, exemplified by the TV series *The Jewel in the Crown* and by such films as *Staying On* (1980), *Passage to India* (1984), *Gandhi* (1982), *Heat and Dust* (1982), and *Kim* (1984), was denounced by Salman Rushdie as a transparent Thatcherite attempt to refurbish the image of empire, forming the "artistic counterpart of the rise of conservative ideologies in modern Britain."[64] Although Forster's novel *Passage to India* helped crystallize the beginnings of a change of attitude toward the British presence in India, David Lean's adaptation tones down the cautious anticolonialism of the novel in the name of "balance." Richard Attenborough's *Gandhi*, as a spectacular epic about an ascetic, a *Triumph of the Will* for pacifists, pursues the "Great Man" view of history, subtly prettifying the British role. Some of the few critical colonial "nostalgia" films which, interestingly, have been made by French women (Claire Dénis' *Chocolat*, Marie-France Pisier's *Bal du Gouverneur*, and Brigitte Rouan's *Outremer*, all from 1990), shift their focus from male aggressivity to female domesticity, and to the glimmerings of anticolonialist consciousness provoked by transgression of the taboo on interracial desire.

More often, colonialist imagery has been remarketed under the guise of humor and genre parody. Thus, in a moment of apparent imperial decline, Hollywood resuscitates the imperial romance, where the presumably parodic filmmaker celebrates the extinguished glories of "imperial conquest and dominion, of virtually magical mobility and power, and of exotic life at the outposts of empire."[65] The *Indiana Jones* series recycled Rider Haggard and Kipling for the Reagan–Bush era, resurrecting the colonial adventure genre with insidious charm. Even the films' adolescent qualities recall the pubescent energies of imperial adventure tales for boys. Set in the 1930s, the very heyday of the imperial film, the series, like comic books, is premised on an imperialized globe, in which archeology professors can "rescue" artifacts from the colonized world for the greater benefit of science and civilization. "Indy" operates with ease only in colonized countries, portrayed as ontologically corrupt, awaiting Western salvation. The series assumes an uncontested empire, with no trace of any viable anticolonial opposition. In the Egypt of 1936 of *Raiders*, there is no popular agitation against the British, just as in the

Shanghai of 1935 there is no word of Mao's "Long March."[66] The India of *Indiana Jones and the Temple of Doom* (1984), similarly, betrays none of the civil disobedience against the British that led to the Government of India Act of 1935. In the world of Indiana Jones, Third World cultures are synopsized as theme park clichés drawn from the orientalist repertoire: India is all dreamy spirituality, as in the Hegelian account; Shanghai is all gongs and rickshaws. Third World landscapes become the stuff of dreamy adventure. In a classic splitting operation, the Third World is both demonized and infantilized: non-Western adult characters are evil (Mola Ram, Chattar Lal, Lao Che); children (Short Round and Little Maharajah) are eager, innocent, and pro-Western. In this imperial family order, the modernity embodied by the younger, pro-American children, will replace the hidebound tradition of the older, nationalist fathers. Indeed, the series shows most of the unwashed masses of the Third World passively waiting for Indy to save them from ambitious nationalists like Mola Ram, who constructs his own (religious) domino theory: "The British in India will be slaughtered. Then we will overrun the Moslems. Then the Hebrew God will fall. Then the Christian God will be cast down and forgotten." The blame-the-victim paradigm inherited from the western is globalized: the civilized West is threatened by the savage East, but the imperial family ultimately triumphs.

Postmodern War

That the imperial and Indian war conventions traced here, together with the Eurocentric tendencies of the media apparatus, have not reached an end became strikingly evident during the Persian Gulf War. The ground for the "popularity" of the war was prepared by a long intertextual chain: crusading anti-Islamic tales, captivity narratives, the imperial adventure novel, the "manifest destiny" western, and more recent militaristic films like *Star Wars* (1977), the *Rambo* series (1982, 1985, 1988), and *Top Gun* (1988). An orientalist and imperialist imaginary was reactivated for the ideological purposes of the warrior state.[67] The Gulf War was presented as a macro-entertainment, one with a beginning (Desert Shield), a middle (Desert Sword), and an end (Desert Storm), all undergirded by a fictive telos: the "New World Order." The futuristic overtones of the phrase meshed anachronistically with the medievalist connotations of "shield" and "sword," evocative of a religious substratum of Crusades against Muslim infidels. Network logos – "Countdown to War," "Deadline in the Desert," "America at the Brink" – communicated a throbbing sense of inevitability, of an inexorable slouching toward war; provoking, even, a kind of spectatorial *desire* for war. Talk of peace, following administration cues, was treated not as a hope but as a "nightmare scenario," a kind of "coitus interruptus" within an irresistible orgasmic march.[68]

Multigeneric, the Gulf War mini-series drew on the codes of the war film (soldiers silhouetted against the sky, thrilling martial music, *Top Gun* visuals); of the PBS educational show (military pedagogs with pointers, maps, and video blackboards); of sports programing (instant replay, expert-running commentary); and of the western (lines drawn in the sand, the implacable logic of the showdown). The Gulf War scenario had the elemental, childlike charm of the fable, the awesome pyrotechnics of apocalypse, and the didactic impulses of allegory. With this war, an already powerful media apparatus became "wedded" to another apparatus of the gaze – that of military simulation and surveillance. As a consequence, telespectators were encouraged to "enjoy" a quantum leap in prosthetic audio-visual power. Television news offered its spectator what Donna Haraway, in another context, calls the "conquering gaze from nowhere," a gaze that claims "the power to see and not be seen, to represent while escaping representation."[69] While TV coverage in general allows spectators to imagine themselves at the center of the globe's "hot spots," during the Gulf War the media coaxed spectators to spy, thanks to an almost pornographic kind of surveillance, on a whole geographical region, whose nooks and crannies lay open to the military's panoptic view.[70]

The fact that the military view literally *became* the spectator's view goes a long way toward explaining the massive public adherence in the US to the war. For quite apart from the pleasures of identification with a powerful military apparatus, the Gulf War coverage hyperbolized the normal pleasures of the televisual "apparatus" itself. While the semiotic theory of the cinematic apparatus requires "scanning" for television, since many of the factors that foster the realer-than-real subject effects in the cinema do not apply here, nevertheless TV does have its own pleasuring capacities and its own ways of encouraging spectatorial regression and narcissism. Indeed, TV affords pleasures even more multiform than those afforded by the cinema, for the televiewer identifies with an even wider array of viewpoints: notably those provided by film cameras, video-cameras, and their magnetic residue of images and sounds on tape, along with those provided by tapeless video-cameras directly transmitting images and sounds, all then relayed around the world through satellite transmission. TV thus confers perceptual powers in some ways superior to those of the relatively sluggish cinema, a medium that TV both includes and surpasses in its ability to "cover the world."[71] The smaller screen, while preventing immersion in a deep, enveloping space, encourages in other ways a kind of narcissistic voyeurism. Larger than the figures on the screen, we quite literally oversee the world from a sheltered position – all the human shapes parading before us in TV's insubstantial pageant are scaled down to Lilliputian insignificance, two-dimensional dolls, their height rarely exceeding a foot.

The Gulf War mobilized atavistic passions, as televisual spectatorship became deeply implicated in an attempt to corral multiethnic spectators into a jingoistic communalism. A "feel-good" war became an (ultimately ineffective) electoral ploy, as global and domestic politics became linked to the Nielsen ratings. Much as the encirclement imagery model in the western engages literal point of view – the looking through the sights of a rifle, or through the windows of a fort – Gulf war "spectators" were made to see through the point of view of American pilots, and even through that of "smart bombs." Media coverage endowed the spectatorial eye with what Paul Virilio calls the "symbolic function of a weapon."[72] The Gulf War telespectator, vicariously equipped with night-vision technology, infra-red vision, capable of zapping "enemy" tanks, planes, buildings, and heads of state, was prodded into feeling infinitely powerful. In a war where the same pilot's hand that released the missile simultaneously tripped the camera shutter, spectators were teleguided to see from the bomber's perspective, incorporated into the surveillance equipment, sutured into the sights of high-tech weaponry.

Gulf War media coverage paraded before the viewers innumerable candidates for what Metz calls "secondary identification," that is, identification with the human figures on the screen: the anchors, the correspondents, the generals, the experts, and the people interviewed on the street.[73] As "pivots" of identification, the anchors and correspondents played an especially crucial role. The latter-day descendants of the traveler and scientist heroes of the imperial adventure films, news anchors constitute authentic contemporary heroes. Their words have godlike efficacy; their mere designation of an event calls forth instant illustration in the form of animated miniatures, colorful maps, and live-action footage. As charismatic figures, comparable in power to the great stars of the cinema, the anchors facilitated a massive transfer of allegiance to the war, particularly in contexts where viewers lacked alternative sources of information and analysis.

During the Gulf War the newscasters dropped their usual mask of objectivity and metamorphosed into partisan cheerleaders. The historical inertia of their reputation for "objectivity" functioned in favor of the war. The newscasters' pro-war stance took many forms: adjectival qualifications of the bombing as "beautiful" or "precise," facile references to soldier "heroes," the tendentious use of the word "patriotism" to refer only to pro-war actions and attitudes. Newscasters spoke of Iraq as the "enemy," as if they had personally joined the armed forces. Dan Rather "enlisted" by saluting the troops, Forest Sawyer by donning military fatigues, Howard Threlkel by frisking surrendering Iraqi prisoners. Throughout, the newscasters channeled empathy according to clear hierarchies of human value: at the apex stood Americans and Europeans, then came Israelis, then Arab allies, and lowest on the ladder were Arab enemies. Even the oil-suffocated cormorants in the Persian Gulf and the animals in the Kuwait City Zoo garnered more sympathy than the Iraqi soldiers. The zealous citizens who sported "Nuke Iraq" T-shirts, or who patriotically roughed up people they took to be Arab-Americans (even those from countries allied to the US), intuitively understood the subliminal message sent out by the media: Third World life has no value a European (including an honorary European) need respect.

Although the Gulf War took place in the revised political context of the post-cold war period, many of the tropes, imagery, and narratives deployed were drawn from colonial/imperial discourse. Demonizing Saddam Hussein, the administration not only resuscitated the "just war" paradigm of World War II (thus making the war more amenable to Manichean dualisms of good versus evil than the "messy" Vietnam War), it also invoked the familiar paradigm of the "savage war" and of extermination as morality play. The premise of "savage war," according to Richard Slotkin, is the idea "that ineluctable political and social differences – rooted in some combination of "blood" and culture – make coexistence between primitive natives and Europeans impossible on any basis other than subjugation."[74] The psychological basis of public acceptance of massive force, in a situation of "savage war," is the expectation that a people (or leader) defined as savage will commit unimaginable atrocities, such as rape, massacre, or torture:

Once such a *threatened* or rumored atrocity has been avenged with an actual atrocity, the mechanisms of projection become more (rather than less) powerful. Although we hopefully assert that our vengeance has had a chastening effect on the enemy, our belief that the enemy is "savage" suggests that we may merely have given him an additional motive for vengeance.[75]

The melodramatic formula that cast Hussein as villain (a "Geronimo with Hitler's ambitions," as Slotkin puts it), Bush as hero, and Kuwait as the damsel in distress was a replay of countless colonial – western narratives. Basic to such narratives is the rescue of a White woman (and at times a dark one) from a dark rapist, and a happy conclusion entailing the restoration of a patriarchal – imperial world order and the punishment of the dark disobedient rapist, who must be humiliated in the name of the dishonored female. The Gulf War was fought in a gendered language, where the "rape of Kuwait" – the sexual violation of an innocent, passive, symbolically feminine persona – became the pretext for a manly penetration of Iraq. The metaphor of the rape of Kuwait, the circulating rumors about Iraqi rapes of Kuwaiti women, and the insinuation of possible rapes of American female soldiers by Iraqi captors became part of an imperial rescue fantasy eerily reminiscent of the medieval Crusades, when non-Christian enemies were also portrayed as licentious beasts.[76] At the same time, through a show of phallic vigor in the Gulf War, a senescent America imagined itself cured of the traumatic "impotence" it suffered in another war, in another Third World country – Vietnam.

Permeated by skull-and-crossbones-style male bonding, the Gulf War was machismo-driven from the start.[77] But in their mobilization of a national imaginary, the administration and the media were careful not to make jingoistic militarism the spectator's sole locus of identification. They also provided more warm, more stereotypically "feminine" and "progressive" points of identification. Along with the smart bombs came yellow ribbons, along with the martial fifes and drums came the strains of violins. For those disinclined to identify with military puissance *per se*, less masculinist entries for identification were available – with the "multicultural" army on the ground, with women taking military roles, with the advance for Blacks represented by the leadership of Colin Powell, with the homeside families concerned about their loved ones.

In the Gulf War as western, Iraqi conscripts played the role of the Indians. The western's imagery of encirclement entails not only a particular perspective of siege but also the inflation of the external threat. Thus the Iraqi army, a largely conscript force with mediocre weaponry, unable to conquer Iran much less the assembled might of the world's most powerful armies, was promoted to the "fourth army in the world." When diverse pragmatic rationales for the war (oil, jobs, the American way of life) failed to catch fire with the electorate, the administration tapped into two interrelated cultural strains – idealistic exceptionalism and puritanical vindictiveness. On the one hand, the administration sounded lofty goals of regional peace and the New World Order; on the other, it demonized Hussein as "a man of evil standing against human life itself." Here Bush stood well within the tradition of what Michael Rogin calls "political demonology" – the creation of monsters through the "inflation, stigmatization, and dehumanization of political foes."[78] The "moderate" and "pragmatic" Hussein of earlier political rhetoric, ally of American policy and the darling of American, British, and German corporations, was transformed into a reincarnation of Hitler with the rapidity with which enemies for "Hate Week" were fabricated in Orwell's *1984*. It was also within the logic of the Manichean allegory that Bush, invoking the venerable tradition of the righteous massacre, would ask for divine blessing for American armed forces in a National Day of Prayer, just as he thanked the pilots in the January 1992 bombings for "doing the Lord's work."[79] And since the Manichean allegory does not allow for two competing evils, or for lesser and greater evils, or for minor and major thugs, but only for good against evil, it also allows for only one legitimate outcome: the annihilation of evil in a ritual sacrifice or exorcism that "cleanses" the accumulated iniquity. "Allah creates," said one Gulf War ditty, "but we cremate."

While the media on the one hand forced a "dirty-handed" complicity with the war by positioning viewers among the soldiers – Ted Koppel placing us in the cockpit of a Saudi fighter, Diane Sawyer putting us inside a tank – they also symbolically cleansed those very same hands. The spectator was prompted to indulge infantile dreams of omnipotence, made to feel allied to immense destructive forces, but also to feel fundamentally pure and innocent. Any word or image implying that the American spectators or their tax dollars were somehow responsible for mass suffering would have destroyed the shaky edifice of non-culpability, an unflattering implication that might have hurt ratings. Despite its lethal violence (estimates of over 150,000 dead, with an equal number dying later due to disease and malnutrition), the Gulf War was fought in the name of American victimization, in the tradition of the many wars in which reiterated claims of self-defense have masked overwhelming, disproportionate power.

In "'Make My Day': Spectacle as Amnesia in Imperial Politics," Michael Rogin anatomizes the role of real and imaginary massacres in justifying military interventions. Citing Reagan's role-playing as Dirty Harry, Rogin recalls the context in which Clint Eastwood uses the phrase "make my day" in *Sudden Impact* (1983). In the scene, Eastwood is "daring a black man to murder a woman...so that Dirty Harry can kill the black." In other words, "white men show how tough they are by resubordinating and sacrificing their race and gender others."[80] Running like a thread through North American history is the similar notion, recycled by countless westerns, that Indian "outrages" justified Euro-American massacres and appropriations. In 1622, in "A Declaration of the State of the Colonie and Affaires" in Virginia, Edward Waterhouse wrote with relief that "our hands which before were tied with gentleness and faire usage, are now set at liberty by the treacherous violence of the Savages [so that we may] invade the Country, and destroy them who sought to destroy us."[81] Waterhouse's declaration anticipates what one might call the "make my day" syndrome, a desire for an outrage to justify even greater violence. The Gulf War reiterated the trope of "regeneration through violence" (in Slotkin's words), the process whereby the fictive "we" of national unity is reforged through salutary massacres. That President Bush had been figuratively in bed with the dictator Hussein merely betrays the binaristic splitting off of one's own impulses on to a phantasmic other that is so typical of colonialist thinking.

Our point is not that some national essence induces the American public into war – obviously antiwar protest and antimilitarism are equally part of American history – nor to suggest that Hussein is an innocent Third World victim, but rather to map the ways point-of-view conventions and a powerful media apparatus can be mobilized to shape public opinion for militaristic purposes. But these televisual tactics would not have "worked" so effectively had spectators not already been thoroughly "primed" by innumerable westerns, adventure films, and imperial epics.

The Gulf War revealed not only the continued reign of the imperial imaginary, but also the limitations of certain variants of postmodernism. Jean Baudrillard's account of the implosive collapse of boundaries in a mass-mediated global society, for example, is exhilaratingly apt in its rendering of the "feel" of life in the simulacral world of the postmodern, but his conceptions are ultimately inadequate for a phenomenon such as the Gulf War. In an article in the *Guardian* a few days before the outbreak of the war, Baudrillard treated the impending conflict as an impossibility, a figment of mass-media simulation techniques without real-world referents.[82] And on March 29, 1991, shortly after the end of hostilities, playing with the Giraudoux title *La Guerre de Troie n'aura pas lieu* (The Trojan War Will Not Take Place, 1934), Baudrillard declared in *Libération* that "The Gulf War Has Not Taken Place."[83] On one level, there is no denying the descriptive canniness of Baudrillard's account. The representation of the most media-covered war in history did indeed seem to shift from classical realist representation to the brave new public-relations world of hyperreality. Not only was the war packaged as a spectatorial video-game, it also proliferated simulacral strategies – computer simulations, fake bomb damage, fake missile silos, fake attacks, even fake heat to attract heat-seeking missiles. War on the electronic battlefield became a media experience *par excellence* even for its participants, demanding what Paul Virilio calls a *"dédoublement"* of observation – both an immediate perception and a media-inflected perception through video, radar, and computer simulation.[84]

But if the Gulf War revealed the descriptive aptness of the Baudrillardian account of postmodernism, it also signaled that paradigm's political vacuousness, its disempowering combination of extreme cognitive skepticism and political quietism. For what the Gulf War revealed were fundamental asymmetries in how the depthless surfaces of postmodernity are lived; asymmetries not only between the experiences of television and the experience of war, but also between the experiences of the combatants and the spectators engaged on different sides of the war. Some groups watched the war from an antiseptic distance, while others lived it in the company of death, dismemberment, disease, and famine. Technology facilitated seeing and hearing on the one side, and obliterated it on the other. While Americans, as Jonathon Schell puts it, waged war in "three dimensions," the foe was trapped, "like the creatures in certain geometrical games, in two dimensions ... we kill and they die, as if a race of gods were making war against a race of human beings."[85]

If postmodernism has spread the telematic feel of First World media around the world, in sum, it has hardly deconstructed the relations of power that marginalize, devalue, and time and time again massacre otherized peoples and cultures.[86] Baudrillard's radically ahistorical account misses the fact that time is palimpsestic; we live in many times, not just in the "new" time of advertising and the media. In the case of the Gulf War, the most sophisticated technology was used in the service of ideas drawn from millennial sources, from Christian Crusades against Muslims to "savage wars" against Indians. With the Gulf War, the fact of mass death itself, the radical discontinuity between the living and the dead, reveals the limitations of a world seen only through the prism of the simulacrum.

NOTES

1   See Jan Pieterse's chapter on "Colonialism and Popular Culture" in his *White on Black: Images of Africa and Blacks in Western Popular Culture* (New Haven, CT: Yale University Press, 1992), p. 77.

2   Robert Baden-Powell, *Scouting for Boys*, quoted in Joseph Bristow, *Empire Boys: Adventures in a Man's World* (London: HarperCollins, 1991), p. 170.

3   Bristow, *Empire Boys*, p. 19.

4   Patrick Brantlinger, *Rule of Darkness: British Literature and Imperialism 1830–1914* (Ithaca, NY: Cornell University Press, 1988), p. 11.

5   See John McClure, *Late Imperial Romance: Literature and Globalization from Conrad to Pynchon* (London: Verso, 1994).

6   Hayden White, *Tropics of Discourse* (Baltimore, MD: Johns Hopkins University Press, 1978), p. 58.

7   Etienne Balibar writes: "The histories of nations are presented to us in the form of a narrative which attributes these entities the continuity of a subject." See Etienne Balibar

and Immanuel Wallerstein, *Race, Nation, Class: Ambiguous Identities* (London: Verso, 1991), p. 86.

8   Benedict Anderson, *Imagined Communities* (New York: Verso, 1983), pp. 41–6.

9   For more on the extrapolation of Bakhtin's notion of the chronotope, see Robert Stam, *Subversive Pleasures: Bakhtin, Cultural Criticism, and Film* (Baltimore, MD: Johns Hopkins University Press, 1989); Kobena Mercer, "Diaspora Culture and the Dialogic Imagination," in Mbye Cham and Claire Andrade-Watkins, eds., *Blackframes* (Cambridge, MA: MIT Press, 1988); and Paul Willemen, "The Third Cinema Question: Notes and Reflections," in Jim Pines and Paul Willemen, eds., *Questions of Third Cinema* (London: BFI, 1989).

10   Movie theaters in the colonized world were at first built only in urban centers such as Cairo, Baghdad, Bombay. For early responses to the cinema in Baghdad, Ella Shohat has conducted a series of interviews with old Baghdadis from her own community, now dispersed in Israel/Palestine, England, and the US.

11   Christian Metz, "The Imaginary Signifier," in *The Imaginary Signifier: Psychoanalysis and the Cinema* (Bloomington: Indiana University Press, 1982), p. 51.

12   For more on the "mobilized gaze" of the cinema, see Anne Friedberg's discussion in *Window Shopping: Cinema and the Postmodern* (Berkeley: University of California Press, 1993).

13   This photograph and the others discussed in this section can be found in Maria Hambourg, Pierre Apraxine, Malcolm Daniel, Jeff L. Rosenheim, and Virginia Heckert, *The Waking Dream: Photography's First Century*, Selections from the Gilman Paper Company Collection (New York: Metropolitan Museum of Art, 1993).

14   For a critical study of anthropological discourse see for example, Talal Asad, ed., *Anthropology and the Colonial Encounter* (Atlantic Highlands, NJ: Humanities Press, 1973); James Clifford and George Marcus, eds., *Writing Culture* (Berkeley: University of California Press, 1986); James Clifford, *The Predicament of Culture* (Cambridge, MA: Harvard University Press, 1988); Trinh T. Minh-ha, *Woman, Native, Other* (Bloomington: Indiana University Press, 1989); Edward Said, "Representing the Colonized: Anthropology's Interlocutors," *Critical Inquiry*, vol. 15, no. 2, pp. 205–25.

15   Jean Rouch in his critique of ethnographic filmmaking suggested that anthropologists should not observe their subject as if it were an insect but rather as if it were a "stimulant for mutual understanding." See "Camera and Man" in Mick Eaton, ed., *Anthropology-Reality-Cinema* (London: BFI, 1979), p. 62. Ousmane Sembene, ironically, accused Rouch himself of filming Africans "comme des insectes." See special issue on Rouch, *Cinemaction*, no. 17 (1982).

16   For more on the question of science and spectacle, see Ella Shohat, "Imaging Terra Incognita: The Disciplinary Gaze of Empire," *Public Culture*, vol. 3, no. 2 (spring 1990), pp. 41–70.

17   Etienne-Jules Marey, a French physiologist interested in animal locomotion and in wildlife photography, called his 1882 camera a "fusil cinématographique," because of its gunlike apparatus, which made twelve rapid exposures on a circular glass plate that revolved like a bullet cylinder. The same notion was later trained against the colonial powers themselves in the Third Cinema notion of the "camera gun" and "guerrilla cinema."

18   Donna Haraway, *Primate Visions: Gender, Race, and Nature in the World of Modern Science* (New York: Routledge, 1989), p. 52.

19   Egyptians at an orientalist exposition were amazed to discover that the Egyptian pastries on sale were authentic. See Tim Mitchell, *Colonizing Egypt* (Berkeley: University of California Press, 1991), p. 10.

20   Robert W. Rydell, *All the World's a Fair* (Chicago: University of Chicago Press, 1984) p. 236.

21   Ibid.

22 See Pieterse, *White on Black*. On colonial safari as a kind of traveling mini-society see Donna Haraway, "Teddy Bear Patriarch: Taxidermy in the Garden of Eden, New York City, 1908–1936," *Social Text*, 11 (winter 1984–5).

23 See Phillips Verner Bradford and Harvey Blume, *Ota Benga: The Pygmy in the Zoo* (New York: St. Martin's Press, 1992).

24 The African name of the "Hottentot Venus" remains unknown, since it was never referred to by those who "studied" her.

25 For further discussion on science and the racial/sexual body, see Sander Gilman, "Black Bodies, White Bodies: Toward an Iconography of Female Sexuality in Late Nineteenth-Century Art, Medicine, and Literature," *Critical Inquiry*, vol. 12, no. 1 (autumn 1985); and in conjunction with early cinema, see Fatimah Tobing Rony, "Those Who Squat and Those Who Sit: The Iconography of Race in the 1859 Films of Félix-Louis Regnault," *Camera Obscura* no. 28, 1992 (a special issue on "Imaging Technologies, Inscribing Science," ed. Paula A. Treichler and Lisa Cartwright).

26 "Flower and Murie on the Dissection of a Bushwoman," *Anthropological Review*, no. 5 (July 1867), p. 268.

27 Richard Altick, *The Shows of London* (Cambridge, MA: Harvard University Press, 1978), p. 272.

28 Stephen Jay Gould, *The Flamingo's Smile* (New York: W. W. Norton, 1985), p. 292. On a recent visit to the Musée de l'Homme, we found no traces of the Hottentot Venus; neither the official catalog, nor officials themselves, acknowledged her existence.

29 Mitchell, *Colonizing Egypt*, p. 13.

30 The lure of the breast found its way even to the cover of a book on ethnographic cinema, Karl Heider's *Ethnographic Film* (Austin: University of Texas Press, 1976), which features a cartoon of a "native" woman breast-feeding. Trinh T. Minh-ha's *Reassemblage* (1982), meanwhile, reflexively interrogates the focus on breasts in ethnographic cinema. The I-Max big-screen presentation *Secrets of the [Grand] Canyon* also reproduces the paradigm of Native American nudity/Euro-American dress.

31 Interestingly, Méliès' early fascination with spectacle dates back to his visits to the Egyptian Hall shows directed by Maskelyne and Cooke and devoted to fantastic spectacles.

32 For an analysis of the cinematic treatments of North Africa and the Arab world (especially in French films), see Pierre Boulanger, *Le Cinéma colonial* (Paris: Seghers, 1975); Abdelghani Megherbi, *Les Algériens au miroir du cinema colonial* (Algiers: Editions SNED, 1982; and also the section on "Arabian Nights and Colonial Dreams," in Richard Abel, *French Cinema: The First Wave 1915–1929* (Princeton, NJ: Princeton University Press, 1984).

33 For a survey of the British imperial films see Jeffrey Richards, *Visions of Yesterday* (London: Kegan and Paul, 1973).

34 From "Trinidad Government Principles of Censorship Applied to Cinematographic Films," internal circular in 1929, quoted in Ruth Vasey, "Foreign Parts: Hollywood's Global Distribution and the Representation of Ethnicity," *American Quarterly*, vol. 44, no. 4 (December 1992).

35 Memo to United Artists, March 8, 1928, from the MPPDA (Motion Picture Producers and Directors of America, Inc.) Archive, quoted in Vasey, "Foreign Parts."

36 A 1928 Resumé from the MPPDA Archive, cited by Vasey, "Foreign Parts."

37 Hala Salmane, Simon Hartog, and David Wilson, eds., *Algerian Cinema* (London: BFI, 1976). See also Ella Shohat, "Egypt: Cinema and Revolution," *Critical Arts*, vol. 2, no. 4 (1983).

38 See Abel, *French Cinema*, p. 151.

39 See Jeffrey Richards, "Boys Own Empire," in John M. Mackenzie, ed., *Imperialism and Popular Culture* (Manchester: Manchester University Press, 1986.)

40 ABC's *A Line in the Sand* was broadcast on January 14, 1991, a day before the US "deadline" for Iraqi withdrawal from Kuwait.

41   The statistical figure is from Edward Buscombe, ed., *The BFI Companion to the Western* (New York: DaCapo, 1988), p. 35.

42   See Ward Churchill, *Fantasies of the Master Race: Literature, Cinema and the Colonization of American Indians*, ed. M. Annette Jaimes (Monroe, ME: Common Courage Press, 1992), p. 232.

43   Cited in Ralph Friar and Natasha Friar, *The Only Good Indian: The Hollywood Gospel* (New York: Drama Book Specialists, 1972), p. 188.

44   See Churchill, *Fantasies of the Master Race*, p. 232.

45   "There's a hell of a part here for you," Raul Walsh would tell prospective actors, "you get to kill eight Indians," Raul Walsh interviewed by Richard Schikel in *Harper's* (October 1970).

46   Thomas Farnham, *Travels in the Great Western Prairies* [1843], in Thwaites, ed., *Early Western Travels*, vol. XXVIII, pp. 123–4, quoted in Roy Harvey Pearce, *Savagism and Civilization* (Berkeley: University of California Press, 1988) p. 65.

47   In a pro-indigenous documentary entitled *To Protect Mother Earth* (1987), Native American women repeatedly lament what they call "the rape of Mother Earth."

48   Quoted in Noam Chomsky, *Year 501: The Conquest Continues* (Boston: South End Press, 1993), p. 232.

49   On Indian names, see Jack Weatherford, *Native Roots: How the Indians Enriched America* (New York: Ballantine, 1991). On Native American names in New York City, see Robert Steven Grumet, *Native American Place Names in New York City* (New York: Museum of the City of New York, 1981).

50   Passage from Henry Blackman Sell and Victor Weybright's *Buffalo Bill and the Wild West*, cited in Friar and Friar, *The Only Good Indian*, p. 74.

51   See Thomas Schatz, *Hollywood Genres* (New York: Random House, 1981).

52   Tom Engelhardt, "Ambush at Kamikaze Pass," in *Bulletin of Concerned Asian Scholars*, vol. 3, no. 1 (winter–Spring 1971).

53   Ibid.

54   See Richard Drinnon, *Facing West: The Metaphysics of Indian-Hating and Empire-Building* (New York: Schocken, 1980).

55   See Richard Slotkin, *Gunfighter Nation: The Myth of the Frontier in Twentieth-Century America* (New York: Atheneum, 1992), p. 110.

56   Drinnon, *Facing West*, p. 221.

57   Quoted in ibid, p. 314.

58   See Francis Fitzgerald, *Fire in the Lake: The Vietnamese and the Americans in Vietnam* (New York: Vintage, 1973), pp. 491–2.

59   See Slotkin, *Gunfighter Nation*, p. 3.

60   Drinnon, *Facing West*, p. 404.

61   On imperialism in Disney, see Ariel Dorfman and Armand Mattelart, *How to Read Donald Duck: Imperialist Ideology in the Disney Comic* (New York: International General, 1975); Julianne Burton, "Don (Juanito) Duck and the Imperial–Patriarchal Unconscious: Disney Studios, the Good Neighbor Policy, and the Packaging of Latin America," in Andrew Parker, Mary Russo, Doris Sommer, and Patricia Yaeger, eds., *Nationalisms and Sexualities* (New York: Routledge, 1992); Eric Smoodin, *Animating Culture: Hollywood Cartoons from the Sound Era* (New Brunswick, NJ: Rutgers University Press, 1993).

62   Paul Sellors, "Selling Paranoia: *Gilligan's Island* and the Television Medium," unpublished paper.

63   The Arab League protested the film for this very reason. See *New York Times* (April 29, 1985), p. C13.

64   Salman Rushdie, "Outside the Whale," in *Imaginary Homelands* (London: Penguin, 1992).

65   The words are John McClure's, from *Late Imperial Romance* (London: Verso, 1994).

66 Our discussion here is indebted to Harel Calderon's unpublished paper, "I'm Goin' Home to Missouri, Where They Never Feed You Snakes before Ripping Your Heart out," written for a course in Third World cinema at New York University.

67 Ironically, General H. Norman Schwarzkopf himself speaks of this intertext in his recently published memoirs, where he complains of the pressure of the "hawks": "These were guys who had seen John Wayne in *The Green Berets*, they'd seen *Rambo*, they'd seen *Patton*, and it was very easy for them to pound their desks and say: 'By God, we've got to go in there ... gotta punish that son of a bitch!' Of course, none of them was going to get shot at." Quoted in *New York Times* (Sept. 20, 1992), p. 10.

68 The recurrent trope of the war being "on schedule" was as much narratological as military. January 15 was set as the date for war, as Serge Daney pointed out, much as a date is set for the opening of a Hollywood blockbuster. See Serge Daney, "Mais que fait la Police," *Libération* (Feb. 15, 1991), p. 16.

69 Donna Haraway, "Situated Knowledge: The Science Question in Feminism and the Privilege of Partial Perspective," included in Haraway, *Simians, Cyborgs and Women* (New York: Routledge, 1991), p. 188.

70 We focus here on the mechanisms of promoting identification; we do not suggest that these mechanisms were experienced in identical ways by, for example, Baghdadis or New Yorkers, Kuwaitis or Israelis, Christians or Muslims, leftists or rightists. Although the experience of war is mediated, there are differences within spectatorship. These spectatorial differences will be the subject of our last chapter.

71 See Robert Stam, "Television News and Its Spectator," in Ann Kaplan, ed., *Regarding Television* (Fredricksburg, MD: AFI, 1983).

72 See Paul Virilio, *War and Cinema: The Logistics of Perception* (London: Verso, 1989).

73 For Metz on "secondary identification," see *The Imaginary Signifer*.

74 Slotkin, *Gunfighter Nation*, p. 12.

75 Ibid.

76 The media also painted Hussein in the colors of orientalist fantasies of sexual perversity and excess. Entertainment magazines and television shows luxuriated in voyeuristic projections about Hussein's putative sexual perversions, including still photos of his bunker bedroom, his harem, and stories about his presumed penchant for killing his lovers, especially those who could testify to his failures in bed. The cover of a *National Examiner* (March 12, 1991) carried the headline "Saddam Hussein's Bizarre Sex Life: A Recent CIA Report Reveals," with a photomontage of Hussein as a crossdresser in a mini skirt. Geraldo's talk show (March 4, 1991) featured a series of so-called experts' titillating descriptions of torture, all delivered up to an insatiably repelled audience. Close-ups emphasized the responses of good Americans shocked by this cruel dark-skinned leader, compared to Idi Amin, Qaddafi, Noriega, Hitler, and Stalin. Hussein was frequently nicknamed the "Butcher from Baghdad" and "The Thief from Baghdad." See Ella Shohat, "The Media's War," *Social Text*, no. 28, vol. IX, (1991).

77 Pilots reportedly watched porn videos before ejaculating their bombs over Iraq, thus turning pent-up sexual energy into military aggression, and recapitulating the transmutation of sex into violence that Leslie Fiedler, in *Love and Death in the American Novel*, discerned as characteristic of the American novel.

78 Michael Rogin, *Ronald Reagan: The Movie* (Berkeley: University of California Press, 1987), p. xxi.

79 See William Alberts, "Prayer as an Instrument of War," *Z* (April 1991).

80 Michael Rogin, "'Make My Day': Spectacle as Amnesia in Imperial Politics," *Representations*, no. 29 (winter 1990).

81 Quoted in Pearce, *Savagism and Civilization*, p. 11.

82 Jean Baudrillard, "The Reality Gulf," *Guardian* (Jan. 11, 1991).

83 Jean Baudrillard, "La Guerre du Golfe n'a pas eu lieu," *Libération* (March 29, 1991).

84 See Paul Virilio, "L'Acquisition d'objectif," *Libération* (Jan. 30, 1991), p. 15.

85 See Jonathon Schell, "Modern Might, Ancient Arrogance," *Newsday* (Feb. 12, 1991), p. 86.

86 For more on the Gulf War, see Robert Stam, "Mobilizing Fictions: The Gulf War, the Media, and the Recruitment of the Spectator," *Public Culture*, vol. 4, no. 2 (spring 1992). This passage was written before the appearance of Christopher Norris's *Uncritical Theory: Postmodernism, Intellectuals, and the Gulf War* (Amherst: University of Massachussetts Press, 1992), which takes a parallel, although not identical, approach to the same topic. We are in full sympathy with Norris's critique of the "ideological complicity that exists between ... extreme anti-realist or irrationalist doctrine and the crisis of moral and political nerve among those whose voices should have been raised against the actions committed in their name" (p. 27).

9

Complicities of Style

David MacDougall

I will begin with what may turn out to be one of the stranger footnotes in the history of visual anthropology. A number of years ago a researcher in psychology was devising an experiment to measure castration anxiety among American men (Schwartz 1955). In order to trigger the anxiety he hit upon the tactic of putting his experimental subjects in a theater and subjecting them to screenings of film footage of Aboriginal subincision operations in Central Australia. We may find this disturbing for several reasons, not least of all because we are unused to seeing culture shock being dealt out quite so cavalierly. It tends to alarm whatever remains of our sense of cultural relativity.

But in retrospect the researcher's methods may have a crude irony for us. For quite some time, and again in a recent study (Martinez 1990), we have seen mounting evidence that many films designed *not* to shock, but to bridge cultural differences, have quite the opposite effect when shown to at least some audiences. Most anthropological and ethnographic films are not made exclusively for anthropologists, and if one of the underlying metaphors of the anthropological endeavor is to cure the disease of cultural intolerance, then it is clear that for some recipients the medicine may be wrong or too strong. We are finally beginning to take more seriously how audiences interact with films to produce meanings. But that is only one of the issues. We need to pay equal attention to the prior issue of how the implicit discursive forms of filmic representation overlap and interact with the cultures they seek to portray.

It is a commonplace that when Flaherty went to Samoa and the Aran Islands he failed to find the dramatic conflict of *Nanook of the North* (1922) and had to invent it. Granted that he may have invented much of the drama of *Nanook* as well, this is the kind of obvious, large-scale observation that may keep one from going on to ask related questions, such as why some societies (the Inuit, for example) are so heavily represented in ethnographic film as compared to anthropological writing; why some societies are represented largely by films on ritual and material culture; and to what extent ethnographic films are influenced by their search for (or creation of) strong central characters. In this regard one thinks immediately of the "stars" of the ethnographic cinema, among them Nanook, Damouré, N!ai, and Ongka.

The relation between knowledge and aesthetics is always tricky, and that between anthropology and film especially so, in part because the legitimacy for anthropology of a kind of knowledge expressed in images has yet to be fully addressed. Defining the world in writing may appear better understood, but that is often because this older method assumes a literary and linguistic tradition in common with a cultural one. When the subject is another culture, a different and less well explored set of problems arises.

Gilbert Lewis, in a paper called "The Look of Magic," has described how in *The Golden Bough* Frazer's accounts of unfamiliar cultural practices give them an oddness bordering on the surreal, making them more likely to be ascribed to magical beliefs than to everyday rationality. Indeed, he suggests that anthropological writing may make the ordinary strange simply because it *is* writing, unable to contextualize certain details sufficiently to prevent them from emerging in a lurid isolation. Pictures can help to solve this particular problem but they will inevitably introduce problems of their own. For each form of representation, Lewis says, "the conventions may need to be modified for new and unfamiliar subjects" (Lewis 1985: 416).

Film Style vs. Cultural Style

One of the difficulties in developing a coherent discipline of visual anthropology has been pinning down basic principles from a filmmaking practice that is both slender in output and that undergoes a major technological and stylistic shift every few decades. These shifts occur because ethnographic film is not simply an alternative technology for anthropology but has its own history as part of a larger cinema culture. Compared to the rate of chopping and changing in ethnographic filmmaking, the methods of anthropology sometimes appear to have remained in a steady state.

For all that, the fickleness of ethnographic film method is in many ways illusory. Despite certain injections of anthropological ideas, its origins lie in the essentially European invention of documentary cinema, which embodies in its stylistic conventions still earlier European inventions and assumptions about behavior and discourse. Compared to the stylistic diversity of human cultures, and even considering the variations in documentary film style, this makes it quite consistent and specific in its cultural outlook. If new subjects require new conventions, it can be said that ethnographic film has often failed to find them. This stylistic narrowness has led to an unevenness in how films represent the social reality of other societies, rather like the troughs and ridges that a particular wave system creates by reinforcement and cancellation as it passes over other wave systems beneath it. Such an imbalance may also mean that as documentary film conventions are diffused into an international film language, particularly by television, they are likely to have a differential effect on the self-expression and survival of local cultures.

I would suggest that the dominant conventions of ethnographic film make some societies appear accessible, rational, and attractive to the viewer, but applied to a society with a very different cultural style they may prove quite inadequate and inarticulate. They may indeed make the society look strange, and in terms even stronger than Gilbert Lewis describes. And no amount of external explanation or contextualization may make much difference.

This is not simply a matter of the cultural gap between filmmaker and subject or subject and audience. The cultural incompatibility is more deeply embedded in the representational system itself, including its technology, and without radical changes, the result will be much the same whether it is used by a First, Third, or Fourth World filmmaker, most of whom share a global film culture.

Film has a psychological plausibility that tends to naturalize many of these conventions into invisibility. Filmmakers may be aware that alternative approaches to filmmaking are possible – Sol Worth, John Adair, Eric Michaels, and Vincent Canelli have been at pains to show this – and yet not be fully aware how their own filmmaking practice channels their efforts in certain directions and frustrates them in others. This not only affects the success or failure of individual films but may predispose filmmakers (and need I add, television companies) to make films in certain kinds of societies rather than others, or if they have less choice in the matter, to focus on a particular selection of cultural features, such as ceremonial events and technology. These can take on an exaggerated importance simply because they appear more "filmable," just as language and kinship have perhaps figured more prominently in anthropology because they are more easily written down.

The problem is often declared by an absence, or by an awkward or bizarre stopgap solution. Many films give evidence of the bafflement that has confronted their makers – films that suddenly resort to romantic imagery, narration, or a 1940s Hollywood montage when they are unable to follow a subject where it might otherwise lead them. Other films betray a hollowness behind the devices they employ. People are followed almost by reflex, doing things as though those things had a cumulative significance, but the significance never materializes. The camera zooms in on a face which reveals precisely nothing. Worse than just showing nothing, these false emphases contribute to an image of a world that is mute and off balance.

Such strangeness is the overriding quality to me of a considerable number of films on Australian Aboriginal society, including some films of my own and some made by Aboriginal filmmakers themselves. They give off a characteristic cultural tone, like a tuning fork, but it is like a sound heard at a great distance, or the spectral signature of a star. Sometimes the filmmaker's unfamiliarity or lack of sympathy with Aboriginal society can be blamed, but often it seems to have more to do with complexities in the subject and styles of cultural expression unmatched by a comparable cinematic style.

William Stanner, probably the most perceptive and politically engaged anthropologist writing about Aboriginal society in the 1950s, linked the problem to Aboriginal frames of reference. "[The] fundamental cast [of Aboriginal thought]," he wrote, "seems to me to be analogical and *a fortiori* metaphorical . . . I am suggesting that the association of European and aboriginal has been a struggle of partial blindness, often darkened to sightlessness on our part by the continuity of the aborigines' implicit tradition" (Stanner 1958: 108–9). That sightlessness, he might have added, extends as well to the implicit presuppositions of our own habits of description and depiction.

If such difficulties cripple some ethnographic films, it is also true to say, without belittling the filmmakers, that other films have benefited from cultures that seem positively to lend themselves to the codes of Western filmmaking. Peter Loizos has praised the special cogency of the interviews in Melissa Llewelyn-Davies's film *The Women's Olamal* (1984) and has noted how, without intruding on events, the film observes the unities of time, place, and person of classical Greek tragedy (Loizos 1993: 133). We get just the information we need to interpret the events, and these explanations come from the Maasai themselves, either in direct address to the camera or in observed interactions. The drama is Aristotelean and the Maasai are found to be superb explicators of events in their own lives and social system. Other filmmakers, including myself, have found a similar openness and eloquence in the cultural style of East African pastoralists, at a time when the aim was to get away from *ex cathedra* explanations and rely instead upon the self- revelation and social interactions of the people portrayed.

That aim reflected a Western realist tradition dependent upon a certain literalness of words and deeds and a focus upon events that crystallized deeper social issues. But for this to work requires that the social actors conduct themselves in the world in somewhat the same terms. It requires a society in which there is a positive value placed upon explicitness of speech, the expression of personal emotion and opinion, and the public resolution of conflict – although not necessarily to the extent of public adversarial debate, as in *The Women's Olamal*.

But I think these assumptions penetrate to another level as well. Even when ethnographic films do not follow models of classical dramaturgy – and most in fact do not – they make use of certain formal conventions of camerawork and editing that derive from it. Thus even a film guided by an anthropological commentary and concerned with economics or politics will do so in visual terms that reflect Euro-American expectations of causality, chronology, and interpersonal behavior.

The Look of Documentary

If ethnographic writing assumes that we can be told, even if we cannot always experience, ethnographic films, even when they include explanatory commentary, assume that we will learn something experientially from the images, and in some sense make them our own. Films attempt to create a trajectory of understanding, beginning with images that make certain claims upon us. These claims are typically produced through acts of disclosure that create a sense of obligation in the viewer toward the viewed, and this can be compared to a form of submission or display of vulnerability in which the subject invites our protection or interest. That is why the term "exposition" must be taken not only in the sense of setting out the subject and its context but in the literal sense of self-exposure. From the privileged knowledge that results, the audience embarks upon a problem or a journey.

The repertoire of shooting and editing techniques in both fiction and nonfiction films is employed in the first instance to gain the viewer's complicity, by disarming and penetrating the subject from every angle. It is a repertoire of exaggeration, overstepping the bounds of normal vision. There are wide-angle shots and close-ups for expansion or intimacy; montage and continuity editing to condense and intensify significant actions; and sequence-shots to direct an unwavering gaze at nuances of behavior. In documentary, various kinds of direct and indirect address have been added to these expository techniques, perhaps in recognition of the fact that although self-disclosure can be written into a script, special conditions such as the interview must be created to extract it in real life.

Some conventions seem related to implicit expectations about behavioral style, such as the assumption that characters will assert their personalities and desires visually, in ways that can be registered in close-ups of the face. The reaction shot, the over-the-shoulder shot, and the point-of-view shot all show a preoccupation with expressive behavior and response, designed to convey information about inner states and invite identification. These techniques reflect the Western interest in developing an ideology and psychology of the individual, usually in preparation for some test. As cinema relies more and more upon easily recognizable "types" (and this seems a trend in international action movies), it rejoins other theatrical traditions and is capable of wider shots, just as the masks and costumes of Kabuki theater and Greek tragedy, and of certain sports, permit a huge stage and viewing at great distances. A further implication of the close-up – as it is used in interviews with experts, and especially in the case of television "talking heads" – is the assumption of a hierarchical and specialized society in which certain persons have the authority to define social realities and speak for others.

Interiority and the character-narration of Western cinema are encoded not only in the close-up but also in devices such as the shot/counter-shot, or reverse angle, designed to construct an imaginary geography in which the characters can move and which can become the temporary home of the viewer, or what Nick Browne (1975) has called the "spectator-in-the-text."

Other kinds of structures, such as sequence construction, point to cultural assumptions that perhaps have more general implications. For example, it seems to me that the condensation of time characteristic of classical Hollywood continuity editing, and the similar reduction of physical processes to a series of key steps in much documentary editing, point to an essentialist rather than an elaborative view of knowledge, which may have repercussions in how films represent the discourse and activities of other societies. It may well be that what is important to members of those societies lies between the shots, or in the unbroken continuity of part of the action, even if the whole process is never shown. The linearity of such editing may also go against the grain of a way of thinking that is fundamentally multidirectional in recognizing the different manifestations of objects and events. Western conceptions of causality are also implicated in such structures, as well as in the emphasis upon strict chronology in reporting events, which we can see in the predeliction for characters making formal entrances and exits from the frame, and in elapsed-time markers such as the fade and dissolve.

An exception, but a significant exception to this temporal linearity, is the convention of parallel action cutting, in which the film alternates between two actions so that they appear to be happening simultaneously. On the micro-level this kind of editing results in the simple cutaway, whose overriding purpose is commonly to bridge a temporal gap. But when it is used on a larger scale, parallel cutting tends to imply a convergence of the two lines and an eventual collision. This can be taken as the visual analogue of the conflict structure around which so much of Western filmmaking revolves.

For Western filmmakers, conflict is an almost essential discursive principle – if not in an obvious form, then in the form of issues or problems requiring resolution. It is like the carrier frequency of all other matters. Conflict structure in ethnographic films tends to mean filming events in which conflict – real or potential – brings cultural imperatives to the fore. An initiate passes a test and reconfirms a hierarchy. An episode of childhood rivalry explains how personalities are formed. Whether or not Ongka's *moka* ever comes off, or Harry ever turns up, events have occurred that reveal the principles by which people live. At a deeper level, such events reveal the unresolved paradoxes within a society that generate conflicting messages about the management of authority, allegience, and desire.

The strategies of ethnographic filming often involve seeking out significant rents in the social fabric, such as N!ai's sense of rejection and alienation in !Kung society. There is an echo in this process of the propensity of observational cinema to lie in wait for the moments in life when people let their social masks slip and literally "give themselves away." The emphasis may be upon traditional sources of tension, or contradictions between "correct" and actual behavior, or even upon a person who is so specialized or marginal in the society as to provide a revealing perspective on it. These approaches may sometimes make more sense to the anthropologist/filmmaker than to the people being filmed, but in many societies conflicts are perfectly legitimate topics of attention and often focus issues for people. They may even be seen in some sense as therapeutic eruptions which provide opportunities to readjust the social landscape.

But the reliance upon conflict structure also presupposes a society in which people traditionally get embroiled in contradictory sets of obligations and in which some benefit is seen in living through the consequences. In another society this might be deemed sheer foolishness. My experience of Aboriginal society leads me to think that it systematically resists approaches based on conflict structure and most of the expository conventions of cinema. This is partly due to a style of discourse which, as Stanner noted, is highly allusive and, when not formal, often laconic and multi-pronged. Speech here does not provide an open channel to personal feeling and opinion, nor does the close-up of a face. Personal reticence is deemed a virtue, and language is only one of the surfaces of the complex spiral of art, reference, and ritual that I have increasingly come to think of as a "heraldic" culture.

Thus, from a filmmaker's perspective it would perhaps be hard to find a greater contrast to the outspoken and skeptical pragmatism of East African pastoralists than the style of Aboriginal social interaction. Conflict is carefully contained behind the scenes, and should it break out of formal control is considered far from therapeutic and highly dangerous. Contentious issues are systematically avoided or dealt with in parables. This is not to say that Aboriginal people are not personally ambitious or contentious, but the public weal resides in the constant reinforcement and repair of personal relationships.

It could also be said that the form of Aboriginal self-expression is more typically one of inscription than explanation. A film consistent with Aboriginal culture would tend to be enumerative rather than comparative and might typically consist of a demonstration of rights to land, knowledge, or other cultural property. For Aboriginal people, *showing* is in and of itself a sufficient act and can constitute a transmission of rights. Thus a film in these terms need not explain anything or develop any argument or analysis; rather, by simply existing it has the potential to be a powerful political or cultural assertion.

The Voices of Ethnography

To be helpful, recognition of the interactions of different cultural styles must be seen in relation to the larger purposes of ethnographic representation. Ethnographic film is different from indigenous or national film production in that it seeks to interpret one society for another. Its starting point is therefore the encounter of two cultures, or as some would put it, two "texts" of life; and what it produces is a further, rather special cultural document. Increasingly, though, ethnographic films cease to be one society's private notes or diaries about others. They reach multiple audiences and I think must now be made with this in mind. They will certainly be seen and used by the societies they portray. One conclusion, therefore, is that they should become more precise – and perhaps more modest – about what they claim to be. (There is a corresponding obligation on viewers to read these limits more accurately.) Another is that they should begin looking in two directions instead of one.

This is really a question of how ethnographic film conceives and frames its subjects. Since 1898 ethnographic filmmaking has undergone a series of revolutions, introducing narrative, observational, and participatory approaches. With each, a set of assumptions about the positioning of the filmmaker and the audience has crumbled. Now it is the single identity of each of these that is under review. If we are in the midst of a new revolution, as I believe we are, it is one that is interested in multiple voices and that consists in a shift toward an *intertextual* cinema.

I think we are already seeing the changes in a new emphasis on authorship and specified cultural perspectives. Films are less often posed as omniscient or definitive descriptions, but equally, filmmakers are less likely to claim a spurious oneness with their subjects. Societies are no longer portrayed as monolithic, or unpenetrated by external and historical forces. But this is only the beginning of changes that could affect both the conventions and larger structures of ethnographic filmmaking.

The focus on authorship has two important consequences: first, in clarifying the provenance of films, and second in making the search for new directions in film strategy more understandable and acceptable to audiences. (A film with declared interests can more easily afford to be unusual.) Other modifications of film conventions will come from cultural borrowing or from explicit responses to conflicts in cultural style. I think we will increasingly regard ethnographic films as meeting places of primary and secondary levels of representation, one cultural discourse seen through, or inscribed upon another. In place of the usual centered and linear models may come more films employing repetition, associative editing, and nonnarrative structures. The decentering of subject matter could result in films that look at the unexamined or peripheral aspects of what were previously taken to be the significant events.

The other implication of these shifts, and probably the more important one, is the recognition that ethnographic films for multiple audiences must confront contending versions of reality. Further, they must acknowledge historical experiences which overshadow any text and which inevitably escape from it. I think we shall therefore see films that become repositories of multiple authorship, confrontation, and exchange. We shall see more ethnographic films that redeploy existing texts and incorporate parallel interpretations. We shall see more films that begin from separate directions and converge upon a common subject.

In recent years ethnographic films have become less insular in opening themselves to the voices of their subjects. Increasingly, too, ethnographic films concern themselves with the crossing and mingling of different cultural traditions. This need not, in my view, lead to an indiscriminate cultural relativity, of mirrors within mirrors and unending nesting boxes, nor does it imply an abandonment of anthropological analysis. It may instead help us to recast the problem of Self and Other more productively as a set of reciprocal relations in which film, when all is said and done, plays only a very small part.

REFERENCES

Browne, Nick. 1975. "The spectator-in-the-text: the rhetoric of *Stagecoach,*" *Film Quarterly* 29 (2): 26–38.
Lewis, Gilbert. 1985. "The look of magic," *Man* (n.s.) 21: 414–47.
Loizos, Peter. 1993. *Innovation in Ethnographic Film: From Innocence to Self-Consciousness, 1955–1985.* Chicago: University of Chicago Press.
Martinez, Wilton. 1990. "Critical studies and visual anthropology: aberrant vs. anticipated readings of ethnographic film," *Society for Visual Anthropology Review* (spring): 34–47.
Schwartz, B. J. 1955. "The measurement of castration anxiety and anxiety over loss of love," *Journal of Personality* 24: 204–19.
Stanner, W. E. H. 1958. "Continuity and change among the Aborigines," *Australian Journal of Science* 21 (5a): 99–109.

Part III

Representing Selves

If media representations of Others reiterate and reify difference, do media representations of Selves promote commonality? The chapters in part three vary widely on this issue. What "representing Selves" entails ranges from locally based media productions to an injection of local content into national or global productions. Eric Michaels, an American anthropologist who worked for a number of years with Australian Aboriginal television producers, analyzed this question and its attendant assumptions after the Australian Broadcasting Tribunal decided to devote two hours of television time per week to "Aboriginal content" as a gesture of cultural and national inclusivity. Would "Aboriginal content" be restricted to programs about Aborigines by Aborigines, or would programs made by Europeans about Aborigines count? Conversely, would programs made by Aborigines about non-Aboriginal topics count? Would nationally syndicated programs that for an episode or two included an Aboriginal character fit the bill? (Michaels 1994c: 20). Michaels asserted that "the problematic of Aboriginal content expands in a number of interesting directions that allow us to consider not just the media text, in its narrow sense, but the production contexts and institutional practices that ultimately reach into the much broader social and cultural facts of the ascription and inscription of Aboriginality in Australia" (ibid: 21). In other words, the project of self-representation, although conceptually opposed to the project of representing Others, may in fact evoke similar processes of stereotyping and reification (which is why Michaels concluded that concern about "Aboriginal content" should be replaced with concern for local community programming). But for others, media self-presentation constitutes an opportunity to level the playing field, a radical means of upsetting the comfort of familiar media representations and offering alternatives to the representational status quo.

Upsetting the status quo is a rare occurrence in Hollywood, according to Hortense Powdermaker (chapter 10). In *Hollywood the Dream Factory* Powdermaker analyzed Hollywood during the 1940s as an industry that, beyond entertainment, mass-produces apolitical mindsets, conformism, and formulaic dreams. Powdermaker exposed a disjuncture between the actions/ambitions of Hollywood personnel and the film texts they produce. Films camouflage Hollywood's profound emptiness and materialism and although they are American products targeting primarily American audiences they cannot be viewed as promoting an internal sense of community.

Yoruba photography, on the other hand, does reflect communal Yoruba concerns and priorities. Stephen Sprague found that 1970s Yoruba photographers and clients appropriated photography in profoundly Yoruba ways. Photography offered a new medium for perpetuating, while modifying, local aesthetic and cultural values. Chiefs and other important personages readily embraced photographic portraiture (introduced during the colonial period) as a means of representing their social status. A certain stylized pose marks these portraits as distinctly and uniquely Yoruba. But Yoruba portraiture cannot be reduced to a single variety. Different poses and photographic styles emerge in Sprague's data that highlight the diversity of social status, personal style, and ideological orientation within Yoruba communities. Composition is but one aspect of Yoruba photography addressed by Sprague (chapter 11), who extends his discussion from photography as a mode of representation to photographs as material objects. An intriguing example is of the recent substitution of twin photographic portraits for traditional twin statues.

Daniel Miller and Don Slater (chapter 12) similarly focus on the Trini-ness of Trinidadian engagements with the Internet in their book *The Internet: An Ethnographic Approach*. The Internet, perhaps more than any other media technology thus far, constitutes the fulfillment of McLuhan's vision of a "global village." Via the Internet, people who have access to a computer stay in continual contact with each other across multiple time zones; interest groups share and disseminate strategies; and businesses increase their clientele. The global nature of this medium often obscures analysis of the significant degree to which local initiative and priorities remain relevant. Miller and Slater (2000: 8) make an important contribution in their "refusal to treat the Internet independently of its embeddedness." Not simply celebrating the local domestication of a global technology, these authors focus on "how Trinidadians put themselves into this global arena and become part of the force that constitutes it, but do so quite specifically as Trinidadians" (ibid: 7). In chapter 12 they examine how social relationships are constructed and maintained through cyber connections and how exchanges in offline and online life jointly contribute to the active production of Trini-ness.

In chapter 13 Faye Ginsburg assesses the revisionist possibilities of indigenous media. Well aware that indigenous media straddle an uncomfortable position between, as she puts it, "Faustian contract" and "global village," Ginsburg nevertheless advances the position that these efforts constitute necessary cultural interventions against increasingly hegemonic global media forces. She supports her argument with material drawn from a range of Australian Aboriginal media productions that, taken together, illustrate the diversity of Aboriginal concerns and strategies. As with American filmmakers and filmgoers, Yoruba photographers and photographees, and Trinidadian cyber-communicators, we find in Part three a tremendous amount of diversity that is supported, rather than erased, by media.

SUGGESTED READINGS

Dowmunt, Tony, ed. 1993. *Channels of Resistance: Global Television and Local Empowerment*. London: BFI Publishing.

Eickelman, Dale F. and Jon W. Anderson, eds. 1999. *New Media in the Muslim World: The Emerging Public Sphere*. Bloomington: Indiana University Press.

Faris, James. 1992. "Anthropological transparency: film representation and politics," in *Film as Ethnography*, ed. Peter Ian Crawford and David Turton. Manchester: Manchester University Press.

——1993. "A response to Terence Turner," *Anthropology Today* 9 (1): 12–13.

——1996. *Navajo and Photography: A Critical History of the Representation of an American People*. Albuquerque: University of New Mexico Press.

Gerdes, Marta Lucia de. 1998. "Media, politics, and artful speech: Kuna radio programs, *Anthropological Linguistics* 40 (4): 596–616.

Ginsburg, Faye. 1992. "Television and the mediation of culture," *Visual Anthropology Review* 8 (1): 97–102.

——1993. "Aboriginal media and the Australian imaginary," *Public Culture* 5 (3): 557–78.

——1994a. "Culture/media: a (mild) polemic," *Anthropology Today* 10 (2): 5–15.

——1994b. "Some thoughts on culture/media," *Visual Anthropology Review* 10 (1): 136–41.

——1994c. "Embedded aesthetics: creating a discursive space for indigenous media," *Cultural Anthropology* 9: 365–82.

——1995a. "Mediating culture: indigenous media, ethnographic film, and the production of identity." Pp. 256–91 in *Fields of Vision: Essays in Film Studies, Visual Anthropology, and Photography*, ed. Leslie Devereaux and Roger Hillman. Berkeley: University of California Press.

——1995b. "The parallax effect: the impact of aboriginal media on ethnographic film," *Visual Anthropology Review* 11 (2): 64–76.

Hall, Stuart. 1981. "The whites of their eyes: racist ideologies and the media," in *Silver Linings: Some Strategies for the Eighties*, ed. George Bridges and Rosalind Brunt. London: Lawrence and Wishart.

Hamelink, Cees. 1983. *Cultural Autonomy in Global Communications*. New York: Longman.

Heider, Karl G. 1991. *Indonesian Cinema: National Culture on Screen*. Honolulu: University of Hawaii Press.

Imam, Ayesha M. 1991. "Ideology, the mass media, and women: a study from Radio Kaduna, Nigeria." Pp. 244–52 in *Hausa Women in the Twentieth Century*, ed. Catherine Coles and Beverly Mack. Madison: University of Wisconsin Press.

Ivy, Marilyn. 1988. "Tradition and difference in the Japanese mass media," *Public Culture* 1 (1): 21–9.

Lull, James. 1991. *China Turned On: Television, Reform, and Resistance*. New York: Routledge.

Manuel, Peter. 1993. *Cassette Culture: Popular Music and Technology in North India*. Chicago: University of Chicago Press.

Marcus, George E., ed. 1996. *Connected: Engagements with Media. Cultural Studies for the End of the Century*. Late Editions 3. Chicago: University of Chicago Press.

——1997. *Cultural Producers in Perilous States: Editing Events, Documenting Change*. Late Editions 4. Chicago: University of Chicago Press.

Michaels, Eric. 1994a. *Bad Aboriginal Art: Tradition, Media, and Technological Horizons*. Minneapolis: University of Minnesota Press.

——1994b. "Hollywood iconography: a Warlpiri reading." Pp. 80–95 in *Bad Aboriginal Art: Tradition, Media, and Technological Horizons*. Minneapolis: University of Minnesota Press.

——1994c. "Aboriginal content: who's got it – who needs it?" Pp. 20–46 in *Bad Aboriginal Art: Tradition, Media, and Technological Horizons*. Minneapolis: University of Minnesota Press.

Miller, Daniel. 1993. "Spot the Trini," *Ethnos* 58 (3–4): 317–34.

——2000. "The fame of Trinis: websites as traps," *Journal of Material Culture* 5 (1): 5–24.

Miller, Daniel and Don Slater. 2000. *The Internet: An Ethnographic Approach*. Oxford: Berg.

Naficy, Hamid. 1993. *The Making of Exile Cultures: Iranian Television in Los Angeles.* Minneapolis: University of Minnesota Press.

Naficy, Hamid, ed. 1999. *Home, Exile, Homeland: Film, Media, and the Politics of Place.* New York: Routledge.

Pinney, Christopher. 1997. *Camera Indica: The Social Life of Indian Photographs.* Chicago: University of Chicago Press.

Powdermaker, Hortense. 1950. *Hollywood: The Dream Factory. An Anthropologist Looks at the Movie-Makers.* Boston: Little, Brown.

Sprague, Stephen F. 1978. "Yoruba photography: how the Yoruba see themselves," *African Arts* 12 (3): 52–9, 107.

Sullivan, Nancy. 1993. "Film and television production in Papua New Guinea: how media become the message," *Public Culture* 5 (3): 533–56.

Traube, Elizabeth G. 1992. *Dreaming Identities: Class, Gender, and Generation in 1980s Hollywood Movies.* Boulder, CO: Westview Press.

Troy, Timothy, 1992. "Anthropology and photography: approaching a Native American perspective," *Visual Anthropology* 5 (1): 43–61.

Turner, Terence. 1992a. "Defiant images: the Kayapo appropriation of video," *Anthropology Today* 8 (6): 5–16.

—— 1992b. "The Kayapo on television," *Visual Anthropology Review* 11 (2).

—— 1995. "Objectification, collaboration, and mediation in contemporary ethnographic and indigenous media," *Visual Anthropology Review* 11 (2).

Urla, Jacqueline. 1995. "Outlaw language: creating alternative public spheres in Basque free radio," *Pragmatics* 5 (2): 245–61.

Weiner, James F. 1997. "Televisualist anthropology: representation, aesthetics, politics," *Current Anthropology* 38 (2): 197–235.

Wong, Deborah. 1994. "'I want the microphone': mass mediation and agency in Asian-American popular music," *The Drama Review* 38 (3): 152–68.

Worth, Sol and John Adair. 1997 [1972]. *Through Navajo Eyes: An Exploration in Film Communication and Anthropology.* Albuquerque: University of New Mexico Press.

10

Hollywood and the USA

Hortense Powdermaker

Why an Anthropologist Studied Hollywood

I spent a year in Hollywood, from July 1946 to August 1947, a more normal year than those which followed. I went there to understand better the nature of our movies. My hypothesis was that the social system in which they are made significantly influences their content and meaning. A social system is a complex coordinated network of mutually adapted patterns and ideas which control or influence the activities of its members. My hypothesis is hardly original, although it has not been applied before to movies. All art, whether popular, folk, or fine, is conditioned by its particular history and system of production. This is true for Pueblo Indian pottery, Renaissance painting, modern literature and jazz as well as for movies. These are a popular art concerned with telling a story. They differ from folk art in that while consumed by the folk, they are not made by them; and they are unlike the fine arts, since they are never the creation of one person. But although movies are made by many people in the setting of a big industry, certain individuals have power to strongly influence them, while others are relatively powerless.

My field techniques had some similarities to and some differences from those I had used on an island in the Southwest Pacific and elsewhere. As in other communities, I had to establish and maintain the same role: that of a detached scientist. While in Hollywood I was a part-time visiting professor of anthropology at the University of California in Los Angeles, a useful local sanction for this role. More important, however, was the absence of any desire on my part to find a job in the movie industry or to become a part of it. This was unique for anyone living in Hollywood for a year. Then, too, I had no ax to grind in a situation where everyone was very busy grinding his own; instead, I was trying to understand the complicated system in which they worked and lived. I saw people neither as villains nor heroes, but as playing certain roles in this system.

I took the inhabitants in Hollywood and in the South Seas seriously, and this was pleasing to both. To me the handsome stars with their swimming-pool homes were no more glamorous than were the South Sea aborigines exotic. All, whether ex-cannibal chiefs, magicians, front-office executives, or directors, were human beings working and living in a certain way, which I was interested in analyzing. . . .

In analyzing the data, the most important criteria were, first, the degree to which the Hollywood system of production was oriented to maintain and strengthen the qualities essential to its product, which is storytelling, and, secondly, how well the system utilized its resources. This kind of analysis is necessary from the point of view of movies both as a big industry, and as a popular art form.

Obviously, no anthropologist could study Hollywood as an isolated phenomenon. It is part of the United States. But Hollywood is no mirrorlike reflection of our society, which is characterized by a large number of conflicting patterns of behavior and values. Hollywood has emphasized some, to the exclusion of others. It is the particular elaboration and underplay which is important for this study.

Although an expedition to Hollywood has some resemblance to other field trips, it is not quite the same as studying a tribe of headhunters in New Guinea, who have never before been observed. Much is known about Hollywood and much has been written about it. But no anthropological lens had been focused on it. This brings a certain frame of reference – namely, the social system – as well as the knowledge, techniques, and insights gained from comparative studies of the human species from the Stone Age until today. The purpose of the study is to understand and interpret Hollywood, its relationship to the dreams it manufactures, and to our society.

I am concerned with opening up the general problem of movies as an important institution in our society. A unique trait of modern life is the manipulation of people through mass communications. People can be impelled to buy certain articles and brands of merchandise through advertising. Columnists and radio commentators influence political opinions. Movies manipulate emotions and values. Just as advertising can and does promote anxieties to increase consumption, movies may increase certain emotional needs which can then only be satisfied by more movies. In a time of change and conflict such as we experience today, movies and other mass communications emphasize and reinforce one set of values rather than another, present models for human relations through their portrayal by glamorous stars, and show life, truly or falsely, beyond the average individual's everyday experiences. The influence of the movies touches the lives of 85,000,000 American men, women, and children who sit in the audience and likewise extends into remote corners of the earth. The inventions of printing press, radio, and movies have probably been as revolutionary in their effect upon human behavior as were those of the wheel and the coming of steam.

Opinions on the influence of movies range from viewing them as the hope for a better world to the fear of their degrading mankind. Some critics hold them responsible for practically everything they disapprove of, from juvenile delinquency to drunkenness and divorce. These problems, however, have a long a involved history in the life of individuals and society, and the causal factors are complex and not completely known. More important are the millions of people who weekly and monthly go to movies and who do not become delinquents, criminals, or drunkards. These more or less normal everyday people may over a period of time be influenced subtly, but deeply, in their ideas of human relations, and in their values.

Movies are successful largely because they meet some of modern man's deepest needs. He has long known increasing insecurity. He is filled with apprehension about the present and the future. The atomic bomb brings fear of destruction, and the struggle between democracy and totalitarianism throughout the world is truly frightening. Even before these two epochal happenings, the anxieties of modern man had increased because of his growing feeling of isolation and consequent loneliness. This feeling occurs not only in big cities with their intensive concentration of people and industry; it has spread even to agricultural areas, where the traditional rural attitudes have been replaced by those usually associated with the city.[1] Anxieties are further deepened by difficulties in understanding national rivalries, the conflicts in ideology, the complex theories of psychoanalysis and of relativity and so on, which whirl about the average man's head. The popularity of any book which attempts to relieve this situation gives further evidence. Joshua Liebman's book, *Peace of Mind*, was on the bestselling list of nonfiction books continuously for several years after its publication, and so also was the latest Dale Carnegie volume, *How to Stop Worrying and Start Living*. But the book-buying public represents only a small fraction of the population; for the masses of people, the reading of books is not the way out of their confusion and apprehension.

In this age of technology and the assembly line, many people wish to escape from their anxieties into movies, collective daydreams themselves manufactured on the assembly line. To some people, the word "escape" connotes a virtue; for others it is derogatory. But escape, *per se*, is neither good nor bad. All forms of art offer some kind of escape, and it may well be that escape is a necessary part of living. The real question is the quality of what one escapes into. One can escape into a world of imagination and come from it refreshed and with new understanding. One can expand limited experiences into broad ones. One can escape into saccharine sentimentality or into fantasies which exaggerate existing fears. Hollywood provides ready-made fantasies or daydreams; the problem is whether these are productive or nonproductive, whether the audience is psychologically enriched or impoverished.

Like all drama and literature, movies extend the experiences of the audience vicariously, and translate problems which are common to mankind into specific and personal situations, with which identification is easy. Results from some preliminary research with audience reactions provide the hypothesis that audiences tend to accept as true that part of a movie story which is beyond their experience. A low-income group of workers, for instance, were very critical of part of one movie which touched their own experiences, saying, "That's just Hollywood!" – but in the same movie they accepted as completely true the portrayals of a successful girl artist and her two wealthy boy friends, the counterparts of whom they had never met. Those whose associations are restricted to lawabiding respectable members of a community will get their picture of gangsters, thieves, and "bad" women from their movies. This happens even to quite sophisticated people. In a graduate school seminar on case work, a social worker reporting on the case of an unmarried mother said that the mother spoke very casually of being pregnant again. The instructor asked what she had expected, and the student replied: "W – ell, I thought she'd act more like the way they do in the movies!" For people who have never traveled, the movies give them their ideas of what foreigners are like; and the latter may get their pictures of Americans in the same way. The ideas of young people with relatively limited experience about love and marriage may be influenced by what they see in the movies: a young girl in a small Mississippi town complained about the local beaus as compared to the movie heroes....

Hollywood and the USA

The anthropologist sees any segment of society as part of a whole; he views Hollywood as a section of the United States of America, and both in the larger frame of Western civilization. The problems of the movie industry are not unique to it. But some characteristics of the modern world have been greatly exaggerated in Hollywood while others are underplayed. Hollywood is therefore not a reflection, but a caricature of selected contemporary tendencies, which, in turn, leave their imprint on the movies. It is a three-way circular interaction between Hollywood, USA and movies.

Many people would agree with the characterization of our society by the poet W. H. Auden as "The Age of Anxiety." The present generation has known two world wars and is worried about the possibility of a third, even more devastating. We won the last war and are probably the strongest nation, and yet we are insecure in our relations with former enemies and allies. Our country is prosperous and we have demonstrated an enormous capacity for production, but we are worried about a possible recession and unemployment. We live in a fast changing world but have lost faith in our belief that change is always for the better, and that progress is inevitable. We are not so sure of the happy ending.

Man has become increasingly lonely. Although people live in close physical contact, their relationships have become more and more depersonalized. We have a sense of being with people, and yet do not feel in any way related to them. In cities we are accustomed to having strange people beside us in street car, bus, or uncomfortably close in the subway. The technique of business and many other organizations, in trying to personalize their selling relationships, such as by announcing the name of employees to customers, really fools no one. The fact that the name of the post office clerk, the bank teller, or the person who handles complaints in the department store, is posted, does not really influence their relationship with customers. The market place is still basically impersonal. Over the radio, we listen to the voices of strangers relating intimate domestic stories or giving us their opinions about the latest national or world event. All these factors give an illusion of companionship which, however, only increases the feeling of being alone. This loneliness is particularly striking when we compare modern to primitive man with his web of personal relationships within his clan. From birth to death he was tied through reciprocal duties and responsibilities to his clan kindred. Clan membership could not be lost and was as fixed for the individual as was his sex. He belonged to his group through basic biological ties and isolation was rare.

Many other factors contribute to modern man's anxiety. The traditional American belief that anyone, by working hard and industriously, may rise in the social hierarchy and become rich and successful is being questioned. There is considerable evidence that the American worker realizes that social mobility is decreasing. Workers increasingly believe that hard work no longer counts for as much as it did and that opportunities for advancement are restricted.[2] Many employees do not even understand the immediate aspects of their work situation. A study made at an electric company, which had an unusually good relationship with its employees, showed that there was much that the worker did not understand about his job, even including the method of payment. The author thought that this lack of understanding caused a feeling of exasperation and sense of personal futility on the part of the workers.[3] Modern man lives in a world which is difficult to comprehend. He is prosperous or unemployed in recurring economic cycles about which economists talk in learned words of cause and effect. But the average man sees only the effect, and is confused as to the causes.

In Hollywood there is far more confusion and anxiety than in the society which surrounds it. Even in its most prosperous periods when net profits were enormous, far surpassing those of other businesses, everyone was scared. Now, when diminishing foreign markets, increasing costs of production, competition with European pictures, and changing box-office tastes threaten the swollen profits of past prosperity, fear rises to panic. Anxiety grips everyone from executive to third assistant director. The happy endings of at least 100 percent net profit for the studio and a relatively long period of employment at high salaries for employees, are becoming less common. Yet, although this is well known, many individuals still cherish the fantasy for themselves. In the movies the happy ending is still almost universal. Perhaps the people who make the movies cannot afford to admit that there can be another kind of ending, and many of those who sit in the audience prefer this fantasy, too. But an increasing number are becoming dissatisfied with the so obviously contrived nature of these endings. The neat and unrealistic movie solution to all problems is neither satisfying nor entertaining.

Attitudes stem from the past and change slowly. In a rapidly changing society such as ours, some attitudes born out of a past situation continue under new conditions, even when inappropriate. Today there are people who will still believe in the *laissez-faire* economy of the frontier days and are hostile to planning designed for a country which no longer has a frontier. But many who stubbornly cling to the old *laissez-faire* thinking are uneasy lest they fight a losing battle, while many of those who plan are afraid that the planning may go too far. Neither side is really very sure of itself. In Hollywood the lack of planning and extemporizing has been carried to extremes probably not known even on the frontier, and greater certainly than in any contemporary industry. Even more important, extemporizing without a plan has long been regarded by many as a necessary and inherent part of movie making. However, the proper accompaniment, the frontier self-confidence and courage in taking chances, is very rare in Hollywood. The distinguished director–producer William Wyler appeals for

"'men of courage' in Hollywood to reach out for a wealth of picture material which the industry has shunned so far." He continues, "We need men of courage in high places who will not be intimidated or coerced into making only 'safe' pictures – pictures devoid of any ideas whatsoever." Too often he has bunked up against a situation where the top men were forced to decide between two stories and asked the question, "Which is the safest?" Mediocrity in films is the direct result of playing it safe.[4]

The men who make these decisions do not trust the public to like a picture which has ideas in it, Mr. Wyler says, in the same interview. It might be added that the men who do not trust the public usually do not trust themselves.

From the frontier past comes also the tradition of individual aggressive behavior. This persists although industry has become increasingly regimented and cooperation more essential. In the movie industry which depends on the collaborative effort of many people, the aggression is more ruthless than any described on the frontier, although, due to the insecurities of most people, it is masked under "Darlings" and "Sweethearts" and costly presents and parties. In the movies, however, the hatred and aggression comes through with a bang. Here is undiluted violence. This may meet the needs of the makers of our daydreams, as well as of those who consume them. Many people in our society experience a high level of frustration but are unable, either because of social pressures or inner fear, to express their resentment. In the movies they may find comfort and encouragement for their fantasies. . . .

Traditions, however, have a habit of living on in the deeper levels of our consciousness, even when they are overtly denied. Comparatively few people give the impression of really enjoying their wealth or their good times. Many of them appear to be consumed with an obsession to merely fill up time with more and more activity, and space with more and more costly objects. The frenzied and compulsive activity in the studios and outside of them is one of Hollywood's most striking characteristics. Another is the evaluation of not only objects, but people too, in terms of how much they cost. In making movies, this is reflected in the idea that the more a picture costs the better it must be. The tendency towards lavish sets, costumes, and other extravagances is now being curtailed because of the need for economy and the trend to shooting on location. But, with a few exceptions, the correlation of the value of pictures with their budgets is still the prevalent type of thinking in Hollywood. The greater the cost the more sure the studio feels of success, and hence high costs become one way of reducing anxiety. Actually, money can no more guarantee dramatic values than it can insure accuracy or significance in research.

The USA has been labeled by many students as a business civilization as contrasted to a religious one. This is obviously true, but not the whole truth. Roger Butterfield has described the dominant themes of American life as "the desire to see all men free and equal, and the desire to be richer and stronger than anyone else."[5] This conflict between human and property rights has, as this author points out, generated much of the drama of American life. The political idealism and humanitarianism of the eighteenth and nineteenth centuries, as well as the earlier Puritanism, still influence our business civilization. In our Declaration of Independence is the quintessence of idealism, expressing for the first time the idea that all men have a right to happiness. If the anthropologist interested in our contemporary society digs under the top layers of people's beliefs, he will find still surviving the archaic concepts that money is not the road to happiness, or, at least, not the main one. If he is historically minded, he will note that when private capitalism was developing, the man who accumulated wealth through his own hard work was respected and admired; but that later when private capitalism changed to a corporate form, the corporation was regarded as an enemy of the people. Theodore Roosevelt became famous as a "trust-buster." No man in the USA becomes a national hero just through making a lot of money. He must have made some contribution to the welfare of his fellow men; most of the nation's heroes have been humanitarians.

In Hollywood the concept of a business civilization has been carried to an extreme. Property is far more important than man and human values have to struggle hard to exist at all. But, while the heroes in Hollywood are those with the most money, in the movies we find the opposite extreme. The wealthy tycoon is almost always the villain and the hero is the man of good will. The hero or heroine may be rich, but wealth does not give them their status. Often we are asked to admire the poor little rich girl who breaks away from her luxurious environment to marry the poor hero whom she loves. Hollywood leans over backward to sentimentalize love, which in the movies is always more important than wealth. Earning a living is never shown with any sense of reality and making a fortune is rarely portrayed sympathetically. True, most of the characters in the movies are better dressed and live more luxuriously than do their counterparts in real life. The secretary dresses like a wealthy debutante and the female psychoanalyst like the popular concept of a Hollywood star. But neither they nor any other heroine or hero are shown as fundamentally interested in or concerned about the problem of making a living or becoming rich. It is only possible to speculate on the reasons for this almost complete negation of economic motives which are so prevalent in our society. The very extremes to which most movies go in the negation may mean that the executives who control the contents of the movies have themselves some hidden ambivalence about their goals. After all, the executives, as well as the actors, do belong to the human species and are not completely unaffected by the conflicting values of our society. Or, they may think that this underplaying of economic motives in the movies is desired by the audience. Neither reason precludes the other, and both could be true, as well as other unknown ones. Whatever the reasons, Hollywood represents a caricature and overelaboration of the business motives and goals of our society, while the movies consistently underplay the same characteristics.

Art and aesthetic goals have always been less important in our society than either business or humanitarian ones. The artist in all societies has traditionally been a kind of barometer, more sensitive to nuances and changes than others, because he is more deeply immersed in his culture and more interested in its meanings. Since he rarely completely accepts all the conventions, he has a certain degree of objectivity and freedom, which of course also makes him seem different from other men. While the artist's status declined in all Western societies after the Industrial Revolution, many of the European countries with their older traditions of painting, music, and literature, accorded him a higher position than he enjoys in the United States. Here, he is still considered peculiar, abnormal, sometimes feminine, and unimportant unless he achieves a commerical success comparable to that of a businessman. A Hollywood caricature of this concept is portrayed in the movie, *A Kiss in the Dark*. The hero, a successful concert pianist, played by David Niven, is scared, nervous, withdrawn, and obviously infantile. He is saved by noticing, with appreciation, a model's legs (those of Jane Wyman). She has no interest in his music and leads him to her world of jazz and trombones. He finally frees himself from being an artist and wins his girl by using his muscian's hands to knock down the heroine's fiancé, a former athlete. The hero is now a he-man, throws his practice keyboard away, and embraces the heroine as the train carries them away on a honeymoon.

So in the actual production of movies in Hollywood, the American concept of the unimportance of the artist is magnified. Those who know most about storytelling, who are gifted with imagination, and who have a knowledge of human beings, all raw materials which the camera transforms into a movie, do not have sufficient status to use their abilities. As one director expressed it, "the environment is hostile to them." The environment favors the latest developments in sound and color, but discourages new ideas from its artists. These men, who traditionally have known considerable freedom in expressing themselves, work under the direction of businessmen.

The movies have to earn their living. Unlike some of the fine arts, they are not privately endowed nor are they an esoteric medium for the enjoyment of the few. The goals of business and art are each justifiable and not necessarily irreconcilable. When art meets the needs of a large number of people in our society, it inevitably makes a profit. Some of our most creative popular artists, such as Chaplin, Gershwin, Walt Disney, and Irving Berlin, have made fortunes. The problem is not the simple one of art versus business. The artist can contribute to business. But his stock-in-trade is not only his technical know-how: it includes the ability to interpret man to himself. This is true in folk art, popular art, and fine art. But it makes little difference to the businessman whether he assuages man's anxieties by interpretation, or whether he exploits them; but the latter is easier. Or, if phoniness brings in money easily, why bother about the details of honesty? The front-office executives are not completely blind to humanitarian issues, but they seem far more interested in profits than in man. Most of them are not conditioned to be otherwise. Artists have a different kind of conditioning. While they are concerned about money, they must also, in order to be reasonably contented, use their gifts to give their interpretations. It has already been indicated that while only relatively few of the Hollywood writers, directors, and actors are artists in this sense, they are far more important than the host of mediocre people.

The social organization of Hollywood has, however, permitted the businessman to take over the functions of the artists and to substitute his values for theirs. The movies are the first art form of any kind, popular, folk, or fine, to become a trust. Quite early the major companies combined in their efforts to restrain competition and to blacklist those who would not do their bidding. The struggle between the Independents and the organization of the major studios still continues. At the same time movies increasingly make use of a developing technology and of the heritage from theater and literature. Under any circumstances such a combination would create complex problems. In this particular situation, the men with power have known how to exploit the advantages of a trust better than they could utilize the assets of literature and drama. They have not seemed to realize that the efficiency of the factory is possible because it turns out identical products, whether automobiles or coffeepots, and that this principle cannot be applied to the making of movies. Since these businessmen have neither understanding nor respect for the artists' ability, they attempt to negate or destroy it, partly out of ignorance and partly from a desire to satisfy their urge to dominate men. It is only an exceptional executive who does not give the impression that he would have been equally satisfied as a tycoon in any other industry.

Outside of Hollywood there is a certain freedom in choice of goals. A man can decide to be an artist, a scientist, or a college professor, which means that most likely he will never be rich. Or he can plan to be a big business executive and have the possibility of acquiring great wealth. In Hollywood the same freedom of choice does not exist, because whatever role the individual plays, the goals of business are paramount. In the country as a whole there is the combination of humanism and materialism. But in Hollywood, money is always more important than man. It is this difference in goals which accounts for much of the deep hostility between the front-office and the artists' group. People with the same goals may argue and differ on how to achieve them, but they speak the same language. People with conflicting goals speak a different language. The real artist in Hollywood cannot be completely satisfied, even though he earns a fortune, if he is not functioning as an artist, and this the head of a trust cannot understand.

Another trait of our civilization is its high level of ingenuity and inventiveness in the mechanical skills. Our heroes include men like Thomas Edison, Alexander Graham Bell, Eli Whitney, and Henry Ford as well as the humanitarian, political figures. We are justly famous for the enormous number of additions to material culture which make life more comfortable. Movies are themselves a remarkable invention in their integration of electricity, photography, color, sound, and acting. The history of inventions from the first stone ax is a fascinating story and one peculiar to our species. For only man is a tool- making and tool-using animal. Each succeeding example of his ingenuity and cleverness has brought, however, its own problems. This has always been true, but only recently has atomic energy forced a public recognition of the serious social consequences of technological developments.

The control of machines and of all our inventions for the benefit of man is one of the most pressing problems of our time. Machines can enslave people or free them. The Industrial Revolution brought young children into sweatshops and kept them and their parents for long hours at machines. Gradually changes in the social and economic organization reduced the hours of work, set age limits for workers, and enabled them, as well as other people, to enjoy the higher standard of living which machines made possible. But even the most casual observer of our society today recognizes its machinelike character. Not only do machines increasingly replace human labor, but what is left of it grows more mechanical. The role of the individual worker on the assembly line tends to be more and more automatic and he has less and less understanding of its relationship or his own to the whole. The ironic climax is his attempt to escape into fantasies and daydreams, themselves manufactured on an assembly line, far more concerned with technology than with meaning.

The way in which Hollywood has mechanized creativity and taken away most of its human characteristics again exaggerates the prevailing culture pattern, which gives little prestige to creativity not technological. This, of course, does not apply to the genius: an Einstein, Picasso, or a Rachmaninoff is given due honor. But we do little to bring out the creativity which lies in all human beings. Most people – just the everyday garden variety, not the geniuses – have far more potentialities for being creative than they use. But very few of them have the courage or desire to carry through their own ideas, big or little, because they have been conditioned to think routinely and follow the crowd. Our society tends, particularly today, to prize uniformity in thinking more than originality. The concern with the "know-how" rather than the "why," with technology rather than meaning, permeates much of the thinking even in the social sciences when method becomes more important than problems. The use of the most exact scientific methods on a sterile and meaningless problem is not too different from the employment of the most technically advanced camera work to produce a banal movie. It is the same when our educational system stresses the accumulation of facts rather than the meaningful relationship between them, and the taking of so many courses that there is little time for thoughtful reflection. The radio with its "Information, Please" and other quiz programs continues the emphasis. It is not that factual knowledge or scientific methods are unimportant, but rather that they are of use only in the larger context of problems and meanings. Hollywood expands these two features of our society to such an extent that it discourages and sometimes even forbids creativity in the very people whom it presumably pays to be creative. ...

Hollywood represents totalitarianism. Its basis is economic rather than political but its philosophy is similar to that of the totalitarian state. In Hollywood, the concept of man as a passive creature to be manipulated extends to those who work for the studios, to personal and social relationships, to the audiences in the theaters, and to the characters in the movies. The basic freedom of being able to choose between alternatives is absent. The gifted people who have the capacity for choice cannot exercise it; the executives who technically have the freedom of choice do not actually have it, because they usually lack the knowledge and imagination necessary for making such a choice. Much behavior is compulsive, springing from fears, hidden and open. The careful planning and good judgement of the exceptional people have been already described and are in dramatic contrast to the hysterical behavior of the others.

The Hollywood atmosphere of crises and continuous anxiety is a kind of hysteria which prevents people from thinking, and is not too different from the way dictators use wars and continuous threats of war as an emotional basis for maintaining their power. As the late Dr. Harry Stack Sullivan pointed out, there is considerable difference between fear and anxiety. Fear, he said, is often provoked by a new or novel situation and wears off as one becomes accustomed to it. Anxiety, however, arises out of relationships with other people which are disturbed, and "from its mildest to its most extreme manifestations interferes with effective alertness to the factors in the current situation that are immediately relevant to its occurrence, and thus with the refinement and precision of action related to its relief or reduction."[6] Put more colloquially and applied to Hollywood, this means that a stage director who directs a movie for the first time might have some fear which would disappear as he became more accustomed to the new situation. In the meantime, the fear would not inhibit his learning as much as possible about the new situation and applying his knowledge and talent to it. But the anxiety of the average producer who has been in movies all his adult life springs out of his character and interpersonal relations, and the Hollywood situation calls forth and increases what is already there. Nor is it possible to become accustomed to anxiety-provoking situations. The very anxiety prevents an awareness of the factors which call it forth and of realistically doing something about them. These anxiety-ridden producers and executives of Hollywood try to reduce anxiety by spending more money, buying a bestseller whether or not it is appropriate for a movie, using ten writers instead of one, having three "big name" stars in a movie, and so on. But none of these formulas rids him of his anxiety. Even where a picture is a big success, he knows the same anxiety on the next one.

In *Mein Kampf* Hitler wrote about Fate as sometimes cruel and other times loving. Whether it is called Fate, destiny, or breaks, the underlying concept is the same: man gives up the attempt to exercise some control over his life through his own intelligence, because he thinks forces beyond his domain completely direct it.

The totalitarian concept of man is not limited to human relationships in Hollywood, but is reflected in many movies. Life, success, or misfortune is usually portrayed as caused by luck or an accident. Only rarely does a movie show the process of becoming successful or the process of disintegration. Either one is treated as a *fait accompli* in the beginning of the picture or as caused by accidents during the course of the movie. Most movie characters, whether hero or villain, heroine or jade, are passive beings to whom things happen accidentally. Rarely do they even try to think through the situation in which they find themselves. They are buffeted about and defeated; or Fate smiles on them and almost magically they are successful. A few pictures have freed themselves from this formula. In *Home of the Brave* the Negro hero is shown as suffering realistically from prejudice. His escape is not on a magic carpet into a never-never world but through a painful psychological process, which the movie plainly says is kaleidoscoped. The Negro problem is seen as part of a larger human one. Nor is the problem over at the end of the picture. The hero merely understands it better and has a way of handling it.

The totalitarian concept likewise extends toward the audiences, often regarded as suckers whose emotional needs and anxieties can be exploited for profit. Hollywood producers are, of course, not the only people with undue anxieties and many of the movies cater to the same kind of anxieties in their audiences, strengthening rather than reducing them, and contributing nothing to understanding. Only men who are not completely ridden with anxieties and who have some understanding of their own, as well as mankind's problems, can make other kinds of pictures. "The people," however, are always used as a rationalization – by dictators who say they rule for the good of the people, and by Hollywood producers who say they give the people what they want.

NOTES

1 Cf. Carey McWilliams, *Factories in the Field* (Boston: Little, Brown). Also Walter Gold-schmidt, *As You Sow* (New York: Harcourt, Brace).
2 William Lloyd Warner and J. O. Low, *The Social System of the Modern Factory*, p. 182 (New Haven, CT: Yale University Press).
3 Elton Mayo, *The Human Problems of an Industrial Civilization*, 2nd edn., pp. 119–20 (New York: Macmillan).
4 *Variety*, October 12, 1949.
5 *The American Past: A History of the United States from Concord to Hiroshima*, p. 5 (New York: Simon & Schuster).
6 Harry Stack Sullivan, "Multidisciplined Co-ordination of Interpersonal Data," in *Culture and Personality*, p. 179. Proceeding of an Interdisciplinary Conference held under the auspices of the Viking Fund. Published by the Viking Fund, New York.

11

Yoruba Photography: How the Yoruba See Themselves

Stephen F. Sprague

Photographers and photographic studios are prevalent throughout many areas of Africa today, and particularly in West Africa many indigenous societies make use of this medium. The Yoruba, though not unique, are certainly exceptional in the extent to which they have integrated photography into many contemporary and traditional aspects of their culture. Some Yoruba photographs reflect traditional cultural values, and some are even utilized in certain traditional rituals. These more conventional-ized forms of photography seem to exist in the smaller, more isolated Yoruba towns and villages. In the large cities such as Ibadan and Lagos, where contemporary Western photography is more influential, the work exhibits a greater sophistication and a wider range of styles and techniques.

Photography is no newcomer to Africa. Three months after Daguerre publicly announced his daguerreotype process in 1839, the French romantic painter Horace Vernet wrote from Alexandria, Egypt, "We keep daguerreotyping like lions, and from Cairo hope to send home an interesting batch..." (Bensusan 1966: 7). In colonial South and East Africa, the first studios were opened in the 1840s (ibid: 11), and photography immediately became a part of colonial life. In West Africa it is likely that photography was introduced more slowly and coincided with the later nineteenth-century expansion of permanent European colonies and political rule. It was past 1900, for instance, before the interior of Nigeria was completely under British rule, and 1895 before some of the first photographs of the River Niger were made (ibid: 82).

Considering the long history of photography in colonial Africa, it seems reason-able to assume that many indigenous societies would have had ample opportunity to become familiar with the medium and to make it as much a part of their own cultures as seemed appropriate. Indigenous photographers have indeed been working in West Africa at least since the 1930s and probably very much earlier, as their actual existence would likely predate by a considerable number of years their recognition and documentation in the literature. A picture by a Gold Coast photog-rapher appeared in a pre-World War II British book on commercial photography with the condescending comment that "crude though the result is it had virtues which showed that the mind of the photographer was at work" (Charles 1938: 17). A possibly much earlier example is the large framed photograph hanging over the doorway to a traditional *abiku*[1] shrine in the Yoruba town of Ila-Orangun. It depicts the mother of the old priestess who is presently head of the society, and it could date from as early as pre-World War I. The Yoruba may have been substituting photographs in place of traditional sculpture since the 1930s and probably much earlier, provided the substance of this ethnocentric quote is correct: "The *Oba* was constrained to relax his patronage of the artists' works: very much like other African chiefs he thought he could hand on his image to posterity more beautifully by means of an enlarged photograph than by a wooden statue" (Westerman 1939: 102).

Most of the material for this article was collected in the Igbomina Yoruba town of Ila-Orangun during the summer of 1975. Some comparative material was collected in the Ijebu-Remo area and in the large cities of Lagos, Ibadan, and Kano. Ila-Orangun is a typical Yoruba community of about 30,000 inhabitants, which did not have either electricity or running water at the time of this investigation. In spite of the lack of modern facilities, the town supported ten flourishing photographic studios. I investigated the negative files of each studio and requested ten to fifteen postcard-size prints ($3\frac{1}{2}$ " × $5\frac{1}{2}$ ") from each. These were selected on the basis of criteria established, in part, from a stylistic and subject matter analysis of 300 sample postcards kept by Sir Special Photo Studio for prospective clients to view. Briefly, these criteria were: (1) the photograph was a good example of a distinct subset of Yoruba photographs as previously defined by the analysis of Sir Special's postcards; (2) the photograph was unique in some way or did not fit into any previously defined category; (3) the photograph seemed to contain anthropological information useful to Marilyn Houlberg, who was also in Ila-Orangun continuing her research on Yoruba sacred children; and (4) the photograph particularly pleased my own aesthetic tastes.

All ten photographers were interviewed, and they willingly discussed their profession and demonstrated their personal camera and darkroom techniques.[2] In addition, members of the community contributed information about the subject matter and function of photographs they owned. Finally, I myself took pictures of the photographers, their studios and darkrooms, and the use and display of Yoruba photographs within the context of the community. Yoruba photography in Ila-Orangun was studied, then, from the points of view of the producer and the consumer, and by looking at the photographs themselves. Although this investigation was primarily restricted to Ila-Orangun, observations in other areas of Yorubaland strongly suggest that the use of photography in Ila-Orangun is typical of many Yoruba communities and probably has much in common with other areas of West Africa.

The photographers of Ila-Orangun claim that practically any subject may be photographed except for those ritual objects, masquerades, and ceremonies that some segments of the public are traditionally prohibited from viewing. Also, they say that a good photographer will take a picture of whatever the client requests. However, a study of the kinds of photographs most commonly produced indicates that the actual practice of the profession is generally much more restricted than is claimed.

Yoruba photography in Ila-Orangun and elsewhere is, almost exclusively, posed portraiture of individuals or groups of people, which are often commissioned in order to commemorate an event of some importance to those depicted. Though an important ritual object or prized possession, such as a traditional sculpture or a new car, might occasionally be photographed, general subjects such as landscapes, architecture, or ordinary objects and events are seldom taken by local photographers.[3] In short, the Yoruba have developed unstated but clearly discernible conventions regarding appropriate subject matter; those governing posing and presentation of the subject matter have also developed. Together, these conventions offer a codification of a range of Yoruba cultural values.[4]

Yoruba photography certainly shares similar categories of subject matter and formalistic conventions with other West African societies and with Western cultures, particularly British. But cultural patterning exists, not only in subtle differences in these conventions but more importantly in the unique, culturally derived symbolic meanings and specific functions attributed to these seemingly similar forms. It is beyond the scope of this essay to analyze all the diverse external and indigenous factors that might have contributed to the development of Yoruba photography. Instead, I simply seek here to establish Yoruba photography as a genuine expression of the culture by discussing several specific examples with respect to how their subject matter, formal and stylistic conventions, symbolic meanings, and function within Yoruba society are in part a reflection of Yoruba cultural values and perceptions of the world.

Older Yoruba in traditional dress often sit in a particular stylized manner at traditional ceremonies and events. This pose has become visually codified through photography and now seems to be the accepted way for traditional Yoruba to present themselves in a formal photographic portrait. What I call the "traditional formal portrait" is highly conventionalized both in the manner in which the subject poses and the manner in which the photograph is composed (plate 11.1). The subject always wears his best traditional dress and sits squarely facing the camera. Both hands are placed on the lap or on the knees, and the legs are well apart to spread the garments and display the fabrics. The face has a dignified but distant expression as the eyes look directly at and through the camera. Symbols of the subject's position in Yoruba society are worn, held, or placed conspicuously near by. The photographer enhances the sense of dignified stateliness by a camera viewpoint either level with the subject's waist or looking slightly upward, as if from the position of one paying homage. The entire body is always included within the frame, and a neutral vertical background immediately behind serves to isolate the subject in a shallow three-dimensional space. The figure gives a feeling of sculptural massiveness and solidarity, and the whole pose is one of symmetry and balance.[5]

It might be argued that the traditional formal portrait is in part a synthesis of certain traditional Yoruba cultural values, the inherent attributes of nineteenth-century photography, and nineteenth-century British attitudes toward the medium. Its formality might be partly explained as a convention that developed out of the practical difficulties of making portraits when photography was first introduced. The early technology (the large view cameras, slow lenses, and insensitive emulsions) made taking a photograph a laborious process and forced the sitter to assume a rigid pose that could be held for the duration of a long exposure. Consequently, in the hands of an inexperienced operator, many portraits turned out unnaturally serious and stiffly formal.

However, the particular style of posing represented by the Yoruba traditional formal portrait is almost never seen in nineteenth- and twentieth-century British portrait photography.[6] In the latter, the subject does not squarely confront the camera but usually turns asymmetrically to one side and looks out of the

Plate 11.1 This chief and Babal Awo (Ifa diviner) requested that I make a portrait of him. He had his family set up the mats and background, and proceeded to pose in the traditional manner.

frame and away from the lens. The whole body is seldom shown; most British portraits range from three-quarter length to extreme close-ups that include only the head. Also, studio props are often cropped by the frame rather than being entirely included in the picture. If a painted studio background is used, it often visually interacts with the subject. These visual codes are, of course, common to photographic portraits in many socieites, and they often appear in many Yoruba examples as well, with the significant exception of the traditional formal portrait.

Both nineteenth-century British and traditional Yoruba cultures placed great emphasis on tradition, proper conduct, and the identity and maintenance of one's social position. Early British portraits and Yoruba traditional formal portraits visually codify these commonly held values: the dignified pose, proper clothes, and

Plate 11.2 The Orangun of Ila-Orangun in his private sitting room in the palace. The horsetail flywhisk, necklace, beaded crown, and the other beaded objects surrounding him are all symbols of his position. The traditional formal pose and many of the same symbols are repeated in the free-standing cut-out photographs on display.

Plate 11.3 One of the free-standing cut-out photographs.

often the display of symbolic objects identify the subject's profession and social station. British portraits, however, also emphasize the Western values of individuality and even eccentricity, while the traditional formal portrait emphasizes how well the subject fulfills his traditional role in Yoruba society.

The traditional formal portrait, of all the forms of Yoruba photography, most clearly embodies in its composition not only certain traditional Yoruba cultural values, but also their aesthetic values as outlined by R. F. Thompson in his discussion of Yoruba sculpture (1971: 374–81). The concept of *jijora* – mimesis at the midpoint – implies the work should exist somewhere between complete abstraction and individual likeness. It should resemble the individual and at the same time embody all the ideal Yoruba characteristics without over-emphasizing any one. The extreme stylization of pose and facial expression of the traditional formal portrait is an attempt to achieve this state by circumventing to a degree the inherent specificity of the photographic portrait. *Odo,* depiction midway between infancy and old age, at the prime of life, is seen in the strength of the pose and in the facial expression, both of which seem to imply the subject's maturity and wisdom. *Ifarahon,* "visibility," implies clarity and definition of form and line, and a subsequent clarity of identity. This is emphasized in the photograph by the isolation of the subject against the neutral background, in the sculptural dimensions and symmetry of the figure, and in the inclusion of objects symbolizing the subject's position in Yoruba society.

A comparison of much Yoruba sculpture with the traditional formal portrait reveals two obvious similarities in form: in both, the head invariably faces forward with respect to the body, and when the sculpture is viewed from directly in front (the point of view at which the traditional formal portrait is taken), both characteristically appear bilaterally symmetrical. Another relationship between photography and the sculptural tradition can be seen in the practice of mounting a photo of a person on a thin sheet of wood, then cutting out the subject and adding a flat base to make a freestanding, three-dimensional portrait. Any style of photographic portrait may be treated in this way. A studio in Ibadan features an entire display case of freestanding portraits ranging from a very Westernized close-up of the head to the traditional formal portrait. Yesufu Ejigboye from the Ijebu-Remo area, in addition to carving traditional sculpture and silver airplanes (Houlberg 1976a), has cut-out and mounted full-color magazine portraits of two lovely ladies. These are displayed in his parlor surrounded by photographs and other fascinating items. The Orangun of Ila-Orangun has at least three cut-out portraits of himself in the traditional formal pose displayed in his sitting room (plate 11.3). When I requested permission to take his picture, he posed in the sitting room in an identical manner. He wore a traditional gown and included similar symbols of his office: the horsetail flywhisk, beaded crown and large beads around the neck (plate 11.2).

The traditional formal portrait, then, seems to have been functioning as an integral part of Yoruba culture for a significant length of time. It is meant to memorialize the subject not so much as a unique individual, as in much British portraiture, but rather in terms of how well he has embodied traditional Yoruba ideals and fulfilled his given position in society. When the subject dies, this portrait might be carried in his funeral procession to particularize the ancestral Egungun (Schiltz 1978: 51). It is the portrait that might be hung in his crypt or laminated to his tombstone, and published in memoriam each year in the Lagos *Daily Times*.

The memorial pages of the *Daily Times* are a manifestation in contemporary Nigerian culture of traditional respect for, and veneration of, ancestors. Every day the *Daily Times* has several pages of memorials to the deceased, many of whom have been dead ten or twenty years or longer. Each memorial almost always includes a photograph and a brief tribute and description of the person's accomplishments and social position.[7] A limited survey of a few recent editions of the Lagos *Daily Times* indicates that those Yoruba whose accomplishments could be identified with the traditional culture were often pictured in traditional dress in the traditional formal pose, while Yoruba whose accomplishments could be identified with contemporary Nigerian culture were often pictured in modern dress in a variety of more casual, Europeanized poses. An extended survey should show a definite correlation, which might change over time, between dress and pose in the memorial photograph and the subjects' wealth, social position, and education.[8]

There are many other styles of formal, informal, and even humorous portraiture; and many reflect more directly Western conventions in their manner of posing than does the traditional formal portrait. However, as a particular pose is adapted into Yoruba culture, its meanings may also be modified. What I call the squatting pose is one such example (plate 11.4). This pose seems restricted to young Yoruba ladies dressed in modern styles, and may be in part a fusion of the deferent behavior traditionally required of young women toward their social superiors with the rather innocent, physical allure shown in American "cheesecake" pin-up photographs circa 1950. A painted studio backdrop from Ila-Orangun featuring such a pin-up girl squatting on top of a modern skyscraper is but one indication of this Western influence. This pose might be seen to express the ambiguous position of Yoruba women in a changing society: the impression is that of a young lady who, while maintaining her proper place in traditional society, has turned her fascinated eyes to the modern world.

Many conventions that reflect Yoruba cultural values are independent of any particular subject matter or style of posing. One is that both of the subject's eyes must always be visible in a portrait. This convention again relates to the concept of *ifarahon* – of visibility and clarity of form, line and identity. Both older, traditional Yorubas and younger, more Westernized Yorubas expect this convention to be upheld. In one case, an American photographer made a series of photographs of a contemporary "juju" musician and offered him a profile view as being the best. The musician, however, rejected the photograph, saying that it was "not clear." In another case, Houlberg asked an Ijebu-Remo priestess to evaluate and rank in order of preference eight photographs of herself previously taken by Houlberg. The priestess ranked lowest the one portrait that showed her in profile.[9]

Many photographs are made to commemorate a particular ceremony or event, and another convention is the prominent inclusion in the photograph of the proper symbolic objects to adequately identify this event. In a group photograph the social hierarchy must also be made clear by the positions of individuals within the frame. The most important person is seated (often in the traditional formal pose) in the center of the first row, with the next most important seated to his left. Persons of least status stand furthest toward the back and edges of the frame. Children are exceptions, being allowed to squat or sit anywhere in the foreground. The poet George Awooner-Williams expresses this status ordering in the second stanza of his poem "Song of Sorrow" (1967): "I am on the world's extreme corner I am not sitting in the row with the eminent. But those who are lucky sit in the middle and forget I am on the world's extreme corner I can only go beyond and forget."

These few examples establish Yoruba photography as a genuine expression of the culture by showing how some cultural values have been given visual form in certain kinds of photographs. Many Yoruba would not consciously know, or be able to articulate, how their photographs reflect commonly held values and myths – and many members of our own culture would find it equally difficult to explain the symbolic

Plate 11.4 The squatting pose. Postcard-size prints collected from photographers in Ila-Orangun.

meanings of their family photographs. Instead, photographically unsophisticated members of both cultures assume that the photographic image is simply a visual record, which serves as a device to bring to mind at some future time the people and events depicted. The actual structure and symbolic meaning of the photographic image are not consciously considered; it serves only to trigger the viewer's memory of the subject. Even the traditional formal portrait, though meant to invoke a specific, culturally determined image, still functions basically as a memory device.

The Yoruba photograph itself, as an object, also serves specific functions in the community. Photographs are prominently displayed in the parlor or sitting room of homes, and at the front of many shops and offices. Family members, relatives,

PHOTO AS MEMORY DEVICE

friends, and important gatherings are the dominant subjects. The largest and most elaborate photographs are of senior family members and distinguished ancestors. Local and national leaders and other famous people are often included in either original photographs or in magazine and poster reproductions. By displaying these photographs, the owner publicly acknowledges his respect for, and his involvement with, the subjects. There is often an additional implication of status. A person of relatively little wealth will own a few photographs, and they will be mounted and displayed in a simple fashion. Those of greater wealth and social standing will have more and larger photographs on display, and many of them may be elaborately hand-colored and framed, and occasionally made into a freestanding cut-out.

Educated Yorubas and wealthy families who have been exposed to Western culture often own photograph albums that can date back a number of generations. These albums contain mostly postcard-size photographs and other memorabilia arranged in a rough chronological order, forming a culturally conditioned visual history of the family or individual. Again, there is the implication of status; it is considered progressive and modern to own photo albums, and the mere fact that a visual record has been kept validates one's importance. Wealth is also implied. Since the concept of the amateur family snapshot is not prevalent among the Yoruba, only the relatively well-off could afford over the years to hire a photographer for practically every occasion of any importance.

There are fascinating exceptions to the general function of the photograph as literal record, memory device, and an object symbolizing respect and status. The photograph is sometimes believed to possess additional power and spiritual meanings and can be used in traditional rituals. A few instances appear to be simply individual beliefs, while others are widely accepted practices. The most fascinating and widespread example is the integration of photography into the traditional beliefs and rituals surrounding twins. Because twins are sacred children with connections to the spirit world, it is especially important to show them proper respect. Photographs are often made of twins and other children to hang in the parlor with the photographs of other family members. Then, if a child dies, there is a portrait by which to remember him. The procedure becomes more complex when one twin dies before their photograph is taken. If the twins were of the same sex, the surviving twin is photographed alone, and the photographer prints this single negative twice, so that the twins appear to be sitting side by side in the final photograph. If the twins were of opposite sexes, the surviving twin is photographed once in male clothing and once in female clothing. Sometimes these two exposures are made on separate negatives, which must then be printed together; and sometimes they are made on opposite halves of a single $3\frac{1}{2}'' \times 5\frac{1}{2}''$ glass plate negative, which can be printed without any darkroom manipulation. In either case the photographer attempts to conceal the line blending the two separate exposures in order to maintain the illusion of twins sitting together in a single photograph.

Though twins are quite common, not only among the Yoruba but throughout Africa, the incidence of triplets is much lower, and a photographer would seldom be confronted with the problem of representing triplets. In one unusual case the two brothers died, and the surviving girl was photographed once as herself in girl's clothes and once in matching boy's clothes. The two exposures were made on the same $3\frac{1}{2}'' \times 5\frac{1}{2}''$ glass plate. The photographer then printed the "boy" image twice, once on either side of the girl, to give the proper illusion of triplets (plate 11.5).

Plate 11.5 A rare representation of triplets. The two boys died, and the surviving girl was photographed as herself and in matching boy's clothes to represent her brothers. The male image was printed twice, once on either side of the girl's image to show the triplets sitting together. By Simple Photo.

The traditional procedure when a twin dies is for the parents to commission the carving of a twin figure, or *ibeji*, which then participates in the twin ceremonies along with the living twin. In some areas, it is now accepted practice for the photograph to be substituted for the *ibeji*. This picture is then kept on the twin shrine and participates in the traditional ceremonies.

The exact function of these twin photographs seems to depend in part on the religious convictions of the parents. Houlberg (1973) states that the Christian and Muslim prohibition against the use of Yoruba traditional sculpture has been a major influence in the simplification of *ibeji* forms used by Christian and Muslim Yoruba, and in the substitution of other objects, such as plastic dolls, for *ibeji* in the traditional twin rituals (1973). She suggests in a more recent article (Houlbergh 1976a) that this prohibition has been a major influence in the substitution of photographs for *ibeji*. Through the use or possession of a twin photograph, Christian and Muslim Yoruba seek to distinguish themselves from believers in the traditional religion. The cycle of substitution can, on occasion, come full circle when both twins die before their pictures have been taken. Then, if the traditional *ibeji* are carved, these are sometimes photographed and the photo of the carvings is hung in the parlor in place of the usual twin photograph.

The photographers themselves and the craft of Yoruba photography deserve some discussion. Photography enjoys a respected position within the community similar to hairdressing, barbering, or tailoring. It is considered a good modern profession for young people to enter, and though the vast majority of photographers are men, there are no restrictions against women. In Ila-Orangun the ten photographers included eight young men, one young woman, and one older retired photographer who served as head of the photographers' union. Though it tends to be a young person's profession and is seldom handed down from father to son, there are often family connections between photographers in the smaller towns. In Ila-Orangun four of the ten photographers belonged to the same family compound, and the younger three had all been apprenticed to their senior brother.

To become a photographer a young person must first complete primary six (sixth grade). He then must apprentice to a master photographer for a period of one to three years. If he has learned well, he is given his freedom in a special ceremony at the end of his apprenticeship. He can then open a studio and eventually attract his own apprentices. Photographers are highly organized. There is a union in each town to which every photographer automatically belongs, and which meets at least once a month. These local unions form regional unions, which meet about every six months. The unions regulate such things as the price structure of the various types of photographs and services, the details of apprenticeship, and the professional conduct of its members.

Plate 11.6 The backdrop of Oyus Photo Studio is particularly interesting, with its varieties of foliage and architecture, inconsistent perspective and mixture of contemporary and traditional motifs.

The typical photography studio, such as those in Ila- Orangun, is usually small but efficiently laid out. Double doors swing open to reveal to the passerby samples of the photographer's work. A backdrop hangs a few feet inside the studio, with a bench for the sitter placed immediately in front of it. These backdrops are painted by sign painters in various shades of black, white, and gray. They often show a fascinating but naive use of Western perspective, and usually mix traditional and contemporary motifs (plate 11.6). Behind the backdrop is a tiny darkroom, often without either electricity or running water. Along one wall is a narrow table on which are set the processing solutions in enameled bowls from the market. A kerosene lantern with a red cloth surrounding the globe serves as a safelight. An old postcard-size view camera is installed with its back to a window for use as a solar enlarger, and a mirror, located outside the window, is titled to reflect the sunlight through the system. An enlargement is made by placing a negative in the back of the camera and projecting its image onto a sheet of photographic paper clipped to a vertical easel. Except for minor variations, this makes up the photographer's entire facilities.

The traditional view camera that takes postcard-size glass plates has been increasingly relegated to the darkroom as an enlarger. Since about 1960 there has become available a wide variety of more flexible, twin-lens reflex cameras that take twelve $2\frac{1}{2}''$-square negatives on inexpensive 120-roll film. The success and status of a photographer are often indicated by the camera and other equipment he owns. A beginning photographer will own a cheap plastic Russian Lubitel or Chinese Sea Gull; the majority own Japanese Yashicas, and a few photographers in the large cities own expensive German Rolicords or Rolliflexes.

From the $2\frac{1}{2}''$-square negative of these cameras, the photographers offer standardized photograph sizes based on the old British view camera negative formats. These are passport ($2'' \times 2''$), postcard ($3\frac{1}{2}'' \times 5\frac{1}{2}''$), half plate ($3\frac{1}{4}'' \times 4\frac{1}{4}''$), and full plate ($6\frac{1}{2}'' \times 8\frac{1}{2}''$). The larger sizes of $11'' \times 14''$, $16'' \times 20''$ and occasionally $20'' \times 30''$ conform to the sizes of photographic paper available.

Many photographers offer additional services, including multiple-printing and hand-coloring, and mounting techniques ranging from simple cardboard mounts to elaborate frames and freestanding cutouts. Some photographers have a specialty. Sir Special Photo of Ila-Orangun is known for his skill in mounting a portrait behind a mirror. He says the technique came to him in a dream. He scratches away the mirror coating in the shape of the subject and then places the photograph behind the mirror, allowing only the subject to show through.

If the customer does not like what the studio has to offer, other frames are available in the market and from the sign painters. Sign painters make very popular frames by painting a design and a proverb in English or Yoruba on the back of a sheet glass while leaving room for one or more postcard-size photographs to show through.

This brief introduction to Yoruba photography suggests some broader implications and questions.[11] One of the first questions that might be asked is why certain groups in West Africa, like the Yoruba, have integrated photography into their cultures, while other groups, such as the Hausa, appear to make little use of the medium.[12] It is suggested that societies with a strong tradition of figurative art, such as the Yoruba, have aesthetic values and a need for representation that could be satisfied and understood in a photograph. For example, the Yoruba were initially introduced to the medium of photography by the British, whose photographic portraits appeared to display values important to the Yoruba. This made the usefulness of the photography immediately apparent. On the other hand, societies such as the Hausa, which have a more abstract aesthetic tradition involving decorative pattern and design, would have less use for, or even understanding of, the photographic image. Also, any society that has a long history of dominant Muslim influence, again the Hausa, would be less likely to make use of the medium because of the strong Muslim prohibition against graven images, which specifically includes photographs. Another important consideration is that a society with an economic system that could accommodate the commissioning and production of photographs would be more likely to make use of the medium. The Yoruba have a long history of urbanization with a developed tradition of individual enterprise in the production of goods and the marketing of specialized skills.

The large number of photographs available from individual Yorubas and from photographers' negative files form a vast visual data bank that is unique because it has been generated entirely by members of a non-Western culture. This material might be utilized in a number of ways. The most obvious would be simply to study the subject matter of photographs available in a particular community in order to discover the existence of people, ceremonies, events, and even objects and masquerades, which otherwise might not be known. Copies of these photographs could be used to elicit more information from other members of the community.

More importantly, as this essay has shown, these photographs are "coded in Yoruba" and can also give us much information about how the Yoruba see themselves; about their cultural values and their view of the world. But understanding all the implications of this wealth of visual information will not be easy. A coherent methodology does not exist for extracting cultural and historical data from even our own heritage of family snapshots and anonymous photographs, and the formulation of a methodology for interpreting the photographic heritage of a non-Western society has never been attempted as far as I am aware. One hopes that continued investigation will eventually lead not only to a better knowledge of the Yoruba view of themselves, but also to a better cross-cultural understanding of how we communicate through mediated visual images of the world, and to the formulation of a methodology to deal with these images.

NOTES

1　*Abiku* means, literally, "we are born to die." Children who are discovered to be *abiku* must be paid special ritual attention in order to keep them in this world; otherwise they will surely die and return to their spirit world. See "The Concept of Abiku" (Mobolade 1973) for more information.

2　I would like to thank the photographers in Ila-Orangun, and especially Sir Special Photo, for their cooperation in providing information and in allowing me access to their negative files.

3　Newspaper photographers in the cities have adapted a more candid journalistic approach, but their range of subject matter is much the same, predominantly people at ceremonial or other newsworthy events. Many news photographs typical of Western papers, such as accidents, disasters, or action pictures of sports, seldom appear.

4　I am particularly indebted to the thinking and research of Sol Worth, who in his book *Through Navajo Eyes* (Worth & Adair 1972) has demonstrated that members of a culture or subculture who learn to use a new medium of communication (in this case, film) will produce work that is structured in part by their own cultural values and by their culture's perception of the world.

5   This describes the ideal form; sometimes the figure will be cut by the edge of the frame, and occasionally the subject will be smiling. Although minor variations are common, the traditional formal portrait always maintains its distinct identity.

6   Many types of nineteenth-and early twentieth-century British photographic portraits were looked at in detail. This included the work of artistic photographers such as Julia Margaret Cameron (Gernsheim 1975), commercial studio photographs (Hillier 1976), and colonial British photographs of India (Aperture 1976).

7   The concept of the memorial pages may have been adapted from the obituaries in the *London Daily Times*. But the emphasis on the photograph, the brief tribute in different type faces, and the de-emphasis on text mark this as a distinct form.

8   Betty Wass (1975) has shown that Yoruba dress, as depicted in 600 photographs dating from 1900–74, does relate to the event photographed and to the social position and education of the subject, and that the percentage of indigenous dress increases from 1900 to 1974 as a function of increased national consciousness and pride.

9   The full results of this research were presented by Houlberg in a paper, "Image and Inquiry: Photography and Film in the Study of Yoruba Art and Religion" (Houlberg 1976b). The profile portrait rejected by the priestess was selected for publication in *The 1973 World Book Yearbook* (p. 95).

10 Additional photographs taken by me and by the Yoruba photographers of Ila-Orangun, along with a brief statement of methodology, are being published as a photographic essay entitled "How I See the Yoruba See Themselves" (Sprague in press). These photographs visually present the main point of this present paper as well as show more of the photographers themselves, their studios, and the display of photographs within the context of the community.

11 A week of searching throughout Kano, a predominantly Hausa area, revealed very few photographic studios or photographs on display. When questioned about this, Hausa traders repeatedly said that I must go to the Yoruba area of Kano, that all of the photographers were either Yoruba or Ibo.

REFERENCES

Aperture Books. 1976. *The Last Empire: Photography in British India 1855–1911*. Millerton, NY.

Awooner-Williams, George. 1967. "Songs of Sorrow," *West African Verse*, annotated by Donatus Ibe Nwoga. London: Longman Press.

Bensusan, A. D. 1966. *Silver Images: The History of Photography In Africa*. Capetown: Howard Timmons.

Charles, David. 1938. *The Camera In Commerce*. London: Pitman Greenwood.

Field Educational Enterprises. 1973. *The 1973 World Book Yearbook*. Chicago.

Gernsheim, Helmut. 1975. *Julia Margaret Cameron*. Millerton, NY: Aperture.

Hillier, Bevis. 1976. *Victorian Studio Photographs*. Boston: David Godine Publisher.

Houlberg, Marilyn. 1973. "Ibeji Images of the Yoruba," *African Arts* 7, 1.

——. 1976a. "Collecting the Anthropology of African Art," *African Arts* 9, 3.

——. 1976b. "Image and Inquiry: Photography and Film in the Study of Yoruba Art and Religion," paper given at the panel "Methods in Visual Anthropology – Recent Research in Yoruba Art and Religion," 19th annual meeting of the African Studies Association, Boston, (Nov.).

Mobolade, Timothy. 1973. "The Concept of Abiku," *African Arts* 7, 1.

Schiltz, Marc. 1978. "Egungun Masquerades in Iganna," *African Arts* 11, 3.

Sprague, Stephen F. in press. "How I See the Yoruba See Themselves," *Studies in the Anthropology of Visual Communication* 5, 1.

Thompson, Robert. 1971. "Aesthetics in Tradition Africa," *Art and Aesthetics in Primitive Societies*, edited by C. Jopling. Dutton.

Wass, Betty M. 1975. "Communicative Aspects of the Dress of Yoruba: A Case Study of Five Generations of a Lagos Family," paper presented at the panel "The Social Significance and Aesthetics of African Dress," 18th annual meeting of the African Studies Association, San Francisco (Nov.).

Westerman, D. 1939. *The African Today and Tomorrow*, quoted in *Yoruba Culture*, by G.J.A. Ojo (1966, p. 200). University of Ife and University of London Press.

Worth, Sol and John Adair. 1972. *Through Navaho Eyes*. Bloomington: Indiana University Press.

12

Relationships

Daniel Miller and Don Slater

A recent advertising campaign for a British beer company proclaimed that real men go out to the pub and relate to females, not just to emails. It reflected a widespread assumption (shared by some academics) that the Internet generates a culture of 'nerds' who substitute virtual relationships for 'real' ones, a charge that is inadequately met by the opposite argument that virtual relationships are themselves real. The opposition of real and virtual in both cases completely misses the complexity and diversity of relationships that people may pursue through the communicative media that they embed in their ongoing social lives. The point is made clearly by thinking back historically to the times when 'old (media) technologies were new' (Marvin 1988). Worries about the reality of telephone or telegraph relationships and their impact on 'real' (i.e. face-to-face ones) may have been rampant at the time of their introduction (Stein 1999), but it is no surprise that the bulk of present-day telephone advertising can take it for granted that the telephone is widely accepted as a means of enhancing and developing relationships, not for replacing them. Where public concern re-emerges – as with the introduction of mobile phones – it is articulated in far less global, far more contextualized terms.

Hence, we will pursue the present discussion as if the Internet technologies were older, reflecting the alacrity with which Trinidadians have indeed embedded them in relationships, ignoring the issue of 'real' versus 'virtual'. This is particularly evident in looking at the family, especially the diaspora family, with which we begin. The second section examines the use of the Internet in friendships, including those that develop into love and marriage, and the third section deals with the immediate spaces in which Internet use and relationships take place, using as examples our studies of cybercafés and of Internet use amongst schoolchildren. Finally, in the conclusion some of this evidence will be considered in terms of the history and theory of Trinidadian society.

From Diaspora Family to Internet Family

Prior to the arrival of the Internet, the family was indeed under threat as the core institution of social life in Trinidad. The Caribbean family is highly distinctive, as is indicated by the anthropological literature discussed in the conclusion to this chapter.

Most anthropological accounts have been conservative in emphasizing continuities or a well-established normativity in expectations about the family. To understand the use of the Internet, however, we need to focus on a radical disruption that has been of huge importance for more than a generation: the impact of widespread Caribbean emigration on the Trinidadian family (see Basch, Glick Schiller and Szanton Blanc 1994; Chamberlain 1998; Ho 1991). Migration from Trinidad has been very extensive, even if it has not matched other Caribbean contexts where the majority of those who identify with an island now live abroad (e.g. Olwig 1993). Miller (1994: 21) found in his earlier survey that in the majority of families at least one member at the nuclear level (that is either parents, siblings or children) was living abroad. Therefore the following discussion of the use of the Internet by diasporic families[1] actually applies to the vast majority of Trinidadian families overall.

Email was taken up readily as an intuitive, pleasurable, effective and above all inexpensive way not only for families to be in touch, but to be in touch on an intimate, regular, day-to-day basis that conforms to commonly held expectations of what being a parent, child or family entails. It appeared as an obvious way of realizing familial roles and responsibilities that had been ruptured by Diaspora, and even of reactivating familial ties that had fallen into abeyance. Email contrasted on the one hand with letter-writing, which was seen as proverbially problematic to Trinis (perhaps the most common generalization people made during fieldwork was that 'Trinidadians hate writing letters') and stymied by what was regarded as an inefficient postal service. In practice letter-writing was important to some of those living in the UK, but they were a minority.

On the other hand, while the phone has dominated contact amongst family members it was viewed as inordinately expensive. It tended to be associated with less frequent use and therefore with a very different temporality, appropriate for the exchange of news rather than casual communication. Telephones were also considered to be more suitable than email for special occasions and lifetime events such as births, marriages, deaths and other rites of passage, but as far too expensive for enacting what are held to be the more 'Trini' forms of communication, involving liming, banter and ole talk, which were pleasurably performed through email and chat, where time could flow more naturally without an eye on the phone bill. But this connects to a wider sense of why email and chat could so easily serve the purposes of re-establishing normal or normative family relations: conversation could be mundane, everyday, intimate in a household way, in both style and content. Internet communication could shift contact from once a month to three times a week. This was sufficient to turn these into quite different types of relationship, because of the sense of the present it allowed. Email could allow constant, taken-for-granted communication, engaged in without great thought. It was informal or playful in style, and filled with everyday trivia (what we had for dinner, or bought at the shop, or who said what to whom) or with nothing much at all except a sharing of each other's 'voices'. Email could also encompass the exchange of mundane 'objects' such as scanned photos, addresses of websites the other might like, jokes found online and forwarded to a family member with the thought – clearly expressed by informants – of bringing a familiar smile to the other's face. Indeed, it was rare for people to talk about email without a smile.

This use of email extended into the hugely popular practice of sending each other e-greetings or virtual postcards (as well as electronic flowers and chocolates). This applied to many relationships besides family ones. Websites offering greeting card services were amongst the most frequently visited by Trinidadians, who invested a lot of time in finding ones that were animated, multimedia or simply unusual, often sentimental. This use of cards was interesting not only as an extension of a long Trini tradition, but also in making explicit the latent sense that an email was in some ways itself a gift, though one that could be offered at any time, not merely special occasions. And yet it demanded a response, and therefore created the conditions for sustaining relationships through reciprocity (see Carrier 1995; Mauss 1954).

Approximately half the Trinidadians we contacted in the UK primarily used the Internet for such mundane and constant email contact with their families. Given the nature of the diaspora this could as well be family living outside Trinidad as within. If only one side of the family had online access they often exerted considerable pressure on the other end of the family also to go online, in some cases buying and sending the equipment. For example, several older people came into one of our ethnographic sites (a little shop with an online computer) brandishing letters from relatives abroad instructing them to set up an email account, and giving their own address. Someone in the shop (sometimes one of us) would help them register on a web-based email site. The ability to engage in routine contact through the Internet had two primary effects: the first was to re-establish the kinds of family contact that would have existed in a non-diaspora context and the second was sometimes to actually expand the family as a viable unit of sociality. Ann-Marie may exemplify the first point. Perhaps the important relationship that emerges in Trinidadian discussions of the family is mother–daughter relations, and the sundering of these in the diaspora family had often been a cause of anxiety, especially for the mothers. But with the Internet Ann-Marie reports the following norms of contact:

Q: So your mother emails you every day? What kinds of things does she talk about?
A: Nag.
Q: What kinds of things does she nag you about?
A: Motherly things – like eat properly, dress well and she checks out everyday the weather in London. And she would say all right you are going to have a little bit of sun next week. And then she will talk about whatever she has done. . . . My dad is not into it at all, you will not get a letter from him at all. But Mummy she is home and she got time to sit down.
Q: How long has she been doing this for?
A: For a year. She likes to know everything that is going on so she can tell you how to take your vitamins and how to do this. It is almost as if you are talking all the time because she is always giving advice, she would do a paragraph at a time.

Others who reported such regular connections with parents revealed how this reconstructed the common ambivalence of living together as a family. For example a UK-based student noted on the one hand:

By speaking to my family every week, I do feel that they still have quite a strong hold on me. I feel that they do need to know where I am and what I'm doing. For instance I wanted to quit my Ph.D. about six months ago. I felt that I needed to consult them as it was common that I did when it came to big decisions. They were not very happy about the decision and used the guilt factor to make me continue. I'm still doing the Ph.D.

On the other hand a moment later she notes: 'I do feel that it's keeping them close and despite differences in opinions at times, I don't feel alone here in England knowing that I could contact them at any time.' Just as when people are actually living together within a household, parents could be regarded as oppressive and constraining, but this coexisted with the sense that one had returned – thanks to the Internet – to the security and support of this fundamental family relationship. It was also not uncommon for the relationship to work the other way around, so that a Trinidadian parent who had left her or his child in Trinidad used the Internet to continue to provide support to their children, though in most cases returning at times when more support was required, such as exam-taking. The Internet assuaged some of the problems and sense of guilt of leaving the children behind, since it made possible a new mediated parenting.

The impact of the Internet is not restricted to the nuclear family. In the case of the extended family, and in particular in relationships between cousins, there is the possibility not only of repairing the rupture caused by emigration, but also long-term relationships between cousins are made viable in a way they had not been before. For example George has settled in the UK for many years, but keeps in contact through the Internet:

A: The only person I contact with in Trinidad is my cousin. Every weekend Saturday 5 p.m. in UK time we hook up and have a little chat. . . . We speak for about three hours. All my aunts and cousins and everybody coming down. They want to speak to this one, that one. I will call my cousins and they will come to him. They are of the same household. But everyone will speak. Some of my cousins who can't afford PCs in Trinidad will come on weekends and have a little chat.

Q: So you are quite close with that family?

A: Yes. What we do as well is that all of the cousins, I got most of my cousins as well in Canada, we do link up together on weekends and all of us have a little family reunion every week. It's just an hour. Just a family thing.

As in this case it was common for an online relative to then communicate news to other relatives who are not online. Group cousin chatting could also take place through chat sites: 'I met six of them and we chatted. We were on the chat site for about three hours on a Sunday. It was quite good though – everybody use a different colour.' As well as this collective sense of family, cousins were also very often the 'friends' one confided in, confidants for discussing intimate problems such as reactions to the death of a relative. Equally for those in Trinidad the most common use of the Internet for contacting people abroad was related to aunts, uncles and cousins. Of course not every cousin turns out to be a natural friend. As a UK-based Trinidadian noted: 'Stephen would send email, but he has got a weird sense of porno-graphic humour, I do not reply. I don't even open the attachment because I did once and I said O God! He sent about a hundred disgusting jokes.'

In general Trinidadians found that their 'cousinhood' is now viable as a much larger phenomenon, bringing back into the fold relatives that would not otherwise have been included. Discovery of a cousin in New York they had not heard from in ten years would re-create the relationship, or on returning for Carnival they might meet a cousin settled in Japan who had also returned to Trinidad. They would then exchange email addresses and strike up the relationship on their return to their respective homes. It is possible that these contacts will decline as the cousins grow up, just as one would expect in the conventional developmental cycle of the domestic group. It is also possible that one result of the Internet will be a longer maintenance of such relationships, since the factors that often break up 'cousinhoods', such as moving away, will no longer have the same effect. However, the time depth of our study is too shallow for confident predictions.

The possibilities for actually expanding the family were most dramatically illustrated by George:

A: Both my parents split up 28 years ago. I had contact with my Mom but I never had contact with my Dad. Twenty-eight years and I never knew what he look like, I never knew where he was, what he did, or anything. And through the Internet I decided, I saw these search engines. So I was going to fiddle around and see to try and get a worldwide one, which there wasn't. Then I thought America is the biggest country on the Internet. I'll try a search there. I came up with nothing. I then tried one in Canada, and half an hour later I came up with 25 names and I thought every week I would send out one letter and see what happens. So the first name I pick from the list and four days later, about four o'clock in the morning the phone rang, and it was my Dad. He couldn't believe it himself, I couldn't believe it too. I thought it was a joke or something. But what happened about this letter I send out. I sent a photo of me and I send a photo of him. His wife phones me back, and that caused a bit of problem there.
Q: She never knew...?
A: She never knew if I existed. That was a shock to her.
Q: So he is in Canada?
A: He is in Canada. He phones me every two weeks.
Q: So he phoned you first to check it out?
A: She phoned me and she thought it was a joke as well. Because she is looking at my photo and she is looking at his photo and she is saying to me where did you get this photo from? This is my son and this is his Dad. I said no, it isn't. That's me and that's my Dad and she thought it was a hoax and I thought she was a hoax as well.
Q: Did you ever meet?
A: We met last year. One of my brothers or sisters were suppose to come but financially they weren't able to. I think I am going to make an effort go across to them actually.

Internet use by the elderly is more rarely encountered but is perhaps an important pointer to the future. One example was a widow who seemed to have lost much of her reason for living when her husband died. In order to keep in touch with a particularly close grandchild who had gone abroad, she was persuaded to educate herself in Internet use. Subsequently she contacted many other relatives abroad and in Trinidad, and has taken to the net to such a degree that the younger members of her family swear it has given her 'a new lease of life'. This might offer a partial resolution to the increasingly common problem of elderly people who had previously tended to live in the homes of their descendants but are now being encouraged to live by themselves: the Internet keeps the new physical separation but in some other respects can keep them in the heart of family life. However, this is currently rare, and there are worries that the effective family might become restricted to those that are online, which would particularly exclude the elderly. On the other hand, a UK Trini noted that although the Internet tended to determine which of his cousins he continues to be close to, it would in no way affect the close personal relationship he has with his grandmother, who happens not to be online.

Friends and Partners

In contrast to family relationships, friendships, acquaintances, and chat partners point to less well-defined relationships that can be more ambiguous when pursued online. Establishing their character and status as relationships may need more reflection, since they may take novel forms that have to be assessed in terms of new normative concepts of friendship. Moreover, in addition to being a means for pursuing established relationships (school friends, boy-and girlfriends, colleagues), the Internet – particularly chat and ICQ – routinely opens up the possibility of engaging online with people from anywhere in the world whom one has not and probably will not meet face-to-face; and these contacts are likely to be made through interests or even through random meetings and coincidences.

The situation is made more complicated by the dynamics of Internet mediation. People tend to experience the Internet as a battery of related but separate possibilities for pursuing relationships, which they assemble in different ways according to their particular preferences. One individual who has his own personal website abhors the use of chat-lines and makes all his new friendships through signing the guestbooks of personal web-pages that happen to appeal to him. He will make a comment about that website, and hope for a reply from which further contact can ensue. Another uses chat but hates using email, while a third only uses email and extends his range of contacts by being put in touch with friends of his current email friends. Sometimes this is just conservatism; an individual is 'taught' one method, takes to it, and is resistant to alternatives. A UK Trini suggested that he continued to phone friends where the relationship predates the Internet, but emails those who have become friends through the Internet, though this was a rare distinction.

Chat and ICQ, however, are the Internet media that were most fashionable in pursuing relationships, and ones that corresponded more to what we have called 'expansive potential' than to the 'expansive realization' that marked family relationships. Especially for the young within Trinidad, Internet chat and ICQ marked their entry into an expanded possibility of new encounters, including immediate, unexpected and volatile styles of encounter. Chat can be used as a straightforward extension of pre-existing relationships, or of ones related to the immediate locale (as with the schoolchildren discussed below), or it can be a vehicle for developing relationships that were initially made on ICQ itself. Or it can be a mixture, as in the case of one teenage informant who carried with him a list of fifty ICQ friends, most of them from other parts of Trinidad but all first encountered online, some of whom he then met offline, some not. ICQ software includes the ability to make lists of ICQ contacts and categorize them as one wishes (e.g., home versus away, work versus personal), a feature that recognizes the desire to be flexible in ordering, or even separating out, the variety of possible relationships.

In fact, many people claimed that they only put a very few people on their lists. This generally indicates that people make strong distinctions about which relationships are valuable and therefore should be closely integrated into their online activities, and which are not. This distinction – which we encountered across many observations and interviews – was closely tied to the issue of time, of dividing online relationships between those considered short, casual and 'light' and those that are more serious, enduring and emotionally weighty. This tallied very closely with Slater's (1998) previous observations of 'trading sexpics on IRC': chat comprises a larger number of short-term casual encounters, which can be exciting, interesting, boring or lunatic, but are treated as relatively weightless as relationships. They may be valued and sought for many reasons, but they are in a different category from the serious relationships into which a very few of them will develop, which are characterized by the kinds of trust, investment and intimacy that are only possible over a longer term: 'Every time you go online, you'll always find some crazy fool out there, talking rubbish...there for theirself, just to be on the net, that's all they're there for. You talk shit to them and that's about it but you don't take them on, you don't get down to anything. With a long-standing relationship you talk to them for *looooooong*, [i.e.] you start to share stuff between each other.' In Trini chat, just as in the chat studied by Slater, 'long term' is not necessarily all that long in comparison to offline relationships of a similar seriousness. Because of the dynamic character of these social settings and because of their intensity, three months is very good going, but this might mean three months of spending as many hours of the day as possible locked into the highly internalized modality of chat. This intensity also means that chat very much takes place in the moment: people frequently talk about current relationships as if they were several years rather than weeks old, while earlier similar relationships are all but forgotten.

Short-term encounters of a largely random nature are primarily a form of mutual entertainment. Their essential characteristic – that the other person could turn out to be more or less anyone, and one can never know – already gives it something of the *frisson* of gambling. In addition it commonly has the additional *frisson* of sexual banter. While this is no difference in principle from non-Trini chat (again see Slater 1998) the role of flirtation and sexual language in Trini culture (see Yelvington 1996) gives it a very particular salience for Trinis who use it. While some users will talk to same-sex others, most readily admit that almost all their chat is with opposite-sex others (reflecting a pervasive assumption of heterosexuality offline). For example a man notes he chats to: 'Mostly women! The only time I would chat to men is when I want information on music, games and stuff. When I want to download something from the Net and they might know where it is.' Once a partner has been located then the encounter sets up a challenge where there is relatively little to lose, given the cover of anonymity, but much to be gained:

Yes, you learn a lot from them, especially the different types of expression for stuff....It's like when you go on, the first time, uh talking to a female over the Net, it's kind a like if you meet a female on the street, uh tackling her. You're not seeing what she looks like unless you have video conferencing, but she sounds good. What she said really catches your attention and you're able to hold that attention. It's kinda like a thrill, the longer you could talk to this person, keep them excited as well as they keep you excited and sometimes the things they say to you, well....It surprised me the first time. After a while I started to get used to it.

Quite apart from this art of banter, at which Trinis know they are particularly proficient, for many users the experience of playful sexuality is clearly a major part of the pay-off of the time spent online, even if some of the stories are apocryphal:

There was one time we actually got a girl sent us twelve different video clippings of her while she was talking and then she started to take off her clothes. She stopped when she reached half way. And I bet you it was real. There are chances it might not have been real but it was fun. It's like you being able to do what you want and knowing that the person doesn't have to know who you are, because you could never meet them at all.

For women, in particular, however, there is the problem that Trinidadian forms of sexual banter can be quite different from many of the societies of those they are chatting with, so the scope for being misconstrued is endless. A girl who went by the 'nick' Miss Sexy simply could not see why she kept having such problems:

I know, it does: it simply does attract a lot of people, because basically most of them come on and say 'what your name goes with, why are you calling yourself Miss Sexy?' and I simply tell them, that to me, I'm very beautiful and to me, I think I'm sexy, but it's nothing more than that. Most of them think I want to do stuff. I simply said, no my name is not Miss Sexy, just my nickname 'cause I'm friendly, I'm kind-hearted and understanding. Basically I want to chat with them, and there where the conversation goes they find I'm intelligent and what they think I was with my nickname is not what I am.

While sex dominated, there are other concerns in short-term chat. These include simply the interest in each new person. For example, 'every time I go on ICQ it's somebody new, something new, some different story, some guy claims he's having family problems or with some woman, this sort of thing. Each time I get ICQ it is a unique story.' There is also a kind of mediated but personal tourism, where the interest is in meeting people from different countries and learning about the countries. More female chatters seem to follow this route, and they often seem particularly interested in interweaving it with discussions about personal problems such as dealing with their parents. The result confirms for them the general sense that 'underneath our differences we are all the same', so that an aura of global sentimentality can be one product of these kinds of encounter.

Given the 'lightness' of these short-term encounters, when did Trinidadians ascribe them 'weight'? We argue that 'virtuality' needs to be treated as a social accomplishment rather than an analytical assumption, that we need to understand when, why and how particular people come to treat online relationships as 'real' or not. Slater has previously argued that, in the apparently extremely disembedded context of 'sexpics trading on IRC', this was crucially related to the ways in which one could establish sufficient trust in the authenticity of the other to warrant the risk of investing in them emotionally, and that this was related to the persistence of the other's online presence over time, as well as to ways in which they could be 'embodied' through encountering them through additional media.

Similar dynamics were clearly at play in Trinidadian chat relationships, and a range of social and technical possibilities were used to sort out which relationships mattered and how they should be conducted. Firstly, just as with email in a family context, there was a great stress on sharing a mundane life with the other both on- and offline. That is to say, people could spend a great deal of very intense time chatting online, over the course of which they felt that the other had a clear idea of their daily lives, thoughts and attitudes. One informant, Jason, had some unusually long-lasting relationships (one of over two years' duration), which he placed at the same level as face-to-face relationships on the basis that they knew him well, were stitched into his everyday life and had been tried and tested over time by a variety of means:

A: Yeah I would say I take them seriously. 'Cos they ask me, how ya going today? They knew when my baby was born. They all got the news that my baby was born – send cards of congratulations, everything. When I go online they say, how's ya baby going today? What's she doing da? It's like regular people, regular conversations . . . they're just a part of your friendship group: you still consider them the way you consider the friends who you see everyday.

Q: They feel part of your everyday life?

A: Yeah – also part of your everyday life, 'cos basically I get an email from them every day, chat with them every day . . .

This sharing of mundane life included everyday exchanges of electronic jokes, pictures, e-greetings and postcards, electronic boxes of chocolates and bouquets of flowers that people scoured the net to find for their friends. Sites for e-greetings were amongst those most commonly visited by Trinidadians, and are offered by Trinidadian companies and found on Trinidadian portal sites. These new electronic gifts are indeed new material forms that constitute relationships in new ways: that is to say, they should be treated seriously as mediations or material culture (Jaffe 1999). Virtual postcards, as noted, extend to the Internet the immense and long-term popularity of such cards in Trinidadian society generally. However, in going online, postcards have now slipped out of their previous more formal frame of being used for marked events and special occasions. They have become a regular means for maintaining general contact, acquiring – like email – the informality of a gesture or spontaneous moment of acknowledging the other. Moreover, people seek out cards with animations, music or other such accompaniments so that they can also feel they are part of a 'coolhunt', and they accept the gift of cool (one teenager talked with zest about the recent receipt of 'the frog in the blender swimming, and he's insulting you and you have to press each knob on the blender and in the end, it just blend him up . . . cool!').

Stitching the other into a shared everyday world rapidly extends to the sharing of intimacies, problems, perspectives and values, so that you not only feel that the other really knows you, and vice versa, but also that they are reliably 'there for you' as a persistent and embodied ethical other.

Q: How much do you value a [long-term] relationship like that; how real does it feel?
A: You have to think about how well you know the person, what you talk about, things like that . . . . We exchange ideas about what's going on in her life and what's going on in my life, and we put together what we think about it and how it should be and how it shouldn't be. We learn from each other.
Q: So part of being a real relationship is getting into real issues?
A: Real issues, yeah. Because I tell her what's up with me and she tells me what's with her. I know her family, what's going on with her. How she handles going to school and her family, being with them. Her mum is separated from her Dad so she tells me how different her life is from living with her Dad from living with her mum cos I'm the same, I'm living with my Dad and I told her about it.
Q: You feel she understands you and shares your values? You trust it?
A: Yes, everything, yes.

People could describe this sharing in nearly therapeutic terms, as in the case of one woman who actually was a counsellor and transferred her listening skills and values to ICQ.

This intimacy can be treated and treasured as something that is largely detached from offline consequences and costs and at the same time differentiated from 'the usual stupidness' of casual chat encounters. Although we encountered almost no talk that corresponded to cyberutopian expectations about a radical break between offline and online identities, Jason talked about his serious online relationships through a notion of 'just communicating':

A: Sometimes it's more meaningful, right, 'cos they know you're not taking them on any other level but the mind, it's like a kinda brain to brain kinda thing . . . yeah, just communicating, looking out for each other. Talking, being friends, without the hangups.

Q: So there's almost something pure about it?
A: Yeah, yeah [he agrees with that]. That's the exact term: there is something pure about it.

The nature of the 'impurities' from which his serious chat relations released him in order to be treated as 'real' relationships were quite clear:

A: Even though we try not to be, we all have our prejudices, right, and there will be people who automatically on sight you see them and you categorize them. On the Internet it is not like that. Right. Especially the chat sites or whatever: you actually see into people's minds, their personalities, right there.
Q: But you can be wrong about people, taken in by them?
A: If you're stupid, yeah. You are what you type. Especially the way people type in the chat groups you could actually get a hint of their accents, of the way they speak, everything from the way they type, the word structures, everything. You got good feeling for people. And you know if they are lying, hands down – 'cos a lot of them saying, well I am 5'11″, the usual stupidity. But when you get, like you meet people seriously, and ya talking to them, it's a whole different level. You don't consider what they look like, whatever: it's a mind-to-mind contact kind of thing. It's entirely different, and you actually find yourself making a good few friends online. 'Cos I got four or five people that I can really kick with regularly. And I just met them over the net.

Jason – like most people who take seriously any online relationship – felt he had reliable strategies and instincts for assessing these relationships. In fact he was pragmatic in sorting out the real – trustworthy, serious, weighty – relationships, and therefore in deciding where to place his trust:

But the way I'm made up, I always give everybody, no matter who, right, that comes into my space and touch my life, they always get a chance to screw me up – but they only get one chance to screw me up. You tell me this and you say this is the truth, I take it as ok. But when you're online and you're getting to learn somebody you do proceed with a little more caution. In this case you can see somebody's eyes and you know – well yeah, he lying to me, or – he pulling a fast one. Online you track what they say – me, I track what they say. The trust comes from normal banter, because when you first meet somebody online you're usually talking some stupidness or the other. You're not really into anything serious. Most of the times it's a lot easier to trust someone online because they can't hurt you as much as someone who you trust face to face.

Finally, Jason not only sorted the light from the heavy relationships, but he placed them in quite different ethical universes of responsibility and commitment. As we have argued previously, the issue here is in no sense a distinction between the 'real' and the 'virtual', but rather the ways in which Jason chose to frame online relationships as significant and what consequences he then attached to them:

The thing is when they say stuff, say in the general chat rooms, etc., stuff is said, whatever goes. But when you're on a one-on-one with somebody, and [when] you get past the bullshit and the jokes, people really reveal a lot of their soul to you. And you are entrusted to keep what you have there as sacred property, 'cos they share a piece of theirselves with you. And if you sharing you expect that they return the sentiment, and they do.

Whereas Jason tended to see chat relationships as a potentially very pure form of what he valued in offline relationships, a surprising number of people framed special chat relationships as very literal forms of the most conventional primary relationships. They talked to us of boyfriends or girlfriends or even fiancées who turned out to be entirely online correspondents living in another part of the world. In an even more surprising number of cases we could confirm that these relationships, formed through random chat encounters, had in fact been pursued into serious offline encounters, including living together or marrying. For example, in one family visited, the daughter, a university student, had met a Buddhist from Brazil online. The relationship developed, and the Brazilian twice visited Trinidad; but finally the religious divide from the staunchly Catholic daughter proved too great a barrier to a permanent relationship. While the daughter has since fallen in love with a Trinidadian, she has also managed to develop a sufficiently deep friendship with a Danish male that he also planned to visit her in Trinidad. So common is this kind of occurrence that we would predict that for the young the tradition of anonymous tourism may increasingly be replaced by holidays being taken on the basis of a previous long-term Internet-based friendship.

Serious relationships and indeed marriage developed from online meetings. These can be framed in quite diverse ways, as could be seen in the case of several relationships within one family. The mother had actually married an American whom she originally met online. However, she still not only expressed worry about the online relationships that her children were concurrently developing, but also doubted the reality and seriousness of their relationships as opposed to hers. She pointed out that although there were several months of purely online communication before she met her husband face to face, she did not and would not characterize it as friendship, let alone as developing on to love, until they had actually met in person. It was not 'real', and there was too much possibility for deception. In this and other respects, such as her distaste at the very idea of cybersex, she clearly distanced her own actions from her children's, who fell in love and got serious without meeting the persons concerned. A further irony here was that her children's practice was condemned mainly on the basis of her own ideals, that a couple should live together before marriage. It seemed in talking to her own children separately that one of them had internalized his mother's strictures and was clear that the eight-month relationship he had had online was only to be understood within the confines of the medium. It was also clear that his brother and sister were much less constrained or influenced by her scepticism, and saw their online relationships in terms of love and possible marriage. This is a clear example of the different ways in which people can construct or assess the 'virtual'; not as an assumed property of Internet relations but as a criterion by which they understand them.

On the same day and at the same cybercafé at which these interviews were conducted, an 18-year-old girl had just announced to us that she was getting engaged to a man in Australia whom she had never met, on the basis of almost daily ICQ contact supplemented by occasional phone calls to him and to his parents. As one of the company pointed out, it is 'mostly girls and those who are rather sheltered at home. You know they have problems, they don't agree with their parents, and they are looking for getting out of the house and maybe out of the country.' It was implicit that this remark particularly applied to Indian girls living in the local villages. As in this case, such relationships could be unusually public in their development. Another large group reported eagerly awaiting the first visit to Trinidad of one of their friend's ICQ correspondents from Dominica, and their delight when the couple subsequently married.

Sometimes these relationships start as unintended consequences of short-term random chats, with conversations about their respective countries and common popular culture leading to an exchange of photographs, and then a mixture of flirting and discussing personal problems. In most such cases the Trinidadians have a clear normative model of how such relationships should develop, and a rich language to describe this. Their correspondents are commonly accused of being too *maco* (nosy) or too *fass* (fast); they give one the horrors and fail to keep cool. In short Trinidadians do not like people who come on too fast and too strong. Many users had stories about dropping people from chatlists because they were incapable of taking things at the pace the Trinis wanted. On the other hand there are some who go online with the specific intention of looking for long-term rather than short-term relationships, which they expressly state on the information forms attached to their names on ICQ. Since already many Trinidadians know of others who have found partners this way, the Internet has quickly become a specific option for those in search of love, with the additional implication of leaving for another country through marriage. This is a possibility that many Trinidadians, young and old, view with what might be termed an interested ambivalence. Another option is to establish long-term online relationships without either partner's having any particular expectation of this ever turning into a face-to-face relationship.

Once established, these relationships can have many of the characteristics of any other long-term relationships. When those involved discuss them, often with rich details about quarrels and making up and issues of different degrees of commitment, it is very hard to discern any tangible difference from their discussion of offline relationships. When a woman storms into the room in a fury of 'God that man drives me to . . .', the man in question may be in the room she has just stepped out of; but equally he may be on the screen in that room. Sometimes there is an online version of a common offline scenario. For example, one woman noted that: 'I have this boyfriend and I caught him sweet-talking somebody else in a next chat room. I dumped him. I don't remember her name, but I found him out. Well, I tell him it's over. I stop talking to him.'

This implies that those involved do not perceive as problematic what to outsiders might be the 'obvious' constraints of online romance. This is important not only in new relationships with those living abroad, but also to ongoing relationships between Trinidadians. Internet use in respect of long-term friendships follows a similar pattern to that with relatives: partly recovery, partly maintenance, partly expansion. Indeed, there is a close similarity in the use of the Internet to 'repair' the specific problem of relationships that would have been sundered when one partner went abroad to study and the other remained at home. A common speculation was that a particular relationship would have subsequently broken up, but thanks to the Internet was maintained until the couple could be together again. It was very common for those who had not gone online while at school to purchase a first computer or to go to a cybercafé when their school friends went abroad to study or work. So here the Internet comes across as the saving of such relationships. For example, a married couple had known each other since they were fifteen, but had had to spend three years apart, as she was in the UK and he remained in Trinidad. During this time they would email every day, and go on a chat line every two or three days. As they noted this was: 'Fantastic. It was more effective than a phone call. It was harder to say goodbye than when I was on the phone. Strange enough, it was as good as actually sitting down and talking to the person. When you are on the phone you just don't get that sort of . . . probably because we write and that sort of triggers off all the emotions. We get more time to think, I guess.'

This was a rare statement; most couples wanted to complement their online chat with telephone calls, and ideally with visits. This was a clear difference from short-term use, where the other is viewed specifically as an online correspondent. But for long-term relationships the medium does not define the partner; rather, it is merely the means by which the partner is encountered. Some users never seem to be that comfortable with chat and email as a means to express deep emotions; but it is striking that most users have quickly taken these new media for granted as entirely appropriate for expressing emotions, running the gamut of love, anger, jealousy, guilt, and intimacy. This is evident not only from discussing online relationships, but also from watching people online getting riled by but also intensely involved in their communications, or waiting around in agitation (particularly at cybercafés) when there is a technical problem that delays them from finding out if the significant he/she has left a message.

Chat and ICQ lend themselves to floating and unstable populations; ICQ encounters are commonly fleeting. However, within the institutional facilities created to make chat possible there are provisions for photographic and personal archives and message boards, which may be used to support relationships in a more enduring, visible and material form. A more formal and perhaps more socially consequential example of this would be the lists of alumni posted on their websites by some of the prestige schools. These often list names, email addresses, websites and graduation years of any school graduates who are online. This was clearly a significant resource for a body of alumni that largely disperses to further studies around the globe immediately on graduation. There remains a strong sense of 'old boy' and 'old girl' affinity with their 'alma mater' fostered by the schools. Perhaps the most conscpicuous example of this diaspora effect was Fatima College. Because of its long-term association with computer and Internet teaching, this school seemed to have a presence on the Internet well beyond its relative size. As well as the alumni listed on its own site, there is a separate website developed in Canada. Broken down by current place of residence, this reveals the following spread of ex-students, which in turns explains the immediate significance of the internet: USA 170; Trinidad and Tobago 148; Canada 87; UK 13; country not entered 10; Jamaica 3; together with two each for Australia, Grenada, Scotland and Venezuela and one each for Bermuda, Botswana, Brazil, Denmark, Ireland, Japan and Switzerland.

The significance of such lists goes beyond renewing friendships. Simply by hyper-linking between the websites of all these graduates, the Internet comes both to represent and to replicate a key aspect of Trinidadian social structure. The Internet not only maps it but plays a part in reproducing it through the practical interconnections it enables. Some of our research developed by following such links and email addresses, which have become an effective means of tracing the Trini elite.

Places of Sociality

In so far as Internet studies have shifted their gaze from what happens online, they have started to investigate the microsociological contexts of Internet use, such as cybercafés or domestic spaces (Crang, Crang and May 1999; Furlong 1995; Wakeford 1999). The immediate social locations of Internet use both frame and set limits on the kinds of relationships that take place through them. For example, workplace access could range from minimal to extensive, and from extremely liberal attitudes to personal use to a restrictive, 'business use only' policy. Hence some people could treat their office as a place for pursuing family contacts on behalf of their entire household, for chatting and even for cybersex; others could not relate workplace access to any kind of sociality.

Just as important as the impact of social spaces on the way relationships were pursued through the Internet was their impact on relationships around the computer. Two places of sociality that brought out quite different possibilities for relationships were cybercafés and secondary schools.

Cybercafés

The global usage of cybercafés is diverse, as Rao (1999) has noted. In Trinidad, they were largely unstable and in most cases unprofitable enterprises. They were generally either adjuncts to other businesses (computer sales or maintenance, private IT courses) or on the verge of transforming into other businesses (webdesign and Internet technologies). They also ranged from scams (one charged people TT$5 for each email sent or received) to dynamic community centres.

In the event, we were able to visit six operating cybercafés, each of which was very different in style and in the kinds of sociality it generated. For example, of the two in which we spent a good deal of our research time, Café A had a strong emphasis on an informal and convivial ambience. There was always music, loud conversation, bustling activity. It was also literally a cybercafé, in that it served food and drink. The eight computers were placed along the outside walls of the main rooms so that anyone sitting at the spare tables in the centre could see what was going on at the monitors. It was a very public space and a friendly liming spot. This reflected the personality and strong beliefs of the couple who owned it, especially the husband, who was regarded by many users as a kind of father-figure, who calmly dispensed advice, support and encouragement, as well as keeping both order and excitement. He combined entrepreneurialism and nationalism in typical Trini measure, doing his utmost to develop his users' Internet expertise and enterprise. He also gathered about himself talented and enthusiastic young people who could use the facilities to develop commercial projects in webdesign and programming.

The second cybercafé – B – was an adjunct to a computer retail business that also had an extensive programme of computer courses. This was distinctly a business premises, with white and undecorated walls. Partly for teaching purposes, the computers were sited in three different rooms, and within them machines were positioned to give much privacy to the user. There was no area for general liming, and the consumption of food and drink was forbidden. Despite the different style, the social ambience was very friendly and supportive, but this was entirely due to a core of employees, their relatives and some regulars.

In each case there were probably a majority of people who used the spaces as individuals, without much apparent connection to the cafés as institutions beyond finding them more or less congenial. This included people stopping by to check their email or research a particular topic or just surf or chat for a while. The population was mainly, but not exclusively, young. They related to the staff mainly for technical support and help in using software.

On the other hand, both places had a core of one or two dozen regulars who came in very frequently and spent a lot of time there. One person we knew seemed to live there, chatting non-stop to her cyber-fiancé in Australia, to a degree that staff expressed some concern to us. Hourly charges were laxly enforced, and in some cases the most regular visitors paid for little of their online time, but in return helped the employees sort out 'newbies' and generally added to the ambience of the place. Even though Café B had little in the way of atmosphere, and certainly did not put itself forward as a liming spot, regular users still strongly identified with it, and another cybercafé noted that most of their Christmas decorations were put up by users. Café A went much further. A few people said that they came there even though they had online computers at home or work; others hung out after school with no apparent desire to use a computer at all: 'Nearly every day after work I come up here, even if is not to use the PC, if I buy something from the cybercafé downstairs and I'll come up and eat, or just chill. People come up here to study too. It does be a real nice lime.'

Sociality comprised a wider variety of collective uses of the space than simply hanging out. At this point, the styles of the two places diverged more markedly. A lot of the activity in cybercafé B was oriented to chat. Partly because of the privacy afforded by the room and monitor arrangements, people could both pursue their own activities and at the same time form small groups, sharing their experiences. This might mean that regular users found their on-and offline worlds merging in interesting ways: for example, they might pass chat friends on to each other, or gather round a screen as a chat progressed. The girl mentioned above, recently engaged to a man in Australia, encouraged him to find Australian girls who would chat to a boy she had come to know at the café. Equally his interests in certain games led him to make friends both with café regulars and with some online contacts. Often young users would want to make sure there were friends around to appreciate some sexual adventure or the excited danger of encountering a hacker online. Regulars would rush over to a friend's screen to take over their keyboard and latch on to some event, in between juggling half a dozen open windows and conversations on their own machine.

The private spaces possible in Café B (especially, but not exclusively, its 'back room') also allowed looking at pornography, alone or in groups (pornography was banned at Café A, because of the public view of all monitors rather than for reasons of principled disapproval). For example, a group of gay Trinidadians collectively used the back room to look at sexual material – an important opportunity in Trinidad, which has tended to be highly homophobic. The staff are clearly aware of the pornographic material being used, and themselves suggested that this repre-sented some 70 percent of all usage (we felt this was an exaggeration, although some users claimed the same figure); but their concern was primarily to ensure that such activities be carried out in privacy and not be directly exposed to chance encounters with schoolchildren and others who would be offended. Our observations would then certainly support Wakeford (1999: 188–94) in noting the importance of spatial order within the cybercafé to understanding the kinds of interaction that take place there.

Coming into the café as a group generally tended to have an impact on machine use, creating the bravado for illicit activities. In addition to porn, this might include schoolchildren who would impress each other with their ability to work as hackers. Another example was:

Sometimes me and my friend will come as a group and just sit at a computer and go into ICQ and just diss everybody and get thrown out from the chat room. Well, we just like to interfere with people. Like harmless, just embarrass, just jump in, listen to a particular conversation and then we chose this one and decide that we going to harass this one. Out of kicks and then everybody just get involved. Only as a group, until we got banned, restricted, eventually: got kicked out a couple of times, then we got banned.

Sociality in Café A was rather different. As opposed to the groups huddled around monitors in Café B, people were either liming at the tables or engaged in more purposeful (but still sociable and pleasurable) development of their skills or projects. There was a great emphasis on helping each other learn ever more ambitious skills and on projects. Finally, and rather unusually for Trinidad, where computer game culture is not as important to Internet use as in North America and Europe, there were a number of people at Café A, many of them core staff and regulars, who were heavily into networked games such as Quake. There were occasional all-nighters, and some investment of time in downloading the paraphernalia of Quake clans.

One final case of cybercafé sociality that indicates how unexpected the relationships formed around the Internet can be: a cybercafé recently opened up in an up-market mall by a young woman turned into a kind of virtual crèche. She started by offering basic training in Internet use to younger children and found that not only did the children love it, but their mothers loved leaving them there, in safety and worthy educational pursuits, while they shopped for several hours. One particularly wealthy family regularly left their son there with his personal bodyguard, and both would play for hours.

Secondary schools

One of the traumas of Trinidadian life is the common entrance exam, which separates children between the more prestigious Church-founded secondary schools and the ordinary government schools. The striking difference between the two was that the Internet had already become an integral part of school culture for students of the prestige schools. This was as much a reflection of the fact that they tended to come from wealthier families with Internet access at home as from the much improved online facilities at school (clearly evident in their school websites). Provision for boys and for girls was radically unequal, though this did not seem to make the Internet any less of a feature for girls' school culture or schoolwork, at least at the schools we visited. Home use was more equal, with several individuals and groups suggesting a figure of around a third of schoolchildren having online access at home, though those without access might come and use the computers of those with. Schoolchildren with online computers at home tended to receive 5–20 emails a week. There was much sharing of online culture, with people forwarding jokes and cards but also friends to each other. Chat and ICQ were very common for younger children. One noted how she had stopped using ICQ, since she had found it so addictive during the four months she had used it. For boys music was the most common use after chat and ICQ, followed by email, and then porn, with rather less use for sports and games.

Perhaps in schools more than anywhere else one has a sense of the Internet as something that already has a history, and also a relationship to the school as a life course. For example, there is the sense of a pre-ICQ phase or a pre-personal webpage phase. There is already the expectation amongst schoolchildren that members of a certain school form would go through a phase of heavy involvement in Internet pornography or cybersex, but that by the next school year this was already seen as immature and not really cool. In one year children might come into school and call each other by their ICQ nicks instead of their real names; but again this would be scorned by the more senior years. As one pupil put it: 'Some get out of the phase faster than others, others are still into it. They are the minority. The other forms are in it right now. When we were in lab in Computer Science everybody had their own porno section. I had 300 pictures, a friend had about 400 pictures. Now if you go back only the lower forms have their porno sections. The school doesn't really know.'

Schoolchildren constituted one of the only groups that extensively exploited the Internet for socializing with other Trinidadians in Trinidad. One example of this was the extension of playground gossip and interaction. ICQ seemed to have replaced the telephone as the privileged medium for continuing school conversations after school, letting each other know about or comment on events that day, in the privacy of their one-to-one chat. Already the patterns of spitefulness, cliquishness, sentimentality and making-up that are familiar genres offline were finding their online equivalents. Also there was the concomitant rise of the particularly Trinidadian sense of bacchanal and *commess* (disorder caused by gossip). For example, schoolgirls relished the story of a boy who published gossip about his friends on his personal website. News of this event spread quickly, so that they too had visited the site. During the one week before the boy's mother closed the site down, it had been hacked – we were told – by some of those concerned to publish counter-accusations about the website author. Another story concerned a boy watching a screen with his girlfriend while gossip about this girlfriend was being relayed. A more direct relationship was established in San Fernando, where there is a concentration of secondary schools. Many pupils used an IRC-based chat room where they tended to congregate online, especially on Friday nights continuing through into the morning hours while the parents were asleep. They also arranged to meet occasionally for a group lime at the food court of the local mall. Email and ICQ might also be used to plan a weekend lime or other gathering.

The Internet was also providing schoolchildren with a major conduit to offline relationships. Chat was seen as an ideal precursor to dating, since both boys and girls could be less reticent and feel their way towards a relationship while staying relatively anonymous:

'Before, the girls are shy kind of way, so it would take a fellow to go over and meet a girl and talk. But with ICQ it's easier. You speaking to them like you know them kind of thing, before you actually know them. And when you meet you already know them.' Another boy noted of a friend: 'He met her on one of the open chat lines and then he met her in real. They going strong now, haven't had a fight yet. It's a good way of meeting girls. It's easier than walking up to someone and talking.'

Internet content becomes common school culture as easily as television programmes such as *South Park*. In the morning people would report new sites or software. The Internet could be used to constitute the non-school sociality of children, as: 'A place to get away from school, that's what the Internet is for my class. They look at it as liming on the net. They are all in one big chat room and lime.' But this was the least academic class in the year. For most students the relationship between the Internet and school culture clearly integrated both sociality and also educational activities, such as sharing Internet resources for schoolwork. One group of schoolgirls laughed at our adult naivety when we discussed using books for essay-writing, since they pointed out the great store of previously written essays existing on the Internet that could be mined as the basis for their own essays. They all claimed that they themselves (of course) only ever used ideas and snippets of these essays, but that others in their class had submitted entire essays taken from the web without as yet ever being caught out by the teachers. One group did suggest, however, that their teachers were asking more obscure questions in subjects such as literature partly in response to the threat of their pupils' merely presenting public-domain essays. Books and libraries were seen as *passé*: according to the girls, even teachers accepted the inability to find information online as a reasonable excuse for not handing in a homework project.

Almost all these children will at least investigate the possibility of further education abroad through researching the net; indeed throughout Trinidadian society this has become a far more frequent use of the Internet than pursuits such as sports and games. This was confirmed by inspection of many 'histories' recorded on web-browsers in cybercafés. At Fatima College around half the students were expected to take SAT exams for US colleges, of whom around half were expected to obtain full scholarships to prestigious universities in the US. The evidence from the alumni lists on the school websites suggest this is not unrealistic. The schools themselves clearly recognized that Internet skills were becoming an integral part of general education. Some were quite liberal in opening up their banks of computers to after-school use, even when finding on occasion that a schoolchild was still online when they returned for school the next morning! Fatima funded its computer laboratories partly through putting on annual courses for the public. IT remains integral to the social relations of its alumni.

The personal websites of schoolchildren are themselves clear expressions of school culture. They also make far more inventive use of the technology than even the most expensive commercial sites. 'Maria's So Called Life', with the address 'sullengirl', has words like 'pathetic' and 'wasting away' that come and go within a frame. Instead of the simple 'about me' found in most personal websites, this one states 'Stuff on me, WARNING! – Before you proceed to waste your time by reading this page I should warn you . . . it SUCKS!!! I don't know why I'm doing this really, guess it's because I have a lot of time on my hands.' Sullengirl thereby illustrates the effectiveness of a website in conveying the typical sense of the teenager as alienated: even visually, she mainly appears on the site as an alien. Other teenage sites also present themselves as stupid and pathetic and tell us how they really shouldn't be working on this site one week before taking their examinations but . . .

What is impressive is not just the sheer dynamics and creativity of these sites, but the techniques they use to entrap surfers and draw them in. For example, there is the brilliant way one site exploits a conventional form of computer link to suck in the passing surfer. The crucial factor in all these sites seems to be not just the ability to attract surfers but also to engage in the act of exchange represented by the (usually mutual) signing of their guestbooks. It is this that attests to the fame/name of the website creator, and is analogous to the circles of exchange that create the name and fame of those who transact Kula (Munn 1986). Surfers are drawn to share the offerings of the site, for example their jokes, their MP3s, their friends, or their links to other sites as long as they sign the guestbook and attest thereby to the fame of the creator.

The Internet was also at the centre of school cultures of heroes and outlaws that focused on technical feats and knowledge, generally possessed by boys (this was not confined to schools, but certainly prevalent there). While some of this involved relationships formed between technically proficient boys who were developing small website businesses or helping manage school IT facilities, the thrilling stuff involved various kinds of organized outlawry, often mythological, directed against school or each other. One school had allowed a highly skilled 15-year- old to develop their website and other computer facilities for the school. The fact that the same pupil was reputed to then hack into the system at will led to a subsequent parting of ways. All the students had a repertoire of stories about master hackers and hacking feats, of particularly devastating viruses and ingenious 'trojans' that could take control over anyone's computer. It was hard to confirm any of these stories, and many of them were pretty outlandish (the shared ultimate ideal was for some schoolboy to hack into the Trinidadian banking system); but it was clear that reports of such exploits were a guaranteed addition to peer status. As one 15-year-old put it:

Normally they brag about how good they are at hacking, or blowing up somebody's system, shutting them down. Some instances – they are true. People that they do it to come back and talk about it. They does be real vex. They quarrel a lot. Why you do me that? They have this fella, he left school now, he was in form five with us, he could shut down somebody even on the net, or disconnect, he's real good.

Hacking involved competitive bravado between the boys. By contrast, a 15-year-old schoolgirl noted that girls would commonly send viruses to each other, often in the belief that they were already victims of a virus sent by the girl in question. Girls would come to school also moaning about how their computer had been messed up and how they would wreak revenge on the girl they believed had sent the virus. Again, the mix of truth and lore is both undecidable and revealing of school culture, but the comment that 'this is their mentality' strongly suggested that the stereotypes that are developing about how schoolgirls and schoolboys respectively use their skills closely follow older gender stereotypes.

Continuities

Much of the first half of this chapter could have been written under the rubric of kinship studies. At first glance the material appears very different from what one might expect to encounter in kinship studies; but we want to suggest that there may be much more continuity here than meets the eye. This becomes more apparent when it is recognized that the relationships discussed throughout this chapter are, like kinship itself, an idiom for the expression of core Trinidadian values. The central argument of Miller (1994) was that there existed a historical logic that could confer on Trinidad a vanguard position in arguments about the nature of modernity. It was suggested that the relevant values – termed there 'transience' and 'transcendence' – were historically first developed and expressed through the idiom of kinship. After the oil boom of the 1970s the same contradiction in values was also expressed through the meanings given to the objects of mass consumption, perhaps now through the medium of the Internet.

The key author for understanding the distinctive character of West Indian kinship is R. T. Smith (1995). Trinidad had equivalent norms of kinship to those Smith describes for Jamaica, although they have recently moved closer to international norms and ideologies as a result of affluence and cosmopolitan aspirations. Smith (1988: 49) found that Jamaicans typically recognized a large number of people as relatives (a mean of 284 in 51 cases). As in Trinidad, these became a kind of potential network rather than, as in other countries, a series of concentric circles representing decreasing degrees of contact and obligation. Closeness or affection is almost an independent variable one establishes with some kin but not with others. Connections with kin are rather less tied to a sense of obligation based on relative closeness of blood than would be true elsewhere. As a potential network these connections grow in particular ways. For example, in Trinidad the birth of a baby signifies the creation of new bonds irrespective of the continued presence of the baby's father. This relative separation between a sense of connection and a sense of obligation may be understood in part as an act of resistance to historical pressure from groups such as the Church to develop more institutionalized norms of kin. For example, there was resistance to marriage prior to demonstrating the ability to have children and most especially the ability to own and run a house.

Instead, kinship included a strong element of pragmatism. One might be only vaguely aware that a particular relative lived in a locality until the decision to send one's son to school in that area, in which case that relative's house becomes the obvious place for him to live. Similarly if one wanted to extend a business link to a new region. The same applied to affection in general. Cousins were more like a pool of potential close relations; but only through mutual attraction does a very close friendship develop with one particular cousin. So what mattered was not the distance between any two relatives, but rather the realization of particular pragmatic and affective relations out of a pool of possible relationships. Even in the practice of sexuality there is a stress on the mutual act of exchange, for example of giving one's labour in clearing the yard of one's sexual partner as part of mutual recognition of the relationship. There is also an antipathy to forms of marriage in which partners can take each other for granted in providing either sex or labour.

In effect kinship represents a potential pool of people, while circumstances are allowed to determine whether or not there develops a bond of affection or whether or not a relative becomes an important node in solving some logistical problem. In Miller (1994: 168–93) it was argued that all of this expresses the value of transience, in which institutions are prevented from limiting the sense of freedom and voluntarism basic to what are seen as authentic relationships. Its roots in the particular history of the region are therefore clear.

Such a perspective is very different from the 'baggage' that usually comes with terms such as 'community' and 'family' if used as models for Internet use. Usually such terms tend to assume a commonalty of sentiment in which community as a symbol and focus of commitment transcends the relations that constitute it. If, however, West Indian kinship of this transient variety is taken as the model for Internet use, other possibilities arise. The first analogy is found in the way people use the Internet to create networks. One common concern is simply to expand the number of people one knows or knows of. Once one has had a communication with them it could in future be extended if that were mutually desired. This evolution occurs through a number of different routes. These include creating networks of potential correspondents, for example through contacting distant kin on the Internet, developing a list of 'nicks' on one's ICQ link, or signing a website's guest-list. A prime example of this would be the 'de Trini Lime', an ICQ list that grew as we were doing fieldwork to 2,215 people. The only criteria that mattered as far as most people were concerned were that the other person on the lime was a genuine Trini and then also usually that they were of the opposite sex.

As in the transient family, one finds with Internet relationships that larger appeals to sentiment or obligation on the basis of nearness or proximity often have little authority. Rather, there is a large pool of potential contacts that can be realized for either or both of two main reasons, one being to create bonds of affection, some-times including deep intimacy and acts of confession. The other is to engage in mutual communication in order to fulfil some largely pragmatic and perhaps fortuit-ous need, such as a common desire for computer games cheats, though such a need might also be represented by something one might think of as more personal. Many of the random chat links are based around discussions of such things as how to deal with nagging parents or teachers, or persistent ex-boyfriends.

As a result the presence of the correspondent cannot be taken for granted. It follows that there is a constant need to recreate the mutuality of the relationship. This works for both short- and long-term relationships. As some young men noted in trying cybersex, they simply had to show more sensitivity and concern for the pleasure of their female partners than they had in offline sex, since otherwise their partners would just leave them standing (as it were). So, as in transient kinship, Internet relationships are more dyadic, voluntaristic and based on the continuity of their reconstitution through constant acts of exchange. This is not to say that the relationships are more superficial or less normative or lacking in the possibility of affection; but rather it makes these compatible with using relationships to objectify a project of freedom as a central value of modernity.

The final point is that contrary to expectations such uses of the Internet are not to be opposed to 'traditional' forms of relationship and especially kinship (Castells 1998: 340–51). In this case, by contrast, such attributes would make the Internet strongly continuous with those values that were developed first in kinship and later through the experience of mass consumption (see Miller 1994: ch. 5). So while it is too early to know to what degree these Trinidadian uses of the Internet are highly specific, if they are, there will be a local historical trajectory that might help us account for that specificity. Once again there may be elective affinities at play; but most importantly, the argument suggests that the relationships outlined here cannot be assumed to mere creatures of the Internet developed in opposition to or replace-ment of something else called 'traditional kinship'.

Conclusions

The evidence in this chapter suggests that online and offline worlds penetrate each other deeply and in complex ways, whether people are using the Internet to realize older concepts of identity or to pursue new modes of sociality. With respect to the family the Internet is used largely to roll back changes that were dissolving some family relations. It is used to bring people back to what they think of as 'proper' family life. As such it is a prime example of what we call the expansive realization. Chat and ICQ can further new kinds of social contact, which then have to be assessed and related to a normative sense of what a 'real' relationship is. They may also be reframed as, or even literally lead to, the most traditional forms of sociality, such as marriage. Apparently quite mundane new media, such as virtual postcards, can both transform older gifting practices and materially reconstitute the relationships in which they are embedded. Spaces of sociality emerge around Internet use in cybercafés and schools, with their own norms and variations based on a complex interweaving of online and offline worlds, frequently more significant in their intensification of offline rather than online relationships, or in the way they integrate the two.

'Virtuality' is unhelpful or even misleading as a point of departure in sorting out this complexity. Ethnographically, it is at best a special case that emerged in Jason's valuation of 'just communicating' in chat relationships – yet even he did not use the term 'virtual'. Rather he stressed that the value of these relationships hinged on the way in which they were stitched into his everyday life, exemplified in their know-ledge and participation in his family life. Similarly, although it is tempting to treat the alumni lists of prestige schools as a kind of virtual social structure, they evidently arose from and maintained an intricate relationship with a quite conventional sense of social structure, and had an eminently practical function in reproducing that structure, alongside other modes of formal and informal practices (for example careers, travel, and business contacts).

These conclusions are tied to local circumstances. It need not follow that ICQ will necessarily have the same consequence for another society or diaspora. The 'elective affinity' by which a particular Internet technology can be developed to enhance a particular genre of relationships is highly contextualized. Indeed, it was suggested at the end that there may be strong continuities with earlier forms of kinship, partly because both kinship and the Internet are being employed as idioms to express particular values that connect with what we have termed normative freedom. To try and separate our material into the 'real' and the 'virtual' would thus seem to us to lose almost everything that can be learnt from studying relationship on and through the Internet.

NOTE

1   The term 'Diaspora' here is used to include not only Trinidadian families that live overseas but also families that are split between residence in Trinidad and overseas. Obviously this does not accord with the usual definition of the term diaspora, but we feel the text would lose rather than gain clarity by trying to specify the degree of transnationalism in each case. With respect to the issue of Internet use we are concerned with all situations where some members of a family that was once from Trinidad now live outside Trinidad. It would also seem to be pedantic to try to be too precise about the semantics of migration, since most accounts show just how fluid identities and residence can often be for Caribbean migrants (e.g. Basch, Glick Schiller and Szanton Blanc 1994; Chamberlain 1998).

REFERENCES

Basch, L., Glick Schiller, N., and Szanton Blanc, C. 1994. *Nations Unbound*. Amsterdam: Gordon & Breach.

Carrier, J. 1995. *Gifts and Commodities*. London: Routledge.

Castells, M. 1998. *End of Millennium*. Oxford: Blackwell Publishers.

Chamberlain, M. 1998. *Caribbean Migration: Globalized Identities*. London: Routledge.

Crang, M., Crang, P., and May, J. 1999. *Virtual Geographies*. London: Routledge.

Furlong, R. 1995. 'There's no place like home,' in *The Photographic Image in Digital Culture*, ed. M. Lister. London: Routledge.

Ho, C. 1991. *Salt-Water Trinis: Afro-Trinidadian Immigrant Networks and Non-Assimilation in Los Angeles*. New York: AMS Press.

Jaffe, A. 1999. 'Packaged sentiments: The social meaning of greeting cards,' *Journal of Material Culture* 4: 115–41.

Marvin, C. 1988. *When Old Technologies Were New*. New York: Oxford University Press.

Mauss, M. 1954. *The Gift*. London: Cohen and West.

Miller, Daniel. 1994. *Modernity: An Ethnographic Approach*. Oxford: Berg.

Munn, N. 1986. *The Fame of Gawa*. Cambridge: Cambridge University Press.

Olwig, K. F. 1993. *Global Culture, Island Identity: Continuity and Change in the Afro-Caribbean Community of Nevis*. Chur, Switzerland: Harwood.

Rao, M. 1999. 'Bringing the net to the masses: cybercafes in Latin America,' *Cybersociology* 4 22/04/99: http://www.cybersoc.com/magazine

Slater, Don. 1998. 'Trading sexpics on IRC: embodiment and authenticity on the Internet,' *Body and Society* 4 (4).

Smith, R. T. 1995. *The Matrifocal Family*. London: Routledge.

Stein, J. 1999. 'The telephone: its social shaping and public negotiation in late nineteenth-and early twentieth-century London.' Pp. 44–62 in *Virtual Geographies*, ed. M. Crang, P. Crang, and J. May. London: Routledge.

Wakeford, N. 1999. 'Gender and the landscapes of computing in an Internet Café.' Pp. 178–201 in *Virtual Geographies*, ed. M. Crang, P. Crang, and J. May. London: Routledge.

Yelvington, K. 1996. 'Flirting in the factory,' *Journal of the Royal Anthropological Institute* 2: 313–33.

13

Mediating Culture: Indigenous Media, Ethnographic Film, and the Production of Identity

Faye Ginsburg

And tomorrow? . . . The dreams of Vertov and Flaberty will be combined into a mechanical "cine-eye-ear" which is such a "participant" camera that it will pass automatically into the hands of those who were, up to now, always in front of it. Then the anthropologist will no longer monopolize the observation of things.

Jean Rouch

Aboriginal communities are ensuring the continuity of their languages and cultures and representation of their views. By making their own films and videos, they speak for themselves, no longer aliens in an industry which for a century has used them for its own ends.

Michael Leigh

Many Aboriginal people have said, "let's have our own rights concerning TV. We must have equal time on air, showing our own people, our own culture and our own language. And it must be done in our own way!"

Central Australian Aboriginal Media Association

Over the last ten years, indigenous and minority people have been using a variety of media, including film and video, as new vehicles for internal and external communication, for self-determination, and for resistance to outside cultural domination. Yet the use of such visual media by indigenous people has also raised serious questions for them. Is it indeed possible to develop an alternative practice and aesthetic using forms so identified with the political and economic imperatives of Western consumer culture and the institutions of mass society? In the most hopeful of interpretations, these new media forms are innovations in both filmic representation and social process, expressive of transformations in cultural and political identities.

Alternative "multicultural media" have become both fashionable and more visible since the mid-1980s: exhibitions and film festivals in the United States,[1] the Black Film workshop sector in the United Kingdom,[2] and a Special Broadcasting Service (SBS) in Australia are just a few examples of this increased interest.[3] Until quite recently,[4] support for and exhibition of such work focused on productions by ethnic minorities rather than on the indigenous groups who have been dominated by encompassing settler states such as the United States, Canada, and Australia.

This essay will focus on what I am calling indigenous media – with a particular focus on Aboriginal Australians – as a distinct if problematic form of cultural activism and an emerging genre. To recognize indigenous media in this way acknowledges the fact that most indigenous people have a sense of how their political, historical, and cultural situation differs from that of ethnic minorities and how that difference might shape their use of media. As Rachel Perkins, the head of Australia's SBS Aboriginal Unit, explains, in relation to her work in developing Aboriginal television programming:

They [SBS management] would probably consider us another ethnic group . . . like the Italians, the Greeks, the Yugoslavs, etc., but . . . we've got a definitely different role than all the other people. . . . First of all, we have to educate the whole country about the history of the place and we've got to try and maintain our culture and also build an economic future for ourselves through employment in the television industry; we're not trying to assimilate as much as them, we're trying to promote our differences.[5]

Indigenous media also should be distinguished from the national and independent cinemas of non-Western Third World nations in Africa, Latin America, and Asia, which have developed under quite different historical and institutional conditions, and about which there is considerable scholarship.[6]

More positively, the term "indigenous media" respects the understandings of those Aboriginal producers who identify themselves as members of "First Nations" or "Fourth World People," categories that index the sense of common political struggle shared by indigenous people around the globe. "Media," on the other hand, evokes the huge institutional structures of the television and film industries that tend to overwhelm local specificities and concerns for relatively small populations while privileging commercial interests that demand large audiences as a measure of success. Thus, to use the label "indigenous media" suggests the importance of contextualizing this work within broader movements for cultural autonomy and political self-determination. These movements exist in complex tension with the structures of the dominant culture. In a recent article on Aboriginal media, Philip Batty describes these social relations as a process of "negotiation" with the settler nation, a kind of intercultural bargaining that has shaped the emergence of such work.[7]

In general, efforts to produce indigenous media worldwide[8] have been relatively small-scale, low-budget, and locally based. Much of this work is shown in events organized for indigenous peoples, such as the Native American Film Festivals held regularly in San Francisco and New York City, the Pincher Creek World Festival of Aboriginal Motion Pictures (now known as Dreamspeakers) held every summer in Alberta, Canada, and the Inter American Film Festival of Indigenous Peoples held every two years in South America, most recently in Peru in 1992. For many indigenous producers, these festivals, as events that reinforce indigenous identities, are venues that are preferred over more "high profile" mainstream institutions such as the Museum of Modern Art in New York, which has made some effort at showcasing indigenous work.

There is very little written on these developments, and what exists comes mostly in the form of newsletters, reports, brochures, and catalogues that are useful but difficult to obtain. Only occasionally do such writings address broader theoretical questions regarding how indigenous media alter understandings of media, politics, and representation. It is particularly surprising that there is so little discussion of such phenomena in contemporary anthropological work, despite the fact that VCRs, video cameras, and mass media are now present in even the most remote locales. In part this is due to the fact that the theoretical foci anthropologists carry into the field have not, until very recently, expanded sufficiently to keep up with such changes.[9] The lack of analysis of such media as both cultural product and social process may also be due to our own culture's enduring positivist belief that the camera provides a "window" on reality, a simple expansion of our powers of observation, as opposed to a creative tool in the service of a new signifying practice.

My work is a preliminary effort to address what Aboriginal cultural activist Marcia Langton has identified as the "central problem" that has accompanied the development of Aboriginal media – that is, "the need to develop a body of knowledge and critical perspective to do with aesthetics and politics, whether written by Aboriginal or non-Aboriginal people, on representation of Aboriginal people and concerns in art, film, television, or other media."[10]

In order to open a new "discursive space" for indigenous media that respects and understands them on their own terms, it is important to attend to the *processes* of production and reception. Analysis needs to focus less on the formal qualities of film and video as text and more on the cultural *mediations* that occur through film and video works. This requires examining how indigenous media are situated in relevant discursive fields in order to understand how this work gets positioned by those practising it and by those in the dominant culture with some interest in it.

The initial section of this essay addresses at a general level how indigenous media might be positioned analytically in relation to ethnographic film as a form intended to mediate across cultural boundaries. The second section concerns the relationship of indigenous media to identity production among Fourth World peoples in the late twentieth century, examining claims for both its destructive and productive possibilities. The third section examines ideas about identity production in relation to recent developments in media production by Australian Aboriginal people. Specifically, I discuss several media groups in Central Australia that I have been following since 1988. These are the Warlpiri Media Association (WMA) in the Central Desert Aboriginal community of Yuendumu; CAAMA – the acronym for the Central Australian Aboriginal Media Association, located just outside the town of Alice Springs; and Imparja Television, based in Alice Springs but serving all of the Northern Territory and large parts of South Australia as well. I also will briefly discuss some of the efforts since the late 1980s to bring Aboriginal producers and production into national television.

It is difficult to consider indigenous media outside of some version of one of two dominant tropes, which I summarize as the Faustian contract and the global village. Each scenario has its virtues and shortcomings. The model of the Faustian contract, most clearly articulated in the work of the Frankfurt School, regards "traditional culture" as something good and authentic, as something that is irreversibly polluted by contact with the high technology and media produced by mass culture. This view is very clear about what cultural domination can mean, but social actors are absolutely overdetermined; both kinds of societies are frozen into paradigmatic positions that essentialize features that distinguish them. By contrast, the model of the global village optimistically suggests that new media can bring together different cultures from all over the earth, recreating a local sense of community associated with village life through progressive use of communications technologies. Here, social actors are active agents, and societies are recognized as constantly changing rather than determined by state, economic, and technological imperatives. However, the important, specific ways in which cultures differ and people experience political and economic inequality are erased in a modernist and ethnocentric utopian vision of an electronic democracy.

New discursive possibilities, I argue, might be found in models emerging from anthropology and cultural studies; these models call on metaphors of hybridity and self-consciously reject notions of "authenticity" and "pure culture" as ways of understanding contemporary identities. For example, Stuart Hall, a central figure in British cultural studies, argues that identity is a production that is never complete, always in process, and always constituted within, not outside, representation.[11] Accordingly, these studies tend to focus on the creative aspects of cultural production, where questions of representation are central.[12] Similarly, an area of primary concern for those concerned with indigenous identity is the mediation of politics and identity through the signifying practices of film and televisual forms; such practices cannot be considered apart from the political economies of the dominant cultures in which they are embedded. Ideally, from the point of view of indigenous producers, the capabilities of visual media to transcend boundaries of time, space, and even language can be used effectively to mediate historically produced social ruptures that link past and present. In so doing, producers are engaged in a powerful new process of constructing identities on their own terms but in ways that address the relationships between indigenous histories and cultures and the encompassing societies in which they live. As Stuart Hall expresses it, identities are the "names we give to the different ways we are positioned by, and position ourselves within, the narratives of the past."[13]

Genre Positions: Indigenous Media and Ethnographic Film

Ethnographic film was originally conceived of as a broad project of documenting on film the "disappearing" lifeworlds of those "others" – non-Western, small-scale, kinship-based societies – who had been the initial objects of anthropology as it developed in the early twentieth century. Whatever its colonial origins, the field of ethnographic film took on definition and shape as a genre during a critical period, the 1960s and 1970s, when efforts to "reinvent anthropology"[14] were produced by a variety of historical, intellectual, and political developments. Briefly stated, these include:

- the end of the colonial era with the assertions of self-determination by native peoples;
- the radicalization of young scholars in the 1960s and the replacing of positivist models of knowledge with more interpretive and politically self-conscious approaches; and

- a reconceptualization of "the native voice" as one that should be in more direct dialogue with anthropological interpretation.

Some have called this constellation of events "a crisis in representation" for the field, a crisis that required new, experimental strategies for transmitting anthropological understandings.[15] It is not sufficiently appreciated that, in fact, many people working in ethnographic film already had responded to this "crisis." Often less constrained by the academy than those working in written ethnography, ethnographic filmmakers offered a variety of creative solutions. Following the experimental turns in the arts in general, they developed dialogical and reflexive strategies to mark the films as encounters contingent on the particulars of a historical moment. For example, questions of epistemology, ethics, and the position of the native interlocutor were being addressed in the 1950s by ethnographic filmmaker Jean Rouch in works such as *Les Maîtres fous* (1955), *Jaguar* (1955), and *Chronique d'un été* (*Chronicle of a Summer*, 1960). By the mid-1970s the list included (to name a few) Tim Asch, David and Judith MacDougall, John Marshall, Gary Kildea, Barbara Myerhoff, and Jorge Preloran. A number of these people also articulated arguments in print for what David MacDougall has called more participatory methods and styles of representation.[16] This increasingly collaborative approach to ethnographic filmmaking foreshadowed and encouraged the development of indigenous media.

An early effort to get the camera into native hands was carried out by Sol Worth and John Adair in the 1960s. Their project, discussed in the book *Through Navajo Eyes*, attempted to teach film technology to Navajos, without the conventions of Western production and editing, to see if their films would be based on a different film "grammar" based on a Navajo worldview. However, the experiment focused overmuch on the filmic rather than the social frame. Worth and Adair failed to consider seriously potential cultural differences in the social relations around image making and viewing, even though these concerns were brought up clearly in the initial negotiations with Sam Yazzie, a leading medicine man and elder.

Adair explained that he wanted to teach some Navajo to make movies.... When Adair finished, Sam thought for a while and then... asked a lengthy question which was interpreted as, "Will making movies do sheep any harm?"

Worth was happy to explain that as far as he knew, there was no chance that making movies would harm the sheep.

Sam thought this over and then asked, "Will making movies do the sheep good?" Worth was forced to reply that as far as he knew making movies wouldn't do the sheep any good.

Sam thought this over, then, looking around at us he said, "Then why make movies?"[17]

The lack of consideration for how movies might "do the sheep good" meant that the Navajo Eyes project was rather short-lived; in retrospect it is seen as a somewhat sterile and patronizing experiment. Still, the notion of distinct indigenous concerns for cinematic and narrative representation was prescient.

By the 1970s indigenous groups and some ethnographic filmmakers were questioning not only how conventions of representation are culture-bound; they also concerned themselves with central issues of power regarding who controls the production and distribution of imagery. Indigenous peoples who had been the exotic objects of many films were concerned increasingly with producing their own images, either by working with accomplished and sympathetic filmmakers[18] or by entering into film and video production themselves, for example Hopi artist Victor Masayesva, Jr., or Inuit producer/director Zacharias Kunuk.[19]

These developments were part of a more general decentralization, democratization, and widespread penetration of media that emerged with the growth of new technologies that simultaneously worked the local and global fronts. On the one hand, inexpensive portable video cameras and cable channels open to a spectrum of producers and viewers gave new meaning to notions of access and multicultural expression. On the other hand, the broad marketing of VCRs and the launching of communications satellites over Canada in the 1970s and Australia in the 1980s suddenly brought the possibility or menace, depending on one's point of view, of a mixture of minority/indigenous and mainstream Western programming entering into the daily lives of people living in remote settlements, especially those in the Canadian Arctic and central Australian desert.

Given these developments, I would like to consider the position of indigenous media in relation to ethnographic film. Some simply want to abandon or declare "colonialist" any attempt to film "the other" since indigenous media production makes it clear that "they" are capable of representing themselves. For example, critiques coming out of some branches of cultural studies, while raising important points about the politics of representation, are so critical of all "gazes" at the so-called other that, to follow the program set forth by some, we would all be paralyzed into an alienated universe, with no engagement across the boundaries of difference that for better or worse exist.[20]

Underlying these responses, of course, is the idea that "we" and "they" are separate, which in turn is built on the trope and mystique of the noble savage living in a traditional, bounded world, for whom all knowledge, objects, and values originating elsewhere are polluting of some reified notion of culture and innocence. The movie *Crocodile Dundee* presented a witty commentary on such misapprehension in an encounter between New York journalist Sue Charlton (Linda Kozlowski) and Dundee's (Paul Hogan) Aboriginal friend Neville Bell (David Gulpilil). "Creeping through the bush, looking authentic but sounding up-to-date, he is painted from the waist up but wears jeans and a watch. Sue then wants to take his photo. He solemnly tells her she can't. She wonders whether it is because it will steal his spirit. 'No,' he informs her, 'the lens cap's on.'"[21]

Questions about the legitimacy of one's presence in a foreign setting (especially in which power relations are unequal) as an outsider with a camera should *always* be raised and generally have been in most successful projects. The fact that the people one is dealing with also have cameras and choose to represent themselves with them should not diminish that concern. The making of images by "outsiders" is illegitimate when ethical and social rules have been violated in the process. Conversely, the fact that one is an "insider" does not guarantee an untroubled relationship with one's subject, as is dramatically clear in Navajo filmmaker Arlene Bowman's problematic encounter with her traditional grandmother in *Navajo Talking Pictures*. Filming others and filming one's own group are related but distinct parts of a larger project of reflecting upon the particulars of the human condition; each approach raises its own sets of issues regarding ethics, social relations, power, and rights to represent.

Another response considers indigenous production as an altogether separate category from ethnographic film, with different intentions and audiences. The sense of differences is exacerbated by the academic or media positions of one set of producers, as opposed to the community-based locations of the other, a point raised cogently by Marcia Langton regarding more academic anthropology.[22] One might, for example, view indigenous work as not intended to cross over so-called cultural boundaries but rather as made for intracultural consumption and therefore not satisfying some minimal definition of ethnographic film as images of some other, "B," taken by people identified as "A" and presented back to people "A." However, "ethnographic film" has never been bounded by its potential audience. To name only one prominent example, for nearly half a century Jean Rouch has argued that he considers the primary audience for his ethnographic films to be the people who are in them.[23] And recently, native groups all over the world have been reappropriating colonial photography and films for purposes of cultural revival and political reclamation.[24]

Clearly, indigenous media and ethnographic film are related but distinct projects. *Because* of the differences, I believe it is crucial that those interested in ethnographic film be informed and aware of developments in media being produced by those who might be their subjects. But beyond this ethical/political concern for an inclusive pedagogical frame, I would like to explore the basis for incorporating ethnographic film and indigenous media within the same analytical frame.

Mediating Culture

In considering what I call indigenous media, I use the word "media" not simply because it embraces video and television, which play an ever-increasing role in these concerns, but also because of other meanings of the word. The *American College Dictionary* defines it as "an intervening substance, through which a force acts or an effect is produced; [2] an agency, means or instrument." It is related to "mediate": "to act between parties to effect an understanding, compromise, reconciliation." Using these definitions, "indigenous media" as a term points to the common (and perhaps most significant) characteristic that the works I have been describing share with more conventional understandings of ethnographic film. They are all intended to communicate something about that social or collective identity we call "culture," in order to mediate (one hopes) across gaps of space, time, knowledge, and prejudice. The films most closely associated with the genre (ideally) work toward creating understanding between two groups separated by space and social practice, though increasingly they are calling attention to the difficulties of comprehension, as in Dennis O'Rourke's *Cannibal Tours*.

Work being produced by indigenous people about themselves is *also* concerned with mediating across boundaries, but they are directed to the mediation of ruptures of time and history. They work to heal disruptions in cultural knowledge, in historical memory, and in identity between generations occasioned by the tragic but familiar litany of assaults: the taking of lands, political violence, introduced diseases, expansion of capitalist interests and tourism, and unemployment coupled with loss of traditional bases of subsistence. Among some of the groups most actively engaged in media production – native North Americans (including Inuit), Indians of the Amazon Basin (especially Kayapo), and Aboriginal Australians – the initial activities with the camera are almost always both assertive and conservative of identity: documenting injustices and claiming reparations; making records of the lives and knowledge of elders whether through dramatizing mythic stories, explaining traditional food gathering and healing practices, or recreating historically traumatic events with those who witnessed the often violent destruction of life as they had known it.

What these works share with the current practices of ethnographic filmmakers such as David and Judith MacDougall, Gary Kildea, Dennis O'Rourke, and Jean Rouch is that they are not about recreating a preexistent and untroubled cultural identity "out there." Rather they are about the *processes* of identity construction. They are not based on some retrieval of an idealized past but create and assert a position for the present that attempts to accommodate the inconsistencies and contradictions of contemporary life. For Aboriginal Australians, these encompass the powerful relationships to land, myth, and ritual, the fragmented history of contact with Europeans and continued threats to language, health, culture, and social life, and positive efforts in the present to deal with problems stemming from these assaults.

More generally, I am proposing that when other forms are no longer effective, indigenous media offers a possible means – social, cultural, and political – for reproducing and transforming cultural identity among people who have experienced massive political, geographic, and economic disruption. Yet, as in Worth's study with the Navajo, perhaps the real question remains, "Will it do the sheep good?" Or, in the case of satellites and VCRs, the question might be, "Can the sheep be kept alive?" As Rosemarie Kuptana of the Inuit Broadcasting Corporation succinctly phrased it: "As you know, the history of the Inuit people is a history of adaptation; to climatic change, to cultural threat, to technological innovation. Television had clearly arrived to stay; a way had to be found to turn this threat to our culture into a tool for its preservation."[25]

For some scholars of Third World broadcasting (following on the gloomy predictions of the Frankfurt School theorists) the Faustian contract is the discursive frame. They believe that people such as Rosemarie Kuptana are, at best, simply bargaining with Mephistopheles. They conclude that the content and hegemonic control of mass media irreversibly erode traditional languages and cultures, replacing them with alien social values and an attraction to Western consumer goods.[26] Others argue that the very *form* of Western narratives may undermine traditional modes but take this as a mandate for supporting more indigenous production. As David MacDougall recently pointed out,

The dominant conflict structure of Western fictional narratives, and the didacticism of much of Western documentary, may be at odds with traditional modes of discourse. The division into fiction and documentary may itself be subversive. Or differences may arise in the conventions of narrative and imagery. At a film conference in 1978, Wiyendji, an Aboriginal man from Roper River, argued against the Western preoccupation with close-ups and fast cutting, saying that Aborigines preferred to see whole bodies and whole events. This may not be borne out by Aboriginal preferences when viewing non-Aboriginal material, but it is a common complaint about films by outsiders which portray Aboriginal subjects. Such objections obviously cry out for more Aboriginal filmmaking.[27]

Last, and most significant, indigenous filmmakers, scholars, and policy makers have been advocating indigenous use of visual media as a new opportunity for influence and self-expression. In their view, these technologies offer unique potential for the expansion of community-generated production and for the construction of viewing conditions and audiences shaped by indigenous interests and, ultimately, cultural regeneration.

Transmitting Identity: Aboriginal Media

In the following section I discuss particular instances of indigenous media production by Aboriginal Australians. I propose a preliminary analysis of how such work is engaged in the construction of contemporary Aboriginal identity in a way that attempts to integrate historical and contemporary lifeworlds for both Aborigines and the wider society.

The development of Aboriginal work in film and video is as diverse as the Aboriginal population itself, which includes both traditional groups and urban people who are relatively acculturated to Euro-Australian culture and whose history of contact may go back as far as 200 years. Urban Aborigines such as avant-garde filmmaker/photographer Tracey Moffatt may have been raised in a thoroughly assimilated manner and produce work comfortably within the structures of the dominant culture's independent film community, albeit addressing issues of Aboriginal identity, usually confronting problematic relations between Aborigines and the dominant culture.[28] At the other end of the spectrum are traditional people living in remote areas of central and western Australia whose contact history may be as brief as a decade and who have been experimenting with video production strategies to suit their own local concerns. While to Euro-Australians different "traditional" groups may seem indistinguishable, linguistic variation alone makes it clear that they are not a monolithic block; of the 200 Aboriginal languages originally spoken, approximately sixty are still in active use today.[29] Unfortunately, this diversity is frequently ignored by whites setting broadcast policy. As media scholar Helen Molnar points out: "This cultural diversity is important to stress as it can be ignored when discussing Aboriginal media and usually results in inappropriate planning. For Aboriginal programming to be effective, each community's requirements have to be addressed. A pan-Aboriginal solution is inappropriate."[30]

While Aboriginal media is barely a decade old, it is part of the ever-increasing involvement of Australian Aboriginal people in visual media production over the last twenty years. Different aspects of this involvement are summarized nicely in essays by film historian Michael Leigh,[31] filmmaker David MacDougall,[32] as well as the late Eric Michaels[33] and communications scholar Helen Molnar,[34] who reminds us that many remote living Aborigines have been producing their own radio programming since the 1970s, "leaping over the print generation to begin recording their languages, stories, music, and culture."[35] Underscoring the connection of such indigenous media to political consciousness, Michael Leigh links the upsurge of collaborative productions with Australian Aboriginal people to the Labor government's liberal left policy toward Aboriginal "self-determination" from 1972 to 1975.[36] For example, since the early 1970s, at the Australian Institute for Aboriginal and Torres Straits Islanders Studies Film Unit, new projects were based increasingly on interest expressed by Aboriginal communities, resulting in outstanding films such as *Waiting for Harry* (dir. McKenzie, 1980) or *Good-Bye Old Man* (dir. MacDougall, 1977). Paralleling a similar shift in ethnographic writing, these changes in ethnographic film practice that accommodated indigenous interests were, according to David MacDougall, a shift away from "reconstruction of pre-contact situations towards an examination of the realities of contemporary Aboriginal experience. Initially this took the form of supporting and documenting

Aboriginal moves for cultural reassertion."[37] In 1979 the institute began taking on occasional Aboriginal trainees in film and video, such as Wayne Barker, who is now an independent filmmaker. That same year saw the debut of *My Survival as an Aboriginal*, the first film directed by an Aboriginal woman, Essie Coffey of Brewarrina (made with Martha Ansara and Alec Morgan of the Sydney Filmmakers Cooperative).

Indigenous Media at Yuendumu

In the early 1980s questions of Aboriginal involvement in televisual media were raised in relation to the planned launching of Australia's first communications satellite, AUSSAT.[38] With it would come the possibility of the introduction of commercial television to remote areas of the nation for the first time, including many Aboriginal settlements and communities whose geographic isolation had protected them from such intrusions. To assess the impact of majority culture media on Aboriginal viewers, the (then) Australian Institute of Aboriginal Studies hired American researcher Eric Michaels in 1982 to conduct a long-term study in Central Australia.[39] He chose to work with Warlpiri-speaking Aboriginal people at the community of Yuendumu in the Central Desert, northwest of Alice Springs. He also helped train people from Yuendumu to produce videos based on Aboriginal concerns that might be programmed in place of the imagery of standard commercial television. The WMA grew out of this activity.[40]

The fifty tapes produced by Warlpiri videomakers between 1982 and 1984 demonstrated how media could be fashioned and used in ways appropriate to native social organization, narrative conventions, and communicative strategies. Originally intended for use in their school, the works covered subjects ranging from traditional dances, to a piece memorializing a massacre of Warlpiri people by whites, to recording of local sports events. In April 1985 WMA established its own low-power TV station via a homemade transmitter, which pulled in the signal of the state television channel, the Australian Broadcasting Corporation (ABC) and also provided a broadcast outlet for locally produced tapes. (This and other similar operations, in a Kafkaesque twist of bureaucracy, are considered illegal because the state had not managed to authorize a new, appropriate licensing category.)[41]

By 1992, when I visited Yuendumu for the second time, the activities of WMA had expanded to include a new and very successful project, *Manyu-Wana*. Loosely translated as "just for fun," *Manyu-Wana* was initiated in 1989 by Aboriginal and white school teachers at Yuendumu to develop a kind of homegrown Aboriginal *Sesame Street* for Warlpiri-speaking communities. Made with local children for local use, the half-hour programs are intended to help Warlpiri youngsters learn about numbers and stories in their native language rather than in English, which is used in much formal schooling. The creative process is collaborative and improvisational; community members come up with ideas for the program and local children are the "stars" of the show. The show is shot and edited by David Batty (a veteran of CAAMA), who works with a wind-up Bolex 16 mm camera that allows for simple special effects such as fast forward, slow motion, and claymation. The result is a delightful kind of visual style in which cardboard toy cars magically become Toyota trucks or children's drawing become the background for animated versions of Warlpiri mythic stories.

As of April 1992, a new *Manyu-Wana* series is in production, funded by the National Aboriginal Languages Programme, with additional funding from the Australia Council and London's Central Television. The six completed shows have become extremely popular not only for Warlpiri people, children and adults alike, but also for other Aboriginal and white audiences who are drawn to the quirky, local, and altogether charming sensibility of the work, despite the fact that it is all in Warlpiri language. In addition to its regular and frequent use at Yuendumu and other Warlpiri communities such as Lajamanu and Willowra, the work was broadcast on Imparja television and is scheduled to be aired on the national Special Broadcast Service.

Most recently, Yuendumu helped organize the Tanami Network, a video conferencing network that uses the satellite to link four Aboriginal communities in the Tanami area of the Northern Territory (Yuendumu, Lajamanu, Willowra, and Kintore) to each other and to Alice Springs, Darwin, and Sydney. The state-of-the-art compressed video technology that they are using allows groups of people to see and hear each other, what some have called a "space-age picture telephone." The communities jointly contributed over $350,000 in mining royalties and other community funds to establish this communication system, an indication of their view of its usefulness to them. Their sentiments were articulated at a communications workshop at Yuendumu in 1990 when the technology was first demonstrated to the community. At that meeting, two paintings by a Warlpiri woman, Jeannie Nungarrayi Egan, were used to show alternative models of communication. In one, Warlpiri communities depend for information on *kardiya* (white people's) centres such as Alice Springs, Katherine, or Darwin, a difficult and expensive situation; the other painting provides a decentralized, interactive model in which large white settlements are not privileged over smaller Aboriginal ones.

At a communications conference in March 1992, shortly after the network had been put in place, Peter Toyne, a former principal of the Yuendumu school who has been active in helping organize the network, put the network's goals in cultural and historical perspective from a Warlpiri point of view.

The establishment of the Tanami communities over the last fifty years severely disrupted the traditional network of information and personal contacts which existed amongst people in the area. The Aboriginal people have responded by attempting to reassemble the earlier network through the use of motor vehicles... outstations... and through such telephone and radio links as have escaped the restrictive control of non-Aboriginals in the communities.... Aboriginal community members have stated repeatedly that they want the links to work out family things and help keep the traditions and Aboriginal law strong.... The Tanami Network is being developed in the belief that it offers a completely new line of approach to many of these problems by changing the basic dialogue through which the services are planned and delivered.[42]

The network has already been used for purposes as diverse as "sorry business" (funeral arrangements); driver's education; and long-distance marketing of Aboriginal art. Other possible services include community-based secondary courses, enhanced adult education aimed at professional and semiprofessional employment for Aboriginal people; community detention as an alternative to jail; inservice support for agency employees; enhancing processes of consultation and representation; and secondary education.[43]

While some are skeptical of the expense and specialized nature of the technology at a time when so many basic needs – health, nutrition, shelter – are not adequately served, others find in the Tanami Network global-village possibilities. Consider the newspaper headlines that announced its debut: "Tribal business has gone space age in the outback" read the Alice Springs paper;[44] "Resourceful Aborigines use latest technology to preserve tribal life."[45] Whatever the outcome or relative utility of this experiment, what is clear is that there is an increasing self-consciousness and initiative on the part of remote living Aboriginal people to develop these media technologies in ways appropriate to traditional patterns of social organization.

Other local media associations similar to Yuendumu have developed in a number of other remote areas, most notably at Ernabella, a Pitjantjatjara community in South Australia.[46] There, in 1983, local people began producing video programs reflecting their cultural practices and daily activities. The videos immediately became quite popular. By April 1985 Pitjantjatjara Yankunytjatjara Media Association established Ernabella Video Television (EVTV) when "EVTV commenced local broadcasting on the world's cheapest community television transmission system (less than $1,000 worth of equipment purchased from a 10 cent surcharge on cool drinks in the store)."[47]

Since then EVTV has produced over 100 hours of community television each year, which is strictly regulated by the local media committee in terms of both timing – so that it would not interfere with the social activities of the community – and substance. Rather than competing with traditional practices, EVTV's strong focus on recording the songs, dances, and ceremonies performed at the places associated with the mythic *Tukurrpa* ("Dreaming Stories") for the area has had a revitalizing effect on these beliefs and values – for example, generating traditional dance festivals at Ernabella and throughout Australia.[48]

EVTV and WMA became models for government efforts to introduce televisual technologies into other communities, in particular the Broadcasting for Remote Aboriginal Communities Scheme (BRACS). This plan was the government's response to the recommendations of *Out of the Silent Land*, the 1984 report of its Task Force on Aboriginal and Islanders Broadcasting. BRACS provides equipment for receiving and rebroadcasting the satellite signal as well as for producing video and radio programs to approximately eighty remote Aboriginal communities. It was conceived as a way to protect and promote local culture and languages against the intrusion of national or commercial television; the intention was to give Aboriginal communities the capacity to interrupt the satellite transmission with their own programming.[49] With a few exceptions, however, BRACS has not operated in that way for a number of reasons: there was almost no consultation with Aboriginal communities and no provision for maintenance, training, repairs, upgrades, suitable buildings, electricity, or cassettes. Also, the quality of the equipment is so poor that BRACS productions have very short life spans and limited circulation. Given these problems, it is not surprising that, for the most part, the only successful BRACS programs are those that are developed at communities that are already experienced in media production.[50] In comparing BRACS to the success of groups such as WMA and EVTV, Philip Batty suggests that the key to effective Aboriginal "resistance" to the imposition of television is not to ban it altogether but rather to figure out how to integrate it on their own terms.[51]

In this model information can travel easily to government centers but
it is more expensive and indirect to contact your family in other
communities.

Lajamanu with its kardiya
(whitefella) and yapa (Warlpiri) inhabitants

Lajamanu outstations

Main communication routes
(roads, telephones)

Kardiya towns (Darwin,
Alice Springs, Katherine)

Willowra and its outstations
yapa and kardiya inhabitants

Yuendumu and its
outstations yapa and
kardiya inhabitants

Plate 13.1 Jeanie Nungaarrayi Egan, two paintings of intercommunity communication (1990). Yuendumu Community Education Centre reproduces two large color
paintings made by Jeanie Nungaarrayi Egan, a Warlpiri schoolteacher, painter,
and activist, who painted them specifically for the October 1990 conference at Yuendumu, where the future of communications for Aboriginal people in the Tanami
region was under discussion. As in her other painting, she used Warlpiri iconography
that traditionally has been used in ceremonial settings to visualize stories
about the relationship of mythic ancestors to the land in the "Dreamtime"; in
this case, however, the meanings of some of the abstract signs have been transformed
to indicate specific places that are linked through satellite information technologies
in order to clarify the differences between *kardiya* (whitefella) and *yapa*
(Warlpiri) models of communication. These paintings demonstrate that the rethinking

This model is a true network. It is just as easy for information to be
shared between families and communities as it is between
communities and government centers.

Lajamanu surrounded by its
outstations

Willowra surrounded by its
outstations

Pathways join all places
together and are of equal
importance

Yuendumu surrounded by
its outstations

Alice Springs

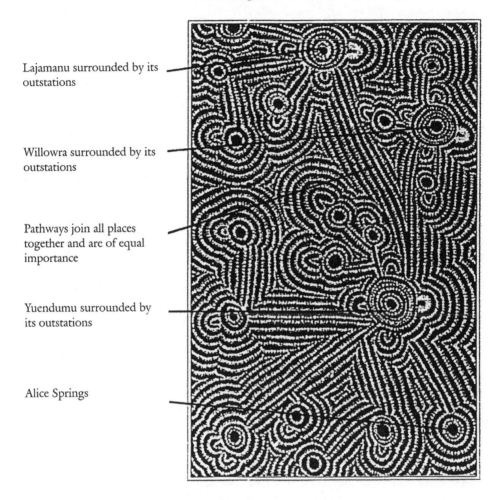

of Western media technology from an Aboriginal perspective is coming out of discussions and ideas in local Aboriginal communities such as Yuendumu that have successfully incorporated television and video on their own terms. I have used it here with the permission of the painter because it makes graphically clear (contrary to conspiracy models of media in which indigenous people are implicitly cast as innocent victims) that Aboriginal people are not only creating their own media, but are integrating it into their own theories and ideas about communication and information networks. The arguments in this essay, for example, are drawn in large measure from those I heard articulated by a range of Aboriginal media activists, whom I have quoted and named throughout. Photograph: Yuendumu Community Education Centre © DACS 2002.

Aboriginal Media in Central Australia: CAAMA and Imparja

The Central Australian Aboriginal Media Association, or CAAMA, is one of the most successful of Aboriginally controlled media projects. Like many of the other Aboriginal media associations in Australia,[52] it started as an FM radio station. CAAMA was founded in 1980 by two Aboriginal people and one "whitefella," whose private record collection was the basis of most of the original programming. It quickly became one of the most popular radio stations for both blacks and whites in the Northern Territory. Its format combines country western, Aboriginal rock, call-ins, and discussion of news of concern to Aborigines in six native languages and English for nearly 15 hours a day. It later expanded to AM and shortwave broadcasts, a prize-winning educational show called *Bushfire*, and a recording studio for Aboriginal bands whose tapes are sold along with other Aboriginal art products in the CAAMA shop. In addition, a video unit was established in 1984; originally, it produced a series of one-hour video newsletters in English and other major Aboriginal languages to circulate to communities without radio access.

In 1985, when the Australian government launched AUSSAT and it became clear that, eventually, commercial TV was going to be available to the remote Aboriginal settlements in CAAMA's radio broadcast area, CAAMA's leaders were concerned about the destructive potential. Freda Glynn, the former director of CAAMA, made the argument clearly. As an Aboriginal woman who was taken from her family in childhood to be educated in Western schools, she is keenly aware of the impact of such interventions and sees TV as part of a continuum of assaults on Aboriginal life that must be dealt with in as positive a manner as possible.

TV is like an invasion. We have had grog, guns and diseases, but we have been really fortunate that people outside the major communities have had no communication like radio or TV. Language and culture have been protected by neglect. Now, they are not going to be. They need protection because TV will be going into those communities 24 hours a day in a foreign language – English. It only takes a few months and the kids start changing. We're trying to teach kids you can be Aboriginal and keep your language and still mix in the wider community and have English as well. At least they will be seeing black faces on the magic box that sits in the corner, instead of seeing white faces all day long.[53]

Out of this concern for mass media's impact on traditional Aboriginal languages and culture, CAAMA made a bid for the satellite's downlink licence to Central Australia as a symbolic assertion of the presence and concerns of that region's Aboriginal people. Much to their surprise, their proposal for taking on this multimillion dollar operation was taken seriously. In January 1987, after a prolonged battle agaisnt bigger commercial interests as well as opposition from the Northern Territory government, CAAMA won the Regional Commercial Television Services (RCTS) licence for the television downlink to the Central Australian "footprint" (so named because it describes the general shape of the signal patterns to earth given off by satellites). They were able to make the acquisition with financial assistance from a variety of government sources.[54] The private commercial station they now own, Imparja (which means "tracks" or "footprint" in the Central Australian language Arrernte), began broadcasting in January 1988, serving approximately 100,000 viewers in Central Australia, over a quarter of them Aboriginal (though some put that figure as high as 40 percent).[55]

Thus far, in addition to public service announcements, logos, wrap-arounds, and the like, which are directed to Aboriginal concerns such as bush foods or the Central Land Council, Imparja has been broadcasting regular Aboriginal programs produced by CAAMA. In 1988 they carried twenty-six 30-minute current-affairs programs, broadcast twice a week in prime time: *Urrpye* (*Messenger*), an English-language "magazine and current affairs style program helping to promote awareness about the concerns and issues of Aboriginal people" (cancelled in 1989); and *Nganampa – Anwernekenhe* (*Ours* in Pitjantjatjara/*Our Way of Culture* in Arrernte), a magazine show in different Aboriginal languages – Arrernte, Luritja, Pitjantjatjara, Warlpiri – with English subtitles, intended to help maintain and represent Aboriginal language and culture through art, music, storeis, and dances. In 1989 Imparja broadcast a thirteen-part language series, an Aboriginal music program, and a late-night show featuring Aborigines talking in their own languages, telling their history, and "dreaming" stories.[56] In 1991, in addition to *Nganampa, Talking Strong*, a series of independent films by or about Aboriginal people, was telecast over a seven-month period on Saturday nights. Currently, *Nganampa* continues to be produced and broadcast on Thursday nights at 8:00, and Aboriginal programs produced for other RCTS stations (programs such as *Milbindi*) are re-broadcast as well. As part of their support for Aboriginal health concerns, Imparja does not sell commercials for alcohol.

In its first two years Imparja was viewed with great optimism. For example, writing in *Art in America* in 1989, cultural critics Tony Fry and Anne-Marie Willis presented Imparja optimistically as

a cultural space in which innovation is possible; it has a future. This is a new symbol of power in a culture dominated by the media. It doesn't override the effects of the damaged culture in which it functions, but creates a fissure in which a new set of perceptions can seep in. Such comments do not imply such an operation is free from either the reach of ethnocidal agency or of more direct effects of unequal exchange – it is not judged by authority as a mainstream commercial channel and is dependent on government funding. It is neither beyond nor lacking in criticism, especially over the nature and quantity of Aboriginal-made content.[57]

More recently there have been complaints, especially from other Aboriginal people, that 2–3 hours out of 70 hours a week, even at prime time, is insufficient Aboriginal programming. Others are concerned about Imparja's stress on "broadcast quality" – an elusive and problematic term, for somewhat arbitrary technical standards for productions used by television stations, that effectively keeps low-budget and unconventional work off the air. The result has been to limit Imparja's use of material produced by Yuendumu and other local Aboriginal media associations. It also restricts CAAMA's ability to produce programming for Imparja because of the costs involved in "broadcast quality" work. A 30-minute piece could cost between $10,000 and $20,000, while imported American shows can be purchased inexpensively.[58]

The question of advertising also has an impact on programming content for any commercial TV outlet. Imparja, like the other Australian satellite downlinks, struggles to meet the $4.5 million satellite rental fee (rising at 12 percent a year) via advertising revenues, which will never grow significantly because the population numbers (and therefore potential consumers) are low. Aboriginal programming is particularly not lucrative because there is a dropoff in European viewers, and advertisers – most of whom are local business people – do not view Aboriginal people as consumers.

Finally, while Imparja is the only large-scale commercial television station owned by Australian Aboriginal people, only 10 percent of the television staff is Aboriginal. To help correct for this problem, in 1988 CAAMA and Imparja made a training agreement with the Department of Education, Employment and Training to train 33 Aboriginal people as videotape operators, editors, recording assistants, TV present- ers, radio journalists and broadcasters, translators/interpreters, sales representatives, researchers, and bookkeepers. All trainees were supposed to be taken on as perman- ent employees by CAAMA and Imparja at the end of their training; the fact that this did not happen was in part responsible for a change in leadership at CAAMA in 1992 and ongoing criticism of Imparja.

Imparja, as the only indigenously owned commercial television station in the world, has received considerable attention by critics and supporters alike. However, to comprehend the significance of indigenous media production, it is important to look at the *range* of media projects being carried out by Aboriginal Australians (of which this only touches on a few). Together, WMA, CAAMA, and Imparja (and others of course) might instruct us as to the costs and benefits of the introduction of media technologies in different settings. Small groups such as WMA, compared to CAAMA and Imparja, are fragile in economic terms *and* because they rely heavily on the unique talents of a few individuals. For example, WMA's central figure, Francis Jupurrurla Kelly, is able to juggle and use both Australian and traditional Aboriginal language and knowledge. Eric Michaels captured a sense of this in his description of Francis:

Jupurrurla, in his Bob Marley T-shirt and Adidas runners, armed with his video portapak, resists identification as a savage updating some archaic technology to produce curiosities of a primitive tradition for the jaded modern gaze. Jupurrurla is indisputably a sophisticated cultural broker who employs videotape and modern technology to express and resolve political, theological, and aesthetic contradictions that arise in uniquely contemporary cir- cumstances.[59]

Such individuals, however, occupy a historically unique intergenerational position that is unlikely to be replicated unless a conscious effort is made to do so. So, the departure of just one of them is a serious blow to the operation of these small-scale media groups.

On the positive side, the local scale of WMA has allowed for community control over media both artistically and politically – for example, through the "illegal" satellite downlink into which they insert their own programming. More important, WMA has developed an innovative production style (in aesthetic matters and in work relations) that is embedded in local concerns and social organization and traditions. Eric Michaels, in his report *The Aboriginal Invention of Television*, based on his work at Yuendumu, argued that the substance and formal qualities of the tapes have a distinctly Warlpiri sensibility, marked for example by an intense interest in the landscape as filled with specific meaning. In contrast to the free- floating signifiers that characterize televisual semiotics, traditional Aboriginal knowledge is made meaningful by associations with particular geographic locations. But, he went on to point out, of equal if not more importance is the social organiza- tion of media production; the ways in which tapes are made, shown, and used reflect

Warlpiri understandings of kinship and group responsibilities for display and access to traditional knowledge.[60]

The complex control of cultural information in Aboriginal society has been of much interest to scholars of Aboriginal society. A number of ethnographic inquiries (e.g., Bell, Dyers, Sansom)[61] demonstrate how ceremonial and other kinds of knowledge ("law") critical to cultural identity are transmitted, and the power inherent in such social relations. Elders impart their knowledge at appropriate times over the life cycle, most dramatically through initiation rituals. Such knowledge transmission is organized not only by generation but by gender and kin classifications. Thus, in traditional communities, knowing, seeing, hearing, speaking, and performing certain kinds of information is highly regulated; violation of norms can meet with severe sanctions. Groups such as WMA, because they are locally based, are able to develop rules for video production and viewing appropriate to such community standards.

In contrast to the WMA, Imparja is a large multimillion dollar station in which information flows follow the imperatives of commercial television oriented toward mass audiences. The need for advertising always supersedes investment in programming for Aboriginal viewers. In keeping with the management's Euro-Australian orientation, Imparja's Aboriginal programs such as *Nganampa* use the conventions of television; yet Aboriginal people, news, and languages are heard and seen twice weekly on commercial television in Central Australia. The two other RCTS stations (satellite downlinks), though not owned by Aborigines, also offer programming for the Aboriginal populations in their areas. The Golden West Network in Western Australia (excluding Perth) produces *Milbindi*, a weekly current affairs magazine in prime time. The half-hour program, which is rebroadcast on Imparja, has Aboriginal presenters and stories stress positive aspects of Aboriginal life and culture. They also produce a twice-weekly news insert on Aboriginal issues, *Marnum*, and once a month screen an Aboriginal special as well as the government-produced *Aboriginal Australia*.[62] Queensland Satellite TV (QSTV) works with an Aboriginal and Torres Straits Islander program committee to provide about an hour a week of Aboriginal programming and also offers monthly broadcasts of *Aboriginal Australia*. Their thirteen-part Aboriginal affairs program, *My Place, My Land, My People*, about the various Aboriginal communities in the QSTV viewing area, was cancelled due to budget cuts in 1991.

Do the formal conventions of Western TV that these shows use turn off more traditional Aboriginal viewers, or do they seduce them into watching other non-Aboriginal programs? Are more European viewers inclined to attend to things Aboriginal when they appear in the "flow" of broadcast? Indeed, in settings such as Central, Western, and Northern Australia, where different cultural models for communication intersect, questions about media reception are complex. As Helen Molnar points out:

European mass media with its homogenized messages transmitted from a central source are at odds with Aboriginal information patterns. Aborigines see their local areas as the centre from which information emanates. Their information/communications model is completely the reverse of the European model which sees the urban cities as the centre and the remote communities as the periphery. The mass media not only ignores local boundaries (Aboriginal countries), it also makes information accessible to all viewers.[63]

However, the development of Aboriginal video production is significant not only to their own communities. "Aboriginal people, both individually and collectively, are turning to film, video and television as the media most likely to carry their messages to one another and into the consciousness of white Australia."[64] Given this situation, how can efforts to increase the visibility of Aboriginal people in the mass media also respect Aboriginal rules of representation – such as the taboo on viewing images of people who have recently died?

Over the last five years a number of efforts have been initiated to meet the demand for more Aboriginal participation and visibility in television, not only for local access to video in remote areas of Australia, but also for more Aboriginal representation on mainstream national television. While the state-controlled and funded Australian Broadcasting Corporation (ABC) had been training Aborigines since 1980, by 1987 only seven Aborigines were employed there. That same year, the prime minister established the Aboriginal Employment and Development Policy (AEDP), which requires all industries to have 2 percent Aboriginal employment by 1991.[65] Consequently, the ABC set up an Aboriginal Programs Unit in 1987; their first Aboriginally produced and presented program, *Blackout*, began broadcasting in May 1989 on a Friday-evening time slot. Additionally, in 1991, the unit programmed a Thursday-night eight-part series of independent documentaries on Aboriginal topics, *The First Australians*.[66]

In April 1989 the Special Broadcast Service initiated a thirteen-part TV series devoted to Aboriginal issues. Called *First in Line*, it aired Tuesday nights at 7:30 p.m. The producers and crew were primarily Aboriginal and consulted with communities throughout Australia for items stressing the positive achievements of Aborigines.[67] Eventually, *First in Line* was discontinued, and an Aboriginal Program Unit was established with Rachel Perkins (a former CAAMA trainee) at the head. For 1992–3, she is purchasing programming from groups such as WMA and CAAMA (Nganampa-Anwernekenhe), as well as commissioning four independent documentaries on different aspects of Aboriginal history and culture.[68]

Mediating Identities

The range of media generated with and by Australian Aborigines since the 1980s operate at distinct levels of social, political, and economic organization, yet increasingly they intersect. In some measure, they correspond to the diverse social positions occupied by Aboriginal Australians and the various ways they have attempted to gain visibility and cultural control over their own images. And it is important to remember that some remote Aboriginal communities still regard television as "the third invader" following Europeans and alcohol.[69] Yet the imposition of Euro-Australian televisual forms and technology on relatively intact traditional Aboriginal communities has also catalyzed locally controlled, innovative, community-supported video production that has had a revitalizing effect in some venues. It is important, then, to consider what distinguishes groups such as EVTV and WMA, who have maintained local control and creativity in developing television and video. As Philip Batty assesses it:

They had managed to establish their own local television service funded through their own local resources and became familiar with the basic processes of television production, long before the arrival of global television.... So when we talk about "resistance" to global television, it seems that this can only be accomplished in any effective way, by gaining an active if basic knowledge of television technology, and applying that knowledge in locally relevant and meaningful ways, and thereby be in a position to develop the confidence and the community consciousness to deal with global television on an equal footing.[70]

To return to Marcia Langton's argument, such work is necessary but not sufficient if it occurs in a vacuum of political and aesthetic sensibility toward Aboriginal cultural production.

The conflict between black and white in Australia about representations of "aboriginalities" cannot be resolved by demanding that Aboriginal people have control of those representations. Self-determination does not work at this level of social life. Rather the resolution is to be found in the development of a body of critical theory and knowledge about representations of Aboriginal peoples and concerns.[71]

The problematic placement of new forms of cultural expression has been noted by other scholars of Aboriginal Australia. It was the concern of Eric Michaels's later works on Aboriginal art and Warlpiri Media.[72] Recently, Fred Myers has written on the place of art criticism in the global circulation of Aboriginal acrylic paintings.[73] These works in Aboriginal studies have profited from an arena of discursive production in anthropology and cultural studies that has been emerging during the late 1980s, a discourse that transcends the static essentialism of the Faustian bargain and the cultural and political myopia of the global village. For example, in his essay on ethnic autobiography, Michael Fischer offers insights that also seem appropriate to understanding indigenous media (recognizing that Aboriginal identity and ethnic identity are not to be equated with a depoliticized domain of multiculturalism):

What the newer works bring home forcefully, is, first, the paradoxical sense that ethnicity is something reinvented and reinterpreted in each generation.... The search or struggle for a sense of ethnic identity is a (re)invention and discovery of a vision, both ethical and future oriented. Whereas the search for coherence is grounded in a connection to the past, the meaning abstracted from that past, an important criterian of coherence, is an ethic workable for the future.[74]

With these insights in mind, what are we to make of MTV-inspired indigenous productions with well-known Aboriginal country western and rock groups that are so popular with a range of Aboriginal audiences? These are perhaps the metalanguage, the poetry of indigenous media, *performing* what is implicit in other kinds of productions that might follow more conventional lines. In one particularly popular segment featuring a band led by Aboriginal singer Ned Hargraves, the video-processed image, clearly a Western form, might be interpreted as contradicting the message of the song the group sings:

> Look at us, look at the price we have paid.
> Keep your culture, keep your land.
> Will you stop before your ways are dead?

As the group performs against a dramatic desert background, visions of men doing traditional dances, images of desert animals and sites, fade in and out. By the end of the piece, the lead singer, Ned Hargraves, falls down, apparently dead. It seems to be the fitting image to the end of the piece as the last line is repeated: "Will you stop before your ways are dead?" Then, suddenly, Ned revives with a wink and a "thumbs up" signal to the audience, suggesting a different perspective that inverts the usual jeremiad over cultural loss. Such unexpected bricolage, borrowing freely from a range of available expressive resources (rock music, video, Aboriginal language and landscape) is in the service of Aboriginal cultural assertion.

For Aboriginal producers, the goal of their media work is not simply to maintain existing cultural identities, what some Aborigines have called the "cultural refrigeration" approach.[75] The production of new media forms is also a means of cultural invention that refracts and recombines elements from both the dominant and minority societies. Art critics Fry and Willis try and capture that sense of "hybridity" in the language of postmodernism. They update Lévi-Strauss's image of bricolage with more contemporary metaphors, combining popular understandings of recombinant DNA and telecommunications.

Making a new culture which knowingly embraces the future is a more viable form of cultural bricolage (by this we mean the making of a culture by a process of the selection and assembly of combined and recombined cultural forms). Resistance to ethnocide is not seen as trying simply to defend an existent cultural identity but the forging of a new one which rejects the models sought to be imposed. Radio, television and video have become significant media in this cultural strategy. And what is particularly significant is that these media break the circuit of producing products for circulation and consumption within the culture of dominance (as opposed to works of art). Aboriginal radio, video and TV producers are producing ideas and images that circulate in their own cultures.[76]

Mass mediation of indigenous culture is certainly not a global village, as Imparja's subsuming of Aboriginal interests to commerical imperatives makes clear. Yet, when indigenous media is under local control, it seems to have a revitalizing potential, suggesting a more positive model than the Faustian one. Young Aboriginal people who are or will be entering into production are not growing up in a pristine world, untouched by the dominant culture, nor do they want to assimilate to the dominant culture. They are juggling the multiple sets of experiences that make them contemporary Aboriginal Australians. Many want to engage in creating images and narratives about their present lives, which nonetheless connect them to their history, and direct them toward a future as well. For this generation, Aboriginally produced stories and images about Aboriginal life in Australia are increasingly visible in the flow of images seen by *all* audiences.

At its best, indigenous media is expressive of transformations in indigenous consciousness rooted in social movements for Aboriginal empowerment, cultural autonomy, and claims to land. Many would argue that there is a continuum of activities for Aboriginal self-determination *vis-à-vis* the state that links land rights to air rights. Like the ethnic autobiographies that Fischer discusses, one can see in this work a new arena of cultural production in which specific historical and cultural ruptures are addressed and mediated, and reflections of "us" and "them" to each other are increasingly juxtaposed.

INTERVIEWS

Batty, Phillip, assistant director, CAAMA, Alice Springs, July 5, 1988.
Glynn, Freda, director, CAAMA; chair, Imparja, Alice Springs, July 6, 1988.
Perkins, Rachel, director, Aboriginal Programs Unit, SBS, Sydney, April 29, 1992.
Peters, Frances, Aboriginal Programs Unit, ABC, Sydney, April 30, 1992.
Sandy, David, Aboriginal Programs Unit, ABC, Sydney, April 30, 1992.

FILMOGRAPHY

Bowman, Arlene 1986. *Navajo Talking Picture*.
Cavadini, Alessandro and Carolyn Strachan 1981. *Two Laws*.
Coffey, Essie, with Martha Ansara and Alec Morgan 1979. *My Survival as an Aboriginal*.
Elder, Sarah and Leonard Kamerling 1973. *At the Time of Whaling*.
—— 1973. *Tununeremiut*.
—— 1976. *From the First People*.
—— 1976. *On the Spring Ice*.
—— 1988. *The Drums of Winter*.
Kanuck, Zacharias 1977. *Goodbye Old Man*.
—— 1987. *From Inuit Point of View*.
—— 1989. *Quaggig*.
Macdougall, David and Judith Macdougall 1980. *Familiar Places*.
—— 1980. *Takeover*.
—— 1980. *The House Opening*.
Mckenzie, Kim 1980. *Waiting for Harry*.
Msayesva, Victor 1984. *Itam Hakim, Hopiit*.
—— 1988. *Ritual Clowns*.
Moffatt, Tracey 1987. *Nice Coloured Girls*.
—— 1990. *Night Cries: A Rural Tragedy*.
Olin, Chuck 1983. *Box of Treasures*.
O'Rourke, Dennis 1976. *Yumi Yet*.
—— 1978. *Ileksen*.
—— 1987. *Cannibal Tours*.
Rouch, Jean 1954. *Les Maîtres fous*.
—— 1955. *Jaguar*.
—— 1960. *Chronicle of a Summer*.

NOTES

All illustrations to this chapter can be found at http://ethnonet.gold.ac.uk

1   For example, in the summer of 1990, "The Decade Show: Frameworks of Identity in the 1980s" was hosted by a consortium of three New York City museums: the New Museum

of Contemporary Art, the Studio Museum in Harlem, and the Museum of Contemporary Hispanic Art. The accompanying brochure to the show describes the issue uniting the diverse visual, video, and performing artists in the exhibition: "Through their examination of familiar issues – homelessness, gender, racism, sexism, AIDS, homophobia, media politics, the environment, and war – these artists demonstrate that identity is a hybrid and fluid notion that reflects the diversity of American society.... The work included in this exhibition may be seen as material evidence of alternate viewpoints. Many artists of color, for example, in their philosophical, aesthetic, and spiritual linkages to precolonial societies of Asia, Africa, and America, legitimize diversity, resist Eurocentric domination and create a foundation from which to analyze and explain contemporary social phenomena. Feminist, gay, and lesbian artists similarly affirm that there are other ways of seeing, ways equal to existing cultural dictates."

2 As part of a commitment to multicultural awareness, Britain's Channel 4 and the British Film Institute developed the Workshop Declaration of 1981, which gave nonprofit media-production units with four or more salaried members the right to be franchised and eligible for nonprofit production and operation money. These workshops are expected to provide innovative media and educational programs in the communities where they are situated.

   In the racially tense climate of Britain in the early 1980s, and especially after the 1981 Brixton riots, the Labour Party initiated progressive cultural policy through the establishment of a race relations unit and Ethnic Minorities Committee. Money was made available for film and video from the Greater London Council and local borough councils. Based on these funds, the future members of two influential and ground-breaking black film groups, Sankofa and Black Audio Film, financed their first works and organized workshops; see Coco Fusco, "A Black Avant-Garde? Notes on Black Audio Film Collective and Sankofa," in Coco Fusco, ed., *Young, British and Black* (Buffalo, NY, 1988), 7–22.

3 The Special Broadcast Service (SBS) in Australia was set up initially as an ethnic broadcasting service. Until 1989 it viewed Aboriginal people as outside its mandate because they are indigenous rather than ethnic minorities.

4 The following two examples illustrate the growing interest in indigenous media work in well-known "high culture" institutions. In the spring of 1990 the New Museum hosted "Satellite Cultures," a showcase of experimental and alternative video from Australia that included screenings of work by Tracey Moffatt, an urban Aboriginal filmmaker and artist who is relatively well known in art circles, as well as a reel of work by CAAMA, and a documentary on Aboriginal land rights, "Extinct but Going Home." Unfortunately, the video was poorly contextualized and badly exhibited. Lacking any background, most American observers watching the CAAMA programs seemed intrigued but bewildered.

   In June 1992 the Association on American Indian Affairs, the National Museum of the American Indian, the American Indian Community House, the Learning Alliance, and the Film Society of Lincoln Center jointly sponsored "Wind and Glacier Voices: The Native American Film and Video Celebration." This was the first such festival ever held at the Walter Reade Theater, part of New York City's prestigious "high culture" Lincoln Center.

5 Quoted in Philip Batty, "Singing the Electric: Aboriginal Television in Australia," in Tony Downmunt, ed., *Channels of Resistance* (London, 1993), 114.

6 For a recent comprehensive work, see Roy Armes, *Third World Film Making and the West* (Berkeley, CA, 1987).

7 Batty, "Singing the Electric," 3.

8 The main centers of indigenous media production (besides Australia) are among the Indians of the Amazon Basin, especially the Kayapo, among Native North American Indians. See the following sources: Deborah Lee Murin, *Northern Native Broadcasting*

(Runge Press [Canada], 1988); Terence Turner, "Visual Media, Cultural Politics and Anthropological Practice: Some Implications of Recent Uses of Film and Video among the Kayapo of Brazil," *Commission on Visual Anthropology Review* (spring 1990): 8–13; Elizabeth Weatherford, ed., *Native Americans on Film and Video*, vol. 1 (New York, 1981); Elizabeth Weatherford and Emelia Seubert, eds., *Native Americans on Film and Video*, vol. 2 (New York, 1988).

9   This is beginning to change. For example, at the 1991 American Anthropological Association meetings in Chicago, there were two panels on Television and the Transformation of Culture that examined the social processes of production, distribution, and consumption/reception of television in Great Britain, Nigeria, Papua New Guinea, Nigeria, Indonesia, the United States, Colombia, China, and Japan.

10   Marcia Langton, *Well, I Heard It on the Radio and Saw It on the Television: An Essay for the Australian Film Commission on the Politics and Aesthetics of Filmmaking by and about Aboriginal People and Things* (Sydney, 1993), 6.

11   Stuart Hall, "Cultural Identity and Diaspora," in J. Rutherford, ed., *Identity, Community, Culture, Difference* (London, 1990), 222.

12   Some key figures in these discussions include Homi Bhabha, "The Other Question: Difference, Discrimination and the Discourse of Colonialism," in Russell Ferguson, Martha Lever, Trinh T. Minh-Ha, and Cornel West, eds., *Out There: Marginalization and Contemporary Cultures* (Cambridge, 1990); Michael Fischer, "Ethnicity and the Post-Modern Arts of Memory," in James Clifford and George Marcus, eds., *Writing Culture: The Poetics and Politics of Ethnography* (Berkeley, CA, 1986), 194–233; Hall, "Cultural Identity and Diaspora"; Stuart Hall, "Cultural Studies and Its Theoretical Legacies," in L. Grossberg, C. Nelson, and P. Treichler, eds., *Cultural Studies* (New York, 1992), 277–94; Lucy Lippard, *Mixed Blessings: New Art in Multicultural America* (New York, 1990).

13   Hall, "Cultural Studies and Its Theoretical Legacies," 285.

14   Dell Hymes, "The Use of Anthropology: Critical, Political, Personal," in Dell Hymes, ed., *Reinventing Anthropology* (New York, 1972), 3–79.

15   For example, George Marcus and Michael Fischer, *Anthropology as Cultural Critique: An Experimental Moment in the Human Sciences* (Chicago, 1986).

16   David MacDougall, "Beyond Observational Cinema," in Paul Hockings, ed., *Principles of Visual Anthropology* (Chicago, 1975), 109–24.

17   Sol Worth and John Adair, *Through Navajo Eyes* (Bloomington, IN, 1972), 5.

18   These projects include works such as *Familiar Places* (1980), *Goodbye Old Man* (1977), *The House Opening* (1980), and *Takeover* (1980), by David and Judith MacDougall with various Aboriginal groups in Australia; *Two Laws* (1983), made by Carolyn Strachan and Alessandro Cavadini with Aboriginal people in Boroloola; *Ileksen* (1978) and *Yumi Yet* (1976), made by Dennis O'Rourke in New Guinea; and Sarah Elder and Leonard Kamerling's work with the Alaska Native Heritage Project, including *At the Time of Whaling* (1973), *From the First People* (1976), *On the Spring Ice* (1976), *Tununeremiut* (1973), and *The Drums of Winter* (1988).

19   Hopi video artist Victor Masayesva's works include *Itam Hakim Hopiit* (1984) and *Ritual Clowns* (1988); Inuit producer Zach Kanuck's work includes *From Inuit Point of View* (1987) and *Quaggig* (1989).

20   See, for example, Annette Hamilton's excellent discussion of this and related issues in her review of *Communication and Tradition: Essays after Eric Michaels in Canberra Anthropology* 14, no. 2 (1991): 112–14.

21   Peter Malone, *In Black and White and Colour: A Survey of Aborigines in Recent Feature Films* (Jabiru, Northern Territory, Australia, 1987), 114.

22   Marcia Langton, "Some Comments on Consultative Anthropology in Aboriginal Australia," paper presented at the Australian Anthropological Society meetings, Canberra, 1982.

23 "What reason could we as anthropologists give for the glances we cast over the wall at others? Without a doubt, this word of interrogation must be addressed to all anthropologists, but none of their books or articles has ever been questioned as much as have anthropological films.... Film is the only method I have to show another just how I see him. In other words, for me, my prime audience is... the other person, the one I am filming." Jean Rouch, "The Camera and the Man," in Hockings, *Principles of Visual Anthropology*, 83–102.

24 For example, the film *Box of Treasures* (1983) shows how contemporary Kwakiutl Indians are utilizing a number of resources – including colonial photography – to facilitate cultural revival.

25 Rosemarie Kuptana, "Inuit Broadcasting Corporation," *Commission on Visual Anthropology Newsletter* (May 1988): 39.

26 A recent example of this argument is Neil Postman's *Technology: The Surrender of Culture to Technology* (New York, 1992), in which he argues that we have surrendered our social institutions to the "sovereignty of technology" so that traditional culture has become invisible and irrelevant.

27 David MacDougall, "Media Friend or Media Foe," *Visual Anthropology* 1, no. 1 (1987): 58.

28 Anne Rutherford, "Changing Images: An Interview with Tracey Moffatt," in Anne Rutherford, ed., *Aboriginal Culture Today* (Canberra, 1988); Scott Murray, "Tracey Moffatt," *Cinema Papers* 79 (1990): 9–22.

29 P. Black, *Aboriginal Languages of the Northern Territory* (Darwin, 1983), 3.

30 Helen Molnar, "The Broadcasting for Remote Areas Community Scheme: Small vs. Big Media," *Media Information Australia* 58 (Nov. 1990): 148.

31 Michael Leigh, "Curiouser and Curiouser," in Scott Murray, ed., *Back of Beyond: Discovering Australian Film and Television* (Sydney, 1988), 78–89.

32 MacDougall, "Media Friend or Media Foe."

33 Eric Michaels, *The Aboriginal Invention of Television: Central Australia* 1982–86 (Canberra, 1986).

34 Helen Molnar, "Aboriginal Broadcasting in Australia: Challenges and Promises," paper presented at the International Communication Association Conference, March 1989.

35 Molnar, "Broadcasting for Remote Areas Community Scheme," 148.

36 For anthropological analyses of Aboriginal "self-determination" and the production of Aboriginal identity in relation to the state, see "Aborigines and the State in Australia," a special issue of *Social Analysis* 24, edited by Jeremy Beckett.

37 MacDougall, "Media Friend or Media Foe," 55.

38 Molnar, "Broadcasting for Remote Areas Community Scheme," 149.

39 While Yuendumu and many other Aboriginal communities had not received the steady flow of broadcast television, it is important to point out that they were acquainted with Western filmmaking practice through community viewings of rented films, attending cinemas in towns, and, most recently, through the circulation and viewing of materials through their own or resident whites' video cassette recorders.

40 Most of this information is compiled from my interviews with Philip Batty and Freda Glynn and from Eric Michaels's report *The Aboriginal Invention of Television* (Canberra, 1986).

41 Molnar, "Aboriginal Broadcasting in Australia," 34.

42 Peter Toyne, "The Tanami Network: New Uses for Communications in Support of Social Links and Service Delivery in the Remote Aboriginal Communities of the Tanami," paper presented to "Service Delivery and Communications in the 1990s" conference, Darwin, 1992.

43 Ibid.

44 Jenny O'Loughlin, "Tribal Business Has Gone Space Age in the Outback," *The Advocate* (March 8, 1992): 12.

45 *Canberra Times*, 1992.

46 Molnar, "Aboriginal Broadcasting in Australia," 25ff.; Neil Turner, "Pitchat and Beyond," *Artlink* 10 (1990): 43–5.

47 Neil Turner, quoted in Philip Dutchak, "Black Screens," *Cinema Papers* 87 (March–April 1992): 48.

48 Batty, "Singing the Electric," 9.

49 Dutchak, "Black Screens," 49.

50 Molnar, "Broadcasting for Remote Areas Community Scheme," 149–53.

51 Batty, "Singing the Electric," 11.

52 In addition to CAAMA, there are now four large Aboriginal regional media organizations: WAAMA (Western Australia Aboriginal Media Association); TEABBA (Top End Aboriginal Bush Broadcasting Association); TAIMA (Townsville and Aboriginal Islander Media Association); TSIAMA (Torres Straits Islanders and Aboriginal Media Association). These organizations produce radio and in some instances video programs for broadcast in remote Aboriginal communities (Molnar, "Broadcasting for Remote Areas Community Scheme," 148).

53 Freda Glynn, interview with author, Alice Springs, July 6, 1988.

54 Imparja's initial funding came from the Australian Bicentennial Authority ($2.5 million), the Aboriginal Development Commission ($1.8 million), the National Aboriginal Education Commission ($1.5 million), and the South Australian Government ($1 million). Batty, "Singing the Electric," 121.

55 Cliff Goddard, "Imparja Gears up to Bring TV to the Bush," *Land Rights News* 2, no. 4 (1987): 12.

56 Molnar, "Aboriginal Broadcasting in Australia," 23.

57 Tony Fry and Anne-Marie Willis, "Aboriginal Art: Symptom or Success?" *Art in America* 77, no. 7 (winter 1989): 163.

58 Molnar, "Aboriginal Broadcasting in Australia," 23.

59 Eric Michaels, *For a Cultural Future: Francis Jupurrurla Makes TV at Yuendumu*, Art and Criticism Monograph Series, vol. 3 (Melbourne, 1988), 26.

60 Michaels, *Aboriginal Invention of Television*, 30.

61 Diane Bell, *Daughters of the Dreaming* (Melbourne, 1983); Fred Myers, *Pintubi Country Pintubi Self: Sentiment, Place and Politics among Western Desert Aborigines* (Washington, DC, 1986), and "The Politics of Representation: Anthropological Discourse and Australian Aborigines," *American Ethnologist* 13 (1986): 138–53; Basil Sansom, *The Camp at Wallaby Cross* (Canberra, 1980).

62 Dutchak, "Black Screens," 50.

63 Molnar, "Broadcasting for Remote Areas Community Scheme," 8.

64 MacDougall, "Media Friend or Media Foe," 58.

65 Molnar, "Broadcasting for Remote Areas Community Scheme," 36–8.

66 Francis Peters and David Sandy, Aboriginal Programs Unit, Australian Broadcasting Corporation; interviews with the author, Sydney, April 30, 1992.

67 Molnar, "Broadcasting for Remote Areas Community Scheme," 38–9.

68 Rachel Perkins, director, Aboriginal Programs Unit, Special Broadcasting Service; interview with the author, Sydney, April 29, 1992.

69 Alexander McGregor, "Black and White Television," *Rolling Stone* 415 (1988): 35ff.

70 Batty, "Singing the Electric," 11.

71 Langton, *Well, I Heard It on the Radio*, 6.

72 Eric Michaels, "Bad Aboriginal Art," *Art and Text* 28 (1988): 59–73, and *For a Cultural Future*.

73 "Representing Culture: The Production of Discourse(s) for Aboriginal Acrylic Painting," *Cultural Anthropology* 6, no. 1 (February 1991): 26–40.

74 Fischer, "Ethnicity and the Post-Modern Arts of Memory," 195, 196.

75 Molnar, "Aboriginal Broadcasting in Australia," 151.

76 Fry and Willis, "Aboriginal Art: Symptom or Success?" 160.

Part IV

Active Audiences

The conceptual revolution in the 1980s that transformed audience members from passive receptacles into active agents elicited a vast amount of research aptly titled "audience studies" or "reception studies." Much of this literature, beginning with Ien Ang's pioneering *Watching Dallas* (1982), focused on how encoded media texts frequently change meaning during the process of being decoded by audiences (Hall 1980). This understanding led many to proclaim victory for the local over the global, the purportedly powerless viewers over powerful producers. Although initial enthusiasm has since been tempered with attention to concerns we will explore in Part five of this book, the original source of optimism remains: no longer can audiences be denied their agency.

How many of us sing along with the radio or employ radio as a means of waking up in the morning or easing us into slumber? Although it is a deceptively solitary activity, Jo Tacchi (chapter 14) shows how radio listeners construct social lives for themselves through engagement with radio broadcasts. Analyzing different degrees of engagement, from radio as an escape from silence (aural silence and/or "social silence"), to radio as background texture, to foregrounded radio sound, Taachi shows how radio contributes to the construction of a sense of self and constitutes a mode of real (not vicarious) social interaction.

Just as audiences vary widely in how they interact with radio, so too with films. In chapter 15 Elizabeth Hahn considers the cultural specificity of media experience by way of moviegoing behavior in the Kingdom of Tonga. She explores how the Tongan way of going to the movies is structured and pursued in a manner akin to that of other Tongan performance genres. Tongan public performances require a person who facilitates and in many ways makes the event as a narrator and master of ceremonies, directing and commenting upon the performance, filling in any performative gaps. Tongan moviegoers similarly required narrators to "interpret" (liberally defined) the films which typically were in languages unknown to most Tongans. The presence of a narrator and the extension of his traditional role to the movie event – commenting on the behavior and appearances of the characters on screen, embellishments, rendering the narrative comprehensible according to Tongan parameters – transformed film attendance into a highly local event. Audiences assumed their typical performance roles as well by participating in the drama on screen (offering advice to characters, warning them of danger, etc.) and engaging in a repartee with the narrator.

From the cultural specificity of media experience we move to the cultural specificity of media interpretation via Don Kulick and Margaret Willson's analysis in chapter 16 of *Rambo* as understood by Papua New Guinean audiences. Papua New Guineans may watch the same films as those shown in the West or other urban centers, but how they understand them and the meanings they give to them would surprise many a film producer. Papua New Guineans construct parallel narratives that subvert supposedly dominant narratives. These parallel narratives reflect their own cultural concerns, such as the need for establishing clear kinship relations and adding any that are deemed lacking. In the end, Papua New Guinean audiences transform the films they see into locally relevant texts.

When American television programming hit Belizean airwaves in 1981, it was greeted with great controversy. Newspaper editorials and government officials voiced fears of cultural imperialism and the eventual demise of local autonomy. In talking with people about television, Richard Wilk (chapter 17) explored the social and political consequences of the debate and discovered how they approached, assessed, and experienced the new medium. What he found was a wide range of opinion. In newspapers, television was blamed for all societal ills and marked a perceived shift between a positively evaluated past (characterized by social justice, good morals, and respectful children) and a negatively evaluated present (American-induced materialism, rampant crime, increased violence, and degenerate children). In interviews similar concerns arose but were complemented with some positive evaluations of television as a form of entertainment and source of knowledge about world events. Thus it is less audience interpretation of media content that is examined here than interpretation of the medium as a new social phenomenon.

Chapter 18 by Purnima Mankekar concerns her work with television audiences in India. Mankekar researched how television was watched in households (who watched, when, how, and with whom), as well as how viewers interpreted and related to what they saw on the screen. State-produced and state-selected serials dominate prime-time slots in Indian television and are designed to inculcate nationalist sentiment in their viewers. In discussing the characters, their crises and their decisions, viewers displayed a range of interpretations that shed light both on their variegated engagement with television and ongoing projects of constructing national and gendered identities.

SUGGESTED READINGS

Ang, Ien. 1982. *Watching Dallas: Soap Opera and the Melodramatic Imagination*. Trans. Della Couling. London and New York: Methuen.

——1990. "Culture and communication: towards an ethnographic critique of media consumption in the transnational media system," *European Journal of Communication* 5, nos. 2–3.

Corner, John. 1991. "Meaning, genre and context: the problematics of 'public knowledge' in the new audience studies." Pp. 267–84 in *Mass Media and Society*, ed. James Curran and Michael Gurevitch. London: Edward Arnold.

Crawford, Peter I. and Sigurjon Baldur Hafsteinsson, eds. 1996. *The Construction of the Viewer: Media Ethnography and the Anthropology of Audiences (Proceedings from NAFA 3)*. Hojbjerg, Denmark: Intervention Press.

de Lauretis, Teresa. 1984. *Alice Doesn't: Feminism, Semiotics, Cinema*. Bloomington: Indiana University Press.

—— 1987. *Technologies of Gender*. London: Macmillan.

Dickey, Sara. 1993. *Cinema and the Urban Poor in South India*. Cambridge: Cambridge University Press.

Douglas, Susan J. 1999. *Listening In: Radio and the American Imagination, from Amos 'n' Andy and Edward R. Murrow to Wolfman Jack and Howard Stern*. New York and Toronto: Random House.

Drummond, Phillip and Richard Paterson, eds. 1988. *Television and Its Audience: International Research Perspectives*. London: British Film Institute.

Fiske, J. 1987. *Television Culture*. London: Methuen.

—— 1989. "Moments of television: neither the text nor the audience." Pp. 56–78 in *Remote Control: Television, Audiences, and Cultural Power*, ed. E. Seiter, H. Borchers, G. Kreutzner, and E.-M. Warth. London: Routledge.

Gamman, Lorraine, and Margaret Marshment, eds. 1989. *The Female Gaze: Women as Viewers of Popular Culture*. Seattle: Real Comet Press.

Hahn, Elizabeth. 1994. "The Tongan tradition of going to the movies," *Visual Anthropology Review* 10 (1): 103–11.

Hall, Stuart. 1980. "Encoding/decoding." Pp. 128–38 in *Culture, Media, Language: Working Papers in Cultural Studies, 1972–79*. London: Hutchinson.

Jhally, Sut and Bill Livant. 1986. "Watching as working: the valorization of audience consciousness," *Journal of Communication* 36: 124–43.

Kottak, Conrad. 1990. *Prime-Time Society: An Anthropological Analysis of Television and Culture*. Belmont, CA: Wadsworth.

Kulick, Don and Margaret E. Willson. 1992. "Echoing images: the construction of savagery among Papua New Guinean villagers," *Visual Anthropology* 5 (2): 143–52.

—— 1994. "Rambo's wife saves the day: subjugating the gaze and subverting the narrative in a Papua New Guinean Swamp," *Visual Anthropology Review* 10 (2): 1–13.

Liebes, Tamar. 1984. "Ethnocentrism: Israelis of Moroccan ethnicity negotiate the meaning of 'Dallas'," *Studies in Visual Communication* 10(2): 46–61.

Liebes, Tamar and Elihu Katz. 1990. *The Export of Meaning: Cross-Cultural Readings of Dallas*. Oxford: Oxford University Press.

Livingstone, Sonia M. 1991. "Audience reception: the role of the viewer in retelling romantic drama." Pp. 285–306 in *Mass Media and Society*, ed. James Curran and Michael Gurevitch. London: Edward Arnold.

Mankekar, Purnima. 1993a. "National texts and gendered lives: an ethnography of television viewers in a North Indian city," *American Ethnologist* 20 (3): 543–63.

—— 1993b. "Television's tales and a woman's rage: a nationalist recasting of Draupadi's 'disrobing'," *Public Culture* 5 (3): 469–92.

—— 1999. *Screening Culture, Viewing Politics: An Ethnography of Television, Womanhood, and Nation in Postcolonial India*. Durham, NC: Duke University Press.

Martinez, Wilton. 1990. "Critical studies and visual anthropology: aberrant vs. anticipated readings of ethnographic film," *Society for Visual Anthropology Review* (spring): 34–47.

—— 1992. "Who constructs anthropological knowledge? Toward a theory of ethnographic film spectatorship." Pp. 130–61 in *Film as Ethnography*, ed. Peter Ian Crawford and David Turton. Manchester: Manchester University Press.

—— 1996. "Deconstructing the 'viewer': from ethnography of the visual to critique of the occult." Pp. 69–100 in *The Construction of the Viewer: Media Ethnography and the Anthropology of Audiences (Proceedings from NAFA 3)*, ed. Peter I. Crawford and Sigurjon Baldur Hafsteinsson. Hojbjerg, Denmark: Intervention Press.

Michaels, Eric. 1994. "Hollywood iconography: a Warlpiri reading." Pp. 80–95 in *Bad Aboriginal Art: Tradition, Media, and Technological Horizons*. Minneapolis: University of Minnesota Press.

Miller, Daniel. 1992. "The young and the restless in Trinidad: a case of the local and the global in mass consumption," in *Consuming Technology*, ed. R. Silverstone and E. Hirsch. London: Routledge.

Miller, Daniel and Don Slater. 2000. *The Internet: An Ethnographic Approach*. Oxford: Berg.

Morley, David. 1988. *Family Television: Cultural Power and Domestic Leisure*. London: Routledge.

—— 1992. *Television, Audiences and Cultural Studies*. London: Routledge.

Press, Andrea. 1991. *Women Watching Television: Gender, Class and Generation in the American Television Experience*. Philadelphia: University of Pennsylvania Press.

Pribram, E. Deidre, ed. 1988. *Female Spectators: Looking at Film and Television*. London and New York: Verso.

Seiter, E., H. Borchers, G. Kreutzner, and E.-M. Warth, eds. 1989. *Remote Control: Television, Audiences, and Cultural Power*. London: Routledge.

Silj, Alessandro et al. 1988. *East of Dallas: The European Challenge to American Television*. London: British Film Institute.

Silverstone, Roger. 1994. *Television and Everyday Life*. London: Routledge.

Silverstone, Roger and Eric Hirsch, eds. 1992. *Consuming Technologies: Media and Information in Domestic Spaces*. London: Routledge.

Taachi, Jo. "Radio texture: between self and others." Pp. 25–45 in *Material Cultures: Why Some Things Matter*, ed. Daniel Miller. Chicago: University of Chicago Press.

Wilk, Richard R. 1993. "'It's destroying a whole generation': television and moral discourse in Belize," *Visual Anthropology* 5 (3/4): 229–44.

14

Radio Texture: Between Self and Others

Jo Tacchi

In 1967 Needham was struggling with the "problem" of where, in the categorical processes of anthropology, to place what he saw as the clear link between percussion and transition, i.e., the use of drumming or other percussive sounds in the ritual contexts of *rites de passage*. Trying out a few approaches, which included an attempt to define both percussion and transition in broad terms, he found it difficult to assimilate two apparently distinctive, yet conjunctive "primary, elementary, and fundamental features: (1) the affective impact of percussion, (2) the logical structure of category-change" (Needham 1967: 612). The problem was that empirically, he saw the connection, yet theoretically, they resided in "disparate modes of apprehension"; the emotional and the rational (ibid). Needham was asking why the noise of percussion was so widely used to communicate with spiritual powers, with the "other world." Needham found it difficult, in the face of a lack of analytical terms and ideas around sound within anthropology, not only to frame his problem, but also to analyze it in more depth.

When thinking about a framework for analysis of a study of radio sound in the home, there is a distinction to be made between the mundane context of domestic media consumption, and the ritualized use of percussive sounds in *rites de passage*. Here, the focus is on the everyday use of sound, and how sound acts to create an environment for domestic living. Radio sound can be seen to fill "empty" space and "empty" time with a familiar routine, so familiar that it is unremarkable. In this way, radio sound is a presence in domestic time and space, which can be viewed as setting a pattern for domestic living, but a pattern that is naturalized to the extent that, as in Needham's focus on percussive sound and rituals, there are few academic pegs from which to hang it. Additionally, it can be seen to provide a frame, not only for social interactions in Goffman's sense, but also for avoiding, or making up for, a lack of social interactions.

Like Needham, I too am faced with elementary features that can be viewed as residing in "disparate modes of apprehension" – the emotional or affective qualities of, and reactions to, radio sound, and the rational and logical business of everyday life. Their empirically observed connection is expressed theoretically, in terms of radio sound providing a texture in which everyday life can take place. Radio is not an essential component for everyday living, but it is one that many use on a regular basis.[1] My starting point is the idea that radio sound creates a textured "sounds-cape" in the home, within which people move around and live their daily lives.[2] Rather than connecting with other worlds in a supernatural sense, these sounds, on both a social and a personal level, can be seen to connect with other places and other times. Linked with memories and with feelings, either experienced or imagined, they can evoke different states of mind and moods. From the perspective of material culture studies, the soundscapes themselves can be seen to have no intrinsic value or meaning; these are established and reestablished continually in each domestic arena, through each individual instance of use.

Miller suggested that "the very physicality of the object which makes it appear so immediate, sensual and assimilable belies its actual nature" (Miller 1987: 3). Mater-ial culture "is one of the most resistant forms of cultural expression in terms of our attempts to comprehend it" (ibid.). One of the problems with material culture is that its meaning is not experienced linguistically, and therefore any attempt to explain its significance which relies on language as a communicative medium, is bound to fall short of full explanation. Radio as a medium is immediate, intimate, and direct. Translating this quality of radio into language, people often speak of it as a "friend", as "company". Such clichéd expressions of the relationship between listeners and radio are used by both producers of radio sound and consumers, because of the experiential nature of listening, which is difficult to define in words. Something that is experiential and a part of everyday life does not normally require explanation. Radio is not a friend in the way that a person whom we are close to is a friend, and it is not the same as the physical company of another person; these terms are used as metaphors to express a particular (and usually unexpressed) relationship with a medium that we are not normally asked to talk or even think about. Thinking of radio sound as textured allows the possibility of considering how it operates, and how people operate within it. As a researcher, it allows me momentarily to "fix" something that is dynamic and flowing. Yet this is true also of objects and artifacts more generally. As already mentioned, their meanings are not static, as one might assume from their concrete physicality. To think about sound as material culture is not intended to translate it artificially into something it is not. Rather, I would suggest that radio sound is experienced as a part of the material culture of the home, and that it contributes greatly to the creation of domestic environments.

Radio sound can be used as a filler of space and of time. It can act as a referencer of memories and feelings, of other places and other times. It can serve to ground someone in the present. It can help to establish and maintain identities, and it is often used as a marker of time. It moves through time; it is a time-based medium. While listening to the radio is predominantly an individual occupation, and radio is seen by both consumers and producers as an intimate medium, I would contend that in this context of the domestic environment, which it helps to create and maintain, it serves a social role.

In this chapter I shall concentrate on the role that radio in the home plays in the establishment and maintenance of relationships, between the self and others. These relationships may be imagined or real, a distinction that underpins the main suppos-ition of this chapter. Radio can be used in this *pseudo* social way to create a self that could, or would like to be, social. This makes listening to the radio a social activity, in that it can act to reinforce sociality and sense of social self, and at the same time has the potential to fill perceived gaps in one's social life. Radio sound can be used to create a non-public social space, making it a safe environment in which to work on one's sociality. Radio sound, as part of the material culture of the home, is viewed as a texture. The use of radio adds to the sound texture of the domestic environment. Unlike the "solid" material culture of the home itself and the objects within it, or the more "fluid" aspects of the material culture of everyday life, such as clothing, radio sound can be seen to add a dimension of sociability to the lives of individual listeners in their homes. Degrees of sociability will be examined here, beginning with the sometimes feared, sometimes desired, silent environment, moving on to the use of radio as a background texture, in some instances creating a rhythm by which to live, to a consideration of foregrounded radio sound, and its potential creation of an image of a desired society, which is closer to, but essentially and importantly different from, real face-to-face social exchange. I shall demonstrate that it is nevertheless part of "real" sociality.

In order to paint a coherent picture of the gradation between silence at one end of a scale of sociability, and face-to-face interaction at the other, based on my fieldwork data,[3] some generalizations have been made. I have case studies that would dispute some of my findings, but looking at my data in broad terms, there are clear patterns emerging, that lead to the arguments put forward in this chapter.

Silence

When talking about *silence* many informants displayed an appreciation of the difficulties of definition. For some, silence appeared to mean absence of speech or music, although for some it meant complete absence of sounds. Absolute silence was recognized as being either "very rare" or "not possible". The more generally accepted definition of silence, as used in everyday speech, was seen as a lack of intrusive or obvious noise, perhaps better described as "quiet". When I use the word "silence" here, I am thinking of a state that is not necessarily to do with sound at all. That is, silence is seen here as one end of a scale of sociality. *Social* silence indicates a lack of social interaction, but not necessarily a lack of all noise. Working in the realm of philosophy, Dauenhauer (1980) notes that, while silence occurs most obviously in conjunction with sound, it is "a rich and complex phenomenon" which, with minimal investigation, can clearly be seen to occur, also without the context of sound. Dauenhauer sees silence as necessary in many, if not all, forms of human communication and performance. Sign language, for example, would not be an effective language without the presence of silence, in this case not dependent on the presence of contrastive sound, but a contrastive communication or language that does not involve sound at all. Silence here means a break or pause in communication, which highlights or enhances what is being communicated.

Dauenhauer also cites the performing arts, and activities such as silent reading or viewing works of art, to make his point that silence itself is an active performance (ibid: 3–4). Not only is it an active performance, but also it involves *conscious* activity. Therefore, according to Dauenhauer, "the occurrence or non-occurrence of passively or spontaneously encountered noise, of itself, can neither prevent nor produce silence" (ibid: 4). My research supports the notion that silence can be actively created, and actively avoided. The question of levels of consciousness, however, poses certain problems. Given the already-mentioned immediate and experiential nature of material culture, in this case radio sound and silence, it is difficult to be precise about levels of consciousness employed. With the viewing of art works in a gallery or museum, one can perhaps be more accurate. The site with which I am concerned, however, is the home, where radio sound (and silence) is interwoven into the larger fabric of everyday life, to the extent that it is often hardly thought about consciously at all.[4] It is often routinized, and naturalized, so that conscious consideration is not necessary. It is very firmly a part of everyday life, and as such, works on both conscious and unconscious levels. *Electric Radioland*, a report on research among radio listeners, prepared for the Radio Advertising Bureau, demonstrates how listeners find it very hard to describe the ways in which they listen to the radio, and what "makes their ears prick up," and concludes that this is because it is "a behavior which is only semi-conscious (and often unconscious)" (Navigator 1993: 11).

Dauenhauer calls any type of active human performance an utterance, an utterance being any part of any form of language which, when placed with other utterances, forms a discourse. My use of the term "silence" sees each occurrence, or instance of use, employed or experienced on whatever level of consciousness, in the larger context of the sociality of the individual. This in turn is constitutive of social relations, and of the self. Silence can be an activity, and a *condition*, using the notion of *social silence*, as employed in this chapter. A lack of, or low level of, noise for some of my informants was seen as sometimes offering a positive state, where reflection and relaxation could take place. In some of these cases I would argue that silence is used to allow contemplation of sociality. It can be a necessary part of defining sociality for those who have a very demanding job and/or lifestyle. That part of their lives that involves high degrees of sociability is seen more clearly when observed from a situation of non-sociability and without definition and contrast, sociability may be hard to appreciate. Alternatively, a high volume of radio sound was sometimes used by informants to block out distractions, thus creating a form of social or anti-social silence. Sue, for example, listens to a music radio station, and told me how she sometimes "blasts" the radio, that is, she plays it at a very high volume level, "it clears things . . . to clear your mind of what's bothering you and put something else in there . . . I find it very therapeutic."

For other informants, who see their lives as lacking in sociability, silence can offer a reminder of their undesired social situation, and so it is to be avoided (see Gullestad 1992). Some informants will leave their radios on whether or not they are listening, or even present in the home at the time, and some leave it on through the night while sleeping. It is used by some to distract them from their feelings of loneliness and from other unhappy thoughts or worries, yet is not necessarily consciously listened to. In this way, it is an utterance in Dauenhauer's terms, which is primarily used to prevent silence, with silence being the focus of attention and impetus for action, rather than the radio sound itself.

Thus, social silence can be both a positive and a negative thing. Some informants longed for, or at least welcomed it, others feared it. For some, silence could be experienced in both ways, depending on context and timing, or had been at different times in their personal histories. Some of the most negative thoughts on silence were expressed in relation to the evenings and night-times, when the rest of the world is apparently sleeping. For some, the availability of silent times that hold this capacity to highlight other aspects of their lives was to be feared, because of their unease, or discontent with, the quality of their social lives, or their feelings of isolation or loneliness:

Researcher: Do you ever like silence?
Deborah: Not really, I used to but not now, it is because I'm by myself I know that, whereas before I used to read a lot more, now I watch telly and the radio a lot more because it is company...
Researcher: How long have you been on your own?
Deborah: Two years.
Researcher: Before that you wouldn't have listened to radio in bed?
Deborah: No, I'd have read a book, it is the silence, that's why I stick the radio on...it is company, the reason I do like talk shows rather than listening to Radio 1 [contemporary popular music] is that it is someone talking rather than music, that's why I like it when I go up to bed, because I suppose it is a way then of knowing that someone else is around.

Deborah is a 27-year-old divorcée with two young children. She has what she described to me as a virtually non-existent social life. When she is not caring for her children or doing housework, she will be at work (part-time) in a supermarket, or attending college, where she goes twice a week to try and improve her job prospects. If an individual like Deborah is not happy with her social life, silence would surely emphasize this. Silence as a commentary on sociality can therefore exist in the elements of one's life: in the sounds, for example, that remind us of our mundane and perhaps lonely existence. These will be very individual connections – for some, the ticking of a clock, or the sound of church bells. Silence can reside in certain sounds, or circumstances. In these situations, radio can, and for many of my informants, does, cover up such silences. It creates an alternative activity or a distraction, an alternative textured soundscape with which to surround oneself. In doing so, it can be seen in some instances to create an alternative form of silence, one that is more acceptable because it silences the troubling silence, and takes the edge off the contrast between different aspects of sociality. In such a case it may be that the sound of the radio is not listened to for itself; instead, it can be listened to as a reminder that there is a world of sociability out there, creating a link with it that does not actually require risk-taking, as face-to-face social interaction often does.

A Background Texture

Although the *content* of the radio transmission may not always be heard, it does not necessarily follow that the content is therefore irrelevant. With the growth in commercial radio there are many new stations to listen to, offering different styles of music and speech, delivered in different ways. There are now nine national, three local, one regional, and at least two pirate stations at any one time available to listeners in the Bristol area.[5] For the purposes of this chapter, I take radio sound as a generic group, in order to investigate the qualities that radio sound possesses in more general terms, which nevertheless allows me to address some of the most basic questions about radio sound and its use in the home.

One of the ways in which almost all of my informants talked about radio use was as a "background" to activities in the home. When Anne is at home on her own she says she would feel that there was something missing if there was no sound from the radio or the television.

I tend to have it as background around the house, I've got music in virtually all rooms, so, it's always on...I'm not necessarily listening to it as such, but it's on.

Anne is a 32-year-old charity coordinator who lives alone and finds that having the radio on at home helps her to relax.

I see it as something to relax to, even the debates, I just, it's nice to hear it going on and have a smile, but I wouldn't turn it up loudly, I don't, probably I don't necessarily wanna hear it but I just know it's there.

The radio itself is seen by Anne as the creator of an environment that means relaxation. She will listen to stations as different as Radio 1, local pirate stations, or local BBC. As a very busy person she sees the radio as an aid to taking "time out" from her hectic life, yet the stations she will most often listen to in order to relax relate very directly to her working and social environment. Anne is a Black woman working in a job that involves her with many local Black families' lives, in a very direct and intimate way. The pirate stations that she tunes to when wanting to relax are seen by her and many others as the sounds of the Black community. So when Anne listens to these stations she does so to keep "in touch" but at the same time she takes "time out."

I'm a person who likes my own company and I'm very grateful when there's very little going on, because this job keeps us really busy you know...so I do look forward to time at home just to chill out, and that's the radio and TV...like I said, on Friday it's like, Yea! this is the weekend, put the radio on, puts you in the mood, I mean, if they're playing decent music, yea – it's just a bonus I tell you.

Joe is 29, married with a 10-year-old daughter. He will sometimes listen to the radio with his family, but it is rarely the focus of attention, more often it provides a background so that

We'd chat through some of the less important bits...it would be shhh for the news slots, there might be a bit of informal stuff in between, a bit of music, so we'd talk over that, but just listen out for the more formal bits.

This would be when they are listening to *Asian Hour* on the local BBC station, otherwise they will be listening to one of two local pirate stations that play mainly music. Like Anne, Joe is African Caribbean and he likes to keep in touch with the wider Black community. One of the ways he does so is through his listening to Black stations (these are "pirate" stations which Joe prefers to call "community" stations). With these stations the volume is often turned up quite loud, but Joe still explains it as providing a background to what he is doing:

If I'm using it as a background, doing something else, it will be right up, I wouldn't use radio as a background to a conversation or anything like that, or writing a report or letter...but cleaning windows and things like that, and then cooking...turn the volume up...it's to create an atmosphere really, you know, the sort of dance hall atmosphere. It sounds crazy to create it while you're cooking but it's a bit of nostalgia really, you know, because we don't get out as often as we used to...so it's like, sometimes you create as near to a dance hall atmosphere as you can, it just reminds you of when you used to go out dead regular.

Both Anne and Joe have very full social lives. Radio for them is often used as a way of "switching off" from social aspects of their lives, while retaining a link. They, like many others, use radio as a background of unfocused sound, that provides them with an environment that is nevertheless social and thus reassuring, but demands nothing of them. As the site of their sociality, the social world is very important to them and it is reassuring to know that it is continuing, but they need some silence, or break from it, in order to better define and appreciate their sociality.

Two studies that come out of the tradition of ethnomusicology have a particular relevance to the notion of sound as texture, and point to ways in which we can think about the materiality of sound. Waterman (1990) looked at the relationship between music, identity, and power in a modernizing African society, specifically at *juju* musical style as performed among the Yoruba in contemporary Nigeria. He concentrates mainly on performance of this popular musical style in the context of the national environment, seeing the diverse range of stylistic systems as an opportunity for individuals to place themselves on a map of shifting identity patterns in an urban setting that is culturally heterogeneous and densely populated. Feld (1990) looked at sound as a symbolic system among the Kaluli of Bosavi, Papua New Guinea; specifically at what he sees as the most important myth among the Kaluli, the boy who became a *muni* bird, and its role as mediator between ritualized performance of weeping, poetics, and song, and culturally specific personal emotions. Feld comments that the way in which the Kaluli use these sounds in ceremonies relates to their larger cosmic world (their origin myth) and to culturally specific personal emotions, which in turn are related to their conceptions of death and sadness.

Feld concludes from his ethnography that the human ability to organize and think about things – in other words, the classificatory process – is "complexly symbolic" (ibid: 218). It is a creative process that depends on the pragmatic needs of any situation, but is broadly defined in social ways, and is deeply felt on an individual basis. Looking at Western cultures in their heterogeneity is clearly a different exercise from the study of a particular myth in Bosavi, yet any generalizations that one would want to draw from Feld's work can be tested for their applicability to the current research. The point I wish to make here is that the use of radio sound in the home in Bristol does seem to have some analogous links with Feld's research, in that it is clear that personal uses and preferences of radio sound are structured both on an individualistic and a social level. Feld's analysis of the social, ceremonial use of sound is related directly to everyday sounds, which in fact are seen to ground the ritualized uses of sound, that is, everyday understandings of sounds affect the production and use of sound in a social context. The wider world is not shut out when we listen to the radio in the home; in fact it has a very direct channel into this most private sphere. The important thing to try to understand is how it is woven into that private existence. Looking at sociality and the use of radio sound, we can begin to understand the weave of domestic life and links between self and others.

Waterman focuses on the historical and contemporary performance of *juju*, a popular music style, and one of many in Nigeria. According to Waterman (1990: 8), musical style may articulate and define communal values in a rapidly transforming, heterogeneous society. *Juju* is one of many musical styles that are popular, and the very naming of such a style is seen as a declaration of "cultural consolidation." The choice of radio stations could be seen in a similar way – the classic gold stations, for example, which offer popular music predominantly from the 1950s, 1960s, and 1970s, is a choice that is related to taste and position in society. One of my informants seemed to use a classic gold station because of the era it recreated for him:

Of course, when I grew up all that was sort of starting to die out, the traditional family you know, the neighborhood feel, and all get-togethers and parties at each other's house, I mean that was starting to go in the '70s and '80s, well as I say it's practically non-existent today I think... it used to be a close-knit society and, they [his parents] said to me a couple of years ago, "you would have really loved it in the '60s because it was it each other's houses, always having parties" so it really was a lovely time. So I mean that's probably why, I mean I love get-togethers and things like that you see so perhaps in my mind I'm wishing I was in the '60s.

The interesting thing about Paul is that he is aged only 29, and so the past that he looks to as a "lovely time" is an imagined past. He is thereby creating a certain nostalgic soundscape that evokes an idealized past that he was too young to experience. Such stations perhaps offer the opportunity for nostalgia and a syncretism of past and present, analogous to Waterman's exploration of the syncretism of tradition and change in modern Nigerian musical style. This is a particular characteristic in Nigeria, where rapid change and heterogeneity are firmly rooted in tradition among the Yoruba. For Paul, the textured soundscape created by his choice of radio sound provides an environment in which he feels comfortable, and links him with what, for him, is an imagined society, part of which he feels he has experienced through the tales of his parents, and through past experiences such as his stints as a Red Coat during summer months. This work at a holiday camp is, for Paul, analogous to the 1960s, because of the particular form of sociability it recreates. He wants to live in such a social environment, and radio sound in his flat, where he lives alone, helps him to imagine this. His ideal social life is made real through his recreation of it as a backdrop to his domestic life, and elements of his imagined and experienced past are brought into play in his present.

Waterman (ibid: 9) shows how it is the people in a heterogeneous setting, rather than the musical style, or the culture, that accept or reject new ideas and practices. Equally, it is the listener who, as the radio sound enters the "moral economy of the household" (Silverstone and Hirsch 1992), accepts or rejects ideas and practices from the radio. Gretta, when I first met her in 1995, also listened to classic gold radio, and had done for some time, although, as I pointed out to her, at the age of 37, she is quite young to call the music of the 1950s and 1960s, which she particularly liked, of her "era":

No, when I was growing up it was all the Jacksons and the Osmonds, all that sort of stuff, but as I got older this was the sort of music that I could relate more to... I like all the old stuff... it's just the people who introduce it as well, they're good, but I can't say I'd ever go to another station again, I don't think I'd ever go back to Radio 1, it's just not my music at all.

Three months later, Gretta had changed her station. She had started to listen to a different ILR (Independent Local Radio) station that played contemporary pop music alongside pop music from the 1970s and 1980s. Later, her listening habits were to change again. These changes were directly related to relationship changes in her life. Gretta has been divorced for almost two years, and she has two sons, aged 12 and 19, the elder living away from home when I first met her. She lives in a top (fourth) floor council flat and receives Income Support. She sometimes works part-time as a catering assistant.

Over the previous year, Gretta had developed four different relationships with men, and each time her listening had changed with her changing emotional situation. The interpretation or reception of radio is not predictable, but individual, so that the same radio output would not necessarily create the same, or even similar, soundscapes for different people, or in different contexts, or at different times. Within the home, as Gretta demonstrates, other factors come into play, such as changing relationships and work patterns. For Gretta, radio's importance and presence in her life has fluctuated along with her emotions. It has, at different times, provided a link to an outside world, which she has felt somewhat excluded from when she has been alone. At other times, it has provided a link with someone she has been romantically involved with, so that on more than one occasion, she has changed her station to one that her current boyfriend listened to. Nevertheless, her preference for what radio stations would define as classic gold music has always remained important to her, and this is the sound that has dominated her listening choices, and to which she has always returned.

Gretta demonstrates how radio sound can be used to provide a changing backdrop to social relationships. Radio sound can also reinforce a routine; it can provide a rhythm to prepare oneself for social life. Bob, a 46-year-old financial adviser, switches Radio 4 on as he gets ready for work, as he puts on his suit and tie. It is a preparation for the day, which keeps him in touch with what's going on in the world, and puts him in the right frame of mind. He will surround himself with the sound of the radio, so that both of the sets in his house can be on at the same time; he will

turn it on first thing in the morning in the bedroom and listen to it, if I'm moving around the house then I've often got both sets on [the other set is in the kitchen] quite loud so I can hear it all over the house.

When he returns home after work, it is put on again, always on Radio 4. This is his routine that he says has not changed for many years, and he predicts that it will remain the same in the future. It is a part of his life. It keeps him in touch with a world that interests him and helps him to define who he is in such a world.

Foregrounded Sound: A Moving Soundscape

A soundscape is not a static, two-dimensional thing. Waterman writes of a "densely textured soundscape" created by "Juju music, with voices, guitars, and talking drum amplified at high decibel levels . . . which conditions the behavior of participants in Yoruba neo-traditional life-cycle celebrations" (Waterman 1990: 214). He sees the possibilities of investigating music not simply in its context – the usual ethnomusic-ologists' approach – but as a context "for human perception and action" (ibid). Thus, the concept of a textured soundscape produces a means of looking at the effect of sound on the actors involved, and on their effect on that sound.

The choice of the type of radio output – music, speech, and combinations of both – seems to depend in part on what activities the listener is engaged in, what state of mind or mood the listener is in or wants to achieve, and what level of backgrounding or foregrounding is required: in other words what sort of textured soundscape. Feld found that sound was used as an expressive means for articulating shared feelings and emotions, and he uncovered a pattern linking activities, myths, feelings, gender, and expressive performance. This pattern pointed to "linkages between sounds, both human and natural, and sentiments, social ethos and emotion" (Feld 1990: 14).

While Feld's emphasis is on the symbolism of sound in a ritual context, in a postscript he concentrates on his informants' reactions to his findings and relates how his informants felt that he should have paid more attention to more mundane daily sounds:

the ones that tell the weather, season of year, time of day. They asked why I told so much about birds but so little about frogs, insects, different animals. They asked why I had told about the *muni* bird myth, and not told many others. They asked why I had not told about how all sounds in the forest are mama, "reflections" of what is unseen. (Ibid: 264)

Taken in isolation, his analyses of certain uses of sounds were seen by his informants as providing only a part of a much wider picture. This led Feld to look again at sound in the ritualized context, relating it more to "the kind of practical and feelingful everyday interaction with environmental sound" (ibid: 265) in everyday life. His informants had made it clear to him that "every sound was a 'voice in the forest'" (ibid) and that he should pay attention to them all. He found that everyday sounds serve to ground the ceremonial performances. To look at radio sound as texture in the domestic sphere requires an understanding of the ways in which a soundscape can operate to link the social and the private. Within the texture of a domestic soundscape, listeners can work on their sociality, keeping the outside world firmly in the background, or bringing it closer and surrounding oneself with it. The domestic universe, with its particular soundscape, can thereby provide some sort of validation, company, stimulation, or simply a background texture in which to embed, or against which to relate, oneself. This could be seen as an exercise in "grounding" the listener.

Radio sound, and sound in general, has the capacity to become foregrounded or backgrounded. To look at a soundscape as some sort of two-dimensional entity would be to miss the ways in which different sounds appear to integrate to create it. Waterman makes the point that sound is, in itself, textured. Both Feld and Waterman see the soundscape as consisting of interacting and overlapping sounds. Feld names this constantly changing soundscape a spatio-acoustic mosaic, a term that offers a perception of the depth and motion of soundscapes.

To look at it more closely, this mosaic has potential for developing an understanding of the use of radio sound, because it allows for the ways in which sounds can be brought forward or pushed back, depending both on their particular form, and on the uses the listener has in mind, or credits them with: "all sounds are dense, multilayered, overlapping, alternating, and interlocking" (Feld 1990: 265) discrete sounds do not appear in nature. The Kaluli have a concept for this which they call *dulugu ganalau* or "lift-up-over-sounding." This is the most general term used to describe the natural sonic form of the forest, and explains Feld's conception of the Kaluli soundscape as a mosaic:

The constantly changing figure and ground of this spatio-acoustic mosaic is a a "lift-up-over-sounding" texture without gaps, pauses or breaks. The essence of "lift-up-over-sounding" is part relations that are simultaneously in-synchrony while out-of-phase. The overall feeling is of synchronous togetherness, of consistently cohesive part coordination in sonic motion and participatory experience. Yet the parts are also out-of-phase, that is, at distinctly different and shifting points of the same cycle or phrase structure at any moment, with each of the parts continually changing in degree of displacement from a hypothetical unison. (Ibid: 265–6)

Feld makes the point that this is the case, both in the ritualized, ceremonial context, and in the context of the everyday, natural soundscape. The idea that sounds and textures "lift-up-over" one another is an interesting way of looking at radio listening. Stockfelt (1994) talks about our ability to "disharken" sounds that we see as "normal in the situation," but irrelevant to what we are listening to or doing, so that in a concert hall we disregard, or disharken, the sound of our neighbor's rumbling stomach. Poysko (1994) writes about radios in cowsheds in Finland, where the sounds of cowsheds in recent years have been transformed by mechanization. In their use of radio in the cowsheds, it "is as though the workers resume possession of the acoustic space by covering it with their own music" (ibid: 85). The noises they are covering are mechanical: "music in a cowshed is a form of soundscaping, and its function is to humanize and personalize" (ibid: 88). *Electric Radioland* reports that "Radio is . . . being used primarily as a backdrop: therefore it follows that whatever the primary activity is, it may intrude further onto the radio station and then drop out again" (Navigator 1993: 10). Written for the Radio Advertising Bureau, this report is aimed at advertisers, and seeks to explore ways in which their messages can better be heard. It sees radio as a good medium for advertisers (as opposed to TV) because it sees listeners as "zoning, not zapping." This means that listeners will mentally switch off, or zone out from, what they are not interested in, rather than physically switch stations, as a TV viewer would more likely do. Later on, they would zone back in again. This ties in closely with the ways in which my informants talked about their listening. While radio sound provides a background to activities, it also has the capacity to suddenly become the central activity in itself.

Ear Contact

For the Kaluli, weeping and song are about confirming shared emotional states. They are "expressive codes" that reference "items and events to a lived world of actual people, places, actions, and behaviors. At the same time they reference the same items and events to abstract qualities and values, precisely described by the Kaluli notion of *hega* or 'underneath'" (Feld 1990: 222). This concept of "underneath" is most readily translated into English as "meaning." These referencing systems, as Feld describes them, where the real world and the abstract world are brought into play, are able to create a "momentary social and personal 'inside' sensation in which the weeper or singer can be seen, heard, or felt to be a bird" (ibid). To stretch an analogy, we might consider what referencing systems come into play when we listen to the radio: what role does such an activity play in our conception, and perception, of what is public and private? What effect does it have on our personal identities, and on our creation of our social selves? Does radio allow a momentary "inside" sensation that the listener is a part of something else, perhaps outside of the home, or encompassing it, and does radio sound possess an abstract quality that might somehow get "underneath"?

One of my informants talked to me about his choice of radio listening, which has been fairly consistent throughout his adult life, in terms of the "type" of radio he listens to. He is aged 57 and works for a local utility company. His preference is Radio 4, which he will listen to up until around six o'clock in the evening as often as he can. Other times, he might listen to Radio 3, but this is "only a standby, it's not something I would listen to regularly, it would only be a standby if there was something I wasn't terribly interested in on Radio 4." While he likes radio that stimulates, interests, and educates, he prefers Radio 4 to Radio 3 because although he enjoys the music on Radio 3, "the speech tends to get a little bit above my head." According to Roy you have to "have a certain feeling for it," and although he cannot account for his history of choice in radio listening, he knows what he has a feeling for and what he does not have a feeling for.

Trisha, who is 37, and works part-time as a care assistant, has five radios in her three-bedroom house. She lives with her husband, an engineer (previously a professional sportsman), and three teenage sons. When I first met her, she was a very dedicated listener of an ILR station that plays chart music from the 1970s, 1980s, and 1990s.

I usually have the music on wherever I am in the house . . . sometimes I have it on in the kitchen and in here [lounge] because I like to hear music loud you see, that's me personally, not that I would disturb the neighbors, not to that extent, but I actually do like it quite loud, so if I sometimes have it on in the kitchen and in here it sounds wonderful. . . . If there's a particular record on that I really like I will come back in and turn it on really loud, because I like to hear, I love the bass of the music coming through you know, so if there's a particular record I like, I'll do it then.

For Trisha, music is an important part of her life. Her husband and three sons are all very interested in sport, and do not share her interest in music or radio. She feels isolated in her family and listens to radio when she is on her own at home. This is usually for around seven hours a day. She has a very large collection of CDs, and buys books about pop music, which she uses to research competitions set by the station and to reinforce her extensive knowledge of popular music. She sees herself as "passionate" about music, and about radio. Her passion is not shared by her immediate family or by her friends:

I don't really mix with anybody who's particularly interested in music, oh, apart from my brother, I mean if my brother was here now we'd be talking shop . . . people are aware where I work that I'm really into music and radio so they'll say to me sometimes, for instance, "there's this record on at the moment and I don't know what it is" and they sing it to me, and I say "Oh, that's . . ." but I don't actually mix with anybody that actually has the same interests.

Trisha will listen to her own music collection on CD sometimes, usually when she is having an "off day," as it can lift her out of a mild depression, in a way that radio cannot:

I just look through my selection and I would know what was the appropriate one to put on, and I play a song and I know I'll feel a lot better after that . . . You rely on it don't you [music], I couldn't be without it I know that.

Researcher: So what is it about radio that makes you want to listen to that rather than play your own music all the time?

Trisha: I like some of the slots, particularly that Gary Vincent has in his show, for instance the 10 at 10 which is at the start of his show . . . this is ten songs with a connecting theme in some way and Gary Vincent devised a slot in his show whereby we get the opportunity to send in our suggestions so that's played approximately 10 o'clock till about 20 to 11 it takes about that time, and I really look forward to that every day . . . sometimes I'll set my alarm, shows how silly I am, I'll set my alarm after I've been on nights for my radio alarm to come on at 10 for me to listen to it and I'll lie in bed dozing and listening to it and go back to sleep after, because I really do like it.

For Trisha, radio was important because she felt she was sharing her passion with other people. She joined a listener panel, organized by the station, and enjoyed the quarterly meetings and her involvement in the station. She felt "very privileged to be chosen to go on it." She was unsure, however, about how the others at the meeting saw her. She worried that she may have been viewed by them as "over the top" with her enthusiasm and interest. This meant that she often wanted to make suggestions to the station, but did not through lack of confidence.

I think I can present as being a little bit over the top and I think sometimes I need to stand back a bit...a bit too enthusiastic. And I think you can frighten some people off and sometimes I wonder and question whether that's probably how I presented myself, but I mean it's genuine....I don't know if there's anybody who's as over the top as I am.

In her home she was faced with a similar situation, where she felt that if only she could win a top prize (£1,000) she could justify her involvement with radio to her husband. When alone, she was able to indulge her interest in a way that was not possible when the rest of her family were there. The children preferred to watch television when they got home from school, and her husband would ask her to turn the radio down when he was at home:

My husband doesn't actually like listening to the radio very loud, if I've got it on ever, so if he ever comes in sometimes and I've got it on the first thing he will say is "could you please turn that down" it's not acceptable to him hearing-wise, but to me it doesn't seem particularly loud...so there's a conflict sometimes between us...

It causes conflict between our relationship sometimes because I mean, he's into cricket and football and my sons are as well and so I'm on my own regarding my music, I suppose that's why I've taken it on board as being a friend as well because I sometimes feel isolated, I feel I'm up against it really with them being so much into sport and everything, it actually has caused conflict sometimes. As I said before, the noise level sometimes when my husband comes in is unacceptable to him and so sometimes he'll say to me "could you please turn that down Trisha" and inevitably I end up switching it off.

Music plays a central part in Trisha's life, and music radio enabled her to think that she was not alone in this, despite her family isolation. When she saw other people wearing station sweatshirts, she felt relieved and excited that she was not the only one who was proud to walk around with her favorite station's logo displayed on her chest.

Trisha is unusual among radio listeners in that she was very actively involved in radio, either through phoning-in for competitions and attending listener panel meetings, or through other events organized by the station. She is unusual in the way in which she engaged with the station, in a face-to-face way, moving beyond using the radio to create a background, to making eye contact, or "ear contact," thus forming a "real" relationship with it. Her case, however, emphasizes the problems that can emerge when the "feeling" for radio, and the particular soundscape created by it in an individual domestic environment, is taken outside of the home and tested against other interpretations of radio relationships.

Trisha was aware that the station representatives who attended the listener panel meetings did not understand her involvement with and passion for radio, and felt a need to explain this to them, but did not know how to do this. She had invested a lot in the station, which had helped her to define her sense of self, and practice her interest in music, but to the station, she was just another listener, and worse than that, she was seen by them, she felt, as "over the top." She felt that her input during meetings was criticized by the station staff, that they did not appreciate her abilities and knowledge of music: "I really feel deep down that I've got something I could offer [the station]," but her qualities were not recognized. She found herself in a situation where she was looking for ways of improving her relationship with the station, but not finding them. Nevertheless, she was happy to attend the meetings, as this kept the possibility of being recognized for who she was, and developing the relationship on that basis, alive.

After about two years of membership, the listener panel was disbanded by the station, and for Trisha this marked the breakdown of a real relationship. Trisha had sensed the end of the relationship at the last meeting, although the members of the panel were not told at that time that it was to be the last meeting. She told me how she had "picked up vibes" and knew something was wrong, and had "come home really upset." She felt personally let down by the station.

In a way, Trisha could be seen, metaphorically, to have been having an affair with the radio. It provided her with an escape from the oppression of her family and her feelings of isolation, but did not contain the risk of a "real" affair. As an affair it was accompanied by guilt, so that she was continually trying to justify her "passion." It also involved collusion with others who shared her "passion." In the safety of her domestic environment all was well, but as the relationship moved outside of the home and entered the realm of face-to-face social relationships it became fraught with problems, causing her to question her own self-image. While initially her relationship with the station had acted to reinforce her commitment to it at home, gradually it challenged it. Eventually, she became like a jilted lover and was left feeling upset, insecure, and misunderstood. When I last talked to Trisha she was trying out other stations in an attempt to find one that was right for her. Although the sound of her previous station had not changed, her relationship to it had.

This interpretation, however, could be oversimplistic and superficial. In the music radio industry there has been a long-standing notion of a stereotypical female listener who invites the male presenter into her home, as "romantic visitors descending on a bored housewife" (Baehr and Ryan 1984: 8). Yet there has been no research to investigate this perceived relationship on a deeper level. The fact that the target audience of Trisha's preferred station is female, and in their thirties, because this is the most prominent section of their audience as shown by ratings, does not make the stereotypical image of the housewife, fantasizing about the male presenter, true. The relationship, if Trisha's case is used as an example, is much more than this. Trisha fits the station's profile of the target listener, but they do not really know who she is.

Trisha was not "having an affair" with an individual male presenter or with the station as a whole. She was "having an affair" with her self, in relation to a world that can, and does, exist in the soundscape that she was able to create when alone at home. Her father, whom she remembers with affection and sadness, died when she was a young girl. He was a trumpet player, and it is to him that she attributes her interest in and love for music. She is not a musician and cannot play an instrument, and she regrets this. If her father had lived he would, she thinks, have taught her this.

The soundscape she creates on a daily basis has, as a major contributor, a radio station that tells her, and all of its listeners, through their station rhetoric, that it cares about music and about its listeners. It tells them how it listens to them, and gives them only what they want to hear. It respects the music it plays, not allowing presenters to talk over records. This particular station is very predictable in its sound – it is therefore very reliable. Its tight format means that Trisha can be sure that it will sound the way she expects it to sound, at all times. It therefore contributes, in a very reliable way, to the domestic environment that she creates in everyday life.

On the surface, radio can appear to be an unremarkable thing, yet once it is viewed in the complex environment of everyday lives it can be seen to act in many different and meaningful ways. There are qualities of radio sound that seem to touch people in a very immediate and intimate way. Perhaps the feeling that Roy describes works in a similar way to the abstract quality described by the Kaluli as "underneath," in the way in which it (momentarily or not) creates a social and personal "inside" sensation. Trisha demonstrates how radio sound can act in the home, to create relationships between self and others that are not the same as face-to-face relationships, but that are nevertheless important in the constitution of a self that is, or would like to be, social. The way in which her construction of self was threatened, when she took her experience of radio sound outside the home, and found that others failed to see her relationship with radio in the way that she did, demonstrates the way in which the home as context provides a safe and manageable environment, for explorations of relationships between self and others that are personal and unique.

What the examples used in this chapter have in common is the use of radio sound to conceptualize social relationships. That is, it is used to contribute to an individual's sociality. For example, it can be used to create silence (social silence) when there is too much sound (social activity), or it can be used to create sound when there is too much silence. Equally, it can act as a reminder of social life outside of the home, when one is too busy, or unable, to take part in it. And as Trisha demonstrates, it can, on a very personal and intimate level, provide a form of sociality that allows for the creation of an alternative environment for living from her perceived, domestic oppression. It is one that draws on many referencing systems, as Feld proposes, referencing a lived world and abstract qualities and values. Trisha is able to create a personal reality that reflects on, and affects, notions of her own sociality.

The research I have undertaken, in order to explore the ways in which radio sound is used in the home, provides many avenues for exploration. This chapter aims to recognize the ways in which radio sound in the home adds to the textured environment (or material culture) within which everyday lives are lived, and social selves are created, recreated, and modified. Thus, upon entering the home, radio sound becomes both material and social – it is social in its materiality. Looking again at the example of Trisha, who uses radio to create a sociality that is different from face-to-face social relationships, we can see that it is, nonetheless, real. What she is engaged in is not a vicarious pursuit. The relationships established between self and others are significant, and complementary, in a larger scheme of sociality, and they are present within real lives, not merely imagined. These relationships may exist in part in Trisha's imagination, but they have a very direct impact on her as a person, a wife, a mother. They are made material, tactile even, through her creation of her own textured, domestic soundscape. To paraphrase the words of another informant, radio stimulates the imagination, and imagination gives substance to sound. And sound can be seen to gives substance, in its materiality, to relations between self and others.

NOTES

1 RAJAR (Radio Joint Audience Research Limited) figures show that each week 86 percent of UK adults aged 15 and over listened to radio between January and April 1995, with an average listening per week for those adults of 21 hours (RAJAR/RSL, Quarter 1/95).
2 The term "soundscape" is fairly commonly used in discussions of music and more general sounds. Its definition (although not its invention) as the sonic environment consisting of oth natural and human-made sounds is generally attributed to R. Murray Schafer (1980).
3 The fieldwork for this study is ongoing at the time of writing and is being carried out in and around Bristol using qualitative research methods. Bristol is a city in the southwest of England with a population at the last Census (1991) of approximately 506,000 (Greater Bristol). An Independent Local Radio station based in Bristol serves an adult population of 1,231,000. I have lived in Bristol since 1988. A pilot study followed by the main fieldwork involving 55 informants took place between 1993 and 1995. I have used several methods of obtaining data, including informal questionnaires, follow-up interviews, diary keeping, sound mapping of the home, and participant observation. In addition I have looked at the radio industry, both commercial and BBC, in particular at how they research audiences and assess audience need. The methodology employed and the problems encountered will be described elsewhere.
4 See Silverstone (1989, 1994) on the use of theories on everyday life and domestic television consumption; Morley (1986, 1992) on the need to contextualize television consumption in the home; Silverstone and Hirsch (1992) on the consumption of information and communication technologies in the home.
5 Pirate radio is the name widely used to describe stations operating without a license. I shall discuss such stations and their listeners elsewhere.

REFERENCES

Bachr, H. and M. Ryan 1984. *Shut up and listen! Women and local radio: a view from the inside*. London: Comedia.
Dauenhauer, B. P. 1980. *Silence: the phenomenon and its ontological significance*. Bloomington: Indiana University Press.
Feld, S. 1990. *Sound and sentiment: birds, weeping, poetics and song in Kaluli expression*, 2nd edn. Philadelphia: University of Pennsylvania Press.
Gullestad, M. 1992. *The art of social relations: essays on culture, social action and everyday life in modern Norway*. Oslo: Scandinavian University Press.
Miller, D. 1987. *Material culture and mass consumption*. Oxford: Blackwell Publishers.
Morley, D. 1986. *Family television: cultural power and domestic leisure*. London: Comedia.
Morley, D. 1992. *Television, audiences and cultural studies*. London: Routledge.
Navigator 1993. *Electric Radioland: report on research among radio listeners*. Prepared for the Radio Advertising Bureau.
Needham, R. 1967. "Percussion and transition." *Man* 3 (2).
Poysko, M. 1994. "The blessed noise and little moo: aspects of soundscape in cowsheds." In *Soundscapes: essays on vroom and moo*, H. Jarviluoma (ed.). Tampere, Finland: Tampere University.
RAJAR/RSL 1995. Quarterly summaries of radio listening. Quarter 1/95.
Schafer, R. M. 1980. *The turning of the world*. Toronto: McClelland & Steward.
Silverstone, R. 1989. "Let us then return to the murmuring of everyday practices: a note on Michel de Certeau, television and everyday life." *Theory, Culture and Society* 6 (1), 77–94.

Silverstone, R. 1994. *Television and everyday life*. London: Routledge.

Silverstone, R. and E. Hirsch 1992. *Consuming technologies: media and information in domestic spaces*. London: Routledge.

Stockfelt, O. 1994. "Cars, buildings and soundscapes." In *Soundscapes: essays on vroom and moo*, H. Jarviluoma (ed.). Tampere, Finland: Tampere University.

Waterman, C. A. 1990. *Juju: a social history and ethnography of an African popular music*. Chicago: University of Chicago Press.

15

The Tongan Tradition of Going to the Movies

Elizabeth Hahn

The Cinema

HOLIUTI [Hollywood]...
the glaring letters
sprawl across the unpainted walls;
The laughter and noise
Of children half-naked
In body and mind
Waiting...anticipating
The hideous eyes of guns
And blood
The lens bringing these
Closer to their young
Innocent eyes.

Inside they giggle and tickle
One another
Embarrassed by the embracing,
The long drawnout kisses
Rehearsed many times
But the children do not know;
Words...what do they mean?
The sounds of guns and sirens
Make sense...
Well done! Malie!
Deafening shouts
Annoy Europeans who sit upstairs
Drinking cokes, frowning at
The ignorant natives
And fanning themselves impatiently.

The show is over
And there is a faint murmur...
"Ti'eni" [The End];
There is a rush for the only exit

The children, half asleep
Hurry home to the warmth of
Their soft tattered tapa [bark cloth]
Under which they will dream
Of rich palangis [Europeans] and brave cowboys
And will wake, laden with the wounds
Of time

Konai Helu Thaman

In the Polynesian country of Tonga, movie screenings tend to be raucous events of intense audience participation. The action film (e.g., *Rambo*, *Ninja* films) reigns supreme in Tonga. Konai Thaman, a Tongan poet, captures the mood of contemporary Tongan cinema with her poem (Thaman 1974: 12) about a theater in the capital Nuku'alofa. On first hearing, this poem's sole theme seems to be the corrupting influence of the cinema's content. Many media researchers (e.g., Schiller 1976; Tunstall 1977) have commented upon the cinema's enormous capacity to import foreign ideas and fashions. The Pacific region in particular suffers from the dominance of Western culture in local movie houses (Takeuchi 1977; Thomas 1984; Mercado and Buck 1981). Such observations have spawned many ideas concerning the one-way flow of information, a power imbalance known in the field of mass communication research as "media imperialism." However useful, this insight is only the first and most obvious layer of theorizing about culture and communication. In many ways the current emphasis upon detailing instances of media imperialism is one more extension of the Western tradition which tends to isolate and reify the messages, the content, of communication processes. In the mass media model, audiences are defined as *receivers* of information. Devising sophisticated measurements of what is absorbed by mass media audiences is one of the cornerstones of mass communications research. Though the cultural studies of today typically focus upon the audience's active "reading" of media texts, audiences remain defined in terms of their relationship to the media message. This concern with text is so central that it is hard for us to imagine what this approach to mass media processes excludes. To discover the more subtle nuances of the Tongan encounter with Hollywood, the peculiar non-Western frame of reference for the Tongan cinema experience must be explored – not in terms of its design for receiving and processing media messages but rather as a preexisting system of communication in its own right. To fully appreciate Konai Thaman's poem, the Tongan context of her imagery, i.e., the Tongan tradition of going to the movies, needs to be made explicit. We need to move beyond the assumption that Tongans are raucous because they don't understand English and can only revel in the action scenes. We should not automatically assume that the glamorous messages contained in foreign films eclipse traditional values and seduce the young. Granted, to some extent, audiences *are* caught up in the glamor and excitement of the clothes and other accessories of the lifestyles portrayed on the screen. This general observation has been thoroughly documented and commented upon by previous communications research. And granted, the language barrier *is* a factor in creating a tendency towards paying attention only to action scenes. Tongan theatergoers vary widely in their comprehension of what they see on the screen; many Western allusions *are* lost on the unsophisticated. But to allow poor viewing conditions and poor comprehension to stand as explanations for the form of the Tongan cinema experience is to adopt a rather condescending and vacuous view of Tongan culture, concentrating on what Tongans lack and what they wish to acquire instead of also considering what aspects of Tongan culture they *bring* to the theater. The Europeans mentioned in Konai's poem mistakenly attribute the rowdiness to a general lack of manners, failing to understand that it occurs *because of* the manners of the locals, because of their Tongan training in the proprieties of attending a performance. The focus of anthropologically sensitive media studies has already shifted from asking how much an audience understands the given media message to more sophisticated analyses of what the audience "makes" of the cinematic text. I would like to push this approach a bit further by putting culture squarely in the center of analysis in order to consider how Tongan audiences use cinema to reference and reinforce being Tongan. To answer such a question, cinema must first be construed as one *medium* of Tongan entertainment. Of course the movies themselves, consisting of 100 percent imported material, do not fit the standards of Tongan performance. However, audiences experience the movies in the larger context of various *faiva* (dance, music, poetry), oratory, and storytelling, Indeed, in the Tongan language, movie entertainment is generally referred to as *faiva*.

Tongan Performance

On November 30, 1985, a celebration was held at St. Andrew's, a private secondary school in the capital Nuku'alofa, commemorating the school's 80th anniversary and the completion of a new meeting hall. The guests possessing written invitations began arriving around 9:30 a.m. in their best church attire. They were seated in rows of chairs set out under several large awnings. The school band played the national anthem upon the arrival of the king and his entourage at 10 a.m. He was greeted by the bishop of Polynesia and seated upon a throne on the speakers' platform.

The program that followed was conducted partly in Tongan and partly in English and consisted of a hymn, prayers, a brief scripture lesson, the school anthem sung by the students, words of welcome by dignitaries, and the dedication of the new hall by the bishop. The program culminated with the royal address. Each event was carried out according to strict protocol, from the seating, to the agenda, to the opening acknowledgments of the speakers, and reflected the hierarchical structure of Tongan society. The king unveiled a plaque behind a fine Tongan mat and cut the ribbon spanning the threshold of the building. After his inspection of the hall (which was out of sight of the crowd still seated on the lawn), a subgroup of guests consisting of the king's *matapules* (talking chiefs), members of the royal family, diplomats, church leaders, school officials, and nobles were seated inside the hall for the premiere of a special school play entitled "One Friendly Island."

Across the road in a large playing field, elaborate *polas*, long wooden trays of feast foods covered with colorful canopies of crepe paper and balloons, had been arriving all through the morning on small flatbed trucks. The clamor and excitement of the unloading area rivaled the formal proceedings as the center of activity. A typical *pola*, measuring 3 × 12 feet, and laden with a couple of roasted pigs, baked fish, yams, raw fish with *miti*, shellfish, fruits, watermelon, and sweets, was quite a production to move. Several people were needed to steady the *pola* in transit and then lift it out of the truck bed to its designated place on the green. Each arrival was a spectacle unto itself with a colorful *pola* extending precariously out the back of the truck bed and exuberant guests perched along the sides.

Once the play began, the crowd seated outside began to make their way over to the feast. The king arrived shortly after 1:00 p.m. and was escorted to a large *pola* in a raised covered platform opposite the dozens of *polas* under makeshift coverings which formed a column the length of the field. Grace was said and everyone began to eat. Speeches were made by *matapules* and various officials. The St. Andrew's students began lining up *en masse* in dance costume at the far end of the field for the *lakalaka*.

The *lakalaka* is a traditional Tongan dance performed in rows facing the audience. The drama is expressed in poetic song and interpreted by lines of dancers moving in unison. Fluid hand movements tell the story, augmented by precision stepping and slight discrete tilts of the head. The meaning of the story is paramount in the *lakalaka*. In fact, Kaeppler (1983: 90) defines the *lakalaka* as "metaphorical sung and danced speech." Yet dancers do not strive for clear, unambiguous interpretations which can be understood by all. Accomplished performances test and tease the audience with many levels of artful allusions, following the Tongan aesthetic imperative known as *heliaki*. Thus, one *lakalaka* praised Queen Salote repeatedly, but her name is never mentioned; she is referred to as "the sun" or "the dove of the tower." The dancers always interpret these motifs figuratively, adding yet another layer of allusion that is not as readily recognizable.

All of the school proceedings were artfully orchestrated by a master of ceremonies with a microphone in the center of the field. He introduced each speaker and directed the lines of students performing the *lakalaka*. At times, the stylized pitch of his voice was almost whining, a style characteristic of Tongan comedians. He became more prominent as the afternoon wore on and the gathering became increasingly exuberant and informal. In the words of one man who attended the festivities, "he told good *Tongan* jokes." Pressed for an explanation, the informant added, "the meanings were . . . 'e, camouflage(d)!"

The entertainment culminated in a *tau'olunga*, a traditional dance performed by a few select female dancers. By the time the individual dancers began performing, the master of ceremonies had entered into a dialogue with the audience, making comments, jokes, and egging people on as they came up to the dancer to stick paper money on her oiled body. A line formed as people waited in turn to put bills on the dancer. This part of the ceremony was the most spirited, and by then everyone seemed to be caught up in the feeling (*mafana*).

People participated by (1) applauding the dancers and shouting "*Malie, malie!*" (Well done!) (2) Placing money on the dancer, with the bolder ones dancing up to the dancer with their donation (all of which was ultimately for the school.) (3) Dancing alongside the dancer, or off to the side (which is characteristic of older women who, overcome with *mafana*, spontaneously "get happy" and join in.) (4) Watching who donates and being entertained by the *spectators'* clowning and dancing. (5) Listening to the inside comments made by the master of ceremonies, relishing comments with their neighbor, explaining the reference to their neighbor, or having their neighbor fill them in as to what the master of ceremonies means.

Although there were hundreds of people present who were spread out over a large area, the gathering maintained an intimate quality. Not everyone had a clear view of the speakers and dancers from their *pola*. And people milling about walked up and down the long column of *polas* rather than forming a semi-circle around the activities. Nonetheless, the group had definition. The master of ceremonies deftly "played" the audience, picking up cues from the audience and adjusting his commentary accordingly. Chuckles, comments, laughter arose from scattered pockets of people. The audience was not responding as a mass, for the comments hit home for some and not for others, and not everyone understood the reference of particular comments.

By Western standards the afternoon was long, with verbose speeches and repetitive dances. The donor line seemed endless; people stepped up to place a bill on the dancer one by one by one. (Many resident expatriates roll their eyes at the prospect of sitting through yet another Tongan feast.) But for those who knew enough about Tongan dance to understand some of the poetic allusions, or knew enough about the relationships of the people involved to understand some of the jokes being made, quite a bit was going on. The master of ceremonies interjected comments in the same way dancers added style to the repetitive movements of the dance itself by moving their heads cleanly and crisply in an unexpected manner or direction:

The head movements do not play an important part in interpreting the words, but they have a great deal to do with the dancer's personal interpretation of the dance. The head is moved by a quick tilt to the side and serves to give style to the dancer. This is occasionally done at prescribed places in the dance, but is usually added when the individual dancer wishes. The ambition of the dancer is to have all observers' eyes on him, and one of the ways to achieve this is to move the head in such a way and at such unexpected times as to compel attention. (Kaeppler 1967: 519–20)

Such small finesses are the hallmark of master storytellers, whether executed in speeches, song, or dance. Compare the following comment by a Tongan orator on the art of speaking:

You must not have too sweet a quality because everyone will doze. You must go in with good quality and must remember a little something, a little amusement, to keep the people's eyes open.... There are people who know that and they go and inject in a little joke or something... they keep them [the audience] giggling and they keep them awake. And when they finish, people say, "Aaah, too short, sir!" (Ve'ehala, personal communication)

There basic aspects emerge from the details of the St. Andrew's Day celebration which are characteristic of the form of Tongan entertainment in general:

1   Oral performances are tailored for the occasion. A good story has timely references and multiple layers of meaning. The allusions are often obscure or ambiguous and not understood by all. Comments are often personal and invite audience involvement and interaction. More correctly stated, the audience expects to be brought to a vigorous response.
2   Events have a leisurely quality with peaks of interest. Activities can be repetitious and last for hours. Pacing is critical and is accomplished by interspersed witty comments, a change in tempo, or a change of focus.
3   Events are spatially spread out and are not experienced by an undifferentiated mass audience. There are many different ways to participate around a center of interest with numerous side "rings." People are not expected to observe or celebrate in equivalent ways since they are not individuals, but members of a particular group distinguished by rank, sex, age, and affiliations.[1]

Tongan Cinematic Traditions

Tongans have a long acquaintance with cinema, beginning with the introduction of silent films in the 1920s. In fact, cinema technology in Tonga has never been more than a few years behind that which is found in small American towns. From the beginning, Tongan moviegoing exhibited many striking indigenous qualities. In the 1930s, when large Western-style theaters were constructed with separate balconies, the mezzanine was immediately identified by Tongans as being reserved for nobility. Often the audience was composed of defined groups such as church congregations or classes of high school students.

Religious movies and Westerns were extremely popular in Tonga for several decades. Middle-aged and elderly informants always mentioned these two movie genres, and a few elderly men still could recall the names of Tom Mix's and Buck Jones's horses. Movies such as *The Ten Commandments* and *Ben Hur* were seen by audiences seated in their respective church groups, and left equally vivid impressions. As a man in his seventies explained,

In one movie about Jesus Christ, people sat in different groups and sang hymns inside the theater according to the church they belonged to – Free Wesleyan, Catholic, Free Tongan, Seventh Day Adventists, Mormons, and so on. They sang a hymn when a particular event occurred on the screen such as the crucifixion. Everyone wore their church clothes to such movies . . . the *ta'ovala, tupenu*. (73-year-old male informant)

Here the cinema context was clearly subordinate to the larger social context of Tongan churchgoing.

The audience's presence brought the religious *faiva* into full fruition. Going to the movies has never been a family outing in Tonga. Relatives of the same sex frequently go together, but one would never go to the cinema with an opposite-sex sibling because of the brother–sister *tapu*. The brother–sister relationship is the most sacred bond in Tongan kinship and, as such, is observed with great respect. To respect is to set apart, and in Tonga siblings learn avoidance behavior at an early age. Movies usually contain some material or reference to sexual matters (e.g., kissing, courtship, scantily clad women . . . never mind the more explicit scenes found in later movies) and to attend with one's brother or sister would be extremely embarrassing and a gesture of great disrespect. To be absolutely proper one should not even go to the movies if an opposite-sex sibling is going with others on the same night. However, this has been customarily "overlooked" in the darkened theater. Opposite-sex siblings sit far apart, seemingly unaware of the other being present in the audience. For anyone to call attention to this fact would activate an actuely shameful situation. In small village cinema it is almost unavoidable that some relatives will be present. Propriety depends upon the kind of movie being shown and the degree of closeness of the relative. An entire family may see the movie but at different times. For a special village showing a large crowd would come and sit dispersed in the same manner they would segregate themselves at a village dance. Nevertheless, dispersed seating is only a partial solution, most especially in close quarters. The inevitable presence of relatives in small movie houses reinforces the conservative nature of village audiences.

Interpreters were used widely until about fifteen years ago; a few villages still use them on occasion. "Interpreter" is a misleading term because the task involves much more than translating the English dialogue into Tongan. Perhaps "narrator" is a more accurate term, since this person embellishes and personalizes the story of the movie, cracks jokes, and makes comparisons with local people in much the same manner that a comedian, a master of ceremony, or storyteller would use to entertain a group in a traditional setting. Prior to the 1970s the cinema, in parallel with traditional Tongan entertainment, was usually a several-hour event with many things going on in addition to the movie. People sat in distinct groups and paid attention to the movie in varying degrees of intensity, entertained by the wit of a narrator's comments rather than by a faithful rendition of the dialogue. In the case of biblical movies Tongan audiences were very familiar with the stories and characters, and a brief summary at the beginning was sufficient for plot details. Some narrators made additional comments, peppering them throughout the movie as a dancer would embellish a well-known *lakalaka*.

There is an often-told story about a narrator who upon finishing his tale with a flourish discovered to his embarrassment that the projectionist had one more reel to show. This story may be just an entertaining tale but the joke works because of the nature of the narrator's role as a storyteller. As Ve'ehala, a leading native authority on Tongan tradition, explained to me, "People would ask, 'Who is the interpreter?' first, 'What is the film?' second."

A man named Tava is still well remembered in Nuku'alofa as being one of the best film interpreters, though he has not worked for many years and is now living in New Zealand. A Tongan woman had this to say about Tava:

He would make comments from the projection booth to keep himself awake. "Isn't that girl beautiful? So beautiful . . . as beautiful as the flower of the . . . (let's say) the *heilala* tree."

She explained that depending upon his whim or the mood of the film, the actress could be very pretty or ugly, and the tree he named could be renowned for its beautiful flowers or for its lack of flowers. She also recalled a movie scene in which several men were courting a woman. To the audience's delight, Tava shouted out the name of a weed in reference to the suitors. She explained that "this grass is hurtful to stand on, it spreads rapidly in your yard, and it is very hard to get rid of . . . you do not want it in your yard." As one of my assistants put it, Tava translated "half and half" – sometimes he would follow the conversation on the screen and sometimes he would make things up.

In the late 1970s one theater company in the capital found out just how important this style was to village audiences. They hired a distinguished middle-aged man who was well-educated and fluent in English to narrate movies in the villages. He tried to translate what was being said on the screen literally. "He did not have the flair of Tava, but no one had," explained the manager who hired him. Evidently his plodding literal commentary so annoyed audiences that they shouted at him to be quiet. He was soon fired. The audience was not so interested in fully understanding what was being said in the movie, i.e., its content, as in an evocation of the Tongan form of entertainment. He was unable to create an *extra*-cinematic context, that of a *faiva*, and the movie remained flat.

The Social Dimension of Cinema Technology

In any sort of gathering the audience unavoidably forms a public that becomes a part of the event. Live performances, however, impart a qualitative difference. In the case of theater, the physical presence of the actors creates a tension which we, the audience, *actively* participate in: we must put them into the imaginary world of the story by using our imagination. In the process of being spoken to, the audience becomes part of, or a partner in, that imaginary world. The audience participates in a *public* journey with the actors.

In comparison, the cinematic context is rather peculiar and much less demanding. The plot moves irrespective of audience comprehension or viewing contexts. A cinema spectator "eavesdrops" on people who are removed in time and space. The characters are represented by a visually dense, highly realistic, flow of images. Each audience member watches the screen and identifies with the *characters* as the story unfolds before him or her. This identification is a *private* act of interiorizing the story. (Alfred Hitchcock capitalized upon this insight and mastered the subjective camera angle which became his film signature: viewers could only see from the point of view of a particular character, transforming them from voyeurs to accomplices in the screen action.) The film scholar Bazin points out that in the case of cinema "crowd" and "solitude" are not antinomies: the audience in a movie house is made up of solitary individuals. "Crowds" should be taken here to mean the opposite of an organic community freely assembled (Bazin 1967:99). Bazin is describing nothing less than the social dimension of cinema technology. The cinema story is designed to play directly to the individual. Audience participation is epiphenomenal, and in a strict sense impossible. Bazin is also describing the essence of the social environment of Western cinema. In this case, the vision that is contained and promoted by the cinematic context of entertainment dovetails with prevailing Western ideology to underscore the primacy of the individual in the communication process. Western audience behavior is grounded in the normative Western conception of how to absorb information: the process of understanding is an *individual* act. Here, movie entertainment involves a celebration of the individual as surely as Martin Luther's Protestant movement.[2] Moreover, in Western ideology, meaning is contained primarily in the message or text itself. Herein lies the heart of the concept of "mass" media. Messages are designed to transcend context, to be understood anywhere by anyone. Clear, direct transmission is the ideal. Editing is directed towards refining the message so that it stands on its own. Ideally the transmitted message plays as well to an audience of one as it does to a large number of individuals. Almost always, the (intended) audience is physically absent from the actual performance. With the invention of cinema, especially sound films, entertainment was able to approximate the emerging ideal of mass communication, the reification of the message, more closely than it ever had before. While plays are performed anew each time with no two performances alike, movie screenings, like books in print, are exact duplicates unfolding with or without an audience. The bias of the cinematic context converges with Western cinema practice to form a coherent vision.

In the Tongan tradition, the self-contained, highly defined completeness of the cinema story becomes a feature to be surmounted. A good Tongan narrator takes the elements of the story flashing on the movie screen and fashions a personalized commentary that makes the audience a partner in the *faiva*. In keeping with Tongan performance, the audience expects a recasting of the movie into a lively exchange which is appropriate for the assembled gathering and pertinent to the events and people of their world. Audience members respond to the movie in relation to each other, creating an entertainment context which is essentially public.

A former film interpreter and prominent orator recounted how he had translated the words of Friar Tuck, who was administering the last rites in a dramatic death scene: "I said [in a most reverent voice], 'In the name of the Father, Son, and Holy Ghost,' as someone died on the screen, and the audience, many which were Catholic, said, 'Amen.' They asked, 'We are not praying?' 'No,' I said, 'I am just telling you what is in the movie!'"

Playing upon expectations, the interpreter had teased the audience. He drew in the gullible audience members for just a moment, but long enough to chide them for their silliness. Clearly the exchange epitomizes not *naïveté* concerning the reality of media images, but the Tongan sense of humor and delight in repartee.[3]

Contemporary Tongan Cinema Practice

Today, movie houses no longer provide the only glimpse of LA culture and fashion. Many Tongans have experienced European culture directly; almost every Tongan family has a member living and working abroad. The present population is more cosmopolitan than the one of the 1970s. English comprehension has undoubtedly improved with increased exposure to the language. Yet the disappearance of cinema narrators has less to do with rising levels of English proficiency than it does with an erosion of the traditional entertainment context at Tongan movie houses. The more elaborate elements of the movie *faiva* have disappeared. Many factors have contributed to its decline.

Most importantly, audiences are increasingly composed of small independent clusters of friends. Today's cinema audience is predominantly teenagers and young adults. Today's movies are also increasingly geared for this same age group, fast-paced fare that increasingly relies upon violence and titillation over plot and character development. The majority of the audience is there to escape scrutiny and social constraints, to watch an action movie, and to hang out with friends.

These changes were accelerated by the arrival of large numbers of VCRs in 1984 (see Hahn 1992). While men, teenagers, and most especially male teenagers, continue to frequent the cinema for the outing it provides, many women, children, and elderly are content to stay home and watch "video." This audience shift contributes to the narrowing of social contexts found in contemporary Tongan cinema.

The result of all of these changes is that Tongan audiences, most especially the more urban, Nuku'aloha audiences, are beginning to respond as a mass media audience. Religious movies have significantly waned in popularity and are perhaps the canary of the coal mine. While, according to a cinema manager, *The Ten Commandments* played to standing room only throughout the 1960s, *King David* lost money for one cinema house in the 1980s. The church is still a very important institution in everyday life and the congregation remains the main arena for local politics. What has changed is the social context in which these movies are seen. The patronage of religious movies appears to be dependent upon a fully constituted traditional *faiva* context. Only those few individuals who have, to use Walter Ong's term, *interiorized* the structure of church teachings or have become mass media consumers will buy a movie ticket to watch biblical characters in a darkened room with an atomized anonymous audience of various denominations.

The Tongan audience is not yet composed of a crowd of solitary individuals. The hot issue among Tongans themselves is the effects of moviegoing on the brother–sister *tapu.* The issue is not new. Observances of the *tapu* and moviegoing practices have coevolved over the years, but two recent developments have heightened Tongan concerns. Sexually explicit movies (uncut "R" films) are now getting past the Tongan film censor board and have become regular fare in Tongan theaters. Secondly, the new video context of moviegoing takes the movies out of the public realm and into the semi-private context of people's living rooms, creating a whole new set of viewing situations which must be negotiated in accordance with the *tapu.* Such concerns demonstrate that the Tongan movie audience remains an explicitly social entity.

Today, in the absence of narrators, a member of the audience may informally translate certain passages for his companions. Banter among the audience, especially in the small showings in the villages, is still common. For example, a movie I watched one evening in a village banana shed featured an actor with a particularly big nose. Whenever his face appeared on the screen, someone would call out the name of a man in the village who also had a big nose. The close relatives of the man being mocked eventually came to his defense and muttered for everyone to shut up even through everyone knew that the comment was "just a joke."[4] Such comments made by the village wags of today continue to utilize the same principles as traditional Tongan storytelling.

In Nuku'alofa "deafening shouts" still "annoy the Europeans who sit upstairs drinking cokes." Though the audience has lost much of its internal coherence, small clusters of Tongan viewers still enjoy the movie *in terms of* the overall gathering in the theater. The audiences are no longer praying along with the priest on the screen, but they do collectively cheer on their Ninja heroes and warn them of imminent danger. Action films seem to evoke a lively *faiva* context more easily than other genres. Tongans still speak of the movies in terms of "the *faiva* at Superstar's or some other theater house" with no mention of the particular feature.[5] The phrasing suggests that for many the social event still takes precedence over the content.

As their fathers and grandfathers did before them, young unmarried men retire with their friends to the boys' houses after the movies. These clubhouses now carry names such as *Star Wars, Ninja, Bronx Warriors, Black Hole Hotel,* and *Vietnam.* These starkly Western labels evoke the feelings and fears expressed in Thaman's poem. But "the wounds of time" that cut deeply into traditional life may have less obvious manifestations. The Tongan cinema experience has lost much of its grounding in traditional Tongan entertainment and now more closely follows the implicit bias of the cinematic context. These simpler forms of Tongan moviegoing attentuate the traditional *faiva* context directly by their increasing emphasis upon the message or content of the performance over the context embeddedness of the social event, and indirectly by displacing other kinds of entertainment which mirror the explicitly social Tongan ideology. Simply put, boys have been taking colorful names home with them from the cinema for generations, but going to the movies is not what it used to be. Indeed, they dream of Hollywood under their *tapa* and wake to a new morning.

NOTES

1   Far from being particular to Tongan society, these characteristics are commonly found in oral cultures. For a discussion of ideology, performance, and the mass media, see Ong (1982).

2 Certainly there are exceptions to this depiction. One famous exception to standard Western cinema audience behavior developed around *The Rocky Horror Picture Show*. The groups of friends who attended, in costume, knowledgeable of the songs, dance steps, and dialogue, and armed with the appropriate props, turned the screenings into social events. As such, their behavior was so remarkable in the US as to be dubbed a phenomenon by the national news media. (Significantly, this cult event arose among the younger TV generation.) The cinema practices of cultural minorities may also not fit this archetype, but the point remains that the social dimension of cinema technology matched mainstream Western predilections to form a particularly influential viewing style that prevails today. All other cinema practices exist in its long shadow. For instance, the very design of movie theaters reflects this individualistic orientation.

3 Compare this Tongan style of interaction to Carpenter's descriptions of the initial reactions to radio and photographs in Papua New Guinea where the new media were interpreted in mystical terms. When cinema was just a novelty, Tongans said things like "Briggs [the cinema owner], you are going to kill us!" during the screening of a black and white Western when the train barrels straight ahead towards the audience (Ve'ehala, personal communication). Such comments, though parallel in content to the Papua New Guinean responses reported by Carpenter (1976), are made in an entirely different cultural context and should not be interpreted literally. In Tonga, mass media never had the instant authority and potency that they commanded initially in Papua New Guinea. Rather such exchanges are suggestive of the Tongan tradition of ritualized repartee, the *fetau* in *lakalaka* poetry and the *talanga* of the *kava* ceremony. See Shumway (1977) for a full discussion of the artistic conventions of Tongan *faiva*.

4 In a discussion of the ambiguities of Tongan social interaction and conversation in the context of social control, Berstein (1983) demonstrates that there is rarely such a thing as "just a joke" in Tonga. Undercurrents are invariably present, most especially in public contexts such as a cinema screening.

5 I am indebted to Tamar Gordon for this observation.

REFERENCES

Bazin, Andre 1967. *What Is Cinema?* trans. Hugh Gray. Berkeley: University of California Press.

Berstein, Louise Myra 1983. Ko E Lau Pe (It's just talk): Ambiguity and Informal Social Control in a Tongan Village. Ph.D. dissertation, Department of Anthropology, University of California, Berkeley.

Carpenter, Edmund 1976. *Oh, What a Blow that Phantom Gave Me!* London: Paladin Books.

Hahn, Elizabeth P. 1992. The Communication of Tongan Tradition: Mass Media and Culture in the Kingdom of Tonga. Ph.D. dissertation, Department of Anthropology, University of North Carolina, Chapel Hill.

Kaeppler, Adrienne L. 1967. "Preservation and Evolution of Form and Function in Two Types of Tongan Dance." In *Polynesian Culture History: Essays in Honor of Kenneth P. Emory.* Genevieve A. Highland, Roland W. Force, Alan Howard, Marion Kelly, and Yoshiko H. Sinoto, eds. Honolulu: Bishop Museum Press. pp. 503–36.

—— 1983 *Polynesian Dance: With a Selection for Contemporary Performances*. Honolulu: Alpha Delta Kappa.

Mercado, Orly S. and Elizabeth B. Buck 1981. "Media Imperialism in Philippine Television." *Media Asia* 8 (2): 93–9.

Ong, Walter J. 1982. *Orality and Literacy: The Technologizing of the Word*. London: Methuen.

Schiller, Herbert I. 1976. *Communication and Cultural Domination*. White Plains, NY: International Arts and Sciences Press.

Shumway, Eric B. 1977. *Ko E Fakalangilangi: The Eulogistic Function of the Tongan Poet*. Pacific Studies 1: 25–35.

Takeuchi, Floyd 1977. A Status Study of Commercial Cinema in the Pacific Islands. MA thesis, Pacific Islands Studies Program, University of Hawaii.

Thaman, Konai Helu 1974. *YOU, the Choice of My Parents*. Suva, Fiji: Mana Publications.

Thomas, Pamela 1984. "Through a Glass Darkly: Some Social and Political Implications of Television and Video in the Pacific." In *Transport and Communications for Pacific Micro-states*. Christopher C. Kissling, ed. Suva, Fiji: Institute of Pacific Studies.

Tunstall, Jeremy 1977. *The Media are American: Anglo-American Media in the World*. New York: Columbia University Press.

16

Rambo's Wife Saves the Day: Subjugating the Gaze and Subverting the Narrative in a Papua New Guinean Swamp

Don Kulick and Margaret Willson

Introduction

One of the most central and enduring concerns in film and communications theory has been the relationship between "audience," or those who watch a film, and the projected image and sound of the film itself. This relationship was initially explored in terms of the effect of the film upon a viewer, or of the film working as an active agent upon a reactive and submissively passive audience. Feminist film discourse, beginning with Laura Mulvey's pioneering article "Visual pleasure and narrative cinema" (1971), is renowned for its analysis of this active/passive relationship in terms of filmic gaze. In the early literature inspired by this approach, dominant cinematic forms were characterized as male, white, heterosexist, and active; female spectatorship was Other and passive: females could position themselves either as alienated, temporarily masculinized consumers, or as masochistic/narcissistic spectators who are compelled by the filmic narrative to identify with the masculine objectifying fantasy constructed within the narrative.

Current feminist film theory is fragmenting these earlier models of female passive subjectivity by positing and exploring multiple spectator positions, by highlighting the fluidity of and self-contradictory tensions in film, and by emphasizing the female spectator's ability to respond to, rather than just consume, the film gaze (Clover 1992; Doane 1982; de Lauretis 1984, 1987; Gamman and Marshment 1989; Mulvey 1975; Roof 1991). In pursuing such explorations, feminist scholars have come to share many of the same concerns that guide the research of those involved with communication and British Cultural Studies. Indeed, throughout media studies as a whole, there has been a firm and steady shift away from texts as a privileged site of meaning, towards a view of texts as "dynamic sites of struggle over representation, and complex spaces in which subjectivities are constructed and identities contested" (Spitulnik 1993: 296).

The emphasis has thus shifted, as Livingstone (1989: 287) has recently noted, "from an analysis of meaning 'in' the text...to an analysis of the process of reading a text." Most of this newer research has been with Euroamerican audiences, but a number of scholars have begun to look at audience reception to film in non-Euroamerican contexts. Some of these studies continue to focus on the "effect" of television on audiences (Kottak 1990, 1991), while others interpret alternative readings as resistance and empowerment (Hodge and Trippe 1986; Mattelart 1980).

A problem we see in these studies, however, and to which we wish to draw attention here, is that even though it is nowadays widely recognized that the production of meaning involves active spectatorship, and even though analysts commonly employ terms such as the "negotiation" of meaning between spectator and film, viewers' interpretations are still commonly evaluated against what is taken to be the "reality" of the filmic text. This text is presented and analyzed as what Nichols (1981: 74) has called "a closed system" – an entity bounded by space and time which actively guides and structures interpretation and which, therefore, is subject to *mis*interpretation. An example of this is Tamar Liebes's study on how Israelis of Moroccan origin negotiate meaning while watching the American television show *Dallas* (Liebes 1984). Here, sensitive observations about how viewers construct meaning out of their own experience, their conversations with other viewers, and their understanding of the filmic narrative, are constrained and subtly displaced by authorial pronouncements by Liebes on whether the viewers have correctly understood the plot and the situational contexts that she sees encoded in the narrative (see also Liebes and Katz 1990). The filmic narrative, in studies such as this, remains squarely in the center of analysis. The narratives may allow for relatively more "open" or "closed" readings (Fiske 1987), but they are accorded an *a priori* status as bounded, discrete objects.

In this essay we want to show how an audience, through an alternative reading of cinematic signifiers and of the "meaning" of the medium itself, can not only subvert the cinematic gaze, but also destabilize the notion of a bounded filmic narrative. The audience we will be exploring lies in a remote jungle swamp in northern Papua New Guinea. It is thus a very different kind of audience than the ones that feminist film critics and most others have in mind when they write about the power and constraints of gazes and filmic narratives. We will demonstrate, however, how this very differently constituted group of spectators speaks to the same sorts of issues that these critics are addressing, even as they direct us to examine other, related, issues of cultural processes of interpretation and colonial discourses about the Other.

As far as the latter topic is concerned, we find it striking and predictable that in the sparse and sketchy literature that discusses non-Western (and particularly non-urban and non-literate) interpretations of Western-made films, the same kinds of arguments and assumptions as those mentioned above in relation to gendered spectators dominate any analysis. Just as females, because they are not males, have been interpreted as signifying a lack in relation to the cinematic object, so are non-Western, non-literate spectators commonly portrayed as also lacking: their reactions to Western films are said to be based on their lack of Western knowledge; on their lack of familiarity with cinematic signifiers and conventions; on their lack of understanding, education, "sophistication" (Wilson 1983: 31), and so on (e.g., Carpenter 1975; KVB 1956). What we hope to show here is that deficiency analyses which emphasize what these non-Western viewers lack are really only a prop for Western self- imagery that capture nothing about spectators' engagement with film. Furthermore, what becomes very clear in examining the ways in which these Papua New Guinea villagers have interpreted cinematic images is that they – in sharp distinction to many Western film theorists – do not see film as a closed system imbued with an inherent interntionality and truth. For these spectators, filmic narrative is inherently open, temporally unchained, and replete with possibilities. For the villagers we will be discussing here, as for other non-Western viewers of film (see Fiske 1991 and the recent literature on "indigenous media," e.g., Ginsburg 1991), filmic narrative does not so much "inhabit a space and time of its own" (Nichols 1981: 81), as it exists with and becomes embedded within the space-time of social relationships and cultural imaginings.

Telling Stories

Gapun is a small village located in northern Papua New Guinea, about 10 kilometers from the coast. The village is difficult to get to from most places. Getting there from Angoram, the largest town in the area, involves a six hour trip down the Sepik river by motor-powered canoe, then a two-to-four hour journey through clotted waterways and swamps often swollen with chest-deep mud. The hundred or so villagers who live in Gapun are largely self-supporting through a combination of swidden agriculture, sago-processing, and hunting.

Gapun villagers spend a great deal of time in each others' company, and much of that time is spent exchanging news about one another and about people and places they hear about from others. The villagers do not own radios, read newspapers, or have access to other depersonalized sources of information, so whatever they know about other people and other places, they know through their own experiences or through the stories of others. In this way, information is always contextualized, and it is always tightly bound up with whomever passes it on. Villagers' talk is not taken up with discussions of issues like politics, religion, or economy abstracted from social relations. People in Gapun occasionally talk about the papally bestowed "power" of Michael Somare, Papua New Guinea's first prime minister; about miraculous happenings linked to a statue of the Virgin Mary in a Ramu village; or they may discuss why the price they get paid for their coffee beans keeps going up and down for no discernible reason; but these topics are never discussed apart from the fact that someone has seen or experienced them him/ herself, or has heard about them from someone else. Talk about anything in Gapun is ultimately anchored in the talkers, and the social contexts in and about which they speak.

Men and women in the village spend a tremendous amount of time and energy observing and gathering information about the activities of others. Most homes are built so that villagers can survey large sections of the village from their verandahs or through small peep-holes poked through the thatch of their walls. Acoustics in the village are good, and Gapuners have sharp ears, so most conversations inside a house are readily audible to one's nearest neighbors and to anyone happening to stroll by. In addition to more surreptitious means of getting news, villagers constantly ask each other questions about their destinations and purposes, and they depend heavily on their children (who up to about age fifteen are free to come and go in a large number of village houses) to provide them with information about others.

The information that villagers gather about one another is most commonly dispersed throughout the village by means of a verbal genre known in Gapun as *stori*. A *stori* is a narrative account, in the words of one villager, of "where you went and what you saw." *Storis* offer accounts of events which the teller has either experienced him/herself or has heard about in a *stori* from someone else. The content of *storis* ranges from telling about that morning's hunting trip, to retelling what one woman said that another woman did with the sago grubs that a third woman had announced were for herself, to explaining what one of the young men in the neighboring village of Wongan claimed to have heard on the radio about the imminent second coming of Christ. *Storï*ing occurs in any size group, from between two to several dozen people. Gapuners feel uncomfortable with silence between people, which they interpret as a sign of conflict or hostility. So whenever members of a gathering suddenly run out of things to say, it is not long before somebody launches into a new *stori*, or anxiously begins urging others to *stori*.

Villagers in Gapun *stori* to inform, entertain, and to pass the time. *Storis* are highly participatory events, and listeners are invited to draw on their past experiences and their knowledge of particular people and settings and to contribute to both the telling of the *stori* and the subsequent evaluation of the action described in the *stori*. Listeners are expected to freely interrupt the *stori*-teller, questioning facts or challenging detail. They are also expected to decenter and imagine themselves as part of the *stori*, facing the same situation or predicament as the characters in the *stori*. Listeners pepper the telling of a *stori* with short evaluatory comments such as "*mi les/ŋa mnda*"[1] (how awful; literally, I'm sick of that) whenever the protagonist of the *stori* finds him/herself in a sticky situation, such as meeting up with a spirit in the rainforest or being clawed by an irate cassowary, or "*em nau/ gumɛ aŋgi*" (that's right), when the protagonist acts in a way the listeners agree with and approve of. The active role that an audience is expected to assume in the course of a *stori*-telling episode means that in the course of the telling, *storis* become retold and reworked, sometimes so dramatically that the version of an event that is discursively negotiated by speakers often bears little resemblance to the event which prompted the *stori* in the first place.

For example, once, in 1987, when a baby in the village was so sick that everybody was convinced that the child was about to die, the baby's aunt and her husband left Gapun with him and his mother, saying that they were going to the Sepik village of Singrin (about a seven hour journey from Gapun by paddle canoe), where they would pay a renowned old diviner to reveal the cause of the baby's illness. Before they came back, an old man named Agrana arrived in Gapun, returning from a short trip he had made to the neighboring village of Wongan. He brought with him the *stori* of what the diviner in Singrin had said about the baby. Agrana *stori*ed in a characteristic Gapun way which made it impossible to know whether or not he had actually been present at the divining session (it later turned out that he had been in another village at the time). He said that the diviner had disclosed that the baby's mother, Jari, had had sex with a man from the far-off Ramu-rive-village of Tarengi several months previous to her baby's illness, and that she had laid her baby at the base of a tree while engaged in intercourse. During the time the baby was on the ground, Agrana recounted, a tree spirit (*devil bilong diwai/kandap*) had stolen the child's spirit. The illness was a result of this loss.

Upon hearing this explanation, Agrana and the people to whom he *storied* began to discuss the details of Jari's indiscretion. Everyone present began to think back and retrace all happenings that they had seen during the past few months that might shed light on this event. When had Jari left her baby alone long enough for her to rendezvous with a visitor from Tarengi? One woman remembered that one evening she heard Jari's older sister shouting at her because she wasn't around to feed her baby. This woman recalled that Jari's sister had shouted at Jari through the village: "Is it my baby that I should be carrying him around?!" Where could the couple have had sex? Another woman present at this telling thought that they must have done it "in the cemetery by the trunk of the tree there," but then suddenly realized that the diviner "was speaking in riddles" (*tok bokis*) and that the two must have had intercourse not at the base of a tree, as he had said, but near a patch of a particular kind of grass that the woman speaking had long maintained was used by sorcerers to kill people.

A collaborative reconstruction of this event continued as each person present dredged their memory and contributed observations that gradually became connected and crystallized into an account of Jari's encounter with the Tarengi man and the theft of her child's spirit. Of course, it was agreed, Jari's sister's shouts at Jari occurred when Jari was away having sex.[2] And yes, wasn't that when John, the man from Tarengi, was in Gapun? And no, "he never sat down a little bit in the men's house," someone recalled meaningfully at this point: "He was always going and coming, going and coming. Going and coming from what?"

As it turned out in the end, Jari and the others never even went to the old diviner, since the baby had begun to get better as soon as it left Gapun. This fact, although it became known after Jari's return to Gapun a few weeks later, became unimportant in face of the collectively constructed account that had crystallized in her absence. Today, seven years later, ask Jari or her sister if they went to the diviner. "No," they will answer. Ask anybody else the same question. "Yes," they will respond, and proceed to tell you exactly what the diviner divined.

Episodes like this occur continually in village life, and they underscore the fact that villagers do not merely describe events in their narratives; they actively *produce* them. Events get authored in the telling, and it is in this authoring that meaning emerges. Once villagers decided that the cause of Jari's child's illness was her sexual indiscretion near a patch of magical grass with a visitor from another village, for example, several meanings emerged. Not only was the "meaning" of the child's illness suddenly revealed – the long-suspected nature of the grass and the Tarengi man's frequent absences from the men's house also all became mutually illuminating and illuminated. Meaning in Gapun thus emerges as events are contextualized and embedded in the ongoing flow of social life. Meaning does not exist in decontextualized isolation. Events are, in effect, meaningless until the contextualizing voice of village narrative negotiates their structure and their significance.

Rambo in the Bush

In June 1991 we transported video equipment into Gapun. With the video equipment we showed the villagers a video of themselves that had been made several years previously by a tourist acquaintance of Kulick's who visited him briefly in Gapun during his final week of fieldwork there (see Kulick and Willson 1992). The video screening provided us with an opportunity to talk to the villagers about film, and before we showed the video we conducted a survey by going from household to household asking people whether they had ever seen a "moving picture" (*mubin piksa*) before. While the majority of the villagers had "heard stories" of moving pictures, many had never actually seen one. A total of 45 villagers – 32 males and 13 females (of 44 males and 40 females interviewed) – had seen, in various settings away from the Gapun, one or more moving pictures, which for most of them meant either a movie (sometimes specifically called *mubi, mubin piksa*), video (*wideo*), or slide presentation (*ol slait*).

Whenever a villager had seen a moving picture, we asked him or her to tell us the details surrounding it; where they saw it, who had shown it, who had seen it with them, and why they had gone to see it. We also asked people if the images had a "story" (*i gat stori tu?*). We collected seventeen of these stories on audio tape.

In analyzing the villagers' stories we discovered that whenever villagers talk about the films they have seen they treat them as they treat real-life events, and they rework them, just as they rework real-life happenings. Just as the descriptions and evaluations of events in their lives that Gapuners construct are shaped more by their interaction with their interlocutors and the prevailing mood of the village than by what, on some level, "really" happened (e.g., Jari's aborted trip to the diviner), so are their descriptions of the films they have seen cheerfully independent of the cinematic gaze. Despite the claims that film critics may make about spectator positions, there is no passivity here: villagers effectively author the films they watch. They decline to take up a particular position in relation to the film – they are not enmeshed by anyone's gaze. Instead, it is *they* who do the structuring. When a villager sees a *Rambo* film, he does not become positioned by a gaze structured through overwrought masculine signifiers and racist stereotypes of Vietnamese. Instead, his look reframes the film as being about 'rascals' (the Papua New Guinean name for violent young bandits who do great damage but who are becoming steeped in a kind of heroic lore throughout the country), and about how a tough old woman rescues her limp and ineffectual husband (Rambo) from imprisonment by sneaking into rascal encampments and blasting their helicopters out of the sky:

	Mangai:	Rambo fights with rascals.
		He was sitting and rascals came and
		held him up.
		They held his legs and hands and took
5		him away.
		Took him away to a place in the jungle
		where the rascals lived.
		Put him there/
		And Rambo has a wife too.
10		His wife was looking for him, they
		were watching, after a long
		time they knocked out one of
		[his? her?] teeth (*tit bilong en*).
	DK:	One [what?]
15	Mangai:	Rambo's tooth.
		They knocked it out, his wife was
		looking for him, his wife/

his wife she was old, she got her
husband, the two of them ran away.
20   Ran away onto the road where rascals
had/they came in a car.
Came, the two of them found their car,
fire broke out. The rascals.
The rascals bombed Rambo's.
25   Bombed it/the wife didn't die, just her
husband died.
And [she? they?] turned back and got
an airplane, OK it blew up, they came.
Looked for her – the woman shot,
30   they shot.
They went on [like that], the woman
blasted this helicopter and it
crashed. Blew up on top of them (all).
The rascals didn't die, they scattered
35   about (*kalap nambaut*).
( ) the woman walked around in the
jungle ( ) went, held this woman
and killed her dead.

When villagers recount film narratives, they embed them in local concerns and everyday understandings. Mangai's *Rambo* story is typical of the narratives about film that we recorded in the village, and several discursive features, present in all our examples, stand out in this telling.

One of these features is the way in which this narrative focuses on action. With the single exception of Mangai's parenthetical description of Rambo's wife (line 18 – she is old [*wanpela hap meri*]), his narrative contains no description of people or places. Neither does it contain any discussion of affective states or the motivational concerns of protagonists. The narrative focuses very tightly on actions, and it describes these as an observer watching them might. This narrative style is characteristic of the way villagers talk to one another about events they have seen or heard about. In the *stori* genre, speakers present their listeners with a series of events and descriptions of actions, which are later collectively evaluated and interpreted. When telling a *stori*, speakers tend to use a minimum of description and speculation about the thoughts, feelings, and motives of others. These speculations follow the telling of the *stori*, as the teller and his/her listeners together discuss and evaluate the behavior of the protagonists in the *stori* (Kulick 1992: 234–47).

The other feature to notice in this narrative is the way in which its form works to embed it in village concerns. Mangai's *stori* is patterned on a type of narrative that is becoming increasingly common in Gapun, and which is referred to by the villagers as a *stori bilong ol raskol* – a rascal tale. These stories, most frequently told by young men to impress and disquiet others, recount the exploits of famous rascals as they steal, murder, and pillage. Typical of these stories are assertions or hints that the rascals have access to virtually unlimited resources and weaponry, that they shoot and kill people for no reason, and that they are rarely captured or killed (Kulick 1993). In Mangai's telling of the Rambo film, all of these features are present: the rascals have seemingly inexhaustible supplies of cars, airplanes, and helicopters; they capture Rambo for no other reason than he "fights with" them; and at the end of the carnage wreaked on them by Rambo's wife, the rascals emerge completely un-scathed. Both Rambo and his much more resilient wife get killed by the rascals. The rascals, on the other hand, do not seem to suffer any losses, and they survive even when a helicopter crashes on top of them. In characteristic form, the rascals do not die. The most that happens to them is they get "scattered about" (only, so the assumption goes, to regroup later).

In describing films they have seen, villagers talk about the things that interest and compel them. Narratives about the Papua New Guinean-made film *Tukana*, for example, focus dramatically on a sequence in which a man performs sorcery on a young woman. A young woman named Akwaria describes the film like this:

Tukana married two women. The first didn't like him and the second wanted to live with him. He didn't want the first to stay with the second. And his father told him/he asked him: "Do you want the second to stay with the first, or what?" And Tukana said: "It's up to the two women." And the two women got up and/the second one got up and went to the house of the first one. And the father of the first went and made magic on her. Like sorcery magic. He worked magic, put her dirty things into the fire. He made a huge fire and chanted on the side of the fire. Time went and the father of the first, he came and speared the second's/the second wife's father. He speared him and he died at the side of the fire. And they took his body and buried it.

A second narrative, from another young woman named Awpa, sums up the film this way:

One it's/a man whose name is Tukana, it was all black people who acted.[3] I don't know where he's from, what place/it must be Madang province, a man from there.

He acted/his child married a man. And she said/her husband was away at work: "When he comes I'm gonna marry him." And another [woman] said "I'm gonna marry him." Time went and another man married her and another boyfriend of hers was mad. The father of her boyfriend. He just went and did sorcery the child/this woman. Josefin. Tukana's wife. ( ) worked sorcery on her.

Josefin and her mother went to work in the garden. They went to work in the garden, but that man had already worked sorcery. He covered his buttocks with leaves, went and got flowers to cover his buttocks with, he made a huge fire and was heating up the sorcery magic. He was heating up the sorcery magic, he wanted to kill Tukana's wife. He was talking; "Tukana's wife has to die, Tukana's wife has to die." He made a fire and was singing like that. Fanned the fire. His ass was going round and round the fire. When he was doing like that, Tukana's wife's mother and her (his?) mother went back to the house. When they were going to the house, a car sped by, hit the woman, the woman fell down and died. She didn't live. The car didn't hit her, it just went by her quickly, but this [sorcery-generated] wind got her and the woman died.

Tukana came and saw his wife, and he cried really hard. He's black, when he cried, white came up/tears gushed out, his mouth was wide open. Tukana finished crying over his wife, he went and buried her. And he thought that he has to find another woman and marry her. And he went and/Tukana's father, he went, he saw the man who was heating up the sorcery magic for the woman. He asked: "What are you doing?" He said: "Nothing. My skin is cold and I'm warming it up by the fire." He lied to him.

After this, the talk became known that the man had worked sorcery. They took the man to court, and the police took him away.

In *Tukana*, which is a film over two hours long, the sorcery sequence described in these narratives lasts exactly 63 seconds. Despite its brevity, in the villagers' telling of the film, this scene becomes central. The numerous other messages intended by the film[4] become displaced by the villagers' looks and *Tukana* emerges as a film about sorcery and about what happens to sorcerers. This foregrounding of the sorcerer as what *Tukana* is about is similar to Wilson's account of how an African audience responded to a film about malaria prevention:

We showed this film to an audience and asked them what they had seen, and they said they had seen a chicken, a fowl, and we didn't know that there was a fowl in it: So we carefully scanned the frames one for one for this fowl, and, sure enough, for about a second, a fowl went over the corner of the frame. Someone had frightened the fowl, and it had taken flight through the righthand, bottom segment of the frame. This was all they had seen. The other things we hoped that they would pick up from the film they had not picked up at all, and they had picked up something which we didn't know was in the film until we inspected it minutely. (Wilson 1983: 31)

Wilson's explanation for this look is a deficiency analysis: seeing the film with an "unsophisticated, untutored eye" (ibid), the audience of "primitive African[s]" (ibid) was able to take in only part of the picture, not the whole.

In many ways, Gapuners go well beyond what Wilson describes his African viewers as doing. In their engagement with film, as in their engagement with real-life, villagers, in their narratives, freely alter, expand, substitute, transform, and add characters, actions, sounds, plots, and moral implications to those that are present in the event itself. The sorcery sequence in *Tukana* is an exceptionally powerful one for villagers, because even though everybody in Gapun knows that sorcery exists and exerts an unrelenting influence on their lives (all serious sickness and all deaths in Gapun are attributed to sorcery, for example), few viewers of *Tukana* would ever have seen a sorcerer actually at work. In the village discourse on sorcery, it is evil, and sorcerers should be punished (traditionally they were often the targets of retaliatory raids). And so, in the film, the sorcerer, we are told, is indeed punished – in one version he is speared to death; in the other he is taken away by the police. The fact that in the film itself none of this happens and the sorcerer lives on happily untouched is unimportant – just as the fact that Jari did not take her baby to the diviner became unimportant after it had become decided that she did. Films in Gapun, like real-life events, constitute only the raw material of their own existence. The filmic narrative is only one element of the constructed narrative; it is only one element of what becomes, for the individual spectators, *the* narrative. Films become discursively embedded into village life through the telling, and unlike Wilson, we do not interpret the villagers of Gapun, in their tellings, as lacking sophistication; we interpret them, instead, as deftly subverting the narrative gaze by encompassing it with their contextualizing voice.

"Piksa i no save kamap nating"

Cinematic narratives are thus embedded into village life through the contextualizing voice of village narrative – in their telling, the cinematic narrative becomes transformed and reconfigured as commentaries on village life and village ideas. Through this absorption and transformation, film in Gapun is multiply embedded into the community. Not only the narratives constructed through film, but the technology of film itself is swept up into the contextualizing voice and impressed into village discourse in a very particular way.

Gapuners tell one another that cinematic technology is an "eye" (ai/ginɔ). It is an opening, an elaborate mechanism of voyeurism to other countries, other spaces, and other times. Villagers believe that anyone in possession of a *draivisen* (television), for example, can direct it to see anything they want to. When Kulick first arrived in Gapun in 1985, villagers wondered if the people in "the countries" were watching him on their television sets. One villager told others in an authoritative voice that "when the Pope came to see us [i.e., came to Papua New Guinea in 1984], all the countries used these things [television] to watch him." Another recounted that once in the town of Madang, he and others had seen "the Queen in the flesh" (*mipela lukim skin bilong Kwin*) on a *draivisen*.

It is taken for granted that *draivisen* can penetrate the space of death and see into it. One reason why villagers assume this is because they believe that white people inhabit that space. Gapun is a community of quiet but exuberant millenarian ideas, and the villagers spend a great deal of time trying to be fervent Catholics, in the hope that this will one day bring on the millennium and transform them all into white people (Kulick 1992). Pictures of white people in their native countries are therefore in reality pictures of the space that villagers themselves will inhabit after the millennium or after they die (whichever comes first). Before we showed the video we brought to Gapun to the villagers, they steeled themselves, with these ideas in mind, to see pictures of their dead ancestors. We were repeatedly asked about specific family members – long-dead mothers and fathers, recently deceased children – would they appear on the video screen? Would they speak to their descendants/ parents from the afterlife? Mothers prepared their small children to see their ancestors, telling them in excited voices, "Ooo, you're gonna see your ancestor now. She's gonna appear and talk to you." Just prior to the screening of the video there was a spate of dreams in the village about ancestors with white skin, and near a waterhole on the edge of the village, two villagers claimed to have seen the spirit of a woman who died in the 1960s, and who, it was hoped, would be making an appearance in the video.

One important consequence of seeing cinematic technology in terms of an organ of vision is the idea that what is pictured is actually seen, and therefore actually exists somewhere. "Pictures aren't just invented" (*Piksa i no save kamap nating*), villagers tell one another: pictures exist because what they picture exists. Sitting in his men's house one evening, old Kruni and a group of adolescent boys were talking about rascals:

Kruni:	They pray to Satan and Satan gives them power.
Jim:	Man, Satan is nearby.
Kak:	They can see him.
Kruni:	Eh heh.
Kak:	He talks to them.
Kruni:	Mm.
	You're the big man [addressing Satan as rascals would].
Kruni:	He's the big man. <u>True</u>. (. . .) <u>I saw him in Marienberg</u> [mission station].
	Man, he was really close. He had really good decorations on his body. Good decorations, but he had wings like flying fox.

Mangai:	Good looking man but wings just like a flying fox.
Kruni:	Mm.
Kak:	Nice.
Kruni:	<u>You'll see him and think he's a king</u>. A big man. You'll see him and think he's a king. But he has wings like a flying fox.
Kak:	Two horns.
Kruni:	Two horns, a spear. Man, to plunge into people.
Mangai:	A barbed spear.
Kak:	It's a fork.
Kruni:	His spear, it's a fork. Moving pictures don't lie. Things are there and they photograph them.
Wake:	Pictures aren't just invented. They photograph something, they put it/
Kruni:	We'll look at this and be afraid. And so we'll have good ways.

"Moving pictures don't lie. Things are there and they photograph them." For villagers, what is shown with film technology is unquestionably authentic. Satan, resplendent with his fork, his horns, and his big black bat's wings, is pictured in the movie in Marienberg because Satan, like other Christian deities, exists to be pictured. Some villagers, like Kruni, take this idea even further, and they seem to consider that film technology bodily materializes the image that it reveals. In this conceptualization, the movie screen (which in Tok Pisin is called *banis* – a word commonly used to denote a fence or partition, carrying with it strong connotations of concealment and prohibition) appears to be not so much a surface onto which images are projected as it is a barrier blocking entrance to and direct contact with the actions and people who are understood as existing immediately behind or beyond the screen. This is what we interpret Kruni to mean when he tells the boys listening to him that Satan "was really close" when he appeared in Marienberg, conjured up by the power of the missionaries.

Kruni returned to this theme of the physical proximity of filmic images in a later conversation with Kulick about the same film, when he explained about another sequence that, "... Jesus appeared. All right, Satan told him to go up a really big mountain. Jesus went to the top. We saw this. But I saw the picture sitting like where you are and here [Kruni taps the floor in front of him], the screen was like here. Now you're there. And I'm like Jesus, where I'm [sitting] now."

The villagers' looks do not acknowledge cinematic images to be "just pictures," in content or in form. And neither do they allow film and the technology which produces it to exist in a socially bounded, "closed" space. Instead, film becomes a site of convergence where many of the phenomena that are absolutely central in village life, such as Christian teachings, ancestral beings, modernity (those who have not seen videos referred to themselves only half-jokingly in our interviews as "*bus kanaka*," i.e., country bumpkins), missionaries, white colonialists, and the government all coalesce into commentaries about one another. Because film technology is controlled by white people, for example, and because it routinely peers into biblical lands and presents the villagers with images of deities like Satan and Jesus, villagers continue to believe that white men and women can travel to places like Heaven and Hell, and that they have more or less direct access to the Christian pantheon. One story linking most of these things together was that told by an old village man named Raia, as he pointed to the black and white painting of a fair-skinned Madonna and child, portrayed in a kind of mist, that appears on the last page of the Catholic hymn book *Niu Laip* (New Life). "A *masta* (a white man) in an airplane snapped that picture," Raia explained:

He was flying in his airplane and he snapped a picture of the sky. All right, he took it home, washed it, and the picture [of the Virgin and child] appeared. The government wouldn't let him go (*holim pasim em*) and they asked him about it – where did he get it. He said he didn't know. All right, they bought it from him for lots of money, and now the missions bought it off the government and put it in this book.

Conceived of as an eye, film and cinematic technology becomes for the villagers an instrument of knowledge and revelation whose narratives interweave with and comment upon the present, the past, and what is to come. Film technology permits the villagers access to spaces from which they are normally firmly interdicted. In doing so, the technology presents the villagers with a whole new range of possibilities and opportunities, and the people of Gapun imagine themselves in a vigorously active subject position in relation to it: villagers anticipate being able to use film technology to communicate with their dead, and one villager who explained to others that *draivisen* "is used to look at things that are far away and see what is happening" wanted to obtain a television set and use it to spy on sorcerers.

This subject position into which the villagers comfortably settle in relation to film is also apparent in the way that the villagers appropriate filmic narratives and rework them into commentaries on village life. It is now clearer why they should do this. Since, for the villagers, what is seen in moving pictures constitutes real-life events, the images are treated in the same way as are actions observed in real-life. And because film is life, it is freely available for reauthoring. Just as events that occur in the village get continually reworked until some consensus is established about them, so do filmic narratives become reworked. As such, film blends with life and shapes it, even as it is shaped by it. One of old Kruni's most memorable experiences was a cinematic one that occurred at the government station of Angoram in the late 1950s. A moving picture that he saw there was about a big bucket:

...A big round bucket with white medicine in it. It was going round and round. Round and round. It was going around and they put the carvings, the *kandibwan*, they put the *kandibwan* inside this bucket. All right, they weren't *kandibwan* anymore. The *kandibwan* had become like you. A white man. White skin. It became/they all got out of this water, and they took a knife like a razor. All right, put it in the chest of one. They cut into [the chest], but they were talking. They were talking, walking around, and the long traditional hat (*kawt*), the kind like we make, it turned into a cap. I saw it with my own eyes.... White skinned people. They were talking, laughing. Men/white men (*ol masta*) held the hand of white women (*ol misis*), they walked around. I saw it with my own eyes.

Haunted by the image of traditional carvings emerging from a machine as living white men and women, Kruni has been pondering them for over three decades, convinced that they have revelatory meaning that he should somehow be able to decipher and utilize. One of Kruni's earliest conversations with Kulick, in 1985, was a secretive and hushed summary of this film followed by the hopeful questions: "Do you know about this machine?" and, most importantly, "If I went into this machine, would my skin turn white too? Would I become a *masta*?" This film, and others like the one in which Satan appears that he discusses with the youths in his men's house, have informed and profoundly affected his understanding of his own life, the afterlife, and the look of what is to come. In this way, film in Gapun folds back upon itself – pulled loose of its decontextualized, bounded space by the power of the villagers' contextualizing voice, film narratives and film technology become absorbed into village life as events that have occurred somewhere. And because these events coexist with what goes on in Gapun, they contain within themselves the potential to reveal new meanings and establish new connections – just as new meanings emerged when the story of Jari's baby's illness was constructed – for any villager attentive enough to put the pieces together and assemble them.

Conclusion

Like other technology that has been introduced into Papua New Guinea by white people,[5] film technology is understood by the villagers of Gapun to present them with novel possibilities for which they can think of all sorts of practical uses. The technology does emphatically not make them passive. Villagers position themselves in a subject relationship to film, and they are very articulate about how they would like to get it to work for them. In addition, because they have understood film in the ways they have, the technology does not overwhelm them either. On the contrary. One of the more unexpected findings of our video survey was that people were not especially excited about film. Many villagers who had had various opportunities to see a video in the past in various mission stations or towns told us they didn't go, simply because they just couldn't be bothered (cf. KVB 1956, which documents a similar lack of interest for filming among New Guineans living in the town of Jayapura). Since what the villagers consider they see in moving pictures are scenes from life, they do not appear to experience themselves as doing anything particularly unusual when they watch a film. While the technology allows them to peep into other time-spaces and see things that they normally would be unable to see, they are not unduly surprised by the images they see there, since they have, in an important sense, already authored them.

In interpreting the films they see and embedding them in village life, villagers actively subvert the cinematic gaze. Narrative, as the constructed fiber of a film, is integral to the filmic gaze. The camera and director of a film create a narrative, but what Gapun villagers demonstrate so clearly is that this narrative certainly does not preclude other narratives from existing simultaneously in the same collection of images. Gapuners fail to acknowledge the intended narrative in films like *Rambo*, *Tukana*, or whatever film it was that Kruni may have seen at the Angoram government station. They dislodge the filmic narrative with parallel narratives of their own, fragmenting and then reassembling the film to satisfy *their* desire and *their* gaze. While this kind of narrative subversion will readily and quite clearly occur when spectators watch films produced for an unfamiliar audience, the process is an integral part of every film experience, because the intertextual resonances of film imagery are differently constrained and differently generative for different audiences and different spectators. The question that our analysis of Gapun viewers' engagement with film leads us to pose, then, is not so much "How are people positioned by meaningful structured narratives?" as it is "How do people *make meaning* from the chaos of cinematic images and voices?"

This question, of course, is far from new, and those involved in film and communication studies cited at the beginning of this essay are currently formulating answers to it as they explore the dimensions and possibilities of active spectatorship. What concerns us as anthropologists, however, is that analyses of non-Western audience reception often are not grounded in in-depth ethnographic research. Information on people's interpretations of film in many of these studies is gathered mostly through decentextualized interviews or discussions between people that have been arranged and set up by the researcher. While the data gathered in these kinds of settings are interesting, they tell us very little about how people actually talk about films with one another and how their understandings of film are shaped through situated interaction with others. We agree with Spitulnik (1993) that despite a great number of studies that focus on the consumption of media representations, we still know very little about the "everyday life" of such representations. We also agree with her that much more attention needs to be paid to the local practices and discourses of reception which envelop media and embed them into local life. We hope that this essay contributes to that endeavor. We found the villagers' talk about film – both in response to our questions, but more importantly in their talk about film to one another (e.g., during quiet gatherings in the men's house or on household verandahs after nightfall) – to be an excellent source of primary data about their assumptions about film and the interpretations they make of it. We hope that future research pays more attention to people's talk; that is, how individuals use talk to construct, together with others, narratives from cinematic images, and how that talk is bound up with other discursive events in their community.

Of course, the question which may arise sooner or later in the minds of some readers on the basis of the ethnography and analysis we have presented here is: Haven't the villagers, on some level, simply misunderstood film? That is the question we would now be hastening to answer if we accepted the assumptions that underlie most of the literature on the topic of how non-Western groups interpret Western cinema. If we privileged the filmic narrative as the sole source and site of meaning, and if we disregarded the active and assertive role that the villagers assume in their engagement with film, then it would be possible – indeed, it would be inevitable – to answer yes: Gapuners' lack of experience, sophistication, education, viewing skills, and understanding condemn them to misunderstanding the films they see.

The shallowness and hardly-disguised ethnocentrism underlying this kind of approach is remarkable, however, and we are disturbed that scholars who have dealt with this topic in the (recent) past seem more interested in smugly dishing up stereotypes of bug-eyed savages cowered in awe before the marvel of modern technological wizardry, than they are in trying to discover what these people actually are doing when they watch and discuss Western films. Thus, we read Carpenter's (1975) observations on the "terror" and "trauma" that Papua New Guineans are supposed to feel when they see film (or themselves!) for the first time as telling us much more about Carpenter's desire for wildmen than about what the Papua New Guineans he writes about (who are described relentlessly in his paper as "totally innocent tribesmen," "bedecked in barbaric splendor," who have "no private consciousness, no private point of view," and so on) are doing. And Wilson's explanations of "primitive African[s]" who are "confused" and not "sophisticated" enough to watch the whole screen (they supposedly only "scan the picture" and see unimportant details, not what Wilson (1983: 32) feels they are supposed to see) sound to us more like colonial paternalism than satisfactory accounts of what his Ghanaian spectators were watching, and why. Eyeing supposedly "primitive" people through vision clouded by colonialist and racist stereotypes, analyses like these serve no other purpose than to bolster Western images of itself. It is this kind of analysis, more than the films themselves, that creates specific spectator positions for non-Western viewers of Western-made films. What we neglect to notice when we accept the assumptions that lie behind these kinds of analysis is that the gaze we attribute to others is in fact our own.

NOTES

1   The people of Gapun are multilingual, but two languages, Tok Pisin (a creole language spoken throughout the country) and Taiap (the village vernacular – a Papuan language spoken only in Gapun) predominate. Throughout this essay, non-English words in italics are words in Tok Pisin, and underlined italicized words are words in Taiap. In the translations, which are in roman script, underlining signifies that the words were spoken in Taiap. Non-underlining means that the words were spoken in Tok Pisin. The video interviews discussed in this essay were conducted in Tok Pisin. In the transcribed narratives and conversations appearing here, a slash after a word indicates interruption by another speaker or self-interruption, segments of text joined by vertical lines indicates overlapping talk, parentheses indicate unintelligible talk, and square brackets contain our comments or information that is not explicitly stated but known to both speaker and hearers.
2   The contradiction here between the observation that Jari's sister shouted at Jari about being burdened by her baby when Jari was off having sex, and the contention that the baby's spirit was stolen by a *kandap* when Jari lay the child at the base of a tree during sex, was not considered by anybody at this gathering.
3   This young woman, who is unusual in Gapun in that she is one of the very few villagers who has spent a year in high school, is the only one who uses the word "act" (*aktim*) when she describes film. From this and other narratives we collected from her, it is clear that what she means by "act" is not "play a role" or "pretend," but rather "appear in a film."
4   See *Bikmaus* (1983) for a number of reviews of the film *Tukana* (written by Albert Toro, directed and photographed by Chris Owen in 1982). It is interesting in this context to note that out of eight reviews of the film in this collection, only one of them mentions the fact that sorcery occurs in the film. Most reviewers seem to have read *Tukana* as being "about" traditional versus modern values. Graeme Kemelfield's review is typical. He states that "*Tukana* deals with conflicts between youth and older people in the community, and between modern and traditional lifestyle: problems of marriage, and alcohol abuse, and the impact of towns and industry on people's lives."
5   Other examples are literacy, which villagers perceive to represent a link between white people and the Christian gods; planes and ships, which are believed to regularly travel to Heaven; and radio technology, which represents a direct line of communication with God. The Pope, it is said in Gapun, is connected up to Heaven and hears the voices of God and Jesus through loud-speakers in his house in Rome (Kulick 1992; Kulick and Stroud 1990).

REFERENCES

Bikmaus 1983. Reviews of *Tukana: husat i asua?* 1: 44–55.
Carpenter, E. 1975. "The tribal terror of self-awareness." In *Principles of Visual Anthropology*. P. Hockings, ed., pp. 451–67. The Hague: Mouton.
Clover, C. J. 1992. *Men, Women, and Chainsaws: Gender in the Modern Horror Film*. London: British Film Institute.

Corner, J. 1991. "Meaning, genre and context: the problematics of 'public knowledge.'" *Mass Media and Society*. J. Curran and M. Gurevitch, eds. London: Edward Arnold.

Curran, J. and Gurevitch, M., eds. 1991. *Mass Media and Society*. London: Edward Arnold.

de Lauretis, T. 1984. *Alice Doesn't: Feminism, Semiotics and the Cinema*. Bloomington: Indiana University Press.

—— 1987 *Technologies of Gender: Essays on Theory, Film and Fiction*. Bloomington: Indiana University Press.

Doane, M. A. 1982. "Film and the masquerade: theorizing the female spectator." *Screen* 23 (3–4): 74–87.

Fiske, J. 1987. *Television Culture*. London: Metheun.

—— 1991 "Writing ethnographies: contribution to a dialogue." *Quarterly Journal of Speech* 77: 330–5.

Gamman, L. and Marshment, M., eds. 1989. *The Female Gaze: Women as Viewers of Popular Culture*. Seattle: Real Comet Press.

Ginsburg, F. 1991. "Indigenous media: Faustian contract or global village?" *Cultural Anthropology* 6 (1): 92–112.

Hodge, R. and Trippe, D. 1986. *Children and Television*. Cambridge: Polity Press.

Kottak, C. 1990. *Prime-Time Society: An Anthropological Analysis of Television and Culture*. Belmont, CA: Wadsworth.

—— 1991 "Television's impact on values and social life in Brazil." *Journal of Communication* 41 (1): 70–87.

Kulick, D. 1992. *Language Shift and Cultural Reproduction: Socialization, Syncretism and Self in a Papua New Guinean Village*. New York: Cambridge University Press.

—— 1993. "Heroes from Hell: representations of 'rascals' in a Papua New Guinean village." *Anthropology Today* 9 (3): 9–14.

Kulick, D. and Stroud, C. 1990. "Christianity, cargo and ideas of self: patterns of literacy in a Papua New Guinean village." *Man* 15: 286–304.

Kulick, D. and Willson, M. 1992. "Echoing images: the construction of savagery among Papua New Guinean villagers." *Visual Anthropology* 5 (2): 143–52.

KVB (Kantoor voor Bevolkingszaken) 1956. *Papoea en film: verslag van enn filmenquete*. Hollandia: Landsdrukkerij.

Liebes, T. 1984. "Ethnocentrism: Israelis of Moroccan ethnicity negotiate the meaning of 'Dallas'." *Studies in Visual Communication* 10 (2): 46–61.

Liebes, T. and Katz, E. 1990. *The Export of Meaning*. New York: Oxford University Press.

Livingstone, S. 1989. "Audience reception: the role of the viewer in retelling the romance drama." In *The Female Gaze: Women as Viewers of Popular Culture*. Gamman, L. and Marshment, M., eds. Seattle: Real Comet Press.

Mattelart, A. 1980. *Mass Media, Ideologies and the Revolutionary Movement*. Brighton: Harvester.

Mulvey, L. 1971. "Visual pleasure and narrative cinema." *Screen* 16 (3): 6–18.

—— 1975 "Afterthoughts on 'Visual pleasure and narrative cinema' inspired by 'Duel in the sun'." *Framework* 15–17.

Nichols, B. 1981. *Ideology and Image*. Bloomington: Indiana University Press.

Roof, J. 1991. *A Lure of Knowledge: Lesbian Sexuality and Theory*. New York: Columbia University Press.

Spitulnik, D. 1993. "Anthropology and mass media." *Annual Review of Anthropology* 22: 293–315.

Stacey, J. 1989. "Desperately seeking difference." In *The Female Gaze: Women as Viewers of Popular Culture*. Gamman, L. and Marshment, M. eds. Seattle: Real Comet Press.

Stadler, H. 1990. "Film as experience: phenomenological concepts in cinema and television studies." *Quarterly Review of Film and Video* 12 (3): 37–50.

Wilson, J. 1983. "Comments on work with film preliterates in Africa." *Studies in Visual Communication* 9 (1): 30–5

17

"It's Destroying a Whole Generation": Television and Moral Discourse in Belize

Richard R. Wilk

Have you ever sat down and watch T.V.
Well, it has happened to me.

I don't smoke weed
but I get a natural high
watching the Jeffersons
get a piece of the pie.

Do you know that it's ABC
getting addicted to watching T.V.
and even worse you've got to pay a fee
if you want to have Cable T.V.

The Children come from school
turn on the T.V. and watch cartoon
Later in the evening the parents
join in and watch movies like

the Blue Lagoon.
Well, this is good
but it is also bad
kids failing the
problem is sad
making the teachers and parents extremely mad.

"Television," by Karl Burgess (age 16)

People watch television, but they also talk about television. Most studies of television in Third World countries have looked at the content and origin of the messages carried by television, to detect the social effects and cultural content of programs. In this essay I argue that the connection between TV and society is less direct, and that television cannot be understood without listening to the ways people *talk about* television.[1]

Recent work in communications and mass media studies tells us that we cannot understand television as a medium without considering this discourse. Watching television and talking about television are inseparable parts of a single process. Accordingly, the viewing experience should be seen as an active and social activity, and the content of messages as a matter of dispute and contention rather than being simply given.

This essay argues that an anthropological approach to television must look at discourse about television if we are to understand the place of the medium in social process at a local and global scale. Television transforms social discourse, and this may be as important as its psychological influence, its informational content, or its displacement of other forms of social interaction. This essay suggests some ways that TV has changed social discourse in Belize, a country where TV is a relatively recent arrival.

The Invasion

Taped television was a medium held privately in the hands of the economic elite of Belize for several years before public broadcasting began. During this time there was no hue and cry or alarm raised about its impact, though thousands of videotapes circulated. It was only when private entrepreneurs began to rebroadcast pirated satellite signals in December of 1981 that the newspapers and magazines announced the beginnings of "Television Mania" and "The Video Invasion" (Anon. 1981). Commenting on the euphoric feeling of freedom that swept the capital, one local writer said "The 'tube' has hit Belize like a heady wine" (Ewens n.d.: 4).

Controversy followed, as Belizeans debated both the cultural and political ramifications of the new medium. The government first turned a blind eye, then cautiously tried to regulate the new industry (under pressure from the United States, where the signals originated). With the approach of the 1984 elections the government took stronger steps to control television, and began to raise alarms about its cultural impact. The Minister of Education proclaimed that television was more dangerous than an invading army of 10,000 soldiers.[2] The perception that the government was going to clamp down on television broadcasting was one of the issues that led to their crushing electoral defeat. There has been no such restriction, and today there are at least six cable networks and nine transmitters, mostly providing US programming direct from satellites.[3]

Shortly after the television invasion, another invasion began, this time of foreign scholars. Most of their work followed a diffusionary paradigm, portraying Belize as a victim of cultural imperialism and the neocolonial world information order. They studied the impact of the new medium on politics, social organization, psychology, consumption patterns, and migration (Barry 1984; Bolland 1987; Everitt 1987; Lent 1989; Oliveira 1986; Petch 1987; Roser et al. 1986; Wilk 1989). Few showed any knowledge of local history or culture.

On my return to Belize in 1989 much of the initial furor had died down, and the media scholars had moved on to newer pastures. But the local debate about television continued; everyone I spoke with had an opinion about television. I should mention that my fieldwork was not focused specifically on television. I was led to the topic by my informants' responses to my questions about the meanings of consumer goods, the nature of Creole culture, and the state of the Belizean economy (Wilk

1990). It became clear that in eleven years of broadcasting, television has become important in the ways Belizeans define themselves and their relationships to each other and to the outside world.

This essay is based mostly on conversations and interviews, on some survey responses, and on printed discussion of television in newspapers, magazines, government publications and campaign literature from the 1989 elections.[4] Rather than joining in the debate about television's direct impact on the country, I would like to step back from it and examine the social and political consequences of the debate itself.

The Local and the Global

One striking aspect of both local and academic discussion of television in the Third World is the way it objectifies the concepts of "local" and "global" culture. In its crudest form, seen best in anthropology in the literature on acculturation, or in media studies in the "cultural imperialism" school, the "local" is the passive recipient or victim of a benign or malign outside force. This point of view can easily be modified to accommodate "oppositional" forms that intensify or revitalize local culture to resist the external. The world drama, in this view, is one of global hegemony and local resistance.

This is a common perspective among Belizeans. I was told almost every day, in some way, that local Belizean culture was in jeopardy, and the problem came from outside, usually from the USA. The opposition between "local" and hegemonic "global" cultures, of cultural imperialism as a world drama, is now folk-knowledge. The academic model and the folk model coincide quite well. Belizeans, like foreign scholars, often prescribe intensified production of local television as the best cure.

But as explanation there are both logical and empirical problems with the cultural imperialism model. As Daniel Miller (1990, n.d.) and Ulf Hannerz (1987) point out, the "global" is no longer a unitary category; simply everything outside of the local. Belizeans, like most other Third World people, make clear distinctions between different products from and areas in the outside world. They are happy to discuss English versus American culture, or the cultural differences between LA and New York. The "local" is a similarly flawed concept for a nation fragmented by language, culture, class, and rural–urban divisions.[5]

Hannerz and Miller argue that rather than being opposed, the local and the global are in many ways interdependent, dialectically related to each other. In his analysis of soap operas in Trinidad, Miller finds that Trinidadians' image of *their own* culture is best exemplified in their interpretation of a *foreign* television program, *The Young and the Restless*. In reverse, many local productions express foreign cultural values of seriousness and formality (Miller 1990: 31–2). He says this shows that the products of local and global culture must be understood in the context of their consumption, not of their production. Foreign objects and messages are naturalized into a local context through consumption. And local productions are similarly regenerated when they enter global culture, as with the Trinidadian steel band or Jamaican reggae. This process, called "creolization" by Hannerz (1987), breaks down boundaries between cultures and makes the concept of local culture an obsolete impediment to perceiving the new global reality.

Television Theory: Reading the Text

This new global economy of meaning has become an important topic in the anthropological study of commodities and consumerism. Goods are also recontextualized and reinterpreted at their locus of consumption (Friedman 1990; Lofgren 1990; McCracken 1988; Arnould and Wilk 1984; Wilk 1990; Belk 1988). I think we need to apply these same critical insights to the study of television in the Third World. Just as a McDonald's hamburger means something very different in Moscow from what it means in Dubuque, so the drama of *Dallas* has been found to convey very different meanings to Israelis, Algerians, and Italians (Katz and Liebes 1984, 1986; Silj et al. 1988). Australian aborigines interpret television dramas in ways that would be unintelligible to those who produced the drama in the first place (Michaels 1988). Fiske (1986) argues that even in the countries where they are produced, television programs are open texts subject to a variety of interpretations. The very popularity of television rests on polysemy and ambiguity, on the ability of different groups to find different things in the same program.[6]

Existing studies of the television audience have some very important ramifications for our understanding of the global traffic in objects and meanings, of the process whereby the global becomes localized. One finding is that the message of television is interpreted and absorbed socially, rather than individually. Television messages are mediated in the social context of talk *about* television. (For example, violent programs do not make children prone to or inured to violence when their parents and friends talk about television violence with disapproval [Drummond and Paterson 1988].) Studies consistently find that conversation is an essential part of television watching; the meaning of the program acquires cultural and social relevance through interpretive discourse (Katz and Liebes 1984, 1986; Lee and Cho 1990; Miller 1990). In asking about the impact of television on families around the world, Lull (1988) finds the most universal change is that television creates a new genre of "television talk" within existing family interaction.

But what does this genre of talk do to the messages from the box? Most theorists agree that television talk allows viewers to negotiate different poses, or distances in relation to the program. The various classifications of these poses can be combined into a set of three (based on works by Hall 1981; Livingstone 1990; Morley 1980, 1988; Ang 1985; and Katz and Liebes 1984, 1986):

1　A viewer who is *dominated* places no distance between himself and the program, identifying closely with the characters and situation in a completely uncritical way (Hall 1981). Katz and Liebes (1984, 1986) focus on the emotional fix of the viewer on the program, while Ang (1985) sees an element of fantasy that Livingstone (1990) would call "romantic." The viewer confuses the program with reality, relating to the characters as real people, sometimes as even *more* real than the mundane. This implies that dominated viewers uncritically absorb and internalize the hegemonic messages from the box, accepting and integrating them into their lives. To Leal (1990) this position is also mystical, and the television becomes a fetish imbued with human characteristics.

2　At the other extreme is Hall's (1981) *oppositional* stance, where the viewer has a critical distance from the program that allows judgment about truth, the motives of its producers, and the impact of the medium itself. The position has been labeled "ironic" (Ang 1985), "cynical" (Livingstone 1990), and "moralistic" (Katz and Liebes 1984, 1986). Viewers perceive a message in the box and reject it, or they extract a meaning from the program that was not intentionally coded there, for example that *Dallas* is about the evils of patriarchy, or of capitalism.

3   In between there is a *negotiated* position, where the viewer does not dispute the meaning of the program, but interprets and adapts it in light of his own experience and interest. This "pragmatic" (Katz and Liebes 1984) and "realistic" (Ang 1985) position allows the viewers to relate the events in the program to their own lives. They accept the program as a fantasy, but one that resonates and reflects; they are willing to identify with some things and reject others in a creative process of engaged participation. The way they use and reintegrate meanings has been likened to "poaching" [Silj et al. 1988].

If these three options cover a real range of relationships to television, how can they be mapped onto the local and global audience? Most tempting are transpositions onto social or geographical maps. A proponent of cultural imperialism can argue that viewers in the metropole have critical distance while those on the periphery are dominated and deceived. Some studies in Britain have argued that for specific program categories, gender is the best predictor of reading; women are dominated by soap opera, while men are more distanced (Morley 1988). Katz and Liebes (1984, 1986) found cultural differences that explain viewers' readings of *Dallas*; Israeli Arabs were moralistic and distanced, while Moroccan Jews were pragmatic, and American Jews were engaged (see Silj et al. 1988).

Another tempting map links types of reading to social rank; the educated upper classes are capable of critical distance, while the poor have a direct and uncritical relationship to the program that leads to their domination (Fachel and Oliven 1988; Ang 1985; Leal 1990). This hypothesis can be supported by several studies, including Kottak's in Brazil, that find greater criticism of television at higher income and educational levels (as well as with longer length of exposure to the medium [Kottak 1990: 140–2]).

The idea that the poor are dominated while the rich and educated have critical distance is a folk model of television consumption that I often heard in Belize. Middle- and upper-class people there worried about the effects of television on the gullible poor, whose close, uncritical involvement was going to lead to dire cultural effects. The commonly voiced fear was that the poor were taking television "too literally," that they mistook entertainment for reality. Even many of the poor and uneducated people I spoke with said that their neighbors and children were taking television too seriously, were believing what they saw and were emotionally affected. Government officials see themselves as stuck between a critical elite who want the media controlled, and an engaged, dominated populace interested only in more entertainment.

When folk models and academic models coincide so neatly, there is good reason to be cautious. I personally was never able to find even one of those dominated viewers who simply mistook TV for reality, who uncritically accepted the messages in the programs they saw. All viewers, of every social category, were capable of multiple poses and distances from television. Even the least educated person takes a critical stance towards TV programs in the right circumstances, and even the best educated member of the elite is susceptible to a "dominated" immersion in the medium. As Miller (1990) and Buckingham (1988) have argued, the whole audience is capable of all levels of engagement, and can get enjoyment out of each of them. At the same time, everyone contrasts his or her own position with people who have been duped and manipulated, with someone who believes what he or she is seeing. This may be a rhetorical device rather than an objective social judgment (Seiter 1990). Miller (1990: 7) suggests that the elite seem more critical and distanced because they feel more need to legitimize themselves in the eyes of the scholarly researcher.

Television Discourse in Belize

If there are no simple social maps to different readings of television, these categories of distance are still useful. They suggest that television discourse (1984, 1986) has meaning on a number of levels, and we should expect people to take different positions towards the medium in each social context. In Belize, in the context of the family, dominated and negotiated distances seem to be most common. In the rum-shop and the workplace, negotiation and critical distance appear in conversation about television. I have little ethnographic data on these areas; in the public and political discourse I studied, critical distance and moralistic debate were the rule.

To describe this type of debate, I will start with the print media, based on 14 months of clippings from five weekly newspapers. Belizean newspapers represent different constituencies. In general, papers supporting the conservative, pro-American United Democratic Party are uncritical of television, and stress its positive educational value and its role in promoting free political debate and democracy. These newspapers see television primarily as a source of information, and if Americanization results, that is not seen as such a bad thing. They express some mild misgivings about depictions of drugs and violence, but see this as a matter for parents to control, or for self-censorship by broadcasters (*Beacon* 4/27/1985).

In contrast a newspaper controlled by the left-leaning People's United Party is much more critical of television. The *Belize Times* reflects the government's position that foreign television is a danger to national culture and identity that must be controlled. Television increases foreign domination of the economy by developing tastes for foreign goods, and by promoting a vision of the "good life" in material terms, making Belizeans dissatisfied with their country and culture. Television seduces Belizeans into "an alien way of life." On the positive side, television makes Belizeans more politically sophisticated and, by showing people how poor they are, it makes them want better. Government organs frequently call for more local television production, and more educational television to further the development process, but little practical action has resulted.

The one politically independent newspaper, *Amandala*, tends to be left of center and strongly Afrocentric. It has been openly and vocally critical of television for the last five years. The commentary in *Amandala* comes from both middle- and working-class sources.

Middle-class commentators try for objective balance, arguing for both positive and negative effects of television. The positive include making Belizeans more educated and sophisticated, especially about the outside world, and providing positive models of family life (citing the Cosby show), of health, democracy, art, and patriotism. The editor of *Amandala* told me that by exposing viewers to a wider and more sophisticated world, television had helped Belizeans to feel more confident, less isolated and backward. They have become more sophisticated consumers, less likely to be cheated. Because Belizeans see the problems of the USA on television, the drugs and violence, they know better what to expect if they migrate.

But the negative influences are legion. In various columns television has been blamed for rampant Americanism in sports, food, fashion, music, speech, and even body language. Belize is losing its culture as television undercuts local institutions and communications. This "cultural colonialism" and consumerism lead to greater emigration, less appreciation for education, and the glorification of drugs, sex, and violence. Television shows "people all dressed up in silk lounging on luxurious furniture in air conditioned comfort, driving expensive cars on smooth highways and dancing the nights away in expensive discos frequented by movie actors, drug dons and the beautiful people" (*Amandala* 5/4/1990).

Several feminist columnists add that television is leading to greater child neglect and a lower social position for women. It is invoked as the culprit in discussions of poor school performance by children, low participation in local sporting events,[7] and increasing crime and gang membership. Television is also blamed for increasing racism, homosexuality, adultery, and youthful promiscuity. An editorial claims, "American Television has become a cancer for our children who are not in school, because they are not sophisticated enough to filter out the filth and enjoy that which is entertaining. With American television and its emphasis on sex and violence replacing the sports programs in Belize City, the outlet for the excess energies of our delinquent young has become involvement in what sex and violence they can find or create, hence the young gangs roaming the streets." In the editor's view, America has become decadent – and Belizeans want to copy that decadence, a situation he finds both comic and tragic (*Amandala* 10/20/1989). In a macabre exchange, the USA gave Belize television entertainment, but took ownership of the country's land and resources.

Letters to the editor, and the columns by a working-class commentator ("Smokey Joe"), give few positive opinions about television. Instead, they focus on the effects of television on children, especially the decline in studying and poor school perform-ance. Smokey Joe accuses the parents of being so involved in television, they don't have time for their children anymore. This focus on youth extends to the activities of a working-class "concerned parents" group, who blame television for "disrespect, destructiveness, rebelliousness, and lawlessness" (*Amandala* 12/31/1989).

Smokey Joe also makes some more subtle points about television influence on Belize. Because people are so concerned with the imaginary world of soap operas, he says, they have lost their work ethic, their concern for local issues, and the social conscience that once made them help their poor and homeless neighbors. "Most of you align yourselves with Days of Our Lives and filthy Santa Barbara . . . living in another world. They forget that our street people are their problems" (*sic, Amandala* 3/16/1990). "We must stop believing what we hear on television. Soap Operas are filthy – you should be reading a good book. They keep your brains filled with filth so you cannot think about anything else. Children follow in your footsteps instead of going to school" (*Amandala* 12/29/1990).

Television thus becomes a cultural and historical watershed, allowing people to create a new and mythical past when children respected their parents, and social justice and good morals were the rule. Television has given Belizeans a temporal fix, a spot to mark the beginning of modernity and the passing of the old.

Interviews with Belizeans found a similar range of positive and negative commen-tary. Some people stressed the destructive influences of television; a rural preacher told me that television was the primary cause of immorality in his village: it filled children's heads with "filth," made them disrespectful, and led to rampant sex, drugs, crime, loud music, and organized crime. Worst of all, he said, children lost their capacity to dream, to imagine a future for themselves – all they could see ahead was the image of America on the screen. You could hear this same sermon in churches all over the country almost every Sunday. Television is a malign force, allied with other kinds of evil that are hastening the coming of the Day of Judgment.

Meanwhile, some of those same youth who are becoming so degenerate told me that television had made them more aware of the dangers of drugs and crime, more conscious of the poverty and social decay of the USA. They argued that for most people, television was harmless entertainment that kept them off the streets and out of trouble. Preaching about the dangers of television belonged in church, along with moral condemnations of the other things that most people do – fornicate, drink, and get into trouble.

In two surveys of working-class television viewers, I found similar differences of opinion about the positive and negative effects of television.

- The following represent the range of positive effects:
- people know more about the world today;
- there is better access to preachers and religious programs;
- you learn a lot from watching;
- it is entertaining and fun, something to do with friends;
- it is a good alternative to going out, which can cause trouble;
- news tells you what is going on in the world;
- rural life is less boring, so people don't have to move to the city;

and on the negative side,

- children watch instead of studying;
- shows are often dumb and uninteresting;
- programs are too "wordly" (instead of Christian);
- you do not know what to believe in the advertisements;
- children learn the wrong things.

While the rural working class tends to criticize the moral content of programs and the direct effect of viewing on their children, the middle class is more likely to see negative *social* and *cultural* effects. They speak of cultural dependence and American imperialism, of consumerism, street violence, and emigration. The middle class has had television longer and, unlike the poor, for whom viewing is a social event, they now complain that television decreases social interaction and isolates people (as Kottak [1990: 145] found in Brazil).

To summarize, I found a profound ambivalence about television at every level of society, in every context. This ambivalence allows a space for moral issues to enter.

Leftist politicians and journalists tend to be more critical, while those of the right are much less so. Middle-class critics tend to focus on national and cultural issues, while working-class people were more concerned about their children and community. The middle class blame more problems on television, but they also saw more benefits. Everyone seemed capable of both engaged enjoyment of the medium and critical distance, though rural people spoke more frequently and enthusiastically about the pleasures of watching. And more importantly, everyone seemed to agree on what television was doing to Belize – changing the country profoundly; the disagreement was merely over whether this was a good or a bad thing.

The Effects of Television Discourse

My next question is, has the *debate* about television changed Belizean society? Television discourse has certainly changed some aspects of political behavior. Politicians are wary of making statements about the medium these days because television is seen as a populist issue. Being perceived as "anti-television" now means being an elitist. So their positions during the 1989 campaigns were limited to accusations of censorship and bias, and pious statements about the need to improve television and make it better serve national interests. Between the two parties, television is part of a long-standing debate about Belize's economic and cultural relationship with the US, and about the dangers or attractions of cultural imperialism. The issue is not one-sided, since many Belizeans admire the United States.

This debate about Belizean autonomy and dependence has its roots in the anti-colonial nationalist movement of the 1950s (which was led by the present prime minister, George Price). Pro- and anti-television arguments are based on the political positions taken by the nationalist and loyalist factions during that time. The nationalists built their political power on a coalition between the poor working classes and educated public servants, an alliance that lasted through the struggle for self-rule to independence in 1981. But then television arrived, and the alliance foundered. One issue was that the educated middle class regarded television as a danger to their political and cultural power, and sought to control it (Wilk 1989). The poor wanted television and so resisted that control.

Among the rural and urban poor and working classes, in churches and to a lesser extent among educators, television has become part of a general *moral* discourse that existed long before the television invasion. Television takes its place as one of the many external factors that are corrupting and destroying Belizean families, explaining cultural changes that many perceive as destructive. Television enters moral discourse because its message contradicts or supports ethical positions about what is right, and about what "should be." It opens up options that explicitly and implicitly challenge the moral order (Ang 1985). It also enters moral discourse because it is conveniently exogenous, and could therefore be kept out. Television provides an explanation for the source of evil – and is classified with existing sources of evil like the United States, the devil, money, sex, and drugs.

While television could be seen as merely adding new fuel to old fires, the new linkage between these old discourses about morality and politics is important. Television brings political and moral issues together in a new and powerful way, widening the field of discourse and involving people from different factions, classes, and ethnic groups in a common debate. Where religion was once concerned mostly with the individual and the community, it now speaks to issues of Belizean cultural identity and influence from the United States.

In blurring the distinction between political and religious discourse, television has imbued political debate with a new moral content, and has taken traditionally moral issues and secularized them. In the process it has taken many issues that were once seen as Belizean, local and even familial, and moved them into a global context. The problems of youth, social welfare, ethnicity, and gender roles, for example, are now cast in a global context, of "our way" or "our Belizean traditions" as opposed to "those seen on television." Now that television has presented Belizeans with an objectified "other," the problem of defining the self has a new dimension. Differences between Belizeans seem to fade away when confronted with the light from the box. There is now more common language for the discussion of otherness and sameness, and a visible standard of comparison. In the past, images of foreign culture were received indirectly, with the colonial elite acting as selective agents, the gatekeepers to the outside world (Wilk 1989, 1990).

In a real sense, some of those differences *have* faded away. Belize is still a multi-ethnic and multilingual country with great disparities in wealth and education. But television has proven a unifying force in two ways. At the level of content, all Belizeans with television now share access to some of the same sources of news and entertainment, even if those sources are CNN and Tom Brokaw. Now all Belizeans have a common conversation about NBA basketball, Alf, and the Cosby show. At a second level, television has engaged Belizeans in a common debate about the impact of television on the country, and in the process has made everyone aware of "the local and the global" as a matter of concern. If we liken Belizeans to voyeurs watching America through an electronic peephole, we find they are united by both the common knowledge of what goes on in America and by the shared experience of voyeurism.

I don't want to overemphasize this unity. The country remains highly factionalized and divided. But television discourse has also changed existing social divisions and the alignment of factions. For example, religious organizations, which used to have a very close relationship with political conservatives, now find themselves sharing important common ground with the left. Both are concerned about the danger of foreign television. The Baptist minister and the nationalist student have a new shared agenda, the control of foreign influence. The old nationalist program of building local cultural institutions now finds a much broader constituency.

Another important effect of television discourse among these new coalitions is that it changes the *terms* of the debate about local and foreign. Instead of being about political autonomy from the British, or about local economic development, debate is now carried out in *cultural* terms. In Belize after television, people talk about "culture" constantly, in ways that were not possible before. Television has made Belizeans focus on the autonomy of local culture – on music, cooking, dance, and language – rather than on political or economic autonomy. Thirty years ago when Belizeans spoke about Britain, they talked about the Empire,[8] about wealth and power. Today when they talk about America, they talk about culture and fashion. So while Belizeans make different moral judgments about what is good and bad on television, they share a common language when they debate those moral issues.

One of the most lasting effects of television in Belize, then, is a particular form of what Miller (1987) has called "objectification," building on Hegel's concept of "alienation." The intimate awareness of otherness, presented by the image of America on television, has led Belizeans to objectify a new concept of *culture*. Once culture was inchoate lived practice, and all differences between people were submerged in color, ethnicity, and class. Today Belizeans perceive that there is a thing out there called culture; differences that were once organized and classified in other ways are now recast as "cultural." The objectified other prompts the emergence of an objectified self. Belizeans actively disagree about just what constitutes Belizean culture, but twenty years ago this controversy could not have existed because the concept of Belizean culture was absent.

Conclusions

To conclude: I have argued that the best place to start to talk about television in Belize is with the ways that people talk about television. I suggest that television has become a social, cultural, and political issue that is integrating with ongoing discourse, and is being used by existing groups to further their own positions and agendas. In the process, "television talk" subtly transforms that discourse. It creates new coalitions of common interest. It changes the content and terms of social debate, moving them away from the economic and political and towards the cultural.

Most importantly, television affects Belizean ideas about time and cultural distance. This new medium has created a temporal watershed, a dramatic change in the nation that allows for new interpretations of the past. The beam from satellites provides a new image of the foreign "other" that furthers an emerging consensus about the content and identity of *Belizean* culture. Paradoxically, television imperialism may do more to create a national culture and national consciousness in Belize than forty years of nationalist politics and eleven years of independence.

NOTES

1 It is encouraging that anthropologists who have studied TV *have* shown an interest in the way people talk about the medium from the very start; see Kottak (1990: 127–8, 140–2), Michaels (1988), Kent (1985).

2 This remark has been widely quoted and misquoted since 1984. The opposition claimed it was an elitist position, an attempt to deny access to the media to the poor majority. It must be remembered that at the time there was a serious danger that an army of more than 10,000 Guatemalan soldiers would invade at any moment.

3 The north part of the country gets TV broadcasting from Mexico, and the south from Guatemala and Honduras. Other areas of the country get some Spanish-language broadcasts from American networks, that in turn use Mexican and South American programming.

4 I incorporated some questions about television viewing and program popularity in my surveys on consumer preferences, but this will be reported elsewhere. Here I want to concentrate not on measuring the objective impact of television on Belize, but on who says what about the impact of television on Belize.

5 A number of empirical studies have recently been done of the "cultural imperialism" hypothesis of global television. There is little or no discernible cultural effect of high levels of imported local media on local economies or culture (Meyer 1987). Instead there is good evidence that national governments have used television to bolster their own popularity and political control (Karthigesu 1988).

6 Fiske argues that a number of alternative meanings are *intentionally* coded into the television program to begin with, and that the very popularity and success of a program is in fact a product of this structured ambiguity. This argument returns, in a way, to the imperialism argument, but with more subtlety. Now instead of forcing a single message down our throats, the producer slyly allows us to make several readings, but the options

are still dictated within the form of the message. We get the illusion of autonomy without its substance.

7   One editorial observed that a local football match was called off when a number of players stayed home to watch a basketball playoff game.

8   Belize was formerly British Honduras.

REFERENCES

Ang, Ien 1985. *Watching Dallas: Soap Opera and the Melodramatic Imagination*. London: Methuen.

Anonymous 1981. "The Video Invasion." *Brukdown: The Magazine of Belize*, 5 (6): 15–21.

Arnould, E. J. and Richard Wilk 1984. "Why do the Indians Wear Adidas?" *Advances in Consumer Research*, 11: 748–52.

Barry, Jessica 1984. "The Belize Dilemma." *Media in Education and Development* (March): 11–13.

Belk, Russell 1988. "Third World Consumer Culture." Research in Marketing, Supplement 4, *Marketing and Development*, pp. 103–27. Greenwich, CT: Jai Press.

Bolland, Nigel 1987. "United States Cultural Influence on Belize: Television and Education as 'Vehicles of Import'." *Caribbean Quarterly*, 33 (3–4): 60–74.

Buckingham, D. 1988. *Public Secrets: East Enders and Its Audience*. London: British Film Institute.

Burgess, Karl L. 1990. *Belize Poems*. Belize City: Cain's Press.

Drummond, Phillip and Richard Patterson (eds.) 1988. *Television and Its Audience: International Research Perspectives*. London: British Film Institute.

Everitt, J. C. 1987. "The Torch is Passed: Neocolonialism in Belize." *Caribbean Quarterly*, 33 (3–4): 42–59.

Ewens, Debbe n.d. "Television Hits Belize." *Focus*. Belize City: Caribbean Publishers.

Fachel, O. and R. Oliven 1988. "Class Interpretation of a Soap Opera Narrative." *Theory, Culture and Society*, 5 (1): 81–100.

Fiske, John 1986. "Television: Polysemy and Popularity." *Critical Studies in Mass Communications*, 3 (4): 391–408.

Friedman, Jonathan 1990. "The Political Economy of Elegance." *Culture and History*, 7: 101–25.

Hall, S. 1981. "Notes on Deconstructing the Popular." In *People's History and Social Theory*. R. Samuel, ed., pp. 227–39. London: Routledge and Kegan Paul.

Hannerz, Ulf 1987. "The World in Creolization." *Africa*, 57 (4): 546–59.

Karthigesu, Ranggasamay 1988. "Television as a Tool for Nation Building in the Third World: Post-Colonial Patterns, Using Malaysia as a Case-Study." In *Television and Its Audience: International Research Perspectives*. Phillip Drummond and Richard Patterson, eds., pp. 306–26. London: BFI Publishing.

Katz, E. and T. Liebes 1984. "Once Upon a Time, in Dallas." *Intermedia*, 12 (3): 46–72.

—— 1986 "Patterns of Involvement in Television Fiction: A Comparative Study." *European Journal of Communication*, 1 (2): 151–71.

Kent, Susan 1985. "The Effects of Television Viewing: A Cross-Cultural Perspective." *Current Anthropology*, 26 (1): 121–6.

Kottak, Conrad 1990. *Prime Time Society*. Belmont, CA: Wadsworth.

Leal, Ondina E. 1990. "Popular Taste and the Erudite Repertoire: The Place and Space of Television in Brazil." *Cultural Studies*, 4 (1): 19–29.

Lee, Minu and Chong Heup Cho 1990. "Women Watching Together: An Ethnographic Study of Soap Opera Fans in the US." *Cultural Studies*, 4 (1): 30–44.

Lent, John 1989. "Country of No Return: Belize since Television." *Belizean Studies*, 17 (1): 14–36.

Livingstone, Sonia M. 1990. "Interpreting a Television Narrative: How Different Viewers See a Story." *Journal of Communication*, 40 (1): 72–85.

Lofgren, Orvar 1990. "Consuming Interests." *Culture and History*, 7: 1–36.

Lull, James 1988. "Constructing Rituals of Extension through Family Television Viewing." In *World Families Watch Television*. James Lull, ed., pp. 237–60. Beverly Hills, CA: Sage.

McCracken, Grant 1988. *Culture and Consumption*. Bloomington: Indiana University Press.

Meyer, William 1987. "Testing Theories of Cultural Imperialism: International Media and Domestic Impact." *International Interactions*, 13: 353–74.

Michaels, Eric 1988. "Hollywood Iconography: A Warlpiri Reading." In *Television and its Audience: International Research Perspectives*. Phillip Drummond and Richard Patterson, eds., pp. 109–24. London: BFI Publishing.

Miller, Daniel 1987. *Material Culture and Mass Consumption*. Oxford: Blackwell Publishers.

—— 1990. "Fashion and Ontology in Trinidad." *Culture and History*, 7: 49–78.

—— n.d. The Young and the Restless in Trinidad: A Case for the Local and the Global in Mass Consumption. (Ms. in possession of the author.)

Morley, D. 1980. *The Nationwide Audience*. London: British Film Institute.

—— 1988. "Domestic Relations: The Framework of Family Viewing in Great Britain." In *World Families Watch Television*. James Lull, ed., pp. 22–48. Beverly Hills, CA: Sage.

Oliveira, Omar 1986. "Satellite Television and Dependency: An Empirical Approach." *Gazette*, 38: 127–45.

Petch, Trevor 1987. "Television and Video Ownership in Belize." *Belizean Studies*, 15 (1): 12–14.

Roser, Connie, Leslie Snyder, and Steve Chaffee 1986. "Belize Release Me Let Me Go: The Impact of U.S. Mass Media on Emigration in Belize." *Belizean Studies*, 14 (3): 1–30.

Seiter, Ellen 1990. "Making Distinctions in TV Audience Research: Case Study of a Troubling Interview." *Cultural Studies*, 4 (1): 61–84.

Silj, Alessandro et al. 1988. *East of Dallas: The European Challenge to American Television*. London: BFI Publishing.

Westlake, Donald 1982. "The Box Rebellion." *Harper's Monthly*, July: 22–26.

Wilk, Richard 1989. "Colonial Time and T.V. Time: Media and Historical Consciousness in Belize." *Belizean Studies*, 17 (1): 3–13.

—— 1990. "Consumer Goods as Dialogue about Development." *Culture and History*, 7: 79–100.

18

National Texts and Gendered Lives: An Ethnography of Television Viewers in a North Indian City

Purnima Mankekar

Recent trends in anthropology reflect an increasing acknowledgment of the significance of mass media to processes of identity formation (see, for instance, Appadurai and Breckenridge 1988; Ivy 1988; Russell 1991; Traube 1989). In this essay I analyze the ways in which men and women in New Delhi actively engage with and interpret Indian television, and I explore the place of their interpretations in their constitution as national and gendered subjects. Given the tendency of some scholars to depict audiences of mass media as passive consumers and, in the case of women who live in the "Third World," as helpless victims of a totalizing patriarchal "system," my approach to popular culture and subjectivity represents important theoretical and political gains.

Studies attempting to link television with the construction of identity have tended to focus on the effects of popular texts upon the lives of those who interact with them. For instance, Modleski (1979, 1983) stresses the centrality of the pleasures of television's texts to the construction of femininity. Similarly, Colin MacCabe has emphasized the various ways in which the "terrain of the political is being redefined" by television in the establishment of "enormous machineries of desire" (MacCabe 1986, cited in Caughie 1986: 165). Such studies have far-reaching implications for those of us concerned with the relations of power that suffuse everyday life and the constitution of subjectivities. For when mass media such as television are treated as part of a whole range of cultural products, as texts to be "read" according to interpretive strategies, we see that literary conventions and forms have greater sociocultural significance than we might first suspect: analyses of mass media thus enable us to see how we are fashioned by our interactions with what we read, watch, and listen to.[1]

However, in the analysis that follows I extend these propositions by *ethnographically* examining viewers' variable and active interpretations of televisual texts. I hence highlight the fact that meaning is unstable and is frequently contested by viewers, historical subjects, living in particular discursive formations, rather than positioned by any single text.[2] I go beyond approaches that focus exclusively on the implications of specific viewing conditions (for example, Brunsdon 1984; Modleski 1979, 1983), on the construction of subject positions by televisual and cinematic texts (as in Lakshmi 1988; Mulvey 1989; Thomas 1985; Vasudevan 1989),[3] or on the relationship between texts and the sociopolitical conjunctures in which they are embedded (Krishnan and Dighe 1990; Punwani 1988; Taylor 1989). The questions I raise in this essay emerge from my understanding of the gaps in primarily textual or sociological analyses. What is the place of television in the construction of viewers as national and gendered subjects? How do audiences, themselves historically and spatially located, simultaneously "submit" to and "resist" the texts produced by a hegemonic state apparatus such as Indian television?[4] By examining viewers' *active* interaction with television's texts, we can envision popular culture as a site of struggle and not simply of domination, as an "arena of consent and resistance... partly where hegemony arises, and where it is secured" (Hall 1981: 239).[5]

My analysis of television enables me to situate viewers in particular sociohistorical contexts, to demonstrate that subject positions vary according to the conjunctures in which viewers are interpellated,[6] and to show how class, community, gender, age, and household position mediate people's interactions with televisual texts.[7] Thus, while previous research on Indian television has dwelt on the political and cultural effects of *texts* (see, for instance, Krishnan 1990; Singhal and Rogers 1989), I have focused on the ways in which *viewers* interpret specific themes and images. Because I am interested in tracing connections between responses to television and the continuous constitution of national and gendered subjectivities, I situate viewers' interpretations in the context of life-narratives that those viewers constructed in conversations with me. I am concerned with relationships between the narratives of television and those that viewers weave of themselves, between popular culture and the viewers' perceptions of themselves as Indian men and women.

In what follows I analyze the manner in which men and women living in New Delhi interpret serials on Indian television, in particular those reflecting and reconstructing discourses of gender and nationhood. This constellation of discourses is of crucial significance because the Indian state has attempted to use television to construct a pan-Indian culture (Krishnan 1990: Women's Studies supplement [WS] 103). In particular, I examine the consequences of the state's projects of national integration and development for the *re*constitution of notions of "Indian Womanhood" predominant in popular discourse.[8] "Indian Womanhood" is an indigenous symbolic construct that predates the contemporary nation-state. Although it became a major site of contention in colonial and nationalist discourses, in which women were often represented as icons or "carriers" of tradition (Mani 1987) and nation (Chakravarti 1989; Sangari and Vaid 1989), notions of Indian Womanhood, modified in the postcolonial context, continue to have profound significance for the construction of identity.

The Historical and Political Context

In this section I outline the contexts in which television's discourses were produced and received by the people I worked with. I do so by delineating the historical and political specificity of television as a medium of mass communication and by analyzing the implications of the state's programming policies for the production of culture in postcolonial India. The notion of ethnographic context, usually conceived in terms of a "thick description" of "local communities," is hence expanded to include the broader political–economic conjuncture.[9] Next, I sociologically locate the core of Indian television's target audience, the expanding middle class, and attempt to describe the immediate context in which the viewers I worked with interpreted their favorite serials: the city and neighborhoods in which they lived, their class positions, and the household politics that framed their understandings.

Television neither simply "reflects" nor "reinforces" discourses: it is, in and of itself, a "cultural form" (Williams 1974) and must be analyzed as part of a larger discursive field.[10] Outlining the history of television in India enables us to better understand the politics of representation underlying constructions of gender and nationhood in a postcolonial context. Indian television (officially and popularly known as Doordarshan) is state-owned and state-controlled. It was first introduced in September 1959 as an experimental service for schools and rural audiences ("rural" meaning villages in the immediate vicinity of New Delhi). The only station was the Delhi Kendra (Center), which broadcast programs for a couple of hours a day on one channel. The Ministry of Information and Broadcasting (under whose aegis television continues to function) next began expanding the reach of television: centers were set up in Bombay (1972), Srinagar (1973), Amritsar (1973), Calcutta (1975), Madras (1975), and Lucknow (1975). Concurrently, transmission times were lengthened, and the telecasting of entertainment programs increased. But for the most part television was, and continues to be, primarily geared to what the Indian nation-state clearly sees as a major objective of mass media: the project of nation building (Joshi 1989). Thus, the major themes in most television today include communal harmony and national integration (as in serials such as *Tamas* and *Sanjha Choola*), national development (exemplified by the countless public information spots promoting family planning or public health education), the reconstruction of anticolonial movements (as with serials like *Kahan Gaye Woh Log*), and the need to improve the status of women (illustrated in serials like *Yugantar*).

The Asian Games of 1982, when teams from different nations assembled in New Delhi for sports events, functioned as a major public relations exercise for the Indian state, both within and outside the country. They marked a turning point in the history of Indian television. As Pendakur has pointed out, the state wanted to capitalize on the pomp and pageantry of the Games; to enable wide reception, it relaxed import restrictions not just on television sets for individuals but, more important, on television technology kits for manufacturers (Pendakur 1989a: 182). Television sets appeared in countless homes across the country, and the skylines of Indian cities were soon filled with the scraggly silhouettes of antennas.

The setting up of low-power transmitters in various parts of the country to relay programs beamed from metropolitan centers by satellite dramatically increased both the reach of television and the hours of transmission. Today, over 75 percent of the population is "covered" by television.[11] Further, whereas audiences in the early years could watch television for two hours in the evening, audiences in many parts of the country can now watch from 7:30 to 9:00 a.m., 2:00 to 3:00 p.m., and 5:30 to 11:00 p.m. on weekdays and from 9:00 a.m. to noon on Sundays on Channel 1, and from 7:30 to 10:00 p.m. on Channel 2.

Until the advent of commercial sponsorship in 1980, most programs were produced by employees of government-owned television centers. Media critics, producers, and indeed television officials often contended that the introduction of private production and sponsorship promoted artistic "freedom" and generated the financial resources required for the production of entertainment serials. At the same time, public discourse on television repeatedly emphasized that a poor country like India could not afford the luxury of "pure" entertainment, that what it needed, instead, were programs such as soap operas harnessed to the (modernist) project of national development (see, for example, Government of India 1985). In keeping with the Indian government's anti-West, pro-Third World stance, the source of Indian soaps was said to be not the United States but Mexico, where *telenovelas* supposedly entertain as well as educate people about the benefits of family planning, modern education, and the rights of women as citizens.[12] From this paradigm of "social change through entertainment" was born the new, hybridized form of the *Indian* television serial.

Today, despite the fact that many serials are privately produced, state-appointed selection and screening committees play a powerful role in the formulation of television's discourses.[13] Discourses about nation building and national integration are directly incorporated into and, in fact, underlie the structuring of transmissions. Prime-time segments (from 8:40 to 11:00 every evening and from 9:00 to noon on Sunday mornings) are all part of what is known as the "National Programme." The National Programme is beamed by satellite to small towns, district headquarters, and villages with electricity. About three-fourths of its programs are in Hindi; the remainder are in English. Variations exist only where regional protests have been vociferous: for example, in Tamil Nadu there is no Hindi news, and because attempts to dub Hindi serials in Tamil have failed, a relatively large number of locally produced serials are shown during prime time. Very few entertainment programs (a maximum of two or three per week) are imported. Some local programs produced in metropolitan centers are in regional languages. But all programs seen during prime time – when people are home from work – and an overwhelming majority of the serials are part of the National Programme. The National Programme is a major component of the effort to construct a pan-Indian "national culture," and at present, when relations between the national and the state governments are particularly turbulent, it is part of the center's attempt to exert hegemonic control over the regional governments.[14]

In this essay I focus on teleserials shown during prime time – that is, as part of the National Programme – from July 1990 through March 1991. A cross between American soap operas and popular Hindi films, they speak the "metalanguage" of the popular Hindi film (evident, for instance, in the types of sets, dialogue, costumes, and music used [Krishnan 1990: WS 104]), while they resemble soaps in terms of audience engagement and narrative structure: multiple plots, the deferment of narrative closure, and the build-up of suspense are important aspects of their narrative tone and texture. Further, like the audiences of American soaps, those of Indian serials deeply identify with characters on the screen; unlike their more distant (although still passionate) attachment to film heroes and heroines, viewers' regular and relatively extended interactions with television characters foster familiar, even intimate, relationships.[15] However, because most serials are telecast in the evenings rather than the afternoons, they are targeted not exclusively at women or at people who stay at home but at families. The family, then, is the basic viewing unit, a fact evident from the design of advertisements and confirmed by my observations and by what I inferred from conversations with television officials and the directors of serials.[16]

Serials have ranged in genre from the mythological (*Ramayana* and *Mahabharata*) and the epic (*The Sword of Tipu Sultan*) to the comic (*Yeh Jo Hai Zindagi*). Many serials, such as *Hum Log* and *Buniyaad*, resemble the Hindi film genre known as "the social" in their use of melodrama and social realism (cf. Chakravarty 1989; Vasudevan 1989), and in their focus on the destinies of families, neighborhoods, and communities as well as those of individuals.[17] Most serials on Indian television have explicit "social messages," with themes related to family planning, national integration, and the status of women woven into the narratives. And at any given moment, more than half of the eight to ten serials shown per week during prime time deal explicitly or implicitly with nationalist themes. Although the social messages woven into the narratives have varied according to political contingencies (such as particular national crises or the needs of a ruling party), an astonishing number continue to deal centrally with women's issues. More important, even where gender is not an overt theme, it features prominently as a critical subtext. In nationalist serials the nationalist metanarrative is reinforced by its appropriation of discourses on gender. In *Param Veer Chakra* and *The Sword of Tipu Sultan*, for example, the male protagonists' relationships with women are *constantly* posed against their devotion to their country, and the female characters' attitudes and behavior complement or serve as a foil to the men's heroic patriotism.

From 1990 to 1992 I conducted numerous interviews with viewers living in two neighborhoods in New Delhi: Vikas Nagar and Basti.[18] Working with urban women in multiethnic neighborhoods enabled me to see how reactions to nationalist discourses were mediated by the ways people negotiate and construct their identities in such contexts.[19] Moreover, New Delhi was a particularly appropriate setting for the study of nationalism: the presence of the state is more overwhelming there than in any other Indian city I have known. The state is a major employer in New Delhi. The city's landscape is dotted with government buildings, government housing colonies, ministerial bungalows, and other reminders of the nation-state. And, like Washington, DC, New Delhi does not belong to a regional state; it therefore has no regional roots of its own and its population is composed largely of migrants. People from Old Delhi characterize themselves as laid-back, courteous, and cultured in comparison with the allegedly brash, rude, aggressive residents of New Delhi. Old Delhi, they say, has "tradition"; New Delhi is a place where everything is in disarray. New Delhi's identity ultimately issues from its role as the capital of the postcolonial nation-state. For all these reasons, it has the ambience of a quintessentially "national" city.

Nationalism has been characterized as a middle-class phenomenon (Chatterjee 1989), and the relationship between "middle-classness" and nationalism is a fundamental one.[20] Personal observations and conversations with Doordarshan officials and media critics have led me to believe that the middle and lower middle classes form the core of the target audience for Indian television (as opposed to, say, popular Hindi films, which are aimed at all classes).[21] The past two decades have witnessed a dramatic expansion of the Indian middle classes: they now constitute over 20 percent of the population. This demographic change has created an enormous market for consumer goods. The new middle classes that once invested in bicycles, transistor radios, scooters, and refrigerators now want to buy color television sets (Pendakur 1989a: 186). Indeed, owning a color television is itself a mark of being middle class.

As mentioned above, the relaxation of restrictions on the import of television technology around the time of the Asian Games of 1982 promoted an enormous rise in the production and purchase of television sets. This change in policy reflected a major shift in the allocation of financial and technical resources, from community-owned television sets in rural areas to those owned by urban middle-class and lower-middle-class households (Pendakur 1989a). Programming priorities changed accordingly, from the dissemination of development information to entertainment (although, as noted, sustained efforts are still made to weave social messages into serials). The expansion of television thus indicated the power of the growing middle classes (Krishnan 1990; Pendakur 1989b), a power also evidenced by the launching of color television in 1982, the introduction of advertisements and commercial sponsorship (whereby private companies finance the production of entertainment programs), and the subsequent establishment of a second channel.[22] Television's discourses are designed to draw these upwardly mobile classes – "captured" simultaneously as a market for consumer goods advertised by the sponsors of programs and as an audience for nationalistic serials – into the project of constructing a national culture.[23]

The interpretations provided by the lower middle and upwardly mobile working classes are also significant because of those groups' interstitial, comparatively fluid location. The people I worked with felt they were struggling to cross the threshold of "middle-classness." They were acutely aware of their vulnerable position, and the various ways in which that awareness surfaced in their self-presentation made it clear to me that financial insecurity was a major part of their discursive consciousness.[24]

Vikas Nagar is a lower-middle-class government "colony" that houses junior clerks and stenographers occupying the lowest rungs of the state bureaucracy. Each flat in Vikas Nagar consists of an 8' by 10' room, which functions as a living room by day and a bedroom by night, and an even tinier kitchen. Residents share common latrines and bathrooms. Basti was a village until the city of New Delhi engulfed it from all sides. Like many other "urban villages" forced to coexist with middle-class neighborhoods, Basti has "developed" unevenly. Pressure on land and housing has resulted in the sale of about one-fourth of the plots to middle-class people who have gone on to build new, relatively fancy homes with modern plumbing and other trappings of upward mobility. All the people I worked with lived in older, ramshackle houses. Much poorer than their middle-class neighbors, they all sublet tiny rooms within larger units. Yet most of them were somewhat upwardly mobile: while many of the older generation were employed as household help in adjacent upper-middle-class neighborhoods, most of the younger men and women worked on assembly lines in factories or as clerks in private corporations. Unlike upper-middle-class viewing groups, in which servants watch television with the rest of the household, these lower-middle-class and upwardly mobile working-class viewing groups, just a generation away from poverty, were fairly homogeneous in terms of class composition.

I see the household (loosely defined to include not just the extended family but, in many cases, neighbors and their children) as a politically, hence emotionally, charged context in which people watch television. Although I noticed few conflicts over which show should be watched (as mentioned above, most of the serials were telecast on one channel as part of the National Programme), age and gender influenced people's preferences. Women particularly enjoyed the serials, and even though all the men I met also watched the serials with great relish (and usually made no bones about it), they told me that they made it a point to watch the news. Indeed, watching the news was considered an adult, usually male, activity. Most schoolchildren I met would try to watch as many television programs as the demands of homework and the reprimands of parents would permit. Parents often tried to censor the films their children, particularly their young daughters, watched: they made sure the youngsters were asleep before the weekly late-night film, usually an imported one with relatively explicit "love scenes," came on.[25]

In general, gender, household position, and age were the crucial factors influencing viewers' styles of interaction with what they watched. Power relations within families were sometimes reflected in how people arranged themselves around the television set: the older generation (usually men but sometimes older women as well) would be seated on the few chairs; the children would squat on the floor. Very seldom did I see women, especially daughters-in-law, sitting with the rest of the family: not only was it considered inappropriate for them to sit with the men (particularly in North Indian families), but more important, they were the ones responsible for the housework.[26] The men of the household were usually the most avid viewers because they could afford not to be distracted by household tasks, which kept the women busy in the evenings when dinner was being prepared and served or on Sunday mornings when the house had to be cleaned, clothes washed, and water buckets filled. While the men and children kept up a running commentary on the show, the women were usually silent, instead discussing it among themselves the next day.

One woman told me that she made up for all the evening hours she was unable to sit in front of the television set by insisting on watching the Sunday morning shows undisturbed. Another woman, much to the irritation of the rest of her family, kept her television set at its loudest so she could listen to the soundtrack over the din of her housework. These women were relatively successful in their attempts to gain some control of their time. But not all the women I worked with were in a position to be openly assertive: very often, the younger women (daughters-in-law, in particular) would keep up with their favorite shows by listening to the soundtrack and by getting fleeting glimpses from the kitchen as they cooked or from the veranda as they washed clothes. But despite the fact that most of the women half-watched, half-listened while cooking, serving food, doing dishes, or sweeping the floor, they were nonetheless able to engage intimately with what they "viewed."

Most women I worked with did not have the luxury of sitting "glued to the television set"; the following analyses are therefore predicated on the premise that notions of "viewing" have to encompass more than the visual act of watching television. Further, the cultural and political significance of viewing has to be seen in terms of its restructuring of social relations within the family. As Morley has pointed out, viewing has to be conceptualized simultaneously as a "ritual whose function is to structure domestic life and to provide a symbolic mode of participation in the national community" and as an "active mode of consumption" (Morley 1991: 5). The processes of engagement that I describe were, therefore, necessarily inflected by the fields of power in which people watched television, for they watched not only in the setting of the household – that is, in the immediate context of the politics of the family[27] – but also in settings embedded in the larger sociopolitical conjunctures of community and nation.

What role did the viewers' intense engagement with television play in their constitution as national and gendered subjects? I spent a fair amount of time trying to get a sense of how they related what they watched to their own lives, and of how they identified with characters as their favorite narratives unfolded before their eyes. I will now address the viewers' interpretations of representations of "Indian Woman-hood," the slippery presence of "oppositional" readings, and the significance of interpretive processes to the conceptualization of popular culture.

Notions of Indian Womanhood

Discussions with viewers helped me obtain a glimpse of their engagement with the ideologies of nationalism and gender inscribed in *everyday* discourses on "appropriate behavior" for Indian women: on women's place in the family, their relationship with men, and, most powerfully, their duties to the nation.[28] Creating a sort of double bind, the convergence of discourses of cultural nationalism and gender sometimes fostered particularly oppressive subject positions for women. It raised the expectations women had of themselves and, equally important, those their men had of them. This double bind was most obvious when their "woman-hood" was seen to both contribute to and detract from their role as patriotic citizens.

Selapan and his wife, Padmini, came from Tamil Nadu. Selapan worked as a junior clerk with an army intelligence organization. Tall and broad-shouldered, he sported a bushy, somewhat theatrical, military moustache. He loved to talk and was one of the warmest, most articulate people I met. Like many South Indians raised in the North, Selapan spoke very *filmi* Hindustani (a somewhat melodramatic Hindu-stani imbibed from Hindi films).[29] He often distressed me by passing rude comments about his wife in her presence. Yet I knew that he spent days and nights nursing her when she was sick (which was quite often). Padmini was tall and skinny. She was usually silent when her husband held forth, but when she and I were alone together, she unhesitatingly contradicted and sometimes belittled him. Selapan's favorite serial was *Param Veer Chakra*: he felt it showed "real stories" of men who died for their country. Hence, he said, viewers could see what "real patriotism" (*sacchi deshb-hakti*) and sacrifice were all about.[30] He continued: "Young people who see this program can know that instead of frittering their energies, they can do things that will prove they are worthy of the wombs of their mothers."

One morning soon after an episode of *Param Veer Chakra* had ended, I asked Selapan what he thought of the heroine's courage in persuading her reluctant husband to go to the battlefront on the morning after their wedding night. Selapan had been impressed by her. "But," he went on to say, "Indian women are not all like that. If all women were like that, no one would be able to look disrespectfully at India [*koi bhi aankh utha kar dekh nahi payega*]." His statements reveal an elision, an imperceptible slide from "mother" to "motherland": women are "subjectified" as mothers and held responsible for inspiring their children to safeguard India's honor; at the same time, India is feminized as the mother and made the object of protection-ist discourse.

How did these notions affect Selapan's behavior toward his wife? I found that he seemed to apply similarly exacting standards to her. In one episode of *Param Veer Chakra* the mother of the hero, Abdul Hamid, persuades his father to get him married by saying, "Put a ring through the bull's nose. That will prevent him from roaming around." I had been deeply offended by this metaphor and, while the episode was still on, asked both Selapan and Padmini (Padmini was sitting quietly after serving us tea) what they thought of it. Selapan replied that he agreed with

Hamid's mother: "Women these days cling to their husbands' feet and don't allow them to go anywhere. My wife even stops me from going by bus these days, let alone allows me to go to war."[31]

I silently turned to Padmini, willing her to reply. She did not contradict her husband directly. Instead she pointed out that Hamid's wife, despite all her fears, had run after him to bid him farewell. "When he was so keen to go, what could she do? She had to submit to his wishes," she replied, her voice heavy with resignation. But both Abdul Hamid's mother and Selapan saw women (more specifically, wives) as sources of constraint: while she had implied that they helped rein in the restlessness of young men, Selapan seemed to feel that men had to curb their "courageous" impulses because of women's cowardly fears for their safety. In both cases, women were conceived as obstacles to masculine heroism.

Selapan felt that *Param Veer Chakra* might have a beneficial effect on women because after watching it, they might also become "brave" (*bahadur*) and encourage their husbands to fight and sacrifice for the country. "Don't you think there are already women who are brave, women who themselves do brave things?" I persisted. He replied that there were, only they were very rare. He gave an example of a soldier's wife in South Arcot whose husband had died in Operation Bluestar (the Indian government's 1984 raid on the Golden Temple in Punjab). When the government organized a function to honor him and presented her with a check, she returned it, saying that the glory her husband had earned defending his country was compensation enough for her. And what was more, he continued, she had insisted on wearing her *mangalsutra* (the necklace worn by some Hindu women that signifies their married, as opposed to single or widowed, status). According to Selapan, she had said, "My husband is not dead, he is a martyr [*shaheed*]." Selapan was so moved by this sentiment that he repeated the sentence at least three times. Then, after keeping quiet for a few seconds, he shook his head and said in a low voice, "Indian women are great."

I asked him if he blamed women for worrying about their husbands and sons going to war. When he replied that he would be proud to admit his son into the army, I turned to his wife and asked her what *she* thought of that. She smiled ruefully, put her son's head against her chest (he was sitting between his parents on the bed), and started to stroke his hair. For a minute she was silent. Then after pausing awhile, she turned to me and said: "He is my only child. How can I put him in the army?"

Selapan burst out laughing. "See!" he exclaimed genially. "See how cowardly [*buzdil*] she is! If all mothers start getting scared like this, who will protect the country?"

I felt horrible that I had exposed Padmini to her husband's derision. It was all right for men, whose position in society was relatively secure, to be "brave," I protested, but how could he blame women, who were so socially vulnerable, for being worried? Referring particularly to the plight of women whose husbands die in war, I asked if their fear was unfounded given the low status of widows in Indian society. In any case, I continued, was militant nationalism the only context in which women could be courageous? Ignoring my second question, he replied that while it was true that widows had a hard time in India, if one conducted herself "properly" (*sahi tarah*), even criminals (*goondas*) would fold their hands and call her "sister" (*behenji*). Obviously the onus was on the widow to prove that she deserved respect!

I then asked him what he thought of television's depiction of Indian women in general. His answer, an anecdote, was only apparently off-track. He said that one day, while going somewhere by bus, he had seen a girl wearing a "very short" skirt. She was being teased by some men. "Now, how can you blame boys for teasing her?" he asked, continuing:

Being modern is all right, but there are some rules [*niyam*] in this culture. This is not the way Indian women should dress. . . . Look at what happens with foreign women. They divorce five, six times. What is the meaning of marriage then? What happens to the children, to the family, then? If there is no family, where is society? Indian women have different rules.

He insisted that the most important "duty" (*kartavya*) of an Indian woman to her country was to protect her family and "see that it never falls apart."

"But what happens if the man is bad, if he ill-treats her?" I asked. "Should she still stay with him?"

"Everything is in the wife's hands," he replied. "If she wants, she can save him, she can put him on the right path [*sahi raaste par*]. It is her responsibility to do so."

In Selapan's view, clearly, women's place in the nation is analogous to their place in the family: it is their duty to protect and to sacrifice for the family. As with the family, so with the nation. But in this scheme women do more than play a supporting role: it falls to them to protect the integrity of family and nation and to do so by inspiring and, if necessary, inciting their men to fight for the motherland. And women alone have the strength (the *shakti*) to do so.[32] Indeed, this is why only heroic sons can be "worthy of the wombs" of their mother/motherland.

This response has to be seen in light of the "mythicizing" of motherhood in nationalist ideologies. Its continuing potency is evident in the prevalence in popular discourse of the notion of *Bharat Mata* (Mother India), which, being rooted in the Hindu concept of the Mother-Goddess, has created a space for notions of women's energy as active and heroic (Bagchi 1990: WS 69). Politicized by Hindu nationalists like Bankim Chandra, who thus forged one of the most powerful icons of the nationalist struggle, this concept has been appropriated by mainstream nationalist ideology.[33]

The conception of Indian Womanhood in terms of heroic motherhood is evident both in Selapan's discourse and in that of *Param Veer Chakra*, which dwells on the motif of women inspiring their sons to fight for the motherland. Nationalists during colonial rule spoke of how the mother(land) was ravished by the British, but Selapan and many other viewers I talked with appeared to have picked up a major theme of *Param Veer Chakra*, that of the mother(land) threatened by hostile neighbors. The purported heroism of the ideal Indian Woman (the *bhartiya naari*) is thus measured by her capacity to incite or inspire her children to fight for their country, and not simply by her ability to bear patriotic sons.

Discussions about popular female characters also revealed a fascinating convergence between discourses of gender and those of nationalism. In July 1989 I witnessed a public controversy over the depiction of two mythological heroines on television, Sita of the *Ramayana* and Draupadi of the *Mahabharata*. Everyone, from vegetable vendors and cab drivers to upper-class intellectuals who usually dismissed television serials, was discussing it. A leading newsmagazine ran a poll to ask which of the two better represented "the modern Indian Woman." Many comparisons and contrasts were drawn between Sita, who symbolizes devotion and patience, and Draupadi, noted for her intelligence and fiery strength. Historically, both Sita and Draupadi have served as symbols of Indian Womanhood (ideal types of the *bhartiya naari*). For instance, nationalist ideologues have appropriated both Draupadi's rage and Sita's resilience to encourage orthodox Hindu women to join anticolonial movements (Mankekar 1990). In 1989 the question on many people's lips was: which of the two is more pertinent to *contemporary* Indian Womanhood?

And so it came as no surprise when conversations about Sita and Draupadi led to discussions on Indian Womanhood. Many viewers, both men and women, had strong opinions on which of the two better represented Indian Womanhood. My conversations with women of different ages were particularly interesting because they illustrated how notions of Indian Womanhood were being *reconstituted* (rather than radically transformed) across generations. Uma Chandran lived in Vikas Nagar. Her father was a retired clerk, and her mother, Jayanthi, worked as a stenographer in a government department. Uma had just got a job as a secretary in a private corporation, where she felt out of place because most of the other employees came from much wealthier families. This sense of alienation did nothing to strengthen her fragile self-confidence. While my conversations with all others were in Hindi, she and I spoke English heavily laced with Hindi.

One Sunday morning a couple of weeks after the *Mahabharata* had come to an end, Uma and I were sitting on her veranda. We had been shooed out of the inner room by her father, who wanted to watch the news. Uma talked of how, as a young woman from a poor family, she felt isolated by her wealthier colleagues. She felt she wasn't assertive enough. We soon began talking about the depiction of Sita in the television version of the *Ramayana*. Uma had just started comparing Sita with Draupadi when her mother joined our conversation. This excerpt from the exchange between Uma and Jayanthi illustrates the change and continuity inherent in their notions of volition, suffering, and strength, and it clearly shows the intimate relationship between ideologies of cultural nationalism and those of gender:[34]

Uma: I liked Draupadi better than Sita. Sita was a complete wash-out....
Jayanthi: Why is that? I liked Sita more. I liked her more because she did not have as much glamour. She was simple. You could see devotion [*bhakti*] more clearly in Sita. At every step.
Uma: But why did she submit at every step [*kyon dab jaati hai*]?
Jayanthi: But this was not so in the case of Draupadi.... They did not show her with *pativrata dharma* [roughly translates, in this context, as "duties of a wife"].[35] In this *zamana* [era] there is no *pativrata dharma*. There can't be as much as there was in Sita's time. There shouldn't be less. But people don't see the reality of that *shakti* [strength].
Uma, doubtfully: I don't know. Where will this *shakti* take us Indian women today? [She turns to me.] Aren't American women where they are today because they are more independent than we are?

According to Jayanthi, Sita was much stronger than Draupadi. Her strength, her *shakti*, came from her capacity to suffer for her *pativrata dharma*, that is, her duty toward her husband. But Uma disagreed. She felt that modern times required a *shakti* more akin to Draupadi's rage. And Indian women, she seemed to say, were essentially different from American women, who were more independent. Indeed, another young woman with whom I spoke went so far as to claim that Draupadi seemed "less Indian" than Sita: when I tried to probe her meaning, I discovered that she felt Draupadi was "Westernized" because the heroine questioned and challenged her elders on the propriety of their actions. Explicit contrasts between essentialized "Indian women" and "foreign women" thus reflect the ways in which cultural nationalism, through notions of what constitutes "Indian culture," circumscribes discourses on gender. Ideal Indian Womanhood is constructed in terms of values deemed fundamentally womanly, essentially Indian: modesty, patience, and, above all, a strong sense of duty toward the family, the community, and the nation.

The convergence between cultural nationalism and discourses of gender became clearer when, several months later, Uma compared Indian women with "foreign" or "Western" women. Uma and I usually watched *Phir Wahi Talaash* together. In this serial the heroine is forced into an arranged marriage. After a couple of years of trying to make a go of it, she asks her husband for a divorce so that she can reunite with her lover. Once, just as that episode was drawing to a close, Uma responded with bewilderment and some outrage:

Uma: It's not possible to get a divorce that easily in India. In India a divorce means that it's a very free-wheeling lady, all kinds of things. I don't think there are many women who do that. Okay, the number has increased, but Indian women are still not so keen on divorce.
Purnima: Why is that?
Uma: I think it's because of our culture. Because marriage means it's for keeps; it's not as if you can get a divorce that easily. The thought doesn't come into our minds.
Purnima: You think this is more true of Indian marriages and Indian women?
Uma: Very much so, very much so.

Uma firmly believed that the heroine was at fault because she had not tried hard enough to save her marriage:

Uma: I still feel she didn't try to make the marriage a success. In between, she is so curt with him. I didn't like that. Why doesn't she make an effort to make a go of the marriage? She's got married, now she should try that the marriage stays safe [*sic*]. It seems to me that she was very casual about it all. That's not how it happens.
Purnima: What do you mean?
Uma: Well, you know, it's very unbecoming for an Indian woman.

It was plain that she strongly disapproved of the heroine's actions because she deemed them inappropriate for Indian women and felt that they had no place in what she called "our culture." Uma, like some other young women with whom I spoke, seemed to be caught between two sets of beliefs about women's independence. She felt that it was "unbecoming" for Indian women to divorce their husbands – women's independence should never be allowed to break up an unhappy marriage. Yet in an earlier conversation she had argued that as a young woman she was better off emulating the "independence" of "American women" and that Draupadi's fiery strength was appropriate to contemporary times. Like Selapan, Uma invoked idealized notions of Indian Womanhood in comparing Indian and Western women.

Thus, although heroic motherhood figures as a primary theme in *Param Veer Chakra* and in Selapan's discourse, it represents only one of several constructions of Indian Womanhood in postcolonial India. Indeed, it is important that we acknowledge the *proliferation* of discourses on Indian Womanhood, some more essentialist than others, all of them reflecting what Foucault (1980: 119) has termed the productive aspects of power. This "incitement to discourse" (Foucault 1978: 18) is reflected in television's preoccupation with "women-dominated serials" – that is, those in which the protagonists are women. The Doordarshan Software Committee, set up by the government to formulate guidelines for television programming, has emphasized the significance of the portrayal of women. Its report, significantly titled *An Indian Personality for Television*, proposes that "women be shown in terms of the complex roles they play...as workers and significant contributors to family survival and the national economy" (Government of India 1985: 1, 144–5). However, as seen in the responses of Uma and Selapan, attempts to depict positive and progressive images of women are circumscribed by metanarratives of nation and family. In many serials, for instance, women's anger is portrayed as legitimate only when channeled to the nationalist task of social reform (as in the serial *Rajni*). Marriage is portrayed as the most desirable state for women (as in *Sambandh*; cf. Punwani 1988: 226). Not surprisingly, women are usually portrayed in the context of the family (as in *Hum Log* and *Param Veer Chakra*); those who work outside the home by choice are represented as callous home-wreckers (as in *Khandaan*; cf. Punwani 1988). In serials and in popular discourse in general, Indian Womanhood is now beginning to be conceived in terms of patriotic citizenship, productive labor, and selfless social activism; in short, the ideal Indian Woman is one whose energies are harnessed to the task of promoting national progress in various and multiple ways.

Viewers as Critics

As noted above, viewers' interpretations are profoundly influenced by the broader social discourses in which they are interpellated; they are shaped by events in the viewers' lives and by the relationships in which those viewers define themselves. Thus, there is a two-way relationship between viewers' lives and the narratives in serials: what people watch is mediated by and at the same time helps illuminate developments in their lives. I was astonished by how frequently viewers linked their favorite serials with their lives: it seemed to be the easiest way for many of them to discuss not just what they watched but, more significant, their own experiences. Indeed, in many of our conversations the boundaries between texts and lives often blurred so that I found it hard to discern whether we were talking about a television character or about the viewer.

Aparna Dasgupta was a middle-aged Bengali woman. She had never been to school, and said that she had learned a lot from observing people. I know she thought that I, for all my "foreign" education, was extremely naive about "what really goes on in families." In spite – or perhaps because – of being a silent witness to her husband's and son's brutalization of her young daughter-in-law, Aparna insisted on advising me about how to "shield" myself from the alleged "cleverness" of *my* mother-in-law. (My protestations that I didn't really need her advice served only to make her more protective of me.) Aparna felt that television was powerful because one could learn from it (*shiksha milti hai*). When she was growing up, she said, women were not allowed to go to the cinema. Even though she had been living in Delhi for the past 25 years, she never got to watch films until she started to see them on television. In many ways, she told me, television was her window on the rest of the world. However, she insisted, not everyone could learn from watching television: one had to have a particular *bhaav* (loosely, "feeling" or "emotion"; neither of these words quite captures the meaning of *bhaav*) in one's heart. One morning a couple of days after the last episode of her favorite serial, the *Mahabharata*, had been aired, I asked her what she thought of it. She replied: "When you read the Gita, you should read it with a certain *bhaav* in your heart. It's the same thing when you watch something on television."

But what was this *bhaav*? I pressed her. Did it reside in the heart, only to surface when one watched something touching? Or was it a state induced by what one watched, that is, by the experience of seeing something emotional unfold on the screen? If that were the case, wouldn't everyone learn something, the same thing perhaps, from a particular serial? But *bhaav*, Aparna replied, was not quite so simple. She explained it with reference to her experience of Hindi films:

The first time I watched a Hindi film nothing much happened. But then I saw a second, then a third, then a fourth. Then one day as I watched, *bhaav* came to me [*bhaav aa gaya*] . . . . By then I too had a family. I was watching this film called *Bhabhi*. It was all about how this young woman suffers after she gets married. It was all about how you suffer in the world. How much the *bhabhi* [brother's wife] suffers! I just couldn't stop crying. I thought, suppose I have to face what she is going through, what will happen?

This encounter taught Aparna how to watch films and television serials. According to her, one had to surrender to the mood of what was being watched; to learn from it, one had to be immersed in that state of being. And one had to be at a point in life where what was watched made sense personally, at a level beyond mere empathy. This mode of watching, indeed of interacting, became clearer when Aparna recounted what had happened to her daughter Sushmita when she saw a *Mahabharata* scene in which the female protagonist, Draupadi, is publicly disrobed in her in-laws' court:

My daughter, when she saw [what happened], cried and cried. She cried all morning. Imagine what happened to Draupadi! And in public, in front of her in-laws! A feeling came to my daughter [*bhaav aa gaya*]: What will happen to me when I get married and go to my in-laws' home? Isn't this what happens?

According to Aparna, we learn about life from the emotions (*bhaav*) television's discourses arouse in us. However, interpretation operates within a larger set of discursive practices.[36] As Aparna patiently explained to me, one has to *acquire* the ability to learn from what is watched, and this ability comes from, among other things, frequent exposure. In addition, one must be at a particular point in one's trajectory, in one's development as a person; hence, the film *Bhabhi* would not have aroused *bhaav* in her had she watched it before she was married. She also insisted that not just anyone could learn: only those who, in her words, had an ability to "enter the soul" of what they watched could do so.

However, it is important to emphasize that *bhaav* do not emerge in a vacuum, a result of a text's "impact" on an isolated viewer; we have to foreground the sociocultural bases of these experiences. Aparna was socially "habituated" to read the Gita and to watch the *Mahabharata* with a particular *bhaav* in her heart. Her unmarried daughter's tears at Draupadi's disrobing arose from fear about her own future, a fear reinforced when she saw how other daughters-in-law (including the one in her family) were treated. These *bhaav*, these feelings and emotions, were products of the *social* relations in which they were embedded. In other words, emotions do not emerge from an "inner essence" distinct from the social world; emotions are "social practices organized by stories that we both enact and tell," and "persons are constructed in a particular cultural milieu" of experiences, meanings, relationships, and images, all of which are socially mediated (Rosaldo 1984: 143, 138). I have shown that some experiences, "stories," and representations involve interactions between viewers, located in particular sociocultural contexts, and the texts of mass media such as television: far from being innate, many emotions are themselves produced by the social practices that television's narratives mediate and, indeed, sometimes create.

But are we to think that everyone who watches serials will automatically assume the subject positions created by the discourses of television? I found that even as they deeply identified with characters on television, even as they experienced profound *bhaav*, many viewers were simultaneously able to stand back and criticize what they watched. Neither they nor I saw any contradiction between these two apparently divergent modes of viewing. Viewers loved to critique the acting ability of the cast or the competence of the director. Similarly, they would often comment that, for example, a particular set was "stagey" or the "photographer" had done a "boring job" (in this case I think the person was saying something about camera angles).[37]

Many viewers had definite opinions about what television "ought to" depict – that is, about appropriate or inappropriate subject matter. Surjeet Kaur worked as an unskilled assembly-line employee in a garment factory. An accomplished storyteller, she would narrate the sagas of serials (and of her life) in intricate detail and with great flourish. She had a stormy relationship with her husband, a junior clerk in the Education Ministry, and often said that watching television was one of the few ways in which she could calm herself. But, she complained, some serials encouraged people's "superstitions." She felt that there was no place for "this sort of thing" (*aisi batein*) in serials because "superstition" (*andh vishwas*) was "wrong" (*galt*). She thought television producers were sometimes very careless about how they constructed stories: "You know how they make serials – they pull from here, cut from there, try to patch a story together somehow."

Her thoughts on the appropriate subject matter for television were based on a theory of the relationship between reception and class, a belief that television could lead "certain types" of people astray. For she went on to say:

People shouldn't believe everything they see on TV, but they often do.... Because people are uneducated they believe everything they hear. People should not be guided [she used the English word][38] in this way. Imagine if village women or women who live in *jhuggi-jhopdis* [huts in the shantytown some 20 yards from her house] see all this! They will believe every word.... Someone has to guide [Eng.] them, to explain to them that this is not how things really are.

Herself illiterate and precariously lower middle class, Surjeet Kaur was conscious of what she clearly perceived as the privileges of her class position, which, she felt, gave *her* a critical awareness that poorer people lacked. Her discourse on the effects of television constructed viewers who lived in slums as the "other," the gullible, ignorant masses who had to be "guided."[39]

Further, Surjeet Kaur, like many other women I spoke to, had definite ideas about style and plot, especially the resolution of narrative tensions and conflicts. What she disliked most were the conclusions of many serials.[40] She insisted that they concluded too abruptly, that nothing seemed to be resolved (*koi faisla hi nahi hota*), that one never got a sense of "what really happened" in the end. She speculated that perhaps most of the time they ended before "the original story" (that is, the script) had concluded.

More important, most people I talked with were acutely conscious that the serials they watched had been selected, censored, and shaped by the state.[41] They often commented that when secessionist movements threatened the integrity of the nation-state, there would be a spate of serials dealing with Punjab and Kashmir. One young woman complained that although she enjoyed the stories, she was getting tired of the same old themes. Some people saw even more direct connections between the plots of serials and the political motivations of the ruling party. When I asked one viewer if he enjoyed watching serials, he replied that he had enjoyed them until a few months ago but that ever since V. P. Singh, then prime minister of India, had come to power, the programs had deteriorated. "All they show now," he complained, "is villagers and their problems." The prime minister was then making statements about a need to "bridge the gap" between cities and "the real India," that is, "village India." This viewer, along with countless others who pointed out the same thing, was quite astute in grasping why audiences were suddenly being subjected to a number of hastily produced serials set in villages.

Television watching, I sense, is gradually becoming an opportunity for people to sit around and complain about the power (and, very often, the stupidity: "they must be very stupid [*bewaqoof*] to think we're this gullible!") of the government. However, we need to be extremely cautious about concluding that this critical awareness signifies that people are somehow "outside" the reach of the state or that they simply "resist" dominant discourses received through television. Viewers' responses to what they watch cannot be encompassed by categories such as "resistance" and "submission." Oppositional readings, as I hope to demonstrate, are a great deal more complex and slippery.

For instance, the viewers I interviewed would often "submit" to one of the multiple discourses constituting a serial but would appropriate another to criticize the government. One of my conversations with Surjeet Kaur began with her recapitulation of an emotional episode of *The Sword of Tipu Sultan*, a controversial depiction of an eighteenth-century Muslim king. The main theme of that episode, according to not just Surjeet Kaur but also the others present, was the loyalty and kindness of Haider Ali, a central character. Surjeet Kaur used the episode to contrast Haider Ali with present-day politicians who betrayed their supporters. She launched into a detailed description of the joy experienced by Haider and his friend Ramchander when they reunited after several years, and she pointed out that when he became king, Haider remembered his promise to help Ramchander. She exclaimed: "Haider never betrayed his childhood friendship [*bachpan ki dosti*]; he bridged the huge divide between himself and Ramchander." Surjeet Kaur summarized the story thus: "This story is about a king and his friend, about a poor friend and a king [*yeh kahani hai ek dost aur ek raja, ek garib dost aur ek raja ke bare mein*]." She continued:

Isn't that the way it should be? Not as it is in our country now. That's not how it is now. Whether it's a *raja* [king] or a P.M. [Eng.], they're only interested in keeping their seat [Eng.], their treasury. The people can starve to death, but they don't care. Who cares about the people? When it's time for the election, [politicians] come with their hands folded and say, we'll do this for you, we'll do that for you. What will you [they; that is, politicians] do [*Kya karoge tum*]? You only come to us when you need us. Otherwise who asks about us? Now look, we have to pay Rs. 5 a kilo for onions. Imagine [*Bataiye*]! How are people like us to manage? It's true that the government has increased pay scales. But it doesn't make any difference. I would rather they kept prices down.[42]

Padmini and I once watched an episode of her husband's favorite serial, *Param Veer Chakra*, while he was away visiting an ailing relative. This was one of the few times I saw Padmini actually sitting down to watch television. She had clearly been looking forward to it: she had finished all her work for the morning and was waiting, bathed and ready, when I arrived at her house one chilly Sunday. The episode was particularly melodramatic: by the time it ended I was having a hard time holding back my tears; Padmini was weeping.[43] But was she crying because she was moved by its display of patriotic fervor? I am quite sure she was not. For as soon as the show finished, she turned to me and said, "These men go off. But it's the women who have to suffer because [the men] have gone to fight." It was obvious that she saw the show entirely from the perspective of the wife who had been left behind, and as far as she was concerned, militant nationalism did not seem to be worth the tragedy of war. This response is particularly significant in light of her silence when her husband waxed eloquent on the glories of patriotic Indian Womanhood.

Thus, intense emotional involvement occurs *simultaneously* with a critical awareness that sometimes enables viewers to "see through" the narrative to the state's agenda. "Resistance" and "compliance" are not mutually exclusive categories, and the role of television in the constitution of viewers' subjectivities cannot be conceived in terms of just one or the other. With many viewers, one level of engagement slides into the other all the time. The complexity of resistance has been well demonstrated by Abu-Lughod (1990), who talks of how Bedouin women both resist and support existing systems of power (ibid: 47), and by Radway (1984), who describes how women's resistance is embodied in the act of reading romance novels even as it is sometimes undercut by the content of what they read. This reconception of resistance and compliance helps us see popular culture as a site of *struggle* between dominant discourses and forces of resistance. Popular culture contains "points of resistance" as well as "moments of supersession"; it forms a "battlefield where no once-for-all victories are obtained but where there are always strategic positions to be won and lost" (Hall 1981: 233). Thus, while many of the viewers I met seemed extremely aware of the power of the state, let us not forget Aparna's explication of the role of *bhaav*: it informed viewers, in a frighteningly fundamental way, about their place in the world. They learned about their position as gendered subjects, and as Indians, from *bhaav* as it mediated their interpretations of television's discourses.

Conclusion

My objectives in this essay have been twofold: to analyze the place of television in the constitution of national and gendered subjects and, thus, to arrive at an understanding of how popular texts can be conceptualized. I have tried to argue that nationalism and gender are inherently linked. Discourses on gender seem to crystallize most clearly in discussions centered on the qualities of particular types of women, *Indian* women. Similarly, as evident in the responses of viewers to serials like *Param Veer Chakra*, nationalism is intrinsically both gendered and engendering, creating specific subject positions for men and for women. But, as we have seen, viewers variously interpret, appropriate, resist, and negotiate these subject positions. Discourses of nationhood regulate those of gender and vice versa: I have tried to draw attention both to the multiplicity of interpretations and to the parameters within which those interpretations are made.

Hence, although television plays an unmistakably critical role in the constitution of discursive practices, its cultural and political significance cannot be understood simply in terms of a clear-cut division between the hegemonic text and the passive viewer. By foregrounding viewers' interpretations, we can conceive of popular culture as a site for resistance as well as domination. And by studying the different ways in which viewers actively engage with what they watch, we can break away from theories of popular culture that foreclose the process of interpretation in the production of meaning (for example, Horkheimer and Adorno's (1969) "mass culture" hypothesis, or analyses in which the subject's position is dictated by the text).

I wish to highlight the fact that the viewer is positioned not simply by the text but also by a whole range of other discourses, with those of gender and nationalism being dominant in Indian television. Viewers are reconstituted as subjects not just by the form and content of serials but by the manner in which these texts resonate with the viewers' experiences of dominant social discourses. Viewers' deep emotional engagement with television, the *bhaav* that a text arouses in them, spurs them to introspection about themselves and their lives. For better or for worse, they learn through *bhaav* about their place in the world. Uma's apparently confused views on women's independence, Selapan's ambivalence about women's ability to be "patriotic citizens," and Surjeet Kaur's "submission" to and appropriation of *The Sword of Tipu Sultan* to criticize the contemporary Indian state indicate that television often offers people contradictory subject positions. Foregrounding viewers' active, intimate engagement with television's texts enables us to explore the place of spectatorship in the construction of selves, specifically in the constitution of gender and national identities.

Further, I wish to highlight the importance of delineating the specific contexts in which viewers engage with the texts of television. Morley has described "the average sitting room" as a

site of some very important political conflicts – it is, among other things, one of the principal sites of the politics of gender and age.... The sitting room is exactly where we need to start from if we finally want to understand the constitutive dynamic of abstractions such as "the community" or "the nation." (Morley 1991: 12)

I argue that we must examine the viewing subject's position in particular networks of power within the family as well as in the broader political conjuncture.

Focusing on specific contexts also helps us comprehend television's role in the construction of gender identity, especially that of women. To assume that *all* women are positioned and "manipulated" by the patriarchal discourses of television is to fall into the trap of universal notions of oppression, as well as to underrate women's abilities to "resist, challenge and subvert" relations of inequality (Mohanty 1984:

345). The depiction of women viewers as active subjects is especially important in light of the tendency to depict "Third World" women as passive victims. Hence, instead of perceiving television's role in the construction of gender identities as unvarying, we need to analyze the construction of gendered subjectivities in *particular* political and social contexts. It is therefore important that we also consider the location of men in specific asymmetrical power networks, and that we examine men's interactions with women in varying relations of domination and interdependence.

NOTES

1   For example, feminists have pointed to the significance of representations of romantic love in cultural constructions of gender (Johnson 1986: 59).
2   My positioning of viewers as subjects is based on the premise that "ideologies do not operate through single ideas; they operate in discursive chains, in clusters, in semantic fields, in discursive formations" (Hall 1985: 104; see also Althusser 1971).
3   Feuer (1983) and Modleski (1983) have described some of the factors that distinguish the television experience from that of film: the technological features of the medium itself (for example, the way images are produced and presented); the different texts (commentaries, commercials); the significance of the ties between programs and their commercial sponsors; and the impact of the sites of reception (whether the cinema hall or the living room). Also important are questions of enunciation: Whose voices are being represented in the texts? Who do the texts address? And how are the discourses of television, embedded in specific capitalist relations of production, ideologically charged?
4   Notable exceptions to the preoccupation with textual and sociological analyses are offered by Bobo (1988), Gillespie (1989), Morley (1980), Radway (1984), and Seiter, Borchers, Kreutzner, and Warth (1989).
5   According to the framework used in this essay, popular culture includes folk traditions that may have metropolitan or elite roots, as well as elements of mass culture incorporated into the everyday lives of ordinary people. The concept of "mass culture" formulated by theorists like Horkheimer and Adorno (1969) is modified by the use of Gramsci's notion of hegemony.
6   Drawing on Lacan (1977), Althusser describes "interpellation" in terms of the relationship between ideology and subjectivity: "ideology 'acts' or 'functions' in such a way that it 'recruits' subjects among the individuals . . . or 'transforms' the individuals into subjects (it transforms them all) by that very precise operation which I have called interpellation or hailing. . . . The existence of ideology and the hailing or interpellation of individuals as subjects are one and the same thing" (Althusser 1971: 163). Hall explains interpellation further as the point of recognition between subjects and ideological or signifying chains (Hall 1985: 102).
7   In demonstrating television's place in the discursive construction of subjectivities, I draw on Trinh Minh-ha's (1989: 22) notion of plural, nonunitary subjects. I conceive of subjects as *in medias res*, constantly being formed, never coming wholly to fruition. I thus reject the notion of a unitary consciousness, arguing that each person can be a contradictory subject, "traversed" by a variety of discursive practices (Alarcon 1990: 357, 365).
8   Notions of Indian Womanhood have as much currency and are as central to discourses of cultural nationalism in India as the ideology of the "American Dream" in the United States.
9   See Appadurai (1986) for an excellent critique of the preoccupation with "local" and "face-to-face" communities.

10   Hence, overstressing the dichotomy between television producers and viewers can be extremely problematic.

11   In many parts of the country, "coverage" does not necessarily enable regular viewership. Additional critical factors are ownership of or access to television sets, a reasonably regular supply of electricity, and other infrastructural facilities.

12   In an interview on January 23, 1992, the secretary to the Ministry of Information and Broadcasting, S. S. Gill, confirmed that Indian teleserials were inspired by telenovelas.

13   Selection Committee members Akshay Kumar Jain and Razia Ismail provided this information during interviews in November 1990.

14   I would like to thank one of my anonymous reviewers for emphasizing this point.

15   According to Punwani (1988: 224) the serial *Hum Log* aroused such "intense viewer identification" that producers received regular mail advising them on how the story should develop.

16   This conception of audiences acquires particular significance in light of the fact that audiences do not exist *a priori* but are constructed by discursive and marketing practices. For excellent discussions of this aspect of audience formation, see Ang (1990) and Radway (1988).

17   See Mukherjee (1985) on the unresolved tension between "indigenous" concepts of personhood and notions of the individual in modern Indian fiction.

18   I use pseudonyms to protect the identities of the people I worked with.

19   As an Indian student of anthropology in the United States, I have frequently been startled by how often the typical anthropological discourse on South Asia, craving authenticity, has obsessively attempted to represent "village India" as "the true India" and has stubbornly resisted acknowledging the presence of dynamic, cosmopolitan cultural formations in postcolonial India (scholarship such as that of Appadurai and Breckenridge [1988] is an exception). Hence, my insistence on focusing on urban women is, at least in part, a result of my awareness of the silences in the anthropology of South Asia.

20   The larger project of which this essay is a part details the links between "middle-classness," gender, and notions of national citizenship (Mankekar 1993a).

21   In January 1992 I interviewed both S. S. Gill, the official responsible for the production of the first teleserial (*Hum Log*), and R. Srinivasan, the marketing correspondent of the *Times of India*, a major national daily.

22   Pendakur points out that the state and the middle classes, along with advertising agencies and the growing consumer industries, are highly influential in shaping television policy (Pendakur 1989a: 186). The state competes with producers of television serials (many of whom hail from the Bombay Hindi film industry), private corporations, and advertising agencies for the power to influence cultural production.

23   This point was corroborated by television critic Iqbal Masud in an interview on December 15, 1990.

24   Among my upper-caste interviewees, anxiety about their vulnerable class position reached a peak when the government attempted to introduce the Mandal Commission Bill, which proposed to provide lower and "backward" castes special quotas in educational institutions and state jobs. This bill prompted widespread rioting and street violence all over North India, including New Delhi. My upper-caste but precariously lower-middle-class informants were enraged at the government because they felt their only hope for upward mobility was being snatched; lower-caste people with whom I spoke were, not surprisingly, unequivocally in favor of the legislation. At stake for all concerned was upward mobility.

25   Many parents, however, confessed that such attempts were futile because the children usually slept (or rather pretended to sleep) in the room where the television set was.

26   Because I was generally treated as a visiting "daughter of the house" by most of these families (and, undoubtedly, because of my class position), I would often be made to sit on a chair or, as they became more informal with me, on the floor with the older daughters.

27 I would like to thank Edgar Winans (personal communication, 1991) for emphasizing the significance of this fact.

28 I am indebted to critiques of Anglo-American feminist theory by feminists such as Alarcon (1990) and Lorde (1984), who have shown us the pitfalls of conceptualizing gender as a category *sui generis*.

29 Hence, his speech was rife with words such as *shaheed* (martyr), *buzdil* (cowardly), and *haqiqat* (reality).

30 Once, when I asked him how the theme of the brave wife had been handled in the "last story," Selapan took exception to my choice of words. "It's not a story. It is reality [*haqiqat*]. It is history," he insisted. He was mollified only when I hastened to explain that I did not mean the episode was fictitious but that I was referring to the dramatization of the hero's dilemmas. In an article entitled "Notions of the Real and Indian Television Serials" (Mankekar 1993b), I attempt to analyze discourses about realism that are deployed by the producers and viewers of television serials.

31 Selapan was referring to the public unrest fomented by the anti-Mandal Commission movement. The presence of phrases like "these days," "this era," and "modern times" reflects a certain image of the "traditional" constructed in contradistinction to modernity. This nostalgic reconstitution of tradition is fed by Doordarshan's depiction of "the glorious Indian past" in serials like the *Ramayana*, the *Mahabharata*, and *Chanakya*. The implications of these serials for Hindu nationalism are discussed in Mankekar (1993a).

32 See Wadley (1980) for discussions of the concept of women's *shakti*.

33 The religious origins of notions such as *Bharat Mata* (Mother India) point to the Hindu hegemony of "mainstream" nationalist discourse. This reveals the slippage between Hindu nationalism and Indian nationalism from the outset and is worth a separate investigation.

34 By no means do I intend to assert a "generational cleavage" of any sort: in fact, as I show, Uma herself seemed to be caught between different discourses on Indian Womanhood. This example simply foregrounds the fact that notions of Indian Womanhood are not static, and it highlights the role played by television in their gradual transformation.

35 See Chakravarti (1986) for an excellent analysis of the hegemonic construction of *pativrata dharma*.

36 The *rasasutra* refers to the "aesthetic organization" of a state of being or emotion (*bhaav*) found in classical Sanskrit literature (Gerow 1974: 216), and it singles out the following emotions for aesthetic exegesis: love, mirth, grief, energy, terror, disgust, anger, wonder, and peace. Works of art "transmute" each of these into a corresponding mood (*rasa*) – for instance, grief inspires the mood of compassion – and *rasas* "render the personal and the incommunicable generalizable and communicable" (Ramanujan 1974: 118). Effective realization of a *rasa* depends not only on whether a particular performance or other work of art is "suited" to its construction, but also on the capacity of the viewer or reader to apprehend and therefore affirm the prevailing *rasa* (Gerow 1974: 221). Hence *rasa* refers at once to an aesthetic tradition and to a philosophical state of being. Perhaps the *rasasutra* provided a vocabulary, if not a conceptual apparatus, for viewers like Aparna, who often spoke of the street plays and musical performances she had watched in her village during her childhood.

   However, attempting to identify "indigenous traditions" of spectatorship is tricky because it can sometimes lead one to overemphasize continuity and to underestimate change and borrowing: this danger is particularly acute in the case of popular culture, which necessarily operates in an increasingly transnational world. Therefore, we must pay particular attention to the sociopolitical contexts in which interpretive processes occur. For example, what happens when cultural production is shaped by the modernist discourses of the state? And how are particular themes and images interpreted by viewers who live in a postcolonial, cosmopolitan setting? We must also emphasize the fact that aesthetic categories are neither static nor totalizing and that there is no single "Indian" tradition of aesthetics; instead, many different traditions exist, often in conflict with one another. I explore the relevance of *rasa* theory to analyses of television watching in urban India in "Notions of the Real and Indian Television Serials" (Mankekar 1993b).

37 Pendakur reports that he had a similar experience when he did fieldwork in a small town: when he spoke to lower-middle-class children they demonstrated an astonishing knowledge of production techniques, such as freeze shots and instant replay (Pendakur 1989a: 178).

38 As those familiar with Indian metropolitan centers would know, it is not unusual for even illiterate city dwellers to use English words like "guided."

39 Although a detailed exploration of class consciousness and subjectivity is outside the scope of this essay, Surjeet Kaur's thoughts on how her reception of television differed from that of women living in slums showed clearly how people sometimes construct their identities in relation to prototypical others.

40 Surjeet Kaur's opinion is interesting in light of Modleski's (1983) attempt to link the lack of narrative closure on American soaps with the subject positions of women in suburban US culture.

41 Their suspicion of the state came as no surprise to me: when I was growing up in India, strangers in trains, buses, and other public spaces frequently treated me to long, often vitriolic, discourses on the government's inefficiency, corruption, and so on.

42 Although this particular example tells us nothing about gender ideologies *per se*, it does show how viewers appropriate television's discourses to criticize their own world. It also reflects the creation of certain notions of citizenship that allow viewers to feel they have the right to expect accountability from their elected leaders.

43 For an excellent analysis of melodrama and the construction of gendered subject positions, see Vasudevan (1989).

REFERENCES

Abu-Lughod, Lila 1990. The Romance of Resistance: Tracing Transformations of Power through Bedouin Women. *American Ethnologist* 17: 41–55.

Alarcon, Norma 1990. The Theoretical Subject(s) of This Bridge Called My Back and Anglo-American Feminism. *In Making Face, Making Soul.* G. Anzaldua, ed., pp. 356–69. San Francisco, CA: Aunt Lute.

Althusser, Louis 1971. Ideology and Ideological State Apparatuses (Notes towards an Investigation). *In Lenin and Philosophy and Other Essays*, pp. 121–73. New York: Monthly Review Press.

Ang, Ien 1990. *Desperately Seeking the Audience*, London: Routledge.

Appadurai, Arjun 1986. Theory in Anthropology: Center and Periphery. *Comparative Studies in Society and History* 28: 356–61.

Appadurai, Arjun and Carol A. Breckenridge 1988. Why Public Culture? *Public Culture Bulletin* 1(1): 5–9.

Bagchi, Jasodhara 1990. Representing Nationalism: Ideology of Motherhood in Colonial Bengal. *Economic and Political Weekly* 25 (42–3): WS 65–71.

Bobo, Jacqueline 1988. The Color Purple: Black Women as Cultural Readers. In *Female Spectators.* D. Pribram, ed., pp. 90–109. New York: Verso.

Brunsdon, Charlotte 1984. Crossroads: Notes on Soap Opera. *Screen* 22 (3): 32–7.

Caughie, John 1986. Popular Culture: Notes and Revisions. In *High Culture/Low Theory.* C. MacCabe, ed., pp. 156–71. Manchester, England: Manchester University Press.

Chakravarti, Uma 1986. Pativrata. *Seminar* 318: 17–21.

—— 1989. Whatever Happened to the Vedic Dasi? Orientalism, Nationalism and a Script for the Past. In *Recasting Women: Essays in Colonial History.* K. Sangari and S. Vaid, eds., pp. 27–87. New Delhi: Kali for Women.

Chakravarty, Sumita S. 1989. National Identity and the Realist Aesthetic: Indian Cinema of the Fifties. *Quarterly Review of Film and Video* 11 (3): 31–48.

Chatterjee, Partha 1989. The Nationalist Resolution of the Women's Question. In *Recasting Women: Essays in Colonial History*. K. Sangari and S. Vaid, eds., pp. 233–53. New Delhi: Kali for Women.

Feuer, Jane 1983. The Concept of Live Television: Ontology as Ideology. In *Regarding Television: Critical Approaches – An Anthology*. E. A. Kaplan, ed., pp. 12–22. Frederick, MD: University Publications of America.

Foucault, Michel 1978. *The History of Sexuality. Vol. 1: An Introduction*. New York: Vintage Books.

—— 1980. Truth and Power. In *Power/Knowledge*, pp. 109–33. New York: Pantheon Books.

Gerow, Edwin 1974. The Rasa Theory of Abinavagupta and Its Application. In *The Literatures of India: An Introduction*. E. C. Dimock, Jr., et al., eds., pp. 212–27. Chicago, IL: University of Chicago Press.

Gillespie, Marie 1989. Technology and Tradition: Audio-Visual Culture among South Asian Families in West London. *Cultural Studies* 2 (2): 226–39.

Government of India 1985. *An Indian Personality for Television: Report of the Working Group on Software for Doordarshan*. 2 vols. New Delhi: Publications Division, Ministry of Information and Broadcasting.

Hall, Stuart 1981. Notes on Deconstructing "The Popular." In *People's History and Socialist Theory*. R. Samuel, ed., pp. 227–40. London: Routledge and Kegan Paul.

—— 1985. Signification, Representation, Ideology: Althusser and the Post-Structuralist Debates. *Critical Studies in Mass Communication* 2 (2): 91–114.

Horkheimer, Max and Theodore W. Adorno 1969 [1944]. The Culture Industry: Enlightenment as Mass Deception. In *Dialectic of Enlightenment*. J. Cumming, trans., pp. 120–67. New York: Continuum.

Ivy, Marilyn 1988. Tradition and Difference in the Japanese Mass Media. *Public Culture* 1(1): 21–30.

Johnson, Richard 1986. What Is Cultural Studies Anyway? *Social Text* 6 (1): 38–80.

Joshi, P. C. 1989. *Culture, Communication and Social Change*. New Delhi: Vikas.

Krishnan, Prabha 1990. In the Idiom of Loss: Ideology of Motherhood in Television Serials. *Economic and Political Weekly* 25 (42–3): WS 103–16.

Krishnan, Prabha and Anita Dighe 1990. *Affirmation and Denial: Construction of Femininity on Indian Television*. New Delhi: Sage.

Lacan, Jacques 1977 [1966]. *Écrits: A Selection*. A. Sheridan, trans. New York: International.

Lakshmi, C. S. 1988. Feminism and the Cinema of Realism. In *Women in Indian Society*. R. Ghadially, ed., pp. 217–24. New Delhi: Sage.

Lorde, Audre 1984. *Sister Outsider*. Freedom, CA: Crossing Press.

MacCabe, Colin 1986. Defining Popular Culture. In *High Culture/Low Theory*. C. MacCabe, ed., pp. 1–10. Manchester, England: Manchester University Press.

Mani, Lata 1987. Contentious Traditions: The Debate on Sati in Colonial India. *Cultural Critique* 7: 119–56.

Mankekar, Purnima 1990. "Our Men Are Heroes, Our Women Are Chaste": A Nationalist Reading of the "Disrobing" of Draupadi. Paper presented at the panel "The Body and the Categorization of People", American Ethnological Society Annual Meeting, Atlanta, April 26–29.

—— 1993a. Television and the Reconstitution of Indian Womanhood. Ph.D. dissertation, Department of Anthropology, University of Washington.

—— 1993b. Notions of the Real and Indian Television Serials. MS, files of the author.

Minh-ha, Trinh 1989. *Woman, Native, Other: Writing Postcoloniality and Feminism*. Bloomington: Indiana University Press.

Modleski, Tania 1979. The Search for Tomorrow in Today's Soap Operas. *Film Quarterly* 32 (1): 266–78.

—— 1983. The Rhythms of Reception: Daytime Television and Women's Work. In *Regarding Television: Critical Approaches – An Anthology*. E. A. Kaplan, ed., pp. 67–75. Frederick, MD: University Publications of America.

Mohanty, Chandra Talpade 1984. Under Western Eyes: Feminist Scholarship and Colonial Discourses. *Boundary* 213 (1): 333–58.

Morley, David 1980. *The "Nationwide" Audience*. London: British Film Institute.

—— 1991. Where the Global Meets the Local: Notes from the Sitting Room. *Screen* 32: 1–15.

Mukherjee, Meenakshi 1985. *Realism and Reality: The Novel and Society in India*. Delhi: Oxford University Press.

Mulvey, Laura 1989. *Visual and Other Pleasures*. Bloomington: Indiana University Press.

Pendakur, Manjunath 1989a. Indian Television Comes of Age: Liberalization and the Rise of Consumer Culture. *Communication* 11: 177–97.

—— 1989b. New Cultural Technologies and the Fading Glitter of Indian Cinema. *Quarterly Review of Film and Video* 11 (3): 69–78.

Punwani, Jyoti 1988. The Portrayal of Women on Indian Television. In *Women in Indian Society*. R. Ghadially, ed., pp. 224–32. New Delhi: Sage.

Radway, Janice 1984. *Reading the Romance: Women, Patriarchy, and Popular Literature*. Chapel Hill, NC: University of North Carolina Press.

—— 1988. Reception Study: Ethnography and the Problems of Dispersed Audiences and Nomadic Subjects. *Cultural Studies* 2 (3): 359–76.

Ramanujan, A. K. 1974. Indian Poetics: An Overview. In *The Literatures of India: An Introduction*. E. C. Dimock, Jr., et al., eds., pp. 115–18. Chicago, IL: University of Chicago Press.

Rosaldo, Michelle Z. 1984. Towards an Anthropology of Self and Feeling. In *Culture Theory: Essays on Mind, Self, and Emotion*. R. Shweder and R. LeVine, eds., pp. 137–57. Cambridge: Cambridge University Press.

Russell, John 1991. Race and Reflexivity: The Black Other in Contemporary Japanese Mass Culture. *Cultural Anthropology* 6: 3–25.

Sangari, Kumkum and Sudesh Vaid, eds. 1989. Recasting Women: An Introduction. In *Recasting Women: Essays in Colonial History*. K. Sangari and S. Vaid, eds., pp. 1–26. New Delhi: Kali for Women.

Seiter, Ellen, Hans Borchers, Gabriele Kreutzner, and Eva-Maria Warth, eds. 1989. *Remote Control: Television, Audiences, and Cultural Power*. London: Routledge.

Singhal, Arvind and Everett M. Rogers 1989. *India's Information Revolution*. New Delhi: Sage.

Taylor, Ella 1989. *Prime-Time Families: Television Culture in Postwar America*. Berkeley: University of California Press.

Thomas, Rosie 1985. Indian Cinema: Pleasures and Popularity. *Screen* 26: 123–35.

Traube, Elizabeth G. 1989. Secrets of Success in Postmodern Society. *Cultural Anthropology* 4: 273–300.

Vasudevan, Ravi 1989. The Melodramatic Mode and the Commercial Hindi Cinema. *Screen* 30: 29–50.

Wadley, Susan S., ed. 1980. *The Powers of Tamil Women*. Syracuse, NY: Syracuse University Press.

Williams, Raymond 1974. *Television: Technology and Cultural Form*. New York: Schocken Books.

Part V

Power, Colonialism, Nationalism

Having considered both the power of producers (who create texts that can stereotype and reduce, or alternatively deny stereotypes and counter reductionism) and the power of consumers (to accept, transform, indigenize, or reject texts), we turn now to the importance of *context* that very often tilts the balance in favor of one side over the other. The chapters in Part five all focus on media contexts with particular attention to power relations, ideological agendas, economic motivations, and political objectives. As such, they may be interpreted as updated takes on Horkheimer and Adorno's discussion of "culture industries" in raising awareness of the inequities in media production and distribution. These authors all pay close attention to the processes by which some messages are foregrounded and others silenced.

In chapter 19 Sut Jhally presents a neo-Marxist analysis of Western advertising and the commodity image-system it employs to sell products. Because we are so immersed within the system and incessantly subjected to its distorted messages, Jhally argues that we lose a significant part of our interpretative freedom. Commodity images and messages representing select corporate interests have so colonized aspects of our lives that their transformative reach extends, for example, to electoral politics and gender relations. They substitute artifice for substance and make us all the poorer for it. Jhally ends by suggesting some strategies for countering the commodity image-system, foremost of which is educating people in a "grammar of images" and explicating how they work.

In chapter 20 Annabelle Sreberny-Mohammadi fleshes out the "media imperialism" and related "cultural imperialism" theses, placing them within a rich historical and political–economic analysis. While data on media distribution around the world indicate a significant increase in access to media (an almost 400 percent increase in television ownership worldwide, for example, between 1965 and 1986), distribution remains very uneven and unequal. "Global," Sreberny-Mohammadi points out, "still does not mean universal." Although she describes attempts by a few global media giants to consolidate their control over media production and distribution worldwide, she discusses how non-American, non-European rivals prevent this from happening. Dependency theory, shifting global media flows, trade barriers, piracy, and nationalism all emerge in her analysis as factors that contribute to a nuanced understanding of how media technologies negotiate the global and the local.

From these wide-angle perspectives on media in global contexts, we return once again to specific case studies: Nicaragua during the first Somoza regime and contemporary Egypt. In chapter 21 David Whisnant describes the introduction of and control over media and advertising in Nicaragua from the 1920s to the 1960s. His analysis considers the whims of a dictator, US neocolonial tendencies, corporate America's profound Eurocentrism, and partisan politics in Hollywood. Quaker Oats, Bayer Aspirin, Nelson Rockefeller, and Walt Disney are just a few of the actors who participated in the cultural politics of twentieth-century Nicaragua. Whisnant thus provides us with a stark history of cultural imperialism in practice.

In chapter 22 Lila Abu-Lughod constructs a multi-layered analysis of local media practices and national cultural objectives in contemporary Egypt by way of a state-sponsored televised soap opera. She finds that encoded nationalist messages embracing and promoting a vaguely defined "modernity" are juxtaposed against an equally vaguely defined "traditional" (or alternatively "socialist") past. Questions surrounding Nasser's legacy, the influence of religious revivalism, the importation of American soap operas, and how these are assessed by members of different socioeconomic groups in Egypt, underscore Abu-Lughod's ethnography. Her chapter weaves together many of the strands that define this volume: socioeconomic and political power differentials between and among media producers and consumers, the irreducibility of media texts, audience agency, multinational interests, gendered readings, and nationalist projects.

Media – in all their many facets as technologies, texts, experiences, processes, and contexts – are increasingly commonplace. Anthropologists make important contributions by continually stressing the human agency that underscores their significance and grants them meaning. Media are not autonomous processes. Alarms should go off when they are treated as such. As Raymond Williams states: "Technological determinism is an untenable notion because it substitutes for real social, political and economic intention, either the random autonomy of invention or an abstract human essence" (Williams 1974: 130). Media mediate on a whole host of levels: social, cultural, political, economic, ideological, national, international, and transnational, to mention but a few. Only with increased attention to the people and processes interconnected through media can we further our understanding of these social phenomena.

SUGGESTED READINGS

Abu-Lughod, Lila. 1993. "Finding a place for Islam: Egyptian television serials and the national interest," *Public Culture* 5 (3): 493–513.

—— 1995. "The objects of soap opera: Egyptian television and the cultural politics of modernity." Pp. 190–210 in *Worlds Apart: Modernity through the Prism of the Local*, ed. Daniel Miller. London and New York: Routledge.

Adorno, Theodor W. 1954. "Television and the pattern of mass culture," *The Quarterly of Film Radio and Television* vol. 8, no. 3.

—— 1991. *The Culture Industry: Selected Essays on Mass Culture*. London: Routledge.

—— 1997. "Culture industry reconsidered." Pp. 24–9 in *Media Studies: A Reader*, ed. Paul Marris and Sue Thornham. Edinburgh: Edinburgh University Press. [Originally published in *New German Critique* 6 (1975): 12–19.]

Anderson, Benedict. 1983. *Imagined Communities: Reflections on the Origin and Spread of Nationalism*. London: Verso.

Appadurai, Arjun. 1990. "Disjuncture and difference in the global cultural economy," *Public Culture* 2 (2): 1–24.

Bate, David. 1993. "Photography and the colonial vision," *Third Text* 22: 81–91.

Benjamin, Walter. 1968. "The work of art in the age of mechanical reproduction." In *Illuminations*, ed. Hannah Arendt. New York: Schocken.

Bennett, Tony. 1982. "Theories of the media, theories of society." Pp. 31–55 in *Culture, Society, and the Media*, ed. Michael Gurevitch, Tony Bennett, James Curran, and Janet Woollacott. London and New York: Methuen.

Buckman, Robert. 1990. "Cultural agenda of Latin American newspapers and magazines: is US domination a myth?" *Latin American Research Review* 25 (2): 134–55.

Campbell, Christopher P. 1995. *Race, Myth, and the News*. Thousand Oaks, CA: Sage Publications.

Ching, Leo. 1994. "Imaginings in the empires of the sun: Japanese mass culture in Asia," *Boundary 2*, 21, no. 1.

Croteau, David and William Hoynes. 1997. *Media/Society: Industries, Images, and Audiences*. Thousand Oaks, CA: Pine Forge Press.

Curran, James and Michael Gurevitch, eds. 2000. *Mass Media and Society*, 3rd edn. London: Edward Arnold.

Dowmunt, Tony, ed. 1993. *Channels of Resistance: Global Television and Local Empowerment*. London: BFI Publishing.

Garnham, Nicholas. 1993. "The mass media, cultural identity, and the public sphere in the modern world," *Public Culture* 5: 251–65.

Goffman, Erving. 1976. *Gender Advertisements*. Studies in the Anthropology of Visual Communication (special edition) vol. 3, no. 2.

Hamelink, Cees. 1983. *Cultural Autonomy in Global Communications*. New York: Longman.

Hannerz, Ulf. 1998. "Reporting from Jerusalem," *Cultural Anthropology* 13 (4): 548–74.

Horkheimer, Max and Theodor Adorno. 1973. *Dialectic of Enlightenment*. London: Allen Lane.

Ivy, Marilyn. 1988. "Tradition and difference in the Japanese mass media," *Public Culture* 1 (1): 21–9.

Jhally, Sut. 1990. "Image-based culture: advertising and popular culture." Pp. 77–87 in *Gender, Race, and Class in Media*, ed. Gail Dines and Jean M. Humez. Thousand Oaks, CA: Sage Publications.

Larkin, Brian. 1997. "Indian films and Nigerian lovers: media and the creation of parallel modernities," *Africa* 67 (3): 406–40.

Lawuyi, Olatunde B. 1997. "The political economy of video marketing in Ogbomoso, Nigeria," *Africa* 67 (3): 476–90.

Lull, James. 1991. *China Turned On: Television, Reform, and Resistance*. New York: Routledge.

Malkki, Liisa. 1997. "News and culture: transitory phenomena and the fieldwork tradition." Pp. 86–101 in *Anthropological Locations: Boundaries and Grounds of a Field Science*, ed. Akhil Gupta and James Ferguson. Berkeley: University of California Press.

Mankekar, Purnima. 1993. "Television's tales and a woman's rage: a nationalist recasting of Draupadi's 'disrobing'," *Public Culture* 5 (3): 469–92.

—— 1999. *Screening Culture, Viewing Politics: An Ethnography of Television, Womanhood, and Nation in Postcolonial India*. Durham, NC: Duke University Press.

Morley, David and Kevin Robins. 1995. *Spaces of Identity: Global Media, Electronic Landscapes and Cultural Boundaries*. London: Routledge.

Naficy, Hamid. 1993. *The Making of Exile Cultures: Iranian Television in Los Angeles*. Minneapolis: University of Minnesota press.

—— 1999. *Home, Exile, Homeland: Film, Media, and the Politics of Place*. New York: Routledge.

Notar, Beth. 1994. "Of labor and liberation: images of women in current Chinese television advertising," *Visual Anthropology Review* 10 (2): 29–44.

O'Barr, William M. 1994. *Culture and the Ad: Exploring Otherness in the World of Advertising*. Boulder, CO: Westview Press.

Ohmann, Richard, ed. 1996. *Making and Selling Culture*. Hanover, NH: Wesleyan University Press.

Sarkar, Bhaskar. 1995. "Epic (mis)takes: nation, religion and gender on television," *Quarterly Review of Film and Video* 16 (1): 59–75.

Schiller, Herbert I. 1976. *Communication and Cultural Domination*. White Plains, NY: International Arts and Sciences Press.

—— 1994. "Media, technology, and the market: the interacting dynamic." Pp. 31–45 in *Culture on the Brink: Ideologies of Technology*, ed. Gretchen Bender and Timothy Druckrey. Seattle: Bay Press.

Skov, Lise and Brian Moeran, eds. 1995. *Women, Media and Consumption in Japan*. Honolulu: University of Hawaii Press.

Spitulnik, Debra. 1998. "Mediated modernities: encounters with the electronic in Zambia," *Visual Anthropology Review* 14 (2): 63–84.

—— In press. *Media Connections and Disconnections: Radio Culture and the Public Sphere in Zambia*. Durham, NC: Duke University Press.

Sreberny-Mohammadi, Annabelle. 1991. "The global and the local in international communications." Pp. 118–38 in *Mass Media and Society*, ed. James Curran and Michael Gurevitch. London: Edward Arnold.

Tanaka, Keiko. 1990. "Intelligent elegance: women in Japanese advertising." Pp. 78–97 in *Unwrapping Japan*, ed. E. Ben-Ari, et al. Manchester: Manchester University Press.

Thomas, Rosie. 1989. "Sanctity and scandal: the mythologization of Mother India," *Quarterly Review of Film and Video* 11: 11–30.

Tunstall, Jeremy. 1977. *The Media are America: Anglo-American Media in the World*. New York: Columbia University Press.

Weinberger, Eliot. 1994. "The camera people." Pp. 3–26 in *Visualizing Theory: Selected Essays from V.A.R., 1990–1994*, ed. Lucien Taylor. New York: Routledge.

West, Harry G. and Jo Ellen Fair. 1993. "Development communication and popular resistance in Africa: an examination of the struggle over tradition and modernity through media," *African Studies Review* 36 (1): 91–114.

Whisnant, David E. 1995. *Rascally Signs in Sacred Places: The Politics of Culture in Nicaragua*. Chapel Hill: University of North Carolina Press.

Wilk, Richard R. 1993. "'It's destroying a whole generation': television and moral discourse in Belize," *Visual Anthropology* 5 (3/4): 229–44 (chapter 17, this volume).

—— 1994. "Colonial time and TV time: television and temporality in Belize," *Visual Anthropology Review* 10 (1): 94–111.

Yang, Mayfair Mei-hui. 1994. "Film discussion groups in China: state discourse or plebian public sphere?" *Visual Anthropology Review* 10 (1): 112–25.

—— 1997. "Mass media and transnational subjectivity in Shanghai: notes on (re)cosmopolitanism in a Chinese metropolis." Pp. 287–319 in *Ungrounded Empires: The Cultural Politics of Modern Chinese Transnationalism*, ed. Aihwa Ong and Donald M. Nonini. New York: Routledge.

19

Image-Based Culture: Advertising and Popular Culture

Sut Jhally

Because we live inside the consumer culture, and most of us have done so for most of our lives, it is sometimes difficult to locate the origins of our most cherished values and assumptions. They simply appear to be part of our natural world. It is a useful exercise, therefore, to examine how our culture has come to be defined and shaped in specific ways – to excavate the origins of our most celebrated rituals. For example, everyone in this culture knows a "diamond is forever." It is a meaning that is almost as "natural" as the link between roses and romantic love. However, diamonds (just like roses) did not always have this meaning. Before 1938 their value derived primarily from their worth as scarce stones (with the DeBeers cartel carefully controlling the market supply). In 1938 the New York advertising agency of N. W. Ayers was hired to change public attitudes toward diamonds – to transform them from a financial invest-ment into a *symbol* of committed and everlasting love. In 1947 an Ayers advertising copywriter came up with the slogan "a diamond is forever" and the rest, as they say, is history. As an N. W. Ayers memorandum put it in 1959; "Since 1939 an entirely new generation of young people has grown to marriageable age. To the new generation, a diamond ring is considered a necessity for engagement to virtually everyone."[1]

This is a fairly dramatic example of how the institutional structure of the consumer society orients the culture (and its attitudes values, and rituals) more and more toward the world of commodities. The marketplace (and its major ideological tool, advertising) is the major structuring institution of contemporary consumer society.

This of course was not always the case. In the agrarian-based society preceding industrial society, other institutions such as family, community, ethnicity, and reli-gion were the dominant institutional mediators and creators of the cultural forms. Their influence waned in the transition to industrial society and then consumer society. The emerging institution of the marketplace occupied the cultural terrain left void by the evacuation of these older forms. Information about products seeped into public discourse. More specifically, public discourse soon became dominated by the "discourse through and about objects."[2]

At first, this discourse relied upon transmitting information about products alone, using the available means of textual communication offered by newspapers. As the possibility of more effective color illustration emerged and as magazines developed as competitors for advertising dollars, this "discourse" moved from being purely text-based. The further integration of first radio and then television into the advertising/media complex ensured that commercial communication would be characterized by the domination of *imagistic* modes of representation.

Again, because our world is so familiar, it is difficult to imagine the process through which the present conditions emerged. In this context, it is instructive to focus upon that period in our history that marks the transition point in the development of an image-saturated society – the 1920s. In that decade the advertising industry was faced with a curious problem – the need to sell increasing quantities of "nonessential" goods in a competitive marketplace using the potentialities offered by printing and color photography. Whereas the initial period of national advertising (from approximately the 1880s to the 1920s) had focused largely in a celebratory manner on the products themselves and had used text for "reason why" advertising (even if making the most outrageous claims), the 1920s saw the progressive integration of people (via visual representation) into the messages. Interestingly, in this stage we do not see representations of "real" people in advertisements, but rather we see representations of people who "stand for" reigning social values such as family structure, status differentiation, and hierarchical authority.

While this period is instructive from the viewpoint of content, it is equally fascinating from the viewpoint of *form*; for while the possibilities of using visual imagery existed with the development of new technologies, there was no guarantee that the audience was sufficiently literate in visual imagery to properly decode the ever-more complex messages. Thus, the advertising industry had to educate as well as sell, and many of the ads of this period were a fascinating combination where the written (textual) material explained the visual material. The consumer society was literally being taught how to read the commercial messages. By the postwar period the education was complete and the function of written text moved away from explaining the visual and toward a more cryptic form where it appears as a "key" to the visual "puzzle."

In the contemporary world, messages about goods are all-pervasive – advertising has increasingly filled up the spaces of our daily existence. Our media are dominated by advertising images, public space has been taken over by "information" about products, and most of our sporting and cultural events are accompanied by the name of a corporate sponsor. There is even an attempt to get television commercials into the nation's high schools under the pretense of "free" news programming. As we head toward the twenty-first century, advertising is ubiquitous – it is the air that we breathe as we live our daily lives.

Advertising and the Good Life: Image and "Reality"

I have referred to advertising as being part of "a discourse through and about objects" because it does not merely tell us about things but of how things are connected to important domains of our lives. Fundamentally, advertising talks to us as individuals and addresses us about how we can become *happy*. The answers it provides are all oriented to the marketplace, through the purchase of goods or services. To understand the system of images that constitutes advertising we need to inquire into the definition of happiness and satisfaction in contemporary social life.

Quality of life surveys that ask people what they are seeking in life – what it is that makes them happy – report quite consistent results. The conditions that people are searching for – what they perceive will make them happy – are things such as having personal autonomy and control of one's life, self-esteem, a happy family life, loving relations, a relaxed, tension-free leisure time, and good friendships. The unifying theme of this list is that these things are not fundamentally connected to goods. It is primarily "social" life and not "material" life that seems to be the locus of perceived happiness. Commodities are only *weakly related* to these sources of satisfaction.[3]

A market society, however, is guided by the principle that satisfaction should be achieved via the marketplace, and through its institutions and structures it orients behavior in that direction. The data from the quality of life studies are not lost on advertisers. If goods themselves are not the locus of perceived happiness, then they need to be connected in some way with those things that are. Thus advertising promotes images of what the audience conceives of as "the good life": beer can be connected with anything from eroticism to male fraternity to the purity of the old West; food can be tied up with family relations or health; investment advice offers early retirements in tropical settings. The marketplace cannot directly offer the real thing, but it can offer visions of it connected with the purchase of products.

Advertising thus does not work by creating values and attitudes out of nothing but by drawing upon and rechanneling concerns that the target audience (and the culture) already shares. As one advertising executive put it: "Advertising doesn't always mirror how people are acting but how they're *dreaming*. In a sense what we're doing is wrapping up your emotions and selling them back to you." Advertising absorbs and fuses a variety of symbolic practices and discourses, it appropriates and distills from an unbounded range of cultural references. In so doing, goods are knitted into the fabric of social life and cultural significance. As such, advertising is not simple manipulation, but what ad-maker Tony Schwartz calls "partipulation," with the audience participating in its own manipulation.

What are the consequences of such a system of images and goods? Given that the "real" sources of satisfaction cannot be provided by the purchase of commodities (merely the "image" of that source), it should not be surprising that happiness and contentment appear illusory in contemporary society. Recent social thinkers describe the contemporary scene as a "joyless economy,"[4] or as reflecting the "paradox of affluence."[5] It is not simply a matter of being "tricked" by the false blandishments of advertising. The problem is with the institutional structure of a market society that propels definition of satisfaction *through* the commodity/image system. The modern context, then, provides a curious satisfaction experience – one that William Leiss describes as "an ensemble of satisfactions and dissatisfactions" in which the consumption of commodities mediated by the image-system of advertising leads to consumer uncertainty and confusion.[6] The image-system of the marketplace reflects our desire and dreams, yet we have only the pleasure of the images to sustain us in our actual experience with goods.

The commodity image-system thus provides a particular vision of the world – a particular mode of self-validation that is integrally connected with what one *has* rather than what one *is* – a distinction often referred to as one between "having" and "being," with the latter now being defined through the former. As such, it constitutes a way of life that is defined and structured in quite specific political ways. Some commentators have even described advertising as part of a new *religious* system in which people construct their identities through the commodity form, and in which commodities are part of a supernatural magical world where anything is possible with the purchase of a product. The commodity as displayed in advertising plays a mixture of psychological, social, and physical roles in its relations with people. The object world interacts with the human world at the most basic and fundamental of levels, performing seemingly magical feats of enchantment and transformation, bringing instant happiness and gratification, capturing the forces of nature, and acting as a passport to hitherto untraveled domains and group relationships.[7]

In short, the advertising image-system constantly propels us toward things as means to satisfaction. In the sense that every ad says it is better to buy than not to buy, we can best regard advertising as a *propaganda* system for commodities. In the image-system as a whole, happiness lies at the end of a purchase. Moreover, this is not a minor propaganda system – it is all-pervasive. It should not surprise us then to discover that the problem that it poses – how to get more things for everyone (as that is the root to happiness) – guides our political debates. The goal of *economic growth* (on which the commodity vision is based) is an unquestioned and sacred proposition of the political culture. As the environmental costs of the strategy of unbridled economic growth become more obvious, it is clear we must, as a society, engage in debate concerning the nature of future economic growth. However, as long as the commodity image-system maintains its ubiquitous presence and influence, the possibilities of opening such a debate are remote. At the very moment we most desperately need to pose new questions within the political culture, the commodity image-system propels us with even greater certainty and persuasion along a path that, unless checked, is destined to end in disaster.

Moreover, this problem will be exponentially compounded in the twenty-first century, as more and more nations (both Third World and "presently existing socialist") reach for the magic of the marketplace to provide the panacea for happiness. One of the most revealing images following the collapse of the Berlin Wall was the sight of thousands of East German citizens streaming into West Berlin on a Sunday (when the shops were closed) to simply stare in rapture and envy at the commodities in the windows. Transnational corporations are licking their lips at the new markets that Eastern Europe and China will provide for their products. Accompanying the products (indeed preceding them, preparing the way) will be the sophisticated messages of global advertising emerging from Madison Avenue. From a global perspective, again at the very moment that there needs to be informed debate about the direction and scope of industrial production, the commodity propaganda system is colonizing new areas and new media, and channeling debate into narrower confines.

The Spread of Image-Based Influence

While the commodity image-system is primarily about satisfaction, its influence and effect are not limited to that alone. I want to briefly consider four other areas in the contemporary world where the commodity system has its greatest impact. The first is in the area of gender identity. Many commercial messages use images and representations of men and women as central components of their strategy to both get attention and persuade. Of course, they do not use just any gender images but images drawn from a narrow and quite concentrated pool. As Erving Goffman has shown, ads draw heavily upon the domain of gender display – not the way that men and women actually behave but the ways in which we think men and women behave.[8] It is because these conventions of gender display are so easily recognized by the audience that they figure so prominently in the image-system. Also, images having to do with gender strike at the core of individual identity; our understanding of ourselves as either male or female (socially defined within this society at this time) is central to our understanding of who we are. What better place to choose than an area of social life that can be communicated at a glance and that reaches into the core of individual identity.

However, we should not confuse these portrayals as true reflections of gender. In advertising, gender (especially for women) is defined almost exclusively along the lines of sexuality. The image-system thus distorts our perceptions and offers little that balances out the stress on sexuality. Advertisers, working within a "cluttered" environment in which there are more and more messages, must have a way to break through the attendant noise. Sexuality provides a resource that can be used to get attention and communicate instantly. Within this sexuality is also a powerful component of gender that again lends itself even easier to imagistic representation.

If only one or two advertisers used this strategy, then the image-system would not have the present distorted features. The problem is that the vast majority do so. The iconography of the culture, perhaps more than any previous society, seems to be obsessed with sexuality. The end result is that the commodity is part of an increasingly eroticized world – that we live in a culture that is more and more defined erotically through commodities.

Second, the image-system has spread its influence to the realm of electoral politics. Much has been written (mostly negatively) about the role that television advertising now plays within national electoral politics. The presidency seems most susceptible to "image-politics," as it is the office most reliant on television advertising. The social commentary on politics from this perspective has mostly concerned the manner in which the focus has shifted from discussion of real "issues" to a focus on symbolism and emotionally based imagery.

These debates are too important and complex to be discussed in any depth here, but there is a fundamental point to be made. The evidence suggests that George Bush won the 1988 presidential race because he ran a better ad and public relations campaign. Given the incredible swings in the polls over a relatively short period of time, when media information was the only thing that voters had to go on, it seems to be a conclusion with some substance. The implications of such a conclusion, though, have not really been explored the way they should. The fact that large numbers of people are changing their minds on who to vote for after seeing a thirty-second television commercial says a great deal about the nature of the political culture. It means that politics (for a significant portion of the electorate) is largely conducted in a symbolic realm, and that a notion of politics that is based upon people having a coherent and deep vision of their relationship to the social world is no longer relevant. Politics is not about issues; it is about "feeling good" or "feeling bad" about a candidate – and all it takes to change this is a thirty-second commercial.

The grammar of these images, then, clearly is different to the grammar of verbal or written language. The intrusion of the image-system into the world of electoral politics has meant that the majority of committed voters are held ransom by those who are uncommitted (the undecided or swing votes), and that these groups are influenced differently – and have a different relationship to politics – than those who have an old-style view of politics. These huge swings of opinion, based upon information provided by the image-system, suggest that the political culture is incredibly superficial and does not correspond to what we normally think of as "politics."

Third, the commodity image-system is now implicated, due to changes in the way that toys are marketed, in the very structure and experience of children's play. With both children's television programming and commercials oriented around the sale of toys, writers such as Stephen Kline argue that the context within which kids play is now structured around marketing considerations. In consequence, "Children's imaginative play has become the target of marketing strategy, allowing marketers to define the limits of children's imaginations.... Play in fact has become highly ritualized – less an exploration and solidification of personal experiences and developing conceptual schema than a rearticulation of the fantasy world provided by market designers. Imaginative play has shifted one degree closer to mere imitation and assimilation." Further, the segmentation of the child audience in terms of both age and gender has led to a situation where parents find it difficult to play with their children because they do not share the marketing fantasy world that toy advertisers have created and where there is a growing divide between boys and girls at play. "Since the marketing targets and features different emotional and narrative elements (action/conflict vs. emotional attachment and maintenance) boys and girls also experience difficulty in playing together with these toys."[9]

Fourth, the visual image-system has colonized areas of life that were previously largely defined (although not solely) by auditory perception and experience. The 1980s has seen a change in the way that popular music commodities (records, tapes, compact discs) are marketed, with a music video becoming an indispensable component of an overall strategy. These videos are produced as commercials for musical commodities by the advertising industry, using techniques learned from the marketing of products. Viewing these videos, there often seems to be little link between the song and the visuals. In the sense that they are commercials for records, there of course does not have to be. Video makers are in the same position as ad makers in terms of trying to get attention for their message and making it visually pleasurable. It is little wonder then that representations involving sexuality figure so prominently (as in the case of regular product advertising). The visuals are chosen for their ability to sell.

Many people report that listening to a song after watching the video strongly affects the interpretation they give to it – the visual images are replayed in the imagination. In that sense, the surrounding commodity image-system works to fix – or at least to limit – the scope of imaginative interpretation. The realm of listening becomes subordinated to the realm of seeing, to the influence of commercial images. There is also evidence suggesting that the composition of popular music is effected by the new video context. People write songs or lines with the vital marketing tool in mind.

Speed and Fragmentation: Toward a Twenty-First-Century Consciousness

In addition to issues connected with the colonization of the commodity image-system of other areas of social life (gender socialization, politics, children's play, popular cultural forms), there are also important broader issues connected with its relation to modes of perception and forms of consciousness within contemporary society. For instance, the commodity information-system has two basic characteristics: reliance on visual modes of representation and the increasing speed and rapidity of the images that constitute it. It is this second point that I wish to focus on here (I will return to the first point at the end of the essay).

The visual images that dominate public space and public discourse are, in the video age, not static. They do not stand still for us to examine and linger over. They are here for a couple of seconds and then they are gone. Television advertising is the epitome of this speed-up. There is nothing mysterious in terms of how it arose. As commercial time slots declined from sixty seconds to thirty seconds (and recently to fifteen seconds and even shorter), advertisers responded by creating a new type of advertising – what is called the "vignette approach" – in which narrative and "reason-why" advertising are subsumed under a rapid succession of lifestyle images, meticulously timed with music, that directly sell feeling and emotion rather than products. As a commercial editor puts it of this new approach: "They're a wonderful way to pack in information: all those scenes and emotions – cut, cut, cut. Also they permit you a very freestyle approach – meaning that as long as you stay true to your basic vignette theme you can usually just drop one and shove in another. They're a dream to work with because the parts are sort of interchangeable."[10]

The speed-up is also a response by advertisers to two other factors: the increasing "clutter" of the commercial environment and the coming of age, in terms of disposable income, of a generation that grew up on television and commercials. The need for a commercial to stand out to a visually sophisticated audience drove the image-system to a greater frenzy of concentrated shorts. Again, sexuality became a key feature of the image-system within this.

The speed-up has two consequences. First, it has the effect of drawing the viewer into the message. One cannot watch these messages casually; they require undivided attention. Intensely pleasurable images, often sexual, are integrated into a flow of images. Watching has to be even more attentive to catch the brief shots of visual pleasure. The space "in between" the good parts can then be filled with other information, so that the commodity being advertised becomes a rich and complex sign.

Second, the speed-up has replaced narrative and rational response with images and emotional response. Speed and fragmentation are not particularly conducive to *thinking*. They induce *feeling*. The speed and fragmentation that characterize the commodity image-system may have a similar effect on the construction of consciousness. In one series of ads for MTV, a teenage boy or girl engages in a continuous monologue of events, characters, feelings, and emotions without any apparent connecting theme. As the video images mirror the fragmentation of thoughts, the ad ends with the plug: "Finally, a channel for the way you *think*." The generalization of this speed/fragmentation strategy to the entire domain of image culture may in fact mean that this is the form that thought increasingly is taking at the end of the twentieth century.

Political Implications: Education in Image-Saturated Society

There really is not much to dispute in the analysis I have offered of the history, character, and consequences the commodity image-system may have. The real question concerning these issues has to do with the political implications that one may draw from this kind of approach. Put simply: Is there a problem with this situation, and if so what precisely is it? Further, what solutions may be offered?

In a provocative recent book, Stuart Ewen offers a clear evaluation of the contemporary image-system. He states it succinctly:

The danger is this: as the world encourages us to accept the autonomy of images, "the given facts that appear" imply that substance is unimportant, not worth pursuing. Our own experiences are of little consequence, unless they are substantiated and validated by the world of style. In the midst of such charades, the chasm between surface and reality widens; we experience a growing sense of disorientation. . . . For meaningful alternatives to come into being, however, the dominance of surface over substance must be overcome. There must be a reconciliation of surface over substance, a reinvigoration of a politics of substance.[11]

Beneath his insightful analysis and his many examples from different domains, Ewen maintains a relatively simple division: there is a world of "substance" where real power rests and where people live their real lives (the "material" world of "essence") and there is a world of "style" and surface (the evanescent world of "appearances"). In the history of twentieth-century capitalism the world of substance has been hidden and given a false veil by the world of appearances. People have given up control of the real world and immersed themselves in the ultimately illusory world of appearances. Surface has triumphed over substance.

I am less sure than Ewen of the dichotomy that he works with – after all, appearance is the form in which essence reveals itself – but I am convinced that a modern cultural politics must be conducted on the terrain of the image-system. The question is, how is substance (reality) revealed? Given that our understanding of reality is always socially constructed (that "ideology" is present in any system or situation), visual images are the central mode through which the modern world understands itself. Images are the dominant language of the modern world. We are stuck with them. Further, we have to acknowledge the pleasure that such images provide. This is not simply trickery or manipulation – the pleasure is substantive.

I would focus a cultural politics on two related strategies. First, the struggle to reconstruct the existence and meaning of the world of substance has to take place on the terrain of the image-system. In some progressive cultural politics the very techniques associated with the image-system are part of the problem – that is, images themselves are seen as the problem. A struggle over definitions of reality (what else is cultural politics?) needs to use other mediums of communication. I believe such a strategy surrenders the very terrain on which the most effective battles can be fought – the language of the contemporary world.[12]

The second aspect of the strategy centers less on revealing matters of substance (the underlying reality) than on opening up further the analysis of the contemporary image-system, in particular, *democratizing* the image-system. At present the "discourse through and about objects" is profoundly authoritarian – it reflects only a few narrow (mostly corporate) interests. The institutions of the world of substance must be engaged to open up the public discourse to new and varied (and dissenting) voices.

The other set of concerns are connected to issues of *literacy* in an image-saturated society. As Raymond Williams has pointed out, in the early development of capitalism workers were taught to read but not to write. The skills of reading were all that were required to follow orders and to understand the Bible. Contemporary society is in a similar position. While we can read the images quite adequately (for the purposes of their creators) we do not know how to *produce* them. Such skills, or knowledge of the process, must be a prerequisite for functional literacy in the contemporary world. Basic coursework in photography and video production should be required in all high schools. Moreover, while messages can be read adequately, most people do not understand *how* the language of images works. Just as knowledge of grammar is considered vital in learning foreign languages, so the grammar of images (how they work) needs to be integrated into the high school curriculum. "Visual literacy" courses should be taken right after the production courses.

Finally, information about the institutional context of the production and consumption of the image-system should be a prerequisite for literacy in the modern world. Advertisements, for example, are the only message forms that are not accompanied by credits in terms of who has produced them. In this sense, movies and television programs have a different status within the image-system in that at least *some* of their process of production is revealed. At minimum, we know that they are made by lots of people!

Ads, on the other hand, simply appear and disappear without any credits. A third set of courses could focus on the political economy of the media and advertising industries. Stripping away the veil of anonymity and mystery would by itself be of great value in demystifying the images that parade before our lives and through which we conceptualize the world and our role within it. As Noam Chomsky puts it (talking about the media in general) in his book *Necessary Illusions*: "Citizens of the democratic societies should undertake a course of intellectual self-defense to protect themselves from manipulation and control, and to lay the basis for meaningful democracy."[13] Such a course of action will not be easy, for the institutional structure of the image-system will work against it. However, the invigoration of democracy depends upon the struggle being engaged.

NOTES

1 See Epstein (1982).
2 This is discussed more fully in Leiss, Kline, and Jhally (1986).
3 See Hirsch (1976).
4 Scitovsky (1976).
5 Hirsch (1976).
6 Leiss (1976).
7 See Jhally (1987) and Kavanaugh (1981).
8 Goffman (1979).
9 Kline (1989, pp. 299, 315).
10 Quoted in Arlen (1981, p. 182).
11 Ewen (1988, p. 271).
12 For more on progressive cultural politics, see Angus and Jhally (1989, Introduction).
13 Chomsky (1989).

REFERENCES

Angus, I. and Jhally, S. (1989). *Cultural politics in contemporary America*. New York: Routledge.

Arlen, M. (1981). *Thirty seconds*. New York: Penguin.

Chomsky, N. (1989). *Necessary illusions: Thought control in democratic societies*. Boston: South End Press.

Epstein, E. (1982). *The rise and fall of diamonds*. New York: Simon & Schuster.

Ewen, S. (1988). *All consuming images: The politics of style in contemporary culture*. New York: Basic Books.

Goffman, E. (1979). *Gender advertisements*. New York: Harper & Row.

Hirsch, F. (1976). *Social limits to growth*. Cambridge, MA: Harvard University Press.

Jhally, S. (1987). *The codes of advertising*. New York: St. Martin's Press.

Kavanaugh, J. (1981). *Following Christ in a consumer society*. New York: Orbis.

Kline, S. (1989). Limits to the imagination: Marketing and children's culture. In I. Angus and S. Jhally (eds.), *Cultural politics in contemporary America*. New York: Routledge.

Leiss, W. (1976). *The limits to satisfaction*. Toronto: Toronto University Press.

Leiss, W., Kline, S., and Jhally, S. (1986). *Social communication in advertising*. Toronto: Nelson.

Scitovsky, T. (1976). *The joyless economy*. New York: Oxford University Press.

20

The Global and the Local in International Communications

Annabelle Sreberny-Mohammadi

After three thousand years of explosion, by means of fragmentary and mechanical technologies, the Western world is imploding. During the mechanical ages we had extended our bodies in space. Today, after more than a century of electric technology, we have extended our central nervous system itself in a global embrace, abolishing both space and time as far as our planet is concerned.... As electrically contracted, the globe is no more than a village.

Marshall McLuhan (1964: 11–12)

> A Third World in every First World
> A Third World in every Third World
> And vice-versa
>   Trinh Minh-ha (1987)

Introduction

Contemporary rhetoric suggests that we live in a unitary world in which space and time have collapsed and the experience of distance imploded for ever. The antagonistic blocs of East and West are giving way to international markets, moneys, and media. Germany is unified. A new and expanding 'Europe' looms. The centrifugal force of 'globalization' is the catchphrase of the 1990s. Yet at the very same time, in the same but different world, the centripetal forces of old and new tribalisms and nationalisms are at work and ethnic struggles are breaking out all over. Armenians confront Azarbaijanis, Serbs fight Croats, Mowhawk Indians confront Quebecois, there is violence between Umkatha and the ANC. Race-related violence increases in New York City, with a new Black–Asian dimension. The Soviet Union acts violently against Lithuania, putting perestroika in peril. Iraq invades and annexes Kuwait, and Arab-Americans fear discrimination, as do Muslims in Europe, and the world waits for 'high noon' on January 15, 1991. Far from the 'loss of the subject', identity seems to lie at the heart of politics in the late twentieth century.

The 2000 version of this article came to the editors' attention only after the book went to press. See Sreberny-Mohammadi "The Global and the Local in International Communications," in James Curran and Michael Gurevitch, eds., *Mass Media and Society*, 3rd edn. (London: Edward Arnold, 2000).

Giddens (1990: 64) defines globalization as 'the intensification of worldwide social relations which link distant localities in such a way that local happenings are shaped by events occurring many miles away and vice versa'. For Giddens, what he calls 'time-space distanciation', a theme developed at length in Harvey (1989), helps to create 'complex relations between *local involvements* (circumstances of co-presence) and *interaction across distance* (connections of presence and absence)'. In this stretching process of relations, there are numerous modes of connection between different regions and contexts. Appadurai (1990) has described five such 'scapes' of interaction as the ethnoscape, the technoscape, the infoscape, the financescape and the mediascape – which are interconnected, even overlapping.

Much theoretical debate centres on how the current situation should be conceived and labelled. Some argue that there is a discernibly 'new' kind of economic–cultural structure to be called 'postmodernity' (Harvey 1989), while others argue that the evident changes of the last fifteen years simply reflect the supreme development and natural extension of global capitalism and prefer to call this structure 'late capitalism' (Mandel 1975; Jameson 1984) or 'high modernity' (Giddens 1990). What is significant throughout these debates is that the role of communication and information has been finally and generally recognized as crucial elements in the new world order. Yet the role and shape of communications at the beginning of the 1990s are by no means very fixed or very clear, and neither are our theoretical models for explaining/exploring communications on an international scale. The rapidity and complexity of change in the media environment as we enter the 1990s seems to require a newer set of terms and vantage points than are offered by older perspectives, which often seem frozen in a bygone era. This chapter explores the dynamic tension between the global and local levels of analysis, as suggested by Giddens, as a provocative and useful construct which can help us uncover the deeply contradictory dynamics of the current moment. In the twin yet opposing processes of globalization versus localization, media play a central role and reveal the tensions between the macro and micro levels of socio-economic structures, cultures, and development dynamics.

A Brief Reprise of Older Models in International Communication

Since the 1960s the field of International Communication has been dominated by three successive intellectual paradigms: that of 'communications and development', that of 'cultural imperialism' and currently by a revisionist 'cultural pluralism' which is still searching for a coherent theoretical shape. It will be argued here that this third construct is itself full of contradictions, and that the 'global/local' model at least has the merits of putting 'contradiction' at the core of its construct. A brief reprise of these models is useful, both as intellectual history and to understand the different theoretical bases and implications of the models for current understanding.

'Communications and Development' emerged out of developmentalist thinking in the early 1960s. After the Second World War the emergence of independent national political systems such as India, Algeria, Ghana, out of the grip of varied European colonialisms, spawned debates among Western academics about the nature of 'development' and the obstacles within such newly independent nations to development. Some arguments focused on the lack of capital for investment, prompting such practical solutions as the World Bank and interest-bearing loans, under which results many developing nations are still groaning. Other arguments examined the lack of entrepreneurial vision and trained manpower, spawning education exchanges and training programs. The arguments developed by Daniel Lerner (1958) and Wilbur Schramm (1964) focused instead on the Weberian/Parsonian 'mentalities' or congeries of attitudes that were supportive or obstructive to change. They suggested that the traditional values of the developing world were the central obstacles to political participation and economic activity, the two key elements of the development process. The 'solution' for their analysis was the promotion of the use of communications media to alter attitudes and values, embodied in 'media indicators' (minimum numbers of cinema seats, radio and television receivers, and copies of daily newspapers as a ratio of population necessary for development), which were adopted by UNESCO and widely touted in the developing world. This perspective has been roundly criticized for its ethnocentrism, its ahistoricity, its linearity, for conceiving of development in an evolutionary, endogenist fashion and for solutions which actually reinforced dependency rather than helping to overcome it.

The 'dependency' paradigm, developing initially in Latin America and building on older critiques of imperalism (Gunder-Frank 1964) instead recognized the global structures and interrelationships conditioning the 'development' of the Third World, particularly the multiple and diverse legacies of colonialism. It was particularly critical of the post-independence economic dynamics which kept Third World states in economic hock to the ex-imperial powers, and argued that 'development' could not be mere mimicry of Western structures but had to be conceived as an autonomous, self-chosen path that built on the rich/ancient cultures of the Third World. From within this broad, critical framework, the specific model of 'cultural imperialism' argued that, far from aiding Third World nations to develop, the international flows of technology transfer and media hardware coupled with the 'software' flows of cultural products actually strengthened dependency and prevented true development. The great merit of the models of 'cultural imperialism' (Schiller 1976; Matterlart 1979) and 'media imperialism' (Boyd-Barrett 1977) was their recognition of *global* dynamics and relationships, taking their cue from much older models of imperalism, and the suggested linkages between foreign policy interests, capitalist expansion and media infrastructures and contents. This theoretical model spawned a wide variety of empirical studies which documented the imbalanced flow of media products – from news (Galtung and Ruge 1965) to films (Guback and Varis 1982) to television programming (Varis 1984) – as well as the export of organizational structures (Katz and Wedell 1977) and professional values (Golding 1977) from the developed to the Third World. Behind its structuralist analysis and the descriptive mapping of international communications dynamics, a central assumption was that Western cultural values (often conflated to 'American' values) such as consumerism and individualism, expressed implicitly in a variety of media genres as well as directly through advertising, were being exported to and decisively altering Third World cultural milieux. Fears of 'cultural homogenization' and 'cultural synchronization' (Hamelink 1983a, b) were voiced, and arguments made for Third World 'cultural disassociation' along the lines of Samir Amin's 'delinking' from the global capitalist system as the only way toward autonomous development and protection of indigenous cultures. Criticisms of this position have been made from quite divergent historical perspectives. One argument, looking back in time, suggests that the very term 'cultural imperialism' tends to obscure the many deep and diverse *cultural* effects of imperialism itself, including the export of religion, educational systems and values, European languages, and administrative practices, all of which have long ago and perhaps irretrievably altered the cultural milieux of the colonized (Sreberny-Mohammadi forthcoming). Such an argument questions the utility of terms such as 'authenticity' and 'indigeneity' within a lengthy history of cultural contact, absorption and recreation, and suggests that a cultural debate which focuses mainly on modern media neglects other much older and deeper structures which may embody 'foreign' values but may also be the pillars of modernization.

Another strand of critique, looking forward to the new realities of the 1990s, suggests that, like the earlier arguments for 'communications and development', the 'cultural imperialism' model was based on a situation of comparative global media scarcity, limited global media players and embryonic media systems in much of the Third World. The speed-up of history, evidenced in the rapidity of changes in many areas of social life, is especially evident in the global spread of communication and information technologies and the advent of many new and diverse media actors over the past decade or so. In 1990 it is clear that the international media environment is far more complex than that suggested by the 'cultural imperialism' model whose depiction of a hegemonic media pied piper leading the global media mice appears frozen in the realities of the 1970s, now a bygone era.

Empirically there is a more complex syncopation of voices and a more compli-cated media environment in which Western media domination has given way to multiple actors and flows of media products. More nations of the South are producing and exporting media materials, including film from India and Egypt, television programming from Mexico and Brazil. For example, TV Globo, the major Brazilian network, exports telenovelas to 128 countries, including Cuba, China, the Soviet Union, East Germany, earning export dollars for Brazil, and its productions outnumber those of any other station in the world (Tracey 1988). Indeed the flow of televisual materials from Brazil to Portugal is one example of how contemporary cultural flows reverse the historic roles of imperialism, while Latin American telenovelas on Spanish television channels in the United States has been called 'reverse cultural imperialism' (Anatola and Rodgers 1984). In another region and medium, the Indian film industry has an international reputation as the most productive – more than 900 films in 1985 – with an extensive export market (Dissanayeke 1988). India has also managed to keep a somewhat dualistic yet productive tension between high art film and a popular cinema, creating movies that reflect and reinforce different elements of India's rich cultural past as well as indigenizing invasive foreign elements into a distinctive Indian style (Binford 1988). Television, too, has been successful at translating ancient Indian culture into popular contemporary televisual fare, the Hindu epic, the Ramayana, clearing urban streets and creating a huge demand for additional episodes over the 50 originally planned (Chatterji 1989). These Third World producers have become not only national producers but international exporters of cultural products, a process which revisionists claim has altered any one-way flow of Western material and the 'hegemonic' model of cultural imperialism (McNeely and Soysal 1989). These 'global pluralists' adopt an optimistic voice regarding the diversity of media produ-cers and locales and the many loops of cultural flows that have merged (Tracey 1988; Boyd 1984). But the very rapidity of change on the international media scene makes it hard to discern long-term trends. The 'global pluralists' are correct to note the coming of age of many Third World media producers and the localization of some media production. Yet at the same time even stronger tendencies toward greater globalization and conglomeratization can be discerned, which I will document shortly.

There is also a conceptual challenge to the 'cultural imperalism' model, stemming from new modes of analysing media effects which question the 'international hypodermic needle' assumption proferred by the 'hegemonic' model. Arguments about 'the active audience' and 'polysemy' (e.g. Fiske 1987) inserted into international communications debate suggest that diverse audiences bring their own interpretive frameworks and sets of meaning to media texts, thus resisting, reinterpreting and reinventing any foreign 'hegemonic' cultural products, the details of which we will again explore later. The 'global pluralism' model seems to suggest many independent and happy producers, somewhat evacuating issues of dominance, cultural appropriation and media effects. I think we need a fourth perspective, one that essentially recognizes and does justice to the dynamic tension between the global and the local, as suggested by Giddens, and the shifting terrains that they encompass. After Trinh Minh-ha (1987), I'll call this outlook 'the global in the local, the local in the global' and use the rest of the chapter to explore some of the evident contradictions and tensions between these two poles in different contexts. We could divide globalization in the media sphere into four separable elements: the globalization of media forms, of media firms, of media flows and of media effects. I'll examine them in turn.

Globalization of Media Forms

It is claimed that more and more of the world is wired as a global audience with access to electronic media. The 'success' of the spread of media distribution and reception systems is in evidence: by the end of the 1980s radio signals were globally available and transistors have overcome lack of infrastructure, while nationally based television services have been established in all but the smallest and poorest of African and Asian countries.[1] Globally, the number of television receivers rose from 192 million in 1965 to 710 million in 1986. There are antennae in the Amazon jungle. China is the third largest producer of television receivers. Beyond RTV reception, video players/recorders (VCRs) have *potential* global reach, although a volume entitled *Video World-Wide* actually examines only 22 countries as well as 'the Gulf States', 'West Africa' and 'Southern and East Africa' and argues that there are only four truly 'video rich' areas in the world, Japan and Southeast Asia; the 'Arab countries'; Western Europe, and North America (Alvarado 1988; see also Boyd et al. 1989). Thus, at least in terms of national involvement in electronic media production and distribution of public access to communications infrastructure, there has been significant development over the past two decades.

However, distribution is still extremely unequal. The global 'average' of 145 receivers per 1000 population actually ranges from a high of 783 per thousand in North America to a low of 13 per thousand in the non-Arab states of Africa. The global trend is in place, yet by no means 'achieved'. Global still does not mean universal.

Table 20.1 Television receivers, 1965–1986.

Continents, major areas and groups of countries	Total television receivers (in millions)			Television receivers per thousand inhabitants		
	1965	1975	1986	1965	1975	1986
World total	192.0	414.0	710.0	57.0	102.0	145.0
Africa	0.6	2.5	15.0	1.9	6.2	25.0
Americas	84.0	160.0	268.0	182.0	286.0	397.0
Asia	24.0	57.0	138.0	13.0	25.0	48.0
Europe (incl. USSR)	81.0	189.0	280.0	120.0	260.0	362.0
Oceania	2.4	5.5	9.0	137.0	262.0	360.0
Developed countries	181.0	373.0	564.0	177.0	325.0	472.0
Developing countries	11.0	41.0	146.0	4.7	14.0	39.0
Africa (excl. Arab States)	0.1	0.6	5.7	0.4	2.0	13.0
Asia (excl. Arab States)	24.0	56.0	130.0	13.0	25.0	45.0
Arab States	0.9	3.4	17.0	8.4	24.0	85.0
North America	76.0	133.0	209.0	355.0	564.0	783.0
Latin America and the Caribbean	8.0	27.0	59.0	32.0	84.0	145.0

Source: Unesco Statistical Yearbook, 1988, © UNESCO.

Globalization of Media Firms

Central to any discussion of globalization has been the rise of a global market and the role of transnational corporations (TNCs) in adapting to, producing for and profiting from that. The media sphere has long had its global firms, which tend to become bigger and more powerful as the century winds to an end (Bagdikian 1990). Media moguls such as Rupert Murdoch, Sylvio Berlusconi and Henry Luce with the Warner Brothers have created corporate structures that span continents, combine holdings in broadcast, print and film production and also control distribution facilities such as satellites and cable networks. As an example, the merger in March 1989 between Henry Luce and Harry and Jack Warner made Times-Warner the largest media corporation in the world. It has an assessed value of $18 billion, a workforce approaching 340,000, a corporate base in the United States, with subsidiaries in Australia, Asia, Europe and Latin America (Time Warner Inc. 1990). Its 1989 revenues were over $10 billion during 1989 from activities in magazine and book publishing, music recording and publishing, film and video and cable television. Time Warner is thus a prime example of a growing global corporate structure which is highly vertically integrated – controlling the production process from the conception of a film idea to the building in which it will be shown, for example – and diversifying horizontally to have stakes in other related leisure and information holdings. By Time Warner's own analysis, vertical integration has numerous benefits, including 'creative synergies' and economies of scope and scale; 'optimal levels of promotion' which prevents separate companies having a '"free ride" on the promotional activities of others'; enables companies to 'be responsive to the desires of consumers'; and allows companies to accept greater financial risk than firms which operate in individual industry segments, thus being able to support projects of questionable commercial value. Access to global markets essentially reinforce and multiply the economies of scale.

Time Warner's own materials readily describe the company as 'a vertically integrated global entity' (Time Warner 1990: 47). Indeed, large corporations have not been slow to recognize the positive public value attached to the notion of 'globalization' as a unifying process of recognition of a common humanity, and coolly to adopt it for their own purposes. Thus, as part of its own self-marketing, on Earth Day – April 22, 1990 – a day devoted to global awareness and ecological concern, Time Warner launched a new logo and a new motto: 'The World is Our Audience'. In similar fashion, Sony justifies its development of American-based holdings by appropriating a famous radical grassroots slogan 'Think Globally, Act Locally' for its own purposes. Thus Sony USA writes 'It is Sony's philosophy that global corporations have a responsibility to participate actively in the countries in which they operate, a philosophy of "global localization". This means thinking globally while acting locally – being sensitive to local requirements, cultures, traditions and attitudes' (Sony USA 1990: 1) (Note that Sony employs 100,000 worldwide, enjoys an annual consolidated sales of about $16.3 billion, and has its stock sold in exchanges in ten countries.) These global giants clearly see themselves as part of a current phenomenon and are quick to point out the increasingly international activities of competitors.

Some try to debate the extent of this process of consolidating a few vertically integrated global media giants and their power to control the creation, production and distribution of worldwide information and communication. Thus, Murdoch's News Corporation argues against the notion that the emergent pattern is of 'international media holdings by relatively few media forms', by arguing that 'multinational media companies have emerged but they are too numerous to be characterized as "few" (NTIA 1990: 5). But this appears nothing more than a quibble; of the thousands of corporations active in the media business worldwide, this group of global media moguls is clearly no more than a handful. While accurate and extensive comparative data is still hard to find, a UNESCO-compiled table for seventy-eight firms listed for their total 1987 media turnover (including press and publishing, television, radio and cinema) shows that only seven had turnover of more than 3 billion dollars, with 15 having turnover of more than 2 billion dollars (UNESCO 1989: 104).

Of the seventy-eight firms listed in the complete table, not one was based in the Third World. Forty-eight were US or Japanese, while the rest were Western European, Canadian or Australian. Already in 1988, the combined revenue of five such giants (Bertelsmann AG; News Corp; Hachette; and premerger Time Inc. and Warner) was estimated at $45 billion, or 18 percent of the $250 billion worldwide information industry (see table 20.2.)

Many of these corporations are American, and for many sectors of the American culture industries, international sales are now a crucial source of income. In 1989 foreign revenues accounted for 38 per cent of total revenues for the American motion picture industry and helped to keep the value gap between imported film and film exports at $3 billion. Ted Turner's Cable News Network is received by the Kremlin and the Islamic Republic, and *Dallas* enjoys an international audience in over 90 countries, and US corporations have shown interest in cultural products being included in GATT talks and terms of trade (Time Warner 1990: 62).

Yet clearly by 1990 not all this global expansion is conducted by American or European-based firms, the usual assumption of the 'cultural imperial' thesis. There is considerable inter-capitalist rivalry, and foreign interests have discovered both the lucrative domestic US market, still the single largest in the world, and the global resonance of American popular culture. A few recent examples would be the globalization of Hollywood, involving the purchase of Columbia Pictures and Tri-Star Pictures by Sony, the Japanese giant which had already bought Columbia Records in 1988 (the context for the Sony America slogan discussed above); the purchase of MGM/United Artists by Pathe SA, an Italian company; the purchase of 20th Century Fox by Rupert Murdoch's Australian-based News Corporation, and in November 1990 the purchase of MCA Inc., which includes Universal Studios, Universal Pictures and MCA Records, by the Japanese firm Matsushita.

The dynamic of foreign firms buying US media outlets extends well beyond filmmaking into many other media: Murdoch's News Corporation owns newspapers in Boston and San Antonio, Harper Row books, and Triangle Publications which publishes *TV Guide*, the largest circulation magazine in the United States; International Thomson Group, based in Canada, owns 116 daily newspapers in the United States; the British-based Maxwell Communications owns Macmillan Books; Bertelsmann AG, the West German giant, owns RCA and Arista Records, while the Dutch firm N.V. Philips owns Polygram, Island and A&M Records.

Table 20.2 Selected major information and communication groupings. Total media turnover: top 15 corporations out of 78 listed by UNESCO.

Group	Country	Ranking media	Media sales	Press, publishing, recording (%)	Radio–TV, motion pictures (%)	Period
Capital Cities/ABC	USA	1	4,440	23	77	
Time	USA	2	4,193	61	39	
Bertelsmann	Germany, Fed. Rep. of	3	3,689	54	18	June 87
News Corp	Australia	4	3,453	58	32	June 88
Warner Communications	USA	5	3,404	49	51	
General Electric	USA	6	3,165		25	
Gannett	USA	7	3,079	88	12	
Times Mirror	USA	8	2,994	85	11	
Gulf + Western	USA	9	2,904	37	63	
Yomiuri Group	Japan	10	2,848	63	23	86
CBS	USA	11	2,762		100	
ARD	Germany, Fed. Rep. of	12	2,614		100	
NHK	Japan	13	2,541		100	March 88
Advance Publications	USA	14	2,397	92	8	
MCA	USA	15	2,052	8	92	

Of the 78 firms listed by UNESCO *in the complete table* not one was based in the Third World.
Source: © UNESCO.

The increasing complexity and transnationalization of global media markets has, somewhat tardily, become the focus of a recently launched study by the National Telecommunications and Information Administration (NTIA), a section of the US Department of Commerce in Washington, DC. Entitled *Comprehensive Study on the Globalization of Mass Media Firms*, in February 1990 it invited input in order to 'better formulate US communications policy in a rapidly changing information environment' (NTIA 1990). Culling through the responses which NTIA has provided, and from which much of the above factual evidence is drawn, it rapidly becomes clear that the US-based media/culture corporations are concerned essentially with two phenomena that affect their access to international media markets. The first is the newly defined and instituted European cultural policy which they interpret as a set of trade barriers to the free flow of American cultural products. The second is the problem of media piracy, significantly but not solely in the Third World. Yet it is abundantly clear that Europe is viewed as the most promising media market, with very little interest paid to or in media development in the Third World, other than chagrin at the media free ride that many Third World societies have enjoyed. Thus these frequently cited examples of media 'globalization' actually reveal its very limited coverage. These processes involve corporate actors of the North, interested in Northern media products and audiences, with marginal amounts of the production or circulation occurring among the peoples of the South. It seems quite evident that the production and promotion strategies of these global media firms would do little to alleviate the global imbalance in media availability, and rather exacerbate the global imbalances between the media rich and the media poor.

Global Media Flows

Globalization has often been applied to the spread of Western mediated products across the globe, from which few places seem immune. There is much anecdotal evidence of the use of Western cultural products, sometimes in somewhat improbable and erstwhile 'remote' places. Ouderkirk (1989) describes trekking up the highest Guatemalan mountains in search of some remote and authentic Qeche Indians and hearing some stirring music which as she approached turned out to be old Beatles tapes! Pico Iyer's (1989) travelogue talks about 'video nights in Kathmandu' and elsewhere in Asia, encountering 'Ike and Tuna Turner' sandwiches in the heart of the people's Republic of China, Burmese musicians playing songs by the Doors, as well as countless Asian remakes of Rambo movies. The film *Bye Bye Brasil* amusingly reflects on the public abandonment of traditional performing arts for television as it spread into the hinterland of Brazil. Recent visits to the Islamic Republic of Iran revealed considerable use of American videos such as *Robocop* and *Maximum Overdrive* and audiotapes of Madonna and Michael Jackson, all brought in via the black market from Dubai (Sreberny-Mohammadi and Mohammadi 1991).

As already mentioned, much early work supportive of the 'cultural imperialism' hypothesis provided descriptive mappings of unequal global flows, and much international debate in the 1970s–80s focused on this notion, as an indicator of global domination and threat to indigenous cultural survival. This culminated in the UNESCO mass media declaration, the report of the Macbride Commission and the formulation of a tenet of the New International Information Order as moving from a merely 'free' flow to a 'free and balanced' flow of communication (although no adequate empirical measures of such balance have ever been devised).

Trade barriers and piracy: local strategies vis-à-vis the global

Two different strategies have been devised to deal with the imbalanced flow, one of which involves limitations and trade barriers to cultural imports. Limits on the amount of imported programming and vetting of imported materials exist in Brazil, India, Iran and elsewhere in the Third World. But now that Europe appears to be moving toward an albeit voluntary continental policy for 1992, transnational corporations are extremely worried. Time Warner argues that it faces formidable trade barriers, 'some of which are clothed in the garb of "cultural" measures ostensibly designed to protect the cultural sovereignty and artistic heritage of the country in question' (Time Warner 1990: 48). The corporation proclaims a certain sensitivity: 'Although we must be sensitive to the cultural environment and needs of every locale in which we operate, trade barriers can only be justified to the limited extent that they are truly necessary to protect indigenous cultures that would otherwise be overwhelmed by the cultural products of other countries' but in the very next paragraph the tone changes: 'The cultural issue is appearing with alarming frequency in the international marketplace, and must be roundly rejected' (ibid.). Its main concern, shared by other media multinationals, is the new European initiative in the *Television without Frontiers* directive which suggests a 50 per cent quota on imported programming by October 1992 where possible (although this is non-binding) and defines a 'European' television company as one where the production and control of production is in an EC state or as a majority of the total cost of production is borne by a producer or co-producer from the EC states or those states privy to the Council of Europe convention. Thus even the possibility of transnationals developing co-productions with Europeans is limited to a minority financial and creative capacity, a trade limitation in Time Warner's eyes. There are also European Community initiatives to promote the EC audiovisual industry and cultural uniqueness of member states as well as the development and standardization of hardware such as HDTV. While Koreans are chastized for putting live snakes in cinemas showing US-made films, and Brazil and Egypt are noted for developing policies promoting homemade cultural production, from the statements of Time Warner and other corporations it is evident that essentially they see Europe as the problem, not the Third World. The former presents an already well-developed media market with a substantial population possessing considerable disposable income, a market to which US-based firms want ready access. Thus a closer examination of corporate 'globalization' strategies reveals highly preferred locales and areas of acute uninterest, depending on the already existing level of insertion of the populations within global capitalism.

The Third World is problematic to transnationals mainly because of its video piracy, an ingeniously literal understanding of the 'free' flow concept. Yet while this means lost revenues to multinationals, such piracy often affects embryonic industries at home, and thus undermines alternative national cultural production. It is apparent that the still limited and unregulated media markets of the Third World are not especially attractive to transnational culture brokers, which perhaps ironically gives Third World media systems a chance to produce for themselves and escape the Western cultural net, a *force majeure* for delinking.

Media localization: the newest argument

At the same time as these dynamics of globalization have been established, an opposing tendency is concurrently at work, as a consequence of, and often in reaction to, the former; that is the dynamic of localized production and the indigenization of cultural products already referred to above. The evidence about such trends is patchy and somewhat contradictory. Varis in his two studies of television flows in 1973 and 1984 concluded that few national systems had made major transitions to self-reliance in television programming. Increasing counter-evidence and counter-argument to the few 'positive' cases is being advanced. At a summer 1990 meeting of communication researchers in Brazil, Latin American researchers argued that despite the proliferation of media, television programming has become more North American; that 99 percent of the films shown on Brazilian television are American, and that cheap packages of old movies and TV shows are 'dumped' and thus flood the Latin American media scene (Osava 1990). Oliveira argues that Brazilian homemade television is even more commercial than American programming with 'merchandising' of products a central part of telenovela content, encouraging a consumerist way of life of which the United States is the most advanced example (Oliveira 1990). The same can be said of Peruvian media. India's film industry is being severely challenged by the spread of VCRs and video piracy, the importation of Western movies and the closure of cinemas as running costs rise and audiences dwindle (Mohan 1990). Cross-fertilization between Western cinema and television – predominantly American and British – with the popular Indian cinema is creating more 'hybrid' cultural forms, like a new film genre wryly described as the 'curry eastern' (Jain 1990).

Evidence suggests that when a choice is available, domestic production is preferred over imported, as telenovelas garner larger audiences than imported American soaps not only in Brazil but elsewhere in Latin America (Antola and Rogers 1984). But in such a process fears of hybridization and creolization exist, that the 'authenticity' of a culture is damaged and undermined in its contact with Western culture industries and its adoption of genres foreign to domestic cultural tradition. Some counter that the Latin telenovela is a truly indigenous and independent genre (Straubhaar 1981), building on internal cultural forms and breaking with the mimicry of Western genre that Tunstall forewarned. But Oliveira argues that this 'indigenization' of media often seems to enhance not diversity but domination by corporate concerns. Tunstall in *The Media are American* (1977) pointed out that the importation of media systems to the Third World included not only media hardware but also Western forms and genres, which he suggested would lead to precisely such 'hybrid' concoctions. But we must ask what is this pristine image of culture that lurks behind this argument? Human history is a history of cultural contact, influence and recombination, as is in evidence in language, music, visual arts, philosophical systems; perhaps media flows merely reinforce our mongrel statuses.

More to the point, evidence suggests that this 'newer' model of cultural indigenization may have been severely overstated and certainly presented in a far too naive manner. Much of this so-called indigenous production is created by large corporations, and deeply infused with consumption values, one of the basic critiques of the 'cultural imperialism' perspective. Another point of direct relevance to the 'localism' claim is that the level of this media production is at the level of the nation, either through state-supported or national corporate networks. Thus in such arguments the 'local' is really the 'national', while the truly local (sub-cultural, grass-roots, etc.) is ignored. This 'national' culture may privilege urban life styles over rural, may barely represent minority languages and tastes, even disallowing such diversity in the name of 'national unity'; it may produce mediated culture within a narrowly defined ideological framework that fits the politics of the regime of the day. The case of Iran suggests that tradition required defending at the moment that it was already challenged, so Islam as 'cultural identity' was constructed to oppose the Shah and the influx of foreign cultural values and products, only to be used after the revolution as an ideological weapon against all political opponents (Sreberny-Mohammadi 1991). National agendas are not coincidental with truly 'local' agendas, and real concerns arise as to whether 'national' media cultures adequately represent ethnic, religious, political and other kinds of diversity. In international relations, the 'national' level may be local *vis-à-vis* the global level, but in domestic relations, the 'national' is itself a site of struggle, with a variety of 'local' identities and voices in contention.

Cultural products in the global economy

The *new revisionism* also seems to have exaggerated the size/amount of this 'localized' production, which is perhaps of financial significance for national economies in the Third World, but is barely yet reflected in international statistics. There are immense difficulties involved in cross-national calculations and comparisons of media, information and cultural production and flow statistics. UNESCO has made a major effort to compile international data in *World Communication Report* published in 1989. Taking this information for the moment at face value, it provides important indicators of the extent of the changes the 'global pluralists' suggest. For example, information on 'total turnover for information and communication' for selected major information and communications groupings which includes equipment, services, and cultural products, clearly shows the continuing dominance of US and Japanese firms (see table 20.3).

These comprise 67 per cent of the top 25 companies, 66 per cent of the top 50 companies, and 67 per cent of the top 100 companies; European firms, by contrast, comprise 28 per cent of the top 25, and 26 per cent of the top 50 (with Canada the only other nation included), and 26 per cent of the top 100 companies. Other commonwealth countries begin to appear in the second fifty, while Korean and Brazilian companies appear at positions 83, 91 and 94. Of 304 organizations listed by UNESCO in a ranked table of major information and communication groupings, Globo placed 301. Thus the exemplar of Rede Globo and Brazilian cultural production as a counter to 'cultural imperialism' as a net exporter of cultural products is cut to size. Simply summarized, the US, Japan and Western Europe dominate in this agglomerate category.

If hardware and software areas are parcelled out, does the picture look any different? Not significantly. The table for 'total media turnover' for major information and communication groupings provides a remarkably similar picture to the above.

Half of the first 25 companies, of the first 50, and of the total of 78 companies for which statistics are presented, are US companies (see table 20.2). No Third World

Table 20.3 Selected major information and communication groupings: total turnover for information

Group	Country	Ranking-information and communication	Information and communication sales	Total sales
IBM	USA	1	54,217	54,217
NTT	Japan	2	40,926	40,926
ATT	USA	3	37,458	33,598
Matsushita	Japan	4	24,683	34,832
Deutsche Bundespost	Germany, Fed. Rep. of	5	20,185	28,960
NEC	Japan	6	19,622	19,622
Philips	Netherlands	7	19,253	26,023
British Telecom	UK	8	17,344	17,344
France Telecom	France	9	16,650	16,650
Toshiba	Japan	10	16,106	17,824
Lucky Gold Star	Korea, Rep. of	83	2,791	11,474
CBS	USA	84	2,762	2,762
TRW	USA	85	2,721	6,821
Apple	USA	86	2,661	2,661
ARD	Germany, Fed. Rep. of	87	2,614	2,614
US Sprint	USA	88	2,592	2,592
TDK	Japan	89	2,586	2,586
Toppan Printing	Japan	90	2,584	3,800
Samsung	Korea, Rep. of	91	2,581	14,193
NHK	Japan	92	2,541	2,541
Ford Motor	USA	93	2,500	71,643
IBL	UK	300	501	501
Globo	Brazil	301	500	500
Nippon Telecommunication Construction	Japan	302	500	500
Talt	USA	303	500	500
JTAS (Jydske Telefon)	Denmark	304	500	500

Groups 11–82 and 94–299 have not been included in this table.
Source: © UNESCO.

media corporation penetrates this 'top 78'. Now, of course, such figures represent the total dollar value of communications output, and say nothing specific about *export* dollar values, but they do dampen the optimistic hailing of major Third World cultural producers. While the map of global cultural flows is more complex in 1990, it is not as yet fundamentally realigned. But what about the question of 'effects'?

Global Media Effects?

Media effects is one of the most disputed areas of domestic media research, so there is no reason to expect any greater unanimity about effects at the international level. The 'cultural imperialism' thesis did tend to suggest a 'hypodermic needle' model of international effects, 'American' values being injected into Third World hearts and minds. Recent work, building on reception theory and models of the active audience, is giving a more nuanced view of international effects as mediated by pre-existing cultural frameworks and interpretative schema. Thus, despite their book's title (*The Export of Meaning*) Liebes and Katz (1990) argue that meaning is not exported *in* Western television programming but created *by* different cultural sectors of the audience in relation to their already-formed cultural attitudes and political perceptions. Others (Beltran, Oliveira) argue that it is not so much national American values that are exported but rather more generalized capitalist consumption values (which, of course, America best epitomizes) reinforced by advertising and prevailing development orientations. For them, globalization portends homogenization which, while useful for milk, produces a culture that tastes bland and is not even good for you!

What is often omitted from discussions on effects are the deeper shifts in cultural orientations and patterns of sociability, in modes of perception and information-processing, that the advent of media create everywhere, albeit in different forms relative to the pre-existing local culture; that is to say it is the very 'fact of television', as Cavell (1982) calls it, in our social lives, not so much its content, that is most often overlooked.

The arrival of media in Third World settings is finally being examined by anthropologists (although there is never an index listing for 'media' or 'television' in a cultural anthropology textbook, despite the fact that most Third World societies are now mediated in some way) and communications researchers. Ethnographic studies are beginning to show the rich play between the pre-existing culture and the new quasi-international culture and the shifts in social relations that the latter may foster. In an ethnographic study conducted in various sites across Brazil, Kottak (1990) explored how television alters patterns of sociability, usage of time, creates conflicts within the family and alters the gender balance, themes also explored in the comparative work on family use of television compiled by Lull (1988). Kottak suggests the need to investigate media impact over time, finding in Brazil an early mesmerization with the television set with a later development of selectivity and critical distance, negative attitudes toward television increasing with higher income and years of exposure.

Other ethnographic work suggests the slippery boundaries of the 'global' and 'local'. Abu-Lughod (1990) has studied the impact of what she calls 'technologies of public culture' on the Awlad 'Ali, the Western Desert Bedouin in Egypt. Although these bedouin have been quite marginal to mainstream Egyptian culture, they were by no means culturally or politically untouched before these technologies arrived; indeed, they often made their money from selling postwar scrap metal and from smuggling goods between pre-Qaddafi Libya and Egypt. Abu-Lughod examines the impact of tape-players, radios and television on Awlad 'Ali life, saying that their use does not eliminate sociability but in fact brings people together for long periods of time. Such use does realign social relationships, mixing the sexes and tempering age differences at home, while video shows in local cafes kept young men away from the home and gave them greater exposure to media. In line with reception theory, she argues too that these technologies do not destroy distinctive cultures because 'it is not just that people themselves seem to embrace the technologies and actively use them for their own purposes, but that they select, incorporate and redeploy what comes their way' (ibid.: 8), although she notes that so far at least the amount of truly *foreign* programming available is extremely limited. If anything, new technologies such as cassettes have helped to revitalize Bedouin identity as distinct from Egyptian culture through recordings of poetry and song. The urban middle-class Egyptian lifestyles revealed on soap operas present a different set of options to Bedouin women, especially the possibility of marrying for love and living independent of the extended family, so that the dominant Egyptian mediated culture is used as a language of resistance against the authority of tribal elders. Also embedded in such programming are consumer values, for electronic durables as well as products for a newly sexualized femininity, drawing the Bedouin further into the Egyptian political economy. Yet at the same time, in a contradictory manner, Egyptian radio and television carries more transnational messages about Islam, which is gaining in popularity, and which provides an antidote both to capitalist urban Egyptian values as well as the local Bedouin identity (ibid.: 11)

Hannah Davis (1990) describes life in a small Moroccan agricultural town of 50,000 people and notes how 'symbols from different worlds overlap: a picture of the king of Morocco hangs next to a poster of the Beatles. The sounds of a religious festival outside...mingle with the televised cheering of soccer fans...in the morning we watch a holy man curing a boy, then stop off at the fair where we see a woman doing motorcycle stunts; in the evening we watch an Indian fairy tale or a Brazilian soap opera or an Egyptian romance' (ibid.: 13). She remarks 'it is not the contrast between the elements that is striking; it is the lack of contrast, the clever and taken-for-granted integration' (ibid.: 12). As in much of the Middle East (the world?!) public space is male space, and thus it is the women who gather round the television and VCR at night, watching Egyptian, Indian and 'French' – here the generic term used for Western – films. Egyptian films were romances that reduced the women to tears, while the Western films elicited 'gasps of suprise, horrified hiding of the eyes, fascination or prurience', with American sexual shamelessness being both admired and feared, imitated and denigrated. The transcultural mix of symbols is apparent when one young girl organizes a traditional religious feast yet defiantly appears wearing a denim skirt and earrings; thus, such symbols may be used in personal struggles to 'define, test or transform the boundaries' of local lives (ibid.: 17).

Such examples reveal the complex (re)negotiation of identity(ies) *vis-à-vis* the 'dominant' and the 'foreign' cultures, both of which shift in focus depending on the specific locale of the actor. The above examples pose a number of different pairs of relations in which the site of the 'local' and the image of the 'global' are differently defined: rural/urban; Bedouin/Egyptian; Moroccan/Egyptian; Bedouin/ French; Moroccan/American and so forth. This work reveals again the post-modern 'bricolage' of assorted cultural icons from different locations and time periods which circulate inside the non-industrialized world, yet invites no simple reading of the effects of these encounters. Iran is again a useful example of the way in which cultural icons can become deeply invested with one set of ideo-logical connotations in one moment of political struggle, and invested with com-pletely the opposite connotations at a subsequent but differently defined political moment. Thus religious language, traditional symbolism and mythology were popularly (re-)adopted as part of the revolutionary struggle against the Shah, but with the new repression of the Islamic Republic a popular cultural underground began to produce hard liquor and circulate Western videos as part of a new resistance (Sreberny-Mohammadi forthcoming). Thus a 'sign' of resistance – the veil, for example – at one point in time can become a 'sign' of oppression at another. The details of such anthropological/ethnographic work extend the 'localist' focus, and show the complexity and range of reactions to and uses of contemporary global cultural encounters. They warn us against general-ized assumptions about media/cultural effects, that the 'foreign' may emanate from the urban capital, a Western country other than the US and perhaps even from a Third World media producer of very different cultural background but whose depictions of social life in the process of development can reverberate across the South.

One other basic shift that the global flow of mediated products and the establish-ment of culture industries in the Third World creates, is that documented by Horkheimer and Adorno toward consumption of mass-produced culture. That is culture, from being local lived experience becomes media product, with the implicit danger that what is not reflected on television no longer has cultural worth. One last neglected 'effect' is important to consider. It has been argued that media develop-ment in the West has moved through a set of 'stages' during which one form of communication and its preferred modality of discourse has been dominant. These have been described by Ong as orality, chirography/typography and the period of the dominance of electronic media which he labels 'secondary orality'. Yet in the Third World there is evidence that the middle stage, at least as measured by mass literacy and circulation of printed materials, may be 'jumped', with societies moving directly from a predominantly oral culture directly into the 'secondary orality' of electronic media. We have paid little attention to this new and different kind of cultural formation. The 'communications and development' model tended to col-lapse history, suggesting the development of newspapers, cinemas, radio and televi-sion all at once, while the 'cultural imperialism' model has given most attention to electronic media. Yet if print is connected to the development of rational logical thinking (Ong), to the development of modern ideologies not linked to church or aristocracy (Gouldner), and the growth of a public sphere, open debate and active citizenry (Habermas), then the limited if non-existent development of this mode of communication in developing countries has profound political and social consequences which have barely been acknowledged. Analysis of the uses of differ-ent media by class and gender in Third World societies and the power relations which develop is another rather ignored area of research (Sreberny-Mohammadi 1991).

Conclusion

If nothing else, the chapter has shown the complexity of the global contemporary media/culture spectrum at the start of the twenty-first century, and the range of theoretical constructs that have been used to explain and base policy on the international role of media, particularly in the 'Third World'. The 'mood' of contemporary analysis can be quite varied. One position is that of the happy postmodernist who sees that many kinds of cultural texts circulate internationally and that people adopt them playfully and readily integrate them in creative ways into their own lives, and that cultural bricolage is the prevailing experience as we enter the twenty-first century. Another is the melancholy political economist who sees the all-pervasive reach of the multinationals and wonders how long distinctive cultures can outlast the onslaught of the Western culture industries. Somewhere in between lies the cautiously optimistic fourth-worlder who sees in the spread of media the possibilities for revitalization of local identities (ethnic, religious, class, etc) and their use as tools of political mobilization *vis-à-vis* both national and global forces. But we have also seen the slippery nature of the linguistic terms used in international communications analysis: that 'global' rarely means 'universal' and often implies only the actors of the North; that 'local' is often really 'national' which can be oppressive of the 'local'; that 'indigenous' culture is often already 'contaminated' through older cultural contacts and exists as a political claim rather than a clean analytic construct. The bi-polar model suggests either imbalance/domination, the political-economy perspective, or balance, the 'global pluralist' perspective, whereas the real world reveals far greater complexity.

Cultural boundaries are not etched in stone but have slippery divisions dependent on the self-adopted labels of groups. What seems clear is that, far from an end to history, or the loss of the subject, identity politics and cultural preservation are going to be amongst the hottest issues of the next century that will be fought out internationally and intranationally, with profound political and economic consequences. The apparent triumph of late capitalism in 1989–90 and the demise of the so-called second world of state socialism, suggest that ideological politics in the classic sense is going to be less important than the revival of identity politics in the future. Yet at the same time as the demise of a single master narrative of global progress is trumpeted in some quarters, in others the old indicators of a single path to 'development' are still utilized, and even adopted with greater eagerness by Third World societies yearning for 'progress'. It is likely that in the next decade we shall see a revival of intense debate about development, and the unresolved role of culture within that process, neo-Lernerian arguments for the positive role of media systems as part of national development encountering arguments for more thorough-going Third World economic disassociation and delinking from the global capitalist economy (Amin 1990), as well as fourth world/indigenist culture arguments for the maintenance of local identities (Verhelst 1990). These levels may themselves be in conflict, for a strong 'national' position taken in relation to international economic and cultural forces may lead to repression of 'local' forces and voices in relation to that 'national' level. Inter-state relations are not coterminous with inter-cultural relations, and the political and conceptual agenda of the twenty-first century is going to be how to cope with these various levels of actors and processes. It is here that conceptual leakage in the global/local framework of analysis is most evident, highlighted by the particularly complex set of issues raised by mediated cultural flows which poignantly reveal in their electronic presence the absence or porousness of boundaries. In the bipolar model it is the 'national' level of analysis that becomes invisible. Yet it is national policy-making that helps define a cultural identity, provides the regulatory framework for media organizations – the state providing direct funding and control in many Third World nations – and cultural trade policy, as well as defining the domestic public sphere and the extent to which diverse voices will or will not be heard. As Giddens himself underscores in much of his work, nation-states are the key political systems of the modern world, controlling the structures – legal, administrative, financial, military, surveillance, and informational – in which we all live and which are now involved in transnational dynamics – a capitalist world economy, the world military order, systems of inter-governmental organizations, transnational political movements, etc. – which both press in on and explode the meaning of national boundaries (Giddens 1985). Indeed, as Giddens argues, the worldwide system of nation-states exists in constant tension with the global capitalist economy.

It seems that we require a third term, between the two terms of 'global' and 'local', that recognizes the separate level of 'state' structures and 'national policy-making' which is still the crucial level of political, economic and cultural decision-making. So much of current political cultural struggle centres precisely on (the memories of) the 'imagined communities' of nations and their claims to be 'states' (Anderson 1983). At issue in current political struggles – in the Soviet Union, Eastern Europe, the Middle East, Africa – is whether 'nations' do/should constitute homogenous cultural/ethnic bases or be political structures which allow heterogeneity and civic rights to flourish. While the latter was the basis for modern nation-states (Hobsbaum 1990) we increasingly hear demands for the former, raising questions about the appropriate relation between cultural rights and national boundaries, and whether narrowly conceived ethnic states are really progressive. A bi-polar model such as globalization and localization too readily implies either dominance or balance. A triangular model, with the 'national' reinserted, reflects the multiple and deeper tensions and contradictions that constitute the present world order.

NOTE

1   UNESCO suggests that 39 countries and territories had not yet introduced a television service by 1988: Africa: Botswana, Cameroon, Cape Verde, Central African Republic, Chad, Comoros, Gambia, Guinea-Bissau, Malawi, Rwanda, St Helena, Sao Tome and Principe, Western Sahara; North America: Anguila, Belize, Caymen Islands, Dominica, Saint Vincent and the Grenadines, Turks and Calcos Islands; South America: Malvinas, Guyana; Asia: Bhutan, East Timor; Europe: Holy See, Liechtenstein, San Marino; Oceania: Cook Islands; Fiji, Kiribati, Nauru, Niue, Norfolk Islands, Papua New Guinea, Samoa, Solomon Islands; Tonga, Tuvalu, Vanuatu.

REFERENCES

Abu-Lughod, Lila, 1990: 'Bedouins, Cassettes and Technologies of Public Culture', *Middle East Report*, 159, 4, 7–12.

Alvarado, Manuel (ed.), 1988: *Video World-Wide: An International Study*, London/Paris: Unesco/John Libbey.

Amin, Samir, 1990: *Delinking*. New York: Monthly Review Press.

Anderson, Benedict, 1983: *Imagined Communities*. London: Verso.

Antola, L. and E. M. Rogers, 1984: 'Television Flows in Latin America', *Communication Research*, 11, 2, 183–202.

Appadurai, Arjun, 1990: 'Disjuncture and Difference in the Global Cultural Economy', *Public Culture*. 2, 2, 1–24.

Bagdikian, Ben, 1990: 'Lords of the Global Village', *The Nation*, 248, 23, 805–20.

Binford, Mira Reym, 1988: 'Innovation and Imitation in the Indian Cinema', in W. Dissanayeke (ed.), *Cinema and Cultural Identity*. Maryland: University Press of America.

Boyd, Douglas, 1984: 'The Janus Effect? Imported Television Entertainment Programming in Developing Countries', *Critical Studies in Mass Communication*, 1, 379–91.

Boyd, D., J. D. Straubhaar and J. A. Lent (eds), 1989: *Videocassette Recorders in The Third World*. London: Longman.

Boyd-Barrett, Oliver, 1977: 'Media Imperialism: Toward an International Framework for the Analysis of Media Systems', in J. Curran, M. Gurevitch and J. Woollacott, (eds), *Mass Communication and Society*. London: Edward Arnold.

Cavell, Stanley, 1982: 'The Fact of Television', *Daedalus*, III, 4, 75–96.

Chatterji, P. C., 1989: 'The Ramayana TV Serial and Indian Secularism', *InterMedia*, 17, 5, 32–4.

Davis, Hannah, 1990: 'American Magic in a Moroccan Town', *Middle East Report*, 159: 19, 4, 12–18.

Dissanayeke, Wimal, 1988: 'Cultural Identity and Asian Cinema', in W. Dissanayake (ed.), *Cinema and Cultural Identity*. Maryland: University Press of America.

Fabrikant, Geraldine, 'Studios look to Foreign Markets', *New York Times*, March 7, 1990, Section D1.

Fiske, John, 1987: *Television Culture*. New York: Methuen.

Galtung, J. and Ruge, M., 1965: 'The Structure of Foreign News', *Journal of Peace Research*, 1, 64–90.

Giddens, Anthony 1985: *The Nation-State and Violence*. Cambridge: Polity Press.

—— 1990: *The Consequences of Modernity*. Stanford, CA: Stanford University Press.

Golding, Peter, 1977: 'Media Professionalism in the Third World: The Transfer of an Ideology', in J. Curran, M. Gurevitch and J. Woollacott (eds), *Mass Communication and Society*. London: Edward Arnold.

Guback, Thomas and Tapio Varis, 1982: *Transnational Communication and Cultural Industries*. (Reports and Papers on Mass Communication No. 92) Paris: UNESCO.

Gunder-Frank, André, 1964: 'The Development of Underdevelopment' in *Capitalism and Underdevelopment in Latin America*. New York: Monthly Review Press.

Hamelink, Cees, 1983a: *Finance and Information*, New Jersey: Ablex.

—— 1983b: *Cultural Autonomy in Global Communications*. New York: Longman.

Harvey, David, 1989: *The Condition of Postmodernity*, Oxford: Blackwell Publishers.

Hobsbaum, Eric, 1990: *Nations and Nationalism since 1780*. Cambridge: Cambridge University Press.

Iyer, Pico, 1989: *Video Nights in Kathmandu*. New York: Vintage Press.

Jain, Madhu, 1990: 'The Curry Eastern Takeaway', *Public Culture* 2, 2.

Jameson, Frederic, 1984: 'Postmodernism, or the cultural logic of late capitalism', *New Left Review*, 146, 53–92.

Katz, E. and Wedell, G., 1977: *Broadcasting in the Third World*. Cambridge, MA: Harvard University Press.

Kottak, Conrad Phillip, 1990: *Prime-Time Society: An Anthropological Analysis of Television and Culture*. Belmont, CA: Wadsworth.

Lerner, Daniel, 1958: *The Passing of Traditional Society*. New York: Free Press.

Liebes, T. and E. Katz, 1990: *The Export of Meaning*. Oxford: Oxford University Press.

Lull, James (ed.), 1988: *World Families Watch Television*. Thousand Oaks, CA: Sage Publications.

McLuhan, Marshall, 1964: *Understanding Media*. London: Routledge Kegan Paul.

McNeely, Connie and Yasemin Muhoglu Soysal, 1989: 'International Flows of Television Programming: A Revisionist Research Orientation', *Public Culture*, 2, 1: 136–45.

Mandel, Ernest, 1975: *Late Capitalism*. London: NLB.

Mattelart, Armand, 1979: *Multinational Corporations and the Control of Culture*. England: Harvester Press and New Jersey: Humanities Press.

Minh-ha, Trinh, 1987: 'Of Other Peoples: Beyond the 'Salvage' Paradigm', in Hal Foster (ed.), *Discussions in Contemporary Culture Number One*. Seattle: Bay Press.

Mohan, Anjoo, 1990: 'Cinema Fall Prey to Video Pirates', *Development Forum*, Sept.–Oct.

NTIA (National Telecommunications and Information Administration), US Department of Commerce, 1990: *Comprehensive Study of the Globalization of Mass Media Firms*. February.

Oliveira, Omar Souki, 1990a: 'The Three-Step Flow of Cultural Imperialism: A Study of Brazilian Elites'. Paper presented at ICA Conference, Dublin, Ireland.

——June 1990b: 'Brazilian Soaps Outshine Hollywood: Is Cultural Imperialism Fading Away?' Paper presented at ICA Conference, Dublin, Ireland.

Osava Mario, 1990: 'Foreign Domination of TV Perplexes Latin Americans', *Development Forum*, May–June.

Ouderkirk, Cathleen, 1989: 'Modern-day Mayans', *World Monitor*, 2, 7.

Schiller, Herbert, 1976: *Communication and Cultural Domination*. White Plains, NY: International Arts and Sciences Press.

Schramm, Wilbur, 1964: *Mass Media and National Development*. Stanford, CA: Stanford University Press.

Sony, USA, 1990: *Comments in Response to Notice of Inquiry on Globalization of Mass Media Firms*, NTIA/OPAD.

Sreberny-Mohammadi, Annabelle, 1991: 'Media Integration in the Third World: An Ongian Look at Iran', in B. Gronbeck, T. Farell and P. Soukup (eds), *Media, Consciousness and Culture*, Thousand Oaks, CA: Sage Publications.

——forthcoming: 'The Many Faces of Cultural Imperialism', in P. Golding, P. Lewis and N. Jayaweera (eds), *Beyond Cultural Imperialism: The New World Information Order Debate in Context*, London: Sage Publications.

Sreberny-Mohammadi, A. and A. Mohammadi, 1991: 'Hegemony and Resistance: Cultural Politics in the Islamic Republic of Iran', *Quarterly Review of Film and Video* (special issue on World Television), 12, 4, 33–59.

Straubhaar, Joseph D., 1981: 'Estimating the Impact of Imported versus National Television Programming in Brazil', in S. Thomas (ed.), *Studies in Communication and Technology*, vol. 1, New Jersey: Ablex.

Time Warner Inc., 1990: *Comprehensive Study of the Globalization of Mass Media Firms*, Response to National Telecommunications and Information Administration Request for Comments, NTIA/OPAD.

Tracey, Michael, 1988: 'Popular Culture and the Economics of Global Television', *Intermedia*, 16, 2.

Tunstall, Jeremy, 1977: *The Media are American*. London: Constable.

UNESCO, 1989: *World Communication Report*. Paris: UNESCO.

Varis, Tapio, 'The International Flow of Television Programs', *Journal of Communication*, winter 1984: 143–52.

Verhelst, Thierry, 1990: *No Life Without Roots: Culture and Development*. London: Zed Books.

21

Media and Cultural Politics in Nicaragua, 1920–1956

David E. Whisnant

The Cultural Agenda of the First Somoza Reign: 1936–1956

Broadcast media: spreading the good gospel of American goods

Controlling the radio and television broadcasting industry in Nicaragua was far more crucial to Anastasio Somoza García's political project, than the tiny National Museum (or any specifically cultural institution or program) could possibly be. As it turned out, his drive to control it dovetailed well with both the expansionist aspirations of the nascent US broadcasting industry and the strategy of containment and manipulation being pursued by the US government in Central America.

Somoza's interest was captured first by the radio network built by the US Marine Corps and the National Guard (created by the United States in May 1927).[1] Marine Corps Captain James Smith began training the Guard's first telegraphers in June 1929, using Westinghouse equipment, and eighteen days later they were sent into the field with government troops fighting Sandino's army. During the next two years, technicians created a radio network (*Radio Nacional*) linking Guard installations. In 1931 radio operators who were veterans of the campaign against Sandino returned to form the Guard's Office of Communications (Hernández 1969). In December *Radio Nacional* began transcontinental service from a station located at Bonanza, an American-owned mining center (Millett 1977: 76).

By the time he became head of the Guard in January 1933, Somoza García had a firm sense of both the military necessity and the political potential of the new medium (Millett 1977: 92, 110–11, 132–5). Within a few months he created a formal radio school, headed by former Marine Lieutenant Hugh James Phillips. Phillips's students sat on wooden benches and shared scarce books and equipment during a spartan ten-month course. For political emphasis, Phillips displayed in his office a skull he said came from a person killed by Sandino's men, and a copy of Sandino's own order ordering Phillips's death if he were caught.

Somoza's strategy was to fuse the Marine Corps–National Guard system with Nicaragua's fledgling commercial radio stations, the antecedents of which came to

Nicaragua through the United Fruit Company, which had begun experimenting with radio communications among its Central American producing areas, shipping stations, and ships as early as 1904. By 1906 the company had constructed primitive stations on Nicaragua's east coast (Bluefields and Rama), and in 1911 had formed its Tropical Radio Telegraph Company subsidiary. Political and military developments thereafter (the Panama Canal, the Mexican Revolution, World War I) intensified the US government's interest in controlling the involvement of Central American states in commercial radio. In 1921 (after some years of trying) Tropical Radio Telegraph – by then linked to the new Radio Corporation of America trust – signed a contract to open commercial stations in Nicaragua (Managua, Bluefields, and Cabo Gracias a Dios), and opened the first one in 1925 (Hernández 1969: 96; McCreery 1993: 26–34). The 500-watt commerical station YNOP went on the air in February 1933 as *Radio BAYER*; *Radio Rubén Darío* and *The Voice of Nicaragua* followed within the next year or so.

By 1936 Somoza had fused what were by then the Guard's fifty radio stations with the new private ones to create *Radio GN y Nacional* (Radio National Guard and National) – in order, he said, that "the entire citizenry of our country may feel that they live and vibrate to a single high ideal marked by evolution toward progress, culture, and peace" (Hernández 1969: 49). In fact what the public was being offered was small doses of Latin American programming and large ones of the popular music of Bing Crosby and Tommy Dorsey, Hollywood film-star gossip, "Amos 'n Andy," and the like.[2] Clearly, radio was, as New York Congressman Emanuel Celler reminded President Roosevelt in 1937, "of intense utility and value to us for spreading the good gospel of American goods." Radio could be used, Celler added, "to cement our neighborly relations with South and Central American countries."[3]

Between 1933 and 1968, 135 radio stations were licensed in Nicaragua. The earliest ones were all in Managua, but by 1940 others were operating in Masaya, León, and Bluefields. Matagalpa (in the mountains) and Chinandega (near the northwestern border with Honduras) got stations in 1947 and 1953, but Estelí (in the far north) and Rivas (near the southern border) had none until the 1960s. Several stations were devoted explicitly to cultural programming: Diriamba's *La Voz de Diriangén* (YNDX, 1950) and *Radio Cultural* (YNRC, 1957), and Managua's *Radio Güegüense*.[4]

Commercial radio developed in Nicaragua, it is important to note, within the interwar climate of growing nationalist (and fascist) sentiment. Under the banner headline FASCIST REGIME IMPELS PROGRESS IN ITALY, Granada's *El Diario Nicaragüense* quoted from the *New York Times* Mussolini's taunt that "what we have done is nothing compared with what we are still going to do." During the early 1930s Nicaragua had its own European-style fascist *camisas azules* (blue shirts), trained by National Guard troops who praised the killing of Sandino and held rallies in support of Somoza's emerging power. Luis Alberto Cabrales, former director of the *Camisas Azules*, was appointed inspector of public instruction in 1933. Radio broadcasting schedules published in Managua's newspaper *La Noticia* in late 1934 included four hours of programming (in German and Spanish, via shortwave) from Germany, including an offering called "Why we have faith in our Führer." In the same spirit, Nicaragua's immigration law prohibited entry of any person who "propounds doctrines dangerous to the social welfare, morality or public order," anarchists and those who "teach the destruction of the regime of private property," as well as Chinese, Turks, Arabs, Syrians, Armenians, Negroes, gypsies, and "those individuals called 'coolies.'"[5]

Within such a climate Somoza moved swiftly to control broadcasting over the radio network his National Guard had established. After December 1935 all radio stations were subject to Executive Decree No. 284, based on the international radio broadcasting conventions of 1927 but also altered to serve explicitly political ends. Article 31 of Decree No. 284 allowed the government to prohibit any transmission or to interrupt any private telephone conversation or telegraphic communication "which may be dangerous to the security of the State ... to public order or to good custom." Article 47 specifically prohibited the transmission of "Marxist propaganda concerning the abolition of private property or militant atheism," or other propaganda that "might stimulate strikes having political ends." Nor did control wane with the passing of the years. When Lieutenant Phillips departed in 1943, after heading the National Guard radio school for ten years, Somoza appointed his nephew Captain Rodríguez Somoza as its new director. After Somoza's death in 1956, his sons continued the tradition: of the nine heads of the various operating sections of *Radio Nacional* in 1969, seven were uniformed National Guard officers; all ten of the higher-ranking officials were as well (cf. Walter 1993: 81–2). The National Director of Radio and Television was Lieutenant Colonel Armando Monge González (Hernández 1969: 14–15).

During its early days, Nicaragua's fledgling television industry was not controlled quite so tightly by the Somoza government as radio had been. To an even greater degree, however, it developed as an extension of North American media interests, commercial products, and cultural styles and values.

As early as 1934 the Radio Corporation of America informed its stockholders that "street scenes and studio performances have been satisfactorily transmitted and received by television, on an experimental and laboratory basis."[6] The foreign extension of the US television industry began in 1939 when RCA sold a transmitter to the USSR, but it was nearly twenty years until it reached Latin America (Wells 1972: 94). Emerging first in Mexico, Argentina, Brazil, and Venezuela in the early 1950s, television did not reach Nicaragua until the 1960s (Tunstall 1977: 175). As long as the US market was still not saturated, US commercial television networks were reluctant to invest heavily in Latin America, but by 1960 that market saturation was evident and investments grew rapidly. In the decade after 1955 the number of television stations in Latin America increased from 32 to 217 and the number of sets from 600,000 to 6.6 million. By 1972 there were nearly 17 million sets and close to 80 million viewers (Nordenstreng and Varis 1985: 13; Wells 1972: 174).[7]

Once it began, the merchandising of North American (primarily US) programming moved aggressively into Latin America. Prohibited by FCC regulations from exporting as freely as they would have preferred, US television networks collaborated with major film companies (not similarly restrained) to form such exporting entities as the Motion Picture Export Association of America (MPEA), Viacom International, and ABC Worldvision. Together with Screen Gems, MCA, and Twentieth Century-Fox, these merchandisers supplied the bulk of Latin American television fare: Screen Gems' *Flintstones* and *Father Knows Best*; MCA's *Leave It to Beaver*; Twentieth Century-Fox's *Peyton Place*; Viacom International's *Wild, Wild West* and *Perry Mason*; ABC's *Invaders*; and NBC's *Bonanza* (already by 1965 the network's top export, watched by 350 million viewers in sixty countries)

(Nordenstreng and Varis 1985: 32–3; Schiller 1969: 82). By 1965 US commercial television networks were selling $80 million worth of programs a year in Latin America (80 percent of all programs broadcast there) (Wells 1972: 120–1). Taken together, US television stations were broadcasting some 5 million hours of programming annually by 1972, less than 30 percent of it news or educational programs. Between 100,000 and 200,000 of those hours were being exported to other countries, approximately a third of them to Latin America. Some 26 percent of what Latin American viewers saw on television consisted of commerical advertising (Nordenstreng and Varis 1985: 15, 19, 32).

Managua's first television station (YNSA-TV, Channel 8) became operational in 1956. In 1960 ABC linked Nicaragua to its *Cadena Centroamericana* network, and thence to its larger Worldvision network by buying YNSA-TV. Agreements required the stations to accept whatever ABC offered in programs and advertising. By 1962 a second station (Televisión de Nicaragua) was on the air, and in the late 1960s ABC controlled four stations in Nicaragua. The number of sets in use grew rapidly: from about 6,000 in 1964 to 19,000 three years later, to 35,000 in 1970, and to 68,000 in 1975 when YNTCN (Telecadena Nicaragua, the last of the Somoza-era stations) went on the air. By the time the regime fell in 1979, there were 115,000 sets in the country (Frappier 1969: 1–7; Wells 1972: 102, 177).[8] During the Somoza regime's final days, big- league sports, game shows, soap operas, crime shows, and the newly popular PTL (Praise the Lord) Club of fundamentalist evangelist Jim Bakker were as accessible to Managua viewers as to those in any US city.[9]

Hence Nicaraguan media developed as they did during the Somoza period partly because of the powerful expansionist capacities of the US media industry (supported in many instances by official US foreign policy), but also because of the Somozas' cultural and political sycophancy, their own rapacious drive to reap the economic benefits of a rapidly expanding new technology, and their cynically perspicacious grasp of the media's political usefulness.

Repression and censorship

While the Somoza regime starved the National Museum through neglect and built a broadcast media system tailored to its own interests and those of North American corporations, it also engaged in direct repression and censorship against many writers and artists.

Concern about violation of citizens' rights had arisen as early as January 1933, immediately after Somoza became head of the National Guard, when some members of the National Assembly demanded an investigation of reported torture by the Guard. During the ensuing months President Sacasa repeatedly declared states of siege that limited constitutional freedoms. As the election of 1936 approached, the Guard took an increasingly active role in pro-Somoza rallies, imprisoning supporters of Sacasa. To offset criticism in *La Prensa*, Somoza started his own newspaper *Novedades* in 1936.[10]

Openly declaring his admiration for Mussolini, Somoza projected himself as a "strong *caudillo*" redeemer of Nicaragua, and moved to take over municipal governments. To the National Assembly in January 1937 he proclaimed that his government would prohibit "the expression of *ideas exóticas*." The constitution of

1939 made it illegal to "make statements contrary... to the fundamental institutions of the state," to the established social order, or "to public morality and proper behavior" (*la moral y las buenas costumbres*). It guaranteed freedom of the press, but provided for preventive detention and martial law. As World War II approached, a new Law for the Defense of Democracy prohibited the diffusion of "all ideologies and political and social systems contrary to the country's 'republican and democratic system' and against established social order." It led to the closing of the labor newspapers *La Verdad* and *Hoy* in 1941–2 (Booth 1985: 51–63; Walter 1987: 80–8, 98, 125, 166–95). As soon as Nicaragua entered the war, Somoza declared a state of siege that remained in effect for four years. Anti-Somoza demonstrations in mid-1944 led to the ironically named *Ley de libertad de emisión y difusión del pensamiento* (Law of freedom of broadcast and diffusion of thought) of September 1944, which gave the media free postage and tax exemption but prohibited propaganda to subvert public order, to call for civil disobedience, or to insult the fundamental institutions of the state (Walter 1987: 166, 184, 194–6, 229–42).

The end of the war brought little relaxation in the repression. The National Guard became larger rather than smaller – from about 3,600 in 1946 to nearly 4,400 in 1956, and many Guard members became wealthy through working in Somoza family businesses and participating in the many forms of graft and corruption in which the Guard was regularly involved (Booth 1985: 54–7; Walter 1993: 214–15).[11] The university student newspaper *El Universitario* was harassed continuously by the Guard throughout its short life until it was closed down early in 1947. A new law passed in September 1953 made it a crime for anyone to criticize established authorities or friendly foreign governments, or for anyone belonging to a "political party with international connections" to own a printing shop or newspaper. An executive decree of February 1955 prohibited the circulation of any printed "communist propaganda," and reporters and publishers of newspapers were regularly paid off to hew the regime's line (Walter 1987: 244, 353, 372).

One of the first Nicaraguan writers to feel the repression was Manolo Cuadra (1907–57), who had worked as a journalist in Managua before fighting with Somoza's troops against Sandino. He soon became disaffected, however, and was jailed in León's infamous *La Veintiuno* prison for participating in an uprising in the army against Somoza. Subsequently accused of being a communist, he was confined for ten months to Little Corn Island off the Atlantic coast. He was also jailed for political activity in Managua's *La Aviación* prison in 1943 and on the island of Ometepe four years later (Cuadra 1982: 11, 171).[12]

Following the assassination attempt against Somoza García in April 1954, artists, writers, and intellectuals felt increased pressures to conform or keep silent. Poet Ernesto Mejía Sánchez, rumored to be the "intellectual author" of the 1954 plot, had to leave the country for ten years after Somoza was assassinated in 1956. Father Ernesto Cardenal – a participant in the 1954 plot – found all of his books prohibited in Nicaragua, as were those of virtually any Russian writer (even Tolstoy) and any books by or about Fidel Castro or Che Guevara (White 1986: 38–9, 61). Cardenal's mail was also intercepted and opened, and he was harassed by customs officials when he returned to Nicaragua from travels abroad (experiences recounted in his poem "La Llegada") (Cardenal 1983b: 240–1; Zwerling and Martin 1985: 45; Borgeson 1977: 36, 77).

Cultural Intervention from the North

Both the system of cultural neglect, manipulation, censorship, repression, and trans-formation put into place during the early decades of the Somoza dynasty's rule and subsequent culturally destructive cotton-boom economic development were prob-lematic to the people of Tonalá and scores of other communities across Nicaragua. That was so in the first instance because such transformations were directly inimical to non-elite ways of life. But those transformations were also exacerbated by the increasing cultural intervention of US culture through print and broadcast media, a flood of consumer products, and what in diplomatic parlance was called "cultural exchange." Although the US Marines left Nicaragua in January 1933 and Managua celebrated its own national culture by raising a monument to poet Rubén Darío in September, the presence and influence of US culture continued to increase for the next forty-six years, both because US corporations and the US government urged it, and because of the Somozas' sycophantic attraction to US cultural values.

Consumer culture

North American products, styles, values, and institutions were already abundantly in evidence to travelers who sailed up the San Juan River in the 1850s. By the early 1920s the tide was in full swell. León's *El Centroamericano* of 1922 carried only a few advertisements for US products (Sloan's liniment, Bayer aspirin, and Dewitt's liver pills), but advertisements in other newspapers in succeeding years offered a cornucopia of such products: Arrow shirts and Stetson hats, Johnnie Walker and Black Cat whiskey, Fisk tires, General Electric and Westinghouse electrical appli-ances, Vick's Vaporub and Mentholatum, Gillette razors, Quaker Oats (plate 21.2) and Royal baking powder, Flit insect spray, Victrolas and Atwater-Kent radios, Ford and Nash automobiles, Camel cigarettes, and Waterman pens. "You will dance as you have never danced before," promised an ad for Victrolas in 1926 (plate 21.1); phonograph records reorganized social life ("It is much more comfortable and agreeable to dance at home," said a Victrola ad in a Managua daily).[13] A later Victrola advertisement that offered the "divine art...of the music of the whole world" was illustrated with images of Latin instrumentalists and dancers, but the text referred solely to European performers. By contrast, virtually no analogous products from European countries were to be seen. Writing in the late 1930s, Gratus Halftermeyer spoke proudly of Managua's "beautiful Roosevelt Avenue, where one encounters the Executive Power, the National Bank and the Bank of London, the best department stores...and elegant buildings....This avenue is today the Wall Street of Nicaragua." By 1940 nearly 60 percent of Nicaragua's imports came from the United States (Halftermeyer [1946?]: 117; *Nicaragua, Guía general ilustrada* 1940: 15). Both the products themselves and the advertising that accompanied them were freighted with cultural messages – frequently with subliminal political messages.

With the development of the Pan American highway and direct air links to the United States, the flood of beguiling US products, styles, and values was further reinforced by tourist traffic in both directions. Pan American Airways made its first Key West-to-Havana flight in 1927 and by 1929 was flying to Puerto Rico with intermediate stops in all the Central American capitals.[14] A 1941 edition of the

Plate 21.1 Victrola advertisement. "You will dance as never before...to the new Victrola.... It is as if you had the most famous orchestras in the world at your disposal." From *El Diario Nicaragüense*, July 9, 1926.

airline's Spanish-language public relations magazine (*Caminos del Aire*) was dedicated to Somoza, whom it called a "heroic champion of peace and pure idealist, whose goals...have been to channel...Nicaragua along the paths of progress." By the late 1940s Costa Rican TACA Airlines was offering direct flights to New Orleans and Miami, and $149 roundtrips to Mexico City. Pan Am countered with four flights daily to Guatemala. The Pan American highway, first proposed during the 1920s and developed during the 1930s and 1940s, finally opened completely in 1948.[15]

It was not merely the taste-shaping presence of US products on the market in Nicaragua that had such a cultural impact, however, but the fact that their use inevitably affected long-established cultural practices and values. The availability of patent medicines changed both notions of health (particularly of women's health) and methods for treatment; electrical appliances reorganized domestic design, decoration, and daily routines; baby formula changed both the relationship between mother and child and other traditional aspects of child care. Other advertisements employed remarkably explicit appeals to gender stereotypes to enhance the appeal of products. A series for Bayer's Cafiaspirina in the early 1920s featured one-word large-type imperatives illustrated with images of forceful Aryan-looking males: a sword-wielding gladiator standing triumphantly with one foot on his dead opponent (*MATALO!* [kill him!]) (plate 21.3); a nearly nude, muscular male breaking through a barrier of stone letters (*DESTRUYA!* [destroy!]); and a burly sculptor gazing (hammer and chisel resolutely in hand) at a sculpture of a nude female who is leaning on a rather insistently phallic-looking support (*CREA!* [create!]). A parallel series drew upon explicit and subliminal images of women: three flaxen-haired and begowned maidens stretched upon the rocks in a mountain pass, pouring *La Fuente Primitiva* (the primitive fountain) from their hands into the peaceful valley below; and another naked, muscled Aryan male forcing kneelike rocks apart with his bare hands to allow the Primitive Fountain to flow (plate 21.4).[16]

Plate 21.2 Quaker Oats advertisement as a late example of colonialist themes in advertising. "Don Facundo never penetrated into anywhere without being served Quaker for breakfast." From *La Prensa*, May 18, 1949.

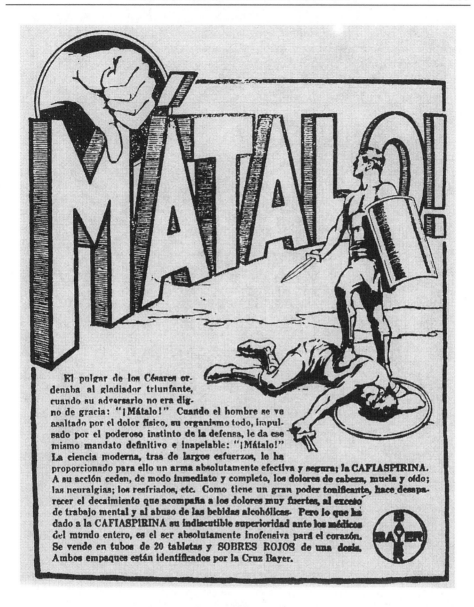

Plate 21.3 "Kill him!" Advertisement for Bayer Aspirin. Text reads in part: "When the adversary did not deserve grace, the thumb of the Caesars ordered the triumphant gladiator, 'Kill him!' When a man is assaulted by physical pain, his whole organism, impelled by the powerful instinct of defense, gives him the same definitive and unappealable mandate, 'Kill him!'" From *Los Domingos*, December 31, 1922.

Plate 21.4 The Primitive Fountain (later version). Advertisement for Bayer Aspirin. From *Los Domingos*, May 22, 1921.

Hollywood film and US policy

In some sectors the aggressive promotion of US commercial culture was bolstered by US government policy. The marketing of US commercial films, for example, depended upon close coordination between Hollywood and Washington, and the proliferation of US comics in daily newspapers benefited from Walt Disney's enhanced prestige as a producer of (and spokesperson for) US cultural and political propaganda from the early 1940s onward.

From at least a dozen years before the advent of the Somoza regime, US commercial filmmakers were peddling their wares successfully in Nicaragua, as they were throughout Latin America. As early as 1926 Managua had at least three movie theaters, and US films were their staple fare.[17] The earthquake of 1931 destroyed some theaters, but new ones (the Palace, the González, Teatro Clamer) opened soon thereafter. It was almost as easy for Managuans as for North American audiences to see Clara Bow ("more beautiful and seductive than ever") in *Savage* ("an impetuous romance, full of passion"). On the same day that El Teatro González was offering viewers Charles Boyer and Olivia de Havilland in *The Golden Door*, and Mickey Rooney in *Harmonies of Youth* with the Paul Whiteman orchestra, Carole Lombard and Victor Mature graced the screen of the América.[18]

With the advent of the Franklin Roosevelt administration in 1933, film and its effects upon public attitudes and its consequent implications for policy began to receive more governmental attention. Only a few months after the inauguration, Senate majority leader Joe T. Robinson wrote to Roosevelt to advise him that "a subtle campaign is being started through the media of moving pictures designed to render the Administration unpopular." Robinson was concerned that former Republican National Committee chairman Will Hayes's increasing power in the film industry promised that more and more clips of out-of-work people would show up on movie newsreels.[19] Roosevelt's papers reveal him to have maintained a keen interest in film: its educational and entertainment value, its potential political uses relative to economic recovery and to partisan politics, and its technological development.

In order to maintain good relations with the motion picture industry, the administration worked to facilitate the distribution of Hollywood films in Latin America. In late 1938 US Vice Consul H. Bartlett Wells wrote to his superiors in Washington about gaining concessions from the Somoza government that would make US films more competitive with films from Mexico, Germany, and Great Britain.[20] His efforts paid off. Of the nearly fifty films shown during November 1941, thirty-six (72 percent) were from the United States.[21] In mid-1941 Managua's Teatro Margot had screened *The Duke of West Point*, starring Joan Fontaine and Louis Hayward – a timely offering in view of the fact that Somoza's elder son would shortly enter West Point as a student.[22] Viewers were promised "a brilliant and grandiose film developed in the famous academy of West Point, with its joys, its nobility, its patriotic ideas, its immortal romances and its impressive parades. By the end of the 1940s Managua could offer Paramount, United Artists, and other US film companies more than a dozen theaters for screening their creations, and the US embassy reported that of nearly 250 feature films shown in Nicaragua during the first six months of 1950, 177 (73 percent) were from the United States.[23]

The US government also attempted to insure that the films screened would reflect favorably upon the United States, especially during World War II. In mid-1942 Coordinator of Inter-American Affairs Nelson Rockefeller chartered as a Delaware corporation Prencinradio, Inc., all of whose officers and employees were Rockefeller's own employees in the Office of the Coordinator. Rockefeller's letter of July 18, 1942 to the general counsel of the Office of the Coordinator argued that forming the corporation was essential "in view of the practical difficulties in having the Government participate directly in foreign countries in activities of a confidential nature designed to improve existing media and to create additional media."

Prencinradio's confidential first annual report described its two principal activities. The first was "to stimulate development of the Mexican motion picture industry" in order to support the war effort and hemispheric solidarity and to "combat Axis Spanish-speaking pictures," and forestall development of the industry in Mexico by interests unsympathetic to the US war effort. The United States sold equipment to two Mexican companies (Azteca and Clasa studios), and provided training, underwrote some production costs, and cooperated in distribution. The second activity was referred to cryptically as "a radio project of a highly confidential nature" for which funds appear to have been laundered through commercial banks. Although the initial film-related activities of Prencinradio were carried out in Mexico, Rockefeller informed its board of directors shortly after it was formed that "this program designed for Mexico is but one of a broad plan to develop the motion picture industry in some other Latin American republics for the same purpose." "It is believed," wrote an official of the Motion Picture Division of the Office of the Coordinator, "that the plan will serve the important purpose of cultural and educational interchange between the other American republics themselves"; that it would be a "local industry" that could do a better job than the United States itself; and that it "would carry their message in the native tongue of the republics."[24]

The US government's interest and involvement in film in Latin America continued unabated after the war's end. A confidential 1950 memo referred to the embassy's interest in gathering "information on newspaper reviews, public criticism and informal evaluation . . . of the effect on local audiences of American motion pictures and in particular in cases where . . . [films] might be offensive to the customs, languages and institutions of foreign peoples."[25] The embassy was concerned, however, not about offending foreign sensibilities but about embarrassing revelations of racism in the United States. At issue were two Twentieth Century-Fox films in particular: Elia Kazan's *Pinky*, and *No Way Out*, both of which treated "the negro question in the United States." The embassy admitted that both films were "remarkably fine productions from an artistic point of view," and that the latter was a "truly fine picture." Moreover, they were "honest portrayal[s] and interpretation[s] of an American problem." Nevertheless, the embassy argued, "both are equally inappropriate for showing in Managua." But why? Weren't local people capable of judging whether or not the films were offensive? The embassy spokesperson argued that *No Way Out* was "a very dangerous picture to be shown abroad in almost any country and certainly in countries where mixed blood, negro or Indian, is the rule." Why? Because racial tensions were so high in Nicaragua? That couldn't be it, because – as the writer admitted – "the problem with which [the film] deals does not exist in this country . . . and racial prejudice is virtually unknown." Then why? The problem, it turned out, was that the film "has been prejudicial to . . . [US] interests . . . [and] can be used as ammunition by communist elements." For their own part, Nicaraguans seemed indifferent to the potentially dire consequences of showing the films; there have been, the embassy admitted in conclusion, "no press reviews or comments." Even back home in the United States, *Commonweal* called *Pinky* one of the year's best films and *Newsweek* noted that "what little press criticism there was . . . was either tactfully oblique or ironic." The film played without incident in many southern cities, although Houston's blacks and whites had to attend separate showings.[26]

Fortunately, the embassy was persuaded, there were safer means of achieving "cultural understanding" than promoting Hollywood films that treated "the negro problem" so candidly – such as promoting a "cultural exchange" of baseball players. Since its introduction to Nicaragua decades earlier, baseball had become the national sport, and earlier US functionaries had been well aware of its pacifying political potential. From his position as Collector General of Customs in Nicaragua, North American Clifford D. Ham commented in 1916 on the "moral influence" of the marines and the political impact of baseball upon Nicaragua. Middle-class working people who initially resented the presence of the marines, Ham said, got interested in watching them play baseball, and then formed their own teams "under the patronage of the President and the Archbishop." "The American marines are now very popular," he reported, and "baseball has done it. It would be a crime to withdraw the marines and stop the baseball craze in Nicaragua. It is the best step towards order, peace and stability that has ever been taken. . . . People who will play baseball and turn out by the thousands every week to see the match games are too busy to participate in revolutions" (Ham 1916: 187–8). "Anything to do with baseball and anything that would tie Nicaraguan and American baseball in the public consciousness," the embassy was still convinced more than thirty-five years later, "would pay off heavily in the promotion of good will."[27]

The cultural planners envisioned a "traveling exhibit" of baseball paraphernalia that could be given as trophies to local teams after exhibition games. "The appearance of two or more well-known baseball names . . . heralded by good advance newspaper and radio publicity," they assured the State Department, "could make a greater sensation in this country than the visits of top ranking movie stars." The problem of the "language barrier" could be easily solved: Nicaraguan players from the Atlantic coast spoke English, albeit of "a somewhat peculiar variety." And US players put off by the lowly "social status" of Nicaraguan players could be mollified by arranging visits "to the Presidential Mansion, to General Somoza's residence, and the like." Visits by US players to Nicaragua would be preferable, moreover, to visits in the other direction, because they "would yield considerably smaller returns on the money invested" and because "many of the top flight local players have colored blood" and (incidentally) would find it "very hard on their finances to provide themselves with suitable clothes for a visit to the United States."

The cultural politics of comic strips

The growing importance of Hollywood movies and the promotion of US big league sports (together with their associated politics) was paralleled by the proliferation of US comic strips in Nicaraguan newspapers.

The contemporary newspaper comic strip's most recognizable predecessors emerged in the 1890s in the Hearst and Pulitzer newspapers. The *Katzenjammer Kids* dates to 1897 and *Mutt and Jeff* to 1907, but many others appeared in the 1920s and 1930s: *Little Orphan Annie* in 1924, *Tarzan* and *Buck Rogers* in 1929, *Dick Tracy* in 1931, *Terry and the Pirates*, *L'il Abner*, and *Flash Gordon* in 1934, and *Superman* in 1938.

Although an early form of *Aventuras de Chico Rosita* ran as early as 1922 in *Los Domingos*, comic strips were rare in Nicaraguan newspapers until the 1930s. *La Prensa*'s *El Agente Secreto X-9*, which appeared on January 1, 1934, ran only a few months, but others soon became staples of the daily newspapers. *Aventuras de Sherlock Porras* and *El Temporal* appeared in January 1935 and were followed by several short series produced by Ed Wheelan for Editors Press, another of whose series created by J. Carrol Mansfield featured US military actions against "redskins" (*pieles rojas*).

Following a hiatus during World War II, the comics became more numerous. *La Flecha* had *Felix the Cat* by late 1947, and by at least the early 1960s, *La Prensa* and *Novedades* readers could follow such characters as Mutt and Jeff (*Benetín y Eneas*), Buck Rogers (*Buck Rogers en Guerra Interplanetaria*), *El Jincho Inteligente* (featuring a stereotypical sombreroed Mexican *indio* [mispronounced "jincho" for a denigratingly comic effect]), Sherlock Holmes, the Katzenjammer Kids (*Maldades de Dos Pilluelos*), Maggie and Jiggs (*Educando a Papá*), Tarzan, Superman, Dick Tracy, Blondie and Dagwood (*Lorenzo y Pepita*), Popeye, and Walt Disney's Donald Duck and Mickey Mouse (*El Ratón Miguelito*).[28]

Especially in countries undergoing socially and culturally destabilizing pressures – rapid urbanization, the disturbance of traditional patterns of rural life, a major influx of consumer culture from outside, or the rise of a dictatorship – so apparently benign a cultural detail as newspaper comics is by no means devoid of political effect. The political and cultural implications of the Walt Disney comics in underdeveloped countries, and especially their links to larger US interests, are particularly suggestive in this regard.[29]

The emerging Disney empire in fact almost died during the late 1930s, and probably would have done so had its resuscitation not been aided by the US government (Schickel 1986: 229–30; Eliot 1993: 81–118). When World War II cut off Disney's lucrative European market (and thus half his income), the government rescued him by commissioning training and propaganda films that became a mainstay for his nearly bankrupt studio. A parallel effort turned Disney toward developing Latin American markets for his films and comics.

At a critical moment when Disney was trying to settle a long and costly strike among his employees, Nelson Rockefeller, as Coordinator of Inter-American Affairs, arranged for him to go on a six-week tour as a "good-will ambassador" to Latin America, which coincidentally helped divert public attention from the strike (Schickel 1986: 263; Mosley 1985: 205; Eliot 1993: 148–50).[30] Disney's subsequent Latin American films *Saludos Amigos* and *The Three Caballeros*, which depicted a stereotypic Latin America of comic parrots and goofy gauchos (together with a lecherous Donald Duck and a sequence of animated phallic cactus plants), were panned by the critics (Schickel 1986: 275; Eliot 1993: 180–3).[31] But the critics had one view, and the public had another: the Disney empire flourished, and by 1962 the monthly circulation of Disney comics had reached 50 million in fifteen languages in fifty countries, including four Spanish language editions.

As Dorfman and Mattelart amply demonstrate, the political and cultural world projected in the Latin American versions of the Disney comics features degrading cultural stereotypes and reactionary politics. Third-world countries (Inca-Blinca, the Republic of San Bananador, Aztecland, Unsteadystan, and Outer Congolia) are burlesqued and trivialized. The typical Disney Latin American, Dorfman concluded after looking at hundreds of examples, is "somnolent, sells pottery, sits on his haunches, and has a thousand year-old culture" (Dorfman and Mattelart 1984: 54). Women are unfailingly subordinate to men; their only power derives from their role as seductresses. In the Unsteadystans of Disney (ruled by leaders with names like Prince Char Ming and Soy Bheen), power relationships are sharply defined by patterns of obedience, submission, discipline, economic domination, and physical repression. When Unsteadystan citizens get up off their haunches and rebel, Dorfman and Mattelart note, their rebellion "is immediately turned into an incomprehensible game of someone-or-other against someone-or-other, a stupid fratricide lacking in any ethical direction or economic *raison d'être*" (ibid: 56).

Disney's own real-life politics mirrored those of his comic strips, and even as he shipped politically and culturally reactionary movies and comics south of the border, he placed those politics directly in the service of the similarly reactionary elements of US life. From late 1940 onward, as Eliot demonstrates from FBI files obtained under the Freedom of Information Act, the openly anti-Semitic Disney was a valued collaborator of the FBI and (later) of the House Un-American Activities Committee. He also served as vice president of the Anti-Communist Motion Picture Alliance for the Preservation of American Ideals from its formation in 1944, working to blacklist "communist sympathizers" in the industry (Eliot 1993: 168–97; cf. Tunstall 1977: 140). Thus within repressive, increasingly anti-communist *Somocista* Nicaragua, the Disney intervention was in no way benign.[32]

NOTES

1 The formal US–Nicaraguan treaty establishing the Guard was finally signed after long negotiations on December 22, 1928. Somoza assumed the presidency in 1936, after a rigged election in which the National Guard counted the votes. He retained the director-ship of the National Guard following his election (Bermann 1986: 223; Millett 1977: 61, 70, 181–2; Walter 1987: 108).

2 Representative radio schedules in *La Prensa*, January 19, 1938, p. 4, and April 29, 1938, p. 6.

3 Emanuel Celler to Roosevelt, 16 November 1937, Official File 3093, Franklin D. Roosevelt Library. From the early 1930s through the opening of World War II, a series of regional and worldwide radio conferences was held to moderate the increasing tension over the allocation of shortwave and broadcast radio frequencies. Nicaragua participated in the 1933 North and Central American Regional Radio Conference in Mexico City. One of the most important conferences for the Americas was the 1937 Inter-American Radio Conference in Havana, which produced the Inter-American Radio Convention, signed in December. Nicaragua was a signatory (Secretary of State Cordell Hull to Roosevelt, 1 May 1934; Roosevelt to Congress, 3 August 1937; State Department memo-randum to Roosevelt, 23 April 1938; all in Official File 2973, Franklin D. Roosevelt Library).

4 Unfortunately I have discovered no published record of the programming of these sta-tions.

5 *El Diario Nicaragüense*, 24 November 1926, p. 1; State Department Decimal File 817.42/33 12 June 1933, National Archives and Records Service; *La Noticia*, 22 September 1934, p. 2, and 16 July 1937, p. 4; *Nicaragua. Guía general ilustrada*, sec. XIII, p. 7. Unfortu-nately, the schedules contain no further details on the pro-fascist broadcasts.

6 Radio Corporation of America, *Report to Stockholders*, 24 February 1934; Official File 1314, Franklin D. Roosevelt Library.

7 Unfortunately, neither Nordenstreng and Varis nor Wells singled out Nicaragua for study.

8 Additional data compiled from *Television Factbook* and *Television Digest*, 1961–79.

9 Also prominent (as throughout Latin America) were the *telenovelas*, produced mostly in Mexico and Brazil.

10 *La Prensa* had been bought in 1933 by Pedro Joaquín Chamorro Zelaya. His son took over the editorship two decades later and became an implacable enemy of the last of the Somoza line before being assassinated in January 1978 (Diederich 1981: 39, 154). Diederich notes (p. 71) that Anastasio Somoza Debayle (younger son of Somoza García) was less concerned about controlling newspapers than radio, because the majority of Nicaraguans were illiterate. Although I draw corroborative evidence from print media, I have chosen to focus on nonprint media instead. A systematic study of culture in the print media during the Somoza and Sandinista periods would require a book in itself. For an excellent analysis of direct political repression during the 1940s, see Walter 1993: 129–63.

11 Walter 1987: 293–6, observes that although government income quadrupled in the decade 1946–56, the percentage used for almost everything but the National Guard declined. Education remained at about 10 percent, but public works declined from 30 to 19 percent.

12 It is important to bear in mind that the evidence concerning censorship and repression is mixed, since the regime used them selectively. During the early 1940s, for example, *Nuevos Horizontes* published some of Cuadra's work and sponsored a daily radio program that broadcast Pablo Neruda's "Nuevo canto de amor a Stalingrad" (*Nuevos Horizontes* 1 [August 1943]: 12, 20).

13 *El Diario Nicaragüense*, 1927–9; ibid., 10, 20, 27 January, 11 February, 19 March 1931; *El Centroamericano*, July–August 1937; *La Prensa*, 7 March 1935. Since files of newspapers from this period available to me are somewhat spotty, I have had to draw upon some from outside Managua. Comparisons with available Managua newspapers suggest, however, that differences were not substantial in this respect. In *Three Gringos in Venezuela and Central America*, 187, Richard Harding Davis reported the presence of two American phonograph salesmen in Corinto in the mid-1890s.

14 A confidential memorandum for the Chairman of the [US] Maritime Commission (ca. 1936) details the means Pan American employed to gain an exclusive concession for air passenger service from the US to Latin America: intense lobbying of Congress, the masking of accident rates, highly profitable subsidies on a monopoly contract for airmail service, and an adroit public relations campaign managed by the Madison Avenue firm of Batten, Barton, Durstine & Osborn (Official File 2875, Franklin D. Roosevelt Library).

15 Black 1981: 62–8; *La Prensa*, 13 March and 4 May 1948.

16 *Los Domingos*, 31 December 1922, p. 20; 25 February 1923, p. 20; 10 April 1920, p. 20; 22 May 1920, p. 20.

17 Advertisements in Managua's *El Diarito*, 16 April 1926, p. 2, indicate that all three (Teatro Margot, Cine el Otro, and the Capitol) were showing US films.

18 *La Prensa*, 3 March 1935; 19 March 1935. The situation was by no means unique to Nicaragua; it was endemic in Latin America (cf. Dorfman and Mattelart 1984: 12, 114).

19 Robinson to Roosevelt's secretary Louis Howe, 24 June 1933; Official File 73, Franklin D. Roosevelt Library.

20 H. Bartlett Wells, "Nicaraguan Measures to Facilitate Introduction of Motion Pictures," 20 December 1938; Record Group 59, 817.4061 Motion Pictures/7, National Archives and Records Service.

21 *La Prensa*, 13 April 1940, p. 4; 2 November 1941, p. 6. Three films were from Mexico, two were from Argentina, and one was Cuban.

22 The convergence of state policy and the dissemination of ideology through popular culture is particularly evident here. In connection with his state visit to the United States in 1939, Somoza importuned President Roosevelt repeatedly for assistance with reopening the National Guard training academy, which he wanted a US military officer to head. Roosevelt agreed to provide the assistance, naming West Point graduate Major Charles L. Mullins Jr. as the academy's commandant. By the spring of 1941, the US had indeed constructed a "Little West Point" for Somoza's National Guard (Somoza

to Roosevelt, 22 May 1939; President's Secretary's File, Box 45; 1 April 1941 memo to Roosevelt, Official File 432; Franklin D. Roosevelt Library).

23 *La Prensa*, 27 December 1933, p. 1; 9 February 1934, p. 4; 17 January 1935, p. 6; 27 January 1940, p. 4; 13 April 1940, p. 4; 29 August 1941, p. 4; 2 November 1941, p. 6; 11 September 1949, p. 2. Foreign Service of the United States to Department of State, 30 September 1950; Confidential US State Department Central Files: Nicaragua, 1950–54: Internal Affairs, Reel 9. A Nicaraguan government report enclosed with the memo listed a total of fifty-seven theaters in fifteen towns and cities in Nicaragua. Tunstall 1977: 142, cites 1948 UNESCO figures that included Nicaragua among the countries in which US films claimed 70 percent or more of the market.

24 *Annual Report of Prencinradio, Inc.*, 30 June 1943; Official File 4512, Franklin D. Roosevelt Library (Rockefeller letters appear as appendices to the report).

25 Foreign Service to Department of State, 30 December 1950; Confidential US State Department Central Files: Nicaragua, 1950–54: Internal Affairs, Reel 9. Subsequent quotations from this document.

26 *Commonweal* 51 (14 October 1949): 15; *Newsweek* 34 (10 October 1949): 89–90.

27 Foreign Service to Department of State, 28 April 1950; Confidential US State Department Central Files: Nicaragua, 1950–54: Internal Affairs, Reel 9. Subsequent quotations from this source.

28 *La Prensa*, early 1935 through mid-1950s.

29 I make no claim about US "domination" of the media in Nicaragua, but rather hope to convey some sense of the ubiquity of US cultural forms in the media, and of the highly politicized content of those forms. Buckman (1990: 193) argues that of some seven thousand cultural articles in two dozen or so "elite" Latin American newspapers and magazines from the years 1949 and 1982 (none of them from Nicaragua, unfortunately), only 10–20 percent originated in the United States. In taking US *origin* as the sole indicator of potential influence, however – hence omitting articles on "local" cultural events patterned on US models (beauty pageants, baseball, Kiwanis or Lion's Club meetings, and the like) and others that although locally written, reflected US cultural values or assumptions – Buckman substantially underestimates the problem.

30 While Disney was in Latin America, his animators – key members of what Mosley has called "the most brilliant and the most overworked and underpaid [staff] in Hollywood" – won their strike (Mosley 1985: 188, 195–97; Eliot 1993: 150).

31 Burton in Parker et al. (1992) presents a detailed analysis of the cultural politics of *The Three Caballeros* in the context both of the Office of the Coordinator of Inter-American Affairs and of Disney's own personal politics and cultural views (pp. 21–41). Burton focuses on "ten perverse propositions of desire" that are the organizing subtexts of the film: Latin America as a war-time Toontown, the packaging of Latin America as pure spectacle, narratives of colonial conquest, hierarchies of willing-and-waiting-to-be-conquered subjects, the reassuring politics of Donald Duck's sexual inadequacy and his ambiguous sexual identity, the sexual dominance promised to Latin American men as a reward for submission to colonial power, the ostensible humaneness of the conquerors, the illusory reciprocities of the exchange, and the hidden agendas of "intercultural understanding."

32 As with most areas of ideology and policy, Somoza attempted to play both ends against the middle with regard to labor and the left. As Gould has pointed out, by intervening periodically on the behalf of striking workers, Somoza portrayed himself as a defender of the working class and strove to unify the labor movement in order to use it against his Conservative opponents. The *obrerista* leadership consequently supported him until the early 1940s. Somoza approved the progressive Labor Code of April 1945, and actually permitted the founding of the Socialist-dominated Confederación de Trabajadores Nicaragüenses (CTN) in early 1946. From its own perspective, the left responded favorably, Gould argues, because the labor movement was "young and potentially expansive...

[but] weakened by internal division, constantly harassed by management, and seriously threatened by the possibility of a right-wing takeover." Ultimately, however, Somocista unionism was "an integral component of Somoza's strategy to foment labor–capital harmony, politically debilitate the landed oligarchy, and establish *somocista* hegemony over the Nicaraguan bourgeoisie." At length Somoza turned to avid anti-communist rhetoric, however, in order to curry favor with the United States, and began to "portray the Left as a foreign-dominated version of what the national labor movement could do more efficiently and authentically under the guidance of the *jefe obrero*." Emerging labor–student opposition forced Somoza to cancel his candidacy for the presidency twice in the late 1940s, and Somoza jailed most leaders of the labor movement in January 1948 (Gould 1992: 243–8, 261, 274).

REFERENCES

Bermann, Karl. 1986. *Under the Big Stick: Nicaragua and the United States Since 1848*. Boston: South End Press.

Booth, John. 1985. *The End and the Beginning: The Nicaraguan Revolution*. 2nd edn. Boulder, CO: Westview Press.

Borgeson, Paul W., Jr. 1977. "The poetry of Ernesto Cardenal." Ph.D. diss., Vanderbilt University.

Buckman, Robert. 1990. "Cultural agenda of Latin American newspapers and magazines: is US Domination a Myth?" *Latin American Research Review* 25 (2): 134–55.

Cardenal, Ernesto. 1983a. *Nueva antología poética*. 4th edn. Mexico City: Siglo Veintiuno Editores.

——1983b. *Ernesto Cardenal Antología*. Managua: Editorial Nueva Nicaragua/Ediciones Monimbó.

Cuadra, Manolo. 1982. *Sólo en la compañia*. Managua: Editorial Nueva Nicaragua.

Diederich, Bernard. 1981. *Somoza and the Legacy of US Involvement in Central America*. New York: E. P. Dutton.

Dorfman, Ariel, and Armand Mattelart. 1984 [1971]. *How to Read Donald Duck: Imperialist Ideology in the Disney Comic*. Translated by David Kunzle. 2nd edn. New York: International General.

Eliot, Marc. 1993. *Walt Disney: Hollywood's Dark Prince*. New York: Birch Lane.

Frappier, Jon. 1969. "US media empire/Latin America," *NACLA Newsletter* 2 (January): 1–11.

Gould, Jeffrey L. [no title supplied]. 1992. In *Latin America Between the Second World War and the Cold War, 1944–1948*, Leslie Bethell and Ian Roxborough, eds. New York: Cambridge University Press.

Halftermeyer, Gratus. 1946? *Managua a través de la Historia: 1846–1946*. Managua: Editorial Hospicio S. J. de Dios.

Ham, Clifford D. 1916. "Americanizing Nicaragua: how Yankee marines, financial oversight and baseball are stabilizing Central America," *American Review of Reviews* 53 (February): 185–90.

Hernández, José R. 1969. *Historia: Radio Nacional de Nicaragua*. Managua: Tipografía Pereira.

McCreery, David. 1993. "Wireless empire: the United States and radio communications in Central America and the Caribbean, 1904–1926," *Southeastern Latin Americanist* 37 (summer): 23–41.

Millett, Richard. 1977. *Guardians of the Dynasty*. Maryknoll, NY: Orbis Books.

Mosley, Leonard. 1985. *Disney's World: A Biography*. New York: Stein and Day.

Nordenstreng, Kaarle and Tapio Varis. 1985 [1974]. *Television Traffic – A One Way Street? A Survey and Analysis of the International Flow of Television Programme Material.* Ann Arbor, MI: UNIPUB.

Schickel, Richard. 1986 [1968]. *The Disney Version: The Life, Times, Art and Commerce of Walt Disney.* Revd. edn. London: Pavilion Books.

Schiller, Herbert. 1969. *Mass Communications and American Empire.* New York: A. M. Kelley.

—— 1976. *Communication and Cultural Domination.* White Plains, NY: International Arts and Sciences Press.

Tunstall, Jeremy. 1977. *The Media Are American.* New York: Columbia University Press.

Walter, Knut. 1987. "The regime of Anastasio Somoza García and state formation in Nicaragua, 1936–1956." Ph.D. diss., University of North Carolina, Chapel Hill.

—— 1993. *The Regime of Anastasio Somoza, 1936–1956.* Chapel Hill: University of North Carolina Press.

Wells, Alan. 1972. *Picture Tube Imperialism? The Impact of US Television in Latin America.* Maryknoll, NY: Orbis Books.

White, Steven. 1986. *Culture and Politics in Nicaragua: Testimonies of Poets and Writers.* New York: Lumen Books.

Zwerling, Philip and Connie Martin. 1985. *Nicaragua: A New Kind of Revolution.* Westport, CT: Lawrence Hill.

22

The Objects of Soap Opera: Egyptian Television and the Cultural Politics of Modernity

Lila Abu-Lughod

Circulating in Cairo in the 1980s was a joke typical for its urban contempt for the peasant from Upper Egypt:

A Sa'idi [Upper Egyptian] came to Cairo and wanted to buy a TV set. He went to the appliance store and, pointing, asked, 'How much is that TV in the window?' The owner yelled, 'Get out of here you stupid Sa'idi!' He went away and dressed in a long white robe and headdress to disguise himself as a Saudi Arabian. He came back to the store and again asked, 'How much is that TV in the window?' The owner yelled, 'Get out of here you stupid Sa'idi!' He went away and changed into trousers and a shirt and tie, coming back disguised as a European. Again he asked 'How much is that TV in the window?' The owner yelled, 'Get out of here you stupid Sa'idi!' Puzzled, the poor man asked, 'How could you tell it was me?' The shop owner answered, 'That's not a TV, it's a washing machine.'[1]

In this joke, lack of familiarity with television was made symptomatic of rural backwardness. Television represents modernity, requiring for its production advanced technology and for reception an expensive instrument. Although introduced into Egypt in 1960, it took the slow spread of electrification and labour migrants' wages in the 1970s to bring television sets to the majority of households, especially outside the major cities.

In the 1950s this new communication technology was celebrated in US discourses on the modernization of the Third World. This was exemplified in Middle East studies by Daniel Lerner (1958) whose classic text, *The Passing of Traditional Society*, argued that mass media opened closed traditional minds by revealing the vast world of difference, facilitating the 'empathy' that was a prerequisite of the mobile, politically participating, opinion-holding personality essential to modernity.

Although Lerner's confident views of mass media have been countered by a more recent critical literature on cultural imperialism, followed by counter-critiques by anthropologists attuned to the creative and self-productive local appropriations of imported television (e.g. Miller 1992; Wilk 1993 [ch. 17, this volume]), in countries like Egypt, India and China with major television production capabilities of their own, the more pressing question may be how the internal cultural politics of government-controlled media articulate with contested visions of modernity. An anthropologist interested in Egypt would want to ask what sorts of differences Egyptian television actually reveals to its audiences and what difference this makes to those exposed to it. What, in fact, is the relationship between television and modernity?

More than any other form of mass media, especially in a place where many remain non-literate, television brings a variety of vivid experiences of the non-local into the most local of situations, the home. So when someone like Nobel laureate Naguib Mahfouz laments the decline of the Cairo coffee house, explaining 'People used to go the coffee shops and listen to story tellers who played a musical instrument and told of folk heroes. These events filled the role played by television serials today', he forgets that this older form of entertainment, with the imaginary non-local worlds it conjured up, was only available to men (quoted in Hedges 1992). Television gives women, the young, and the rural as much access as urban men to stories of other worlds.

In Egypt, I will argue, a concerned group of culture-industry professionals has constructed of these women, youths and rural people a subaltern object in need of enlightenment. Appropriating and inflecting Western discourses on development they construct themselves as guides to modernity and assume the responsibility of producing, through their television programmes, the virtuous modern citizen. Especially in the dramatic serials which are Egypt's most popular television fare, they seek to 'educate' their public. Their faith in the impact of television is spurred by the debates their serials provoke among critics and other parts of the urban intelligentsia.

Yet a look at the place of television in these subalterns' lives suggests that this public subverts and eludes them, not because they are traditional and ignorant of the modern, as the joke about the country bumpkin would have it, but because the ways they are positioned within modernity are at odds with the visions these urban middle-class professionals promote. The nationalist message is broadcast into a complex social space where the very local and the transnational both exert powerful pulls. On the one hand, people live in the local worlds of their daily experience, of which television is only a small part. On the other hand, as multinational companies bombard the Egyptian market with their products, as Islamic political groups with broader than national identifications vie for loyalty, and as elites look to the West, television's nationalists have much to compete with.

Television in a Discourse of the Modern Nation

In the discourse of some key culture-industry professionals in Egypt, television figures in a nationalist and elitist vision of modernity. When film star and director Nur al-Sharif described the beginnings of Egyptian television, he noted that in a general atmosphere of national advancement the government had a plan for using media and art to change people's views on political participation and life.[2] Films and serials of the 1960s were based on literary works in order 'to educate people, enlighten them, and draw them into the policy of the new revolution in transforming Egyptian society from a feudal, capitalist society into a socialist one'. In the same breath, he added that many serials were based on novels by Egypt's great writers 'to help the uneducated Egyptian youth in rural areas, the provinces, and in cities other than Cairo and Alexandria, who had no concern with culture, to become acquainted with those great writers'.

This professed interest in educating and 'culturing' the poor and those outside the urban capitals was echoed by Muhammad Fadil, one of Egypt's foremost television directors, who argued that television in a developing country plagued not just by illiteracy but by cultural illiteracy should not simply entertain; it has to work to eliminate this cultural illiteracy. Linking culture and social responsibility, he defined culture, in terms reminiscent of Lerner's portrait of 'modern man', as 'familiarity with the news, appreciation of art, a taste for art, music, theatre . . . Culture is the concern of the individual with the problems of others, which comes from knowledge.'[3] Fadil concluded that since drama was the most loved form, it had to be exploited to teach people without them sensing it.

Essential to this construction of television entertainment as serious art that is socially or politically uplifting is the contrast with commercial entertainment. Fadil distinguished between serials people enjoyed watching and those whose effects carried on long after they had been broadcast. He criticized colleagues for making pumpkin-seed serials – serials that were fun to watch, like munching on seeds, but gave no real nourishment.[4] Nural-Sharif defended government policy regarding television in the 1960s claiming that it enabled television 'to produce a common national dream, not only inside Egypt but in the whole Arab world. It made people enthusiastic and optimistic.' He contrasted this to what had happened since the mid-1970s when private companies began producing programmes, their only interest being to entertain people and their hands being tied by the necessity of selling their programmes in the conservative Gulf states where political and moral censorship are highly restrictive.[5]

This contest between the idealistic vision of television drama as the producer of a modern cultured citizen with a national consciousness and the competing tendency of Egyptian television to present 'cheap' entertainment was dramatically played out during 1993 in the controversy, not over an Egyptian serial, but over the American soap opera, *The Bold and the Beautiful*. Beginning in late 1992, Channel 2, the channel that broadcasts most of the foreign programmes in Egypt, began airing nightly episodes of this successful American daytime soap that has been running in the USA since March 1987 and has been exported to twenty-two countries.[6] In Egypt, cartoons in a weekly magazine caricatured its popularity; one showed a government minister on the telephone noting that the best time to raise prices on goods without anyone protesting was between 9.30 and 10.30 p.m., the time the soap was being aired.

The Bold and the Beautiful is set in the fashion world of Los Angeles and centres on two key families involved in fashion design and publishing. Nearly all the actresses are blonde and most of the actors are handsome, something that is not incidental to the success of the soap. Cartoons in a weekly magazine *Sabah al-Khayr* suggested that both men and women viewers had become smitten with the characters. One showed a woman viewer watching the female announcer introduce the show as follows: 'Dear Family Members, now is the time for our date with the adorable handsome boy who drives you crazy, damn him – Ridge.' Beside it was a cartoon showing a man strumming on a lute and singing as he watched television: 'O Night, linger over this pretty friend.'

Newspapers participated in and satirized viewers' immersion in the characters and their relationships, commenting on the way characters had become taken for real. A cartoon showed an older veiled woman talking to a friend on the telephone about the surgery of one of the female characters. 'Hey, people are all the same', she says. 'Come on, let's take two kilos of oranges and rush to visit our Aunt Logan, Brook's mother, in the hospital.' In a major magazine a serious article on USAID in Egypt introduced the argument that Egypt was actually subsidizing the USA economy by saying, 'Would you believe that Egypt supports America? And gives it economic aid? ... You don't believe that you subsidize that charming American woman, Brook Logan?'[7]

The contrast between *The Bold and the Beautiful* and the highlight of Egyptian television viewing over the past five years could not be more stark. Since 1988 during successive Ramadans, the Muslim month of fasting and the television season's high point, people had been emotionally riveted by a brilliant Egyptian television serial written by Usama Anwar 'Ukasha. This was the quintessential non-pumpkin-seed serial. Called *Hilmiyya Nights*, it followed the fortunes and relationships of a group of characters from the traditional Cairo neighbourhood of Hilmiyya, taking them from the late 1940s, when Egypt was under the rule of King Farouk and the British, up to the present, even incorporating into the final episodes the Egyptian reaction to the Gulf War.

Although many Egyptian television serials have captured large audiences and generated discussion and affection, and the local productions are generally more popular than foreign imports, the broadcast of this unusually long and high-quality serial was a national cultural event.[8] Its popularity was not confined to the millions who regularly followed the evening serials but extended to the intelligentsia who were provoked by its political messages. The merits of the serial were debated in newspapers and magazines and a leading intellectual, Sayed Yassin, even used it as a metaphor for 'Egypt's real abilities'. In a brief essay in a major weekly magazine, *Al-Iqtisadi*, he contrasted the successful serial, with its excellent text, capable director, talented and devoted actors, and involved audience with the failures of current political activity in Egypt, suggesting that what Egypt needed was a better political text to guide its director (the President), more respect for its citizens, and the introduction of new political actors.[9]

With little daytime television and a state-controlled television industry until recently only minimally supported through advertising, there never developed in Egypt an equivalent of the US daytime soap opera.[10] Instead, since the late 1960s, the form of the evening dramatic serial (*musalsal*) consisting of anywhere from fifteen to thirty episodes broadcast on consecutive days, has dominated Egyptian television entertainment. Although as television critics have noted, the strict definition of television genres is becoming increasingly problematic, serials are distinguishable from daytime or prime-time soap operas in being finite and self-contained, offering viewers some sort of dramatic resolution by the final episode (Geraghty 1991). Like soap operas, however, most Egyptian serials are set in the domestic space, using limited and familiar sets; more importantly, their plots revolve around unfolding personal relationships often presented melodramatically. Much like the USA and British prime-time soaps of the 1980s (e.g. *Dallas*, *Dynasty* and *East-Enders*) that have deliberately sought wider audiences, Egyptian serials are believed to have women as their primary audiences while reaching out successfully to whole families, men included.

Hilmiyya Nights, more than most Egyptian serials, seems to be a hybrid product. Although its talented writer denied in print that he had given audiences an Egyptian *Falcon Crest* (an American prime-time soap that had aired several years earlier), there are numerous aspects of *Hilmiyya Nights* in which the influence of such American programmes can be detected. If the prime-time soap opera can be defined by its peculiar mixing of the aesthetics of melodrama, realism and light entertainment, then *Hilmiyya Nights* fits the description (Geraghty 1991: 25). Strong on emotional drama, the serial focuses on the faces and feelings of its characters and intensifies its effects through dramatic music.[11] As in other Egyptian serials tears are plentiful, if balanced by laughter and anger. Like the British soap operas (and unlike the American) that take realism more seriously, the serial is set in particular neighbourhoods and attempts to depict class differences and regional identities authentically and nostalgically.

What makes *Hilmiyya Nights* seem most like American prime-time soaps is that it partakes of the element of spectacle. The costumes are lavish, the sets sumptuous, and at least some of the women characters extravagantly glamorous and fashionable (Geraghty 1991: 27–8). The aristocratic central characters move elegantly among their villas and luxurious apartments, the key woman character elaborately made up and coiffured and dressed in a different outfit for each of well over a hundred episodes, trading sequined gowns for chiffon and furs, except when going in to the office when she wears stylish suits in striking colours.

In addition, the serial resembles the American prime-time soap operas in certain aspects of plot. As in *Dallas* the central action revolves around the rivalry between two wealthy men and their families, in this case an urban aristocrat and a rural mayor, both of whom become millionaire businessmen in the 1970s and 1980s. The financial wheelings and dealings of these two and the woman who at different times was married to each of them carry much of the narrative along. The adventures and love interests of their children become the focus as the serial moves into the present.

Though by definition serials differ from soap operas in having resolutions, this serial was unusual in deferring its resolution for so long. Drawn out over five years and far more episodes than any previous Egyptian serial, *Hilmiyya Nights* allowed for the development of the kind of attachment to characters that soap-opera audiences relish. Following the tribulations and successes of some of the characters from childhood to adulthood and others through marriages, divorces, losses, imprisonments and careers well into old age, audiences were treated to the pleasurable experience common to American soap-opera viewers: of finding meaning in scenes from their knowledge of the characters' histories (Geraghty 1991: 15). An intimacy was created by the deep familiarity viewers came to have over time with characters' personal histories and tangled relationships, especially since old episodes of the serial were re-run each year before the new instalment was aired and the whole serial, now complete, was being shown on successive Sunday evenings in 1993.[12]

Analysts have noted that among the distinguishing features of the soap-opera genre is the centrality of strong women characters. This too applied to *Hilmiyya Nights* with its important women figures in each generation. Not only do we have at the centre of the drama a *femme fatale* who is also a crafty and financially ruthless aristocrat turned businesswoman, but also the long-suffering and moral wives and mothers of key male figures, the educated daughters of rich and poor pursuing professional careers while trying to manage love lives, and the odd belly-dancer. Although strong women characters are not uncommon in Egyptian dramatic serials, in *Hilmiyya Nights* the richness of the variety of women, their competence in the work sphere, and their dramatic centrality were striking.[13]

Despite these resemblances, however, 'Ukasha was right to deny that *Hilmiyya Nights* was the Egyptian *Falcon Crest*. This is not, as he charged, because *Falcon Crest* was made to dupe Third World people, full of beautiful women and sex, but because the series differed radically from any American soap opera in being historically contextualized. American soap operas have been characterized as a women's genre because they privilege the personal, depicting even the non-domestic work scenes in terms of personal relationships. This Egyptian serial similarly portrayed the personal lives of individuals, but instead of having its narrative pushed along simply by events in the personal relationships among the characters, *Hilmiyya Nights* had the moral themes of loyalty, betrayal, corruption, thwarted desires and tragic errors embedded in an historical narrative that tied individual lives to Egyptian national political events. It did what no American soap would ever do: it provided an explicit social and political commentary on contemporary Egyptian life.[14]

Above all, *Hilmiyya Nights* promoted the theme of national unity. With the exception of a very few truly evil characters, selfish and corrupt individuals out for themselves, the characters of different classes and political persuasions were shown to be basically good and patriotic. Our hearts went out to them as many were led astray, reacting to romantic and political blows. But in the end, they saw the errors of their ways, prevented by their love of Egypt from pursuing the materialistic, immoral or corrupt paths they had taken. Even the young religious extremist (the first to be depicted in an Egyptian television serial) was sympathetically portrayed as part of a generation that had been led astray by the lack of national spirit.[15]

Protecting the Public

Hilmiyya Nights sought to teach and enlighten. In response, intellectuals, critics, politicians and censors sought to protect the public from its messages. Both the writer and his critics, the urban educated elite who felt it incumbent on them to protect others, assumed the power of television serials and the vulnerability of subaltern viewers.

Hilmiyya Nights attempted to inform millions of ordinary Egyptians about their country's modern history. Its characters participated in such activities as anti-colonial raids against the British, the nationalization of factories during Nasser's era, the wars with Israel, political crack-downs in a police state, the rise of Islamic fundamentalism and the scams of the new Islamic investment companies. Characters' lives were deeply affected by the economic liberalization of Sadat's 'open door' policies, the increase in heroin addition and drug trafficking, and the policies of state feminism.

The debates in the press focused on the political perspective presented. As the headline of an article in the centre-right newspaper *Al-Wafd* bluntly asked, 'Does the Author of *Hilmiyya Nights* Have the Right to Write History from the Nasserist Viewpoint?'[16] The serial then provided the occasion for setting the public straight. In the same newspaper, Dr Abd el-Azim Ramadan, the leading establishment historian of the Sadat period, defended himself for not criticizing the serial, noting that *Hilmiyya Nights* was excellent drama, important for raising cultural standards in the Arab world, and that although the writer had glorified Nasser, he had presented the period as those living through it had perceived it. Ramadan explained why the people had worshipped Nasser; they thought he had achieved so many of their dreams: a republic, land reform, socialism, a strong army and Arab unity. They had not realized, he continued, that what Nasser had created was a military dictatorship. And because of media disinformation, they knew little about how many Egyptian thinkers of the left and right he had imprisoned. Ramadan concluded his articles with the two lessons to be learned from the Nasser period: that dictatorship and justice do not go together and that people should distrust the mass media.[17]

The serial was criticized from other political perspectives as well. In the leftist newspaper *Al-Ahaly* 'Ukasha was asked why he made the capitalist pasha such a sympathetic character and ignored the everyday problems of ordinary people. In *Al-Sha'b*, another opposition newspaper that now presents the viewpoint of the Muslim Brotherhood, the paper's editor Adel Hussein defended the serial and 'Ukasha's right to free expression. He praised the new instalment for depicting everyday religiosity, noting that he had earlier criticized the serial, like all television drama, for never showing Islamic religious practices as part of daily life.

Those sympathetic to 'Ukasha's politics wrote articles complimenting the serial for its brilliance, invoking a discourse of art over politics. 'Asim Hanafy criticized those who treated the serial as a political tract rather than a superb artistic achievement that had made people realize the fraudulence and poverty of the past thirty years of television drama. Yet, in enumerating their political criticisms, he made his own position clear. Most pointed was his mockery of one writer who had accused *Hilmiyya Nights* of being anti-Sadat 'because it dealt with the open-door policy and the new parasitical commercial class'. His comment was 'Isn't Egypt suffering because of the influence of this class today?'[18] Alluding to the problems 'Ukasha had faced from the television censors, his article went on to condemn censorship in an age of increasing democracy.

State censorship is exercised in Egypt in the name of protecting the public from the morally, politically or religiously offensive. *Hilmiyya Nights* tested the limits of the more generous freedom of the press that has been President Mubarak's policy. The writer 'Ukasha clashed with the television censors who not only commented on the screenplay but also required cuts after the filming was complete. Many of the cuts requested by the censorship office were finally overridden on the personal authority of the Minister of Information and the head of the television sector responsible for the production of films and serials.

From the internal records of this clash about the third instalment, which covered the period of the 1970s, it is clear that most of the censors' objections were political. They only asked that one sexually suggestive scene be cut but they wanted to cut lines in which President Nasser was praised or defended by sympathetic characters, lines in which lower-class good folk absolved Nasser by blaming those around him, those who 'isolated him from the people and built a wall around him higher than the Aswan Dam' so that 'the people couldn't reach him to tell him what was going on' and so that 'he did not trust the people in the street who loved him and could have protected him'. More tellingly, they objected to scenes suggesting criticism of President Sadat and his policies. For example, they requested more balance in the reaction of the characters to Sadat's visit to Israel in 1977. They asked 'Ukasha to add a scene showing people happy about the visit, a request he refused on budgetary grounds. They also asked him to change the timing of a scene in which the neighbourhood coffee shop of a beloved patriotic character is sold; by having it coincide with Sadat's visit they felt he implied that it was Egypt being sold. Finally they asked that all dialogue be removed from a scene in a mosque, saying 'We don't want any discussion of religion and role of fundamentalists.' Ironically, the censors also objected to a scene in which a newspaper editor cuts part of a journalist's story as too dangerous. They insisted that this was inaccurate; there had been no censorship at the time of Sadat.

'Ukasha bitterly accused them in the press of 'destroying the work on grounds that to criticize the Sadat period is to be against the current regime in the country'. Turning the language of protection on its head, he argued that the state was not in need of protection by these unqualified censors.[19] Invoking his public mission he vowed that if he felt forced to produce Part 4 privately and it was banned from broadcast in Egypt, he would 'go around the streets with a video to show it to people in the coffee shops' so his words could reach the people.[20]

Hilmiyya Nights, a serial that showed how political events at the national level affected the lives of individuals and communities, a serial in which personal histories, fortunes and tragedies were directly related to policies and events, battled with the censors. In contrast, several months into *The Bold and the Beautiful*, the director of censorship responsible for foreign films could still claim that there was very little to censor in the American serial. The characters are free-floating, their only real context being that created by the soap-opera world itself. This was read by many as making it 'human'. The censor, for example, defended the soap, saying: 'The serial carries general human values and debates problems that are not place specific; they are close to many of the problems of Eastern society.'[21] Muna Hilmy, the daughter of the prominent Egyptian feminist Nawal El-Saadawi, defended the serial claiming that what the foreign serial offered that those 'serials irrigated by Nile water' didn't was a look inside people. Instead of external events – political, economic or social – one had people with feelings, desires, weaknesses, strengths, small wickednesses and goodness. She defended the slowness of the serial as necessary to show the vastness of the human psyche and the politics of the serial as feminist.[22]

Critics of the American soap opera, on the other hand, deployed the discourse of protection – this time against bad art, immorality and American aid. 'Ukasha, the writer of *Hilmiyya Nights*, was provoked to analyse *The Bold and the Beautiful* when a major newspaper columnist praised the soap and invited Egyptian writers to watch it in order to learn the art of dramatic writing. Acknowledging its enormous success, 'Ukasha argued that like the earlier popular American imports this serial's popularity was not due to its artistic merit but rather to the fact that 'we in the nations of the Third World like to see the Western lifestyle which is forbidden to us because of the closed societies we live in. We like to watch pretty women in a range of abnormal sexual relationships that would be taboo in our Eastern societies.'[23] He took the moral high ground with his conclusion, 'God preserve us from what we watch on *The Bold and the Beautiful*: children encouraging their mother to get involved with a married man.'

Invoking the elitist discourse of 'art' 'Ukasha then contrasted the soap operas, 'targeted to housewives busy in their kitchens', to the high-quality imports such as *Roots* and *Upstairs Downstairs* so rarely shown on Egyptian television. Admiring the camera work and the casting, he nevertheless went on to criticize the techniques used in the soap opera; were any Egyptian writer to draw out stories over so many episodes or to have so many contradictions or shifts in character (classic criticisms of American soap operas), the critics would hang him. Instead of insulting Egyptian drama writers by asking them to learn from such programmes, he argued, columnists should request that censorship exercised on the work of Egyptian writers be lifted so that their full creativity could be enjoyed.

The final use of a discourse of protection hints that Egypt's inability to protect its citizens from American imperialism is at the root of the problem. 'Ukasha contrasted *Oshin*, the first Japanese serial to be broadcast in Egypt (a high-quality production that valorized honesty and simplicity and 'symbolized the triumph of the Japanese character over the tyranny of nature ... the character that built a civilization and achieved a high standard of technology and economy'), to the American soap operas 'exported to poor Third World countries as part of American aid'.[24] Ahmad Bahgat, a traditionalist writer with Islamic leanings, complaining of the poor quality of *The Bold and the Beautiful* with its repetitions and the stupidity and immorality of its characters, sarcastically remarked in his column in the official government newspaper, 'Since the roulette wheel of the New World Order has stopped at the United States, we have to watch their silliest serials without the right to file a complaint.'[25]

Unenlightened Subjects?

Thus, to justify television as more than entertainment, a socially concerned and politically conscious group of culture- industry professionals who came of age under Nasser have constructed as their object 'a public' in need of enlightenment. Their use of a discourse of protection is part of their patronisation of their public but it also serves to reinforce among the professional classes the faith that mass media have powerful effects.

But can we determine how the television serials produced for them affect these 'unenlightened subjects'? Although the answers to this are complex, on the basis of some ethnographic work in Egypt in the 1990s I will suggest how at least two groups who are the object of these professionals' efforts and discourse – poor working-class women in Cairo and villagers in Upper Egypt – seem to slip through their well-meaning nets.

'Ukasha might be relieved to discover that many of 'the uneducated' are protected from a pumpkin-seed serial like *The Bold and the Beautiful* by its timing and its language. A soap directed at America's subalterns – housewives (although watched by students and many others) – has in Egypt captured instead an elite, or at least middle-class, audience that includes as many men as women. To enjoy it one must know English or be able to read Arabic subtitles and one must not be too exhausted from a hard day's work to stay awake.

Likewise, he can be reassured that many of the Egyptian serials made by his less socially concerned colleagues are so far-fetched or of such poor quality that audiences ignore them.

He would be less happy to discover the ways some viewers resist the nourishing social messages of his *Hilmiyya Nights*, even as they acclaim it as the best serial ever made. An example will illustrate this. *Hilmiyya Nights* had numerous important women characters, most sympathetically portrayed and shown to be facing dilemmas shared by different generations of woemn. Morally good older women put up with mistreatment by husbands, including secret marriages and deceptions.

Younger women struggled with the tensions between career and marriage. The serial glorified education, showing most of the daughters of working-class men going on to university, the daughter of a coffee shop owner and a singer becoming a university professor and the daughter of a factory worker and a dancer becoming a physician. In general the women were independent and able to take decisions on their own. The state feminism of Nasser's era was commended, one tough-minded wife of a factory worker counselling a friend to stand up for the rights 'Gamal' had given her.[26]

However, when asked what they liked about the serial, several poor women who work as domestic servants in Cairo volunteered not the serious political or social messages but the character of Nazik Hanem, the aristocratic, conniving, magnificently dressed *femme fatale* who plays the leading female role. One young woman whose husband had left her with two children to raise suggested, 'Nazik is the reason everyone watches *Hilmiyya Nights*. She's tough; she married four men. She wouldn't let anyone tell her what to do.' An older woman with a disabled husband explained why Nazik was so great: 'She's fickle, not satisfied with one type. She married many times. She represents what? What's it called? The aristocracy? She was strong-willed. And stubborn. Because of her desires she lost her fortune.' After a short silence she added, 'And Hamdiyya, the dancer, did you see her?' She laughed as she imitated a characteristic arrogant gesture of this belly-dancer turned cabaret-owner.

These were the two glamorous women characters with little nationalist sympathy who wrapped men around their fingers and wouldn't act like respectable ladies, despite the pleas of their children, their ex-husbands and their other relatives. These were also the two who took dramatic falls. The dancer became addicted to heroin after being strung along by a man she hoped to marry. By the time she was cured she had lost everything and had nowhere to go. Nazik Hanem's end was more complex but brilliantly played. She was someone who could not accept her age, even after being swindled out of her fortune by her fourth husband, a younger man who threw her aside. She became increasingly temperamental and then began dressing up like someone half her age, with a wig covering her grey hair, to flirt with a 20-year-old student. When scolded for this, she had a nervous breakdown.

None of the poor women who admired Nazik or the dancer ever mentioned the moral lesson of the fall; rather, they seemed to take vicarious pleasure in these women's defiance of the moral system that keeps good women quiet. These domestic workers were women whose respectability was threatened by their need to work outside the home and as servants. They struggled daily to claim and proclaim their respectability. They hid from their neighbours and sometimes even their relatives the actual sort of work they did and they had all adopted the *higab*, the head-covering of the new modest Islamic dress that, in Egypt, has come to be a sign of Islamic piety and middle-class respectability.

'Ukasha might have himself to blame for this resistance to his nationalist feminism and morality. For popular appeal and clarity in creating the righteous, modern, patriotic character, talented television drama producers often reach out to popular images, such as those purveyed in American soap operas, or introduce the debased 'other', usually parodied, for contrast. This can backfire as outrageous characters like Nazek Hanem, or the corrupt ignorant villainess of another successful serial by the same writer, *The White Flag*, steal the show from tiresomely earnest protagonists.[27]

Only one older woman commented on the more explicit national politics of the serial that had so exercised critics. She noted that *Hilmiyya Nights* was 'against Sadat' and that was why it showed what happened with the *infitah*, or open-door economic policy: people started importing all sorts of putrid goods, like canned meat that was actually cat food. Yet she felt free to disagree with 'Ukasha's basic position adding, 'In those days everyone was busy getting rich. There was lots of money around. For all of us.' Various political opinions circulate in Egypt and there is no reason to assume that the 'unenlightened' audiences of shows such as *Hilmiyya Nights* are waiting passively to learn from the serials what to think.

Viewers were selective in their appreciation of the messages of these television dramas. They could disagree with the politics; they could marvel at and take pleasure in the defiant characters who lived as they could not. They accepted the moral stances presented only when they resonated with their worlds. This was clearest in poor women's positive responses to the moral conservatism about family and a mother's role promoted by Egyptian serials generally and *Hilmiyya Nights* in particular. As one admirer of Nazik Hanem noted, to explain why Nazik's daughter Zohra never found happiness, 'The poor thing. It was because her mother didn't take care of her. She abandoned her as a baby with her father. When the girl got sick and had a bad fever, his new wife brought her to Nazik saying, "Here take your daughter and hold her close." But she refused. So Zohra never knew the love of a mother. She had to depend on herself. So the man duped her [tricking her into a shameful secret marriage and a pregnancy]. Poor thing.'

The villagers of Upper Egypt with whom I have worked make no more pliable subjects for the enlightening messages of the serials than these working-class urban women. This is not because they are unfamiliar with television, however. Every household in the village near Luxor where I have been working had a television set. Many were simple black and white sets with poor reception balanced precariously on rickety shelves in corners of mudbrick rooms whose only other wall decorations might be a poster of a favourite soccer club or movie star. The wealthiest families in the village had large colour sets in their reception rooms – rooms that often also boasted padded couches and framed religious calligraphy. On every poor family's wish list, were they to sell a piece of land or somehow save enough for a down payment on the instalment plan, was a colour set.

Only on rare evenings would the television be silent; if there had been a death in the neighbourhood or among one's kin, if someone was ill at home and receiving visitors. The most common reason for televisions to be silent was loss of electricity, something that happened for a few minutes almost every day and occasionally for long frustrating hours. And precisely because electric power in the village was so weak, children often had to do their homework by the light of the television sets.

Rather, the impact of serials like *Hilmiyya Nights* is deflected by the ways villagers consume television. For one thing, like their urban counterparts, villagers I knew were capable of selective readings of dramas. This was often necessary since the distance between the 'realities' dramatized in the serials and the lives lived in the village was vast. The fashionable blonde stars of *The Bold and the Beautiful* in their plush offices and grand mansions are most obviously far from these hardworking people in mudbrick two-storey homes with blue-painted wooden doors wide enough to allow the donkeys, sheep and water buffaloes to pass through into the pens inside; but the characters portrayed in Egyptian serials like *Hilmiyya Nights* are hardly much closer. Most Egyptian serials are set in urban locations and deal with urban, often upper-class problems.[28]

An anecdote about watching television in a relatively poor household can illustrate the gulf between local and television lives and the selective ways women interpret what they watch. One evening, Yamna, the vivacious but exhausted mother of the family, was preparing dinner with the help of her sister when the serial, *Love in a Diplomatic Pouch*, came on. Her sister had been there all day helping this overworked woman who had bread to bake and children to be watched when she went off to get fodder for the animals. The family was miserable that night – between the fever of the eldest son, the measles that had struck all four of the little girls, the three boys' end-of-year exams, the expenses and fatigue of a recent trip to a hospital in Assiut in search of a cure for the chain-smoking father's asthmatic cough, and the government's announcement the previous day that the price of flour was to be doubled, they wondered how they would cope. Yet the serial they watched centred on a wealthy diplomat's family and included characters like ballet teachers, woman doctors, journalists and radio personalities with career problems.

As Yamna cooked, her sister, wrapped in the black cloak women wear when they go visiting, shouted out a summary of the plot for her. She focused on the family dynamics that are the regular stuff of their own forms of telling life stories in the village. Divorces, arguments, absences, thwarted matches. She also picked up the moral message of the serial about women and family – the importance of the mother's role in raising her children and the ill consequences for their children of mothers who abandon them or put themselves or their marriages or careers first.

However, many of the 'women's issues' in this serial, written and directed by one of Egypt's few women directors, were constructed in psycho-social terms that were foreign to these women: 'psychological' problems like psychosomatic paralysis that love could heal, men unable to commit themselves to marry for fear of losing their freedom, mothers who cried because their children were not emotionally open with them, and psychiatrists treating drug addiction among the wealthy and educated. The women simply ignored in their discussions these aspects of the serial that were not part of their experience.

From my ethnographic work in the village, I would also suggest that the villagers make elusive targets for the cultural elite's modernizing messages for a more complex reason: through the very ease with which they have incorporated television into their everyday lives. Although it is difficult to articulate how this happens, I would argue that television created its own world, one that was for the villagers only a part – albeit an exciting one – of their daily lives. What they experienced through television added to but did not displace whatever else already existed. They treated the television world not as a fantasy escape but as a sphere unto itself with its familiar time slots and specific attitudes. It was a realm of knowledge about which people shared information: adolescents often had an encyclopedic knowledge of Egyptian films and serials and people knew a staggering amount about the private lives and previous roles of actors and actresses who starred in the serials. The young people read magazines but everyone had access to this knowledge through hours of viewing and the glorification of stars promoted by Egyptian television itself through interview programmes and celebrity game shows.

In the villagers' attitudes toward the stars is a clue to the larger question of how television serials affect them. The villagers spoke about these stars as 'ours', somehow belonging to them as viewers, but not as 'us'. The same mix of entitlement and distance applied to the serials. They are for 'our' pleasure but they depict the lives of others who have different problems, follow different rules, and do not belong to the local moral community. What these others do, then, has little bearing on what we do or how we conduct our lives. The daily worries of trying to make ends meet, balancing a father's monthly salary of 130 LE (less than USA $40) with work in the fields to grow clover for water buffaloes and sheep, of struggling to get families grown, through school, and married, of asserting rights to inheritances or extracting support from kin, of preserving one's moral reputation and standing in the face of in-laws and jealous neighbours with whom one has had disputes – these consume villagers. So do the pleasures of visits with friends and relatives, of meeting social obligations with generosity, of passing examinations, selling an animal, having a good harvest or wearing new clothes on the religious feasts.

Even when serials try to reflect village lives, as did a 1993 serial called *Harvest of Love* about Upper Egypt written by a politically concerned progressive woman writer, people reject the problems as not theirs. In this case people enjoyed the serial and recognized the dialect and occasional bits of clothing but alleged that its central issue – the problem of revenge killings – was something that happened elsewhere in Upper Egypt. Perhaps this happens in Sohag (a city to the north), some villagers offered, even though I had heard the vivid narratives about just such a revenge killing in their village only a decade earlier.

I was most struck by the suspension of judgement people applied to the compartmentalized television others because it was so different from their critical evaluations of neighbours and kin. This response resembled the villagers' curious but neutral discussions of the foreign tourists, archeologists and researchers who were daily in their midst and had been since the early part of the century.

I am not arguing here that the villagers anxiously compartmentalize the 'modernity' television serials (or foreigners) present in order to preserve a static traditional community somehow untouched by the global or 'modernity'. On the contrary, while the village appears picturesque with its 'traditional' sights like mudbrick homes and swaying palm trees, donkeys and the occasional camel carrying loads of clover or sugar-cane leaves, men hoeing fields or walking barefoot along muddy irrigation canals, and women in long black robes balancing bundles on their heads, there is not an aspect of people's everyday lives that has not been shaped by 'the modern'.

The modern Egyptian state determined that sugar cane be grown in the region, decides on prices, requires permits and licences, conscripts all young men into its army, and runs the Antiquities Organization that employs so many local men, prevents people from building in certain areas, and requires that they build in quaint mudbrick. It runs the schools that most children now attend, coming home weary from carrying the schoolbooks that teach about cleanliness, patriotism and religion.

People suffer from various health problems, the result of chemicals and pesticides, too much sugar in the diet, and waste – including plastic bottles, batteries, and Raid cans – thrown into the irrigation canals. The straight-backed men in their turbans and long pale robes are savvy about the difference between local physicians and specialists who are university professors and practise in Cairo, Mansura and Assiut. The women in black want 'television examinations' of their pregnancies and want to know if you had an ordinary delivery or a caesarian.

How well people eat and whether they decide to uproot cash crops to grow wheat is determined by such faraway organizations as the World Bank and the IMF.

Whether the men are away looking for work depends on the state of the Saudi Arabian economy, the decisions of bourgeois investors in the Red Sea tourist developments, French archeologists, and wealthy Lebanese refugees setting up chicken factories on the desert road to Alexandria, 600 kilometres away. Whether children who have learned to say 'Hello, baksheesh' come running home to give their mothers a few pounds, men who have developed pride in the art of carving pharaonic cats and Horus statuettes find buyers, and those who cook meals for the low-budget tourist groups visiting the tomb of King Tut on donkeys make enough to get new covers for their cushions all depends on whether the *New York Times* has reported 'terrorist' attacks in Cairo.

And contrary to the joke told in Cairo, everyone knows how to operate not just television sets but washing machines, refrigerators, fans and water pumps.

Television is, in this village, one part of a complex jumble of life and the dramatic experiences and visions it offers are surprisingly easily incorporated as discrete – not overwhelming – elements in this jumble.

This is not to say that television in general has not transformed social life or imaginaries. There are at least three areas in which careful ethnographic work might reveal significant transformations. First, in social life: there is less visiting among households in the evenings since families stay home to watch television. More important, television may have increased the number of 'experiences' shared across generation and gender. Television brings families together in the evening and makes it more likely that men and women will socialize together as they sit around the single television set in the house. The focus of attention is the evening serial but families converse with each other while waiting for it, as when the start of the serial is delayed by government ministers droning on during the televized sessions of parliament. Conflicts also arise, though, between generations and genders about which programmes to watch, just as exposure to television differs by generation.

Second, television may have changed the nature of experience itself. Some Egyptian professionals rationalized to me viewers' pleasures using a discourse of continuity, suggesting, for example, that the serials are like 'the stories a grandmother tells her grandchildren to send them to sleep', or 'like *The Thousand and One Nights*, where the story-teller would stop at the most exciting moment to attract the audience to listen to him the next day', or the North African tradition 'where the wandering poet who sings his poetry to the tune of the rababa stops every day at an exciting point in the story of "Antar or Abu-Zeid al-Hilaly"'.[29] But this ignores a distinctive feature of television drama, what Raymond Williams (1989) has called, referring to the frequency with which TV viewers are exposed to it, its possible role in dramatizing consciousness itself.

The third area where television in general may be transforming experience is in its facilitation of new identifications and affiliations. Do the villagers feel part of an imagined community of citizens or consumers because they know they are watching the same programmes at the same time and being offered the same goods as people across the country?

To acknowledge or explore the general effects of television on experience is not, however, the same project as the one I've been pursuing in this essay, which is to track the effects of particular kinds of public-spirited programmes on their objects. Two factors conspire to undermine the impact of serials like *Hilmiyya Nights*. First, of course, the serials appear only as part of the flow (Williams 1975) of programming, sandwiched between films, pumpkin-seed serials, advertising, religious programmes, children's programmes, sports, news, nature programmes and countless talking-head shows. More important, their messages are evaluated from within, and hence often balanced or even contradicted by the powerful everyday realities within which villagers, like poor working women in Cairo, move. These realities are both resolutely local and transnational.

Whereas *Hilmiyya Nights* and related serials condemn the consumerism and materialism encouraged in the 1970s with the renunciation of socialism and the turn to economic liberalization, the proliferating television advertisements that precede the broadcast of evening serials and the middle-to upper-class lifestyles portrayed in most dramatic serials offer different messages. These are reinforced by local circumstances. At least among the schoolchildren, the availability of the goods in the nearby town of Luxor combines with these television messages to instil an insistent desire for specific brands of candy or running shoes (Amigo shoes with Ninja Turtles on them). For urban poor women, the availability of such goods is that much more persuasive.

'Ukasha and the other enlightened professionals also exclude from their storylines any positive depiction of the various guises of the Islamic alternative being offered to Egypt's populace. Yet the Islamic identity and knowledge promoted by religious programmes on television interact positively with adults' experiences in the new or refurbished mosques that are being enthusiastically supported and children's experiences in schools, secular state institutions that are, somewhat ironically, the locus of religious pressure especially in rural areas. In the village where I worked, these children, the girls forced to wear the new Islamic headcovering and all subjected to the lectures of their aggressively religious schoolteachers, even discussed in class the significance of a television serial loosely based on the Koranic story of Joseph.

Furthermore, as for poor women in Cairo, there is little to reinforce the enlightening messages about culture, social responsibility and national unity the politically inspired culture-industry professionals are seeking to disseminate. *Hilmiyya Nights*, with its secular vision of a modern Egypt full of virtuous patriotic citizens, united across class by their love of country, sought to bring these subalterns into its modern fold.

But these subalterns are already folded into Egyptian modernity in a different way. The children who sing every morning the national anthem and memorize countless other nationalist songs from government schoolbooks may be somewhat receptive to the nationalist messages of television serials. Some, like a young village girl completing agricultural school, dream of impossible futures like being given a government plot of land in Sinai to develop. But their elders in Upper Egypt believe that their region has long been discriminated against and exploited by the north; they regularly experience the nation not through songs but through a formidable bureaucracy, a corrupt police force and army service (in which they are badly treated). The unity of rich and poor in national endeavours that *Hilmiyya Nights* idealizes is undermined by their knowledge of how the wealthy buy their way out of the army and around all regulations. For urban women who are the exploited supports of a modern class system, solving the twin demands of work and respectability through 'Islamic' veiling, this vision of the nation must also find little corroboration.

The problem, finally, is that the kind of modernity these television serials depict as a vision for Egypt depends on class position and the availability of certain kinds of educational and career opportunity. The 'uneducated public' at whom these serials are directed participates in the more common form of modernity in the postcolonial world: the modernity of poverty, consumer desires, underemployment, ill health and religious nationalism.

NOTES

1 Given the non-specialized readership for this essay, I have used an extremely simplified system of trnasliteration from the Arabic. To mark the letter *ayn* I use an apostrophe; otherwise all diacritics are absent, as are distinctions between long and short vowels.
2 Interview with the author, 22 July 1990.
3 Interview with the author, 15 April 1990.
4 Interview with the author, 15 April 1990.
5 Interview with the author, 22 July 1990.
6 So popular has it been internationally that its stars have been invited to act in Italian, Spanish and French films. They were treated as VIPs when invited to Egypt's Film Festival in December 1993, and thrilled audiences in India when they came on the air to wish Hindus well on a religious holiday. Many of these details were provided in a major magazine spread by Galal Al- Rashidy, 'The Stars of the Bold and the Beautiful Behind the Camera' (in Arabic), *Sabah al-Khayr*, 25 March 1993, pp. 46–50.
7 Ibrahim 'Issa, 'An American Researcher in an Important Book: Egypt Subsidises America!' in Arabic, *Roz al-Yusuf* 3382, 5 April 1993.
8 It seems frequently the case that national productions are more widely popular than imports. For evidence from Europe, see Silj 1988.
9 Sayed Yassin, 'Cultural Papers: "Hilmiyya Nights" and Political Activity', *Al-Iqtisadi*, 9 July 1990, pp. 96–7.
10 With the increase in products available on the market, competition has become fierce and television advertising considered effective in a country where illiteracy runs high. According to Aida Nasr (*Cairo Today*, November 1992, p. 98), the television advertising industry grossed LE 50 million, gleaned from a 15–20 percent commission.
11 For a stimulating discussion of the politics of television melodrama, see Joyrich (1992).
12 According to 'Abd al-Nur Khalil, 'The Ramadan of Television Captured People in a Bottle' (in Arabic), *Al- Musawwar* 3518, 13 March 1992, pp. 48–9, so wedded did the actors become to their roles that, after the conclusion of the serial, many of them complained that they felt trapped by their roles in *Hilmiyya Nights*. As in American soap operas, stars also quit the show before its conclusion and had to be replaced so audiences had to cope with the separation of character from actor.
13 According to Soha Abdel Kader (1985), based on a content analysis of television dramas and women's programmes in 1980, women are numerically under-represented in Egyptian television drama but often play significant roles (pp. 15–19). She argues, however, that women are 'always portrayed as more morally "good" than men' (p. 61), something that was not true of *Hilmiyya Nights*.
14 The only exception in recent American television was the *Murphy Brown* situation comedy that attacked the Bush family-values campaign in retaliation for Vice President Dan Quayle's attack on the protagonist's decision to have a baby out of wedlock. The fact that it was a *cause célèbre*, reported in newspapers and thought worthy of a BBC documentary, indicates how unusual the explicit inclusion of politics was in American television entertainment.
15 For a discussion of the exclusion of the perspective of the Islamic movement from television serials, see Abu-Lughod (1993).
16 10 June 1990, p. 10.

17   Articles entitled 'The Political Impact of Hilmiyya Nights' (in Arabic) (*Al-Wafd*, 14 May 1990, p. 5) and 'Historical Facts and Hilmiyya Nights' (in Arabic) (*Al-Wafd*, 21 May 1990, p. 5).

18   'Hilmiyya Nights Between Nasser and Sadat', *Roz al-Yusuf* 3233, 28 May 1990, pp. 68–9.

19   Interview by Aynas Ibrahim (in Arabic), *Roz al-Yusuf*, 24 May 1990, p. 56.

20   Interview by Abla Al-Ruwayny (in Arabic), *Al-Ahaly*, 30 May 1990.

21   Dalal 'Abd Al-Fatah (in Arabic), *Roz al-Yusuf*, 3371, 18 January 1993, p. 10.

22   The men, she argued, are not macho and they don't dominate women. The women work and make money. They want to succeed and to make their own futures. They don't give in to fate or circumstances or gossip. They use their minds and all they've got. The pleasure viewers get from *The Bold and the Beautiful*, she continues, is in seeing confrontation and hope ('*The Bold and the Beautiful*: A Serial without Male Complexes' (in Arabic), *Sabah al-Khayr*, 11 February 1993, p. 59).

23   *Roz al-Yusuf*, 3371, 18 January 1993, p. 8.

24   The theme of protection even came up in this article 'Ukasha wrote about *Oshin*. Accusing Egyptian television authorities of conspiring to discourage viewing by placing it in an unusual time slot, he compared *Oshin* favorably to *Roots* and other high-quality serials of the sort they hated to import for fear that people might come to demand programmes that met intellectual standards. No doubt alluding to his battles with the censors, he accused them of perceiving these high-quality serials the way they perceived democracy – as something that Egyptians needed to be protected from and only given in small doses.

      Using a different food metaphor than Fadil's pumpkin-seed munching, 'Ukasha contrasted *Oshin*, a natural drama with no food preservatives or artificial flavours, to the 'hawawshy bread' of *The Bold and the Beautiful*. ('Hawawshy bread' is a kind of meat pie whose strong spices are known to cover poor-quality minced meat.) Instead of striking women showing off their bodies and male mannequins smiling promiscuously, *Oshin* told the profound story of an ordinary Japanese woman who overcomes great obstacles (Usama Anwar 'Ukasha, 'Pay Attention Gentlemen: "Oshin" Confronts the "Bold and the Beautiful"' (in Arabic), *Roz al-Yusuf*, 3385, 26 June 1993, pp. 52–3).

      Ironically, under public pressure, *The Bold and the Beautiful* was eventually reduced from nightly broadcasts and *Oshin* brought back on the air in late 1993. Only a few months later, however, *Oshin* had become the subject of tremendous criticism in the press because of its relentlessly depressing character.

25   *Al-Ahram*, 6 February 1993, p. 2.

26   On state feminism and its demise in Egypt, see Hatem (1992).

27   For more on *The White Flag*, see Abu-Lughod (1993).

28   Abdel Kader's (1985) study showed that there was a bias toward portraying the urban upper classes. Of fourteen serials and twelve short plays sampled during a six-month period in 1980, none were set in rural areas (p. 36).

29   Nur Al-Sharif, interview with the author, 22 July 1990.

REFERENCES

Abdel Kader, Soha (1985) 'The Image of Women in Drama and Women's Programs in Egyptian Television.' Unpublished Report, Population Council.

Abu-Lughod, Lila (1993) 'Finding a Place for Islam: Egyptian Television Serials and the National Interest.' *Public Culture* 5 (3): 493–513.

Geraghty, Christine (1991) *Women and Soap Opera*. Cambridge: Polity Press.

Hatem, Mervat (1992) 'Economic and Political Liberalization in Egypt and the Demise of State Feminism.' *International Journal of Middle East Studies* 24: 231–51.

Hedges, Chris (1992) 'In Cairo Now a Coffee Shop is Just a Shop.' *New York Times*, 3 August.

Joyrich, Lynne (1992) 'All That Television Allows: TV Melodrama, Postmodernism, and Consumer Culture.' In L. Spigel and D. Mann, eds, *Private Screenings: Television and the Female Consumer*. Minneapolis: University of Minnesota Press, pp. 227–51.

Lerner, Daniel (1958) *The Passing of Traditional Society*. Glencoe, IL: Free Press.

Miller, Daniel (1992) 'The Young and the Restless in Trinidad: A Case of the Local and the Global in Mass Consumption.' In R. Silverstone and E. Hirsch, eds, *Consuming Technologies: Media and Information in Domestic Spaces*. London and New York: Routledge, pp. 163–82.

Silj, Alessandro et al. (1988) *East of Dallas: The European Challenge to American Television*. London: British Film Institute.

Wilk, Richard (1993) '"It's Destroying a Whole Generation": Television and Moral Discourse in Belize.' *Visual Anthropology* 5: 229–44.

Williams, Raymond (1975) *Television: Technology and Cultural Form*. New York: Schocken Books.

—— (1989) 'Drama in a Dramatised Society.' In A. O'Connor, ed., *Raymond Williams on Television: Selected Writings*. London and New York: Routledge, pp. 3–13.

Resource Bibliography

The following is intended as a helpful resource for those interested in exploring anthropological approaches to media. No attempt has been made to make this a comprehensive bibliography. For additional references please refer to Debra Spitulnik's (1993) review essay in the *Annual Review of Anthropology*.

Abu-Lughod, Lila. 1993. "Finding a place for Islam: Egyptian television serials and the national interest," *Public Culture* 5 (3): 493–513.
—— 1995. "The objects of soap opera: Egyptian television and the cultural politics of modernity." Pp. 190–210 in *Worlds Apart: Modernity through the Prism of the Local*, ed. Daniel Miller. London and New York: Routledge.
Adorno, Theodor W. 1954. "Television and the pattern of mass culture," *The Quarterly of Film Radio and Television* vol. 8, no. 3.
—— 1991. *The Culture Industry: Selected Essays on Mass Culture*. London: Routledge.
—— 1997. "Culture industry reconsidered." Pp. 24–9 in *Media Studies: A Reader*, ed. Paul Marris and Sue Thornham. Edinburgh: Edinburgh University Press. [Originally published in *New German Critique* 6 (1975): 12–19.]
Allen, Tim and Jean Seaton, eds. 1999. *The Media of Conflict: War Reporting and Representations of Ethnic Violence*. London and New York: Zed Books.
Anderson, Benedict. 1983. *Imagined Communities: Reflections on the Origin and Spread of Nationalism*. London: Verso.
Ang, Ien. 1982. *Watching Dallas: Soap Opera and the Melodramatic Imagination*. Trans. Della Couling. London and New York: Methuen.
—— 1990. "Culture and communication: towards an ethnographic critique of media consumption in the transnational media system," *European Journal of Communication* 5, nos. 2–3.
Appadurai, Arjun. 1990. "Disjuncture and difference in the global cultural economy," *Public Culture* 2 (2): 1–24.
Askew, Kelly. In press. *Performing the Nation: Swahili Music and Cultural Politics in Tanzania*. Chicago: University of Chicago Press.
Banks, Marcus and Howard Morphy, eds. 1997. *Rethinking Visual Anthropology*. New Haven, CT: Yale University Press.

Banta, Martha and Curtis Hinsley. 1986. *From Site to Sight: Anthropology, Photography, and the Power of Imagery.* Cambridge, MA: Peabody Museum of Harvard University, Harvard University Press.

Barbash, Ilisa and Lucian Taylor. 1997. *Cross-Cultural Filmmaking: A Handbook for Making Documentary and Ethnographic Films and Videos.* Berkeley: University of California Press.

Barthes, Roland. 1977. "The rhetoric of the image." Pp. 32–51 in *Image-Music-Text.* London: Fontana.

—— 1981. *Camera Lucida: Reflections on Photography.* Trans. Richard Howard. New York: Hill and Wang.

Bate, David. 1993. "Photography and the colonial vision," *Third Text* 22: 81–91.

Bateson, Gregory and Margaret Mead. 1942. *Balinese Character. Special Publication of the New York Academy of Sciences* II.

Bazin, André. 1967. *What is Cinema?* Berkeley: University of California Press.

Benjamin, Walter. 1968. "The work of art in the age of mechanical reproduction." In *Illuminations,* ed. Hannah Arendt. New York: Schocken.

Bennett, Tony. 1982. "Theories of the media, theories of society." Pp. 31–55 in *Culture, Society, and the Media,* ed. Michael Gurevitch, Tony Bennett, James Curran, and Janet Woollacott. London and New York: Methuen.

Berger, John. 1972. *Ways of Seeing.* Harmondsworth: Penguin/BBC Books.

Berger, John and Jean Mohr. 1982. *Another Way of Telling.* New York: Pantheon Books.

Bhabha, Homi K. 1994. *The Location of Culture.* London: Routledge.

Bhabha, Homi K. 1999. Preface to *Home, Exile, Homeland: Film, Media, and the Politics of Place,* ed. Hamid Naficy. New York: Routledge.

Biella, Peter. 1993. "Beyond ethnographic film: hypermedia and scholarship," *Anthropological Film and Video in the 1990s,* ed. Jack R. Rollwagen. Brockport, NY: The Institute.

Bobo, Jacqueline. 1995. *Black Women as Cultural Readers.* New York: Columbia University Press.

Bourdieu, Pierre. 1990. *Photography: A Middle-Brow Art.* Trans. Shaun Whiteside. Cambridge: Polity Press.

—— 1991. "Towards a sociology of photography," *Visual Anthropology Review* 7 (1): 129–33.

Bowlin, John R. and Peter G. Stromberg. 1997. "Representation and reality in the study of culture," *American Anthropologist* 99 (1): 123–34.

Brady, Erika. 1999. *A Spiral Way: How the Phonograph Changed Ethnography.* Jackson: University Press of Mississippi.

Buckman, Robert. 1990. "Cultural agenda of Latin American newspapers and magazines: is US domination a myth?" *Latin American Research Review* 25 (2): 134–55.

Campbell, Christopher P. 1995. *Race, Myth, and the News.* Thousand Oaks, CA: Sage Publications.

Carpenter, Edmund. 1972. *Oh, What a Blow That Phantom Gave Me!* New York: Holt, Rinehart and Winston.

Carpenter, Edmund and Marshall McLuhan, eds. 1960. *Explorations in Communication: An Anthology* Boston: Beacon Press.

Carson, Diane, Linda Dittmar, and Janice R. Welsch, eds. 1994. *Multiple Voices in Feminist Film Criticism.* Minneapolis: University of Minnesota Press.

Caton, Steven C. 1999. *Lawrence of Arabia: A Film's Anthropology.* Berkeley: University of California Press.

Cherneff, Jill B. R. 1991. "Dreams are made like this: Hortense Powdermaker and the Hollywood film industry," *Journal of Anthropological Research* 47 (4): 429–40.

Ching, Leo. 1994. "Imaginings in the empires of the sun: Japanese mass culture in Asia," *Boundary* 2, 21, no. 1.

Clifford, James. 1988. "On ethnographic authority." Pp. 21–54 in *The Predicament of Culture: Twentieth Century Ethnography, Literature and Art*. Cambridge, MA: Harvard University Press.

Collier, John, Jr. and Malcolm Collier. 1986. *Visual Anthropology: Photography as a Research Method*. Albuquerque: University of New Mexico Press.

Corner, John. 1991. "Meaning, genre and context: the problematics of 'public knowledge' in the new audience studies." Pp. 267–84 in *Mass Media and Society*, ed. James Curran and Michael Gurevitch. London: Edward Arnold.

Crary, Jonathan. 1990. *Techniques of the Observer: On Vision and Modernity in the Nineteenth Century*. Cambridge, MA: MIT Press.

Crawford, Peter I., ed. 1993. *The Nordic Eye (Proceedings from NAFA 1)*. Hojberg, Denmark: Intervention Press.

Crawford, Peter I. and Sigurjon Baldur Hafsteinsson, eds. 1996. *The Construction of the Viewer: Media Ethnography and the Anthropology of Audiences (Proceedings from NAFA 3)*. Hojbjerg, Denmark: Intervention Press.

Crawford, Peter Ian and David Turton, eds. 1992. *Film as Ethnography*. Manchester: Manchester University Press.

Croteau, David and William Hoynes. 1997. *Media/Society: Industries, Images, and Audiences*. Thousand Oaks, CA: Pine Forge Press.

Curran, James and Michael Gurevitch, eds. 1991. *Mass Media and Society*. London: Edward Arnold.

Das, Veena. 1995. "On soap opera: what kind of anthropological object is it?" Pp. 169–89 in *Worlds Apart: Modernity through the Prism of the Local*, ed. Daniel Miller. New York: Routledge.

de Lauretis, Teresa. 1984. *Alice Doesn't: Feminism, Semiotics, Cinema*. Bloomington: Indiana University Press.

—— 1987. *Technologies of Gender*. London: Macmillan.

Devereaux, Leslie and Roger Hillman, eds. 1995. *Fields of Vision: Essays in Film Studies, Visual Anthropology, and Photography*. Berkeley: University of California Press.

Dickey, Sara. 1993. *Cinema and the Urban Poor in South India*. Cambridge: Cambridge University Press.

Dines, Gail and Jean M. Humez, eds. 1990. *Gender, Race, and Class in Media*. Thousand Oaks: Sage Publications.

Douglas, Susan J. 1999. *Listening In: Radio and the American Imagination, from Amos "n" Andy and Edward R. Murrow to Wolfman Jack and Howard Stern*. New York and Toronto: Random House.

Dowmunt, Tony, ed. 1993. *Channels of Resistance: Global Television and Local Empowerment*. London: BFI Publishing.

Drummond, Phillip and Richard Paterson, eds. 1988. *Television and Its Audience: International Research Perspectives*. London: British Film Institute.

Eco, Umberto. 1978. "Independent radio in Italy: cultural and ideological diversification," *Cultures* 5 (1): 122–32.

Edwards, Elizabeth, ed. 1992. *Anthropology and Photography, 1860–1920*. New Haven, CT: Yale University Press.

Eickelman, Dale F. and Jon W. Anderson, eds. 1999. *New Media in the Muslim World: The Emerging Public Sphere*. Bloomington: Indiana University Press.

Escobar, Arturo. 1994. "Welcome to cyberia: notes on the anthropology of cyber-culture," *Current Anthropology* 35 (3): 211–31.

Fabian, Johannes. 1983. *Time and the Other: How Anthropology Makes Its Object.* New York: Columbia University Press.

Faris, James. 1992a. "Anthropological transparency: film representation and politics," in *Film as Ethnography*, ed. Peter Ian Crawford and David Turton. Manchester: Manchester University Press.

—— 1992b. "A political primer on anthropology/photography," in *Anthropology and Photography 1860–1920*, ed. Elizabeth Edwards. New Haven, CT: Yale University Press.

—— 1993. "A response to Terence Turner," *Anthropology Today* 9 (1): 12–13.

—— 1996. *Navajo and Photography: A Critical History of the Representation of an American People.* Albuquerque: University of New Mexico Press.

Fiske, J. 1987. *Television Culture.* London: Methuen.

—— 1989. "Moments of television: neither the text nor the audience." Pp. 56–78 in *Remote Control: Television, Audiences, and Cultural Power*, ed. E. Seiter, H. Borchers, G. Kreutzner, and E.-M. Warth. London: Routledge.

—— 1990. *An Introduction to Communication Studies.* 2nd edition. London: Routledge.

—— 1991. "Postmodernism and television." Pp. 55–67 in *Mass Media and Society*, ed. James Curran and Michael Gurevitch. London: Edward Arnold.

Gaco, ute, Aisha Khan, Jerrie McIntyre, and Ruth Weinberg, eds. 1989. *Women Anthropologists: Selected Biographies.* Urbana and Chicago: University of Illinosis Press.

Gamman, Lorraine and Margaret Marshment, eds. 1989. *The Female Gaze: Women as Viewers of Popular Culture.* Seattle: Real Comet Press.

Garnham, Nicholas. 1993. "The mass media, cultural identity, and the public sphere in the modern world," *Public Culture* 5: 251–65.

Gerdes, Marta Lucia de. 1998. "Media, politics, and artful speech: Kuna radio programs," *Anthropological Linguistics* 40 (4): 596–616.

Ginsburg, Faye. 1992. "Television and the mediation of culture," *Visual Anthropology Review* 8 (1): 97–102.

—— 1993. "Aboriginal media and the Australian imaginary," *Public Culture* 5 (3): 557–78.

—— 1994a. "Culture/media: a (mild) polemic," *Anthropology Today* 10 (2): 5–15.

—— 1994b. "Some thoughts on culture/media," *Visual Anthropology Review* 10 (1): 136–41.

—— 1994c. "Embedded aesthetics: creating a discursive space for indigenous media," *Cultural Anthropology* 9: 365–82.

—— 1995a. "Mediating culture: indigenous media, ethnographic film, and the production of identity." Pp. 256–91 in *Fields of Vision: Essays in Film Studies, Visual Anthropology, and Photography*, ed. Leslie Devereaux and Roger Hillman. Berkeley: University of California Press.

—— 1995b. "The parallax effect: the impact of aboriginal media on ethnographic film," *Visual Anthropology Review* 11 (2): 64–76.

Gitlin, Todd. 1991. "The politics of communication and the communication of politics." Pp. 329–41 in *Mass Media and Society*, ed. James Curran and Michael Gurevitch. London: Edward Arnold.

Goffman, Erving. 1976. *Gender Advertisements.* Studies in the Anthropology of Visual Communication (special edition) vol. 3, no. 2.

Grady, John. 1996. "The scope of visual sociology," *Visual Sociology* 11 (2): 10–24.

Graham-Brown, Sarah. 1988. *Images of Women: The Portrayal of Women in Photography of the Middle East 1860–1950*. New York: Columbia University Press.

Gurevitch, Michael, Tony Bennett, James Curran, and Janet Woollacott, eds. 1982. *Culture, Society, and the Media*. London and New York: Methuen.

Hahn, Elizabeth. 1994. "The Tongan tradition of going to the movies," *Visual Anthropology Review* 10 (1): 103–11.

Hall, Stuart. 1980. "Encoding/decoding." Pp. 128–38 in *Culture, Media, Language: Working Papers in Cultural Studies, 1972–79*. London: Hutchinson.

—— 1981. "The whites of their eyes: racist ideologies and the media," in *Silver Linings: Some Strategies for the Eighties*, ed. George Bridges and Rosalind Brunt. London: Lawrence and Wishart.

—— 1989. "Cultural identity and cinematic representation," *Framework* no. 38.

—— ed. 1997. *Representation: Cultural Representations and Signifying Practices*. London: Sage Publications.

Hamelink, Cees. 1983. *Cultural Autonomy in Global Communications*. New York: Longman.

Hannerz, Ulf. 1998. "Reporting from Jerusalem," *Cultural Anthropology* 13 (4): 548–74.

Heider, Karl G. 1976. *Ethnographic Film*. Austin: University of Texas Press.

—— 1991. *Indonesian Cinema: National Culture on Screen*. Honolulu: University of Hawaii Press.

Hendy, David. 2000. *Radio in the Global Age*. Cambridge: Polity Press.

Henley, Paul. 1998. "Seeing is understanding. Review of *Rethinking Visual Anthropology*, ed. Marcus Banks and Howard Morphy," *Times Literary Supplement*, May 8, 1998.

Hockings, Paul, ed. 1995. *Principles of Visual Anthropology*, 2nd edn. Berlin and New York: Mouton de Gruyter.

Horkheimer, Max and Theodor Adorno. 1973. *Dialectic of Enlightenment*. London: Allen Lane.

Imam, Ayesha M. 1991. "Ideology, the mass media, and women: a study from Radio Kaduna, Nigeria." Pp. 244–52 in *Hausa Women in the Twentieth Century*, ed. Catherine Coles and Beverly Mack. Madison: University of Wisconsin Press.

Innis, Harold A. 1950. *Empire and Communication*. Oxford: Oxford University Press.

—— 1951. *The Bias of Communication*. Toronto: University of Toronto Press.

Ivy, Marilyn. 1988. "Tradition and difference in the Japanese mass media," *Public Culture* 1 (1): 21–9.

Jay, M. 1973. *The Dialectical Imagination: A History of the Frankfurt School and the Institute of Social Research, 1923–1950*. Boston: Little, Brown.

—— 1991. "The disenchantment of the eye: surrealism and the crisis of ocularcentrism," *Visual Anthropology Review* 9 (1).

Jenkins, David. 1993. "The visual domination of the American Indian: photography, anthropology and popular culture in the late nineteenth century," *Museum Anthropology* 17 (1): 9–21.

Jhally, Sut. 1990. "Image-based culture: advertising and popular culture." Pp. 77–87 in *Gender, Race, and Class in Media*, ed. Gail Dines and Jean M. Humez. Thousand Oaks, CA: Sage Publications.

Jhally, Sut and Bill Livant. 1986. "Watching as working: the valorization of audience consciousness," *Journal of Communication* 36: 124–43.

Hockings, Paul, ed. 1995. *Principles of Visual Anthropology.* 2nd edition. The Hauge: Mouton.

Kottak, Conrad. 1990. *Prime-Time Society: An Anthropological Analysis of Television and Culture.* Belmont, CA: Wadsworth.

—— 1991. "Television's impact on values and local life in Brazil," *Journal of Communication* 41 (1): 70–87.

Krauss, Rosalind. 1988. "The im/pulse to see," in *Vision and Visuality,* ed. Hal Foster. Dia Art Foundation Discussions in Contemporary Culture, Number 2. Seattle: Bay Press.

—— 1993. *The Optical Unconsciousness.* Cambridge, MA: MIT Press.

Kulick, Don and Margaret E. Willson. 1992. "Echoing images: the construction of savagery among Papua New Guinean villagers," *Visual Anthropology* 5 (2): 143–52.

—— 1994. "Rambo's wife saves the day: subjugating the gaze and subverting the narrative in a Papua New Guinean Swamp," *Visual Anthropology Review* 10 (2): 1–13.

Lapham, Lewis H. 1994. "Introduction to the MIT Press edition." Pp. ix–xxiii in *Understanding Media: The Extensions of Man,* by Marshall McLuhan. Cambridge, MA: MIT Press.

Larkin, Brian. 1997. "Indian films and Nigerian lovers: media and the creation of parallel modernities," *Africa* 67 (3): 406–40.

Lawuyi, Olatunde B. 1997. "The political economy of video marketing in Ogbomoso, Nigeria," *Africa* 67 (3): 476–90.

Leuthold, Steven M. 1995. "Native American responses to the Western," *American Indian Culture and Research Journal* 19 (1): 153–89.

Levin, David Michael, ed. 1993. *Modernity and the Hegemony of Vision.* Berkeley: University of California Press.

Leyda, Jay. 1972. *Dianying: An Account of Films and the Film Audience in China.* Cambridge, MA: MIT Press.

Lidchi, Henrietta. 1997. "The poetics and the politics of exhibiting other cultures." Pp. 151–208 in *Representation: Cultural Representations and Signifying Practices,* ed. Stuart Hall. London: Sage Publications.

Liebes, Tamar. 1984. "Ethnocentrism: Israelis of Moroccan ethnicity negotiate the meaning of 'Dallas'," *Studies in Visual Communication* 10 (2): 46–61.

Liebes, Tamar and Elihu Katz. 1990. *The Export of Meaning: Cross-Cultural Readings of Dallas.* New York and Oxford: Oxford University Press.

Lipsitz, George. 1986. "The meaning of memory: family, class, and ethnicity in early network television programs," *Cultural Anthropology* 1 (4): 355–87.

Livingstone, Sonia M. 1991. "Audience reception: the role of the viewer in retelling romantic drama." Pp. 285–306 in *Mass Media and Society,* ed. James Curran and Michael Gurevitch. London: Edward Arnold.

Loizos, Peter. 1993. *Innovation in Ethnographic Film: From Innocence to Self-Consciousness, 1955–1985.* Chicago: University of Chicago Press.

Lull, James. 1991. *China Turned On: Television, Reform, and Resistance.* New York: Routledge.

Lutz, Catherine and Jane Collins. 1991. "The photograph as an intersection of gazes: the example of *National Geographic*," *Visual Anthropology Review* 7 (1): 134–49.

Lutz, Catherine and Jane Collins. 1993. *Reading National Geographic*. Chicago: University of Chicago Press.

MacDougall, David. 1991. "Whose story is it?" *Visual Anthropology Review* 7 (2): 2–10.

—— 1998. *Transcultural Cinema*. Princeton, NJ: Princeton University Press.

McEachern, Charmaine. 1994. "The power of the 'real': hegemony and the production of a British soap opera," *Dialectical Anthropology* 19: 81–108.

McLuhan, Marshall. 1994. *Understanding Media: The Extensions of Man*. Cambridge, MA: MIT Press.

Malkki, Lisa. 1997. "News and culture: transitory phenomena and the fieldwork tradition." Pp. 86–101 in *Anthropological Locations: Boundaries and Grounds of a Field Science*, ed. Akhil Gupta and James Ferguson. Berkeley: University of California Press.

Mankekar, Purnima. 1993a. "National texts and gendered lives: an ethnography of television viewers in a North Indian city," *American Ethnologist* 20 (3): 543–63.

—— 1993b. "Television's tales and a woman's rage: a nationalist recasting of Draupadi's 'disrobing'," *Public Culture* 5 (3): 469–92.

—— 1999. *Screening Culture, Viewing Politics: An Ethnography of Television, Womanhood, and Nation in Postcolonial India*. Durham, NC: Duke University Press.

Manuel, Peter. 1993. *Cassette Culture: Popular Music and Technology in North India*. Chicago: University of Chicago Press.

Marcus, George E., ed. 1996. *Connected: Engagements with Media. Cultural Studies for the End of the Century*. Late Editions 3. Chicago: University of Chicago Press.

—— 1997. *Cultural Producers in Perilous States: Editing Events, Documenting Change*. Late Editions 4. Chicago: University of Chicago Press.

Marcus, George E. and Michael Fischer. 1986. *Anthropology as Cultural Critique: An Experimental Moment in the Human Sciences*. Chicago: University of Chicago Press.

Marris, Paul and Sue Thornham, eds. 1997. *Media Studies: A Reader*. Edinburgh: Edinburgh University Press.

Martinez, Wilton. 1990. "Critical studies and visual anthropology: aberrant vs. anticipated readings of ethnographic film," *Society for Visual Anthropology Review* (spring): 34–47.

—— 1992. "Who constructs anthropological knowledge? Toward a theory of ethnographic film spectatorship." Pp. 130–61 in *Film as Ethnography*, ed. Peter Ian Crawford and David Turton. Manchester: Manchester University Press.

—— 1996. "Deconstructing the 'viewer': from ethnography of the visual to critique of the occult." Pp. 69–100 in *The Construction of the Viewer: Media Ethnography and the Anthropology of Audiences (Proceedings from NAFA 3)*, ed. Peter I. Crawford and Sigurjon Baldur Hafsteinsson. Hojbjerg, Denmark: Intervention Press.

Mead, Margaret. 1956. "Some uses of still photography in Culture and Personality." Pp. 79–103 in *Personal Character and Cultural Milieu*, ed. D. G. Haring. Syracuse, NJ: Syracuse University Press.

—— 1968. "Anthropology and the camera." Pp. 166–85 in *The Encyclopedia of Photography*, ed. Willard Morgan. Vol. 1. New York: Grestone Press.

—— 1975. "Visual anthropology in a discipline of words." Pp. 3–10 in *Principles of Visual Anthropology*, ed. Paul Hockings. The Hague: Mouton.

Mead, Margaret and Gregory Bateson. 1942. *Balinese Character: A Photographic Analysis*. New York: New York Academy of Sciences, Special Publications II. (Reissued 1962).

Mead, Margaret and Rhoda Metraux, eds. 1953. *The Study of Culture at a Distance*. Chicago: University of Chicago Press.

Michaels, Eric. 1994a. *Bad Aboriginal Art: Tradition, Media, and Technological Horizons*. Minneapolis: University of Minnesota Press.

—— 1994b. "Hollywood iconography: a Warlpiri reading." Pp. 80–95 in *Bad Aboriginal Art: Tradition, Media, and Technological Horizons*. Minneapolis: University of Minnesota Press.

—— 1994c. "Aboriginal content: who's got it – who needs it?" Pp. 20–46 in *Bad Aboriginal Art: Tradition, Media, and Technological Horizons*. Minneapolis: University of Minnesota Press.

Miller, Daniel. 1992. "The Young and the Restless in Trinidad: a case of the local and the global in mass consumption," in *Consuming Technology*, ed. R. Silverstone and E. Hirsch. London: Routledge.

—— 1993. "Spot the Trini," *Ethnos* 58 (3–4): 317–34.

—— 2000. "The fame of Trinis: websites as traps," *Journal of Material Culture* 5 (1): 5–24.

Miller, Daniel and Don Slater. 2000. *The Internet: An Ethnographic Approach*. Oxford: Berg.

Miller, Toby. 1998. *Technologies of Truth: Cultural Citizenship and the Popular Media*. Minneapolis: University of Minnesota Press.

Miller, W. Flagg. Forthcoming. "Metaphors of commerce: trans-valuing tribalism in Yemeni audiocassette poetry," *International Journal of Middle East Studies*.

Minh-ha. Trinh T., 1989. "The language of nativism: anthropology as a scientific conversation of man with man." Pp. 47–76 in *Woman, Native, Other: Writing Postcoloniality and Feminism*. Bloomington: Indiana University Press.

—— 1995. "'Who is speaking?' Of nation, community and first-person interview." Pp. 41–59 in *Feminisms in the Cinema*, ed. Laura Pietropaolo and Ada Testaferri. Bloomington: Indiana University Press.

Moeran, Brian. 1996. *A Japanese Advertising Agency: An Anthropology of Media and Markets*. Honolulu: University of Hawaii Press.

—— ed. 2001. *Asian Media Productions*. Honolulu: University of Hawaii Press.

Morley, David. 1988. *Family Television: Cultural Power and Domestic Leisure*. London: Routledge.

—— 1992. *Television, Audiences and Cultural Studies*. London: Routledge.

Morley, David and Kevin Robins. 1995a. "Cultural imperialism and the mediation of Otherness." Pp. 228–50 in *The Future of Anthropology*, ed. Akbar Ahmed and Cris Shore. London: Athlone Press.

—— 1995b. *Spaces of Identity: Global Media, Electronic Landscapes and Cultural Boundaries*. London: Routledge.

Morphy, Howard. 1994. "The interpretation of ritual: reflections from film on anthropological practice," *Man* N.S. 29 (1): 117–46.

Mulvey, Laura. 1989. *Visual and Other Pleasures*. London: Macmillan.

Naficy, Hamid. 1993. *The Making of Exile Cultures: Iranian Television in Los Angeles*. Minneapolis: University of Minnesota Press.

—— ed. 1999. *Home, Exile, Homeland: Film, Media, and the Politics of Place*. New York: Routledge.

Naficy, Hamid and Techome H. Gabriel, eds. 1993. *Otherness and the Media: The Ethnography of the Imagined and Imaged*. Langhorne, PA: Harwood Academic Publishers.

Nichols, Bill. 1994. *Blurred Boundaries: Questions of Meaning in Contemporary Culture*. Bloomington: Indiana University Press.

Norris, Pippa, ed. 1997. *Women, Media, and Politics*. New York and Oxford: Oxford University Press.

Notar, Beth. 1994. "Of labor and liberation: images of women in current Chinese television advertising," *Visual Anthropology Review* 10 (2): 29–44.

O'Barr, William M. 1994. *Culture and the Ad: Exploring Otherness in the World of Advertising*. Boulder, CO: Westview Press.

Ohmann, Richard, ed. 1996. *Making and Selling Culture*. Hanover, NH: Wesleyan University Press.

Peters, John Durham. 1997. "Seeing bifocally: media, place, culture." Pp. 75–92 in *Culture, Power, Place: Explorations in Critical Anthropology*, ed. Akhil Gupta and James Ferguson. Durham, NC: Duke University Press.

Pietropaolo, Laura and Ada Testaferri. 1995. *Feminisms in the Cinema*. Bloomington: Indiana University Press.

Piette, Albert. 1993. "Epistemology and practical applications of anthropological photography," *Visual Anthropology* 6 (2): 157–70.

Pinney, Christopher. 1992. "The parallel histories of anthropology and photography." Pp. 74–95 in *Anthropology and Photography, 1860–1920*, ed. Elizabeth Edwards. New Haven, CT: Yale University Press.

—— 1997. *Camera Indica: The Social Life of Indian Photographs*. Chicago: University of Chicago Press.

Powdermaker, Hortense. 1939. *After Freedom: A Cultural Study in the Deep South*. New York: Viking.

—— 1950. *Hollywood: The Dream Factory. An Anthropologist Looks at the Movie-Makers*. Boston: Little, Brown.

—— ed. 1953. *Mass Communications Seminar*. Proceedings of an Interdisciplinary Seminar held under the auspices of the Wenner-Gren Foundation for Anthropological Research, Inc., May 11–13, 1951. New York: Wenner-Gren Foundation for Anthropological Research, Inc.

—— 1962. *Copper Town: Changing Africa. The Human Situation on the Rhodesian Copperbelt*. Westport, CT: Greenwood Press.

—— 1966. *Stranger and Friend: The Way of an Anthropologist*. New York and London: W. W. Norton.

Press, Andrea. 1991. *Women Watching Television: Gender, Class and Generation in the American Television Experience*. Philadelphia: University of Pennsylvania Press.

Pribram, E. Deidre, ed. 1988. *Female Spectators: Looking at Film and Television*. London and New York: Verso.

Rabinow, Paul. 1986. "Representations are social facts: modernity and post-modernity in anthropology." Pp. 234–61 in *Writing Culture: The Poetics and Politics of Ethnography*, ed. James Clifford and George E. Marcus. Berkeley: University of California Press.

Rofel, Lisa. 1994. "Yearnings: televisual love and melodramatic politics in contemporary China," *American Ethnologist* 21 (4): 700–22.

Rollwagen, Jack R., ed. 1988. *Anthropological Filmmaking: Anthropological Perspectives on the Production of Film and Video for General Public Audiences*. Chur and London: Harwood Academic Publishers.

—— 1993. *Anthropological Film and Video in the 1990s*. Brockport, NY: The Institute.

Rony, Fatimah Tobing. 1996. *The Third Eye: Race, Cinema and Ethnographic Spectacle*. Durham, NC: Duke University Press.

Ruby, Jay. 2000. *Picturing Culture: Explorations of Film and Anthropology*. Chicago: University of Chicago Press.

Sarkar, Bhaskar. 1995. "Epic (mis)takes: nation, religion and gender on television," *Quarterly Review of Film and Video* 16 (1): 59–75.

Schiller, Herbert I. 1976. *Communication and Cultural Domination*. White Plains, NY: International Arts and Sciences Press.

—— 1994. "Media, technology, and the market: the interacting dynamic." Pp. 31–45 in *Culture on the Brink: Ideologies of Technology*, ed. Gretchen Bender and Timothy Druckrey. Seattle: Bay Press.

Seiter, E., H. Borchers, G. Kreutzner, and E.-M. Warth, eds. 1989. *Remote Control: Television, Audiences, and Cultural Power*. London: Routledge.

Shohat, Ella and Robert Stam. 1994. *Unthinking Eurocentrism: Multiculturalism and the Media*. London and New York: Routledge.

Silj, Alessandro et al. 1988. *East of Dallas: The European Challenge to American Television*. London: British Film Institute.

Silverstone, Roger. 1994. *Television and Everyday Life*. London: Routledge.

Silverstone, Roger and Eric Hirsch, eds. 1992. *Consuming Technologies: Media and Information in Domestic Spaces*. London: Routledge.

Skov, Lise and Brian Moeran, eds. 1995. *Women, Media and Consumption in Japan*. Honolulu: University of Hawaii Press.

Sontag, Susan. 1990 [1977]. *On Photography*. New York: Anchor Books.

Spitulnik, Debra. 1993. "Anthropology and mass media," *Annual Review of Anthropology* 22: 293–315.

Spitulnik Debra. 1997. "The social circulation of media discourse and the mediation of communities," *Journal of Linguistic Anthropology* 6 (2): 161–87.

—— 1998. "Mediated modernities: encounters with the electronic in Zambia," *Visual Anthropology Review* 14 (2): 63–84.

—— In press. *Media Connections and Disconnections: Radio Culture and the Public Sphere in Zambia*. Durham, NC: Duke University Press.

Sprague, Stephen F. 1978. "Yoruba photography: how the Yoruba see themselves," *African Arts* 12 (3): 52–9, 107.

Spurr, David. 1993. *The Rhetoric of Empire: Colonial Discourse in Journalism, Travel Writing, and Imperial Administration*. Durham, NC: Duke University Press.

Sreberny-Mohammadi, Annabelle. 1991. "The global and the local in international communications." Pp. 118–38 in *Mass Media and Society*, ed. James Curran and Michael Gurevitch. London: Edward Arnold.

Sreberny-Mohammadi, Annabelle and Ali Mohammadi. 1994. *Small Media, Big Revolution: Communication, Culture, and the Iranian Revolution*. Minneapolis: University of Minnesota Press.

Steiner, Christopher B. 1995. "Travel engravings and the construction of the primitive." Pp. 202–25 in *Prehistories of the Future: The Primitivist Project and the Culture of Modernism*, ed. Elazar Barkan and Ronald Bush. Stanford, CA: Standford University Press.

Stevenson, Nick. 1995. *Understanding Media Cultures: Social Theory and Mass Communication*. London: Sage Publications.

Sullivan, Nancy. 1993. "Film and television production in Papua New Guinea: how media become the message," *Public Culture* 5 (3): 533–56.

Tacchi, Jo. "Radio texture: between self and others." Pp. 25–45 in *Material Cultures: Why Some Things Matter*, ed. Daniel Miller. Chicago: University of Chicago Press.

Tagg, John. 1988. *The Burden of Representation: Essays on Photographies and Histories*. Amherst: University of Massachusetts Press.

Tanaka, Keiko. 1990. "Intelligent elegance: women in Japanese advertising." Pp. 78–97 in *Unwrapping Japan*, ed. E. Ben-Ari et al. Manchester: Manchester University Press.

Taylor, E. 1989. *Prime-Time Families: Television Culture in Post-war America*. Berkeley: University of California Press.

Taylor, Lucien. 1996. "Iconophobia: how anthropology lost it at the movies," *Transition* issue 69.

——ed. 1994. *Visualizing Theory: Selected Essays from V.A.R., 1990–1994*. New York: Routledge.

Thomas, Rosie. 1989. "Sanctity and scandal: the mythologization of Mother India," *Quarterly Review of Film and Video* 11: 11–30.

Tomlinson, John. 1991. *Cultural Imperialism*. Baltimore, MD: Johns Hopkins University Press.

Traube, Elizabeth G. 1992. *Dreaming Identities: Class, Gender, and Generation in 1980s Hollywood Movies*. Boulder, CO: Westview Press.

Troy, Timothy. 1992. "Anthropology and photography: approaching a Native American perspective," *Visual Anthropology* 5 (1): 43–61.

Tunstall, Jeremy. 1977. *The Media are America: Anglo-American Media in the World*. New York: Columbia University Press.

Turner, Terence. 1992a. "Defiant images: the Kayapo appropriation of video," *Anthropology Today* 8 (6): 5–16.

——1992b. "The Kayapo on television," *Visual Anthropology Review* 11 (2).

——1995a. "Objectification, collaboration, and mediation in contemporary ethnographic and indigenous media," *Visual Anthropology Review* 11 (2).

——1995b. "Social body and embodied subject: the production of bodies, actors, and society among the Kayapo," *Cultural Anthropology* 10 (2).

Tyler, Stephen. 1984. "The vision quest in the West, or what the mind's eye sees," *Journal of Anthropological Research* 40 (1): 23–40.

Urla, Jacqueline. 1995. "Outlaw language: creating alternative public spheres in Basque free radio," *Pragmatics* 5 (2): 245–61.

Visweswaran, Kamala. 1992. *Fictions of Feminist Ethnography*. Minneapolis: University of Minneapolis Press.

Walton, Kendall L. 1984. "Transparent pictures: on the nature of photographic realism," *Critical Inquiry* 11: 246–77.

Warren, Charles, ed. 1996. *Beyond Document: Essays on Nonfiction Film*. Hanover, NH: Wesleyan University Press.

Weakland, John H. 1975. "Feature films as cultural documents." Pp. 231–51 in *Principles of Visual Anthropology*, ed. Paul Hockings. The Hague: Mouton.

Webb, Virginia-Lee. 1995. "Manipulated images: European photographs of Pacific peoples." Pp. 175–201 in *Prehistories of the Future: The Primitivist Project and the Culture of Modernism*, ed. Elazar Barkan and Ronald Bush. Palo Alto, CA: Stanford University Press.

Weinberger, Eliot. 1994. "The camera people." Pp. 3–26 in *Visualizing Theory: Selected Essays from V.A.R., 1990–1994*, ed. Lucien Taylor. New York: Routledge.

Weiner, James F. 1997. "Televisualist anthropology: representation, aesthetics, politics," *Current Anthropology* 38 (2): 197–235.

West, Harry G. and Jo Ellen Fair. 1993. "Development communication and popular resistance in Africa: an examination of the struggle over tradition and modernity through media," *African Studies Review* 36 (1): 91–114.

Whisnant, David E. 1995. *Rascally Signs in Sacred Places: The Politics of Culture in Nicaragua*. Chapel Hill: University of North Carolina Press.

Wiggershaus, Rolf. 1994. *The Frankfurt School: Its History, Theories, and Political Significance*. Trans. Michael Robertson. Cambridge, MA: MIT Press.

Wilk, Richard R. 1993. "'It's destroying a whole generation': television and moral discourse in Belize," *Visual Anthropology* 5 (3/4): 229–44.

—— 1994. "Colonial time and TV time: television and temporality in Belize," *Visual Anthropology Review* 10 (1): 94–111.

Williams, Raymond. 1974. *Television: Technology and Cultural Form*. New York: Schocken Books.

Willis, Sharon. 1997. *High Contrast: Race and Gender in Contemporary Hollywood Film*. Durham, NC: Duke University Press.

Wong, Deborah. 1994. "'I want the microphone': mass mediation and agency in Asian-American popular music," *The Drama Review* 38 (3): 152–68.

Worth, Sol. 1980. "Margaret Mead and the shift from 'visual anthropology' to the 'anthropology of visual communication'," *Studies in Visual Communication* 6 (1): 15–22.

Worth, Sol and John Adair. 1997 [1972]. *Through Navajo Eyes: An Exploration in Film Communication and Anthropology*. Albuquerque: University of New Mexico Press.

Wright, Chris. 1998. "The third subject: perspectives on visual anthropology," *Anthropology Today* 14 (4): 16–22.

Yang, Mayfair Mei-hui. 1994. "Film discussion groups in China: state discourse or plebian public sphere?" *Visual Anthropology Review* 10 (1): 112–25.

—— 1997. "Mass media and transnational subjectivity in Shanghai: notes on (re)cosmopolitanism in a Chinese metropolis." Pp. 287–319 in *Ungrounded Empires: The Cultural Politics of Modern Chinese Transnationalism*, ed. Aihwa Ong and Donald M. Nonini. New York: Routledge.

Yoshimoto, Mitsuhiro. 1989. "The postmodern and mass images in Japan," *Public Culture* 1 (2): 8–25.

Zaffiro, James. 2000. "Broadcasting reform and democratization in Botswana," *Africa Today* 47 (1): 87–102.

Zha, Jianying. 1995. *China Pop: How Soap Operas, Tabloids, and Best-sellers Are Transforming a Culture*. New York: New Press.

Index